Research Decisions

Fifth Edition

Research Decisions

Quantitative,
Qualitative, and
Mixed Methods Approaches

Ted Palys
Chris Atchison

Simon Fraser University

NELSON / EDUCATION

NELSON / EDUCATION

Research Decisions: Quantitative, Qualitative, and Mixed Methods Approaches, Fifth Edition

by Ted Palys and Chris Atchison

Vice President of Higher Education, Editorial:
Anne Williams

Acquisitions Editor:
Maya Castle

Marketing Manager:
Terry Fedorkiw

Developmental Editor:
Liisa Kelly

Photo Researcher:
Lynn McLeod

Permissions Coordinator:
Lynn McLeod

Content Production Manager:
Hedy Sellers

Production Service:
Cenveo Publisher Services

Copy Editor:
Erin Moore

Proofreader:
Manikandan

Indexer:
BIM Indexing Services

Manufacturing Coordinator:
Ferial Suleman

Design Director:
Ken Phipps

Managing Designer:
Franca Amore

Interior Design:
Eugene Lo

Cover Design:
Jodi Atchison

Cover Image:
Jodi Atchison

Compositor:
Cenveo Publisher Services

Library and Archives Canada Cataloguing in Publication Data

Palys, T. S. (Theodore Stephen)

Research decisions: quantitative, qualitative, and mixed method approaches/Ted Palys, Chris Atchison.—5th ed.

Includes bibliographical references and index.
ISBN 978-0-17-650937-8

1.Social sciences—Research—Methodology—Textbooks.
I. Atchison, Chris, 1971– II. Title.

H62.P34 2013
300.72   C2012-906731-8

ISBN-13: 978-0-17-650937-8

ISBN-10: 0-17-650937-2

For Anne-Marie and Jodi

BRIEF CONTENTS

CONTENTS

PREFACE

We are writing this preface in the summer of 2012, which marks 20 years since the publication of the first edition of *Research Decisions: Quantitative and Qualitative Perspectives*. Who would have thought that the-little-book-that-could that first appeared two decades ago would still be around two decades later? We'd like to start by thanking all those professors, lecturers, and instructors who have chosen the book as their course text over these many years; the succession of publishers who have come back to us with continued requests to go back to the drawing board yet another time to do a new edition; and the students who tell us that they actually read the book and enjoy the way it takes something they thought would be boring and showed just how fascinating and integrated into our daily lives that research methods can be.

We're always honoured by the opportunity a new edition gives us to reconsider what we believe is important for students—the next generation of researchers—to know about research methods in the contemporary world. As we look back on the process of completing the new edition and the reflection we went through in deciding its contents, perhaps the first set of things to emphasize are the core principles that have guided every edition of this book, including the current one.

We begin with our belief that what makes the research enterprise as a whole great is its diversity. Although any single researcher will discover his or her own interests and develop whatever range of expertise best feeds those interests, it is by reaching out and listening to those who differ from us that we learn the most. *Research Decisions* is not the book for those who want to play safe, to do things the way they have always done them, and who

want to continue their academic life in a cocoon. Rather, *Research Decisions* is a book that encourages social and health science researchers to gain at least passing familiarity with a broad range of methodological approaches and have enough of a research methods repertoire to make their choices about how to proceed based on what makes the most sense to do in a particular research context, instead of being forced to do again and again the one thing they know.

Consistent with that belief, you will find as you go through this book that *Research Decisions* is always encouraging researchers to sample those people and situations that are most likely to challenge the way they think about an issue or area or phenomenon because that is how ideas and knowledge develop and grow. Listening only to those who think the same way you do, who have only one method they use to study everything, and who think that the purpose of research is to "prove" some truth that they already "know" to be true are following a path that in our view is ultimately self-defeating, boring, and has more in common with religion than social science. We prefer to engage research allowing for the possibility of and even hoping for the prospect of someone coming along who will give our heads a good shake and offer a new way of looking at some phenomenon that interests us. Understanding is something that arises from looking at any given person, setting, or phenomenon in a variety of different ways, and from a number of different perspectives. Accordingly, this edition of *Research Decisions* sets out to provide an overview of a broad range of qualitative, quantitative, and mixed methods techniques that in our view should be a part of every social and health science researcher's repertoire. It also explains why you will see our commitment to academic freedom surface on numerous occasions throughout the book, particularly when we rail against some of those contemporary influences that aim to rein in, control, and worse—micromanage—the research process, usually to bring everyone in line with their singular view of what research should look like. Whenever we meet someone who feels they have all the answers, we run the other way, and hope you do, too.

A second principle that guides *Research Decisions* is the idea that research starts by asking good and provocative questions—*not* with a particular method in hand that then constrains what questions you *can* ask. The methods you choose to pursue the questions you identify come afterwards, and which are incorporated into your work will depend on any of a number of different factors that we discuss in this book—how much is known about the phenomenon; where and how it occurs; the information you can generate or have access to; and so on. That philosophy is embedded in the title of the book itself—*Research Decisions*—by which we intend to convey that research involves a conscious decision-making process that you go through as you try and figure out what to study and how to study it, sometimes ahead of time but in many cases even *while* you are studying it. It also reflects our belief that there are few "right answers" in life that are *always* right. The answer most times in the world of research as to what methodological technique or procedure or approach is "best" in any given circumstance is "it depends." Accordingly, one of the things we do in *Research Decisions* is to try and make clear some of the factors that research decisions depend on, while at the same time leaving you the responsibility for figuring out how those factors play out in your particular context and then deciding how to proceed.

And finally, a third foundational principle for the book is that we practise what we preach. We find that in many of the research methods books we see it is very easy to determine what the specialty is of the author. There will be one really excellent chapter that seems grounded and offers compelling examples while the rest of the book describes techniques in more abstract terms that just don't ring with the truth of experience. In contrast, every method that you see in this book is a method that we have done at some time or another. The two of us really have done qualitative research, quantitative research, and mixed methods research, and really do value them all equally. At various times one or both of us has/have done interviews, surveys, oral histories, observation, participant observation, ethnography, archival analysis of various media and various sorts of data, lab experiments, field experiments, evaluation research, and participatory action research, and have had to work through all the issues that we discuss. We also have written grant proposals, served on an ethics committee, served on journal editorial boards, and written articles and books. Because of this we believe and hope that you find an authenticity and presence to *Research Decisions* that you are unlikely to find elsewhere because we make liberal use of our experience to try to convey what it is really like to do the types of research we describe.

NEW TO THIS EDITION

While the above explains some of the principles that have remained constant through various editions of *Research Decisions*—its heart and soul, so to speak—there are also many ways that the book has changed from edition to edition and the changes that accompany this new edition are more extensive than usual. We will leave the more detailed view of these changes to the section below we've entitled "chapter by chapter," but will note three major new elements that permeate this edition of the book.

The first is evident in our change of subtitle from "Quantitative and Qualitative Perspectives" to "Quantitative, Qualitative, and Mixed Methods Approaches." When the first edition of *Research Decisions* was published two decades ago, it was the first text that we know of to give qualitative and quantitative methods equal coverage and to talk about both approaches equally positively. The message was always that the two actually had more in common than most researchers at that time were prepared to admit, and had much to learn from each other. And while there are still diehards among each group who insist that the best way to do research is to engage the world with one hand tied behind your back, it is increasingly common for researchers to have a healthy respect for the others' contributions and to include individuals with a diverse array of specialties and methodological proficiencies in any research team when multiple researchers, often from different disciplines, come together in any project.

So while we have always believed in the wisdom of multi-method approaches, and have practised them throughout our respective careers, we approached this fifth edition of *Research Decisions* with the view that the research world is now ready not only to hear the general message that learning more about those who inhabit the other side of the block is a good idea, but to actually show how qualitative and quantitative methods can be combined in a given research project, and what some of the issues are that one will need to address in the process of doing so. Accordingly, from the first chapter onward those who are familiar with previous editions will see less emphasis on the ways in which qualitative and quantitative approaches differ, and much more emphasis on their complementarities and how methods ground in the two perspectives can be combined to symbiotic effect.

The second dimension that you will now see throughout the book involves the impact that the digital revolution is having on the research process. This theme was introduced in the fourth edition of *Research Decisions*, with Chris bringing his pioneering technological expertise to that edition—his first as a co-author—but its appearance was minimal and, as we read that edition now, at times almost appeared as an afterthought. Part of the reason for rewriting *Research Decisions* from one end to the other this time was thus to ensure that the new opportunities, techniques, and tools that we wanted to talk about—which have been and continue to transform how research is and can be done—are integrated into virtually every chapter of

the book in the same seamless manner that digital technologies are now integrated into virtually every aspect of most of our everyday lives.

And finally, a third dimension that has changed in this edition concerns the examples we have used to illustrate the methods and principles we discuss. Although we have always tried to reach out across the social sciences, which is reflected very much in the diverse array of disciplines across the country that use *Research Decisions* as a text, in this edition we have made a more concerted effort to reach out to the health sciences as well—in part to reflect the bourgeoning presence of Health Science departments in many universities across the country, in part to reflect our own research involvements, and in part to reflect the well-established interest of those in the Health Sciences in establishing multi-disciplinary research teams that exemplify well the transition we see to more mixed methods approaches and the benefits to be gained therefrom.

CHAPTER BY CHAPTER

As noted above, the enhanced emphasis we have placed on mixed methods approaches that combine the benefits of qualitative and quantitative approaches led us to seek a different tone in **Chapter 1** than had been the case in previous editions of *Research Decisions*. There is still a discussion that considers differences between qualitative and quantitative approaches, but the emphasis this time has been on providing the foundation for the latter part of the chapter that discusses and gives an example of how the two can be combined in mixed methods projects, thereby better framing the perspective that we wanted to have characterize this edition.

Chapter 2 on "Getting Started" includes the same basic elements that were included in the previous edition of *Research Decisions*—distinguishing deductive and inductive approaches and noting their complementarity; introducing the notion of operationalization; discussing reliability and validity; connecting with the literature and tapping into one's "sociological imagination" to identify the bigger issues that are reflected in one's research questions; and the empirical commitment to both theory and data. The biggest changes are reflected in our discussion of the literature, where we spend much more time talking about the bourgeoning creation of virtual libraries and other Internet-based sources and how software that was developed for qualitative data analysis—such as NVivo, which we use extensively—actually can be used with electronic libraries as an information management tool at every stage of the research process.

Our discussion in **Chapter 3** regarding research ethics continues to reflect our belief in the deserved centrality of ethical considerations to every research project while at the same time lamenting two aspects of the contemporary regime of ethics regulation that came with the federal government's imposition of the *Tri-Council Policy Statement* (TCPS) on ethics in research with human participants. Accordingly, we begin with a broad discussion of some of the main ethical principles one must consider when undertaking any research project—informed consent, confidentiality, conflicts of interest and roles—but also encourage readers to connect with ethical issues that Research Ethics Boards often care little about, such as questions of voice and privilege and how these should influence research and publication processes, the general nature of the relationship we have with participants before and after a project, and so on. Attention is also devoted to some of the new ethical issues that have arisen because of the wide array of Internet-based sources and computer-assisted means of gathering data, such as the more ambiguous boundaries that exist between "public" and "private" forums, and the question of whether data that is transmitted over the Internet can be considered secure and confidential. As to our concerns, the first is regarding the impacts the federal code's huge bureaucratization of ethics review has had on academic freedom for reasons that appear to have nothing to do with "ethics" and everything to do with liability or "risk" management. Second is how this bureaucratization has transformed what we believe should be a consideration of ethical issues at every stage of the research process to little more than a concern by

researchers for jumping through hoops and gaining ethical approval.

Chapter 4 on sampling is another chapter that has changed significantly, in two directions in particular. First is that instead of focusing simply on "sampling" per se, we also spend more time in this edition talking about recruitment, i.e., recognizing that finding people to participate in your research is one thing, but actually convincing them to agree to participate is another. As an example, the chapter includes an extensive discussion of Chris's research with the clients of prostitutes—a group that has been notoriously difficult to engage in research and hence about whom little has been known—and his pioneering work that has allowed him to engage samples of hundreds and hundreds of individuals who have completed his surveys and agreed to be interviewed.

An element that made its first appearance in the previous edition of *Research Decisions* was a chapter dealing with preparation of a research proposal (**Chapter 5**). As we explained then, with greater emphasis on the ability to secure funding in order to be able to conduct research, coupled with more onerous process requirements that must be met prior to getting approval to do one's research, proposal writing has become a requisite skill, and we are aware of more and more courses that require students to write a proposal as their term project rather than undertaking an actual piece of research. The chapter outlines design elements would-be researchers must address that speak to the concerns of those who evaluate such proposals—including their research methods professors! That chapter is back and, other than updating, remains relatively unchanged. We thank colleagues and students we have been engaged with in various projects—especially Bob Menzies, Michelle McGinn, and Tammy Dorward—for their permission to include portions of research proposals we have worked on together in order to illustrate some of the essential elements that need to be addressed in proposals and how one might do so.

In **Chapters 6 through 8** we present some of the main techniques that are used by social and health science researchers to gather qualitative and quantitative data—including surveys, interviews, oral histories, observation, ethnography, participant observation, and various unobtrusive and archival methods. These parallel our discussion in the previous edition but have changed throughout to reflect the enhanced discussion that characterizes this edition regarding new data-gathering opportunities that are now available via the Internet and intranets, new ways that digital technologies can facilitate and enhance the data-gathering process, and ways that the various techniques can be combined with one another to gain the benefits of mixed methods inquiry.

Chapters 9 through 12 then deal with different aspects of causal inference and data analysis. **Chapters 9 and 10** emphasize the idea that the challenge of research design is typically one of gathering information to enhance our understanding of phenomena while at the same time eliminating as many rival plausible explanations as possible for their occurrence. **Chapter 9** does so within the context of classic experimental design in large part because it offers a vocabulary (thanks to Donald T. Campbell) that can be applied to any research design, and because the logic of eliminating rival plausible explanations is clear. This is followed in **Chapter 10**, which merges the previous edition's **Chapters 10 and 11**, with discussions of quasi-experimental design, qualitative case study analysis, and evaluation research in a manner that extends the rival plausible explanations theme to incorporate notions of analytic control. One of the bigger changes that previous readers of *Research Decisions* will see here is a more abbreviated discussion of Campbell and Ross's famous evaluation of the Connecticut Speed Crackdown, which afforded us the opportunity to give expanded consideration to evaluation research and qualitative case study analysis.

Chapters 11 and 12 focus more exclusively on analysis. While **Chapter 12** remains pretty much unchanged from the conceptual introduction to quantitative data analysis that was featured in the previous edition of *Research Decisions*, **Chapter 11** is completely new and illustrates the greater attention we have paid in this edition to the impacts that the digital revolution is having on the research process. This is evident both in the range of source information that is available to researchers via the Internet—where the primarily textual sources of yesteryear are being expanded through virtual libraries and being joined by extensive archives that exist and/or can be created from videos, audio sources, Twitter feeds, Facebook entries, and so on—and in the availability of qualitative data analysis (QDA) software that can be used to both manage and analyze these diverse sources. We introduce readers to an array of qualitative data analysis software but focus most on the program that suits our research best—NVivo—to illustrate just what can be accomplished if one takes the digital plunge. While important to discuss, we were also conscious that many—if not most—universities and colleges have yet to make QDA software available to their faculty and students, and hence have sought at this time mostly to whet your appetites for what they can accomplish in the hope that we will be further along when and if yet another edition of *Research Decisions* is contemplated in the future. In the interim, we encourage students and faculty to download free trial versions of the programs that will give them an opportunity to try out the software first hand, preferably with data you have gathered, and to take advantage of the many tutorials and webinars that are available online to help new users get started and those who are already familiar with the software to expand their proficiency.

We close the book with **Chapter 13**, which offers an updated version of the "writing" chapter that we included in previous editions of *Research Decisions*, and **Chapter 14** on mixed methods approaches, another completely new chapter that serves the function of previous editions' epilogue by bringing closure to some of the book's main themes, while at the same time giving expanded consideration to some of the conceptual issues that researchers contemplating engaging in mixed methods approaches should consider. As usual, heavy emphasis is placed on using illustrative examples from our own research to go beyond abstractions and give a better feel for how these issues play out in the context of real research.

PEDAGOGICAL FEATURES

This fifth edition of *Research Decisions* continues to include numerous pedagogical features to help professors, teaching assistants, and students work through and benefit from the material contained in the book:

- Each chapter ends with a "Summing Up and Looking Ahead" section that reviews the chapter's main themes and sets the stage for succeeding chapters.

- Sets of *study questions* are included at the end of each chapter. These can serve as a source of examination questions and help students focus their studying (either individually or as part of a study group). Included also are questions posing problems that would be useful to discuss in a class, lab, or tutorial group, and/or that could be a basis for student essays and term projects. These have been updated for the new edition.

- A *glossary* appears at the end of the book, listing many of the technical terms and phrases that are inevitably involved in learning about methods. All glossary terms appear in bold type in the text. The glossary at the end of the book now includes page numbers for quick reference.

- Liberal use of *citation* provides numerous literature sources for professors and more advanced students who wish to examine the issues discussed in this book in more detail.

- A series of *appendices* provides supplementary information that negates the need for other sources, particularly with respect to tests of significance. The appendices have been streamlined for this edition, omitting the Table of Random Numbers and article "One Day At A Time: Single-Parent Mothers in Academe" (Appendices A and F in the fourth edition, respectively), as both can easily be located online by students and instructors.

Finally, we are also accessible via the Internet. You can email Ted at palys@sfu.ca or visit his Webpage at www.sfu.ca/~palys/, and/or email Chris at atch@shaw.ca and see his website at www.academic-freedom.ca. Both websites contain links that might be of interest to professors and students.

PERSONAL NOTES

As was the case with the four previous editions of this book, we are indebted to many for their collegiality and feedback along the way. At the top of the list are our fine colleagues and friends who understand how much we appreciate their trenchant criticism and the unconditional affection and encouragement in which it is always wrapped. The list is a lengthy one, but we especially wish to thank Howie Becker, Sheri Fabian, Bill Glackman, Kevin Haggerty, Mark Israel, Darrell Kean, Louise Kidder, John Lowman, Katarina Kolar, Bob Menzies, Michelle McGinn, Russel Ogden, John Russell, Will van den Hoonaard, Patrick O'Neill, Wenona Victor, Dalia Vukmirovich, and the late Donald T. Campbell. They are a large part of what makes going to work worthwhile.

At Nelson, numerous individuals have played a role in making the book what it is, and we have been blessed with a group of incredibly effective and capable people. Maya Castle served as acquisitions editor for this edition, coordinated reviewer feedback, and took us to the point of agreeing among ourselves what the new edition of the book would look like. Liisa Kelly did a splendid job as developmental editor in steering us towards our complete and final manuscript for production. The efforts of copy editor Erin Moore also were much appreciated; it was a pleasure working with someone who became involved with the material and made some great suggestions that improved the book. Thank you also to the production, design, and permissions teams who contributed to this new edition, and the marketing folks who ensured this book made it into your hands.

Mostly, however, we thank the faculty who continue to use *Research Decisions* in universities and colleges across the country, and to the students whose questions and feedback help us speak to them. In the end it is only because of all of you that we get to deal with the challenge and the great fun of figuring out how to make the newest *Research Decisions* even better than the last. Our hope, of course, is that you enjoy this book as much as the two of us have enjoyed collaborating on it.

Ted Palys and Chris Atchison
Vancouver, BC
6 August 2012

INSTRUCTOR ANCILLARIES

Beyond the book itself, further material is available through the publisher to assist professors, students, and other readers.

NETA

 The **Nelson Education Teaching Advantage (NETA)** program delivers research-based instructor resources that promote student engagement and higher-order thinking to enable the success of Canadian students and educators.

Instructors today face many challenges. Resources are limited, time is scarce, and a new kind of student has emerged: one who is juggling school with work, has gaps in his or her basic knowledge, and is immersed in technology in a way that has led to a completely new style of learning. In response, Nelson Education has gathered a group of dedicated instructors to advise us on the creation of richer and more flexible ancillaries that respond to the needs of today's teaching environments.

NETA Assessment relates to testing materials such as Nelson's Test Banks and Computerized Test Banks, but also in-text self-tests, Study Guides and web quizzes, and homework programs like CNOW. Under *NETA Assessment*, Nelson's authors create multiple-choice questions that reflect research-based best practices for constructing effective questions and testing not just recall but also higher-order thinking. Our guidelines were developed by David DiBattista, a 3M National Teaching Fellow whose recent research as a professor of psychology at Brock University has focused on multiple-choice testing. All Test Bank authors receive training at workshops conducted by Prof. DiBattista, as do the copyeditors assigned to each Test Bank. A copy of *Multiple Choice Tests: Getting Beyond Remembering,* Prof. DiBattista's guide to writing effective tests, is included with every Nelson Test Bank. (Information about the NETA Test Bank prepared for *Research Decisions* is included below.)

Supplements to Accompany Research Decisions: Quantitative, Qualitative, and Mixed Methods Approaches

All of the following supplements are available on the companion website for *Research Decisions,* Fifth Edition, which can be located at **http://www.researchdecisions5e.nelson.com.**

- **NETA Assessment**: The Test Bank was written by Sheri Fabian of Simon Fraser University. It includes over 250 multiple-choice questions written according to NETA guidelines for effective construction and development of higher-order questions. Also included are more than 200 true-false and approximately 100 short answer questions. Test Bank files are provided in Word format for easy editing and in PDF format for convenient printing whatever your system.

- **Instructor's Manual**. The Instructor's Manual to accompany *Research Decisions,* Fifth Edition has been prepared by author Ted Palys and his colleague Sheri Fabian, both of Simon Fraser University. This manual contains learning objectives, sample lesson plans and examination questions, suggested classroom activities and other teaching suggestions, and a resource integration guide to give you the support you need to engage your students within the classroom.

- **Image Library**: This resource consists of digital copies of figures, short tables, and photographs used in the book. Instructors may use these jpegs to create their own PowerPoint presentations.

- **DayOne**: Day One—Prof InClass is a handy PowerPoint presentation that you can customize to orient your students to the class and their text at the beginning of the course.

- **Fostering Conversations about Teaching Sociology in Canada**: We invite you to join Fostering Conversations about Teaching Sociology in Canada, a virtual community site built by sociology educators for sociology educators. A dynamic, continually evolving blog that houses dozens of self-reflexive pieces about various aspects of teaching—including student engagement, assessment, course preparation, and teaching with technology—Fostering Conversations is an educator's toolkit and a virtual home for sharing teaching ideas, practices, and complexities. Housing contributions by educators from across the country, including universities and colleges, large and small, Fostering Conversations provides a framework for cross-institutional conversations about the craft of teaching in the 21st century. Join the conversation today! Visit

http://community.cengage.com/Site/ fosteringconversations/

PERSPECTIVES ON RESEARCH

Sociology, psychology, criminology, business administration, education, political science, nursing, social work, communications, health studies, and the rest of the social and health sciences each have a designated academic "turf." But this book deals with something these otherwise diverse disciplines have in common—a belief in the desirability of trying to obtain the best possible answers to research questions that involve describing, understanding, explaining, and sometimes bringing about change through the systematic study and analysis of attitudes, beliefs, behaviours, and artefacts, i.e., research.

You may be one of those students who is interested in research, enrolled eagerly in your research methods courses, and is simply interested in learning something about how it's done. If you fall into this category, then no problem; this book is written by two "keeners" who love teaching and talking about research and are eager to share what we know.

But we've also taught enough research methods courses to know that there are students at the other end of the spectrum as well, i.e., those who have been dragged kicking and screaming into a required course (as research methods courses often are) and wondering what they might have done in a previous life to have been sentenced to this semester of pain. What we have found among this latter group is that they are often people who are not interested in research as a career, are more interested in what they see as a more applied or professional vocation, and, because of that, write off "research" as an esoteric or arcane pursuit that is only of interest to academics and has nothing of relevance to offer them.

We suggest quite the opposite is true, i.e., that "research" is one of the most fundamental things you can learn about, and that it is relevant to absolutely any walk of life you might wish to enter. Surely there is no more basic human process than (a) being curious about something we want to understand or having a question we want to answer; (b) identifying and gathering the information we need to do so; (c) making sense of the information; and (d) forming some tentative conclusions on the basis of it. Who *doesn't* do that? Your physician does that when you go in to complain about the pain in your side and s/he starts asking questions and poking around to try and diagnose the source of the problem. The courts do that when they interview witnesses and examine forensic evidence to try to determine guilt or innocence. Your mechanic does that when s/he tries to figure out why your car is making that pinging sound whenever you accelerate. Journalists do it when they gather information to write stories and engage in analysis about events in the news. You did that when you tried to figure out what university or college to attend and what program of study to pursue. It's also one of the reasons that Google has become one of the most successful companies on the planet.

Asking questions and trying to figure out what is going on and why things happen the way they do is a fundamental part of being human; there seems to be no end to the questions we pose and the information we wish to access. We may not always call these activities "research" or the processes we follow "research methods"—in fact, most of the time we don't—but people and events engage our curiosity, and we try to understand. In doing so we gather information, decide who and which parts of it we believe, form some conclusions, and act on them. The main difference is thus not in what we do—because we all do "research" every day in our own particular way—but in the extent to which we reflect on how we know what we know, and on the rules or principles we use to determine whether what we believe is a "fact," or something else—e.g., a rumour, speculation, hearsay, guess, or simply wrong. Considering what sorts of principles to keep in mind when gathering whatever information you wish to gather is thus actually a very useful thing to do.

NO ROYAL ROADS TO TRUTH

There are many misconceptions people have about research as a way of understanding the world. One of the biggest is the idea that there is only one "right" method of research. Those who subscribe to this view include all those researchers who only learn one method in the first place: e.g., the psychologists who only learn how to do experiments; the demographers, epidemiologists, and econometricians who only learn how to do statistical research with aggregated data bases; the anthropologists who learn nothing but ethnography.

We have a hard time understanding this point of view; it makes as much sense as a carpenter who refuses to use any tool but a hammer, or a painter who will only use the colour blue. Worse yet, instead of deciding what s/he would like to build and then using tools appropriate to the task, the carpenter who only uses a hammer will only look for building projects where a hammer will suffice. The painter whose palette includes only blue will only render that which is blue. A carpenter requires a full set of tools. A painter requires a full palette. And a researcher requires a full range of observational and analytic strategies in order to arrive at the best answers to her/his questions about the world, not because s/he will necessarily use them all on any given job, but because it is the job that should dictate what tools are used to complete it. Similarly, a fundamental premise for us is that it

is one's research questions that should guide one's choice of method and not the other way around.

RESEARCH AS ENGAGEMENT

There is also often more than one way to accomplish any particular goal, and the choices you make when you decide to do something say as much about you as the thing you are doing. A favourite scene of ours occurs in a film called *The Passenger,* directed by Michelangelo Antonioni, in which a journalist visits a remote desert village to make a documentary about one of the tribes indigenous to the area. He is surprised to meet an individual who, after travelling extensively, returned to become a respected Elder in the village of his birth. The journalist asks the man how his view of his people changed after being exposed to life in the industrialized world beyond the dunes. After some reflection, the Elder replies, "Mr. Locke … There are perfectly satisfactory answers to all your questions … But I don't think you understand how little you can learn from them…. Your questions are much more revealing about *your-self* than my answers would be about me." The scene ends when the Elder turns the camera around so that it looks toward the journalist asking the questions.

Something analogous occurs in the world of research. When, for whatever reason, a phenomenon catches the attention of a social or health scientist, s/he must decide how to approach and investigate that phenomenon. Researchable questions can be posed in myriad ways. In this book, we argue that research methods *can* provide us with at least tentative "facts" or "answers" to the questions we pose, but we also maintain that "knowledge" is not an entity, like gold or oil, that merely awaits our discovery of it. The relation between researcher and researched is more complex than that: the questions we ask and the way we ask them reveal a considerable amount about us and necessarily shape and constrain the answers that we can find. As Morgan (1983) states, it is important to acknowledge that,

science is basically a process of interaction, or better still, of *engagement*. Scientists engage a subject of study by interacting with it through means of a particular frame of reference, and what is observed and discovered in the object (i.e., its objectivity) is as much a product of this interaction and the protocol and technique through which it is operationalized as it is of the object itself. Moreover, since it is possible to engage an object of study in different ways—just as we might engage an apple by looking at it, feeling it, or eating it—we can see that the same object is capable of yielding many different forms of knowledge. This leads us to see knowledge as a potentiality resting in an object of investigation, and to see science as being concerned with the realization of potentialities—of possible knowledges. (13)

The view that the research process involves *engaging* a subject or phenomenon of interest has a fundamentally important set of implications associated with it. In particular, it suggests that *what* we find—the "truths" we unearth about the world—is only partly related to how the world *is,* but also is related to *what* questions we ask, *where* we look to find answers to our questions, *what* method(s) we employ in order to record information and observations and *how* we choose to examine or make sense of our research data. Acknowledging these implications leads us to consider the varying perspectives that researchers bring to the research process.

We say *perspectives* (plural) because the first thing to understand about the research enterprise is just how diverse it is. Indeed, in our view, its diversity is one of its greatest strengths. When many different people enjoy the academic freedom to engage many different issues from a wide variety of perspectives, a vibrant research process is the result, with society its major benefactor (e.g., Horn 1999). We consider three in this book.

QUANTITATIVE, QUALITATIVE, AND MIXED OR MULTI-METHOD APPROACHES

Our main objective in this chapter, and for the rest of this book, is to talk about the varied methods

and perspectives of the social and health sciences by introducing you to two research traditions or perspectives—**quantitative approaches** and **qualitative approaches**—and then showing you what can be gained or lost by interweaving them using **mixed methods approaches**.

You should understand from the start that the simple dichotomization of all research into only qualitative and quantitative that we begin with puts us simultaneously on solid ground and shaky ground. It's solid to the extent that there has been a lot written to distinguish the two approaches, there continue to be zealous advocates of each approach who think that theirs is the one and only royal road to truth, and one can still point to conferences and journals that cater to only one group or the other. The distinction is on shakier ground, however, to the extent that, in the day-to-day world of research, the boundary between the two is far less clear. It's a bit like dividing people according to whether they're "short" or "tall": it may be easy to do in the extremes (e.g., assigning basketball players and jockeys to one side or the other), and a useful distinction to make in some circumstances (e.g., when deciding who will paint the ceilings and who will do the baseboards), but any dividing line between the two groups in the population as a whole is bound to be arbitrary and hard to justify beyond the specific circumstances in which it is used.

That said, dichotomies *can* be useful pedagogical devices, and because we think that's the case here, we'll use this one to give you the flavour of each tradition. Keep in mind, though, that in distinguishing between qualitative and quantitative research, we're actually much more interested in forging links of communication between the two approaches than in driving them further apart. The place to begin is with how they have tended to differ, after which we'll consider what they have in common, and how each can complement the other.

Quantitative Approaches

Although quantitative approaches have a long philosophical lineage, their contemporary forms are often traced to the mid-to-late 19th century. Individuals such as Auguste Comte (in sociology and social psychology) and Wilhelm Wundt (in psychology) noted the tremendous theoretical and technological advances in the natural sciences and believed that natural science methods could be of service to the social sciences as well. The metaphors they used to describe the challenge to social scientists were permeated with natural science imagery. For Comte, for example, "societies and groups [are] organisms—analogous to biological or physical organisms—that exist and behave in accordance with objective and external laws" (Faulconer & Williams 1985: 1181).

A POSITIVIST EPISTEMOLOGY

Comte, Wundt, and others embraced an **episte-mological** tradition known as **positivism**. Bhaskar (1986) notes that

> the term "positivism" was first used systematically by Saint-Simon. It was adopted by his erstwhile secretary Auguste Comte, to express the ideas that the world consists of phenomena which are real, useful, certain, precise, organic, and relative and that knowledge consists in and only in the description of the coexistence and succession of such phenomena. (225)

Positivism championed the view that the only way to truly understand the world and develop dependable knowledge was to avoid philosophical reflection and rely solely on observation of concrete phenomena.

A REALIST PERSPECTIVE

An attribute strongly associated with positivism is the **realist perspective**.[1] Most vigorously applied in the context of positivism, realism's more extreme version of **direct** or **naive realism** subscribes to the view that there is a (i.e., one) reality out there that exists independent of the researcher that can be understood and awaits our discovery (e.g., see Chakravartty 2011; Filstead 1979). An implication of this view is that, if reality involves a singular

truth that exists independent of the observer, it should be able to be understood by different observers in exactly the same way. Realists thus aim to uncover *the* facts and to understand *the* laws or principles that account for those facts. The challenge is to think of the "right" theoretical concepts and develop techniques that are sufficiently precise to measure and test them.

JUST ANOTHER ORGANISM

The positivist reliance on a natural science model had implications for the types of theoretical concepts and data considered legitimate for inclusion in any science of human behaviour. References to Charles Darwin's evolutionary theory were frequent among turn-of-the-20th-century positivists. Psychologist John B. Watson (e.g., 1913), for example, was clearly impressed by Darwin's work and its impact on the biological sciences. A prime reason for this advance, said Watson, was that Darwin resisted the temptation to treat humans as a special entity and instead saw them as just another biological organism, subject to the same scientific principles as any other. Regarding psychology's love affair with **metaphysical** notions like "consciousness," Watson asserted that

> it is granted that the behaviour of animals can be investigated without appeal to consciousness … The position is taken here that the behaviour of man and the behaviour of animals must be considered on the same plane; as being equally essential to a general understanding of behaviour. [The social sciences] can dispense with consciousness. (176)

Watson was the vanguard of behaviourist theories that would dominate the social sciences, and especially psychology, for much of the 20th century, governed by a focus on overt behaviour while dismissing any reference to consciousness or mental states and searching for general principles or laws that were true across all organisms. Much of the research on learning, for example, was done with pigeons, which was consistent with the idea that although pigeons and people might well learn different things—pigeons learn to peck a target to get a food pellet while people learn that using Google's search engine will allow you to find out the capital of Brazil—the principles that govern how quickly and well they do so are the same.

This search for broad behavioural principles or laws was consistent with the positivist ideal that **theory** should be both simple and comprehensive, involving concepts that are adaptable to any specific situation, in the same way that the theoretical concept of "gravity" or "gravitational forces" can be used to explain the big (e.g., the movement of the galaxies), the small (e.g., why and how electrons revolve around an atom), and the mundane (e.g., why someone might need to wear suspenders or a belt to keep their pants from falling down). The ideal theory also would limit itself to expressing relationships among variables and to expressing them precisely, preferably in mathematical terms, rather like Einstein's simple but provocative statement that $E = mc^2$. And to their credit, behaviourists enjoyed much success; the principles of reinforcement that make slot machines such a huge source of income for casinos, for example, are exactly the same principles that govern how long a rat will sit and press a bar in order to make a food pellet come its way.

INPUTS AND OUTCOMES

Positivism's mechanistic purity also was sought with respect to the variables that were to be included in any analysis. The world was seen to be made up of causes (or predictors) and effects (or outcomes) like billiard balls being knocked around a table. We see the causes (e.g., the white cue ball hits a red #3 ball), observe the effects (e.g., the red ball moves and bounces into a pocket), and can develop principles to describe that action (e.g., the angle of incidence equals the angle of reflection, as any physicist or pool player knows) without worrying about what is going on "inside" either ball.

Similarly, early positivists felt that organisms could be treated as "black boxes": any invisible processes that might go on inside (such as

thinking in humans) were deemed irrelevant; all that *really* counts is what goes in (the predictors or causes) and what comes out (the effects or outcomes). Only those causes external to individuals were deemed "legitimate" to scrutinize, largely because such forces and processes are most amenable to observation and measurement. We can't see people's thoughts or motives, but we can see what people *do*. And if we can understand the relation between causes and effects, who cares what happens in between?

DON'T GET TOO CLOSE

Natural science perspectives on "objectivity" also were adapted to the quantitative cause. Positivists suggest that the route to objectivity requires investigators to *depersonalize* the research situation, like the proverbial Martian who naively investigates these strange beings called humans (see Lofland, Snow, Anderson, & Lofland 2006). "Good" data are said to be dispassionate data, far removed from their source. The closer one comes to dealing with people on a one-to-one basis, the more dangerous the situation becomes, since one might be tempted to resort to metaphysical concepts such as thoughts, perceptions, attitudes, and values.

Indeed, many quantitatively oriented research textbooks suggest that the worst fate that can befall anyone who engages in field research is for him or her to "**go native**" or **overidentify**[2] with those being studied. This is said to occur when researchers become so attuned and sensitive to the culture or group they're investigating that they take on the perspective of the group's members, leaving their ostensibly more appropriate detached, analytical perspective behind. Hagan (1989) makes the common argument that the appropriate attitude for researchers is studied neutrality; one should neither love nor hate the group one studies, and one should always maintain some social distance. He explains that a problem commonly experienced in fieldwork is

the *tendency of observers to overidentify with groups.* There are examples in the literature of an anthropologist who married a cannibal chief and of other individuals who, without being aware of it, have taken on the mannerisms of the groups they have studied. "Going native" is a situation in which the researcher identifies with and becomes a member of the study group, and in the process abandons his or her role as an objective researcher. (156–57; italics in original)

Hagan also quotes a case in which one social scientist chastised another for "romanticising criminals" and losing his sense of objectivity:

We ought to restrain impulses, including benign impulses, that prevent us from seeing the world realistically. Just as anthropologists cannot be trusted (intellectually) when they "go native" to the extent that they glorify rather than study their preliterate societies, so a criminologist who has gone native cannot be trusted to tell us what criminals are like. (Toby 1986 [1938]: 2, quoted in Hagan 1989: 157)

The ideal of detachment is also consistent with the quantitative preference for **aggregated data**, which compile responses from many persons so that general trends or patterns across people are made visible. This approach assumes that, across many responses, all "exceptions to the rule," whether in a positive or negative direction, will cancel one another out in any group as a whole, making the group "average" the purest statement of how someone in a given situation "typically" or "normally" behaves.

SOCIAL FACTS

The belief in the desirability of aggregation also can be seen in the quantitative attachment to **social facts**. According to Durkheim (e.g., 1968 [1938]), the important social facts of life, and hence the appropriate causal variables to study, were social practices and institutions such as education, religion, the law, and the economic system.[3] We clearly did not cause them; they existed before we did. They influence us all, although the nature of the

effect may vary. And even had we not been born, they still would exist and still would influence whoever happened to be here. For example, if you were born in Canada, you were born into a capitalist economic system; Canada would still be capitalist even if you had not been born here. That system is a social fact of your life; it has affected you in ways that differ from the effects of being born in, say, a socialist or communist country.

Thus, for Durkheim, social facts are the most appropriate causal factors for social scientists to investigate because they exert their influence coercively, and do so even when we try to resist:

A social fact is to be recognized by the power of external coercion which it exercises or is capable of exercising over individuals, and the presence of this power may be recognized in its turn either by the existence of some specific sanction or by the resistance offered against every individual effort that tends to violate it. (1968 [1938]: 250)

He continued,

The most important characteristic of a thing is the impossibility of its modification by a simple effort of the will ... Social facts have this characteristic. Far from being a product of the will, they determine it from without; they are like molds in which our actions are inevitably shaped. (Durkheim 1968 [1938]: 253)

To measure the effects of social facts, Durkheim recommended relying on official **rate data** (e.g., birth rates, divorce rates, suicide rates, crime rates). Such data deal with matters relevant to and affected by "social facts," are outside the influence of researchers or of the individuals the data described, and describe "reality." In addition, they make it easier to compare two areas or to compare an area with itself over time.

Since each of these [rate] figures contains all the individual cases indiscriminately, the individual circumstances which may have had a share in the production of the phenomenon are neutralized and, consequently, do not contribute to its determination. The average, then, expresses a certain state of the group mind. (Durkheim 1968 [1938]: 249)

A DEDUCTIVE APPROACH

For classic positivists, the ability to predict is the acid test of understanding: if you truly understand a phenomenon (e.g., hurricanes, depression, birth rates, sexual safety), you should be able to predict its occurrence. Not surprisingly, therefore, quantitative researchers prefer the **hypothetico-deductive method** (often referred to more simply as deduction, or the **deductive method**), which involves making predictions and assessing their success in an ongoing process of theory refinement.

Chapter 2 discusses this approach in detail; here we need only note that it involves beginning with a theory; deducing a hypothesis (prediction) from the theory; gathering data to test the prediction (and hence also the theory that gave rise to it); and then either looking for another situation in which to test the theory (if the prediction is borne out) or revising or discarding the theory (if the prediction proves inaccurate). In the ideal situation, the effects of certain variables can be assessed with all other influences held constant, making the **classic experiment** the deductivist's method of choice (see Chapter 9).

RESEARCHER-CENTRED

You should see from all the above that, for quantitative approaches, the researcher is the star of the show. The emphasis on taking a deductive approach brings with it the idea that it is theory that tells you what the important variables are to consider. And it is the researcher who will determine which theory to test, pick the situation to test it in, design the study, and do the research to see whether the theory is supported empirically or not. Research participants—often referred to as "human subjects" in more quantitative publications—have a minimal role beyond responding to whatever

stimuli are presented to them. Subjects' thoughts about what they do are not of interest because their motives and perspectives are suspect; they are too close to the situation to view it with the detached objectivity the researcher strives for. Any interaction beyond the standardized set of procedures that comprise the research is considered problematic because it introduces error and thereby contaminates the results. Many quantitative methods—the classic experiment being the foremost example—sometimes even deem it essential to keep subjects completely in the dark as to what **hypotheses** are being tested or even to deceive them about what the "real" purpose of the study is, ostensibly to ensure that subjects' behaviour is "natural" and not a reflection of their desire to respond in a socially desirable fashion because someone is watching what they do.

Qualitative Approaches

The choices that have characterized qualitative approaches historically have been the opposite of those made by researchers who opt to utilize quantitative approaches on every dimension discussed above. Schutz (1970) is illustrative.[4] He disagreed with behaviourists' and other positivists' choice to investigate a mechanistic world from the aloof stance of the knowledgeable social scientist, but his disagreement wasn't based on a belief that such a science would necessarily give "wrong" information. Rather, he felt that in the long run, such an approach would inevitably fall short of a comprehensive understanding of human action.

His position is reminiscent of a story known as "the drunkard's search" (e.g., Farris 1969).[5] It seems that, one night, a researcher is walking down the street when he comes across a rather intoxicated individual who is down on his hands and knees, looking for his house keys on the ground under a street lamp. The researcher joins in to help, but after another 15 minutes, neither has been able to find the keys. "Are you sure this is where you lost them?" asks the researcher.

"Actually … I lost them over there … closer to the house," says the fellow who lost his keys, pointing to a dark spot close to the house, about 50 metres away.

The researcher's jaw drops when he recognizes the futility of what they have been doing. Exasperated, he asks, "Then why are we looking over here?"

"Because this is where the light is," is the response.

Analogously, Schutz argued that, to gain any understanding about humans and human behaviour, the first trick is to look in the right place, and not to choose methods simply because a certain approach is easier, or is associated with some prestigious field of inquiry, or is expedient to adopt in the short term. The choice should be made on the basis of what is, over the long haul, the right thing to do:

> The basic postulate of the methodology of social science, therefore, must be the following: choose the scheme of reference adequate to the problem you are interested in, consider its limits and possibilities, make its terms compatible and consistent with one another, and having once accepted it, stick to it! (Schutz 1970: 270)

A HUMAN-CENTRED APPROACH

Cogito ergo sum—I think, therefore I am—was philosopher René Descarte's famous foundational statement that proved his own existence. How ironic, therefore, that researchers who embrace a fundamentalist variant of the quantitative method would want to ignore this essential element of our humanity and declare it beyond scientific interest. The methodological "right thing to do" for Schutz was *not* to try and understand humans the same way we try and understand the mating behaviour of the gall wasp or the reactions of chemicals in a test tube, but to acknowledge that social scientists, in trying to understand *human* behaviour, face challenges fundamentally different from those faced by the natural scientist:

> The world of nature, as explored by the natural scientist, does not "mean" anything to the molecules,

atoms and electrons therein. The observational field of the social scientist, however, … has a specific meaning and relevance structure for the human beings living, acting, and thinking therein. By a series of commonsense constructs they have preselected and pre-interpreted this world which they experience as the reality of their daily lives. It is these thought objects of theirs which determine their behaviour by motivating it. (Schutz 1970: 272–73)

And while the complexity this cognitive life creates might be challenging, it also creates great opportunity because, unlike gall wasps or the chemicals in a test tube, we can talk to humans, they can consider our questions, and we can learn from what they say. Schutz and others working within the qualitative tradition believe that when we study humans we must view them as thinking, motivated actors, while also acknowledging the challenges that arise because, as humans, social and health scientists are part of the very entity they seek to understand. A philosophy that expresses this view is known as **phenomenologism**.

PHENOMENOLOGISM

Phenomenologists maintain that any effort to understand human behaviour must take into account that humans are cognitive beings who actively perceive and make sense of the world around them, have the capacity to abstract from their experience, ascribe meaning to their behaviour and the world around them, and are affected by those meanings. W. I. Thomas (1928) stated that "perceptions are real because they are real in their consequences"; that is, in many situations the influence of "reality" (if indeed such a thing exists independently of our experience of it) pales in comparison to the influence of our perceptions of the situation—indeed, those perceptions define our "reality."

As an example, suppose that next week you are scheduled to give a class presentation on some topic related to research methods. In the grander scheme of things, such a situation is a fairly trivial event; among the "big" things that will happen in your life, it probably won't even rank in the top 200. Your career, your future happiness, and your ultimate impact on the human race are unlikely to be significantly affected by your performance on that one assignment in that one class on that one day. And yet, if you're like most students, you won't treat it as trivial. You'll do the appropriate preparation at the library or through the Internet; you'll read your presentation a dozen times before the actual day you present, making last-minute changes and trying to learn it by heart; you may not sleep well the night before you present; and you'll probably come to class on "the big day" feeling at least a little nervous. Can we, as social scientists, adequately understand your behaviour without recourse to the way you perceive this situation and the meaning you ascribe to it?

To take another example, many Canadians these days seem deeply concerned about violent crime. Consistent with these concerns, citizens and their elected representatives frequently call for more punitive sentencing, more caution in the granting of parole, and "special measures" that would give courts greater leeway to incarcerate particularly nasty people and habitual offenders for a long, long time. Yet the "reality" of the situation in Canada is that, at least as measured by the rates reported by Statistics Canada, violent crime in Canada hasn't increased at all over the last decade. In fact, the exact opposite has occurred—violent crime rates have been dropping steadily. Notwithstanding these facts, Prime Minister Harper's Conservative party and those who support his party's policies continue to argue that violent crime is worse than ever and that more punitive approaches are required. Which is more important in accounting for Canadians' and the Conservative party's behaviour regarding violent crime: the "reality" of the situation or people's perceptions of it?

Phenomenologists feel that ardent positivists, in their zeal to mimic the natural sciences, did an injustice to the very humans they wanted to understand. As a result, they argue that any science of human behaviour is destined to be trivial and/or incomplete unless it takes people's perceptions into account. Any approach that defines itself as phenomenological makes understanding human perceptions its major research focus: if perceptions are real in their consequences, and if they are a major determinant of what we do, then clearly they are what we must set out to understand.

NUMBERS CREATE DISTANCE

The shift to phenomenologism affected many other aspects of theory and method. For example, a central aim of positivism was to establish functional relations among explanatory concepts, expressed, ideally, in mathematical (quantitative) form. Many phenomenologists believe that imposing a quantitative measurement just removes researchers further from directly understanding human experience. Instead of trying to come to grips with the anger and powerlessness a woman feels when assaulted, for example, the requirements of quantification leave us either merely counting the frequency of such occurrences (with all the attendant technical problems of how to count "correctly") or asking women to describe their experience on a series of ten-point rating scales. Phenomenologists, in contrast, argue that the closer we can come to such experiences, say, by listening to women explain, in their own words, the nature of their experiences, the better.

UNDERSTANDING EQUALS *VERSTEHEN*

Once the variables of analysis are quantified, positivists argue that the language of mathematics makes our statements far more precise. "Explanation" in the positivist sense involves investigating which "big" variables (e.g., social facts) most significantly affect human existence. Being able to identify these factors and to predict their occurrence becomes the acid test of understanding. The rationale is that if you can successfully predict a phenomenon, you must understand it; conversely, if you think you understand a phenomenon, you should be able to predict its occurrence with some degree of consistency.

Researchers who adopt a phenomenological approach reject the idea that a statistical criterion can ever define explanation or understanding. Instead, they are more likely to embrace Max Weber's concept of **verstehen**, which involves the more intimate and empathic understanding of human action in terms of its interpretive meaning to the subject. While researchers who embrace strict positivism seek general principles of behaviour, Weber argued that, in themselves, such principles can't account for action in context:

> An "objective" analysis of cultural events, which proceeds according to the thesis that the ideal of science is the reduction of empirical reality to "laws," is meaningless … The knowledge of social laws is not knowledge of social reality but is rather one of the various aids used by our minds for attaining this end … Knowledge of *cultural* events is inconceivable except on a basis of the *significance* which the concrete constellations of reality have for us in *individual* concrete situations. (Weber 1968a [1949]: 91)

Weber didn't completely dismiss quantitative research or the theories associated with it; he just felt that one had to go beyond blanket assertions made by strict positivists to account for action in context. He wasn't averse to quantification in principle, but he *was* cautious about how useful it might be for articulating subjective meaning:

> Causal explanation depends on being able to determine that there is a probability, which in the rare ideal case can be numerically stated, but is always in some sense calculable, that a given observable event (overt or subjective) will be followed or accompanied by another event … [Nonetheless], statistical uniformities constitute understandable types of action in the sense of this discussion, and thus constitute "sociological generalizations," only when they can be regarded as manifestations of the understandable subjective meaning of a course of social action. (Weber 1968b [1947]: 30–31)

VALIDITY COMES FROM CLOSENESS

Researchers who adopt qualitative approaches believe that understanding people requires getting close to "research participants" or "informants" or "collaborators." You must spend time with them, get to know them, be able to empathize with their concerns, perhaps even be one of them, if you hope to *truly* understand. Key here is the notion of **rapport**—the development of a bond of mutual trust between researcher and participant that is considered to be the foundation upon which access is given and valid data are built. This approach directly contradicts the views often held by fundamentalist quantitative researchers that "objective" understanding requires aloof detachment, lest the researcher "lose perspective." From a qualitative perspective, "detachment" simply makes for a superficial encounter that is unlikely to go beyond image management.

What degree of closeness is "appropriate," however, is a matter of ongoing debate within the qualitative research community. For most researchers, establishing rapport is possible as long as one is respectful, trustworthy, and spends a lot of time with the person or group that will be the focus of the research. Others take a more extreme position, believing that one can never understand a group of which one is not a part—e.g., that male researchers can never truly understand what it means to be a woman, or that non-Aboriginal researchers can never know what it means to "grow up Indian." By implication, therefore, for these researchers only women should research women and only Aboriginal researchers should do research on Aboriginal issues.

While we have some sympathy for these views, particularly as they apply to minority populations who are often misunderstood and miscast by those from the dominant group, our view is that while having had certain life experiences may give researchers special insights, and we should all be aware of the limitations of our experience, there should be no predefined limits on what topics are "appropriate" for any given person to study. That said, one would be foolish not to have trusted colleagues among the minority that can save one from any imperialist excesses.

Much also will depend on the topic under study and characteristics of the research site and participants. In some cases, such as when dealing with very sensitive topics in a closed community, research participants may feel far more comfortable when the researcher is *not* normally a part of the community because the participant can disclose information without worry about further repercussions within the community after the research is completed and the researcher has departed. In other cases, being part of the community or at least having shared similar experiences can give the research participant more comfort that the researcher can empathize with her/him, and thus feel more comfortable disclosing. Unfortunately, there is no general rule or guideline that researchers can follow to determine the optimal degree of closeness they need to have to research participants or communities where research takes place in order to obtain the most reliable and valid observations. Knowing how close we need to be is a product of our ability to assess and understand the individuals and social settings where our research takes place.

AN INDUCTIVE CASE STUDY APPROACH

Associated with the view that closeness is desirable is the idea that researchers should *listen* to their informants, aiming to understand categories and theoretically important dimensions from the perspective of their informants' experience and to incorporate those understandings into their analysis, rather than relying exclusively on predefined measures and theoretical categories imposed from the "outside." Accordingly, more phenomenologically oriented researchers emphasize **inductive approaches** (where observation in the field *precedes* the generating of theoretical concepts; see Chapter 2) and **case study analysis**.

Instead of beginning with theory and assuming that there's *one* theory that will eventually account for everything, a strict qualitative approach typically involves beginning with individual case studies trying to understand each situation on its own terms, and leaving open, for the moment, the question of whether generalizable theoretical concepts can ever be drawn together in anything resembling a grand theory. For many qualitative

researchers, theory isn't something you start with; it's something you build.

A PREFERENCE FOR FIELD RESEARCH

The qualitative preference for case study analysis is accompanied by a priority being attached to doing research in "the field," i.e., where behaviour is examined in context. There are two main reasons for this. First is simply that, according to qualitative perspectives, behaviour only has meaning in context, and hence "in context" is the only place where behaviour can legitimately be observed. This can be contrasted with the quantitative view, most obviously embraced in the laboratory experiment and social surveys, that behaviour can be divorced from its context and still be effectively the same behaviour. Laboratory experiments that ostensibly examine "aggression," for example—such as research by Ed Donnerstein and his colleagues that examined male sexual violence toward women by allowing men to deliver small electric shocks to a woman who made a programmed series of mistakes in a memory task (e.g., Donnerstein & Berkowitz 1981)—makes little sense to qualitative researchers who would argue that delivering a shock in a lab is a fundamentally different phenomenon from committing sexual assault. Quantitative researchers, in contrast, would suggest that while giving a shock in a lab experiment is obviously different from a sexual assault in terms of its severity, the factors that influence the level of shock that a man gives to a female research subject in a lab are assumed to be the same as those that influence the likelihood of engaging in sexual assault out in the world.

A second, related reason for preferring field research is that, if the reason we do research is to understand the behaviour of people in the world, then field research is the most valid option because it is only in field-based research that we duplicate the contextual conditions that shape behaviour and give it its meaning. As noted qualitative methodologist Howard Becker (1996) explains,

> When we watch someone as they work in their usual work setting or go to a political meeting in

their neighborhood or have dinner with their family—when we watch people do things in the places they usually do them with the people they usually do them with—we cannot insulate them from the consequences of their actions. On the contrary, they have to take the rap for what they do, just as they ordinarily do in everyday life. An example: when I was observing college undergraduates, I sometimes went to classes with them. On one occasion, an instructor announced a surprise quiz for which the student I was accompanying that day, a goofoff, was totally unprepared. Sitting nearby, I could easily see him leaning over and copying answers from someone he hoped knew more than he did. He was embarrassed by my seeing him, but the embarrassment didn't stop him copying, because the consequences of failing the test (this was at a time when flunking out of school could lead to being drafted, and maybe being killed in combat) were a lot worse than my potentially lowered opinion of him. He apologized and made excuses later, but he did it. What would he have said about cheating on a questionnaire or in an interview, out of the actual situation that had forced him to that expedient?*

CONSTRUCTIONISM

Recall that classic positivists embraced a philosophical perspective known as *realism*. Phenomenologists, in emphasizing the role of human perception in understanding human behaviour, adopt a contrasting perspective known as **constructionism**. As described by Schwandt (1994),

constructivists are deeply committed to the … view that what we take to be objective knowledge and truth is [actually] the result of perspective. Knowledge and truth are created, not discovered

* Becker, H. S. (1996). The epistemology of qualitative research. In R. Jessor, A. Colby, & R. Schweder (Eds.), *Ethnography and human development: Context and meaning in social inquiry* (pp 62). Chicago: University of Chicago Press. Available online at www.soc.ucsb.edu/ faculty/hbecker/qa.html

by mind. They emphasize the pluralistic and plastic character of reality—pluralistic in the sense that reality is expressible in a variety of symbol and language systems; plastic in the sense that reality is stretched and shaped to fit purposeful acts of intentional human agents. They endorse the claim that, "contrary to common-sense, there is no unique 'real world' that preexists and is independent of human mental activity and human symbolic language." (125; the last sentence quotes Bruner 1986: 95)

To illustrate, suppose we follow Becker's illustration and decide to study the phenomenon of "cheating," known in some universities as "academic dishonesty." A realist approach to studying cheating would affirm that there are behaviours we consensually recognize as "cheating" and that some people are more or less likely to cheat than others. Given this perspective, our attention might turn to trying to measure either "frequency of cheating" or how likely a given person or group of persons is to cheat; investigating why some people are more likely to cheat than others; or why some situations result in more or less cheating than others.

A constructionist looking at cheating wouldn't deny the usefulness of any of these approaches. But s/he also would encourage us to take a step back and look at "cheating" as a socially constructed concept. Why do we consider "cheating" something worth asking about? Why do we consider some behaviours where one person seeks the help of another "cheating" (e.g., looking over another person's shoulder to see what answers s/he puts down in an exam) but not others (e.g., hiring a tutor, or studying together)? We might also want to interview people who have been identified as cheaters about how they perceived their actions: Did *they* consider it "cheating" or did they call it something else? How did they come to engage in that behaviour?

The realist, then, takes the existence of certain behaviour categories as a given, believing that there are such things as "cheating," "aggression," and "crime," along with other supposed givens such as "birth," "death," "taxes," and "murder."

Constructionists, on the other hand, are at least as interested in why these categories interest us, whom or where we decide to sample in order to investigate the phenomenon firsthand, where the boundaries of the phenomenon are, what meanings the terms have for us, and how those boundaries and meanings change over time. To be a constructionist is not to deny that certain phenomena exist, but to insist that their existence cannot be completely understood unless one understands why, how, and to whom they are applied. This perspective, which falls clearly within the phenomenological traditions exemplified by Weber and Schutz, has several implications.

For one thing, many of the research results we take at face value and perceive as enduring may be little more than transient relationships that reflect the prevailing social order. While realists may be content to try to assess *the* effects of race, poverty, daycare, being gay, winning the lottery, or taking illicit drugs, constructionists argue that we can understand such matters only if we also understand something about how they're construed and the context in which they occur.

Consider, for example, someone who is interested in looking at the "effects" of particular family arrangements on developmental outcomes. A strict realist would have no problems with that: s/he would gather information from a huge sample of people concerning both what sort of family arrangement they were raised in (e.g., single-parent families, children of divorce, daycare use) and what sorts of outcomes they experienced later in life (e.g., their level of school achievement, involvement in crime), make comparisons between the groups, and come up with an answer. Next thing you know the researcher is appearing on *Dr. Phil* talking about how children who attend daycare do far better in school than those who don't and recommending universal daycare to ensure everyone can enjoy the benefits associated with going there.

A constructionist would have problems with that conclusion. From a constructionist perspective, there's no *inherent* or "real" effect to being a child of divorce or attending daycare that's true across all time and space. We can understand the effects of daycare only if we understand the context in which daycare occurs and people's perceptions of it. Any positive effects that daycare may have on later school performance, for example, may simply reflect the lack of universal daycare, which means that most children who go to daycare are from professional and better-educated families who can afford the fees and hence are more advantaged and likely to succeed anyway. In sum, the "effects" of daycare (or divorce or whatever) are associated less with the statuses themselves than with the social context in which they exist.

One way to examine the merits of taking a constructionist approach involves making an effort to **de-construct** some process or statistic, as we do in our discussion in Chapter 8 regarding crime statistics. A realist perspective on matters of "criminal justice" would take "the criminal justice system" and the existing *Criminal Code* as givens, starting any analysis with the view that "criminals" are those who violate the *Code* and that the extent to which "crime" and "criminality" exist in a society is best reflected by such data as the official crime rates reported annually by Statistics Canada.[6]

Such an approach may be fine for those who subscribe to mainstream conceptions of justice and the underlying values they represent, but many argue that "the law" and those it deems "criminal" are best seen as socially constructed entities. One way this is evident is to study crime and law historically; upon doing so, some authors find crime statistics contentious from the outset because of how law changes over time and at times seems to be no more than a score card of who gets to make up society's rules and see their views of the world embodied in the power of law. During the prohibition years for alcohol in the United States, for example, those who distilled and distributed alcohol were considered some of America's most despicable criminals; today shares of their companies are traded on the stock exchange and the distillers are valued members of society. Of course, alcohol is a very "European" and "Christian" intoxicant (e.g., Boyd 1991); those from other cultures and religions who prefer intoxicants such as marijuana, peyote, or opium still risk jail for doing so. The same occurs in many other areas: homosexuality was once illegal in both Canada and the United States, but it is now legal to be gay and illegal for anyone to deny opportunity to anyone on the basis of their sexual orientation; abortion was once illegal and now is not; assisted suicide is permissible in some states and not in others.

Our discussion in Chapter 8 regarding crime statistics uses another favoured constructionist technique, which is to de-construct each step in the creation of these statistics to try and understand how social, historical, and other factors contribute to the numbers we often take to be "objective" measures of crime. What we see is that although all crime statistics have some constructionist element to them, different statistics are subject to differing degrees of construction. Murder statistics, for example, for reasons we explain in Chapter 8, are probably better indicators of the number of murders that actually take place in a society than drug statistics are of the number of individuals who consume illicit drugs.

In sum, the *Criminal Code* and crime statistics are anything but neutral descriptions of criminal behaviour and its frequency of occurrence. Instead, crime statistics embody just one of many possible conceptions of justice and can't be understood outside the cultural context that makes them meaningful. And as Gergen (1985) notes,

> similar kinds of critiques have been launched against the taken-for-granted character of suicide, … beliefs, … schizophrenia, … altruism, … psychological disorder, … childhood, … domestic violence, … menopause, … and situational causes … In each case, the objective criteria for identifying such "behaviours," "events," or "entities" are shown to be either highly circumscribed by culture, history, or social context or altogether nonexistent. (267)[7]

EMPHASIZING PROCESS

A distinct difference in emphasis also follows from either seeing the important elements of the world as essentially stable and awaiting discovery (the

realist view) or seeing the world as something that is actively constructed, deconstructed, and reconstructed on an ongoing basis (the constructionist view). According to those who hold the latter view, our constructions of the world—and hence the world itself—are open to change.

As we've seen, positivist/quantitative researchers tend to emphasize the measurement of *outcomes* in their research. This is consistent with the positivist division of the world into causes and effects and with the view that there are real, monolithic forces that rule our lives. But constructionists consider the world a more ephemeral, transient place whose dynamics are more directly contingent on the meanings and understandings we use to negotiate our world. Accordingly, constructionist-oriented qualitative approaches are also characterized by greater attention to *processes,* particularly the processes by which constructions arise and, by implication, the processes by which constructions can be changed.

PARTICIPANT-CENTRED

All of these objectives are well-served by more collaborative approaches in which, ideally, the researcher will begin the research with an open mind and without preconceived theory, will spend much time with participants in the field, and will look to participants to guide her/him in the identification of important questions that will focus the research and possibly assist in interpretation. How far this goes will depend on the individual researcher. Some see the researcher as no more than an instrument whose job is to represent the views of participants in their own words; others believe that researchers have a role to play because while any given participant has a unique history and experience that the researcher does not, the researcher's social position makes it likely that, at the end of the research, s/he will be the only one in the setting who has systematically learned from *all* of the participants in a setting and thus should have the broadest and most comprehensive view.

An important by-product of this connection to participants is that, although in the long run we are free to develop our own explanations on the basis of what we learn, having the benefits of participants' views enable us to at least consider the meanings that people themselves give to what they do instead of us inventing these meanings on the basis of our experience, or on what *we* would do in such a situation, or extant stereotypes. Making a point he attributes to Blumer (1969), Becker (1996) explains,

> The field of drug use … is rife with such errors of attribution. The most common meaning attributed to drug use is that it is an "escape" from some sort of reality the drug user is said to find oppressive or unbearable. Drug intoxication is conceived as an experience in which all painful and unwanted aspects of reality recede into the background so that they need not be dealt with. The drug user replaces reality with gaudy dreams of splendor and ease, unproblematic pleasures, perverse erotic thrills and fantasies. Reality, of course, is understood to be lurking in the background, ready to kick the user in the ass the second he or she comes down.
>
> …
>
> Such descriptions of drug use are, as could be and has been found out by generations of researchers who bothered to ask, pure fantasy on the part of the researchers who publish them. The fantasies do not correspond to the experiences of users or of those researchers who have made the experiments themselves. They are concocted out of a kind of willful ignorance.*

Becker's position is reminiscent of the statement from psychologist George Kelly (1955) that, "if you want to know something about someone, ask them; they might just tell you." This does not mean that researchers should be naive about people's propensity to manage their image or that we should take at

---

* Becker, H. S. (1996). The epistemology of qualitative research. In R. Jessor, A. Colby, & R. Schweder (Eds.), *Ethnography and human development: Context and meaning in social inquiry* (pp. 58 - 59). Chicago: University of Chicago Press. Available online at www.soc.ucsb.edu/ faculty/hbecker/qa.html

face value anything that people say, but giving them a chance to talk and listening to their explanations and justifications is an important part of coming to a comprehensive understanding of any phenomenon, and may just reveal different perspectives that the researcher had not yet considered.

Comparing Research Perspectives

Thus far, we've seen that numerous differences traditionally have characterized quantitative and qualitative approaches to research. Table 1.1 compares these differences more explicitly, at least as they've been associated with each approach historically.

Each element in the table has been discussed in the preceding pages, so you should now be able to define and explain them and understand why and how each is characteristic of one or the other of the extremes of the two perspectives discussed in this chapter and throughout this book.

As a general sketch, you should see that prototypically quantitative research is more likely to begin with theory as part of a hypothetico-deductive strategy, with the researcher choosing (in the field research context) or possibly creating (in an experiment) a situation in which s/he can test hypotheses derived from theory. Procedures are likely to be standardized, sample sizes are likely to be large, and interaction between research subjects and the researcher is likely to be at a minimum in order to maintain social distance to ensure detachment and objectivity. The data will be gathered in exactly the same way from every research subject—to ensure comparability across subjects and to allow comparisons between groups—and, regardless whether the data are physiological, attitudinal, or behavioural, will be collected in a way that they can be summarized and compared or correlated mathematically. When social fact data are collected, they are likely to be drawn from "official" sources and treated as valid, unbiased indicators of whatever they are said to represent; for example, Statistics Canada data will be used to define "crime," standardized IQ tests will be used to define "intelligence," and census data will be used to define race, sex, and

Table 1.1

Comparing Quantitative and Qualitative Approaches

Quantitative Approach	Qualitative Approach
Natural science model: humans are just another organism	Human-centred approach: people's ability to think and abstract requires special consideration
Positivist epistemology	Phenomenological epistemology
Direct realist perspective	Constructionist perspective
Emphasis on observable variables that are external to the individual; social facts	No variables ruled out; internal, perceptual variables expressly considered
Quantitative measures are preferred for their precision and amenability to mathematical analysis	Direct, qualitative verbal reports are preferred; quantifying responses is a step removed from people's words and perceptions
Emphasis on causes and effects: what goes in and how it comes out; predictors, outcomes	Emphasis on processes: perceptions and their meanings and how these emerge and change
Objectivity is achieved through social distance and a detached, analytical stance; human behaviour can be extracted from its context to be studied	Valid data come from closeness and extended contact with research participants *in situ;* behaviour cannot be extracted from its context
The criteria for understanding are the ability to predict and statistically define significant associations between variables	The criterion for understanding is *verstehen*: understanding behaviour in context in terms meaningful to the actor
Preference for larger samples looking for patterns across many cases; paying more attention to "the forest"	Preference for case study analysis; paying more attention to "the trees"
Preference for a deductive approach: start with theory and create situations in which to test hypotheses	Preference for an inductive approach: start with observation and allowing **grounded theory** to emerge
Researcher and theory decide what is important to study and how results will be interpreted	More collaborative approach where research participants can help identify research focus and aid interpretation

class. The goal of the research will be to identify general overall patterns across the human subjects involved in the research that test hypotheses that arise from theory, compare groups, and/or evaluate the effects of particular causal variables of interest.

In contrast, prototypically qualitative research is likely to begin with the researcher identifying a general topic of interest, and then looking for a particular research site in the field where a case study can be performed that will allow him/her to observe the phenomenon in context and better understand the processes that lead to its production and by which it is given meaning by the inhabitants of the site. The researcher is likely to spend a long time with research participants in the field and to involve them in the process of developing a specific research focus. Procedures might involve administering standardized instruments such as an interview, but these will be adapted to the specific situation or person being interviewed to ensure they are meaningful and relevant to the participant or setting, and new sources of information and even new directions for the research will be incorporated into the study if they are relevant even if they were not anticipated ahead of time.

These two sketches of "prototypically" (or perhaps "stereotypically") quantitative and qualitative research show how the two approaches to research *can* be very different, but recall also that the distinctions described thus far have been made for pedagogical reasons—to highlight the differences for you between the two perspectives. *Are* the two sides essentially from different planets? Although it is true there are still diehards who refuse to see any virtue in the other side,[8] it's much more common these days for researchers to pick and choose elements from either or both sides when they are useful for obtaining answers to the specific research questions that motivate them. And indeed, you should understand that there are no rigid dividing lines between the two—no rule says a researcher doing a more quantitative study cannot take an inductive approach, or that someone undertaking a more qualitative project cannot be motivated by a desire to answer theoretically specific research questions and collect aggregate data across numerous respondents—and that methodological mixtures involving aspects of both sides are for a variety of reasons becoming more and more commonplace.

Mixed or Multi-Method Approaches

Although Table 1.1 highlights some of the differences between qualitative and quantitative approaches, difference does not have to imply disagreement, inconsistency or incompatibility. In fact it is quite the opposite: notwithstanding superficial differences between the two approaches, they actually share a similar underlying logic and, when used together, can complement one another very well.

SIMILAR OBJECTIVES

The similarities between qualitative and quantitative approaches begins with their joint commitment to an **empirical** approach to the generation of knowledge, i.e., the idea that our understanding of the world should come not from philosophizing or speculation, but from data that comes from interacting with and observing the world we seek to understand. Similarly, researchers working within each approach seek to find answers to specific research questions that are founded upon systematic observation as opposed to speculation, innuendo,

or commonsense beliefs. Both approaches also value theory *and* data even though they differ in their preferences of which comes first. Both quantitative and qualitative researchers also seek to describe and understand the world, both for its own sake and because of a shared belief that while understanding how the social world operates will not in and of itself make the world a better place, at least it can help ensure that the moral and political debates we engage in about what policies and laws should be enacted to improve the social condition will be based on evidence and not on misinformation, stereotype, or blind dogma.

A SIMILAR UNDERLYING LOGIC

Both approaches also share a similar underlying logic about how arguments about the validity of a particular conclusion will be evaluated, which is that any explanation will be accepted to the extent that it is the best one available, where "best" is defined as the one that does a more complete job of explanation than any **rival plausible explanation**. The way rival plausible explanations are handled will differ within the different traditions—quantitative researchers are more likely to use either experimental or statistical techniques to rule out alternative explanations while qualitative researchers are more likely to go back and gather more data from the same or another context that will address the rival plausible explanation—but a "superior" explanation will be the one that explains the most, does so most simply, and that leaves the fewest or least serious rival plausible explanations (see Palys 1989) in its wake. Stated another way, no matter what methodological approach you employ, your job as a researcher is always to be your own best critic and to anticipate as much as possible what rival plausible explanations might be brought forth to critique your interpretation. If you don't, then certainly someone else will.

COMPLEMENTARY KNOWLEDGE AND UNDERSTANDINGS

We saw how researchers working within a quantitative paradigm tend to emphasize the search for very general descriptions of human behaviour in the hope of unearthing general laws while those working within a qualitative paradigm are more interested in understanding specific cases and how general principles play out in specific contexts. This often leads them to pose different research questions and to look in different places for answers and explanations. But are they not opposite sides of the same coin? General laws are of limited use if they cannot shed light on specific contexts; and context-specific understandings are typically of limited interest unless they somehow exemplify broader principles of human behaviour. Each offers only a partial understanding of the world; any comprehensive understanding of a phenomenon will require us to be able to explain *all* the data that are relevant and not simply cherry-pick that subset of information that serves a smaller purpose.

While qualitative and quantitative data sometimes will point in opposite directions and need to be reconciled, as is often the case whenever multiple methods are employed, the two also often complement one another by shedding slightly different light on the phenomenon of interest in a manner that addresses rival plausible explanations and provides a more comprehensive understanding. For example, Ted was involved in some evaluation research with an urban police department years ago when computer terminals that would create mobile access data bases were first being installed in patrol cars (see Palys, Boyanowsky, & Dutton 1984). The main issues the research addressed included how officers were using the system, how they felt about it, and what differences it was making to them and the way they did their jobs.

The project involved a multi-method approach that crossed the qualitative–quantitative divide in many respects. For example, there were deductive aspects to the study insofar as the federal government and the company who developed the system both had questions they wanted to make sure were addressed, and the existing professional literature of the time raised further issues. But there were inductive elements to the study as well because Ted and his colleagues took the time to talk with

relevant individuals throughout the department and came up with other unanticipated observations that ended up being incorporated into the study as well.

The various data sources that were used ran the gamut from qualitative to quantitative. The four main sources of data were (a) structured observational data that were generated from spending many hours in patrol cars with officers to see how and when they used the system, and with what effect; (b) aggregate archival data that were generated automatically by the system that recorded the different ways that the system was being accessed; (c) semi-structured but largely open-ended interviews with various stakeholders in the department (dispatchers, administrators, patrol officers) who used and/or were affected in one way or another by implementation of the system in an effort to understand their perspectives; and (d) survey questionnaires that were administered to a cross-section of the department.

The various data sources complemented one another very well. For example, while the more quantitative survey data gave a good indication of the distribution of sentiments about the system in the department as a whole, the interview data allowed the team to probe the issues in more detail and find out why officers might have those various points of view. And while the observational data gave a good firsthand look at how officers were using the system and how it performed in a real workday, the archival data that were automatically generated by the system offered a way to compare the way officers used the system when a member of the research team was sitting there watching them as opposed to when they were on their own. This actually revealed there was one aspect of the system officers were not using when the researchers were around, which was a feature that allowed officers to send short texts to each other. However, the interviews gave an opportunity to ask officers about this discrepancy. They explained that patrol officers had been warned by their superiors to avoid "frivolous" use of the system in our presence, and that the email/text function was often used by the officers to send jokes and make comments that one would not want others to hear over the radio. As this shows, while each and every one of these data sets was important and useful on its own, each also had limitations to how completely it could inform us, and it is only because all these qualitative and quantitative data sets were incorporated into the project that we ended up with as comprehensive an understanding as we did. Rather than seeing quantitative and qualitative approaches as somehow in competition with each other, this study encourages us to see them instead as different parts of a broader more comprehensive understanding.

The Time is Right

Now that *Research Decisions* has reached its fifth edition, it has been interesting to look back on the 20-plus years that have passed since the first edition was published (see Palys 1992), and see the changes that have occurred in the research enterprise in that time. That first edition was the first research methods text to bring qualitative and quantitative methods together in one book, and to make the argument that the two sets of approaches actually had much to offer each other. Although there are still researchers in both camps who continue to do research with one hand tied behind their backs, more and more recognize the gains to be had by incorporating a broader spectrum of research methods, and many more are being educated—thanks to a new generation of texts that discuss both qualitative and quantitative approaches—in a way that leaves them at least conversant with the principles in which both sets of approaches are grounded.

We see three main shifts in the research enterprise over the last few decades that make the time right for this edition of *Research Decisions* to do more than simply cite the desirability of mixed or multi-method research and instead treat it as a fundamental theme of this book. These include: (a) a philosophical rapprochement that provides some resolution to what was hitherto a realist/constructionist impasse; (b) shifts in the overall funding and organization of the academy and the research enterprise that have encouraged the growing prevalence of multi-site and multi-disciplinary departments and research teams; and

(c) the many possibilities for data generation and analysis that have arisen through the digital revolution, and particularly since the rise of the Internet.[9]

A PHILOSOPHICAL RAPPROCHEMENT

Although critics of positivist approaches have been around for many years, during the 1960s and 1970s a significant shift occurred when positivists themselves began to express doubts about some of the most fundamental aspects of their approach. Manicas and Secord (1983), for example, cite *Psychology: A Study of a Science* (Koch 1959–63), a monumental six-volume work in which

> one eminent psychologist after another, after many years—or even a lifetime of research—admitted to strong doubts about where they had been and what had been achieved, and some suggested that our most basic assumptions about the nature of psychology as a science and a method had to be questioned. (399)

Not all positivists were so forthcoming, but the reflection and reconsideration were widespread enough that a "crisis of confidence" was acknowledged (see Elms 1975). A flurry of conferences, books, and articles tried to identify and address the perceived inadequacies (e.g., see Israel & Tajfel 1972; Palys 1978; Strickland, Aboud, & Gergen 1976).

One area of transition is with respect to the realist-constructionist dichotomy discussed earlier. Recall that direct realists believe there is an objective world that exists independent of our opinions of it that we can discover if we just cut away as much interpretive clutter as possible. According to this view, constructionism is no more than the sign of an immature research enterprise that has not yet found the "right" definitions upon which everyone can agree. Constructionists, in contrast, argue that knowledge is best understood as a human product that cannot be divorced from our perceptions and experience. According to this view, realism is based on nothing more than an acceptance of the status quo and the imposition of a false consensus that is nothing more than a power play (see Palys 1990 on these points).

A philosophical position that appreciates the kernel of truth residing in both positions is **fallibilist realism** or **critical realism** (e.g., see Cook & Campbell 1979; Manicas & Secord 1983). This perspective acknowledges that we cannot deal with reality directly, but only through our constructions of it. Yet the task of science is to construct theories that aim to represent the world. In doing so, certainly it is true, as the constructionists argue, that there are different ways we can describe the world that are all equally "correct"—for example, surely it is equally "correct" to say "humans are social organisms" or "humans are biological organisms" or "humans are economic organisms"—and which metaphor(s) we pursue will have implications for what kinds of research questions we pose, the theories we develop, and the actions that arise from the understandings we generate (e.g., what kinds of policies or laws or other interventions we implement). But not *all* explanations are equally correct. We also have to acknowledge there are statements we can make about humans that are clearly and demonstrably "wrong"—for example, surely it would be "wrong" to say that "humans are asexual" or "adult humans do not care for their young." But if it's possible for us to be wrong, then there must be something that we can be wrong about, i.e., there must be a reality that exists independent of our analysis of it (see Bhaskar 1986).

Stated another way, although our constructions *are* social and historical products (i.e., knowledge at any given time is "produced" by a community of scientists and flavoured by its historical context), it is *not* the case that "anything goes." We should indeed be able to develop rational criteria by which the adequacy, or at least the utility, of our formulations can be judged. And it is a reasonable endeavour to collect evidence through empirical inquiry; we need only remind ourselves that while "facts" may exist, their meaning and relative importance are negotiable. This is not particularly threatening if one views science as a dynamic rather than a static entity, that is, as an ongoing process, rather than an existing pile onto which more knowledge is heaped.

But to the extent that the future development of knowledge is at least to some extent dependent on who it is that is producing it, then our primary concern turns to who it is that is engaged in the production of knowledge. In that regard, we should feel encouraged by the unprecedented democratization the academy has experienced in the last few decades, which ensures that any debates about the directions that knowledge takes and the interpretations that are made are occurring with as broad a range of voices as possible.

With growing diversity in terms of *who* was doing research, the **consensus model** (which positivist approaches pretty much take as a starting point) that had dominated the social sciences suddenly came in for intense scrutiny. Women, Blacks, homosexuals, Aboriginal peoples, and Third World academics did not see their experience being addressed or their worldviews considered in what passed for "scientific understanding." Allegedly "neutral" and "objective" science was now seen to be anything but. "Social facts" might indeed be "facts," but only in relation to a particular frame of reference. "Knowledge" came to be seen as constrained by the perspective of the research that had generated it. The constructed nature of science and knowledge became obvious when many new participants made clear that they would construct truth another way. Reality became negotiable, and those who gathered under the "constructionist" banner were very often those who entered the academy during its period of diversification and democratization, who shared the political interest of seeing things done differently than they had been (see Hacking 1999) and were ready and able to contribute to that realization.

CHANGES IN THE ACADEMY AND THE RESEARCH ENTERPRISE

There have been changes within the academy itself that have facilitated the growth in interest in mixed and multi-methods research. Perhaps the most significant change we have witnessed within the over the past 20–30 years has been the growth of interdisciplinary fields of teaching and research and the accompanying creation of inter-disciplinary departments such as criminology, epidemiology, public health, and sexology. Alongside the emergence of fields that have been founded upon a conscious effort to bring together people from a variety of disciplinary backgrounds it is also increasingly common to see previously distinct disciplines such as sociology and anthropology, or demography, population, and public health merging into single departments in order to adapt to changes within the academic landscape.

The academy has changed in other ways that have had implications for the kinds of research that is done. As a matter of policy, university researchers have **academic freedom**, which means they can investigate whatever they want, whenever they want, however they want, as long as they don't violate the ethical standards of their discipline. But such an idyllic statement ignores many realities of doing research: any kind of research requires funds for phones, computer hardware and software, photocopying, and possibly assistants, not to mention funds for attending conferences to share and discuss results. There are also reward structures within all universities: certain capabilities—the ability to acquire grants or contracts, to provide a resource base that allows graduate students to do thesis-related research, and to show that one's work has acquired a national or international reputation—are vital for anyone hoping to get tenure, a promotion, and salary increases. Because of this pressure to perform, many researchers feel an associated pressure to frame their work in ways that fit available funding guidelines. Thus research is influenced in the sense that it often goes where the money is.

Universities themselves are subject to many of the same pressures, particularly in contemporary Canada, where fiscal concerns provided federal and provincial governments with the justification for huge cutbacks in educational and research funding. Accompanying this was an exhortation to universities and university researchers to make up for the evaporating pool of funding by seeking "partnerships" with the private sector. More recently

Canada's granting agencies have made a similar push for partnerships with the public sector—agencies, communities, and community groups. The mere existence of such relationships is not itself a problem—there are many people in every university whose curiosity and interests match those in the corporate and public sectors. The problem is how attendant decreases in funding alternatives may constrain those whose research interests lie elsewhere and how the centralization of authority this more managed funding process has created has undermined academic freedom. In the long run, a diversified strategy that includes tolerance for and appreciation of academe's curiosity-guided (and often esoteric) pursuit of knowledge will bring greater rewards than a myopic strategy in which business or any other specific interest attempts to re-create the universities in its own image. (e.g., Palys 1988; Tudiver 1999)

The story is not all one of misgivings and caution, however. The push to provide more funding for community-based research in both the public and private sectors also has created many new opportunities. Particularly noteworthy is the growth in research that involves multi-disciplinary teams of individuals, often in different universities and even in different countries, coming together to investigate collectively some phenomenon of interest. Although her writing is more focused on *trans*disciplinary approaches,[10] Leavy (2011) is among those who see the trend to more inter/multi/transdisciplinary collaborations as a shift with profound and positive implications. For example,

> The deep sharing of information and research tools across disciplinary borders and the development of new conceptual frameworks have been important and fruitful with respect to moving the scientific community forward in three major ways.
>
> First, it has freed researchers from the limits of working with their disciplinary tools alone. This has fostered an enormous expansion of social research. Second, the ability to use additional tools and resources has allowed research

questions to be asked from more diverse perspectives. Third, and perhaps most significantly, the transdisciplinarity of research methods has caused an erosion of the basis upon which disciplinary borders have historically been formed and maintained.[11] This has prompted a series of re-evaluations of research tools as well as scientific criteria for evaluating research. Concurrently, as borders shift, new research collaborations have led to the asking of new research questions and the creation of new, hybrid research tools, designed to address those questions. (14)

A recent project that Chris was involved in exemplifies this trend. His particular research interest has been in the prostitution area, where he has been especially interested in prostitute's clients, about whom very little was known until he began his research a dozen years ago. While his earlier research was done on his own or with collaborators within his home department, his more recent research projects involve multi-disciplinary groups of researchers interested in issues of physical and sexual health, violence and victimization, consumer and labour policy, and legal and social regulation as they relate to people involved in and around Canada's sex industry. In Chris's case the groups he works with include him from sociology/criminology as well as a variety of health care professionals including physicians, nurses, epidemiologists, addictions researchers, community outreach and service organizations, population and public health researchers, and anthropologists. Their methodological expertise includes everything from qualitative methods such as ethnography and interviewing through more quantitative methods such as surveys and computer modelling. The many publications different subsets of researchers have produced have appeared in a wide variety of social science and medical journals.

Although highly successful, the group's experiences have not been without difficulty, much as one would expect when one brings together collections of individuals who come from different scholarly and agency cultures. Nonetheless, just as individual researchers need to ensure they have enough

familiarity with a broad array of techniques so that they can understand the full range of literature in their area even if they do not themselves employ the whole range of methods, so, too, do researchers on multi-disciplinary teams need to be familiar enough with a range of methods to be able to converse with others in team projects. This is a theme we will revisit often in this edition of *Research Decisions*, in order to help readers rise to that challenge.

IMPACTS OF THE DIGITAL REVOLUTION
A third development over the last few decades that continues to have a growing impact on the research enterprise is the monumental shift that has come with the development and proliferation of **digital technologies**. To begin with, although readers of this book are most likely to be students who grew up with the Internet, we remind you it is actually an incredibly recent development (starting in the mid-1990s) that has in and of itself made the shifts to more team-based collaborative research projects possible. How did teams of researchers ever communicate with each other before email and smartphones? How were epidemiologists able to access the databases they need to understand the incidence and proliferation of disease? Quantitative data analysis programs such as *SPSS* have been around for many years and even pre-date the personal computer (which was developed in the 1980s), but how did researchers interested in more qualitative data analyze the fruits of their research prior to the more recent development of programs such as *NVivo*? What did both qualitative and quantitative researchers do for data before the Internet made it possible to see videos on any topic you can think of on *YouTube*, and the archiving of digital data bases made everything from Statistics Canada databases; to police, health, education, and other institutional records; to transcriptions of interviews in secondary databases available? There is so much information available now on the Internet on any topic imaginable that the problem is no longer finding data to look at in relation to any given phenomenon, it's in managing all the information that can be brought to your monitor at the speed of light.

This is not to say that no one ever did team-based research before the Internet, or that qualitative researchers had nothing better to do than look at their reams of data and look mystified before *NVivo* came along, but clearly the Internet and ongoing hardware and software developments in the digital realm make many things *easy* to do that once required a very motivated individual or group of individuals to accomplish in addition to creating alternatives that never existed before. We began talking about these developments and their implications for research in the previous edition of *Research Decisions* and include them throughout this new edition because they are now integral to how one does research in the early 21st century and need to be learned as such.

SUMMING UP AND LOOKING AHEAD

This chapter introduces the qualitative–quantitative dichotomy that underlies this book, as well as the multi-method approaches that are becoming more and more prevalent among social and health researchers working individually and in teams. If you haven't taken a course in research methods before, you might feel slightly overwhelmed by now. But fear not; these themes will crop up on several occasions in the rest of the book, giving you lots of chances to review and understand them.

The chapter describes how quantitative researchers embraced a perspective known as positivism. This perspective borrowed from the natural sciences a direct realist epistemology or way of knowing, and posited that human beings could and should be scrutinized in the manner of any living organism because they are subject to and shaped by the same laws of nature. This viewpoint prefers observable variables—concrete expressions of variables that meet predefined standards of reliability and validity—and eschews unobservables like thoughts and perceptions. Those that adopt a strict interpretation of the quantitative tradition frequently favour social facts—mega-variables whose monolithic impact is felt by all of us—as independent variables, measuring their effects through rate data, where aggregate tendencies are believed to give true indications of social effects unaffected by the idiosyncrasies of any single case. Emphasis is placed on being aloof and dispassionate in the interests of "objective" analysis. The hypothetico-deductive method is the foundation of this tradition: researchers specify a theory, deduce a hypothesis, and then gather data to test the hypothesis and, hence, also the theory. The trick, says the positivist, is to be inventive in our theorizing, to look for general principles or laws that guide and shape human action. "Good" theory is thought to be simple, to be capable of being expressed in precise mathematical form, and to accurately reflect the relationship between causes and outcomes.

Those adopting a purist variant of the qualitative approach to research, in contrast, argued that people's perceptions not only should not be avoided, they should be the *focus* of analysis: "Perceptions are real because they are real in their consequences" (Thomas 1928). We must understand those perceptions if we want to understand human behaviour: what people *think* about the world influences how they *act* in it. Acknowledging that people *construct* reality implies that there are actually many "realities" and possible realities that exist, and that we negotiate on an ongoing basis. "Understanding" or *verstehen* involves being able to explain unique behaviour in context, after investigating the ways in which reality is constructed and negotiated. One must get close to the people one studies in order to understand them. "Good" theory is not imposed; rather, it emerges from direct observation and contact with people in context.

Science is changing, as it has been doing for hundreds, if not thousands, of years, and so are its products (knowledge and "truths"). Researchers from what once were opposing sides now are more likely to see common ground and the benefits of incorporating a multi-method and multi-perspectival strategy. Such research also has benefited by developments in digital technologies that facilitate data gathering and analysis involving a wide array of sources, and allowed members of research teams to communicate more easily in order to exchange views, monitor their collective progress, and write up the results of their research. As science slowly democratizes, with progressively greater representation from women, members of the LGBTQIA (lesbian, gay, bisexual, transgender, questioning, intersex, and asexual) community, Aboriginal peoples, Third World academics, and others, new voices are heard, and the effects of arguing with data, in a public forum, become evident.

STUDY QUESTIONS

1. Morgan (1983) uses the concept of *engagement* to describe what we do in research. What does he mean by that term, and what implications does it hold for the way we conceive of knowledge?

2. Consider the dimensions of difference between the quantitative and qualitative approaches shown in Table 1.1; explain in your own words what each dimension entails.

3. Outline the differences between realism and constructionism as ways of perceiving the world. Give an example of how a person's perspective on this issue might be evident in research. How does critical realism (also known as fallibilist realism) offer a rapprochement to the conflict between those two perspectives?

4. Outline some differences you see between positivism and phenomenologism.

5. Why have qualitative researchers preferred field-based case-study research? Explain how this approach fits into qualitative perspectives.

6. What are "social facts," and what role do they play in positivist inquiry?

7. Compare and contrast the approaches that might be taken by a realist and a constructionist if each set out to study the effects associated with being a child of divorce.

8. Table 1.1 outlines some of the differences between quantitative and qualitative approaches. But what are some of their similarities?

9. Explain how Palys et al.'s (1984) study of an urban police department's patrol car computer terminals showed that the quantitative–qualitative divide shown in Table 1.1 is not a rigid one. In what way(s) was the multi-method approach in that study helpful in addressing the research questions in a way that no single method could provide?

10. What changes in the research enterprise have contributed to interest in and the ability to do multi-method, multi-disciplinary, multi-perspectival research?

NOTES

1. Realist perspectives are commonly distinguished from constructionist or constructivist perspectives, which will be discussed later in this chapter in relation to more qualitative approaches.

2. The term "go native" has a longer history, having originally appeared in anthropology, where it referred to the way anthropologists who study indigenous peoples sometimes—after extensive contact with those peoples—leave their "more appropriate" scientific values behind and take on the perspective of those they're studying. This term's implicit **othering** of indigenous peoples is considered offensive by many, so we use "overidentify" to communicate the same idea.

3. Readers in sociology will no doubt recognize these variables as some of the favourites of sociologists, particularly demographers, namely, variables like race, class, education, and income.

4. Although the article cited here is dated 1970, this is misleading as Schutz was writing his seminal tracts on phenomenology in the 1930s. He was originally from Austria and was writing in German. Translations of his earlier works did not appear in English until the 1960s and 1970s.

5. The origins of the story are unclear. What appears here is our rendition of it.

6. We say "best reflected" here because even realists acknowledge that crime rate data imperfectly represent the amount of crime that exists. For realists, though, such data's imperfections are primarily a technical challenge. To create "better" data, realists maintain, we need only enhance the reliability and validity of data collection procedures, as well as find some way of better estimating that "dark figure" of crime (i.e., how much crime goes unreported and hence never shows up in criminal justice statistics). In contrast, those with a more constructionist bent question the very notions of "crime" and "criminality," arguing that the issue is less *how* to count than *what* is being counted. See Brantingham (1991), Brantingham and Brantingham (1984), Lowman and Palys (1991), and Chapter 8 of this text for further consideration of these issues.

7. The deletions here represent citations to numerous articles and books that report research in the respective areas noted. Because these citations are secondary to our point and make the quote harder to read, we've edited them out. Readers are invited to pursue the original source for references in areas that interest them.

8. An example, of this antipathy can be seen in the exchange between Bonta and Gendreau (1990) and Roberts and Jackson (1991), in which the two sets of authors debate the effects of imprisonment. Although ostensibly a debate about the effects of prison on prisoners, it is clear the authors have very different views about what kinds of data count as "evidence" for the debate. For Bonta & Gendreau, the only data that "count" are physiological measures and scores on standardized tests with demonstrated psychometric properties; for Roberts and Jackson, the only data that "count" are interview and other more qualitative data that get at the *meaning* of the experience for those who are imprisoned. This debate was discussed at length in previous editions of this book (e.g., Palys & Atchison 2008), but has been omitted here because we are more interested in emphasizing areas of convergence between qualitative and quantitative approaches rather than their disjunction.

9. The fact that the Internet did not yet exist when the first edition of *Research Decisions* was published is itself a reminder of how quickly the technological infrastructure of the research enterprise has changed.

10. Leavy (2011) makes a distinction between disciplinary, multi-disciplinary, interdisciplinary, and trans-disciplinary approaches. She defines transdisciplinary research practices as "… issue- or problem-centered approaches to research that prioritize the problem at the center of research over discipline-specific concerns, theories or methods. Transdisciplinary research is responsive to (public) needs." (14)

11. It should be noted that we do not share Leavy's positive view of the demise of discipline-based approaches. Although multi-disciplinary connection and collaboration is for us very desirable, the other benefits of which Leavy speaks—the expansion of methodological approaches and greater diversity of perspective— is for us in part generated by maintaining disciplinary diversity. To the extent it erases disciplines, transdisciplinarity can simply create a new homogeneity. Our best exemplar of this is criminology, which, in our view, was at its healthiest and most exciting when it was a sort of multi-disciplinary discipline with ideas from sociology, psychology, law, history, urban planning, and others all stirring the pot. Now that criminology has been around for some 30 years, it has developed its own disciplinary orthodoxy that leaves it a shadow of its former self.

GETTING STARTED

The fact that you're reading this book suggests that you have some interest in the social or health sciences. You may even have articulated more specific interests for yourself, for example, studying juvenile delinquency, organizational dynamics, the socialization process, or sexual health. Still, that's only the beginning. Doing research involves translating those general interests into specific researchable questions and then designing concrete research procedures that address those questions. Indeed, one of the first truisms you learn about research is that it is not an activity you can do in the abstract—"doing research" ultimately involves gathering very specific information from specific samples of people or files or other objects in particular places at a particular time.

In the current chapter, we will take you through some of the first steps in that process, in which we (a) outline some ways research ideas arise, (b) consider how the different research objectives you might have will influence your research design, (c) discuss the importance of connecting with the literature, and (d) give a first glimpse at some of the options you have for operationalizing concepts that are of interest to you.

SOURCES OF RESEARCH IDEAS

Two Approaches to Theory

In logic, a distinction has traditionally been made between two different processes of reasoning: **deductive** and inductive processes. *Deductive* logic involves reasoning from the general to the particular; that is, one begins with broad theoretical generalizations and tests their ability to deal with specific instances of phenomena. The hypothetico-deductive method that reflects this logic involves (1) developing theories about a phenomenon; (2) expressing hypotheses (predictions) based on these theories; (3) creating or observing instances of the phenomenon to see whether things happen as the theory predicts they should; and then (4) looking for new situations in which to test or expand the theory if it succeeds, or revising the theory or even abandoning it entirely if its predictions are not supported (e.g., Shank 2008). As you know from Chapter 1, this deductive model of science has been preferred by many people who engage in quantitative research who often go so far as to call it "the" scientific method.

In contrast, *inductive* reasoning begins with specifics and uses these to generate general principles. You *start* by observing, in other words, and then move from observation to theory rather than the other way around. This tends to be the approach of choice for many people who undertake qualitative research, who believe that theory should not be imposed from above but, rather, should emerge from or be grounded in the context of everyday life (e.g., see Fox 2008; Strauss & Corbin 1997).

Although at one time there was scathing debate between practitioners of the respective approaches (e.g., see McKinlay & Potter 1987) as to which was "right" or truly worthy of the title "science," more recently there has been recognition of their inherent complementarity. One of the first to make that point was Wallace (1971), who asserted that inductive and deductive approaches are not in either/or opposition, but rather are better seen as opposite sides of the same coin. **Wallace's wheel** (see Figure 2.1) shows an essentially circular (or iterative), and hence

Figure 2.1
Wallace's "Wheel of Science"

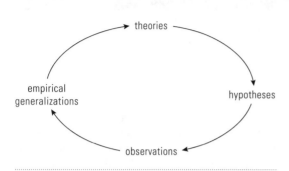

W. Wallace (1971), *The Logic of Science in Sociology* (Hawthorne, N. Y.: Alldine Atherton). Transaction Publishers Inc.

infinite, process that encompasses *both* deductive *and* inductive methods.

Wallace's (1971) "wheel of science" offers an important representation of the scientific process. On the one hand, it acknowledges the different leanings of individual researchers. Deductive researchers emphasize how one should start at the top of that drawing, with theory, while inductive researchers emphasize how one should start at the bottom of the wheel, with observation. On the other hand, it also shows their commonality: regardless whether they emphasize deduction or induction, all scientists are involved in an ongoing dialogue involving both *theory* and *data*, that is, processes that involve the formulation of abstract principles *and* the requirement that one's speculations and theories be subjected to some form of empirical test or validation.

The elegance of Wallace's wheel is that it shows very simply how the question "Which comes first?" is actually quite trivial. Can we ever start with "pure theory," completely devoid of any informal knowledge gained from our earlier observation and experience? Probably not. Can we ever start with "pure data," completely devoid of any prior theoretical organization related to our own naive or "commonsensical" beliefs (as human beings) about how the world works? Probably not. Deciding

where to "start counting" in an ongoing process is ultimately relatively arbitrary.

Deductive Sources of Research Ideas

Returning now to the question of where research ideas come from, the deductive–inductive distinction suggests a number of alternatives.

THEORY AS A SOURCE OF RESEARCH IDEAS

From the deductive orientation, we see the important role that theory can play in guiding and generating research. A theory is essentially a set of *concepts* and a delineation of their *interrelationships* that, taken together, purport to explain a phenomenon or set of phenomena. One function of theory is to help make sense of the world or of a particular class of phenomena. In doing so, theories also guide research, which makes them both powerful and constraining.

Perhaps an example will help here. Suppose we're interested in explaining why some people do not use condoms when they have sex with casual sex partners. An infinite number of variables could potentially "explain" failure to use a condom during casual sex—everything from not having one available, to individual religious beliefs, to lack of knowledge about the "risks" associated with not using condoms.

A theorist takes a particular subset of these variables and tries to offer a convincing explanation of why and how they combine to generate condom use or non-use. These speculations, made public, give theorists and others a research direction to pursue by offering propositions that can be tested. Advocates of the health belief theory (HBT) such as Rosenstock (1974), for example, theorize that health-related behaviours are the result of a decision-making process whereby people evaluate (1) the severity of risk associated with a particular behaviour; (2) the degree to which they believe they are susceptible to such risk; and (3) the benefits and barriers (practical and psychological) they expect to gain from acting in a particular way to avoid or reduce such risks. Researchers interested in explaining why some people choose not to use a condom during casual sexual encounters who are guided by the health belief model in their research thus seek information not only about the type and frequency of sexual activities people engage in, but also (1) the severity of risk they believe they are or would be exposed to if they did not use a condom; (2) the extent to which they believe their own behaviour choice—to use or not use a condom—creates or mitigates risk during casual sexual encounters; and (3) the benefits or other consequences they feel arise from their choices.

But theories have a downside as well insofar as they impose a virtual set of blinders on how you view the world. Because HBT focuses on individual cognitive processes as determinants of sexual safety behaviour, researchers employing this theory focused all their energies on measuring people's opinions and beliefs about their likelihood of risk and completely ignored such phenomena as cultural and social factors that might play a significant role in a person's ability to fully appreciate and understand the risks associated with their behaviour or to act in a particular way to avoid such risks in the first place. As a result of these noted shortcomings some health researchers have begun to look toward social ecology theory (Bronfenbrenner 1979) to help fill in the theoretical gaps in explaining health behaviour in general and condom use in particular. Social ecologists maintain that health behaviour such as condom use is influenced by a combination of personal factors (e.g., individual knowledge, attitudes, skills, and beliefs), one's relationships (e.g., a person's ties to family and friends), organizational factors (e.g., educational, occupational, religious, recreational organizational structures), community factors (e.g., belonging to and participation in organizational activities) and policy frameworks. As this suggests, an important dimension on which theories vary is in their prospective *comprehensiveness.*

In sum, "good" theories are useful devices because they help coordinate research by *providing a research focus* and by *implying hypotheses* that can

be tested empirically. Their weakness is that they may blind you to other variables or other perspectives that are beyond the scope of the theory.

APPLYING THEORY TO SITUATIONS

Many research ideas emerge from theory. If a theory states that some set of events *should* go together, you can test the theory by thinking of a specific situation in which the theory should be able to predict or account for what occurs. For example, a once-popular attitude theory known as dissonance theory (see Festinger 1957) suggested that people will feel differently about things after they have committed themselves to a course of action than before. Knox and Inkster (1968) decided to test that theoretical proposition at their local racetrack. They approached two groups of bettors—some who were in the line-up waiting to place their bets, and others who had just finished placing their bets—and asked them how confident they were their horse would win. Sure enough, those who were asked *after* they had placed their bet how confident they felt about their wager expressed significantly greater certainty about whether their horse would win than those who had not yet made it to the betting window, even though the difference between the two situations was less than a minute.

EXTENDING OR LIMITING A THEORY'S COVERAGE

Another procedure for generating research ideas is to try to *extend the coverage* of an existing theory. One person might have posited a theory that explains a certain social dynamic within business organizations. You'd be making a significant contribution by showing that the same theoretical principles also apply to family dynamics. Conversely, you'd also be making a contribution if you were to *point out limitations* to the applicability of existing theories. Theories of aggression, for example, have typically been developed to account for aggression toward minority groups and/or sources of frustration. But do these theories also account for violent behaviour toward intimates, such as child abuse by parents or wife assault by husbands?

OFFERING ALTERNATIVE EXPLANATIONS

Yet another source of research ideas involves trying to formulate *alternative explanations* for a given phenomenon. For example early criminological theories (e.g., Lombroso 1911) saw those who went through the justice system as "criminals" and tried to ascertain the ways in which "criminals" differed from the rest of us. But later theorists (e.g., Rubington & Weinberg 1968) demonstrated that many, if not most, of us have indulged in "criminal" behaviour at various points in our lives. This finding shifted the research focus of interest from identifying who the "criminals" in society are, which was based on the assumption that some people do criminal things while others do not, to the ways that society reacts to criminal activity and the process by which some persons or actions are labelled "criminal" while others are not.

D. G. Wagner (1984) refers to this process of theory development as *variation* and offers numerous other examples of theorists building on one another's work by offering competing explanatory mechanisms for similar phenomena. Also, note how one role of theory in science is to generate research possibilities; if a theory doesn't suggest research possibilities, it's not a very good theory. Perhaps even more importantly, in order to be considered "scientific," a theory must be capable of being disproved. If there are no data that can possibly lead us to say, "Oh, I guess we were wrong," then we are not talking about theory or science, but about faith, ideology, and dogma.

So theories are an integral starting point for the deductive approach to science. But what about inductive approaches? How might research ideas be derived using them? Inductivists place no less emphasis on theory than deductivists, but they disagree over whether theory should *guide* or *emerge from* the research process. Recall that, for deductivists, one *begins* with theory, and then "good" theory suggests or implies what to research. In contrast, inductivists argue that such theory is unlikely to be profound and may represent little more than a premature imposition of theoretical blinders that says more about the theoretician than about the

phenomenon under consideration. They suggest that ideas and theories should emerge from interacting with and observing the phenomenon itself. Listed below are some ways in which this might occur.

INDUCTIVE SOURCES OF RESEARCH IDEAS

Starting from Where You Are

From within qualitative perspectives, the inductive (grounded) approach to data gathering and theorizing is encouraged, and "intimate knowledge" of the phenomenon under consideration is not considered a sin. Accordingly, while some individuals engaged in quantitative research might be worried if you are "too close" to a phenomenon of interest because of the propensity to "over-identify" and the concern that you might be unable to remain "appropriately" detached and analytical, many researchers working within a qualitative framework recognize that those who have undergone particular life experiences may bring special insights to their research because of having experienced a phenomenon from the "inside" (e.g., Faulkner & Becker 2008).

Consistent with this view, Lofland et al. (2006) suggest that one way to begin research is to "start from where you are"; that is, to begin with your own life situation and the concerns and issues that arise therefrom. Dozens of examples could be cited of researchers who did exactly that:

> For example, Gary Alan Fine's *Gifted Tongues* (2001), a study of high school debate and adolescent culture, was connected to his son Todd's distinguished career as a high school debater. In a similar vein, John Irwin's interest in *The Felon* (1970), in *Prisons in Turmoil* (1980), and in *The Jail* (1985) was intimately related to his own felony conviction at the age of 21 and the five years he spent in a California state prison. And Mary Romero's study of domestic workers

(*Maid in the U.S.A.* 1992) may be said to have had its origins in the fact that as a teenager she had worked as a domestic, as had her mother, sister, relatives, and neighbors. (10)

Starting from where you are has several advantages. You bring: (1) an interest in the research topic, because of its meaningfulness to you, that will help sustain you through the persistence of effort required to actually complete a piece of research; (2) insights into those aspects of the phenomenon with which you are familiar that, ideally, will allow you to ask "good questions" in a manner that is meaningful to the participants; and probably (3) knowledge of at least some others who are in the same position as you, which may help provide access to needed research sites and to an initial sample of people you can approach regarding their experiences.

At the same time, there are also potential potholes in this road that need to be avoided. The first is that, as an insider, you come with baggage—beliefs about "how things work," or "what the problems are," that you will have to get past to ensure that people who do not think like you are included and feel free to express their views. Associated with this is the idea that you have to be open-minded about what you will find and ensure this is not just pseudo-research whose answer is a foregone conclusion because you only look at things and talk to those who will confirm your point of view. Less malevolent, but equally problematic, is that you and your participants' familiarity with the situation may make you less likely to ask questions about things that "everyone knows" to be true, which may or may not be the case: what you believe "everyone knows" may not in fact be shared by "everyone," and it is often the case that what "everyone knows" to be true isn't.

Starting from where you are also can be problematic because of role conflicts that can emerge from making part of your life a research site. Suppose you're employed as a nurse, for example, and want to do a study regarding doctor–nurse relationships. Information derived from interviews with doctors and nurses in the ward where you work might be problematic when and if your role as a researcher creates role conflicts in relation to your duties as a nurse. For example, as a researcher you are normally expected to keep the source of everything you hear confidential; as a nurse, there may be reporting requirements associated with your role in which you are supposed to report certain categories of behaviour to your union, hospital officials, or supervisor. Even if you *are* able to compartmentalize your role for the duration of the study—something you are ethically obliged to do to ensure your primary interests are those of the research participants—once the study is completed, you go back to your former role. But you now have information you might not otherwise have obtained about certain people, information you can't simply "forget."

A third potential problem arises when you are so embedded in a situation that you are unable to rise above it. The trick in starting from where you are is to use the insights to be gained from your own experience, but then to activate the "sociological imagination" (as C. W. Mills [1959] termed it) and be able to see yourself as one instance of many, thereby helping to contextualize your own experience. This is sometimes easier said than done: as Marshall McLuhan is reputed to have said, "The last person to ask how the water is is a fish" (see Hagan 1989: 157). It's sometimes very difficult to see what's "interesting" about our lives, in the social science sense, when we are too wrapped up in experiencing them.

OBSERVATION AS A SOURCE OF IDEAS

As one might expect, research ideas within the inductive framework emerge through observation coupled with the natural curiosity of the social scientist who inevitably asks Why? or How? You might begin with a particular phenomenon that interests you (e.g., unemployment, criminality, depression, the availability of organic food, people buying membership in fitness centres, the surge of interest in "designer" dogs) and then try to suggest and test out factors that might influence it. Where does it come from? Who does it? Is there more of it in the summer than the winter? Are the patterns the same or different in Canada and Australia?

It was observation of this sort coupled with asking Why? that led Emile Durkheim to formulate his classic work (1951) on suicide. He began by observing that countries differ in their predominant religious affiliation, and that they also tend to differ in their suicide rates. This observed covariation ultimately led him to formulate his ideas that suicide is affected by both social regulation (norms) and social integration and group solidarity.

Although more modest in aspiration, the first piece of formal research Ted ever conducted was generated via a similar process. He was walking down a street and saw a movie marquee advertising a somewhat racy (for the time) Swedish movie entitled *I Am Curious (Yellow).* But instead of the usual notations one sees on marquees, in which some obscure critic is quoted as saying that the film is "one of the year's ten best," this marquee said only that the movie had been "banned in Alberta." It made Ted wonder about movie classification and censorship, particularly whether the mere act of banning a movie or classifying it might (ironically) *enhance* interest. Thanks to an encouraging professor, Bob Altemeyer, the result was a field experiment (Palys 1971) in which he advertised a movie called *Prostitution in Denmark* in almost exactly the same way to various groups of people. Each group was given the same general description of the film. The only difference between the groups came near the end of the advertisement, when some of them were told that the film had been rated "G" (General, i.e., persons of any age admitted) by the Provincial Film Classification Board, but told others that it had been rated "Adult" (i.e., one must be an adult or accompanied by one) or "Restricted Adult" (i.e., only those over 18 admitted).[1]

Intensive Case Studies and Experience Surveys

Systematic observation in the context of *intensive case studies* is another useful source of research ideas, still within the inductive framework. Many of Jean Piaget's theories on child development emerged from observing his own children, for example, while many of Sigmund Freud's came from his discussions with clients. Similarly, if you're new to an area of research, an *oral history* or broader *experience survey* may suggest research ideas. If you want to study prejudice and discrimination toward minority groups, for example, you could talk to a Japanese person who lived in the internment camps in British Columbia or California during World War II, a Jew who lived in Germany at the same time, to Muslim women in North America who choose to wear the hijab, or a Maori in New Zealand. Be careful, though, not to let this process steer you away from a review of the relevant literature. Also don't assume that the first person you talk to is necessarily representative of his or her group. When doing this sort of exploratory research, talk to and observe as diverse an array of people and situations as possible.

RESEARCH ITSELF AS A HEURISTIC PROCESS

Other Research as a Source of Ideas

A third general category of sources of research ideas is the actual process of doing and reading about research. Researchers often conclude their papers with *suggestions for further research.* Why not take them up on it?

REPLICATION
Replication of prior research also can serve a useful function. Although most professional journals aren't interested in publishing a straight replication for its own sake, situations may arise where the replication provides interesting information. For example, many older studies that looked at sex differences might be interesting to replicate now that the sex roles in our society have supposedly undergone a major transition over the last few decades. Similarly, American or European studies might be replicated by a Canadian if one had reason to posit that a comparison with the Canadian social context might yield different results.

WHEN TECHNOLOGIES OPEN NEW DOORS

A special occasion arises when new technologies open doors that previously were closed and thereby provide new opportunities for replicating earlier research with newly accessible samples, or moving into areas that were previously inaccessible. There is a wealth of research that was conducted during the mid to late 20th century that needs to be replicated. This research involves looking at the impact of new technologies on social- and health-related phenomena and developing a better understanding about how network and computer technologies have affected the kinds of data available to address our research questions.

Similarly, the Internet and the wide array of computer technologies that surround it have brought together communities of persons, particularly through blogs, podcasts, instant messaging, and social network and media spaces, who otherwise would be very difficult to locate in any significant numbers. Chris does research involving the sex trade, for example; in this field much research has been done on sex trade workers, but very little had been done regarding their clients because of difficulties in locating and contacting them. With the opportunities afforded by the Internet, however (e.g., Atchison 1999; see also Chapter 6), Chris ended up conducting one of the first large-scale studies of sex worker clients when more than 500 clients responded to his solicitations to participate in an anonymous Internet-based survey of persons who had paid for sex (see Atchison 1998; Atchison, Lowman, & Fraser 1998). As new technology develops and becomes more integrated into our daily lives there is no end to the new research possibilities that will arise for members of the social science community to pursue.

CHALLENGING PRIOR RESEARCH

One might also generate new research by *challenging prior research*. For example, earlier research into the day-to-day lives of sex workers found that a very high percentage of women who prostitute had experienced violence on the job. Tamara O'Doherty (see 2011a, b) did not doubt that result, but wondered whether that finding was true throughout the sex trades. She soon had the opportunity to interview a small sample of women who worked in off-street venues such as massage parlours and escort agencies and found that violence in off-street venues was actually quite rare. This suggested that violence is not something that is integral to the trade, but that varies depending on other ecological and situational factors, which she proceeded to investigate in subsequent research.

CLARIFYING UNDERLYING PROCESSES

The idea of "clarifying underlying processes" arises because many treatments or therapies actually comprise multiple interventions. Given an overall finding that a certain treatment or intervention is effective, a useful next step would be to determine *which* aspects of the package of interventions actually produced the observed effect. One researcher might find, for example, that a particular group-therapy program led to some positive social outcome for the participants. But what *specifically* about the program led to that success? Was it the individualized attention? The opportunity to practise new skills? A change in self-concept? The presence of social support? An overall finding that a new therapy is effective can be followed by research that attempts to analyze the processes involved in an ongoing process of program development.

Other Sources of Research Ideas

RESOLVING CONFLICTING RESULTS

Occasionally the literature contains conflicting results, and you may want to do research that attempts to *resolve the conflict*. For example, the business literature that deals with the effects of job enrichment showed mixed results from study to study; sometimes job enrichment would lead to more positive job satisfaction, while other times job enrichment would either have no effect, or sometimes even have a negative effect on job satisfaction. Malka and Chatman (2003) and Saari and Judge (2004) are among those who tried to account for these conflicting results by focusing on the needs and interests of the employees whose jobs were being enriched. They found it useful to distinguish between employees for whom the job or career itself is intrinsically satisfying versus those for whom the job is more instrumental for achieving satisfaction in other domains of life they value more highly. Employees who looked to the job itself as a source of satisfaction became more satisfied with their jobs the more enriched the job became—greater responsibility, more autonomy, and so forth—while increasing extrinsic rewards such as income on its own tended to have little or no effect on their job satisfaction. The proto-type here would be the workaholic, i.e., someone who loves what they do and is happy to do more because of the satisfaction it affords. In contrast, employees for whom jobs were instrumental to satisfaction in other domains responded positively to extrinsic rewards such as more income, while showing reduced job satisfaction in response to job enrichment. If a job is important only because it provides a source of income that allows doing the things that are really important to someone—spending time with family and friends, travelling, or acquiring material possessions of one sort or another—then greater responsibility only gets in the way, while greater income is the key to their heart.

ANALOGY

Research also may be generated on the basis of *analogy* to other domains. William McGuire (1973), for example, took the immunization model from biology and tried to apply it to the realm of attitude change. In biology, organisms are immun-ized against various diseases by giving them vaccines that actually contain weak strains of the disease. When McGuire tested out this same logic in the attitude area, he found similarly that people who were first "immunized" by hearing samples of argu-ments that might be used against their own posi-tion were much less likely to change their attitudes than were those who had not been "immunized" when both were exposed to arguments in oppos-ition to their own opinion.

SURPRISES: ANOMALY AND SERENDIPITY

The terms **anomaly** and **serendipity** refer to research that begins or is redirected because an unexpected and surprising state of affairs arises. Anomalies are situations that should *not* exist according to the theory that's guiding the research. An anomaly is "a fact that doesn't fit" and hence requires explanation for the deviation.

Kuhn (1970) argues that anomaly is a signifi-cant contributor to scientific discovery, although a state of affairs must first be *recognized* as an anomaly before the real process of discovery begins. He provides several examples of anomaly in the nat-ural sciences, but also notes a number of instances where the same state of affairs clearly existed prior to someone's "discovery" of the anomaly. Yet the anomalous situation had been ignored, rationalized away, or otherwise not appreciated by the earlier researchers.

Similar to anomaly is serendipity. While anomaly refers to unearthing disconfirming evidence in the process of an ongoing inquiry, serendipity refers to unexpected findings that are virtually stumbled upon while looking for something else (e.g., the prospector who digs for gold and strikes oil). Once again, Kuhn (1970) notes that recognition of the event precedes "discovery" and that the history of science is replete with examples of individuals who ignored outcomes or considered them a mistake instead of taking the inferential leap required for discovery. The theme is reaffirmed in Barber and Fox's (1958) "case of the floppy-eared rabbits," where the authors compare two researchers who witnessed the same serendipitous phenomenon: one realizes the event's significance, while the other does not.

In sum, new research directions occasionally emerge in the process of doing research when puz-zling anomalies and surprising outcomes occur. It helps to be in the right place when they occur and to be open enough to recognize their significance. A comprehensive understanding of the relevant literature makes both more likely. But there are still other sources of research ideas as well.

THE SUPPLIED PROBLEM

Many studies come about because someone *gives* you a problem. Such is particularly the case in applied settings, where myriad questions require systematic, empirical answers: Is our program effective? How can we better meet our objectives? What will happen if we change our intake criteria? How can we decide who has the best chance to benefit from our program?

For example, the two of us were recently approached by a corporation that publishes magazines in the health and fitness area and was interested in gaining a better understanding of the production, marketing, and consumption of health food products—anything "organic" or "green" and including assorted vitamins and supplements. They envisioned doing a series of studies with health food producers, retail store owners and consumers and asked us to design, implement, and analyze the Web-based survey that retailers from across the country who distributed their magazines would be asked to complete, as well as to advise them on the interview research their employees would be doing with retailers and manufacturers. We agreed to do so in large part because of our interest in how digital technologies can be incorporated into research processes moreso than in their marketing objectives per se. It was actually an interesting example of two different groups—the corporation and us—coming in with different focal interests, but with sufficient common ground that the process and product benefitted both groups. We were fortunate in that respect as finding common ground with the "supplied problem" can sometimes be more difficult to find, as we will discuss in Chapter 10 when we talk about evaluation research.

CULTURAL FOLKLORE, THE COMMON WISDOM, AND "COMMON SENSE"

Much of what we feel we "know" is based on traditional, speculative, or polemical belief that has never been verified empirically. A valuable role of research is to help refute or confirm our beliefs, assuming we believe that truth is a priority and that important social decisions should be based on evidence rather than on speculation or stereotyping.

Immigration policies, for example, have often been the subject of heated debate. Some politicians have even pointed to isolated examples of immigrants getting in trouble, and wondered aloud whether Canada can really "afford" as many immigrants as it takes, given all the social costs and problems allegedly associated with them (e.g., see M. Campbell 1994: A1). A Statistics Canada study entitled *Canada's Changing Immigrant Population* examined census data, addressed that very issue, and concluded that such fears were unfounded:

> Amid widespread fears that Canada's immigration system lets in criminals and layabouts, Statistics Canada has published a study showing immigrants are more hard-working, better educated, and more stable than people born here. (Mitchell 1994: A1)

Clearly, therefore, research has a significant role to play in going beyond stereotype. Gathering data and thereby providing systematic evidence about what "everyone knows" to be true—and often isn't—is an important role for research that attempts to facilitate the development of social policy and/or simply sets out to better inform us about ourselves.

CONNECTING WITH THE LITERATURE

After you choose a topic, making a connection with the literature is a useful next step. Your initial review of the relevant literature will sometimes be cursory and sometimes quite exhaustive, but you do owe it to yourself and to your colleagues (via the literature) to have a look at what's been done in your area of interest. By familiarizing yourself with the literature, you can find out what theory, research and/or policy has been constructed; you can see how others have approached finding answers to particular research questions, the problems and successes experienced by others in the area, and what gaps in theory and research remain.

Take a Broad View of Your Topic

One of the biggest mistakes novice researchers make is that, when they examine "the literature" on a topic, they construe the topic too narrowly and too concretely. Suppose, for example, that you're interested in understanding the decisions made by customs officials at border crossings. How do they decide whether to wave someone through without further scrutiny or pass the person on to their colleagues for more detailed questioning and examination? What makes customs officers suspicious about some people but not others? What makes them decide to look through a person's suitcases, take a person into an interrogation room, or search or even dismantle someone's car?

If you begin your literature search by looking for studies that deal with that specific situation—customs agent decision making with respect to the identification of individuals who warrant further scrutiny—you'll find very few articles beyond an interesting master's thesis by Miriam Currey (1993). Many people would mistakenly leave off searching there, saying, "Gee, I guess there's nothing on this topic, so I'll just have to start off on my own."

But stopping there is quite inconsistent with the spirit of doing research. Any piece of research involves constantly working back and forth between theory and data, that is, between the abstract and the concrete. Seen in this manner, a researcher would rarely be interested in the decision making of customs officers per se. If that's as far as our interest goes, we might as well look at when people choose to mow their lawns or why some people prefer chocolate and others vanilla when they buy ice cream. The question to be asked is, "What makes the decision making of customs officers more 'interesting' (from a research perspective) than one's choice of ice cream?"

Let's first consider what it is that customs officers' work involves. They are government employees whose job involves aspects of social control. They are the first Canadians that a border crosser meets, and their job involves keeping apparently nasty people or other perceived undesirables (e.g., people who are escaping prosecution; people who are trying to bypass "normal" immigration channels; "terrorists") out of the country; keeping nasty things (e.g., weapons, unsafe products) out of the country; and ensuring that the *Customs Act*'s requirements are met (e.g., that people who bring goods into the country pay the legislated duties and fees). In the process of executing their jobs, customs officials have an incredible amount of power: you must answer any question they ask, they can seize your car or other belongings, and they can subject you to processes that most of us consider invasive and undesirable (e.g., interrogation, body scans, strip searches). But if they interrogated, scanned, and searched every would-be border crosser, there would soon be lineups from the Canada–U.S. boundary down to Mexico, and many exasperated people would be calling for their heads. Instead, customs officers are given discretion and are expected to use that discretion wisely. Perhaps only one in ten persons is asked more than a few simple questions (e.g., Where do you live? How long have you been away? Do you have any goods to declare?), and only a small sample is subjected to more detailed searches of their persons or belongings (e.g., people who fit the profile of a "drug mule" or "terrorist"). But where in the literature can we look beyond "customs officers"?

One "trick of the trade" that Howard Becker (1998) calls the "Bernie Beck trick" is a very useful device here. The trick gained its name because Becker had the office next door to Beck's when both were at Northwestern University in Chicago, which led to Becker hearing Beck pose a certain challenge to his students many times over the years when they would come in and tell him there was "no literature" on a topic, or had completed their research and did not know where to go next. The challenge was: "Tell me briefly what your research is all about, but without using any of the identifying characteristics of the actual case." If he were to issue the challenge to someone studying customs officers, it would have been gone something like this: "Tell me what your research is about, but without using the words 'border,' 'customs officers,' or 'screening.'" In response, the researcher might say, "Well, basically I'm looking at a situation where one individual has to form an impression and make a discretionary decision very quickly about another individual in very ambiguous circumstances with very little if any feedback as to whether the decisions they make are 'correct.'"

Given this more general description, you should see that there are now many "relevant" literatures that the researcher might look at, including (a) the various literatures on how people make decisions in an atmosphere of uncertainty (since, after the person leaves without being checked, we can never know for sure whether he or she did indeed smuggle something into the country or import a dangerous weapon); (b) the "impression formation" literature, which deals with factors people take into account when "sizing up" another person; these might include studies that look at both "lay people" and "professionals" (e.g., social workers, clinical psychologists); and (c) the "discretion" literature, which looks at the use of discretion by agents of social control (e.g., police officers, judges, parole boards, psychiatrists). And, of course, this is not to say that you should forget about checking for any existing literature on "customs officers" as well, since the results of such studies might help us understand more about who these people are, how they are trained, how their job is defined, how they perceive their job and their role, and so on, which would be useful in placing them in the larger realm of individuals who make decisions in the theoretical realms you've identified.

You might think of other areas that could be relevant to the study of customs officers and their decisions (e.g., whether and how stereotyping and racist or classist attitudes enter into the decision-making process or a study of interview techniques). But the above discussion should suffice to show that "the relevant literature" for such a study includes far more than just whatever research deals with that specific decision by that specific group.

Belonging to the community of scholars who engage in research means always looking for ways to benefit from the work of others, whether for positive reasons (e.g., to incorporate methods they've used or to include factors shown to be important) or negative ones (e.g., to avoid repeating mistakes and pursuing dead ends). And as this text argues, your search for "relevant" literature should cast a necessarily wide net.

Real and Virtual Libraries

There are two main sources here. One is the library—the heart of every university. If you are uncertain about what to do once you get to the library, ask your librarian about tours of or brochures describing the library or look on your school's library website under the "help" section where you are likely to find a wealth of guides, references, and answers to "frequently asked questions" that will help you familiarize yourself with the physical and virtual resources your library has to offer. Books, journals, and other materials are *not* filed randomly, and a working knowledge of what's available, where things are, and how to find them is invaluable. Knowing the general area in the library that contains material related to your topic of interest provides splendid opportunities for browsing.

Increasingly, library buildings and the physical books and journals they hold are being supplemented and sometimes replaced with virtual materials that you can acquire from your institution's online library catalogue—electronic journals, books, and databases. Many of these library materials overlap, i.e., you can go to the library and find the physical journals or books, but they are also available online. We recommend that your first choice should always be to download the online version. There are several reasons for this. First is the simple ecological reason that far fewer trees are killed to create a digital file than to create something out of paper, so the planet will thank you. Second is that it is far lighter and more convenient to have a library of files at your disposal on your laptop or flash drive than to haul around heavy things like books or stacks of photocopied articles. Third is that the biggest challenge you face these days with all of the information at your disposal is actually going through and managing it, and it is far easier to do so with electronic materials than physical ones. Fourth is that developing your own electronic archive of readings in the substantive areas you are interested in will be an invaluable tool as you move through your undergraduate and perhaps into your graduate academic career.

Ted is old enough to remember the days when "managing your information" meant photocopying articles or books of interest, and then going through with highlighters to underline the important parts, creating a separate index card for each book and article with a summary of what seemed to be the most important information at the time the card was created, and perhaps even jotting down the occasional quote or two. But you learn from the literature as you work through it, and sometimes what you thought was important at the beginning turns out to be less important later on, while something else replaces it on the "important" list that you might have overlooked or considered trivial initially. And then there was always that inevitable feeling that came when you were writing up your project and thought, "Gee, I recall reading a terrific quote that would help me illustrate that point," only to realize that you no longer had the faintest idea who had said it, or where you might find it.

The two of us now manage our materials as much as we can electronically by downloading documents, or scanning and creating our own pdf[2] documents and incorporating them as part of a "project" in a qualitative data analysis program known as NVivo. We will be talking more about NVivo in Chapter 12, which deals with data analysis, where the program is already well-recognized as among the best qualitative data analysis software programs available, but the program's usefulness as an information management tool does not appear to be fully recognized (e.g., Palys & Atchison 2009; in press).[3]

Briefly, incorporating documents into NVivo involves creating an overall "project" into which all "data"—documents in this case—are imported. Two very powerful processes are enabled by doing so. The first is that all of the documents within the project are searchable, which is rather like having your own personal Google that only goes through the materials that you have included within the project shell. The second is that you can do anything electronically that researchers formerly would do with highlighters—tagging particular sections with the concepts they include, noting interesting quotes, making memos or notes (annotations) of your thoughts about particular passages of your material and so on, so that any tagged passage or thought you had about that passage can be retrieved at will.

And, of course, the campus library is not the only place to search for information these days. No search would be complete without also including a search of the information available to you over the Internet. With a computing account, which most universities provide to undergraduate and graduate students for free or a nominal charge, and access to an on-campus lab or home cable or wireless connection, the world is your library. World Wide Web browsers such as Mozilla Firefox, Internet Explorer, Google Chrome, Opera, and Safari, and amazingly powerful search engines such as Google and Bing allow you to check the entire Internet for information about any subject, with return messages indicating what information various universities, government departments, institutes, and other agencies have on whatever subject you've searched for. The only problem is that with a bigger catch comes both more riches *and* more junk. Remember that anyone can host a Web page and make their views and analyses available to the world, i.e., unlike in the academic world, there is no "peer review" or quality control on the Internet, so it becomes more and more critical that you evaluate the quality and perspective of what you read.

The Internet also allows us to get access to information more quickly than ever before. For example, recently Ted and a colleague were engaged in debate with their university administration regarding the ethics of research confidentiality. They were just in the process of finalizing a submission when an article appeared in *The Globe and Mail* about a highly relevant case that had been decided in a United States Court of Appeal the previous day. Ted immediately went to the court's website and was able to download a copy of the decision. An hour later they were incorporating relevant quotes from the decision into their submission. Years ago this would have meant waiting for a hard copy of the decision to be made available and be mailed, which would often take weeks—or to wait for its appearance in legal publications of court decisions, which might take months.

Another wonderful aspect of the World Wide Web is the extent to which it has maintained its character as a place where you can get all sorts of information for free. The Court of Appeal decision noted above, for example, cost nothing, and there are more and more Web-based journals that offer access to articles online regardless of whether your campus library happens to subscribe to the journal or not. And, as many others do, the two of us maintain personal Web pages (Ted's is at http://www.sfu.ca/~palys/, Chris hosts "Academic Freedom" at http://www.academic-freedom.ca) where we have links to other sites of interest and post papers we've written that we hold copyright on or that aren't otherwise available (e.g., conference presentations, submissions to courts, and/or commissions of inquiry), which gives them far better distribution than would have been possible before the Internet. The two of us also host a site that explains some of the computer-assisted work we do on a consulting basis at http://www.sqi.ca.

And finally, although we've concentrated primarily on textual materials thus far, the Internet offers far more than just text in what has become a multimedia extravaganza. Photos, videos, audio, podcasts, twitter feeds, Web pages, chat rooms, and media archives that contain every form of content are available from a wide variety of sites that can be a never-ending source of data for your research. It makes "data management" all the more challenging, and reaffirms again why we use

NVivo, which allows you to code, tag, and manage all the material we collect in relation to any given project—documents, photos, videos,, audio and websites. In fact, recently the company behind NVivo (QSR International) has introduced a new feature to the program that allows researchers to capture all of the posts made to social networking sites such as Facebook and Twitter as a spreadsheet that can then be imported, read, coded, and analyzed right in NVivo.

IDENTIFYING A RESEARCHABLE QUESTION

Having accumulated some background knowledge about your topic, your next step is to translate your interests into specific research questions. Although your search of the literature involves a broadening of vision, your next task involves reining it in again to start translating what will still be a relatively amorphous research idea into a more concrete and specific research question or set of research questions that will form the core of your research project. As with research ideas, these questions can emerge from a number of different sources. Sometimes it is theory that provides us with a research question; other times it arises from our own observations and interests; on other occasions someone will give us a research question they would like us to answer; on still other occasions the identification of a research question is something that will emerge out of a more collaborative interchange between a researcher and some individual, group, or agency. However they arise, the big trick here is to ensure that our research question is indeed "researchable" and that we are open to whatever answers we might find. Some examples of researchable questions include:

1. Why do people buy lottery tickets?

2. How does free access to medical care affect the physical health of a population?

3. Have legislative changes regarding prostitution affected the street trade?

4. What are the effects of long-term incarceration?

5. What understandings and assumptions have guided this nation and its colonial predecessors in their policies regarding the rights of Aboriginal peoples?

6. How does extended exposure to a minority group affect prejudicial attitudes toward that group?

7. Through what verbal and nonverbal means is occupational status preserved and displayed in business organizations?

Each of these questions is reasonably focused and implies some real-world situation that we can look at to ascertain an answer. The first one is probably the vaguest ("why" questions tend to be the toughest), but even here, we might start off by tracking down some people who buy lottery tickets and asking them why they do so, or propose a theory that predicts which individuals or groups will be more or less likely to buy them. We might proceed by comparing those who buy lottery tickets with those who never do, or those who buy frequently with those who buy less often, or those who buy lottery tickets with those who engage in other forms of gambling (e.g., racetrack betting, bingo, playing the stock market). The information obtained may not provide the ultimate answer to our question, but there *is* real-world information that can help inform the answers we do derive. This process of "posing a researchable question" may seem straightforward, but it's actually related to one of the most common mistakes people make when they undertake a piece of research.

The difficulty arises when a would-be researcher chooses a question that is not actually *researchable*, that is, no empirical answer can be derived. Consider the following questions:

1. Is capitalism or communism the better economic system?

2. Is democracy the best political system?

3. What teaching style is best?

4. How should we respond to terrorism?

5. Are quota systems fair?

6. Is rehabilitation or punishment the most appropriate objective for sentencing?

7. What should we do about pornography?

These are *not* empirical questions; they're questions of value, philosophy, law or politics. Answers to such questions cannot be "discovered" without specific criteria by which to identify the "right" answer. Furthermore, these questions are *not* researchable questions with strictly empirical answers.

Research *can* be done in such areas, but these questions aren't researchable in their present form. Look at them again. In each case, the questions are asking you to make value judgments, using words like "appropriate," "better," "best," "fair," "effective," and "should." Although value judgments may well be of interest to us, and the research that we do may lead us to develop opinions about what we believe an "appropriate" course of action would be, researching such questions would require us to specify the criteria that will be used in making those judgments. Specifying criteria *does not* make answering such questions any less of a political, moral, or philosophical process, since the very choice of criteria embodies these dimensions, but it *does* require us to make that aspect of the process more explicit and, hence, more amenable to scrutiny by ourselves and others.

How can we turn a non-researchable question into a researchable question? Take the non-researchable question, "What should we do about pornography?" This question is problematic for several reasons. It suggests that there *is* some inherently "right" thing to do. Clearly, what we should do will involve some basic value considerations concerning what limits, if any, and under what conditions, if any, we feel society has the right to impose on otherwise free patterns of producing and consuming written and pictorial material.

For the sake of argument, let's adopt the classic civil libertarian position espoused by John Stuart Mill (1956): no society should impose restrictions on its citizenry unless allowing the activity to continue would impose greater social harm than the harm that would be realized by curtailing individual freedoms in that realm. Now we have the beginnings of a research question, since we have a criterion—demonstrated harm—that we can address. We might turn our non-researchable question into a researchable question by asking, "To what degree does individual exposure to pornography cause social harm?"

We still need to define "harm" more specifically, perhaps as "encouraging aggression," "encouraging negative attitudes," or "causing reductions in self-esteem." For example, we can ask, Does exposing individuals to pornography lead them to be more physically, sexually, or verbally aggressive? Does it encourage dehumanizing and negative attitudes toward women, men, gay, transgendered, or lesbian individuals? Do people experience a reduction in self-esteem after being exposed to pornography? There's still a long way to go before we actually begin to investigate these questions (e.g., What do we mean by "pornography"? How might we measure exposure? Aggression? Dehumanizing attitudes?), but at least we're off to a good start. We've identified a researchable question, that is, a question for which there *is* information in the world that we can look at and for which tentative answers *can* be unearthed.

The above suggestions aren't, of course, the *only* way we could turn "What should we do about pornography?" into a researchable question. Instead of pursuing the assessment-of-harm option implied by Mill, we might adopt the position that social policy in the pornography realm should be guided by community standards of (in)tolerance. The relevant data would thus involve assessing that standard, and our researchable question might become "What forms of pornographic material, if any, does the general public feel can be tolerated, and which, if any, does it feel cannot be tolerated?"

Although the above examples are policy oriented, not all research questions need be of this type. The research question may be rooted in curiosity and may be little more than "What is the relationship between variable A and variable B?" or "How do relations of power operate within corporate environments?" Both of these questions imply a real-world focus for the research, although further decisions remain to be articulated and resolved. For example, if our question concerns the relationship between personal awareness (variable A) and success (variable B), we'll still need to define these variables further, consider the context or situation in which we will scrutinize them, and be prepared to articulate what these choices say about us and the culture in which we operate (e.g., what do we mean by "success"?).

Similarly, if the social dynamics of some ecological niche (e.g., the business world) interest us, we must still decide where in that niche to focus (e.g., multinational versus domestic corporations; business in relation to other businesses or other elements of the social environment; on the front lines or in the boardroom) and what dimension(s) of that niche interest us (e.g., power relations, socialization, interaction patterns, image management processes).

But the central points here should be clear: (1) although any type of question may have researchable aspects, the approaches considered in this book require that a question be expressed in researchable terms; and (2) researchable questions are specific, limited in scope, related to some empirical "reality" (i.e., there must be some sort of evidence that can be consulted) and should have specific evaluation criteria, so that you can tell whether you are getting closer to an answer. These criteria emerge from social negotiation and debate and will undoubtedly reveal something of the researcher's personal leanings. Any researcher's decisions about "relevant" criteria will necessarily preclude some options in preference for others and, hence, reflect particular values and assumptions about what's "important" to scrutinize.

One recurring problem is researchers' failure to acknowledge the values implicitly embedded in their choice of variables to investigate. The researcher who evaluates organizational interventions on the basis of changes in productivity alone, for example, is effectively adopting a utilitarian status quo approach that implicitly accepts productivity as the only important indicator of a "successful" intervention. Other researchers might evaluate the same interventions by looking at changes in group cohesiveness, worker safety, or job satisfaction. Each approach makes an implicit value statement about what's "important" to observe. As this suggests, the choices you make say something about you and your perception of "the problem." Such implicit statements are inevitable; your obligation is to make "what you say" the result of a conscious decision whose rationale can be articulated. If you are conducting your research in a collaborative environment where you are working with other researchers or community/organizational partners ideally you would consult broadly with "relevant" **stakeholders** in the setting and design a study whose results will "speak" to their interests, perspectives, and concerns.[4] Conversely, when you are working independently you have to ensure that you remain **reflexive**, a process whereby you remain consciously and critically aware of the multiple influences you as a researcher have on the research process while also acknowledging how the research process influences you.

THE ROLE OF HYPOTHESES

Once you've identified a researchable question, the next step for many researchers—particularly those operating within a hypothetico-deductive framework—is to articulate your theoretical conceptions by formulating a hypothesis. Advocates of hypothesis-oriented (deductive) inquiry adamantly maintain that this stage represents a crucial transition in the research process, since the researcher must begin to be extremely specific about what he or she will assess. Talarico (1980) writes that "while general questions may prompt a researcher to turn to a particular subject, and while vague ideas may incite curiosity, no research can properly be labelled scientific without the specific statement of a relationship for testing and scrutiny" (149).

Expressing a hypothesis involves making a specific statement about a state of affairs in the world that is open to empirical test. Your hypothesis may

be seen as your speculative answer to the research question you're posing. In the context of deductive (theory-guided) inquiry, the hypothesis states what one's guiding theory says *should* happen in a particular situation if, in fact, the theory is true and, as such, represents a test of the theory in one particular situation to which, according to the theory, it should apply.

Each hypothesis will mention at least two **variables** and will state how those variables might be related. Here are a few examples:

1. The more strongly that people agree that one should love one's neighbour "because it is God's word," the more racist their attitudes will be regarding visible minorities.

2. A communicator's perceived objectivity will influence the extent to which an audience is persuaded by his or her arguments.

3. Work groups that are run on a democratic basis will have higher worker morale and group cohesiveness than those run autocratically.

4. Educational techniques that emphasize student–teacher interaction will result in higher rates of learning than unidirectional lecture techniques.

5. Providing students with information about safe sex practices will reduce the transmission of sexually transmitted diseases (STDs) in that population.

Each of these hypotheses asserts a state of affairs amenable to empirical test. The first one is based on the well-established finding (e.g., see Altemeyer 1981) that more conservative and fundamentalist religious affiliations are associated with less tolerance and greater hostility toward outgroups. Although everyone may agree that we should "love [our] neighbour," saying that the *reason* we should do so is because it is the "word of God" (as opposed to, say, being a good idea) would be a reasonable way to assess religious fundamentalism. We *can* find a group of individuals and ask them to what extent they agree with that statement, and we *can* use any of a dozen measures that have been developed to assess those same people's attitudes toward visible minorities. By correlating the results of those two measures together across a sample of people, we can see whether the two variables are related (i.e., whether racism increases with greater religious fundamentalism) the way the hypothesis predicts.

In sum, a hypothesis is a testable statement. Any research project will involve recognizing, structuring, or creating a situation in which you can gather information to discover whether the evidence supports or refutes your assertion about the relationship(s) among two or more variables. At times this can be a challenge, particularly when you are at the whim of available data, but the basic idea is to put your money where your mouth is, and place your bets *before* the dice are thrown.

As noted earlier, researchers from the deductive tradition have been the most adamant about the virtues of hypothesis-oriented inquiry. Kerlinger (1973), for example, has asserted that "it can almost be said that the hypothesis is the most powerful tool man has invented to achieve dependable knowledge" (25). Why? Three reasons are cited.

The Strengths of Hypotheses

HYPOTHESES AS INSTRUMENTS OF THEORY

Scientific epistemology necessarily affirms that dependable knowledge requires an ongoing interaction between theory and data. Although authors like Kerlinger sometimes assert emphatically that theory is *the* aim of science, theory is actually judged by its ability to account for data. Hypotheses are thus crucial to scientific inquiry, since they provide a link between theory and data. A theory specifies relationships among constructs in the abstract; the hypothesis applies the theory to a concrete situation, bringing the theory into contact with the real world so that its viability can be assessed.

HYPOTHESES IMPLY A TEST

Since a hypothesis represents a concrete specification of a testable state of affairs, the deductive tradition affirms that one can proceed to gather relevant evidence to establish the truth or falsity of the proposition. This tradition asserts that the true nature of reality can be made to reveal itself unambiguously through empirical inquiry; that is, we can create or observe a situation in which the truth or falsity of a hypothesis (and hence of the theory that gave rise to it) can be assessed (e.g., Stinchcombe 1968).

Others have more reserved views of how much can be accomplished. Popper (1959) argues that, although disconfirming evidence allows us to *falsify* our hypotheses (and hence our theories), *confirmatory* evidence (i.e., results consistent with our prediction) can "provide support for" but *not* "prove" their veracity. There are two reasons for this. First, a supportive datum is only a single victory in a theoretically infinite series of challenges that can be made to the theory; "proof" would require showing that a theory is correct in *all* situations in which it might be used to predict. In contrast, a pattern of disconfirmation is more quickly set. In other words, it takes a long time to get to the Hall of Fame, but not long at all to be banished to the minor leagues. Second, as Cook and Campbell (1979) have explained, although a given result may be consistent with a theory, the theory that gave rise to the prediction may not be the *only* theory that can account for that result. And one of those other theories may turn out to be broader in coverage than the theory at hand and, hence, more preferred in the long run.

HYPOTHESES AVOID FOLIE à UN(e)

A most important quality of hypotheses is that they are public. "Stating your hypothesis" implies an attitude of self-disciplined honesty: putting your money where your mouth is. If you think you understand the dynamics underlying some social phenomenon, tell us *ahead of time* what will happen in any situation you choose. Articulate your theory. Explain what your theoretical constructs mean to you and how you'll observe them. We ask gamblers to indicate their bets *before* the dice are thrown; we chastise pseudoscientific astrologers, whose predictions are so vague that they're always "right" no matter what happens; and we roll our eyes at conspiracy theorists who are able to see conspiracies in any set of facts. Surely the foundations of knowledge are valued more highly than mere money; surely the sciences are capable of more than the vague and self-serving accounts of mystics.

There are numerous fringe benefits to be gained by this attitude. It promotes the communal nature of science by allowing others to comment on our efforts. The possibility of critique and review is afforded only by the public presentation of our research logic. And if we view science as dynamic—as an ongoing process—then we should value components that enhance that process by fostering communication and debate.

Thus, for Kerlinger, "being public" and "expressing hypotheses" are synonymous, and the two together are an excellent way to generate dependable knowledge. As Kerlinger (1973) says, "the investigator who does not hypothesize a relation in advance … does not give the facts a chance to prove or disprove anything … As Darwin pointed out long ago, all observations have to be for or against some view if they are to be of any use" (21–22). In contrast, individuals who do not follow a hypothesis-testing mode of inquiry are seen as pre-scientific throwbacks who are prepared to capitalize on chance events and *post hoc* (after-the-fact) explanations.

Better Living without Hypotheses

Although integral to the hypothetico-deductive method, and clearly (as Kerlinger shows) something that some researchers feel almost a religious fervour about, the formal expression of hypotheses *a priori*[5] is not something that everyone, and particularly researchers taking a more qualitative and inductive approach, would advocate.

DO HYPOTHESES ADEQUATELY REPRESENT THE RESEARCH PROCESS?

One criticism is that the sort of account Kerlinger offers emphasizes a mythical "scientism" that courts triviality and phenomenological injustice if it's true and seriously distorts the process of science if it's

not. You're about to do research in a new area: Is your hypothesis ready? If specifying a hypothesis is a prerequisite to engaging in research, then surely the one you come up with from your office armchair will be superficial and trite. If a hypothesis is generated in the absence of any interaction with the phenomenon in question, then surely it would be miraculous if it were insightful. The legwork must be done first.

Deductivists would counter that even though your preliminary hypotheses might be trivial, coming face to face with reality would, over the long run (like a self-correcting feedback loop), encourage more elaborate and sophisticated revision. But that claim is more an expression of faith than a statement of fact. Once you're committed to the research focus and direction that a hypothesis requires, will further revision simply become mired in variations on the superficial preliminary theme, or will more substantial revision occur? Surely it would make greater sense to more fully explore the phenomenon *before* imposing hypothetical constructs from afar. Thus, while deductivists argue that "real" science starts with the specification of research questions and the delineation of hypotheses for empirical testing, inductivists argue that these things do not simply materialize, and hence the process of generating research questions and hypotheses should itself receive focus.

The implication is that the hypothesis-oriented accounts we see in journals actually represent a distortion of the research process. Silverman (1985) is not alone in suggesting that the specification of hypotheses, methods, and results may look squeaky clean and objective when documented in the journals but that published articles misrepresent the research process by relegating the preliminary skirmishes with research phenomena in the exploratory phase to "non-scientific" (or, at least, not-worth-writing-about) status.

Thus, while Kerlinger might suggest that one is not being forthright if one's speculations are not hung out for *a priori* scrutiny, inductivists would assert that Kerlinger chooses to ignore how his formulations actually emerged—in other words they would say he is not being very reflexive. By acknowledging formulative inquiry as an integral part of the empirical process, inductivists argue that they more adequately and honestly represent the process of science, do not prematurely foreclose on the identification of important research questions, and are in fact more public about the important conceptualization process that deductivists sweep under the rug. In contrast, deductivists would argue that exploratory research that is not explicitly hypothesis-driven is loose science, and hence is best considered a warm-up for "real" scientific activity.

IS PREDICTION THE PRIMARY CRITERION?

The hypothesis-oriented inquiry espoused by the deductivists sees "ability to predict" as the acid test of theory. If you can predict it, deductivists would say, then you must understand it; that is, explanation and prediction are symmetrical. Other philosophers of science (e.g., Manicas & Secord 1983) would agree with this point, but only for closed systems of the type created in a laboratory. Laboratory research is a powerful mode of inquiry because it creates conditions that allow the **ceteris paribus** assumption to operate.

Ceteris paribus is Latin for "all else being equal." In the laboratory, researchers literally create conditions that let them investigate the impact of variable A on variable B with all other variables held constant or otherwise equalized. Given this imposed closure, it makes sense that the researcher can predict effects.

When we move outside the laboratory, though, differences between positivists like Kerlinger (1973) and critical realists like Manicas and Secord (1983) become apparent. For positivists, predicting behaviour in the world requires little more than merely extrapolating from behaviour in the laboratory, although it *is* acknowledged that prediction in the world is a more complex task, because of the multiplicity of variables that operate freely there. Still, prediction is seen as possible; one just needs a larger prediction equation that either takes more variables (and their interactions) into account or more adequately identifies the most potent variables for

scrutiny. The alternative, as Latour (1987) argues happens in the natural sciences, is for scientists to control the world such that they recreate the conditions under which the theorized relationship held, i.e., something that Brandt (1975) argued was deplorable for the social sciences because of the control, deception, and manipulation that seems inherent to laboratory-based social research (see also Palys 1989; Stricker 1967).

But for critical realists, the real world is a whole new ball game. Unlike the laboratory, the real world is an open system, where the *ceteris paribus* assumption that guides laboratory research no longer holds. The problem, as Manicas and Secord (1983) describe it, is that in the real world, *ceteris* is never *paribus*: all else is *never* equal. And because it's typically impossible to predict the particular status that "all other variables" will occupy (except in other closed systems), prediction in the real world becomes an impossible task. Manicas and Secord suggest that it is still reasonable to *explain* how a particular phenomenon was produced, although we may not have been able to *predict* its occurrence; that is, they argue that in open systems, prediction and explanation are *not* symmetrical—one can explain and understand without necessarily being able to predict. Furthermore, they and others (e.g., Becker 1970, 1998; Cook & Campbell 1979; Palys 1989) suggest that it's possible to offer this explanation in a compelling manner that would rise above the pejorative characterizations of positivists such as Kerlinger.

FINDING A FOCUS

For more inductively oriented researchers, the place to start is often in the field at a particular site where you can watch, talk to people, and look for a focus to your research—something "interesting"—that will act as a sort of conceptual hub around which the research will then proceed. Book-length reports such as William Foote Whyte's (1943) classic *Street Corner Society* or Michael Duneier's (1999) more recent *Sidewalk* often describe this process in their early chapters, but it is rare to see it discussed in more article- or chapter-length treatments. An exception is Howard Becker's (1993) "How I Learned What a 'Crock' Was."

Becker's article recounts the beginnings of a study that eventually was published as a book (by Becker, Geer, Hughes, & Strauss 1961) entitled *Boys in White: Student Culture in Medical School.*[6] Becker recalls how the University of Kansas Medical Centre was chosen for what was intended to be a study of the socialization of students into the role of doctor over a four-year period not because it was in any way "special," but because it was for the most part "typical"—or certainly not "atypical"—and unremarkable. The research began with Becker not sure what he would do other than to "hang around" with some of the medical students and observe them in their routines of taking courses, interacting with supervisors, doing rounds, giving examinations, and so on. The turning point came about a week later from a comment that Chet, one of the students, made:

> One morning, as we made rounds, we saw a very talkative patient, who had multiple complaints to tell the doctor about, all sorts of aches, pains and unusual events. I could see that no one was taking her very seriously and, on the way out, one of the students said, "Boy, she's really a crock!" I understood this, in part, as shorthand for "crock of shit." It was obviously invidious. But what was he talking about? What was wrong with her having all those complaints? Wasn't that interesting? (30-31)

One can tell a lot about people from the ingroups and outgroups they identify, who they love and hate, because intense declarations like "She's a crock!" are another way of saying "She is wasting my valuable time" or "How am I ever going to become a doctor with patients like her taking up my time?" But what sort of interests was this patient violating? In response, Becker asked Chet a very simple and straightforward question, which was "What's a crock?" Chet's first reaction was to return with a look that said, "Are you kidding? Any fool knows what a crock is!" But Becker persisted:

"Seriously, when you called her a crock, what did you mean?" Not used to being asked to define so basic a term, Chet fumbled around for a bit, and then came up with the idea that "crocks" were people with psychosomatic illness.

This seemed reasonable, but the next task was to employ the definition. Soon they came to another patient who had a gastric ulcer, at which point the attending physician used that patient as an opportunity to give the students a brief lecture on psychosomatic illness, with ulcers as the example. As this was what Chet had said made someone a "crock," Becker said only, "Crock, eh?"[7] But no, Chet indicated that patient was not a "crock," but why not? Another student overheard and intervened: "He's not a crock. He really has an ulcer." The other students in the group were involved now, too, with discussion ensuing among all of them about what exactly a "crock" was, different definitions being offered, and Becker trying them out as they went from patient to patient until they came to one definition—that a "crock" is a patient that has multiple complaints but no apparent physical pathology—that held up in test after test on succeeding patients thereafter.

But arriving at a consensual definition of a "crock" was not the end of it. As Becker points out in the article, being able to identify a crock was one thing, but he still had to find out "…why students thought crocks were bad. What interest of theirs was compromised by a patient with many complaints and no pathology?" (32) Although we'll leave it to you to read the "crocks" article or *Boys in White* if you are interested in more of the specifics, in general, "crocks" proved to be the doorway that opened discussion into medical students desires to make use of limited time to maximize the amount of "practical experience" they could amass. Given that crocks were time-consuming and you could learn everything you needed to know about how to deal with a "crock"—of whom there were many—from your first one, any successive ones were not a good use of your time. After that your time was better spent with other patients, who would give you an opportunity to get as much varied experience as possible experience with the "sights, sounds and smells of disease in a living person." (33). It also explained much of their other behaviour—the reason they often switched patients with each other (I'll trade my heart attack patient for your diabetic).

Of course Becker and his colleagues were focusing on the would-be doctors in their research, but we can also see how such a concept could open the door to understanding the experience of some patients. How many of us know or have heard about someone who has a long list of complaints and goes from doctor to doctor, no doubt being dismissed as a "crock" by many who then shuffle them out the door, only to be diagnosed at some point along the way by some physician somewhere who finally diagnoses the problem correctly? Looking at it in that way, "crock" becomes a medical shorthand for "I don't have the faintest idea what's wrong with you," with "crock" becoming the way for physicians to rationalize that the problem is not with them and their diagnostic skills, but with a hypochondriac patient who bothers them for nothing.

As you should see, embedded in this way of doing research is very much of a constructionist perspective on how to approach the analysis of any given situation. Our tendency when a teacher points at a student and says, "He's lazy," is to look at the student and ask, "Oh, just how lazy is he?" and we might even develop a "Laziness" scale to measure just exactly how lazy the student is. But as Becker's experience with the medical students shows, the existence of the category and the way it is used tells you as much about the teacher doing the categorizing as it does about the person being categorized. His experience also shows how important it is to *listen* to what people share with you, to pay particular attention to the way they categorize others, and draw boundaries they use to include some people and exclude others. Examples are everywhere. When police call some people "scrots," when prostitutes call someone a "good trick" (or bad one), and when students say that a professor they have is a "great professor" (or terrible one), they are telling you as much about what they think policing, prostitution, or "getting an education" is all about as they are about the persons they are pointing at.

The "crocks" article is a beautifully concise example of that transition moment that comes from extended contact with a person or group and being patient in waiting for that "aha" moment where a pivotal event or comment or dilemma arises that then becomes the focus of study because of the way that it crystallizes the dynamics of the person or group or situation you are trying to understand. It also shows that a form of hypothesizing does often come up in such research. Hypotheses are basically if/then propositions that, in the hypothetico-deductive world are done *a priori* and take the form of "if my theory is correct, then such-and-such an outcome should follow." In Becker's case we saw hypothesizing that took a different form—"if I understand what a 'crock' is for these medical students then I should be able to correctly categorize the next patient we see"—that arises in the context of the research and is driven by concepts that are meaningful to the actors within it.

To Hypothesize or Not to Hypothesize?

As we've seen, the status of the hypothesis is not as clear-cut as the positivist accounts found in most research textbooks would imply. The arguments against always requiring explicit hypothesizing are very compelling, but there is value in the idea of making one's research logic public. The difficulty arises from two sources. First is a misplaced belief that "making public" and "hypothesis testing" are synonymous. Researchers do themselves and science a disservice when they do not formulate their procedures and explanations in a way that allows scrutiny by other scientists. Neither inductive nor deductive researchers would disagree with that point.

As for hypothesis testing per se, a formalized hypothesis may not be appropriate for every research inquiry. Whether it is will depend on such considerations as the work that has already been done in the area in question, your research objectives, and other aspects of your research perspective. This book aims to delineate a methodology that is compatible with both hypothesis-driven (i.e., deductive) and hypothesis-generating (i.e., inductive) modes of inquiry.

A second difficulty arises from the way a hypothesis is defined in more quantitative and experimental types of research (which involves specifying a hypothesis and parallel "null" hypotheses that can be tested statistically) as definitive. Alternatively, one can focus more on the process of *hypothesizing*—maybe "speculating" would be a better word—that permeates all forms of research. In that sense, hypotheses or speculations are the gas that propels and helps guide the empirical bus.

Looking at the relative advantages and disadvantages of hypothesis-oriented and pure induction is beneficial for illustrating how ideological poles operate in relation to informing the formation of research, it is far more common for researchers to take a middle ground and to simply craft their research around answering a particular research question or set of questions. The general question that all deductivists are trying to answer is, "How valid is this theory in explaining a particular phenomenon?" Similarly, an inductivist researcher might want to answer the general question, "What set of processes underlie the occurrence of a particular phenomenon?"

DEVELOPING INDICATORS FOR CONCEPTS

Recall that one thing that both qualitative and quantitative approaches have in common is the commitment to both *theory*—abstract concepts that we think help us make sense of the world—and *data*—real-world evidence that we gather that we feel sheds light on those concepts. Sometimes we start with the concept and look for opportunities to employ it in a more deductive approach—something like "social capital," for example, that one hears a lot about in sociology these days (e.g., Bourdieu 1977; de Vaus 2002); and sometimes we begin by observing and see concepts that the people who participate in our research employ (e.g., some

patients being referred to as "crocks"), which then becomes the launching point for our own conceptualizations of what is going on (e.g., the notion of "crocks" led Becker and his colleagues [Becker 1993; Becker et al. 1961] to talk about "clinical experience" and "medical responsibility" perspectives in the education that the medical students were both receiving and employing in the context of being socialized into the doctoring professions). The notion of "developing indicators for" or "operationalizing" variables addresses the question of how we travel back and forth between those abstract and concrete levels. Normally, this process will see you considering two types of definitions: **nominal definitions** and **operational definitions**.

Nominal (or Constitutive) Definitions

The nominal definition (sometimes called the constitutive definition) involves articulating what you mean by the concept under scrutiny. It's a bit like supplying a dictionary definition, although the nominal definition is often linked to one's theoretical stance. For example, a radical feminist inspired nominal definition of violence might be "any act that is designed to restrict or repress an individual's physical, psychological, intellectual, or emotional well-being." Conversely, researchers working from within a harm-reduction perspective might define violence as "any act that results in direct physical or psychological harm."

Nominal definitions aren't always so straightforward and, because they are socially constructed, they cannot be "right" or "wrong"; they can only be more or less useful. This poses a bit of a problem insofar as, if definitions cannot be right or wrong, does that mean that anyone can define anything any way they want? Yes and no. There *are* times someone comes along and changes the world by arguing that we need to pull the gauze from our eyes and see the world a different way. But for the most part, having a definitional free-for-all makes definitions useless, makes communication between researchers difficult, and often ends up in pointless debate where groups of researchers argue about something when, at the bottom of the debate is the fact that they are simply talking about different things. For example, the extent to which "poverty" exists in Canada clearly depends in large part on how you define "poverty."

The concept "pornography" is also illustrative. Although it has a lengthy tradition of referring only to material that is in some sense sexually explicit (e.g., see Wilson 1973; see also U.S. Commission on Obscenity and Pornography 1970), feminist writing in this area started distinguishing between "pornography" and "erotica" (e.g., see R. Morgan 1980; Steinem 1980). "Pornography" was to refer to materials that portrayed violent or otherwise power-imbalanced relations, and although it was used typically to refer to such relations in the context of sexual activity, it wasn't necessarily limited to that domain. A lack of sensitivity to this different definitional base, as well as considerable self-righteousness among researchers in both theoretical camps about the supposedly inherent "correctness" of their respective definitions, led to considerable superfluous conflict: individuals who argued about "pornography" were actually talking about very different things.

As the preceding paragraphs suggest, variations among researchers in the constitutive definition of theoretical variables may reflect ideological, theoretical, or disciplinary differences among those researchers. It is because a researcher's choice of constitutive definition is often theoretically driven and affects how one goes about conceptualizing one's research strategy that Kuhn (1970) argued that our observations are not *theory-neutral* but *theory-laden*. Variation among researchers is not necessarily unhealthy; what's important is that researchers articulate their definitions, are aware of the values inherent in their choices, and pay heed to any empirical evidence that sometimes can be used to make the claim that one definition is more useful than another. It is also a reason for connecting with the literature relatively early in your research—and especially if you are following a more hypothetico-deductive approach—to see what indicators others have used for the concepts that will provide the foundation for your research.

Operational Definitions

Following from the nominal definition is the operational definition, which is more closely linked to what we will *do*. The operational definition involves giving specific empirical meaning to a concept by delineating the specific indicators or operations that are to be taken as representative of a concept. The trick here is to be specific about how you will derive, create, identify, measure, or record the indicator, and to choose one or more indicators that best approximate your nominal definition. The nominal definition articulated what you were after; the operational definition specifies how you propose to capture it.

INDICATORS

This process might still sound somewhat foreign to you, but it's analogous to processes we engage in every day when we make inferences and draw conclusions about the people we meet. If you meet someone for the first time, the number of questions that person asks about you, the amount of eye contact s/he makes, and his/her tone of voice may be seen as indicators of how interested that person is in you. If the other person laughs at your jokes and the space between you begins to shrink, those may be taken as indicators that you like each other. Or if you hear two people calling each other "Honey" and "Sweetie," you might see this as an indication that they are deliriously in love and/or have been watching too many 1950s Hollywood movies. In each case, you're observing concrete actions (e.g., two people holding hands) and, on the basis of your observation, inferring the existence of some underlying construct or variable (i.e., the two people like each other).

Of course, there *are* times when these indicators may be erroneous. A person may hold another's hand to restrain him or her rather than to demonstrate affection. Someone who asks a lot of questions about you may not be particularly interested in you, but may want to divert attention away from himself or herself. And people sometimes laugh at your jokes only out of politeness or to relieve tension, and the space between you may be shrinking only because the other person can't hear what you're saying. But despite such exceptions, these indicators are probably, in general, fairly accurate ones and, hence, overall, fairly useful, particularly when they are observed in combination.

At the same time, one can also envision bad or poor indicators of a concept. If we took "a person running" to be an indicator of "a crime having just been committed," we would likely be wrong more often than we were right and would probably get on the wrong side of many joggers, soccer players, and people in a hurry. Similarly, many people are so socially insensitive that when someone they are attracted to does anything short of telling them to "get lost," they perceive the other person as "coming on" to them or otherwise encouraging further interaction.

Much the same occurs in the social and health sciences, although the process varies depending on whether the researcher follows an inductive or a deductive approach. Deductive researchers begin with a variable of interest (e.g., liking) and then try to generate a list of indicators that can be used systematically to classify people on that dimension. Researchers taking a more inductive approach may see a behaviour they wish to focus on and then will start to record specific instances of it in all its variation before providing some encompassing concept that unites them, and/or will look to see what persons in the research setting identify as indicators of important concepts that arise (e.g., Becker's efforts to find out who the medical students viewed as a "crock").

In either case, the indicators might be behavioural (e.g., whether two people hold hands or how much eye contact they make with each other); archival (e.g., the content of letters the two people exchange); physiological (e.g., changes in galvanic skin response that occur for one person when a second enters the room); or self-report (e.g., answers to the question "Do you like that person?"). None of these indicators is *itself* "liking"—we never observe pure reality, only our constructions of it—but each can arguably be linked to our understanding of

that construct. Demonstrating this linkage involves assessing the **epistemic relationship** between the theoretical variable and the particular indicator or measure we have chosen to represent it.

So despite the differences between researchers who take an inductive or deductive approach in the way they go about operationalizing variables, *both* sets of researchers *do* operationalize. This is little more than a truism: we use abstract language to describe our concrete world. Deductive approaches involve researchers specifying indicators ahead of time because, within that tradition, the challenge of science is to develop constructs and operationalizations that are generalizable across different situations, with the researcher viewed as the privileged individual who "knows best" and can grasp the bigger picture that few others see. Inductive researchers are prepared for such generalizations to reveal themselves over time, but in the interim wish to ensure that they treat the particular situation at hand with some integrity, which means listening to the understandings that exist among those participating in the research while at the same time having some sense of what the phenomenon they are interested in understanding might look like.

But note that both sets of researchers try to link abstract theoretical constructs and particular empirical attributes that are indicators of those constructs. This textbook adopts a position that is not inconsistent with either mode of inquiry; the main requirement is that researchers articulate their constructs and operationalizations in a way that affords communication between researchers and is amenable to public scrutiny. This says little more than that "being empirical" requires a commitment to both theory (abstract explanatory concepts) and data (real-world evidence) and that researchers are obliged to articulate the links (i.e., the epistemic relationship) they make between the two.

OPERATIONS

Note that all the indicators discussed above involve deciding which real-world events we consider indicative of a particular theoretical construct. Kerlinger (1973) calls these **measured operational definitions**.

At issue is how to capture the variable in some systematic fashion. But not all indicators are of that type.

Some researchers, particularly those involved in experimental research, prefer to create variables of theoretical interest,[8] in which case the way the variable is created operationally defines the variable. For example, in one classic study, Barker, Dembo, and Lewin (1943) set out to test the hypothesis that frustration leads to aggression. They created a situation in which the children who participated were frustrated by being placed in a room where attractive toys were clearly visible but could not be reached. In another classic study, Aronson and Mills (1959) wanted to investigate the effects of the "hazing" rituals that were always being conducted by fraternities, sororities, and many organizations by looking at the relationship between severity of initiation and liking for a group. Clearly the researchers could not shave people's heads or require them to parade across campus in diapers, so they created what they believed was a "severe" initiation by having participants read sexually oriented passages aloud in the presence of others. One simply did not do those sorts of things back in the 1950s, when the sort of books that were being banned were tame relative to anything that is available now on prime time TV, and hence the embarrassment would have been considered "severe."

Both of these are examples of what are known as **experimental operational definitions** (e.g., see Kerlinger 1973). Manipulating a situation to create variables of interest is characteristic of experimental methods, and the operational definition of the construct is the set of experimental procedures used to create it. Thus, frustration was operationally defined by Barker and colleagues (1943) as the emotion a child feels when denied access to an attractive toy. A "severe initiation" was operationally defined by Aronson and Mills (1959) as the experience of university students asked to read sexually explicit passages in front of others in the course of demonstrating their eligibility for group membership.

Clearly, these two examples do not encompass "all" that frustration or a severe initiation involves,

but the two studies *do* seem to create situations likely to produce the desired constructs. Further, note two benefits of this technique. First, creating the situation allows researchers to validate their operations by including other measures, often known as **manipulation checks**, in their procedures. Thus, if asking students to read sexual passages aloud really does embarrass them, and if volunteers for the experiment are asked to rate how embarrassed they feel, then we would expect the group of volunteers who read such passages to rate themselves as more embarrassed, on the average, than a comparable group of students who were not asked to read those passages or who read passages that were not so sexually explicit.

Second, researchers are obliged to describe their operations in sufficient detail for others to replicate their procedures, thereby encouraging debate about the validity and/or limitations of those operations. For example, Gerard and Mathewson (1966) later argued that the students in Aronson and Mills's study may have been "turned on" by the sexually explicit passages and may therefore have rated the group discussion more positively because of the sexual glow they felt, rather than because of the extremity of their initiation.

Evaluating Operational Definitions

There's no reason to believe that researchers are blessed with inherently greater insight about people or human behaviour than anyone else, at least not insight that exists independently of the information they unearth by empirical methods. Developmental psychologists likely have as many "problem" children; marital counsellors likely have as many problem marriages and divorces; and clinical psychologists likely have as many personal problems, overall, as the rest of us. Similarly, social and health scientists are as likely to show the same lack of insight that sometimes characterizes us all in our non-professional lives: occasionally poor decision making, a difficulty in differentiating what we *wish* was true from what *is,* and a difficulty in empathizing with perspectives other than our own. If social and health scientists have *any* special insights, it is because they occasionally get lucky, as we all sometimes do, or because they are particularly creative, as we all sometimes are, or because they subject their insights to the rigours of empirical method before they espouse their beliefs.

Empirical method requires researchers to articulate the bases of their procedures and inferences. Intuitive revelation on the part of researchers—or anyone—is *not* the stuff of science. Accordingly, researchers are expected to present some sort of argument to show why that choice of indicators or operations was a good one. This procedure, referred to as assessing the epistemic relationship or as establishing the validity of your operations or indicators, is generally done in one or (preferably) more of three ways: citing tradition, rational argument, or empirical demonstration.

BY CITING TRADITION

Science is a *communal* enterprise. Thus, establishing connections between you and other researchers—by noting the ways in which your conceptualizations and operationalizations are similar to and/ or different from those of other researchers—is an important responsibility.

For example, for many years, laboratory researchers looking at aggression often used the Buss Shock Apparatus. Participants were told that they could use this apparatus to deliver one of five levels of electric shock to another participant (who was generally an employee of the experimenter's and who never actually receives any shocks). The average level of shock delivered is taken as an index of the aggressiveness of the participant's behaviour (e.g., see Altemeyer 1981; Donnerstein & Berkowitz 1981). Similarly, in the field of interpersonal dynamics, a participant's tendency to engage in cooperative or competitive behaviour was typically assessed with the "prisoner's dilemma" (e.g., see Deutsch 1973).

There are also many standardized measures that are used to define many other variables of interest to researchers. Survey researchers, for example, tend to have fairly standard ways of asking about age, income, education, and other **demographic variables** that are routinely included in surveys to allow the researcher to describe their samples. You can see examples of these and many other types of surveys and survey questions by going online to the Survey Question Bank that is coordinated by the UK Data Archive at the University of Essex in England,[9] the General Social Survey site operated by Statistics Canada,[10] and the Roper Centre site at the University of Connecticut in the United States,[11] while many others can be found online by simple search if any of the previous ones happen to be obsolete by the time you read this book.

On the one hand, there's good reason for researchers to use standard indicators: using similar measures makes it easier to compare results between studies and can encourage the embellishment of knowledge systems across researchers. But such practices also encourage **mono-operationism** (also known as *mono-operation bias*) and **mono-method bias** (e.g., see Campbell 1969a; Cook & Campbell 1979; the concepts are also discussed in more detail later in this chapter), that is, respectively, an overreliance on a particular measure of a construct and on a particular *way* of measuring it (e.g., by self-report questionnaire). By itself, "That's how others did it" isn't sufficient justification for considering a measure to be valid. One also would want to consider at least one, and preferably both, of the other two ways of assessing the epistemic relationship between one's theoretical construct and the indicator that is used to represent it.

BY RATIONAL ARGUMENT

You also should be prepared to explain on a purely rational basis why you feel the indicator you choose is a reasonable one and, in particular, why you feel that it's better for your purposes than others you might have chosen. You might present such arguments through some open-ended narrative or use the schema offered in Table 2.1. Either way, the researcher must explain to others why a particular operationalization "makes sense" in the context in which it is being used and must articulate the relationship between concept and indicator.

Table 2.1

The Four Possibilities Generated by the Cross-tabulation of the Situation as It "Really" Is and as Coded through the Operational Definition

		Is the act "really" aggressive according to nominal definition?	
		YES	NO
Is act categorized as "aggressive" according to operational definition?	YES	1 Correct categorization (true positive)	2 Erroneous categorization (false positive or Type I error)
	NO	3 Erroneous categorization (false negative or Type II error)	4 Correct categorization (true negative)

Table 2.1 uses the example of "aggression" to show some of the possibilities that exist whenever we use an operational definition to categorize an event. Across the top of the table we see the "real" situation according to what we mean by aggression—whether, according to our *nominal* definition, the behaviour we're looking at is "really" aggressive. On the left-hand side of the table are the two possibilities we have open to us: if the indicator *is* present and/or some specified criterion *is* met, the act is labelled "aggressive"; if the indicator is *not* present and/or if some specified criterion is *not* met, we label the act "non-aggressive." The cross-tabulation of these two dimensions yields four possibilities.

We might do any of the following:

1. Label an act "aggressive" when it really *is* an aggressive act (cell 1; a correct categorization). This is also sometimes known as a *true positive,* since one is correctly saying "yes, it is."

2. Label an act "aggressive" when it's actually non-aggressive (cell 2; an error). This type of error is sometimes referred to as a *false positive,* since one is erroneously saying "yes, it is" when really it's not (i.e., it is falsely categorized as a positive); it is also sometimes referred to as a *Type I error.*

3. Label an act "non-aggressive" when it's actually an aggressive act (cell 3; an error). This

type of error is sometimes called a *false negative,* since one is erroneously saying "no, it is not" when really it is; it is also sometimes referred to as a *Type II error.*

4. Label an act "non-aggressive" when it really is a non-aggressive act (cell 4; a correct categorization). This is sometimes referred to as a *true negative,* since one is accurately saying "no, it is not."

Let's say that we've become concerned about how frequently we've been hearing lately about the violent incidents between seniors and between seniors and staff in long-term healthcare facilities. The managers of one facility invite us to do some observational research as a sort of pretest because they are interested in assessing just how often these incidents happen, and also want to use what we find as baseline data that will allow them to test out different protocols and procedures they developed to help reduce the frequency of violent incidents. We begin with the nominal definition of aggression as "any intentional effort by one or more persons to hurt one or more other persons through word or deed." Operationally, we decide to count "any physical contact accompanied by loud vocalizations" as aggressive. We can rationally consider how well such an operationalization would work in this context by working our way through the alternatives expressed in Table 2.1.

First, it is clear that our operational definition may yield many *accurate* classifications. Someone who yells at and strikes another person with the intention of hurting is clearly aggressive according to our nominal definition, and that person will be categorized accurately according to our operational definition (i.e., a true positive; see cell 1). Similarly, many acts that do *not* involve striking and yelling (e.g., telling a joke, asking directions to the washroom, eating a canapé) will correctly be labelled non-aggressive (i.e., a true negative; see cell 4).

But prospective errors of classification are also easily envisioned. Mock fighting and horseplay, for example, would not be aggressive acts according to our nominal definition (because of the absence of intent to hurt), but might well be classified as aggressive according to our operational definition if they were boisterous and engaged in physical contact (i.e., a false positive, or Type I error; see cell 2). This might not be so much of a problem if we are doing the research in a long-term healthcare facility, given that seniors are not known for engaging in horseplay, but would likely be more of a problem if we were to do this sort of research in a daycare or on a school field during recess.

A major source of error, however, would be false negatives, or Type II errors (see cell 3), since there are many acts that are "really" aggressive according to our nominal definition (e.g., insults, surreptitious aggression, intentional embarrassment, or humiliation) that would not be picked up by the operational definition. Obviously, one indicator will be considered better than another indicator of the same concept to the extent that it yields more accurate classifications and fewer erroneous ones in the context in which we are using it.

In sum, operational definitions connect our conceptual variables (theory) to the procedures or operations we use to capture them (data). A good one will correctly classify not only the presence of some attribute or phenomenon, but also its absence. The goal is to define our concepts operationally in a way that allows systematic application of the definition, maximizing accurate classification and minimizing inaccurate classification. Empirically,

the question of how well an operational definition mirrors real differences in the phenomenon under study is a question of assessing the epistemic relationship between concept and indicator. The more accurate the classification, the better the epistemic relationship.

Adequate operationalizations are often hard to generate; no indicator you choose will be perfect. As an example, suppose that we nominally define "suicide" as "the intentional taking of one's own life." An obvious operationalization of suicide would be the "suicide rate" or "deaths proclaimed to be suicides by a coroner or other legitimate authority." But do suicide statistics properly identify all those people who intentionally took their own lives? Probably not. There undoubtedly will be some people who took their own lives but managed to make it look like an accident or a natural death. Similarly, some true accidents—and even some homicides—may be proclaimed suicides because of the circumstances surrounding the death. The greater the prospective loss if the judgment is "suicide," the more likely coroners might be to err on the side of caution before declaring the death a suicide.

Let's take another example. Suppose you want to evaluate whether students who receive a pep talk from the president of the university ultimately become better students than those who do not receive the talk. You would need some way to operationalize student "goodness." What would you propose?

We've asked that question of students in our classes, and they always offer numerous possibilities. Their suggestions have included (a) grade point average, (b) frequency of participation in class discussions, (c) quality of participation in class discussions, (d) involvement in extracurricular activities, (e) frequency of attendance, and (f) hours spent studying.

Each of these proposed operational definitions has strengths and weaknesses. Grade point averages are quantitative and easy to gather. But grades may not be comparable across courses, departments, and faculties, a situation that may pose a problem, depending on our research design. Frequency of participation in class discussions may be a good indicator, since one might argue that "better" students contribute more often than do "poorer" students. But the time investment required to gather those data would be significant. If we go ahead and do so anyway, can we just count the number of times a student says something? If so, should questions be treated the same as statements? Should confused, incoherent comments receive the same weight as clear, insightful ones? And if we want to assess the quality of the contribution, who is the appropriate judge?

BY EMPIRICAL DEMONSTRATION

The third way to evaluate the epistemic relationship between a theoretical construct and its operational indicator is to assess it empirically. When it comes to manipulated independent variables, this assessment is most often done by manipulation checks.

In one classic study, Stanley Schachter (1959) wanted to examine the relationship between anxiety and affiliation; he needed to find a way to manipulate the anxiety level of participants. He decided to do this by telling participants, when they showed up for the study, that they would be receiving painful electric shocks as part of the procedures. That certainly sounds like the sort of thing that might induce anxiety, or perhaps fear, but Schachter went a step further: he asked students to rate (as part of a bigger questionnaire) how they felt at that time. And sure enough, participants who expected shocks rated themselves as significantly more anxious and expressed significantly greater reservations about participating in the study than did other participants.

That is not a particularly surprising finding, nor should it be. But it does increase our confidence that Schachter really did manipulate anxiety levels as he had intended. Once again, the question is, did Schachter really manipulate the variable he *thought* he was manipulating?[12]

Manipulation checks are often easily included in many experimental procedures: participants in a "democratic" group structure should rate the group as more democratic and should believe themselves to have more opportunity for participation and influence than should participants in a group with an "autocratic" structure; participants exposed to an "educational" video should rate themselves as "more informed about the topic" than should another group not exposed to the video; and so forth.

For *measured* indicators, the situation becomes a bit more complex but is generally considered to be a two-stage process. The researcher first demonstrates the **reliability** of his or her operationalizing schema. Having shown the measure to be reliable, he or she would then demonstrate that it is also valid.

Reliability

"Reliability" is generally synonymous with consistency, whether of the same phenomenon over time or of judgments about the same phenomenon across different observers. Many constructs that interest social scientists are considered to be relatively stable. For example, attitudes, aptitudes, personality traits, personal values, cognitive styles, and organizational processes may change to some degree over time but are generally fairly consistent, particularly over shorter periods and in the absence of significant relevant life events.

To use a physical example, our height doesn't change much from week to week. If we have a good measure of height, it should thus show us to be about the same height from week to week. If we measure 1.8 metres (six feet) tall one week, but only 1.4 metres (four feet seven inches) the next, we might suspect that our measuring stick isn't a very good one.[13]

Now imagine that we administer a test of mechanical aptitude to a person one week, and it reveals her to be a prospective Thomas Alva Edison. We administer the same test to the same person one week later, and on this second occasion it reveals that she would probably have difficulty operating a light switch. If this occurred, we hope you would be more than a little surprised. Given that the attribute you're dealing with is a reasonably stable one, any legitimate measurement of that attribute *should* classify the person consistently over repeated measurements. In fact, researchers often test a measure of some attribute by administering it to the same group of persons on two successive occasions. This procedure, known as **test–retest reliability**, reveals whether classifications on the attribute are indeed consistently (i.e., reliably) produced.

A second reliability strategy is known as **inter-rater reliability**. If you've adequately specified what a particular construct means to you, other researchers should be able to read your explanation (or be trained in your procedures) and then proceed to make the same judgments you would. If they cannot, then you haven't explained it clearly enough. For example, in one study, Ted was asked by a federal committee that was looking at pornography and prostitution in Canada to do a content analysis of video pornography that involved scene-by-scene coding of videos according to their sexual, violent, and sexually violent content (Palys 1986). Five different people were to code the videos, so it was clearly very important that they all did so consistently (i.e., reliably).

Ted first read the literature and wrote a coding manual that outlined what *he* understood sex, violence, and sexual violence to be and detailed how he felt they should be coded. After a period of preliminary training, but before actually going ahead with the study, he and his assistants sat down and coded the same set of about 100 scenes without communicating with one another. When they compared notes afterward, it turned out that they were generally quite consistent. But a number of problems also emerged that had not been anticipated when the original manual was prepared. So, it was back to the drawing board, where Ted clarified and elaborated on the initial coding scheme; what began as a 12-page coding manual soon grew to about 35 pages. But it was well worth it. When the five members of the team again sat down to independently code another set of about 100 scenes, they averaged between 80 percent and 90 percent exact agreement in their categorizations, which was sufficient to go ahead.

As a bonus, the coding manual exists as an archival document; any researcher can use the same coding scheme should they wish to replicate or extend that research. And the manual itself is also an elaborate specification of the links between the various theoretical constructs Ted was employing (e.g., sex, violence, sexual violence, aggression, power, consent) and the data his research team were gathering. Finally, the manual can serve as a departure point for researchers who wish to discuss the limitations of the method and to contribute further to the spirit of discovery by offering an alternative.

Validity

Although the demonstration of reliability is considered a prerequisite to **validity**, the two terms are *not* synonymous. Rather, they should be seen as two successive hurdles. If a measure fails the reliability hurdle, there's no use going any further, since in most cases it can't be valid.[14] If the measure *is* shown to be reliable, its validity remains an open question. Consider a variable like shoe size. Shoe size is a relatively stable attribute, at least among adults, and we could develop a technique of measuring shoe size (as shoe manufacturers have) that would let us score individuals consistently (i.e., reliably) both over time (test–retest) and across observers (i.e., inter-rater). But shoe size is probably invalid as an indicator of intelligence or creativity.

Operationalizations are considered to be valid *for some purpose*. To demonstrate validity, you must therefore show that your particular operationalization accomplishes the purpose for which you intend to use it. The researcher's task is to pick a relevant criterion in which the construct is embodied and then show that the operationalization is indeed related to that criterion (**convergent validity**), but *not* related to other constructs you do not want to measure (**divergent validity**).

For example, if you develop an operationalization for a construct like "love" (as did Rubin 1973), people who proclaim themselves to be "in love" should score or be classified differently on your measure from persons who do not declare themselves to be "in love" (as Rubin in fact showed). You'd also want to show that it's loving itself you're assessing most directly, as opposed to either related but different constructs (e.g., liking, infatuation, respect) or clearly· unrelated constructs (e.g., the tendency to respond to questions in a socially desirable manner).

If both the operationalization (e.g., Rubin's measure of "loving") and the independent criterion (e.g., self-reports of whether the persons were in love) are obtained at about the same time, then we speak of **concurrent validity.** In **predictive validity,** administering the operational measure and observing the criterion occur at different times. For example, a researcher who wishes to assess the predictive validity of a measure of "dangerousness" among convicted offenders would administer the measure, make decisions about dangerousness, and then follow up the sample over time to see who had indeed exhibited "dangerous" behaviour in accordance with prediction (e.g., see Menzies 1989; Menzies, Webster, & Sepejak 1985).

Assessments of validity will be dealt with in greater detail later in this book (see Chapters 6 and 9). Here, we need only note that empirical requirements recall the legendary Missourian who says "Show me." Recall also that operationalizations are never considered valid in a general sense, but rather are demonstrably valid (or invalid) *for some purpose* and within demonstrated constraints. Thus, if a procedure is shown to be a valid predictor of success in graduate school, that's all it's good for. A measure that's been shown to differentiate between criterion groups may not be valid for categorizing individuals. And if the validation process involves criterion groups that are clearly different (e.g., a group of neo-Nazis is shown, as expected, to have more authoritarian attitudes than a group of civil libertarians), the measure's validity must still be considered tentative with respect to finer distinctions.

Caveats Regarding Operationism

As we saw earlier, the process of research in the social and health sciences involves a continuing interaction between theory and data. Theoretical constructs are important entities in this scheme,

and the operational definitions we choose represent our pragmatic attempts to gather information about the world that bears on our theoretical conceptions. Listed below are a few final admonitions.

MONO-OPERATION BIAS

Rarely can a single operationalization of a construct fully capture the richness of a theoretical construct. We do a disservice both to our theoretical constructs and to the research process if we repeatedly deal with only a single operationalization of a particular variable of interest to us. This problem is referred to as *mono-operation bias.*

Similarly, since all methods of gathering information have their respective advantages and limitations, we run the risk of producing method-dependent results if we always use, say, self-reports or archival sources. This problem is referred to as *mono-method bias.*

Researchers should use multiple operationalizations and multiple methods whenever possible. If you get the same results even when the theoretical construct is operationally defined in three different ways, you can draw conclusions more confidently than if you've defined it in only one way. And if the results *differ* depending on which operationalization is used, the inconsistency is provocative. Multiple operationalizations may also help resolve previous inconsistencies in the literature, by showing the relationships that exist among the respective operationalizations.

DEFINITIONAL OPERATIONISM

A particularly despicable example of mono-operation bias has been termed **definitional operationism** (e.g., see Campbell 1969a; Cook & Campbell 1979). This process involves essentially imposing a definition by fiat and ignoring the theoretical issues inherent in that choice. Rather than discussing the theoretical construct "intelligence," for example, and attempting to deal with the considerable difficulties of generating measures of that construct, definitional operationists seize on a particular operational definition—such as a particular IQ test—and consider it to be definitive of the construct. The result is a tautological and hence trivial statement: "The scores from the IQ test are my operational definition of intelligence. What is intelligence? It is what the IQ test measures."

Besides being obviously circular, this data-oriented approach must also be considered anti-scientific: it implies a contentment with manipulating numbers without considering the theoretical constructs that underlie them and, hence, deflects rather than encourages embellishment and revision. Operationalizations are a means to an end, *not* an end in themselves.

THE PERILS OF AVAILABLE DATA

The ideal sequence in the development of indicators or operationalizations in more deductive inquiry is first to specify or determine what the construct means to you or involves theoretically, and then to develop indicators that reflect that concept the way it has been defined. Researchers who engage in highly constructed research such as experiments are among the most advantaged in this regard as they exert manipulative control to create the situation and operationalizations they want (e.g., Palys 1989). The same would be true of survey researchers who can pose any question they want and, by creating sets of questions, can create a more comprehensive coverage or **conceptual mapping** of the conceptual domain of interest (e.g., de Vaus 2002).

However, there are many situations researchers find themselves in—such as when they do field research with an agency or government department that gives them access to data that have been gathered internally, or decide to do research using an existing data set that has been compiled by another researcher or agency (such as Statistics Canada)—where they are limited to what is available and must do their best with whatever is there. There is much to be said for this type of research that is based on what is essentially **secondary data**, as we outline in greater detail in Chapter 8. It can be a way to do research for minimal cost; getting access to a data set that has been years in the making or that cost the original researcher or agency tens or even hundreds

of thousands of dollars to compile is not to be dismissed. Nonetheless, researchers in such situations must remain aware of the perils of available data.

Ted is in such a situation at the moment. He has been engaged in research regarding Aboriginal justice issues for many years and is currently working with a Canadian court and an Aboriginal justice program to do a tracking study that will show what currently happens to Aboriginal accused who are brought to that Canadian court. Both parties are interested in the result, but the only data available right now are those that have been gathered by the Canadian court, which reflects its managerial needs and priorities, but only minimally reflects the issues that the Aboriginal justice program wants to know about. Even something as basic as who the "Aboriginal" people are is defined differently by the Canadian court than the way the Aboriginal community would do it. If the project were to be done with existing data, it means the project can be undertaken right now, will not cost a lot, and will provide some information on the issue at hand, but with an injustice to the Aboriginal community's understandings and interests. A better job will require setting up new information systems to begin compiling information that we can analyze a year or two down the road and thus will inevitably keep status quo arrangements—which neither group is enthused about—in place for longer, and will be far more expensive to complete. Ted is suggesting that the ideal solution is to do both: use existing data for short-term analysis but set up different information gathering that also reflects the Aboriginal community's needs and interests as part of the court's routine intake and administration process that will be useful for longer term evaluation of the changes the two groups are intending to implement.

Although programs in "Researcher Heaven" will always have been created in the first place with monitoring systems that will ensure useful data for evaluation, in the real-world the data available likely will reflect a limited agency perspective—usually the managerial interests of administrators—and will have been gathered for purposes other than research. Similarly secondary data sets that are available from other researchers and organizations will reflect their conceptualization of the issues and not necessarily yours, which means that making use of the data will inevitably pull you away from the way that you would have designed the research and asked the questions had you had free rein. Researchers must remain cognizant of these limitations as they analyze, interpret, and write up their reports, and convey these limitations to their readers.

SUMMING UP AND LOOKING AHEAD

In this chapter we have outlined some of the issues that one must address even before beginning the research process. One of the first involves getting an idea of *what* to research. The inductive-deductive dichotomy was introduced not only to explain in more detail a concept introduced in Chapter 1 as one on which researchers' preferences often differ, but also to show the complementarity of the two perspectives in achieving general scientific goals and the role that each can play in generating research possibilities.

We then discussed the usefulness of connecting with the literature—both in the library and through Internet-based sources—and encouraged researchers to avoid conceptualizing their research too narrowly. The "Bernie Beck trick" offered a way to think about your research to take you beyond its concrete specifics to a more conceptual understanding of the phenomena you are investigating.

The next consideration involves researchers taking their concerns and phrasing them in the form of a "researchable question." Although our aim is to do research in the broad sense, getting it done ultimately means concretely addressing a specific, researchable question in a particular setting at a given time. Notwithstanding the fact that some research is done simply to *find out* what a good research question would be, *serious* research cannot begin until the researcher has a focused issue on which to concentrate his or her energies. Put bluntly, it's difficult to search for an answer if you don't know what the question is. Doing research involves engaging reality, partly on its terms and partly on ours.

Once particular variables have been isolated for analysis, a next step in some cases, but not all, will be to specify a hypothesis for test. Although there are often good reasons for asserting a hypothesis, particularly when engaging in the deductive process of theory testing, there are at least as many situations where the researcher and the phenomenon under investigation would be ill served by engaging in such hypothetico-deductive inquiry. This is particularly so with respect to more inductive research approaches, where priority is placed on ensuring that the research question(s) being posed and any hypotheses being expressed have meaning within the context being investigated.

Whether one engages in specific hypothesis testing or not, another issue that must be addressed concerns the links between one's theoretical interests or position and the actual measures or indicators that are taken as representative of the concepts that are implied by her or his research question(s). The literature can be useful in identifying these operationalizations, or they emerge at the site from observation, collaborative strategizing, or the development of valid and reliable instruments. The issue here is one of considering and assessing the epistemic relationship that exists between one's theoretical (conceptual) interests and those concrete indicators that are used in one's research.

The notion of operationalization reflects science's dual commitment to theory *and* data. Deductivists and inductivists may argue about whether one should begin with the theoretical constructs and operationalize them or with exploratory observations from which grounded theoretical constructs can emerge. Researchers engaged in finding answers to qualitative and quantitative questions may argue over whether variables of interest are most adequately described verbally or according to some numerical scale. But all researchers believe in an interplay between theory and data. And part of the turf that invariably comes with this dual commitment is the issue of how to move back and forth between these two levels of interest.

The operational definition is little more than the procedural articulation of a variable of theoretical interest. *All* researchers operationalize, since all are committed to an ongoing dialectic involving both theory and data, and hence must at some point be explicit about the particular data in which their theoretical concepts live.

The question to be posed of *every* theoretical assertion is, What's the evidence for that? And operationalization addresses the links between theory and data. Constitutive (or nominal) definitions and operational definitions, respectively, draw attention to the theoretical and procedural worlds in which social scientists operate. Part of doing research involves being sufficiently detailed and vigilant about one's theoretical constructs and procedures that the links between these two levels can be articulated and examined.

Taken together, the issues described in this chapter offer a conceptual framework for approaching any given piece of research—you find a topic, determine your objectives, devise a particular question or set of questions, connect with the literature, and start thinking about how you will operationalize your terms (where the literature will again offer you some help). For some researchers theory will provide the questions and much of the design can be done from your desk; for other researchers, and particularly those in the field, the whole process may be a more collaborative one that emerges from interaction at the research site. How it happens will differ, but it will happen.

We're almost ready to start talking about gathering data. But before we do so, Chapters 3 through 5 will guide you over a crucial bridge between thinking about research and actually going out and doing it. In Chapters 3 and 4 we review two further foundations: the ethical principles that guide social scientists' efforts, and sampling considerations when deciding on whom or what to focus. At that point we will have enough of the big picture of our research to identify our interests and outline a general strategy of inquiry for addressing them; Chapter 5 describes the elements we need to have considered and will need to explain in a proposal.

STUDY QUESTIONS

1. Practitioners of the *inductive* and *deductive* approaches to science were perceived for many years as being in conflict with one another. Differentiate between these two models of science, and indicate how Wallace (1971), through his *wheel of science,* tries to resolve the conflict between them.

2. What role do *theories* play in empirical research, and in what sense are they both *uplifting* and *constraining?*

3. What do practitioners of the inductive and deductive approaches agree on and disagree on with respect to the role of theory?

4. From the deductive perspective, one begins with a theory, generates hypotheses that are implied by the theory, and then gathers data to test the hypothesis (and hence the theory). If the data do *not* support the hypothesis, we say that the theory has been refuted or disproved. If the data are consistent with the theory, we can say that the theory has been "supported," but we do *not* say that it has been "proved." Why?

5. Some researchers suggest that "starting from where you are" is a good place to begin doing research. What are some of the advantages and disadvantages of "starting from where you are"?

6. Social scientists argue that you should always begin your research by *reviewing the literature* in the relevant area. What benefits are gained by doing so?

7. What is "the Bernie Beck trick" and how is it useful?

8. "Should the use of marijuana be decriminalized?" is a good question, but is it a *researchable* question? If so, explain why; if not, indicate why not and how you might change it into one.

9. Should you feel obliged to specify a formal hypothesis when doing research? What, in

your own words, are the strongest arguments for both sides? Are positions on the inductive–deductive issue related to positions on the hypothesis issue?

10. Because of budget tightening in the healthcare system, a local hospital decides that it will begin a program of research to identify strategies to improve the quality of service they offer in the Emergency area. Before they begin identifying the different strategies they will try out, they know that they will need to operationalize the term that will become the fundamental measure of whether they are successful or not—quality of service. Suggest what you think would be an appropriate nominal definition of "quality of service" as well as three different ways that it could be operationalized in the hospital setting. What are some of the strengths and limitations of each of the potential indicators that you identify?

11. How do *nominal* and *operational* definitions relate to *hypotheses*?

12. On what three bases might one justify the choice of any given operationalization or indicator?

13. At the library, locate two recent empirical articles, one each from two of your areas of interest. What concepts are being scrutinized in each study? How are they operationalized? Evaluate the *epistemic relationships* created. What values are implicit in the authors' choice of variables and operationalizations? On what basis (or bases) do the authors justify their choice of operationalization?

14. Compare and contrast *measured* and *experimental* operational definitions.

15. What is *definitional operationism*, and why is it problematic?

16. Do both inductive and deductive researchers engage in operationalization when they do research? In what ways do they differ in how they do research?

17. What are some of the trade-offs involved (i.e., strengths, limitations) when existing, agency-collected data are used to operationally define one's variables?

NOTES

1. When the day of the movie showing finally arrived, we found that although all members of the audience had heard exactly the same film description, only four of the attendees were from groups that had been told that the film had received a "general" rating. About 40 attendees were from groups who had been told about the film's "adult" rating, and more than 100 had heard the "restricted adult" classification.

2. Every document is encoded in a specific format that is associated with the particular software that created it. The "Portable Document Format," or "pdf," is associated with Adobe Acrobat. You need a copy of the Adobe Acrobat program to create pdf documents, but the most recent version of Adobe Reader that enables you to read any pdf document is always free and available from the Adobe site (http://www.adobe.com). Most documents that you would download are likely to be in pdf format, which has become a universal open standard that can be used with any software, hardware, or operating system.

3. NVivo is not the only program that can accomplish this task, but happens to be the one that we prefer and use and, we believe, is the closest to becoming a world standard. Open source applications at the time of this writing include the Coding Analysis Toolkit (CAT), RQDA, Compendium, Transana, and Weft QDA. Proprietary programs include Annotate, Aquad, Atlas.ti, HyperRESEARCH, MAXQDA, XSight, and Qiqqa.

4. We use the term "stakeholders" frequently in this text to mean people that you, as a researcher, recognize as having a legitimate stake in the outcome of your research. All stakeholders should have a chance to offer input at the design stage. Note, by the way,

that although we refer to the stakeholders as "them," you, too, are a stakeholder in the research, since you, too, have constituencies to whom you must answer (e.g., yourself, colleagues, journal editors).

5. The literal translation of *a priori* from Latin is "from the earlier," which doesn't help us that much, but the general concept here is that it is something that is held ahead of time that is independent of experience.

6. Although it sounds sexist now, in the 1950s when this research was done, most—if not all—medical students at any given medical school were male.

7. According to Becker's account, what he said to Chet was "Crock, huh?" but we thought we should have Becker speaking Canadian in this edition of the book.

8. The reasons behind this preference are not important here but are detailed in Chapter 9.

9. http://surveynet.ac.uk/sqb/

10. http://www.statcan.gc.ca/bsolc/olc-cel/olc-cel?catno=89F0115X&CHROPG=1&lang=eng

11. http://www.ropercenter.uconn.edu/

12. Part of the reason for doing that assessment in the experimental setting is to ensure that one is able to interpret the experiment's results when it is concluded. For example, let's say that Schachter did the experiment and did *not* find the effect he hypothesized. Why might that have happened? One possibility would be that his hypothesis was wrong; that is, there actually is *no* relationship between anxiety and affiliation. But the second possibility would be that he never gave the result a *chance* to happen because his manipulation didn't effectively raise the anxiety level of his research participants; that is, it was not an adequate or fair test of the hypothesis. By including the manipulation check, Schachter not only shows us that his manipulation was a valid one, he also precludes the rival plausible explanation

that any non-significant result was due to his never having really manipulated the variable he wanted in the first place.

13. The height example is an apt one in another way, since it is also the case that height may change significantly over some periods (e.g., between ages 2 and 12 and again between ages 65 and 75) but not others (e.g., between ages 30 and 40). In the former case, a "good" measure would *look* "unreliable" because the phenomenon itself (i.e., the child or elderly person's height) is changing. In the latter case, however, we *would* expect the measure to be "reliable": measurements at the two points in time *should* be similar, and dissimilar measurements would lead us to be suspect about our ruler. The example should also sensitize you to the way in which knowledge from other areas (e.g., child development, gerontology, anatomy) can be used to inform measurement concerns, as well as to the way "commonsensical" knowledge may underlie much of the measurement process. Note that this latter situation can be both a strength *and* a weakness.

14. Note, incidentally, that we are assuming here that the phenomenon with which one is dealing is in fact relatively stable, such that "reliability" (in the sense of consistency) should be expected. If one is dealing with a more dynamic phenomenon, however, a valid method *should* show change, which might *appear* as "unreliability." For example, if we look at the thermometer on the back porch on a hot August day and see that it shows 30° Celsius, and then look at it again on a cool September evening and see that it still shows 30° Celsius, we would be more likely to wonder whether the thermometer works than to extol its "reliability." In such cases, methods of reliability assessment that emphasize inter-rater reliability rather than test–retest reliability would be preferred, and a clear prospective research focus might be to explain the source of these variations. (See also note 13.)

ETHICS IN SOCIAL RESEARCH

After some beginning lessons about "science" and "empiricism," followed by a discussion of the preliminary stages of conceptualizing research, we're almost ready to tackle the procedural aspects of gathering data. Our emphasis thus far has been on the *strategy* of investigation. But as Schatzman and Strauss (1973) remind us, the conscientious researcher "needs both strategy and morality. The first without the second is cruel; the second without the first is ineffectual" (146).

FORMALIZING CODES OF ETHICS

Biomedical Horror Stories

The contemporary formalization of principles of research ethics is most often traced to what was undoubtedly one of the most grotesque examples of experimentation with humans that history can offer: the Nazis and the medical research they performed on the Jews they had incarcerated in concentration camps during World War II. As the postwar Nuremberg trials revealed, the Nazis' "experiments" included such procedures as severing and exchanging limbs between live people, made all the more torturous by a lack of anaesthetic. Or, with clipboards and observational protocols in hand, the researchers would place their captives in ice baths and watch to see how long it took them to die from hypothermia.

The Nuremberg trials resulted in development of the "Nuremberg Code," which was the first contemporary statement of research ethics to articulate ethical standards for conducting biomedical research involving human participants. That code subsequently "became the foundation of the *Declaration of Helsinki*, adopted by the World Health Organization in 1964 and revised in 1975. It was also the basis for the 'Ethical Guidelines for Clinical Investigation' adopted by the American Medical Association in 1966" (Berg 2007: 55).

The Nazis were not the only biomedical researchers to give evil a face. For example, beginning in 1932 the United States Public Health Service (USPHS) undertook the Tuskegee syphilis study, which ended up being a 40-year **longitudinal** study of the consequences of untreated syphilis. The USPHS did not infect anyone with syphilis; rather, it identified a group of men who had contracted the disease and, without their consent, decided it would be useful to observe systematically their deterioration over time. When the study began, there was no known treatment for the disease. However, even after a cure was identified, the researchers made sure that the men in their sample—all of whom were African-American—received no treatment, since doing so would have "spoiled" the study.

Even if we were to assume that the Tuskegee syphilis study initially may have had legitimate aspirations for furthering scientific understanding of syphilis in the 1930s when no cure yet existed,[1] there is nothing that could justify continuation of the study—and simply watching the men degenerate and die—after a cure had been developed. The scientific gains were minimal while the human cost was huge. To continue the study was no less than a denial of the dignity of the participants as human beings, as U.S. President Bill Clinton declared when he made a formal apology to the eight participants still alive in 1997 and the surviving families of the others.

Nor does the list of biomedical horrors perpetrated in the name of science end there. There are the two Brooklyn physicians who injected live-cancer cells into their unsuspecting geriatric subjects; the CIA-sponsored LSD/brainwashing experiments conducted on psychiatric patients in Montreal during the 1960s; Canadian and U.S. pharmaceutical researchers who used convicts as test subjects in risky drug trials; and the government and church authorities who saw Aboriginal children attending residential schools being used as subjects in a variety of experiments without their or their parents' consent. The stories seem to go on and on (e.g., Berg 2007; Bronskill & Blanchfield 1998; Collins 1988; "Native Kids Used for Experiments" 2000). All too often, overzealous researchers have mixed the "noble" motives of science with self-interest, an overblown sense of self-importance, and a dehumanization of their "subjects"—who all too commonly are members of socially vulnerable groups such as Jews, Blacks, Indigenous peoples, women, psychiatric patients, the poor, the drug addicted, the homeless, the elderly, and citizens of the Third World—and have forgotten about such fundamental ethical issues as consent and human rights. Clearly, in these cases, the research never should have been done in the first place; no gain in knowledge can justify the denial of human dignity that is involved when human beings are treated as no more than means to an end.

Complexities in the Social Sciences

In the social sciences, discussion about the formalization of ethics guidelines began in the late 1950s. Unlike the biomedical domain, it did not arise from horror stories of social science research, but from new sensibilities about the sorts of issues that social scientists were facing. Two issues in particular dominated the discussion. The first involved the complexities that were beginning to occur from the growing professionalization of social science fields

of study. In his 1959 presidential address to the American Sociological Association, Talcott Parsons noted the burgeoning interest among sociologists in applied issues and, believing these would create new conflicts of interest, suggested that "perhaps a working code of relationships particularly needs to be worked out" (Parsons 1959: 558). In the 1960s Project Camelot—in which the CIA was surreptitiously funding research devoted to discovering how to generate insurgency that might topple Third World governments and showing they were willing to masquerade as anthropologists if it suited their purpose in foreign lands (Horowitz 1967)— left sociologists and anthropologists concerned about maintaining academic freedom and ensuring independence from government.

Sociology did not jump at the opportunity to develop a formalized code of ethics, however, which was seen as a double-edged sword. Most of the 1960s were spent debating whether or not developing a disciplinary code of ethics was desirable. Some members of the American Sociological Association argued that "ethics regulation" was best left in the hands of individual researchers who would remain accountable for their actions (e.g., Becker 1964; Freidson 1964; Roth 1969). Their worry was that the creation of an external standard—to the extent it took the locus of ethical decision making away from researchers and handed it to bureaucrats who might or might not understand the research process—would mark the beginning of the end of academic freedom both for individual researchers and the academic research enterprise as a whole.

Of particular concern was the impact such committees would have on the **sociology of knowledge**. Although the image people have in mind when generating protective codes of ethics is of the vulnerable welfare recipient, student or prison inmate, Galliher (1973) suggested the creation of codes with those persons in mind would instead make it even more difficult to do research with persons who are not so powerless, and who often have elaborate screening devices to keep researchers at bay until "appropriate" (i.e., often self-serving) agreements for the conduct of research have been put in place:

> The irony of the attempt to protect human subjects through a Code of Ethics is that this very Code encourages an approach to data that can be used to legitimize a highly stratified society. Far from protecting those who are vulnerable, the Code serves to aid those least in need of our concern. (97)

Dorn and Long (1974) agreed, but suggested Galliher's "naive" understanding of the *Code* led him to overlook yet another group protected by its contents, i.e., "mainstream" sociologists and their professional organization, the ASA:

> As a product of professionalism, the *Code* appears to be based on the role of the sociologist as "bureaucratic social scientist." In other words, the *Code* not only proclaims the desirability of ethical conduct, it also proclaims the desirability of a particular kind of sociology and a particular role for the sociologist. The *Code* mainly addresses the problems and dilemmas associated with the "organizational or bureaucratic ethos," that is with the individual researcher who uses human subjects, works with collaborators, relies on grantsmanship and outside financial support, and who believes in a "value-free," objective neutral sociology. (34)

Galliher (1973) summed up the issue well when he cautioned,

> Even after giving due weight to all the likely costs and risks to the profession, the unavoidable question sociologists must answer is whether a sociology that only poses approved questions in an approved fashion is either empirically or morally sound. (99)

Others argued the opposite: far from *impeding* academic freedom, a formalized code of ethics would help *preserve* it by serving as a buffer against third-party intervention into the research process (Schuler 1967). For example, when and if a government were to point to this or that isolated example

of an ethics violation and propose seizing control of the research-regulating apparatus that most codes of ethics represent, researchers could point to their disciplinary code and say, "Thanks, but no thanks; we are already regulating ourselves."

A Shifting Locus of Responsibility

THE RESEARCHER MUST JUDGE

If part of the intention of the development of formalized codes of ethics was that it would keep external efforts at regulation at bay, then the strategy in the long run has proven a colossal failure. In the 1970s, researchers were seen as an accountable group of individuals who were responsible for ensuring that no harm came to their participants. The idea that anyone but the researcher was driving the ethics bus was laughable. How could one possibly predict all the things that could possibly happen during a research project? Who but the researcher would have the knowledge and experience to make responsible ethical decisions as issues arose? How could academic freedom survive any other way?

These issues seemed self-evident when the initial social science codes were formulated. The American Psychological Association's statement of principles (APA 1973) reminded us there are few inherently right or wrong answers to ethical questions. Although each ethical principle is easy to recognize and agree to in isolation, in the real world multiple principles combine and interact, requiring trade-offs that must be decided upon with every choice involving both advantages *and* disadvantages. In the end, the APA recognized that each researcher must choose her/his own resolution to ethical questions. Their ethics "guidelines" were exactly that: advice for researchers to *consider* when designing their research. That they did not carry the force of "commandments" or "rules" was affirmed explicitly by noting that the choice of whether and how to do any given piece of research should reside with the "considered judgment" of the "individual social scientist." Investigators were obliged to take "personal responsibility" for ensuring that ethical issues were considered, and the principles were offered as an ideal to which they should aspire. But the choice of what to do belonged ultimately to the researcher, whose job would be to consider how those principles played out in the specific context at hand.

Three decades later, much on the ethics landscape had changed. Canadian associations that once simply adopted the codes of their U.S.-based counterparts developed codes of their own (e.g., Canadian Psychological Association 1991, 2000; Canadian Sociology and Anthropology Association 1994; Sinclair et al. 1987). The new codes offered nothing original in their inventories of principles but departed significantly from previous efforts insofar as both the Canadian and U.S. associations (1) have (all but one) embraced a more centralized decision-making structure that assumes/gives the discipline/agency regulatory authority, and (2) have emphasized the creation of one-size-fits-all mega-codes that transcend boundaries within and between disciplines.

Also significant was how the disciplines attempted to remove boundaries between professional roles within disciplines. The American Psychological Association, for example, decided in 1997 to stop formulating unique sets of ethical principles for particular roles or settings (e.g., one set directed to researchers and another developed for therapists) and, instead, to generate one overarching set of principles to cover the whole range of roles that psychologists occupy. This obviously made for a lengthier list of principles (15 pages as opposed to 1) and a new order of complexity. A similar approach—essentially a photocopied APA code with few discipline-specific adaptations—was followed by the ASA (1997). Both disciplines moved in the direction of more centralized control—issuing "standards" instead of "guidelines" and soon viewed the respective associations instead of researchers as the final arbiters of ethical practice. And yet, the most recent revision of the Canadian Psychological Association *Code of Ethics* (2000) continues to assert a role for personal conscience, noting in section IV-17, for example, that psychologists should

Familiarize themselves with the laws and regulations of the societies in which they work, especially those that are related to their activities as psychologists, and abide by them. If those laws or regulations seriously conflict with the ethical principles contained herein, psychologists would do whatever they could to uphold the ethical principles. If upholding the ethical principles could result in serious personal consequences (e.g., jail or physical harm), decision for final action would be considered a matter of personal conscience.

The American Anthropological Association (1996) is the only discipline to avoid rather than embrace a centralization of authority. Their *Statement on Ethics* emphasizes educating/sensitizing researchers about ethical issues and offers guidelines for the resolution of ethical dilemmas:

Anthropological research, teaching, and application, like any human actions, pose choices for which anthropological researchers, teachers, or individuals applying anthropological techniques and knowledge individually and collectively bear ethical responsibility. Since anthropological researchers, teachers, and practitioners are members of a variety of groups and subject to a variety of ethical codes, choices must sometimes be made not only between the varied obligations presented in the code, but also between those of this code and those incurred in other statuses or roles. This statement does not dictate choice or propose sanctions. Rather, it is designed to promote discussion and provide general guidelines for ethically responsible decisions. (Sec. VI)

GOVERNMENTAL INTERVENTION

The idea of centralizing ethics regulation and placing government in a watchdog/overseer role seems to have originated in the wake of the Tuskegee scandal at the U.S. Department of Health and Human Services with the establishment of the Office for Protection from Research Risk, which more recently became the Office for Human Research Protections. The Canadian government's formal entry into the ethics regulation business came in the mid-1990s with the development of the *Tri-Council Policy Statement* (TCPS) on ethics in research regarding human participants, which all universities that wish to receive funding from the federal granting agencies are required to follow (see CIHR *et al.* 1998).

It is clear that much of the concern that gave rise to the *Tri-Council Policy Statement* arose in relation to biomedical research and the conflicts of interest that were beginning to arise in an era when money-hungry university administrations were being asked to engage in ethics review of proposals by private benefactors with very deep pockets. In particular, the prospect of big money from pharmaceutical windfalls, genome patents, and the like (large grants to the faculty; large overhead for the university) gave rise to concern about the extent to which universities and university researchers caught up in an entrepreneurial spirit might be tempted to forget their ethical responsibilities to society in general and to their research subjects in particular. In this regard, Michael McDonald, director of the University of British Columbia Centre for Applied Ethics and a member of the Tri-Council Working Group that created the early drafts of what eventually became the TCPS, offered the following reflections:

> In constructing the *Code,* our concern was to address central features of Canadian research involving humans, including:
>
> ♦ Increasing private sector dollars pouring particularly into medical research, much of this in the private sector
>
> ♦ Attendant pressures on REBs [Research Ethics Boards] to issue quick and favourable verdicts on research proposals (McDonald 1998)

Another objective of the federal government presumably was to generate a code of ethics relevant to all researchers in Canada who engage in research with human participants. Citing a growing trend toward multi-disciplinary and multi-site research, which was said to create an inconsistent patchwork of ethics decision making across various institutions using various codes, the interest was in creating a harmonized ethics code that emphasized common ethical principles and to which all researchers in all disciplines in all institutional contexts could be held accountable. Clearly this approach represented a significant departure from a more discipline-driven, localized process of ethics review, replacing it with a more centralized process using a "one-size-fits-all" model to which, presumably, all researchers can and must subscribe.

Unfortunately, there was little effort to accommodate the diversity of methodologies and perspectives that characterize humanities, health, and social sciences. The "one size" that was supposed to fit all reflected a biomedical, experimentalist, quantitative model, with little attention or concern over how these principles would translate into other epistemologies and approaches (e.g., Palys 1996a). Tellingly, there was little or no complaint from researchers who primarily undertook quantitative and experimentalist projects who "saw" themselves in the regulations and found categories and approaches that made sense to them. Others, and especially those who specialized in qualitatively oriented research who engage in field research that takes a more collaborative and inductive approach, expressed grave concern (e.g., see Haggerty 2004; van den Hoonaard 2002). The Social Sciences and Humanities Research Ethics Special Working Committee (SSHWC), a committee established to assess how implementation of the TCPS was affecting the social sciences and humanities and to advise on future developments in the TCPS, consulted with Canada's social science and humanities research communities and found there was good reason for this concern. SSHWC (2004) concluded:

> If there is a fundamental problem we can identify, it is that the granting agencies' desire to create a regulatory structure to deal with the

stereotypical clinical trial has resulted in a document and set of structures that assume different modes of research involving different relationships and different concerns than most social science and humanities researchers seek and encounter. Stated simply, the TCPS does not "speak" to their experience, leaving REBs that may lack appropriate breadth of expertise free to impose default assumptions that threaten free inquiry for no ethical gain. The further one's research gets from the paradigmatic/positivist/experimentalist assumptions and understandings that permeate the TCPS, the more ill-fitting the TCPS's application becomes. As this implies, although the deleterious effects of the TCPS have been felt across the social sciences and humanities, it is the more collaborative, inductive, field- and text-based research traditions that have been the most adversely affected. (10)

These problems with the TCPS and the regulatory system it invokes are not unique to Canada. The centralization of authority in government and federal agencies that the Canadian system involves parallels those taking place in other countries. Not surprisingly, the problems identified by SSHWC in Canada are echoed by researchers from the United States (e.g., see Adler & Adler 2002; Christians 2000; Hamburger 2005), Australia (e.g., Israel 2004a, b), and Great Britain (e.g., Pearce 2002), all of which have similar regulatory systems in place.

More recently, the granting agencies have produced a revised second edition of the TCPS (CIHR et al. 2010) that ostensibly benefited from a decade of experience with the first TCPS, the input of many different committees (such as SSHWC) who consulted with the research community and offered advice to the granting agencies on the problems that had been experienced and made suggestions about how to proceed, and direct consultation with Canada's research community. Many issues remain that we consider later in this chapter but, for now, we discuss some of the core principles of research ethics one must consider when undertaking social and health science research.

ETHICS PRINCIPLES

Is The Research Worth Doing?

The choice at the beginning of any research project involving human research participants is whether to do the research at all. This "basic ethical dilemma" sees the researcher balancing two important and sometimes conflicting obligations: to science and to participants. The first is a *scientific obligation* to *do* research in the *best* way we know how. Being a social scientist involves a commitment to the value of knowledge and understanding. Our social mandate is to understand all aspects of society not only as an end in itself, but also thereby to contribute to the development of rational social policy. Since much of our research involves human participants we also have a *humanistic obligation* to treat people with dignity and to safeguard their interests. When participants are volunteers who are participating only because we enter their lives and ask them to do so, for little or no direct gain to themselves,[2] our obligation only increases to ensure that no harm comes to them. That responsibility rises exponentially when the participants do not even know they are participating in a piece of research, as often occurs, for example, when we do observational research in public settings, in archives, or perhaps even after a person's death.

We have already noted some of the biomedical research that clearly involved greater cost to participants than was justified by the research. Research is not without risks—and some research can pose considerable risk, particularly in relation to maintaining confidentiality—but in the social and health sciences we do not kill people. The more typical situation arises with those studies that challenge us to consider where exactly we should draw the line between ethical and unethical.

Stanley Milgram's obedience research (e.g., Milgram 1963, 1974) is often discussed in this regard. His research dealt with an important social behaviour: blind obedience to a presumably legitimate authority figure. However, to obtain his data Milgram deceived his participants by telling them his experiment was about the effects of punishment on learning, when "really" (from Milgram's perspective) it was about how obedient ordinary people would be when ordered to deliver what they believed were real and painful electric shocks of increasing severity to another human being every time they made a mistake in a learning task.[3]

Many were surprised and disturbed that 65 percent of Milgram's participants were completely obedient to the end, even when every indication was that they had certainly hurt, and may even have killed, the other participant. Perhaps even more disturbing were their rationalizations for doing so, along the lines of "I was only following orders" and "It was not *my* responsibility to decide," which were chillingly reminiscent of the rationalizations of the Nazis charged and tried at Nuremberg following World War II, and of U.S. Lieutenant Calley after his murder of innocent civilians in Vietnam. The guilt and stress that participants felt during their participation was considerable. You get a feeling for what it must have been like for the participants when you read Milgram's (1963) original account of how "real" the situation was for the participants.[4] His general characterization of the atmosphere created is as follows:

> In a large number of cases the degree of tension reached extremes that are rarely seen in socio-psychological laboratory studies. Subjects were observed to sweat, tremble, stutter, bite their lips, groan, and dig their fingernails into their flesh. These were characteristic rather than exceptional responses to the experiment … Full-blown, uncontrollable seizures were observed for 3 subjects. On one occasion we observed a seizure so violently convulsive that it was necessary to call a halt to the experiment. (375)

Milgram presents evidence from the debriefings that always followed participation that his research subjects accepted the deceit and felt they had learned from the experience. But *was* the infliction of deception and stress he routinely induced warranted? Milgram argued that it was and received various awards for his research from such prestigious authorities as the American Association for the Advancement of Science; others (e.g., Baumrind 1964) believed what he had done was despicable and that his research would sully our reputation for many years to come.

Informed Consent

One core ethical principle is that of **informed consent,** that is, the notion that it is important for researchers to get consent from people before involving them in research, and that their consent, when and if they give it, should be based on honest and complete information regarding what their participation will involve. This particular principle is typically highest on the list for those who do biomedical research where the question—when, for example, a patient with a certain disease is given the opportunity to take part in a trial for a new drug or receive some experimental procedure —is whether the patient understands the risks, and is willing to participate nonetheless.

In the biomedical realm, this most often involves a written agreement in the form of a contract that the research participant is expected to sign in order to participate, which is consistent with the accounting culture that exists in the medical community and the highly regulated process of clinical trials necessary to develop and distribute new drugs and treatments. In the social sciences and humanities, and especially with more qualitative forms of research, the process of informing the prospective participant and obtaining consent is more likely to be done orally—which is consistent with the emphasis on establishing a mutually trusting relationship and not on legal contracts—although many researchers often will give a written **information sheet** that outlines what the nature of the participant's contribution would be, any risks involved, and explains any promises and safeguards the researcher offers. The idea is to inform prospective participants, in language they understand, about any considerations a reasonable person would want to know before deciding whether to participate. The researcher should be both clear and realistic about what is being offered, making neither grandiose claims about the prospective utility of the research nor any promises that s/he is not prepared to keep.

But informed consent is not always required in social science research. For example, when observational research is done in public places, the participants might never even know that they were part of a study. Of course, this begs the question of where "public" ends and "private" begins. Consider, for example, the covert participant-observation research Lofland and Lejeune (1960) conducted at Alcoholics Anonymous, where researchers actually joined a group and surreptitiously kept notes of the group's activities and dynamics. Is an AA meeting "public" because anyone can walk in and participate? Or is it "private" because the people who go there for help have an expectation of privacy once they have taken the bold step of sitting down and seeking help for a serious problem? Similarly, is an Internet chat site "public" because anyone can enter? Or "private" because of some tacit social expectation that only those who are serious about the topic will join? Does it make it any more ethically acceptable in either case if the researchers ensure that no one is ever named or otherwise identified?

Perhaps the most famous and controversial study of this type was Laud Humphreys's (1970) *Tearoom Trade,* in which Humphreys played the role of a "watch queen" in order to observe intimate homosexual encounters in public washrooms. Although this choice in itself gave some observers cause for pause because of the intimacy of the behaviour, notwithstanding that it was happening in a "public" place, greater controversy surrounded Humphreys's research when he surreptitiously took down licence plate numbers, found out where the men lived, and then (in disguise) interviewed them in their homes to discover more about who they were in their lives away from the tearooms. Was the lack of consent justified by the knowledge that was produced and/or the confidentiality that was maintained? Would it make any difference to you to discover that homosexuality was illegal in most of North America at the time, and that Humphreys's research went a long way to dispelling many of the homophobic stereotypes that were prevalent?

Even when a researcher *does* set out to secure informed consent, it is sometimes easier said than done. Myriad prospective difficulties present themselves. One worry is that there may be reason to believe that telling participants about the study's objectives may influence the very phenomenon one is trying to observe. For example, in a study commissioned by a federal government committee looking into issues regarding pornography and prostitution (Palys 1986), Ted was interested in ascertaining the social (and particularly the sexual, aggressive, and sexually violent) content of video pornography available in neighbourhood video establishments. Should he have approached video outlet proprietors and told them that he was (in part) interested in determining whether videos involving sexual violence were as pervasive as the media suggested?

Ted felt that if proprietors did indeed have an array of sexually violent material, and if they came to realize that their offerings were under systematic scrutiny, they might withdraw some of their more questionable videos for the duration of the study and thereby invalidate the results. He also reasoned that, in this instance, the videos were "public" materials and that this was a straight economic exchange in which his only obligations were to pay the required fee and return the tapes in good condition. That he and his assistants took the tapes home to code their content was their choice. At the same time, because the proprietors did not know of the study, Ted felt obliged to ensure confidentiality and thus never referred to any particular establishment by name. A record of the establishments was in a file of which only he knew the location, and was destroyed after the study was completed.

Pragmatic problems also may arise in securing informed consent. The information to be conveyed might be too technical or esoteric for prospective participants to appreciate fully, or some attribute of them might virtually preclude the assurance of communication (e.g., in the study of young children or some psychiatric patients). The researcher nonetheless should attempt to communicate those aspects of the study that might reasonably affect willingness to participate and, in the latter case, normally would contact guardians or other advocates of the prospective participant(s).

Further, securing informed consent is sometimes impossible or highly impractical. When coding archival records or photographs of crowds, for example, it may not be possible to identify or contact all the people involved. Lack of identification may not be a problem since it implies anonymity, although one also would want to ensure that subsequent accounts avoid inadvertently providing identifying information through other clues (e.g., personal characteristics, place of work). When people can be identified but not contacted, precautions normally should be taken to ensure confidentiality (e.g., by blurring or pixelating faces if pictures are used).

And finally, although consent is normally discussed and agreed upon before beginning one's research, research that involves more than a one-shot/single-session encounter has the advantage of allowing the development of greater comfort and rapport between researcher and participants, assuming that all is going well and the researcher is treating participants with care. But consent in such research should be seen as more of an ongoing agreement that can be re-negotiated when and if circumstances change. That is what Nancy Olivieri, a medical researcher affiliated with Toronto Sick Children's Hospital and the University of Toronto, intended during a multi-site clinical trial she undertook for a drug that was being developed by multinational pharmaceutical company Apotex. If successful, the drug would have allowed children who otherwise had to stay in hospital and endure frequent and painful blood transfusions to live a more normal and pain-free life. A small preliminary trial showed promising results and Dr. Olivieri signed on to the larger project and began recruiting participants from among her patients. Part of the

informed consent process involved telling them that while the preliminary results were not conclusive, they were at least promising and that the drug was basically safe.

Once the clinical trial actually began, however, problems with the drug started to show up, and there were indications that patients needed to be more closely monitored than was originally expected, with death now a possible "side effect" of the drug. Dr. Olivieri felt obliged to bring these facts to the attention of her patients and their parents—feeling that this was a substantive change that warranted a re-visiting of the information on which their consent had been based—as well as to other researchers in the medical community who were involved in similar trials with this drug. Although such a response would appear to be an ethical no-brainer, given our obligations to participants, the response by the funder and Olivieri's institutional employers was harsh and swift. Apotex threatened to sue Olivieri for breeching the confidentiality agreement she had signed, and the University of Toronto, who had been looking forward to the multimillion dollar donations that Apotex had been prepared to offer the university and Sick Children's Hospital, wilted under the pressure and failed to live up to their responsibilities to ensure that research participants were adequately informed and protected.[5]

Confidentiality

While informed consent is often touted as the primary ethical principle in the biomedical community, **confidentiality** is the principle with more consistent relevance in the social sciences and humanities. People have a right to keep information about themselves private or to share it only with those whom they trust to safeguard it. When we approach people and ask them to divulge information about themselves, and especially when that information could cause them embarrassment or harm if it were to be released, it is incumbent on researchers to take every precaution to ensure that confidentiality as to the source of the information is respected.[6] In order to provide that protection, however, it is important to consider where and how threats to confidentiality might arise and, hence, what we are protecting ourselves and our participants against.

LOOSE LIPS SINK SHIPS

By far the most pervasive threats to confidentiality are those that come from our interactions with people in the milieu we are researching. These are what you might call relatively "low-grade" threats because they disappear most times with a simple "no," but they occur frequently and must be prevented. They arise most commonly when multiple people are being interviewed in one setting—a given organization, community, or family, for example. Some of the participants inevitably will be curious about what another research participant said. It may be quite well-meaning: a concerned parent might fish for hints about what her/his uncommunicative son or daughter divulged to the researcher about illicit drug use or something as apparently innocuous as what they said about their career plans. Or it may be more maliciously motivated: a respondent might give the impression that s/he is an "insider" on some issue and look for confirmation from you that another person divulged a particular opinion, allegiance, or point of view as a way of justifying a vendetta or other campaign of action against the person.

Researchers must be very careful not to say anything to any one person that another person told them, or in many situations even whether some specific other person participated (or did not). This may sound very simple, but guarding against it requires considerable vigilance. The problem arises because we want to appear competent, intelligent, and "in the know" so that people will respect us as interviewers and feel confident giving us information. But if we start sharing what others have told us, even if the information seems innocuous, we begin to tread on very dangerous ground. Our typical status as "outsiders" to the setting means we are less likely to know enough about the internal dynamics of the setting to make good choices about

what is safe to share and what is not. Things that to us seem innocent may have significant consequences within the setting we are researching. The best way to inspire confidence in research participants is to show them how vigilant you are in safeguarding the information that others give you; it tells them that you will show the same vigilance with their information and that they really can trust you. Conversely, if you are sloppy with others' confidences, why would they believe you will be careful with theirs?

LEGAL THREATS

Far less common are more formal efforts by third parties to acquire information from confidential research sources through legal means such as subpoenas. In the litigation-happy United States the literature contains a few dozen examples of legal threats to confidentiality that have arisen in the last 30 years out of what is no doubt hundreds of thousands of research projects that have been carried out in that time (see Cecil & Wetherington 1996 and Lowman & Palys 2001a for a sample of U.S. cases).

In the late 1960s and 1970s these cases most often involved legal authorities (police, grand juries, prosecutors) trying to acquire confidential research information from researchers in order to prosecute the research participant or someone known to the research participant for violations of law. The U.S. federal government recognized the threat this posed to research participants, and ultimately to research itself, and developed statute-based protections known as **Confidentiality Certificates** (for health research)[7] and **Privacy Certificates** (for justice research)[8] that create absolute protections for the confidentiality of identifiable information from being used in any legal proceeding without the permission of the participant. Accordingly, such threats have all but disappeared. When they do appear in court, judges have for the most part been very respectful of the privacy of research participants (see Lowman & Palys 2001a). Since the 1980s and 1990s the more common scenario is for subpoenas to occur in the context of civil litigation, i.e., where one group of people is suing a multinational pharmaceutical, tobacco, oil, or computer company, citing an independent researcher's work in their statement of claim and the company then subpoenas the researcher in order to try to enlist or discredit her/him as part of its legal defence.

RUSSEL OGDEN AND SIMON FRASER UNIVERSITY

In Canada, only one researcher has ever been subpoenaed and asked to divulge information that would identify particular participants, and that is Russel Ogden. Ogden was a criminology graduate student who, for his M.A. thesis, interviewed people who had assisted in the suicides and euthanasia of people with HIV/AIDS. His ground-breaking research illuminated a highly controversial practice to which no one other than the participants would normally ever be exposed. Knowing something about this niche of life—the circumstances of its occurrence and the perspectives of those who engage in it—provides important information that enriches the quality of public debate and our understanding of law in context. Such research is impossible without the assurances of confidentiality, privacy, and anonymity provided for by research ethics policies and the trust that participants have in researchers' and the university's adherence to those principles. Because the very freedom of research participants is at stake, the ethical burden on researchers who undertake such research is high.

All research undertaken at Canadian universities involving human participants requires ethics review, and Russel Ogden's was no exception. Regarding informed consent, Ogden proposed to tell participants there was no obligation for them to disclose identifying information, that there was a small chance he might be subpoenaed, and that he would protect the confidentiality of his sources in any event. Because this research could not be done without a meaningful assurance of confidentiality, Ogden made it clear to the SFU Ethics Committee that he would offer "absolute confidentiality" to his research participants. The committee approved his proposal.

Although few people were interested in the topic of Ogden's research when he was beginning it, it was national news by the time he was completing it two years later because of a woman named Sue Rodriguez. Ms. Rodriguez had a degenerative neurological condition commonly known as Lou Gehrig's disease, and, in anticipation of the day when she would be unable to act, she began petitioning the Parliament of Canada for legislation that would enable her to have an assisted suicide. Media outlets across the country—and a Senate committee established on the topic—looked for an expert in the area of assisted suicide. Russel Ogden was that person. Simon Fraser University bathed in the media spotlight, and the university's media relations department helped him manage the dozens of requests for interviews that were arriving. Ogden's research was a perfect example of the role that university research can fulfill by offering information about certain niches of life to those charged with developing social policy, such as members of Parliament and senators.

All went well until the Vancouver coroner read an article about Ogden's thesis and decided that the information Ogden had gathered might be helpful to him in investigating a death that had come to his attention. Information contained in a newspaper article suggested to him that the death might have been an assisted suicide. But who was she? How exactly had she died? The coroner wondered whether one or two of Ogden's research participants might have attended her death. He asked to see a copy of Ogden's M.A. thesis and subsequently subpoenaed Ogden to give evidence at the inquest.

Ogden appeared and answered all the more general questions that the coroner asked him regarding assisted suicide among people with HIV/AIDS—in the belief we share that part of the role of academics is to share their expert knowledge with the courts when it will assist them in their decision-making—but he refused to answer any questions that would have allowed for any of his research participants to be identified. He then became the first researcher in Canada ever to be threatened with a charge of contempt of court if he did not reveal confidential research information. Ogden claimed **researcher–participant privilege** and again refused.

We will discuss the notion of "**privilege**" in greater detail below, but suffice it to say for now that, to say that some relationship is "privileged" means that persons in that relationship are exempt from the normal requirement that all of us have to testify when asked to do so in a court of law when and if information discussed in the context of that relationship becomes of interest to the court. The lawyer-client relationship is protected by a privilege, for example, so that you can go and talk freely to your lawyer and seek legal advice without fearing that s/he will get subpoenaed and be on the witness stand the next day giving evidence against you. Because privileges can interfere with the court's search for truth—evidence that might otherwise be useful to a court adjudication is not available—privileges are very rarely granted. However, it is recognized that certain socially valued relationships simply could not exist without the confidence that what is said in the context of that relationship will remain confidential. Some of these are recognized in statute; any others have to be asserted in court.

There is no privilege based in statute for researchers in Canada—except for Statistics Canada researchers whose participants are protected through the *Statistics Act*—but one *can* claim privilege on a case-by-case basis in the **common law**. Because the circumstances had never arisen in Canada for such a claim to be tested prior to Ogden, his case was a historic opportunity for SFU to come to Ogden's aid to defend academic freedom and assert researcher–participant privilege for the benefit of research participants and the research community as well. Instead, the university administration dropped him like a hot potato. No one from the university administration or Research Ethics Committee ever testified on his behalf or offered to explain the importance of confidentiality to his research. The university administration also refused initially to assist in any way with his legal fees, but, after pressure by his supervisor, then-president John Stubbs agreed to offer $2,000 on "compassionate grounds" toward legal fees that ultimately mounted to more than $11,000.

Fortunately, Ogden understood his ethical obligations and defended his research participants nonetheless, arguing that his research was done in accordance with the highest ethical standards of his discipline and could not be done without a guarantee of confidentiality, which he was now honour-bound to uphold. After hearing Ogden's evidence in relation to the **Wigmore criteria** (see below), the coroner agreed that Ogden and his participants deserved recognition of a public-interest privilege and "release[d] him from any stain or suggestion of contempt" (*Inquest of Unknown Female* 1994: 10).[9]

The struggle to have the university recognize the error of its decision not to defend Ogden would go on for several years, with the university lambasted along the way by a provincial court judge when Ogden later sued the university for breach of contract. Ogden argued that he was required to do original research as part of the requirements for his M.A. degree, that he did so in a manner that followed SFU's research policies and the highest ethical standards of his discipline, and hence that there was an implicit contract obliging the university to support him in court when the guarantee of confidentiality he made—which the university research ethics committee had approved—was challenged.

There are several respects in which this case is noteworthy, not the least of which is that it allowed Ogden to subpoena then-president John Stubbs as well as Bruce Clayman (a physicist who at that time simultaneously occupied the roles of dean of Graduate Studies, vice-president of Research, and chair of the University Ethics Committee) and require them to explain the basis of their decision to refuse to support Ogden's principled defence of his participants, research confidentiality, and academic freedom. Their testimony revealed the decision had nothing to do with ethics; the primary concerns of the president and vice-presidents who advised him were liability considerations and "image." In the end, Judge Steinberg sided with the university as a matter of contract law—it was up to the university to decide which cases it would litigate and which it would not—but with Ogden on the moral issues that permeated the case:

> The vague statements of personal support as expressed by the president of the University, Dr. Stubbs, and the dean of Graduate Studies, Dr. Clayman, sound hollow and timid when compared with the opportunity they had as leaders of the University, to promote the demonstrated value of academic freedom and academic privilege as evidenced in this case. To set aside this opportunity because of fear that if they were to financially support Ogden by paying his legal fees in this context, some people might misapprehend that they were in favour of euthanasia, demonstrates a surprising lack of courage. (*Russel Ogden* v. *Simon Fraser University* 1998: 68)

An independent review of the university's decision making conducted by SFU professors Nick Blomley (geography) and Steven Davis (philosophy) followed and was consistent with the tenor of Judge Steinberg's decision. Blomley and Davis concluded that the university administration had erred in its decision and should (1) send a letter of apology to Ogden; (2) reimburse Ogden for his legal fees; and (3) guarantee that, in future, any graduate student whose academic freedom was challenged by a third party in the way that Ogden's was would receive legal help. Then-president Blaney accepted all three recommendations (see Lowman & Palys 2000; Palys & Lowman in preparation). Although the episode began as a low point in the university's history, in the end SFU's graduate students went from individuals the university would allow to swing in the wind, to students who probably have the best legal guarantees in the world that such a debacle will not happen again.

Although Simon Fraser University and many other universities in the country started acting as if subpoenas would rain down on researchers thereafter, the fact of the matter is that now, almost 20 years later, Ogden is still the only researcher in the country who has ever been subpoenaed. As this suggests, the likelihood of you or any other researcher being subpoenaed, particularly in Canada, where litigation happens less frequently and where grand juries (the biggest source of subpoenas in the United States in criminal cases) do not exist, is about equal to the likelihood of you being hit by a bolt of lightning on your birthday—theoretically possible but highly unlikely. Nonetheless, since your ethical obligation is to protect your research participants and because in general it is so easy to build some degree of protection into your research, you should do so simply because that is what we do. There are two primary ways to maximize such protection to participants: procedurally and through law.

PROCEDURAL PROTECTIONS

The easiest way to protect the confidentiality of respondents is simply never to obtain or record participants' names in the first place, that is, to safeguard their confidentiality by providing them with anonymity from the moment you begin gathering data. There are many kinds of research—particularly more structured kinds of research such as survey, interview, and questionnaire-based studies in which numerous respondents are all being asked roughly the same questions—where this is the easiest rule to follow. If you have never gathered identifying information in the first place, and if the information you gather is not sufficient to identify specific individuals indirectly, then there is no threat to worry about, and you can simply guarantee confidentiality to your participants when you inform them prior to asking them for their consent to participate.

In situations where you must obtain people's names, either because you need them ahead of time in order to know whom to approach or because the circumstances of the situation lead you to obtain that information, you should **anonymize** your records at the first opportunity and then destroy your original digital recordings or records[10] (or give them to your participants if that is what you promised to do). Sometimes you may need to keep some form of identifier that allows you to distinguish between respondents; in that situation use **pseudonyms,** that is, invented names that are used consistently through your notes so that you can keep together all the quotations from the person you'll call "Kim" and be able to differentiate "Kim" from "Pat." Should your notes ever inadvertently fall into the wrong hands, no one but you will know who "Kim" and "Pat" "really" are, and with the passage of time, your memory of who was assigned what pseudonym will no doubt fade as well.

In the event you are generating more quantified and structured data that are maintained in digital files, your options are simply to delete any identifying information from the file as soon as is practical or to keep identifying information in a separate file, preferably in a different order than exists in the "content" file, but linkable through some designator included in each file that only you know about.[11] In some cases—and the more sensitive the data the more you are advised to do this—researchers save their data in files using encryption programs such as PGP (Pretty Good Privacy) or TrueCrypt, which gives as good an assurance as one can get that no one else will be able to make use of the data to identify particular respondents.[12] Other strategies for anonymizing, encrypting, and hiding computerized data are given by Boruch and Cecil (1979); although the specific technologies they describe are in many cases obsolete, the conceptual guidelines they provide for devising anonymizing strategies are as relevant today as they were at the time that book was written.

Although high-tech, computer-based approaches can create a challenge to third parties who might be interested in your data, another line of defence is offered by going precisely in the opposite direction, that is, the "old school" low-tech solution of using a notebook of sorts (especially for non-quantitative field note data), which can be hidden more easily than your computer's hard drive. The thing to do here is to seek and pursue approaches that are appropriate for the kinds of data you are compiling. The greater the harm that can come to participants if the data were to be revealed, the greater the level of protection you should seek.

LEGAL MECHANISMS FOR PROTECTING RESEARCH CONFIDENTIALITY

Recall that Russel Ogden invoked a researcher–participant privilege when he was subpoenaed. Generally speaking, there are three sources of privilege. The first is statute-based, i.e., where the protections that exist are actually written into law. In Canada, the only research participants whose information enjoys **statute-based protection** are those who participate in research conducted by Statistics Canada. The *Statistics Act* gives Statistics Canada employees a privilege to ensure that identifiable information unearthed by research by one portion of government (Statistics Canada) cannot be used by any other branch of government or in any court or other proceedings in a manner that would violate the confidence of any individual respondent. Researchers in Canada who are not employees or "deemed employees" of Statistics Canada[13] are not so fortunate; they do not have the *guaranteed* privilege that exists via the *Statistics Act*, but in the end may be no less protected because of the possibility for recognition of privilege through the common law (Palys & Lowman 2000).

The two types of privilege that are generated through the common law are known as "class" and "case-by-case" privileges, which differ in how well-established they are and where the onus of proof lies when a challenge arises. An example of a **class privilege** is the lawyer–client privilege that has been recognized by courts in Canada and other countries for a very long time. To say it is a "class" privilege means that the court is prepared to assume it exists without the need for every lawyer and client to prove they deserve it every time their confidences are challenged. Accordingly, if anyone were to argue that any given communication between a lawyer and her/his client should be revealed, the onus of proof would be on the challenger to demonstrate what compelling reasons exist in this case for the privilege to be set aside.

In the event that privilege has not yet been established for a particular relationship either in statute or as a class privilege in the common law, anyone can nonetheless ask the court to recognize a public-interest privilege *in that particular case.* In Canada and the United States, researchers will have the best chance of making a claim of **case-by-case privilege** recognized in common law by designing their research to anticipate the requirements of the Wigmore criteria or Wigmore test, a set of four criteria that the Supreme Court of Canada has stated it will use to adjudicate whether a privilege should be recognized given the circumstances in the case at hand (Palys & Lowman 2000), and that also has been recognized as appropriate for this purpose by the U.S. Supreme Court (Palys & Lowman 2002). The criteria specify that

(1) The communications must originate in a *confidence* that they will not be disclosed;

(2) This element of *confidentiality must be essential* to the full and satisfactory maintenance of the relation between the parties;

(3) The *relation* must be one which in the opinion of the community ought to be sedulously *fostered;* and

(4) The *injury* that would inure to the relation by the disclosure of the communications must be *greater than the benefit* thereby gained for the correct disposal of litigation.* (Wigmore 1905: 3185; italics in original)

A successful claim of privilege requires evidence that speaks to all four requirements (e.g., Crabb 1996; Daisley 1994; Jackson & MacCrimmon 1999; O'Neil 1996; *R. v. Gruenke* 1991; Traynor 1996; Wiggins & McKenna 1996). That is exactly what Russel Ogden did when he was subpoenaed by the coroner, and his research stands as a legacy for researchers dealing with sensitive topics on how to do it right (see especially Jackson & MacCrimmon 1999; Palys & Lowman 2000, 2002; in preparation).

DESIGNING RESEARCH TO ASSERT RESEARCH–PARTICIPANT PRIVILEGE

When engineers learn to design a bridge, they are taught to neither under-build nor over-build. This requires them to have a good understanding of the place the bridge will go—how solid is the ground underneath? what range of weather conditions will it have to endure? how high do the winds ever get? how much traffic does it need to hold at peak time?—and then to design something that is safe within that context. If they under-build they run the risk of the bridge falling down and killing those who are on it. If they over-build they end up spending tens of millions of your taxpayer dollars for nothing.

Researchers face an analogous challenge when it comes to confidentiality protections. The trick is to be thoughtful and careful and to know enough about what you are getting yourself and your research participants into so that you understand the risks without getting hysterical and seeing potential threats in every shadowy corner. When the data are gathered anonymously or anonymized very soon after collection, there is little danger to participants for a violation of confidentiality and hence the researcher should simply guarantee to her/his participants that their identities will be kept "strictly confidential." However, if the source of the information is identifiable and a disclosure would bring harm to the participant, then that is when you need to build a stronger bridge and "Wigmorize" your research. Doing so involves anticipating the requirements of the court, as Russel Ogden did when he was gathering the data for his master's thesis. We outline some of the issues to consider below.[14]

CRITERION 1: ESTABLISHING A SHARED EXPECTATION OF CONFIDENTIALITY The first criterion tells us that a prerequisite for claiming privilege is that the two or more people involved in the relation must have a shared understanding that their communication was, in fact, confidential. As Wigmore (1905) wrote, "The moment confidence ceases, privilege ceases" (3233). In practical terms, this means researchers should ensure there is a clear "expectation of confidentiality" that is shared by researcher and participant and that the research record includes evidence that speaks to that understanding.

In the few U.S. cases where things have gone badly for researchers (e.g., see Lowman & Palys

---

* Palys, T. S., & Lowman, J. (2002). Anticipating law: Research methods, ethics and the common law of privilege. *Sociological Methodology,* 32, 1–17.

2001a; Palys & Lowman 2002), it is noteworthy that none had evidence regarding this first element. For example, neither Mario Brajuha[15] (Brajuha & Hallowell 1986) nor Richard Scarce[16] (Scarce 1994, 1999) had clearly established that their interactions were part of a researcher–participant relationship; neither had completed a formal research proposal, and, consequently, neither had subjected his proposed research to ethics review. No record existed of the pledge they had made to participants, nor was there any formal indication or approval that showed they were engaged in an activity that was university-approved and being executed in accordance with the canons of their discipline. Nor had either of the two kept records of their and the participants' understanding regarding confidentiality in field notes. Brajuha, for example, could say only that he had guaranteed confidentiality to some but not all participants and could not recall to whom he had guaranteed confidentiality and to whom he had not (Brajuha & Hallowell 1986; O'Neil 1996).

In cases where a researcher–participant privilege *was* recognized, the opposite held true. For example, when the Vancouver coroner subpoenaed Russel Ogden (see *Inquest of Unknown Female* 1994; Lowman & Palys 2000) and asked him to identify research participants who may have witnessed the death, Ogden presented evidence showing that he had completed a proposal and undergone a research ethics review, and he produced copies of the pledge of confidentiality he had made to prospective participants. This established that Ogden was indeed engaged in "research," that appropriate officials at the university believed his plan reflected the highest ethical standards of his discipline, and that he and his participants shared the understanding that their interactions were completely confidential. Although no legal authority in Canada had ever subpoenaed a researcher and asked him or her to reveal confidential information, Ogden and his supervisor correctly anticipated that if anyone were to challenge the confidentiality of their information it was likely to be the coroner. Ogden's pledge meant he would refuse to divulge identifying information even if threatened with contempt of court.

A matter of no small legal importance with respect to Ogden's pledge was that it was unequivocal. Although one does not have to guarantee "absolute" confidentiality as Ogden did—and we would actually advise instead that one's promise should state any communications will be "strictly confidential"[17]—anything less runs the risk of being treated as a "waiver of privilege" by the courts. For example, in *Atlantic Sugar* v. *United States* (1980), corporate respondents to an International Trade Commission questionnaire were told that the information they provided would not be disclosed "except as required by law." A U.S. Customs Court later used this exception to justify its order of disclosure of research information from researchers, saying they were the law and "required" the information. The lesson here is that researchers should (1) be prepared to discuss confidentiality issues with participants; (2) make that discussion part of the research record; (3) be clear on what they are prepared to guarantee; and (4) live up to that pledge.

CRITERION 2: ESTABLISHING THAT CONFIDENTIALITY IS ESSENTIAL Because claims of research–participant privilege are decided on a case-by-case basis, general claims about the importance of confidentiality to research are not enough. Researchers also should be ready to demonstrate that confidentiality was crucial to their specific research project (Daisley 1994; Jackson & MacCrimmon 1999; Palys & Lowman 2000, 2002). Traynor (1996) suggests that the necessity of confidentiality should be addressed in research proposals, thereby showing that confidentiality was part of a considered plan and neither capricious nor rote. For example, Ogden's research proposal explained why he believed it would be impossible to gather reliable and valid data and to meet the ethical standards of his discipline unless he offered complete confidentiality to participants.

Claims that confidentiality was "essential" can be weakened by behaviour that is inconsistent with such claims. For example, in the *Scarce* case, the courts seemed skeptical about the researcher's claim of privilege when it became known that he and the research participant who was the prime suspect in the case were friends outside the research context. Was the researcher truly claiming privilege because of the research relationship? Or was he using it out of convenience and his allegiance to a friend? The claim of privilege was undermined further when it became evident the researcher's wife was at a key meeting where a confession may have been made, when the wife had not been shown in evidence to be part of the research team (*In re Grand Jury Proceedings: James Richard Scarce* 1993; O'Neil 1996; Scarce 1994, 1999). If confidentiality is important, then your actions should be consistent with that claim, and "confidential" conversations do not happen when people who are not part of the research team are present.

In contrast, Russel Ogden only strengthened his claim for privilege by asking participants directly—and recording their answers—how important the provision of confidentiality was to their participation. All participants who had witnessed or participated in an assisted suicide or euthanasia stated that confidentiality was vital to their participation. They would divulge information to Ogden *only* if he promised to maintain their anonymity. The coroner found this evidence persuasive, recognizing that the information he sought never would have existed in the first place had it not been for Ogden's guarantee, which he now was obliged ethically to honour (*Inquest of Unknown Female* 1994).

CRITERION 3: ESTABLISHING THAT THE COMMUNITY VALUES THE RELATIONSHIP The third criterion asks whether the relationship under scrutiny is so socially valued that "the community" believes it should be protected. Various "communities" can be considered here, such as the research community; the community of which participants in the research at hand are members; those who engage in policy formulation and implementation and who value independent research that contributes to that task; and the broader citizenry, who benefit from the knowledge created through research. Much of this information would come from expert

testimony when and if the researcher is subpoenaed. However, there is also evidence that can be gathered and material that should be retained as one goes through the process of preparing for and executing the research.

For example, any research that has satisfied peer review, secured funding, and/or undergone ethics review must clearly be valued by the research community. Court decisions, too, often make reference to and reflect the high value that society places on academic research (e.g., *Dow Chemical* v. *Allen* 1982; *In re: Michael A. Cusumano and David B. Yoffie* 1998; *Richards of Rockford* v. *Pacific Gas and Electric Co.* 1976). In Russel Ogden's trial, an internationally renowned criminologist testified about the importance of confidentiality to research such as Ogden's. A nurse who had worked with Vancouver's HIV/AIDS community for years also testified about how important confidentiality was within that community, especially given the hysteria about HIV/AIDS at that time, when a positive test affected one's employability and insurability and made one a social pariah.

CRITERION 4: A BALANCING OF INTERESTS Any well-designed social or health science research on a sensitive topic that anticipates the evidentiary requirements of the Wigmore test should satisfy the first three criteria easily. The fourth criterion sees the court balance the social values upheld in the researcher–participant relationship against the costs that would be incurred by withholding relevant evidence in the case at hand. In Ogden's case, this came down to Ogden's need to maintain his ethical pledge to participants and the impact a disclosure would have on the research enterprise if Ogden complied *versus* the coroner's need for the evidence to make an accurate determination of the Unknown Female's identity and cause of death in the inquest at hand.

But note the asymmetry here: until a "class" privilege is recognized, researchers have to make their decisions ahead of time and can only hope they are correct in their speculation of the range of circumstances that might arise, while the courts make their decisions after the fact on the basis of the concrete facts that are presented to them. The U.S. Supreme Court recognized this paradox in a case involving a claim of therapist–client privilege (*Jaffee* v. *Redmond* 1996):

> We part company with the Court of Appeals on a separate point. We reject the balancing component of the privilege implemented by that court and a small number of States. Making the promise of confidentiality contingent upon a trial judge's later evaluation of the relative importance of the patient's interest in privacy and the evidentiary need for disclosure would eviscerate the effectiveness of the privilege. As we explained in *Upjohn,* if the purpose of the privilege is to be served, the participants in the confidential conversation "must be able to predict with some degree of certainty whether particular discussions will be protected. An uncertain privilege, or one which purports to be certain but results in widely varying applications by the courts, is little better than no privilege at all."

Researchers face exactly this dilemma. We can see what decisions the courts have made and feel some degree of confidence that research can meet the Wigmore criteria and that the judiciary has been very respectful of the rights of research participants, but with the case-by-case analysis that is involved in the Wigmore test, all we really know in advance is that the law will be made after the fact on the basis of a situation we can only guess at. However, researchers must make their decisions ahead of time. One would hope that Canada's ethics powers (see below) will seek to rectify this problem in the manner that it has been done with Statistics Canada's research participants via the *Statistics Act* and in the United States for some kinds of research through Confidentiality Certificates and Privacy Certificates, but as of this writing there has been no visible movement on this issue.

The ideal course of action for any researcher is to do their best to be ethical *and* legal—as the Wigmore criteria allow and as Russel Ogden

demonstrated is possible—but the lack of statute-based protection in Canada and the fact that the law is effectively made up after one's research is over creates the possibility that the "ethical" thing to do—to protect one's research participants and their right to confidentiality—may conflict with the "legal" thing to do—to give identifying information to a court when a legal order is given and all legal means of resistance have been exhausted. Because of this, researchers who want to gather sensitive information from participants must decide ahead of time what they will do if, in that last instant, law and ethics point in different directions. Those who would limit their allegiance to the participant by law and would comply with a legal order to disclose information that would be harmful to participants' interests must inform potential participants of that fact when securing consent.

In our view, the question we need to ask ourselves for any piece of research we do is whether we believe the rights of our participants and the knowledge we are gaining outweigh any other foreseeable concerns or interests that might arise in the research. If the answer to that question is yes, then one proper ethical course is to give an unqualified pledge of confidentiality, and, having made that decision and the promise that goes with it, we are ethically obliged to keep it. If the answer is no, then in our view the proper course of action is to not do the research because you would have to limit confidentiality, and that would be placing research participants at risk—albeit a very small risk because no researcher has ever been ordered to divulge confidential research information to a Canadian court—for your benefit.

If we look to the United States, where there have been more cases and where in at least three instances researchers *have* been ordered to divulge information that would violate particular research participants' confidentiality,[18] a search of the literature that describes the subpoenaing of researchers has yet to reveal a case where we believe violating a research confidence would have been the ethical thing to do. Accordingly, we will continue to ask ourselves the balancing question before we engage in any piece of research and, where the answer is yes, will continue to offer an unqualified guarantee of confidentiality to the participants in our research.

OTHER CONFIDENTIALITY CONSIDERATIONS

THE INTERSECTION OF ETHICS AND LAW The debate about ethics and law with respect to research confidentiality arose in the wake of the Ogden subpoena, ostensibly because his subpoena took something that had, until then, been nothing more than an abstract threat, and made it real. In response, the then-vice-president of Research at SFU, a physicist who chose to be chair of the SFU ethics committee at a time when SFU's ethics policy allowed that, introduced a policy of "**limited confidentiality**" that would be imposed on all researchers who were gathering information that might involve revelations of criminal activity. John Lowman and Ted Palys and most of their colleagues in Criminology rejected this idea, seeing it as a violation of their academic freedom and inconsistent with the ethical standards of their discipline. Criminology as a discipline would not be possible unless researchers were prepared to take a non-judgmental approach to many of the people they study, and the same is true of many other disciplines. How can epidemiologists understand the spread of disease if persons who have them are unwilling to talk to researchers because they will be reported if they admit exposure? How can political scientists understand the development of political attitudes and social policies if members of oppositional groups see the researcher as a prospective agent of the state? If we believe that studying these difficult and controversial areas is a prerequisite to the positive, rational, and humane development of law and policy, ensuring research participant confidentiality is safeguarded so that they do not pay a price for their altruism and our benefit is a fundamental ethical requirement; to do any less seems exploitative.

This stance is reflected in the draft *Code of Ethics* of the Academy of Criminal Justice Sciences, which states,

Confidential information provided by research participants should be treated as such by members of the Academy, even when this information enjoys no legal protection or privilege and legal force is applied. The obligation to respect confidentiality also applies to members of research organizations (interviewers, coders, clerical staff, etc.) who have access to the information. It is the responsibility of administrators and chief investigators to instruct staff members on this point and to make every effort to insure that access to confidential information is restricted.[19]

Other disciplines say much the same thing. For example:

Informants have a right to remain anonymous. This right should be respected both where it has been promised explicitly and where no clear understanding to the contrary has been reached. These strictures apply to the collection of data by means of cameras, tape recorders, and other data-gathering devices, as well as to data collected in face-to-face interviews or in participant observation. (American Anthropological Association *Statement on Ethics* 1986, principle 1c)[20]

[S]cholars also have a professional duty not to divulge the identity of confidential sources of information or data developed in the course of research, whether to governmental or non-governmental officials or bodies, even though in the present state of American law they run the risk of suffering an applicable penalty. (American Political Science Association *Guide to Professional Ethics in Political Science* [2nd ed.] 2008)[21]

Sociologists have an obligation to ensure that confidential information is protected. They do so to ensure the integrity of research and the open communication with research participants and to protect sensitive information obtained in research, teaching, practice, and service....

Confidential information provided by research participants, students, employees, clients, or others is treated as such by sociologists even if there is no legal protection or privilege to do so. Sociologists have an obligation to protect confidential information and not allow information gained in confidence from being used in ways that would unfairly compromise research participants, students, employees, clients, or others. (American Sociological Association [ASA] *Code of Ethics* 1999; reprinted 2008)[22]

However, all these codes also enjoin researchers to understand the law as it relates to their work, to consider possible limitations to confidentiality that may arise from either legal and/or ethical considerations, to make an ethical choice about how these will or will not affect their work, and to be honest and forthcoming to research participants about these choices.

AVOIDING CAVEAT EMPTOR ETHICS People who choose to limit confidentiality have the obligation to tell prospective participants about these limits because in many cases these will affect the willingness of participants to take part in the research. Also, limiting confidentiality is unethical when it involves no more than the researcher downloading risk to the research participant, as well as the responsibility of deciding what is or is not legally appropriate to say. This would make research

participation an unfair and exploitative exchange: the researcher takes no risk but gets all the gains in information and whatever else accrues from it (royalties, patents, publications); the volunteer research participant takes all the risks and, if trouble should ever arise, is greeted by a researcher who says, "Gee, that's too bad, but I told you that might happen." This sort of **caveat emptor ethic**, which we see lampooned in Figure 3.1, is beneath the "highest ethical standards" to which members of the academy are supposed to aspire. Our ethical obligation is to protect our research participants, not to protect ourselves *from* participants by using an ostensibly "ethical" approach that, in our view, is no more than liability management and exploitation in ethics clothing.

Limiting confidentiality does not limit one's ethical obligations. First and foremost is the ethical obligation to ensure research participants know the researcher's commitment to confidentiality is limited, but to do so without causing them to waive any rights they may have, such as their right to assert privilege through the Wigmore criteria. In part, this may involve being crystal clear about what unique set of circumstances might lead to disclosure—so that the courts cannot see the limitation as a general waiver of privilege—and do everything possible otherwise to ensure that the research participant is protected, including exhausting all legal avenues.

For example, in one Canadian case involving a claim of therapist–client privilege, where both

Figure 3.1: Caveat emptor ethics

the therapist and her client considered the fact that a court might subpoena the therapy records (*M. [A.]* v. *Ryan* [1997] 1 S.C.R. 157), the therapist promised to do "everything possible" to defend the confidentiality of the records. She then put this into practice by being vigilant in the way records were maintained so that nothing appeared in the records that would cause the patient harm if they were disclosed in court, not including some information in records in the first place when the therapist and her client agreed that some information was best not recorded, and living up to the promise by defending the privilege all the way to the Supreme Court of Canada.

(UN)ANTICIPATED THIRD PARTY HARM A more difficult issue involves the scenario where a researcher learns of some dastardly harm that will befall some innocent third party. In this case, a researcher might wish to consider violating confidentiality not because of some legal imposition but for ethical reasons. The key thing to consider here is whether or not such revelations of prospective harm are anticipated (e.g., Palys & Lowman 2000). If they are *not* anticipated, then it makes little sense to refer to them in informed consent statements. For example, it would be a tad absurd and somewhat offensive to start off interviews with parents by saying something like, "These interviews about your children's teachers are completely confidential unless you tell me that you are going to kill one of them." We assume the best of our interviewees unless there is reason to believe otherwise, and a pledge of confidentiality about their views of teachers is exactly that, a pledge about their provision of that information. Any plot to kill the principal would be beyond the realm of the research, and the researcher would have to figure out some ethical way to try and prevent that harm without denying the rights of the participant s/he is still obliged to protect.

The decision making becomes a bit more dicey in situations where we might well *anticipate* getting information involving harm to third parties. For

example, in the literature on prisons there has been an ongoing debate regarding the effects of solitary confinement on prisoners. One set of researchers argued that there is really no problematic effect to solitary confinement per se, while another group of researchers argued that the effects of solitary confinement can be very debilitating, and in particular may lead prisoners to become more violent to themselves (i.e., suicidal, self-mutilating) and/or others (i.e., assaultive).

If we wanted to do research in which we assessed what happens to prisoners who are placed in solitary confinement, it seems unlikely that prisoners would tell us about these tendencies if they knew we would inform authorities about anything unseemly they disclose. Imagine you are a prisoner placed in solitary confinement, whereupon a researcher comes up to you and says, "I really want to find out the effects of solitary confinement. I would particularly like to hear whether you have any intention to harm yourself or others. However, I should warn you that if you tell me anything along those lines, I'll be obliged to tell prison authorities."

If you were a prisoner who was planning on doing harm to yourself or someone else, would you tell the researcher about those desires, knowing that the researcher would then go and tell prison authorities? We suspect not. And yet that is exactly the position in which Ivan Zinger and his colleagues (Zinger 1999; Zinger, Wichmann, & Andrews 2001) placed their participants in research conducted in three of Canada's maximum security prisons concerning the effects of solitary confinement on prisoners. In the end, Zinger found that prisoners in solitary confinement were no more likely than inmates in the general prison population to report a desire to harm themselves or others and, because of that, sided with researchers who had argued that there are no terrible effects to solitary confinement. Given that Zinger was at that time an employee of Corrections Canada and that his results place a stamp of approval on Corrections Canada policies—"Problems with the use of solitary confinement? What problems?"—we can only see the limitation of confidentiality in this case as an exercise in self-interest (see Lowman & Palys 2001b; Palys & Lowman 2001).

To the extent that other researchers follow Zinger's lead and routinely limit confidentiality, one can envision a huge credibility gap arising in situations where self-interest leads a variety of authorities to want to find nothing, that is, to do research "with eyes wide shut." Imagine wanting to study police interrogations in order to determine whether and how frequently they violate the rights of accused, and limiting confidentiality by telling officers that any violations will be reported to superiors. Or imagine studying the ways that forestry and mining companies circumvent environmental regulations and telling employees that anything they tell you might be subject to subpoena. We can imagine the headlines now: "Police Always Follow Procedure, Says Study." "Study Finds Resource Companies Always Respect Environmental Regulations." How comforting.

We don't mean to minimize the difficulties and ethical soul-searching that can characterize such situations, but remember again that there are two things we need to consider whenever we undertake a piece of research. One is what it takes to ensure that the data we end up with are valid and reliable—the scientific obligation. If we end up with data whose validity is questionable, then we have wasted everyone's time and perhaps placed people at risk for nothing. Indeed, that is our biggest concern with Zinger's research regarding the effects of solitary confinement; however important the question he addressed and however thoughtful other elements of his research design may have been, his decision to limit confidentiality made the value of the information he gathered questionable. So why gather it in the first place?

The second part of the equation involves the humane considerations that we have for our research participants and those around us. And on that score we have to consider whether hearing about some things and gaining some kinds of knowledge are worth it. Zinger began his research by noting that 19 prisoners died in custody in

Canadian prisons from suicide or homicide in the year preceding his research. To what extent did solitary confinement contribute to that number? Could more humane policies or procedures or the simple banishment of forced solitary confinement reduce that number? Do we want to know or don't we? By limiting confidentiality, Zinger will never know. Is the long-term benefit of potentially saving 19 lives per year worth going into this research with an unqualified guarantee of confidentiality? In our view, that is exactly the question that has to be answered. Because the validity of the data depends on the guarantee of confidentiality, the choice is between deciding that the benefits are worth it and doing the research with full confidentiality, or deciding that it is not and withdrawing from the research. This does not prevent the researcher from taking actions designed to try to avoid the harm that would otherwise result, but s/he must do so in a way that respects the rights of the informant as well.

But what happens if we are simply moving along in our research with the parents of children playing Little League baseball, asking them about the role that organized sports plays in their children's lives, when we come across some piece of disturbing information that might involve harm to a third party that we had not anticipated at the outset of the study? Should we tell someone about it or not?

The answer, we suggest, is "it depends." If we believe confidentiality is a core ethical principle, and that we have a duty to our research participants that is akin to the duty that a lawyer has to their client or that a priest has for the information he hears in the confessional, then it should be only in the rarest and most extreme situations that we should consider violating our promise of confidentiality. But where should the bar be set? One legal case heard at the Supreme Court that addressed these issues in relation to the lawyer–client relationship was *Smith* v. *Jones* (1999).

Briefly, Mr. Jones (a pseudonym) was charged with assaulting a prostitute in Vancouver's Downtown Eastside (DTES). He was intending to plead guilty and his lawyer sent him to a psychiatrist for an evaluation that, it was hoped, would be helpful when it came time for Jones to be sentenced. Because the assessment was being done as part of a legal defence, the communications between psychiatrist Smith (also a pseudonym) and defendant Jones was considered subject to lawyer–client privilege. Perhaps because of this protection, Mr. Jones was very open with Dr. Smith, and started telling him that he had actually developed a plan to kidnap, detain, assault, and kill prostitutes on the DTES and that the assault he was charged with was actually just a "trial run" to see whether he had it in him to kill someone. The plan was already being implemented not only in terms of the trial run, but he had also renovated his apartment—changing locks and doors and such—in a manner that would allow him to imprison women there with no risk of them escaping. Dr. Smith was shocked by these revelations and the potential trail of death that lay ahead if Mr. Jones were let loose, and he let Jones's lawyer know that he wanted to share these details with the court at sentencing. The lawyer balked at this possibility, seeing that such revelations would be contrary to his client's interest, but psychiatrist Smith insisted and the matter went to court. Given that lawyer–client privilege is a class privilege, the onus was on Dr. Smith to show why his concerns were so compelling that the privilege should be set aside and his information be allowed in court.

The case is an important one because it dealt with the very issue we are discussing, i.e., where the bar should be set in order before a violation of confidentiality might be considered permissible given the duty of confidentiality that is reflected in the existence of a lawyer–client privilege. It is relevant to the research enterprise because, as the justices explained,

> [Solicitor–client privilege] is the highest privilege recognized by the courts. By necessary implication, if a public safety exception applies to solicitor–client privilege, it applies

to all classifications of privileges and duties of confidentiality. (at 44)

In the end, the Supreme Court said that three criteria must be met before it might be considered *permissible* for someone who has a duty of confidentiality to violate that confidence: (a) there must be a clear danger to an identifiable target; (b) the prospective harm must involve serious bodily harm or death; and (c) the danger is imminent. Because all three were present in this case—(a) Jones was targeting prostitutes in a specific area of Vancouver's DTES; (b) he was planning on killing them; and (c) the plan was already in motion and being implemented—the Supreme Court decided that it was indeed permissible for Dr. Smith to set aside the privilege and violate the confidence given this set of facts.

Three further observations of the Court are noteworthy. First, the justices made clear they were not setting out any kind of *requirement* for disclosure in such an instance, but rather simply setting out minimal criteria beyond which a disclosure might be permissible. Second, the Court also made clear that it had no rigid formula to offer as to when a decision for disclosure should be made, and that every case must to be considered on a case-by-case basis. How this is done would depend on the time available: if the harm were about to happen, the decision would have to be made then and there; if there was more time before the intended event, as was the case in *Smith* v. *Jones*, then consultation with trusted others (or taking the matter to court, as Dr. Smith did) should occur. And finally, the Court also reminded lawyers (and all others with a duty of confidentiality) that, in the event circumstances such as those described in *Smith* v. *Jones* were to happen and a decision for disclosure made, there are many different ways the situation can be dealt with and the harm prevented—dialing 911 is not the only alternative—and that one's responsibility to the client (or research participant, in our case) does not end with a decision to disclose. Any disclosure must be the minimal possible disclosure needed to effect an outcome, with the rights of the client (or research participant) transgressed as little as possible.

Conflicts of Interest

RESEARCHER CONFLICT OF INTEREST

Being "ethical" as a researcher means that you have a primary obligation to consider things from research participants' perspectives and to ensure participants' rights are safeguarded. In many cases the interests of researcher and participant coincide. Researchers become researchers for many different reasons, but two we frequently hear include the desire to understand something deeply and well for its own sake (whether as a general motive or to understand some specific domain) and to generate knowledge that will help produce some social good. Research participants are also typically altruistic; none of them gets any direct or large reward for participating. So in that sense, both researchers and participants often share the belief that something is important, and both hope their actions will produce knowledge that will benefit the greater good.

However, it would be naive of us to assume that the interests of researchers and research participants always coincide. Occasions may arise when it is in the researcher's self-interest to gloss over the details in order to ensure a ready supply of research participants from whom one can gather information. And these days many university researchers are engaged in entrepreneurial interests in addition to their university "day job": consulting; creating standardized tests that are used in schools, hospitals, prisons, and other institutions; and other product development such as pharmaceuticals, software, and educational materials. Concern arises over the conflicts of interest these activities may bring to the underlying research, for example, where development of a particular product can result in considerable wealth being generated from patents, royalties, fees, and commissions, or where a favourable evaluation may result in an increase in share value. In these situations the university researcher is no longer an "independent" researcher who is simply following

knowledge for its own sake with no stake in the outcome.

This conflict of interest is particularly problematic when the researcher is in a position of power relative to the research participant—or when the **gatekeeper** who has allowed the researcher access to the participants is in a position of power over the participants[23]—and is especially worrisome in the case of captive audiences who depend on the researcher for other rewards. For example, it used to be that many psychology departments would require students—especially the hundreds or even thousands who take Introductory Psychology at some universities—to participate in research in return for partial course credit, in part because it gives students the experience of what it is like to be a research participant but also to keep up the supply of bodies required for faculty member and graduate student research. The practice still continues in many places, but there is now more effort made to ensure that students have reasonable options if they would prefer to decline the opportunity.

Of course, many of those studies entail little or no risk whatsoever; the major one is probably the possibility of dying of boredom. However, other "captive" situations are far more problematic, as the following incident reveals:

> We used prison inmates in a number of research projects and always asked for their consent. However, in retrospect, it seems to me that since I also sat on boards that made recommendations for parole and had other important influences on their prison lives, it might be questioned whether they really felt free to refuse in view of their high need in these areas. (APA 1973: 47)

Ethics problems arise when the power differential between researcher and participant is considerable. They are exacerbated when the prospective risk to participants or the possible cost to them if they refuse to participate is high, for example, where the researcher is also the teacher who hands out grades, the physician who is also responsible for treatment, or the prison authority who is also responsible for

maintaining discipline or making recommendations for positive rewards like day passes or parole.
From an ethical perspective, it is incumbent on
the researcher to seek out independent advice on
how best to deal with any appearance of conflict
of interest—conflict that would be evident to any
neutral third party looking at the situation. The
most common ways of doing so are taking steps
to alleviate the conflict—for example, by divesting
oneself from one side or the other of the conflict,
such as by divesting oneself of shares in the company, or getting an independent decision-maker
involved who has no vested interest in the outcome
and is not in any way dependent on or related to
the researcher.

CONFLICTS OF ROLE

A woman was sitting on a riverbank one day, soaking
up the sun, when suddenly she saw a man in the
river in danger of drowning, calling for help.[24] She
bravely jumped into the water, swam over to the
man, dragged him out, and saved him by giving
him artificial resuscitation. But no sooner had she
sat down to catch her breath when another body
appeared in the water, and she jumped in again and
saved that person as well. Both were thanking her
profusely when suddenly a third body appeared and
in she jumped again. But no sooner than she had
finished saving that person, yet another appeared in
the water! However, this time, instead of jumping
into the water, she began to walk upstream.

"Hey!" called someone who had been watching
all of this unfold. "Aren't you going to save that guy
as well?"

"Hell, no!" she replied. I'm going to go upstream
to find out how all these people are ending up in
the river in the first place!

It is difficult to be in two places at once, as is
the case with the woman in our story. She can
be the front-line person who jumps in and saves
people, or she can don a researcher's cap and head
upstream to find out what is causing the situation,
but she cannot be in both places at the same time.
An analogous situation arises when the individual
doing the research occupies two different roles with

respect to the participant where the duties associated with the two roles come into conflict.

We have already described how the primary
ethical duty of the researcher is to protect her/
his research participants. With respect to confidentiality, this typically means putting one's judg-
mental hat aside and listening to whatever it is
that the participant wants to share with you, and
sometimes what people tell you is not pretty. This
is especially true in regards to many of the social
and health problem areas that are most important
to understand—poverty, addiction, disease, abuse,
oppression, exploitation, bullying, prejudice and
discrimination, corruption. As the preceding section on the *Smith* v. *Jones* case showed, when one
has a duty of confidentiality, the bar that might justify a disclosure is set very high.

However, there are now many professionals—
including, for example, social workers, physicians,
teachers, nurses and counsellors—whose professional codes of ethics call on them to report certain
kinds of behaviour to authorities, with far lower
triggers for disclosure than were outlined in *Smith*
v. *Jones* (1999). These often are "helping" professionals whose inclination and obligation, going back
to our allegory of bodies in the river, is to jump in
the river and save whoever is floating downstream.
There are many situations where their professional
codes of ethics do not clash with codes of research
ethics, but many others where they will, and confidentiality is one of those areas. On this point the
original federal ethics policy, the *Tri-Council Policy
Statement: Ethical Conduct for Research Involving
Humans* (CIHR et al. 1998) stated that

> To preserve and not abuse the trust on which
> many professional relations reside, researchers
> should separate their role as researcher from
> their roles as therapists, caregivers, teachers,
> advisors, consultants, supervisors, students or
> employers and the like. If a researcher is acting in
> dual roles, this fact must always be disclosed to
> the subject. Researchers should disassociate their
> role as researcher from other roles, in the recruit-
> ment process and throughout the project. (2.8)

The newest edition of the TCPS (CIHR et al. 2010) also recognizes the problem but is less prescriptive:

> Researchers and research students hold trust relationships, either directly or indirectly, with participants, research sponsors, institutions, their professional bodies and society. These trust relationships can be put at risk by conflicts of interest that may compromise independence, objectivity or ethical duties of loyalty. Although the potential for such conflicts has always existed, pressures on researchers (e.g., to delay or withhold dissemination of research outcomes or to use inappropriate recruitment strategies) heighten concerns that conflicts of interest may affect ethical behaviour.

> …Conflicts may arise from an individual's involvement in dual and multiple roles within or outside an institution. While it may not be possible to eliminate all conflicts of interest, researchers are expected to identify, minimize or otherwise manage their individual conflicts in a manner that is satisfactory to the REB.*

If left unmanaged, the main problem with these role conflicts is that they can put the researcher in a policing role—as was the case with Ivan Zinger in his study of the effects of solitary confinement—instead of simply trying to understand the situation, thereby violating the following principle:

> Researchers shall avoid being put in a position of becoming informants for authorities or leaders of organizations. For example, when records of

---

*† Excerpt from TCPS 22nd edition of *Tri-Council Policy Statement: 2010*. Pages 59-60 and 91. MR21-18/2010E-PDF http://www.pre.ethics.gc.ca/pdf/eng/tcps2/TCPS_2_FINAL_Web.pdf Canadian Institutes of Health Research, Natural Sciences and Engineering Research Council of Canada, and Social Sciences and Humanities Research Council of Canada, Tri-Council Policy Statement: Ethical Conduct for Research Involving Humans, December 2010. Reproduced with the permission of the Minister of Public Works and Government Services, 2012.

prisoners, employees, students or others are used for research purposes, the researcher shall not provide authorities with results that could identify individuals unless the prior written consent of the participants has been given. Researchers may, however, provide administrative bodies with aggregated data that cannot be linked to individuals for purposes such as policy-making or program evaluation. When seeking consent, researchers shall advise prospective participants if aggregated data from a project may be disclosed, particularly where such disclosure may pose a risk to the participants. For example, aggregate data provided to authorities about research on illicit drug use in a penitentiary may pose risks of reprisal to the prisoners, even though they are not identified individually.† (CIHR et al. 2010, see discussion regarding Article 5.2)

Balancing and Combining Ethical Principles

Although not exhaustive, the list above describes some of the major principles that should be considered prior to undertaking one's research. The role of the researcher is to treat research participants with care. A general rule we always try to apply is to ask what standard we would expect a researcher to follow if the participant was our mother, son, or a close friend.

And of course there are many issues we haven't discussed in this relatively introductory treatise: situations that arise in particular research contexts that pose unique dilemmas and have been the subject of considerable debate. Where does "encouragement to participate" end and "coercion" begin? What ethical safeguards should researchers practise when they are dealing with cultures and groups other than their own? Is concern about privacy outmoded when tens of millions of people put the intimate details of their lives on Facebook and line up to participate in reality TV shows that leave nothing of their personal lives to the imagination?

Our main intention in this chapter thus far has been to try and convey something about some of the main ethical principles that researchers bring to their work. But if "being ethical" involved no more than following a bunch of principles in relatively predictable scenarios, then everything would be easy. We're all intelligent people; we all want to be ethical; we all have a sense of right and wrong. However, problems arise for at least four main reasons, all of which suggest that it's not as easy as it looks.

First is that the very nature of research involves some degree of unpredictability. If we know exactly what is going to happen, there is no need to do the research. The implication is that, instead of relatively *certain* costs and benefits, we are often weighing our best *guesses* of costs and benefits.

Second is that the environment in which we operate is to some degree uncertain, particularly when it comes to the intersection of our research activities and the rights of our research participants with other activities and the rights of other people in society. One area this is particularly true is where issues of ethics intersect with issues of law. We want to be ethical, and of course we want to be legal, and the Wigmore criteria—in relation to confidentiality—give us our best shot at being both ethical *and* legal. But what do we do when and if one of those rare occasions arises when "being legal" points in one direction and "being ethical" points in another? Do you believe it is more important to be ethical? or legal?

A third source of difficulty is that ethical principles do not exist in isolation. All of them operate in any given situation and sometimes they conflict. "Being ethical" thus involves not simply following a set of rules but trying to find a way to resolve competing demands, balancing and trading off different "goods," and making decisions based on the perspective and best interests of our research participants.

An implication of the above is the fourth difficulty, that there are rarely any clear-cut "right" and "wrong" ethical answers. Add to this the fact that researchers and participants are individual human beings who differ from one another, have different belief systems, and value ethical principles differently—because of the value systems they bring to the research—and part of the "problem" is to recognize that there are

potentially different ways to deal with situations, more than one of which can be ethically "correct."

Indeed, far too much time is spent by would-be ethicists arguing about what the "right answers" are, as if these were things that could be determined absolutely once and for all, when (arguably) the more important issue is whether the *process* of ethics consideration engaged in by the researcher has adequately taken into account the perspective of participants and the specifics of the case as they are known. At bottom is the question of whether the research can survive mechanisms of accountability that revere two core principles: whether we adequately consider and protect the rights of the research participant, whose dignity we value and without whose participation the research enterprise would not exist, and whether it is respectful of the academic freedom of the researcher, which is a cornerstone of the research enterprise and without which the social value of research would be undermined.

Beyond some reading that discusses ethics issues and some of the more contentious debates that have raged in the social and health sciences on these issues, your ethics education will come in large part from a front-line involvement with research where you meet real people and, we hope, take the time to know your research participants as people. And notwithstanding the general principles that books like this espouse, ethics considerations always come down to case-by-case considerations that involve a unique mix of the people who are your participants, the specific issue you are researching, your own perspective and interests, the norms and standards of your discipline, the social and legal context in which you are operating, and on and on. There are few simple answers, and you owe it to yourselves and your participants to give these matters deep consideration.

Implications for the Sociology of Knowledge

We continue to be concerned about the regulatory process for ethics that exists in Canada notwithstanding recent efforts to improve the TCPS, particularly because of the impact this highly bureaucratic scheme appears to have had on the sociology of knowledge for reasons that have nothing to do with ethics per se. A recent book by sociologist and University of New Brunswick Professor Emeritus Will van den Hoonaard (2011) adds to the evidence accumulated by others (e.g., SSHWC 2004) that affirm the legitimacy of these concerns. Van den Hoonaard's book documents the changing face of the research enterprise in Canada since the advent of the TCPS. Although it is difficult to disentangle the impacts of the TCPS per se from other changes in the academy, interviews with researchers and REB members across the country reveal REB censorship and, more disturbingly, a growing researcher propensity for *self*-censorship in the wake of REB control. Through archival analysis of master's theses in anthropology and research presentations at conferences that focus on qualitative research methods, van den Hoonaard (2011) revealed that more intensive and involving field research methods such as participant observation and ethnography are done far less frequently since the advent of the TCPS, while studies based solely on interviewing—which was always integral to field methods but often only one element of an inherently multi-method perspective—have increased in frequency.

Other sources make the same observation in Canada and other countries that have seen their governments develop and implement federal codes of ethics (e.g., Fitzgerald 2004; Katz 2007; Shea 2000; SSHWC 2004).[25] While many U.S. authors have emphasized the censorship aspects of ethics regulation (e.g., Hamburger 2005), few have considered the repercussions that contemporary ethics regulation has had for whose voices are being heard and whose are missing in the great social discussion to which researchers are supposed to contribute. Social groups that are most likely to be affected are the socially marginalized and vulnerable who have shown for decades their willingness to speak to social and health scientists who want to learn about their niche of life and point of view as long as their conversations are confidential, but who would be most concerned about prosecution,

suppression, and stigmatization if they were to be identified. This includes not just those who have broken or who are breaking the law that criminologists often talk to, but also those who walk in the shadow between illegal and legal, or who are the whistleblowers that help shed light on injustice or the illegal behaviour of those for whom they work, or who are harassed by legal authorities who themselves are treading the boundary between legal and illegal, or who suffer from health conditions that would affect their reputation, employability, or insurance benefits.

British author Robert Dingwall (2008) draws attention to the role of independent observer that the university has occupied, and the perspectives that would be lost if researchers were to become simple agents of the state:

> In the contemporary world, citizens depend upon a great deal of expert knowledge in order to make good judgments about each other and about the social institutions that they encounter. The quality of that knowledge depends crucially on free competition between information providers. If what has traditionally been the most disinterested source of information, the universities, becomes systematically handicapped in that competition, then all citizens lose out. When we give up doing participant observation with vulnerable or socially marginal groups because of the regulatory obstacles, then a society becomes less well-informed about the condition of those who it excludes and more susceptible to their explosions of discontent. How helpful is it when the only ethnographers of Islamic youth in the UK are undercover police or security service agents? (10)

He also reminds us of some of the functions of deviance, whether with a lower case or capital "d."

> The great English sociologist, Herbert Spencer, drew an important contrast between industrial and militant societies. The latter type, which are well-exemplified by the former Soviet Union and its East European satellites, were, he argued,

doomed to lose out in global competition because their authoritarian structures blocked diversity and innovation. Both socially and economically, they were frozen by their command systems. IRBs and other forms of pre-emptive ethical regulation begin to look like the precursors of the surveillance states that are being increasingly entrenched in the US and the UK. Their incursions into liberty are justified in the name of security, but may well have unanticipated consequences in terms of prosperity. Wherever dissident voices are silenced, innovation eventually dies. (10)

The result is a shallower research enterprise relying more and more on existing public data sets that have been prepared by institutional authorities to serve their own ends, and a progressively greater denial of voice to those most affected by what those institutions do.

SUMMING UP AND LOOKING AHEAD

In this chapter we have attempted to convey some of the many complexities that must be faced whenever one does research with human participants. If there is a central point to this chapter, it is to think about the relations you allow to exist between researcher and researched.

Research participants are a crucial resource to science disciplines that attempt to understand human action, and, particularly when we are in a more privileged position than our research participants, and especially when we are in a position of power over participants, we must live up to our obligation to maintain their dignity and treat them with care. In this regard, several major ethics principles that transcend disciplinary boundaries were introduced. These include the balancing of scientific and human considerations that influence whether we engage the research in the first place, the principles of informed consent and the maintenance of confidentiality, and issues of researcher, REB, and institutional conflict of interest.

A separate focus of the chapter involved examination of the regulation of ethics by third parties:

disciplines, universities, granting agencies, and the federal government. It was argued there has been a trend toward more extensive and more centralized ethics regulation over time. Although general support was expressed for the idea of ethics review because of the opportunity this allows for an independent look at the proposed research by a third party, concerns arise to the extent these third parties are themselves involved in conflicts of interest that lead them to advance views and interests that can be at odds with the rights and interests of research participants and the ethical obligations and academic freedom interests of researchers.

Special heed was taken of the *Tri-Council Policy Statement* (TCPS) on ethics for research involving human participants, now in its second edition (CIHR et al. 2010), that governs all research done in universities across Canada. Some possible strengths of this intervention were noted, as well as possible deleterious effects on research participant rights and the academic freedom of researchers. Particularly worrisome is the negative effect of the biomedically and experiment-driven research mentality that frames the TCPS on other research perspectives, particularly on more qualitative field-based research traditions and more critically oriented research that speaks to some of society's most pressing problems and seeks to give voice to marginalized and stigmatized members of society in order to ensure the broadest possible participation in democratic discussion and debate. Readers of this book are encouraged to keep themselves informed on these matters as the TCPS continues to be implemented and Canada's ethics bureaucracy grows.

STUDY QUESTIONS

1. According to the chapter, what is the "basic ethical dilemma"? Why is it a dilemma?

2. What does each of the following concepts mean, and how can you ensure that they are implemented in your research: informed consent, confidentiality, anonymity.

3. Look up a recent issue of a journal in your area of study, pick an article that interests you, and evaluate it in terms of the ethical principles outlined in this chapter.

4. Is an AA meeting "public" because anyone can walk in and participate? Or is it "private" because the people who go there for help have an expectation of privacy once they have taken the bold step of sitting down and seeking help for a serious problem? Does it make it any more acceptable if the researchers ensure that no one is ever named or otherwise identified? If so, can researchers go anywhere and watch anything as long as no participant is ever identified?

5. Seek out the ethical guidelines of the discipline or career for which you are studying. Are the principles discussed in this chapter included among the guidelines of your discipline? What new issues arise that are not dealt with here?

6. What is the difference between anonymity and confidentiality? What procedures can you follow to ensure confidentiality? What legal mechanisms exist for the protection of the confidentiality of research participants?

7. What are the three sources of privilege? How do they differ?

8. What are the Wigmore criteria, and why is it beneficial to know them? Give some concrete suggestions on how you can integrate your knowledge of the Wigmore criteria into your research.

9. Describe some of the ways ethics regulation has changed over the last 30 years.

10. Go to your university's website and read the university's ethics policy. What does your university do to ensure there is no institutional conflict of interest?

11. How many REBs are there at your university or college? Who are the members of the REB that you would be applying to? Do they represent the full range of research done at your institution? Are there committee representatives who have expertise in both qualitative and quantitative research traditions?

12. The TCPS requires research ethics boards to have at least one "community member" on the board. Who is/are the community member(s) at your institution? In what way might the presence of this/those person(s) be beneficial for researchers and research participants? In what ways might it be detrimental?

13. Discuss the question of the rights of researchers in relation to the rights of participants, and generate your own criteria for how conflicting interests might be resolved (a) when the researcher is in a position of power over participants and (b) when the researcher is dependent on an agency and/or participants for continued funding and access.

14. This chapter has argued that, while researchers should make every effort to be both "ethical" and "legal," situations might arise where those two are placed in conflict, that is, you must choose between acting ethically but in violation of a particular law (e.g., you can live up to your ethical obligation to protect the rights of your research participants only by defying a court order to disclose confidential research information) or to act legally but in violation of an ethical obligation (e.g., follow a court order to disclose confidential research information even though this brings harm to your participant). Put yourself in these situations. Which do you believe is more important?

15. In the 1950s and 1960s when formalized codes of ethics were first being developed in the social sciences, some researchers opined that formalizing a code of ethics was the best thing a discipline could do because it would protect academic freedom and keep third parties who would undermine discipline-based control at bay. Others argued the opposite, i.e., that it was a slippery slope that would ultimately undermine academic freedom and end up with nothing better than socially

approved questions being asked in socially approved ways to the benefit of no one. We now have the benefit of hindsight. Sixty years later, who do you think was right?

16. You are undertaking a study in a psychiatric clinic for which you have signed an agreement guaranteeing confidentiality to the caregivers you are observing. You soon begin to notice cases where patients are apparently being denied their rights to refuse treatment, and you see two instances of what you perceive as physical abuse. Revealing this information to another authority would be a violation of the confidentiality you guaranteed. What would you do in this situation?

NOTES

1. Even this assumption is tenuous, since there is nothing in the facts of this research that would have precluded the researchers ensuring that the men who participated in the study were made aware of the risks and consented freely.

2. While it is deemed acceptable to pay participants with a small honorarium or gift, these are not supposed to go beyond a token thank you or to defray expenses. This is done in order to ensure that the choice to participate is made freely and not solely because of the incentive.

3. Unbeknownst to the "real" subject in the experiment, the "victim" was actually a confederate of the experimenter's—an actor— and never actually received any shocks.

4. Milgram continued doing research along these lines for many years and eventually published a book (Milgram 1974) summarizing his contributions. Since our interest here is not in his substantive findings but in the ethical issues involved in doing such research, we find it most informative to use his earliest reports. These were written with

the enthusiasm of someone who felt he had overcome the reputed artificiality of laboratory settings to discover something important and before controversy broke out.

5. The Olivieri case has received considerable attention and been the subject of a detailed investigation coordinated by the Canadian Association of University Teachers (CAUT). See Thompson, Baird, & Downie (2001).

6. We refer to confidentiality of the *source* because the information itself is not confidential; we set out from the start telling people that the research will be written up in articles and books.

7. For information regarding Confidentiality Certificates, see http://grants.nih.gov/grants/policy/coc/

8. See http://www.nij.gov/funding/humansubjects/privacy-certificate-guidance.htm for information regarding Privacy Certificates.

9. Readers who would like to know more about the *Ogden* case and its repercussions can peruse a Webpage Ted set up that goes through some of the debates that happened at the university and many key documents. It is located at http://www.sfu.ca/~palys/OgdenPge.htm. A key source is the *Russel Ogden Decision Review* by Blomley & Davis (1998), located at http://www.sfu.ca/~palys/ogden.htm. Ted Palys and John Lowman are also now in the process of writing a book about the Ogden case and the ripples it sent through the research community. Tentatively entitled *Going the Distance: The Law and Ethics of Research Confidentiality*, it should be available by 2013.

10. You should specify you are doing this, and the reasons for doing this, in your proposal, and it should be done as soon as possible during the data gathering process. In the United States, most subpoenas have arisen well after the research is done, by which point any identifying information should have been destroyed with only anonymized information remaining.

Once a subpoena arrives, if it ever does, it is too late to destroy the original notes or tape, as any destruction at that point likely would be considered destruction of "evidence," which would leave you open to charges of obstruction of justice or contempt of court.

11. Simply deleting a file from your computer does not actually remove it from your hard drive; it simply removes it from view. Deleted files often can be recovered from hard drives even five years after they have been deleted using file recovery software or hardware.

12. TrueCrypt is free "open source" software, which means that the software is available for free to anyone wishing to modify or use for non-commercial purposes (but it can also be bought in for-profit situations). While PGP was originally distributed as "freeware" by the Michigan Institute of Technology (MIT), it is now only available commercially through the Symantec website (http://www.symantec.com) or directly from the program creator Philip Zimmermann (http://www.philzimmermann. com). At the time of this writing TrueCrypt can be downloaded for free from the organization website (http://www.truecrypt.org/).

13. Section 6 is entitled "Oath of Office." It asserts that "The Chief Statistician and every person employed or deemed to be employed pursuant to this Act shall, before entering on his duties, take and subscribe the following oath or solemn affirmation: 'I, …, do solemnly swear (*or* affirm) that I will faithfully and honestly fulfil my duties as an employee of Statistics Canada in conformity with the requirements of the *Statistics Act*, and of all rules and instructions thereunder and that I will not without due authority in that behalf disclose or make known any matter or thing that comes to my knowledge by reason of my employment.'"

14. This is a good time to remind you that we are social scientists, not lawyers, and while the suggestions we offer here have undergone peer review (e.g., see Palys & Lowman 2000,

2002), it is intended only as general advice and should not be construed as specific legal advice. Researchers who are dealing with sensitive information where the possibility of subpoena is legitimate should consult competent legal help; we emphasize "competent" because we have found there are actually very few lawyers who are up-to-date with the law of privilege *and* who understand the academic enterprise and its ethical requirements.

15. Brajuha was a graduate student doing participant observation at a restaurant where he worked as a waiter while doing an M.A. thesis on the sociology of the American restaurant. One day the restaurant burned to the ground under mysterious circumstances that looked like arson. When the grand jury looking into the matter heard that a researcher was on site and had been maintaining something called "field notes," the grand jury subpoenaed the field notes in the hope they might contain clues on the cause and perpetrator of the fire. Brajuha claimed privilege and refused to share his field notes with the grand jury. In the end, his claim for privilege was not accepted—the Court of Appeal said that while a privilege *might* exist, Brajuha had failed to make the case—but he was allowed to anonymize his field notes before submitting them.

16. Richard Scarce was a graduate student doing research with members of the Animal Liberation Front (ALF), a radical animal rights group that occasionally engaged in "direct action." When Scarce and his family went on vacation one year, a member of ALF took care of his house. On returning from the trip, Scarce discovered that the university's animal care facility had been vandalized extensively and that the ALF member who had house-sat for him was the prime suspect. The grand jury looking into the matter subpoenaed Scarce. Scarce became only the second researcher ever to be jailed (for 159 days) for contempt of court.

17. The word "absolute" is something of a red herring. While it may well reflect the researcher's intention, and may well make sense within the specific context of the research being envisioned, when taken out of context it begs the question of whether anything in life is absolute, which is a tough argument to make. "Strict confidentiality" is similarly strong but without the hook that "absolute" brings.

18. Two of these cases involved subpoenas from grand juries; grand juries do not exist in Canada. The third case was the *Atlantic Sugar* case cited above, where the researchers limited confidentiality, and the court treated the limitation as a waiver of privilege.

19. Online at http://www.acjs.org/pubs/167_671_2922.cfm

20. Online at http://www.aaanet.org/stmts/ethstmnt.htm

21. Online at http://www.apsanet.org/content_9350.cfm

22. Online at http://www.asanet.org/about/ethics.cfm

23. We are thinking here of situations where, for example, the administrators in an organization give access to their employees, or prison officials are the ones giving access to the inmates, or teachers are the ones giving access to their students. Such research often originates with the organization's or institution's needs in mind, which raises the issue of how the interests of prospective research participants are being addressed and/or are in conflict with the desires of the organization.

24. We first came across this story in Stan Cohen's (1985) *Visions of Social Control*. He attributes it to social activist Saul Alinsky. We offer our own version of it here.

25. See also the collection of papers presented at a 2006 Symposium on Censorship and Institutional Review Boards that were later compiled in the *Northwestern Law Review* at http://www.law.northwestern.edu/journals/lawreview/issues/101.2.html. The international scope of the problem is evident when one notes that Katz's and Shea's articles focus primarily on the United States, Fitzgerald's article focuses on the "commonwealth countries" of Britain, Canada, Australia, and New Zealand, and SSHWC's monograph refers primarily to Canada.

SAMPLING AND RECRUITMENT

Research does not happen in the abstract. Although we can talk about research in general terms, and can identify abstract principles that are useful for guiding decisions as the research is being designed, done, and interpreted, in the end any given piece of research involves gathering specific data from specific sources in specific places at specific times. Each one of those choices is a **sample** of all of the choices that we could make in doing our research. To do research, we inevitably sample from among all the possible questions we could ask, all the behaviours (or other attributes) we could observe, and all the people or situations we could approach. Our choice of methods is a sample of all the methods we could use, our analysis of the data is a sample of all the analyses we could perform, and the pattern of findings we choose to focus on in our final report is a sample of all the possible patterns we might have identified.

This fact of research life arises simply because we cannot do everything at once. Although our general interest might be in "healthcare service delivery," in the end out of all the places we could go to study healthcare being delivered—in a clinic; at a physician's office; in a home-care programme; at an out-patient facility—we may choose to study service delivery in a hospital. And because we cannot go to every hospital there is, we decide to go to the one that is located down the street from our university or college. Once we get there, because we cannot watch every single delivery of every single service within the hospital, perhaps we decide to focus on services delivered within the emergency room. And because we cannot use every single method available to us, perhaps we decide to interview people as they are awaiting service and as they leave, or observe them as they go through the process, or simply look at completed files after the

patient becomes a "former" patient and walks out the door. If we have the resources, we might be able to focus on two or three areas of the hospital and incorporate more than one method, but these will still be subsets of all the places that deliver health services and of all the methods we could employ.

In a literal sense, when we get to the end of our research we could write an article about "what happened in the emergency room of Princeton-Plainsboro Hospital when we were there the week of November 13 and talked to 50 of the 333 people who went through that day." But who cares? Will the knowledge of what came of our research in that part of the hospital with those specific people on that specific day be useful to the administrators of Princeton-Plainsboro now that the day is over? Should a hospital administrator sitting in Minneapolis or Halifax be interested in our results? Might the study be of interest to individuals in other kinds of settings where products and services of one sort or another are delivered—prisons, social agencies, the tire installation centre at Costco, the beer vendor at a Toronto Blue Jays baseball game? These are all questions that ask about the **generalizability** of our results beyond the original context of our research. The answers to them will depend on how we have constructed our research, and what theoretical concepts we or others who read our research invoke to explain what we have found. These all involve sampling issues and need to be understood as such.

DECIDING WHOM TO SAMPLE

Earlier chapters discussed our choices (sampling) of perspectives, approaches, and ethics, and should be reconsidered in that light. The rest of this book will see us consider some of the many methods—different ways of posing and answering questions—from which we can sample when designing any given piece of research. The current chapter addresses how we sample people, objects, or places for inclusion in a study.

What constitutes an "adequate" sample depends very much on your research question(s) and objectives, your (and the literature's) understanding of the phenomenon under scrutiny, and on practical constraints. Ultimately, the most important principle is how you connect with the person(s) or other sources of information that best allow you to address whatever research question you pose (Gorden 1980). For example, suppose your research question has to do with how we teach research methods courses at our university. If you want to know how our students feel about their experience, the "appropriate sample" will comprise students who have enrolled in our methods courses. If you want to compare the reactions of our students with the reactions of those who take methods courses from *other* professors, you'll need to sample students from other courses as well. Here, too, the more students the better, but your sampling of other courses will depend on the kinds of comparisons you want to make. If you simply want to compare our students' reactions to those of students taught by "other professors," you might simply sample methods courses taught by other professors. But if you want to compare the way students react to our teaching methods (which tend to be more Socratic) with the way they react to *other* teaching methods (e.g., a more unidirectional lecture style), your sampling of other courses and students must be more strategic: you'll want to ensure that other teaching styles of interest to you and other students taught by professors who favour those styles are represented.

But suppose your research question involves determining *why* Chris teaches his courses the way he does. *No* sample of students, no matter how large or how representative it might be, has access to that information. His students might *speculate* about why he teaches the way he does and might have *partial* information that he has shared with them at one time or another. But the best person to ask is Chris, a sample of one. In sum, "bigger" isn't *necessarily* better, nor is "formal representativeness" a *necessary* requirement. The issue is always what you're trying to accomplish and what sample best suits that task. For example, what do you think would be an appropriate sample for the evaluation of Dilbert's circuit design that is referred to in Figure 4.1?

Procedurally, these issues boil down to two different sets of sampling techniques, known collectively as **probabilistic sampling** and **non-probabilistic sampling**. The former techniques aim primarily to generate formally (or statistically) **representative samples** and are the sampling

Figure 4.1: Which sample is appropriate for any given situation will depend on the research question being asked.

methods of choice when you have a well-defined population from which you want to draw a sample that will allow you to generalize back to that broader population. The latter are the sampling methods of choice when the researcher seeks strategically chosen samples where all participants are not created equal and some participants more than others are particularly well-suited to advance the study objectives. In the former case, generalizability of one's results is more of a statistical issue, and in many cases can be done with an estimable degree of error. In the latter case, generalizability is more of a theoretical/conceptual issue that will have implications for further sampling in subsequent research.

PROBABILISTIC TECHNIQUES

Appropriate use of probabilistic sampling techniques begins with a well-defined population to study, and the challenge for the researcher is to pick some sample from that group that will allow one to generalize back to and make statements about the population as a whole. We see this type of situation most commonly in survey research, and especially the type of research done by national polling organizations. At election time, for example, each of the political parties and every media organization seems fixated on the idea of tracking sentiment toward the various parties in the interest of knowing who is doing

well, who is losing ground and why, what effect last week's leaders debate had on their respective parties' fortunes, who will win the election, and so on.

The "well-defined population" in this instance is the Canadian electorate, which in the end is defined as "all Canadian citizens 18 years of age and older who are eligible to vote," which for the 2011 federal election comprised about 24 million people living in approximately 14 million households in 308 different electoral districts (Chief Electoral Officer of Canada 2011). On the basis of samples of only a few thousand people the national polling organizations did an astonishingly good job of generalizing back from that comparatively small sample to the population as a whole, as the figures in Table 4.1 attest.

The table shows the actual breakdown of votes received nationally by each party (rounded to the nearest whole percent) as well as the predicted results from the polls closest to the election that were conducted by the Angus Reid polling organization, whose predictions fared the best among the seven pollsters for whom information was available, and Compas, the polling organization that fared worst in that group.

For a sample size that was a mere 1/8,000th the size of the population of interest—in a situation where you really don't know for sure which of your survey respondents will actually make it to the polling station to cast their vote—Angus Reid's predictions

Table 4.1
Polling results compared to actual votes in the 2011 federal election[1]

| | Sample Size | Political Parties | | | | | |
		PC	NDP	Lib	Bloc Quebecois	Green	Total Error
Actual Election Results	24 Million	40%	31%	19%	6%	4%	n/a
Best Polling Accuracy: Angus Reid	3,003	37%	33%	19%	6%	4%	5%
Poorest Polling Accuracy: Compas	750	46%	26%	17%	7%	4%	14%

were very accurate. Even the least accurate survey—the one conducted by Compas employing a sample only a quarter the size of the Angus Reid sample—was not completely out to lunch. It still predicted the ordering of the parties correctly, predicted the Conservative majority government that did indeed occur (and which Angus Reid stopped short of predicting), and pointed to the likelihood of what ended up being the surprise second place showing of the NDP over the Liberals.

When a researcher is faced with a research problem of this sort—going from an identified whole population (Canadian voters) and choosing a sample that will allow one to generalize back to the population as a whole—then ensuring a representative sample is one's primary objective, and the best way of doing so is to utilize one of a variety of what are known as probabilistic sampling techniques.

Probabilistic Sampling: The Vocabulary

This family of sampling techniques is known as probabilistic because they are based on probability theory. Understanding them requires that we spend some time reviewing the language that is relevant to this approach.

REPRESENTATIVENESS

Probabilistic techniques are the best ones to use if you want to obtain a representative sample of some target population. A sample is *representative* of some larger group when the distribution of relevant attributes in the sample mirrors the distribution of those attributes in the population. Thus, if our target population is 52 percent female, while 80 percent are right-handed, 23 percent prefer the Conservative party, and 13 percent own Toyotas, then a "representative" sample of 100 people drawn from the target population would contain approximately 52 females, 80 right-handed persons, 23 who say they prefer the Conservatives, and 13 Toyota owners. Probabilistic techniques minimize the difference between the sample and the population; that is, they minimize **sampling error**.

Units of Analysis or Sampling Elements

Any study involves a choice of **units of analysis** or **sampling elements**, that is, the units or elements about which information will be gathered. If we wish to find out how people in North Dakota feel about the state government's approach to education issues, for example, the individual person is our unit of analysis. If we wish to determine the attention given to environmental issues in *The Globe and Mail* by doing some form of newspaper content analysis, individual issues of or individual articles in that newspaper become our unit of analysis. Units of analysis or sampling elements aren't inherent or inevitable divisions among entities; they're defined by the researcher, depending on her/his research interests. Your unit of analysis might be the individual person, family units, larger groupings (e.g., university departments, census tracts, electoral ridings), or even whole countries; it is little more than a statement of what "things" you want to study.

THE UNIVERSE

A **universe** is a theoretical aggregation of all possible sampling elements. If our sampling element is the individual British citizen, our theoretical universe is "all citizens of Great Britain." If our unit of analysis is the newspaper, our universe is "all newspapers." The notion of "universe" is not especially practical, since one's universe is generally so amorphous and huge that it's impossible to define in detail. Its major role, instead, is to keep us attuned to two ideas: that there's often a broader realm to which we might ultimately wish to generalize our results and that we must consider the limitations of our empirical pursuits. To continue with the example of the election survey, the universe would have been "all Canadians eligible to vote."

THE POPULATION

A more practical and perhaps less presumptuous term is **population**. Like "universe," "population" refers to an aggregation of sampling elements, but "population" delineates the exact boundaries that define our sample elements. While "all Ontarians" might be our universe of interest, we might define our population as "all people over 18 years of age who are Canadian citizens and resident in the province of Ontario on January 1, 2013." For the example of the voting survey, the population might be "all Canadian citizens who are eligible to vote in the 2011 federal election." The term "population" is thus more precise than "universe" in delimiting who *specifically* makes up our study's *target group*. Defining our population of interest can be seen as the beginning of our sampling procedures, since it requires us to specify, in no uncertain terms, who or what is "eligible" for participation in our research.

SAMPLING FRAME

The **sampling frame** is a complete list of all the sampling elements of the population we wish to study. If our population of interest is "all students enrolled on a full-time basis at the University of California at Davis as of February 1, 2013," our sampling frame is the list of all students who fit the description. If our population of interest is "all divorce cases adjudicated in Manitoba courts during 2012 in which child custody was contested," our sampling frame is a list of all such cases.

Although the sampling frame's list of all elements would *ideally* reflect our population exactly, it typically does *not*. Many lists are imperfect to begin with, and others quickly become obsolete. For example, in the voting survey example, given that our population was "all Canadian citizens who are eligible to vote in the 2011 federal election," the voters list—all persons whose names appear on the list of registered voters that is maintained by the Chief Electoral Officer—might seem an obvious choice for a sampling frame. But some eligible people will not be enumerated, and some technically ineligible people may be included on the list. So even the voters list starts out as a good but imperfect list of eligible voters.

All lists also decay or become obsolete, some more quickly than others. For example, some

years ago, Ted and Dave Williams wanted to send a questionnaire they'd developed to a diverse sample of local residents (see Palys & Williams 1983). Since a provincial election had been held only two months before the study, they decided to use the voters list as their sampling frame. But even then about 8 percent of the letters came back stamped "deceased" or "moved." Even good lists can become obsolete quickly. Others (e.g., the phone directory) are obsolete even before they're published and delivered, especially when one considers the fact that an increasing number of people use a cellphone as their only means of telephone communication and cellphone numbers are generally unlisted.

In many situations, no appropriate sampling frame exists, and constructing one would be impossible or impractical. A list of "all people in Chicago who were sexually abused during their adolescence," for example, is impossible to construct, as is a list of "all people in Halifax who are consumers of pornography." The same is true of lists of homosexuals, sex trade workers, corporate executives, university students who smoke marijuana, and people who like lemon in their tea. For many groups (or other units of analysis), sampling must occur without a sampling frame.

Probabilistic Sampling: The Techniques

SIMPLE RANDOM SAMPLING

Simple random sampling is the best way to identify a representative sample. It minimizes sampling error (deviation of the characteristics of the sample from the characteristics of the population) and allows us to calculate the degree of sampling error that probably exists. But this precision comes at a price. To perform simple random sampling, in most cases you *must* have a sampling frame in which every sampling element is listed once and only once.[2] Simple random sampling is then accomplished by merely choosing sample elements at random from the list. This can be done by putting all the names (or whatever) into a hat or drum and pulling them out at random, by numbering all elements in the sampling frame and then using a table of random numbers or random number generator to guide your selection, or using a computer program such as Microsoft Excel® or Open Office Calc® to select randomly from the sampling frame.

Other procedures are possible but two criteria are essential for **random selection**: (1) nothing but chance must govern the selection process; and (2) every sampling element must have an equal probability of being selected. If these criteria are met, the resulting sample will be representative of the population included in the sampling frame, within some margin of error, known as "sampling error." Of special importance to note here is how the methodological meaning of "random" is very precise and also very different from the way it is used in everyday conversation, where it is often seen as synonymous with adjectives such as "arbitrary" or "haphazard." It is important to make this distinction because what we might describe as "random" in everyday use often fails to meet the criteria for true randomness in the sampling context. Students often write in their research reports, for example, that they approached a random sample of people waiting in line somewhere, or randomly picked which persons in their residence to survey, when that was not actually the case. Stated simply, humans are very poor at doing things "randomly" in the methodological sense of that word; any process based on anything but a mechanistic impersonal process—using a random number table; rolling a die; employing a random number generator—is unlikely to be truly "random" in the way we mean it here.

SAMPLING ERROR

"Sampling error" refers to the extent to which the sample's characteristics deviate from those of the population. There are two types of sampling error: **systematic error** and **random error**.

Systematic error occurs when aspects of your sampling procedure act in a consistent way to make some sampling elements more likely to be chosen for participation than others. If you're interested in the opinions of *all* the students at your university or college (i.e., the entire population of students enrolled that semester), but place ballot boxes for a referendum only in the buildings where arts classes are held, you've made voting easier for arts students than for science students. This situation introduces a systematic bias to the referendum, all but ensuring that arts students' opinions will be *over*represented while science students' opinions will be *under*represented. Similarly, when we survey city dwellers by using the city's list of homeowners as our sampling frame, we systematically bias the resulting sample to reflect the views of wealthier and possibly older people (i.e., those more likely to own homes) and systematically ignore younger and less wealthy people, as well as all renters, the transient, and the homeless.

Random error has no systematic bias involved, but merely reflects the vagaries of chance variation. If we flip a coin 100 times, we may *expect* (theoretically) to see the coin fall heads-up 50 times and tails-up 50 times, but we wouldn't find it particularly unusual if the coin were to fall heads-up 53 times and tails-up 47 times. Such things happen, purely as a result of chance variation. You may hear such expressions of sampling error when poll results are reported during election campaigns. For example, the Angus Reid pollsters who reported the results of their 2011 election survey based on a national sample of 3,003, stated that, according to probability theory, their results could be expected to reflect the "true" situation plus or minus 1.8 percent 19 times out of 20.

When you use a random sampling method, the amount of sampling error you incur depends on the size of your sample: the bigger the sample, the smaller the sampling error.[3] Suppose your city councillors are trying to decide whether to commission an up-and-coming local artist or a world-renowned artist from another city to create a new sculpture to place in front of City Hall. The council is at a stalemate, with three councillors voting for each alternative; instead of casting the deciding vote, the mayor suggests looking to the citizens for guidance. The council hires you to take the pulse of the city and to report back on what the people want.

Because you're able to acquire a sampling frame that lists all city residents, you're confident that you have a good handle on the population whose views you hope to represent. From this list, you randomly sample 10 people and find that 7 of them, or 70 percent, would prefer to give the job to the up-and-coming local artist. If your 10-person sample was indeed randomly chosen, you can expect (in theory) that these people are representative of your population of interest, within some margin of error. Chapter 6 looks at some of the mathematics associated with computing the sampling error. For now, we need only know that, with a sample size of 10, our estimate that 70 percent of the population would like to see the local artist get the commission must be qualified by stating that the "real" figure could be as low as 34 percent or as high as 94 percent (see Gray & Guppy 1994: 145). Why such a wide range? With a sample of only 10 people, it wouldn't be unusual, simply due to the capriciousness of chance, to get a "weird" result that would be unlikely to repeat itself twice in a row.

If you take such a result to the city councillors, they won't be impressed. Being "95 percent confident" that the "real" figure is somewhere between 34 percent and 94 percent (a range of 60 percentage points) isn't much better than saying that overall, people might agree or disagree with the decision. You might as well have flipped a coin. The council will send you back to the field to draw another sample.

The degree of sampling error you incur relates most strongly to the *absolute* sample size you draw rather than to the *proportional* sample size (e.g., Warwick & Lininger 1975). Table 4.2 shows the relationship between sample size and the margin of error. Each case assumes that 70 percent of the sample indicates a certain preference (e.g., that the local artist should get the job). When we increase the sample size from our original 10 to 50 and find that 70 percent support the local artist, the "real" figure is now 95 percent likely to be

between 55 percent and 83 percent (a range of 28 percent). A sample of 100 reduces the range to 19 percent. Increasing the sample size to 1,000 reduces our confidence interval to a mere 6 percent: if 70 percent of that 1,000-person sample supports the local artist, we can be 95 percent confident that the "real" figure is somewhere between 67 percent and 73 percent (i.e., 70 percent plus or minus 3 percent).

If we push for greater and greater accuracy, and hence require a larger and larger sample, we eventually face the need to acquire a huge sample, which would require equally huge resources to contact and interview. Indeed, we soon reach a point of diminishing returns, where whopping increases in sample size produce only very small gains in accuracy. Gray and Guppy (1994) explain that "the rules of probability theory tell us that we reduce our margin of error by one half if we quadruple our sample size" (144). It follows that, to go beyond the figures shown in Table 4.2, we'd have to increase our sample size from 1,000 to 4,000 in order to reduce our 95 percent confidence interval to 3 percent (i.e., ± 1.5 percent), or to 16 000 to reach ± 0.75 percent, or to 64,000 to reach ± 0.375 percent, and so on.

At some point, such increases simply aren't worth the improved confidence they bring us. Each researcher must determine where that point is, considering such factors as the available resources, how precise the estimate needs to be given the importance and consequences of the answers we seek to our research questions, and how the available funds might otherwise be spent. The researcher must also keep in mind how accurate other elements of the process will be. It would be silly to spend many thousands of dollars to increase sampling accuracy from plus or minus 1.5 percent to 0.75 percent, for example, when small changes in the wording of a question or in the interviewer's demeanour can easily cause results to vary as much as 5 percent to 10 percent. Forgetting those other elements of the process produces nothing but a specious scientism and a spurious sense of precision that simply does not exist (see also Chapter 6).

Table 4.2

Margin of Error by Sample Size

If 70% of a sample agrees, then with a sample size of	the population value might be		Size of confidence interval (high-low)	
	as low as	as high as		
10	34%	94%	60%	(±30%)
50	55%	83%	28%	(±14%)
100	59%	78%	19%	(±9.5%)
250	64%	76%	12%	(±6%)
1000	67%	73%	6%	(±3%)

From GUPPY, *SUCCESSFUL SURVEYING*. © 1994 Nelson Education Ltd. Reproduced by permission. www.cengage.com/permissions.

Another matter to be considered is the extent to which the researcher wants to compare different subgroups of the population. For example, the city council might realize that emphasizing majority opinion sometimes merely opens the door to a "tyranny of the majority," whereby a dominant group consistently uses its majority position to trample over the concerns of others. The council might therefore want you to look at subgroups within the population, for example, to ensure that men and women are equally supportive of commissioning the local artist or that the views of Indigenous people and ethnic minorities are adequately considered. In that case, the question of sampling error changes slightly: because any subgroup will, by definition, be smaller than the overall sample, the degree of sampling error that exists within any of the subgroups will obviously be larger.

For example, public opinion polls published in newspapers are often based on a random sample of 2,000 people from across the country. Such a sample can give a decent approximation of "how Canadians feel" about a social issue, given the question's wording and context, to within plus or minus about 2 percent, 19 times out of 20. The polls also often give breakdowns by province so that you can compare provinces. But with 10 provinces

and an average of, say, 200 respondents per province, the provincial figures are accurate only to within about plus or minus 6 percent, 19 times out of 20. The central point here is this: given random sampling of a population, the larger the absolute size of the sample, the lower the expected sampling error you might incur.

SYSTEMATIC SAMPLE WITH RANDOM START

A type of random sample with a slight twist to it is the **systematic sample with random start**. Like simple random sampling, this technique also requires a sampling frame in which each element is numbered and appears only once. But instead of randomly sampling from the entire list each time, you begin at a *randomly determined starting point,* and then sample every *n*th element on the list.

To illustrate, assume you have a voters list with 10,000 names on it and wish to draw a representative sample of 500 people from that list. Your **sampling ratio,** in other words, is 1:20 (or 1 in 20). To do a systematic sample with random start, you would first randomly choose a number from 1 to 20. Suppose you close your eyes and throw a dart at your random number table, hitting the number 13. That's your random start: the first person you sample is number 13 on your voters list. The systematic part is dictated by your sampling ratio of 1:20; that is, you now systematically pick every 20th person on the list. Thus, given that you began with person number 13, the next one you sample will be number 33, then 53, then 73, then 93, and so on through the sampling frame, until you come to your 500th sample person, who would be number 9,993 on the original list of 10,000 people.

While this technique is effective for acquiring a probabilistic sample from a sampling frame, it's not quite as good as the simple random sample. Recall that one of the criteria that make a selection completely *random* (and hence likely to be representative) is that every sampling element (and type of sampling element) must have an equal probability of being selected. If subject numbers are pulled from a random number table, then no matter how the list is organized, every number (and hence every person or element) has an equal probability of being selected. But in a systematic sample with random start, properties associated with the list itself may result in a biased sample. The most worrisome property is the cyclical nature of many lists, which causes a problem known as **periodicity.**

Suppose we want to generate a 1:5 sample of players in the National Hockey League (NHL). Each team sends us a list of its players, ordered by their jersey number. We add these lists to our master list in the order in which we receive them. Once the whole list is compiled, let's say that we randomly choose number 1 as our starting point and then select every 5th player thereafter, that is, the first on the list, then the 6th, 11th, 16th, and so on. This sounds reasonable, but would get us in serious trouble. The problem stems from the fact that (a) the lowest jersey number on a team is usually number 1, and that number is traditionally worn by goaltenders; and (2) an NHL game roster involves 20 players per team. Our sample would thus overrepresent goalies, since a quarter of the players sampled would be goaltenders, who actually comprise only 10 percent of the players on each team. If we recognized this ahead of time and decided to make our random starting point

some number other than 1, then two things will happen: (1) the starting point is no longer random because not all numbers have an equal likelihood of being selected; and (2) we would now end up *under*representing goaltenders because no one with a number 1 jersey would now be picked.

The main problem with periodicity in systematic samples with random starts lies in recognizing when it's present. Once recognized, periodicity is fairly easily addressed. In the NHL example, the problem is best dealt with by first randomizing the elements in the list to destroy its cyclical nature, and then doing a systematic sample with random start. The process of randomizing a sampling frame is incredibly simple if the list is stored in a spreadsheet program such as Microsoft Excel® or Open Office Calc®. All current spreadsheet programs have a built in RAND ( ) formula function that allows you to assign a random number to each case in the list, once cases are assigned a random number you simply sort the data by the random number and your list will be randomized.

STRATIFIED RANDOM SAMPLING

A third type of probabilistic sample is the **stratified random sample**. In this procedure, the researcher first divides the population into groupings (or *strata*) of interest and then samples randomly within each stratum. This technique is used when there is some meaningful *grouping variable* on which the investigator wishes to make comparisons and where the probabilities of group membership are known ahead of time.

Suppose a researcher wants to survey a representative sample of students who have declared a major in the Faculty of Arts at Brock University. Suppose further that we know that 35 percent of Brock's Arts students are sociology majors, another 30 percent are psychology majors, 5 percent are English majors, and the remaining 30 percent are in other Arts disciplines. Just to keep the numbers easy, suppose there are 1,000 students with declared majors in the Faculty of Arts. They are represented by the "population" drawing in the upper portion of Figure 4.2.

Figure 4.2
Proportional and Disproportional Stratified Random Sampling

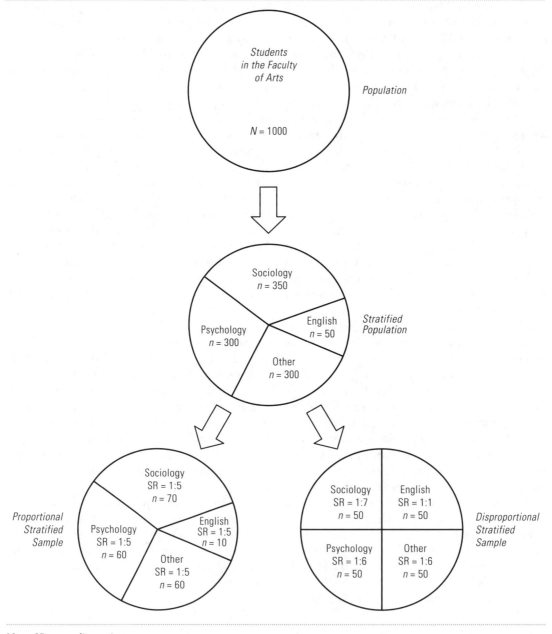

Note: SR = sampling ratio

A researcher who's interested only in "polling students from the Faculty of Arts" could get a list of the 1,000 students from the registrar's office (i.e., a sampling frame) and then draw a simple random sample or a systematic sample with random start. If properly done, the sample should contain, within the limits of sampling error, roughly 35 percent sociology majors, 30 percent psychology majors, and 5 percent English majors, while roughly 30 percent of the sampled students should have majors that don't fall into any of these categories and are therefore labelled "other."

But suppose our researcher wants to *compare* the responses of the four groups (sociology, psychology, English, and other) and hence doesn't want to rely on chance alone to produce the exact numbers of students that would be expected. Since, for example, 5 percent of the students are English majors, we would *expect* to find 10 English majors in a randomly drawn sample of 200 of these students. But the vagaries of chance might leave us with more or fewer than 10 English majors in the sample. If the researcher wishes to ensure that the sample is *exactly* representative of the population with respect to the grouping variable of interest, stratified random sampling is more appropriate than simple random sampling.

The first step in this technique involves stratifying the population according to the grouping variable of interest, as shown in the section of Figure 4.2 labelled "stratified population." The researcher then performs simple random sampling *within* each stratum. Actually, the researcher has another choice to make: whether to use proportional or disproportional stratified random sampling.

PROPORTIONAL STRATIFIED RANDOM SAMPLING

In **proportional stratified random sampling**, the same sampling ratio is used within each stratum. In our example, this approach produces the following result: the proportion of students with different majors in the sample is exactly the same as the proportion of students with different majors in the population; and the students within each stratum of the sample are theoretically representative of

the students within the corresponding population stratum (e.g., the sociology majors in the sample are representative of sociology majors in the population), within the limits of sampling error. At the end of this study, the researcher's conclusions will apply both to "students in Brock University's Faculty of Arts" (since the sample as a whole is proportionately representative of the population, within the limits of sampling error) and "Brock students majoring in sociology, psychology, English, or any other arts discipline" (since each stratum of the sample is representative of the corresponding stratum of the population, within the limits of sampling error).

But in an example like this one, the researcher has obtained stratified samples that are theoretically representative of each stratum within the population; however, her/his ability to make conclusions about each stratum, and especially to compare strata, is impaired. It all comes down to that qualifying phrase "within the limits of sampling error." The main problem arises from including the English majors, of whom only 10 are sampled. As our earlier discussion of sampling error revealed, any result based on a sample of only 10 is bound to be very tentative, since our 95 percent confidence range would require us to specify that the result could be inaccurate by plus or minus 30 percentage points, which is not a very precise conclusion. There are two ways to get around this problem: we can increase the overall sample size, so that even the smallest group is still large enough for analysis, or we can use *dis*proportional stratified random sampling.

DISPROPORTIONAL STRATIFIED RANDOM SAMPLING

When the researcher is primarily interested in *comparing* results between the strata rather than in making overall statements about "students in the Faculty of Arts," or when one or more of the subgroups are so small that a consistent sampling ratio would leave sample sizes in some groups too small for adequate analysis, a **disproportional stratified random sample** might be drawn.

Here, the researcher still begins by stratifying the population into subgroups of interest and then taking a random sample within each stratum. But a different sampling ratio is used within each stratum, so that equal numbers of students end up in each of the strata samples.

So if the researcher wants a sample of 200 students from the population of 1,000 students (i.e., an overall 1:5 sampling ratio), *proportional* stratified random sampling will yield 70 sociology majors, 60 psychology majors, 10 English majors, and 60 students with majors in "other" arts disciplines. But with *disproportional* stratified random sampling, the sample of 200 might include 50 majors of each type (to create an optimal comparison using equal numbers of students from each group), chosen by using different sampling ratios within each stratum. In such a case, overall statements about "Brock University students majoring in arts subjects" would be tenuous (since the sample as a whole is no longer representative of the university's arts students),[4] but the researcher *could* make statements *comparing* the subgroups, since each subgroup (or stratum) of the sample *is* representative of that subgroup in the population. In sum, we end up with the alternatives depicted in the bottom portion of Figure 4.2.

MULTISTAGE CLUSTER SAMPLING

Each technique discussed so far requires a sampling frame. But a sampling frame isn't always available. Does the lack of a sampling frame prevent researchers from drawing a probabilistic (and hence theoretically representative) sample? No. One probabilistic technique *doesn't* require a sampling frame. Known as **multistage cluster sampling**, this technique involves random sampling of clusters within clusters until one reaches the desired unit of analysis.

Suppose we want to acquire a representative sample of people who live in California's Bay Area and that no sampling frame of such people is available. How can we find a sample of people who meet the "representativeness" criterion?

Multistage cluster sampling in this case begins by acknowledging that people (our unit of analysis)

generally live in residences, that residences exist on blocks, that blocks are part of neighbourhoods, that neighbourhoods make up communities, and that "the Bay Area" actually comprises a collection of communities. Thus, if we first prepare a list of communities that make up the Bay Area (i.e., San Francisco, Oakland, San José, Marin County, etc.), and then take a random sample of these communities, that sample of communities is formally representative of the population of communities that make up the Bay Area. We can then get maps of each of our sample communities, divide them into neighbourhoods, and take a random sample of neighbourhoods within each community. Because the neighbourhoods are representative of the population of neighbourhoods in the communities from which they were drawn and because the communities were randomly chosen to be representative of all communities in the Bay Area, the neighbourhoods we've sampled must be representative of all the neighbourhoods in the Bay Area. Neighbourhoods comprise individual blocks, so we can randomly sample blocks within each of our sample neighbourhoods and then randomly sample residences within blocks; finally, we can randomly sample the people within the sampled residences.

By performing a random sampling within each cluster, we end up with a sample of people that is theoretically representative of the population of people in our sample residences, which in turn is representative of the population of residences on our sample blocks, which in turn is representative of the population of blocks in our sample neighbourhoods, which in turn is representative of the population of neighbourhoods in our sample communities, which in turn is representative of the population of communities that make up the Bay Area. Our sample of people is thus theoretically representative of people who live in the Bay Area—and we found them *without* a sampling frame.

While this approach obviously can get somewhat laborious, it *is* a good way to acquire a formally representative sample—an even better way to describe it would be to call it an "unbiased sample"—when no sampling frame is available. To acquire a representative sample of customers of McDonald's restaurants in North America one could sample provinces and states, then counties, then roads within counties, then McDonald's restaurants on those roads, and finally customers in those restaurants.

Multistage cluster sampling can be very useful, but it should be used only when a sampling frame is unavailable, since it's ultimately not as good as the other probabilistic techniques. To appreciate why that's the case we must go back to the concept of sampling error. Remember that there will always be *some* sampling error whenever we draw a random sample, although the bigger the sample, the lower that error is likely to be. For a simple random sample, we sample only once and can easily compute the probable degree of sampling error. But for a multistage cluster sample, we're actually taking samples of samples of samples, and since all sampling involves some degree of error, we thus *accumulate* error with each successive level of sampling.

In the McDonald's example, we take five samples (states/provinces, counties, roads, McDonald's restaurants, and customers), accumulating error at each stage. Thus, while our eventual sample is *formally* or *theoretically* representative, since the sample taken at each stage was random and hence *should* be representative, our *confidence* in the precision of our representativeness is less than it would be if we had sampled only once from some overall sampling frame. Indeed, with multistage cluster sampling, rather than stating that you've achieved a theoretically representative sample, you'd probably be better off stating that you have no reason to believe that your sample is *un*representative.

Can Sampling Problems Be Overcome by Sample Size?

As noted earlier, probabilistic samples receive that name because the sampling techniques used to obtain them conform to the rules of probability theory, particularly its basic requirement that the probability that any given person or element will be selected must be known, or at least knowable. When the population is known and sampling is random, these techniques ensure a theoretically representative sample, within the limits of sampling error.

Sampling error in this context varies according to two factors: the nature of the procedure followed (it must be random) and the sample size. Assuming that the first criterion (random sampling) is met, then the larger the sample size, the smaller the sampling error and the more confident we can be that we've obtained a truly representative unbiased sample.

But if we violate that first criterion by failing to use a random sampling procedure, the principles and mathematics of probability theory cannot be applied because we have no idea of the likelihood that a given element will be sampled. As a result, we can't compute or estimate how much sampling error exists. Thus, as sample size increases, we have no way of knowing whether we can be more and more confident that our estimates of the population's characteristics are getting more and more accurate, or whether we're merely acquiring a bigger and bigger biased sample.

Huge samples in themselves—no matter how big they might be—do not ensure representativeness; it's *how* you sample that's most important. An excellent illustration of this point arose in relation to a 1992 State of the Union address given by then-U.S. President George Bush (senior). After Bush's speech, the CBS program *America on the Line* coupled its post-speech discussion with a "viewer call-in poll." Viewers who owned touch-tone phones[5] were encouraged to call and offer their reactions to the speech through a computerized system that would compile all the responses. A total of 314,786 people phoned to express their opinions.

Now, 314,786 people is a lot of people, far more than the 1,000- or 2,000-person samples used in most national surveys.[6] It's hard not to be impressed when a poll's source states that the poll captures the opinions of more than 300,000 people. But can this particular huge sample genuinely be considered statistically representative of the broader population of Americans?

One way to address that issue considers it on a purely rational basis, asking whether there's any reason to believe that the sample *is not* statistically representative. If there is, we should be able to at least speculate on its deficiencies. The CBS phone-in sample clearly was not chosen randomly; people "volunteered" themselves for participation in a very particular social context. In order to have participated in the poll, a person would have to be home that evening, own a television, have the television on, have enough interest in current affairs to watch the CBS news instead of whatever was on the other channels, be interested enough in politics to listen to a presidential speech, care enough about having her/his opinion heard to actually phone the CBS number, understand English well enough to understand the survey questions, and be free to spend the required time on the phone answering questions. It's doubtful that people who met all these criteria are representative of the general American public. Thus, despite the mammoth sample size, it seems unlikely that a sample of opinion drawn in the manner of the CBS phone-in poll would be representative of the broader population.

We also can address the representativeness issue empirically. The ideal situation would be to have the results of a survey done at exactly the same time, in which the same questions were asked, but with a sample drawn randomly from the general population. Had such a survey been conducted that night using the same questions asked of the *America on the Line* phone-in sample, we could assess just how representative that 314,786-viewer sample might have been.

In fact, exactly such a random sample was drawn. Concurrent with its phone-in poll, CBS also commissioned a survey that used a randomly chosen sample of 1,234 Americans, who were asked exactly the same questions as the phone-in sample. Table 4.3 shows the questions that were asked and the collective responses of both the randomly chosen sample and the much larger phone-in sample.

Monette, Sullivan, and DeJong (1994) note that, given the size of the random sample ($N = 1,234$), we can compute that the probable degree of error involved is around plus or minus 3 percent. Thus, any difference between the random sample and the phone-in sample that was larger than 3 percent is unlikely to be due to chance variation alone, and more likely due to something else—probably the different sampling methods used. As Table 4.3 reveals, only one comparison stayed within the range of 3 percent; the other 13 ranged from 4 percent to as much as 27 percent, with an average difference of approximately 14 percentage points between the two techniques.

Even more disconcerting is the fact that the two sets of results differ not only in *magnitude* but also in *kind*. The call-in results seem more pessimistic and critical. Those who phoned in reported feeling *worse* off than they had four years previously; were *worried* about job loss; wanted *free* healthcare access paid for by taxes; felt that the middle class was *misunderstood;* believed that "America's children" faced an even more *dismal* future; and believed that media portrayals of bad economic times were *not* exaggerated. In contrast, the representative sample of Americans reported feeling that things were pretty much the *same* as they'd been four years earlier; were *not* worried about job loss; were *not* willing to pay more taxes to cover free healthcare for all; and expected *similar* futures for America's children. They agreed with the phone-in sample that the president didn't understand the middle class and that the media weren't exaggerating when they depicted times as tough.

As these results help reaffirm, anyone who claims to have generated a representative sampling of opinion without having used a probabilistic sampling technique is skating on thin ice. Yet such claims appear in the media all the time. Radio phone-in shows, lobbyists who generate letter-writing campaigns, and newspapers that encourage readers to clip a coupon and send it to some local official often argue that the sheer volume of replies allows them to legitimately claim they represent public opinion. Obviously, any issue that can

Table 4.3

Is Bigger Always Better? Comparing Simultaneously Drawn Probabilistic and Non-probabilistic Samples

Question	Alternatives	Viewer Call-In ($N = 314\,786$)	CBS Formal Poll ($N = 1234$)
Are you better off now than four years ago?	(a) better	29%	24%
	(b) worse	54	32
	(c) same	17	44
Are you worried about job loss this year?	(a) yes	64%	48%
	(b) no	36	52
Would you pay more taxes for free health care?	(a) yes	58%	46%
	(b) no	42	53
Does the president understand the middle class?	(a) yes	30%	43%
	(b) no	70	57
Are media exaggerating how bad economic conditions are?	(a) yes	39%	35%
	(b) no	51	64
Future of America's children? Will it be … ?	(a) better	21%	24%
	(b) worse	57	36
	(c) same	22	39

From*MONETTE, KIP: *Applied Social Research*, 3E. © 1994 Cengage Learning

stimulate 100,000 people to send postcards of complaint to their local MP must be more intensely felt and broadly contested than one that generates only 100 cards. But while those 100,000 cards may well indicate that an issue has captured public attention, it's sheer folly to say that the 100,000 people who sent in those cards somehow "represent" public opinion.

Representativeness: An Overrated Concept?

There has been an unfortunate tendency in the literature to treat probabilistic methods as the "gold" method of sampling and the dismissal of non-probabilistic methods as somehow second class. We reject that view. The "best" sampling method in any given situation will depend on the research questions and objectives, the type of research that is being done, and the pragmatics of the situation.

When one has a well-defined population and the research question(s) and objective require that the researcher be able to generalize her/his results back to the broader population, then clearly probabilistic methods are the methods of choice and anything else is second best. But there are many other situations—and we would argue that these "other" scenarios comprise *most* of what social and health scientists do—when probabilistic methods are unnecessary, irrelevant, and clearly the poorer choice. Indeed, if we were to offer a nominee for the "Academy of the Overrated," the "representative sample" would be near the top of our list.

Representative samples aren't useless—far from it. When our research objectives are *descriptive*, that is, when we want to know something like "how Canadians feel about changes to the healthcare system," "how Berkeley students feel about the prospect of tuition increases," or "how Manitobans feel about their provincial government's education policies," representative sampling is clearly the route to take. But social scientists are rarely content with description alone. Our goal is generally theory and understanding, and we can't think of one theory that aspires merely to describe some singular state of affairs. Theories deal with variables (note the plural) and with the interrelationships among them. So if a theory posits that a relationship should exist between variable *A* and variable *B*, all we *really* need in order to test that theory is a sample whose members are heterogeneous with respect to those two variables.

Cook and Campbell (1979) also encourage us to ask what we end up with when we acquire a formally representative sample. They point out that even if one acquires a representative sample and uses it to generate results that can be generalized to the population as a whole, those results *won't* necessarily also hold for all subgroups within the population. For example, even if we find out the overall distribution of attitudes among Canadians about environmental regulation, there are no guarantees that the same distribution would characterize people of varying gendered and sexual positions, people of different religious or political persuasions, or people with different education or income backgrounds. And of course, differences in attitudes among different subgroups of the population are often of greater theoretical interest to us than is mere description of the population as a whole.

Thus, Cook and Campbell (1979) argue that we ought to distinguish between generalizing *to* populations of interest and generalizing *across* subgroups of interest. Ultimately, they maintain, the researcher who samples various "unrepresentative" (i.e., unique) groups of interest and then either demonstrates that the same results hold across all these groups or shows that—and perhaps explains why—results *differ* across groups is in a much more powerful theoretical position than is the researcher who can merely describe, in gross terms, the overall status of a variable in a population of interest.

Finally, many researchers view the emphasis on representative sampling as simply misplaced.

Researchers undertaking qualitative research have been the most vocal in this regard. Huberman and Miles (1994), for example, note that

> sampling choices within and across cases are powerfully determinative of just which data will be considered and used in analysis. Quantitative researchers often think randomly, statistically, and in terms of context-stripped case selections. Qualitative researchers must characteristically think purposively and conceptually about sampling. (441)

Morse (1994) adds simply that researchers should emphasize gathering data that are rich, suggesting that this goal is best achieved when sampling is driven by theoretical aspirations rather than by statistical requirements.

Indeed, we must remember the different role that theory plays in deductive and inductive research; then we must consider how those differences may play out in how we look at things like sampling issues.

In that regard, recall that in more deductive/quantitative approaches, one *begins* with theory; hence it is theory that will tell us which samples and sites are relevant to look at. The universe (in its sampling sense) is defined by theory, and the trick with respect to sampling is to identify one that will be representative of the universe to which we wish to generalize. In contrast, remember that more inductively/qualitatively driven approaches aspire to *develop* theory. Thus, instead of the universe to which we wish to generalize being defined by theory, the whole challenge for the inductive researcher is to *find out* what the universe of generalizability is for whatever concepts emerged in the initial study. Given that there tend to be differences between more quantitatively oriented and more qualitatively oriented researchers with respect to their differential allegiance to deductive and inductive inquiry, you should not be surprised to hear that there are differences between these two groups of researchers in their sampling preferences as well. After noting that "sampling" is something that researchers engaged in both qualitative and quantitative research typically do, Morgan (2008) adds:

> Beyond that similarity, however, the very different goals of qualitative and quantitative research lead to equally different procedures for selecting data sources from a larger population. It is thus important to understand the difference between the logic of purposively selecting a small number of sources for intense analysis in qualitative research, as opposed to the emphasis on randomly selecting large samples for statistical analysis in quantitative research. (799)

The basic point should now be evident: the question of which sampling technique to use and the question of which people or objects to sample are complex ones that depend (like everything else) on your research questions and objectives, the constraints of the situation, your theoretical mission, and the type of phenomenon you're looking at. At those times when a formally representative sample *is* useful and desirable, one or more of the probabilistic sampling techniques discussed above should be pursued. But when a formally representative sample is neither useful nor desirable or when such a sample is impossible to acquire, one of the non-probabilistic techniques discussed below may prove helpful.

NON-PROBABILISTIC SAMPLING

Purposive Sampling

Given the above, you should not be surprised to hear that what is probably the most prototypical non-probabilistic sampling procedure is known simply as **purposive** or **strategic sampling** (Palys 2008). Of course, sampling is always "purposive" to some degree, since identifying a target population invariably expresses the researcher's interests and objectives. Given the diversity of research objectives

that exist, then it follows that there will be many possible purposive sampling strategies. Some of the many that have been noted by Bailey (2007), Morse (1994), and Palys (2008) include:

- **Stakeholder sampling**: This approach, which is particularly useful in evaluation research and policy analysis, involves identifying and interviewing the major stakeholders who are involved in designing, delivering, receiving, or administering the program or service being evaluated. When done properly, it ensures that all relevant views are represented—"all voices have been heard"—and at best may form the basis for a consensual resolution on how to move forward.

- **Extreme** or **deviant case sampling**: Sometimes extreme cases are of interest because they represent the purest or most clear cut instance of a phenomenon we are interested in. For example, if we are interested in studying management styles, it might be most interesting to study an organization that did exceptionally well and/or another that had high expectations but did exceptionally poorly.

- **Intensity sampling:** This involves sampling people whose interests or vocation makes them "experiential experts" because of their frequent or ongoing exposure to a phenomenon. For example, the American Psychological Association (APA) used this technique to develop its first set of ethical guidelines by identifying and interviewing certain "high exposure" people such as journal editors, who review many manuscripts; members of university ethical review boards, who must constantly consider ethical issues; and authors of ethics texts. Similarly, if you want to study techniques of persuasion, the logic of intensity sampling would suggest that you sample people who make persuasion their business, such as lawyers, sales reps, and advertisers.

- **Typical case sampling**: Sometimes we are interested in cases simply because they are *not* unusual in any way. For example, recall the study of a medical school by Howard Becker and some of his colleagues that we described in Chapter 1. They did their research at the University of Kansas Medical School—not a highly prestigious medical school such as Harvard or Johns Hopkins—exactly because there was nothing unusual about it and, for that reason, was probably reasonably typical of the medical school experience.

◆ **Paradigmatic case sampling**: A case is "paradigmatic" when it is considered the exemplar for a certain class. For example, if you were interested in studying the management of professional sports teams, the paradigmatic case in hockey of a successful franchise likely would be the Montréal Canadiens or Detroit Red Wings; for baseball it would be the New York Yankees.

◆ **Maximum variation sampling**: Maximum variety sampling emphasizes sampling for diversity. Suppose the distribution of ethnicity in the general population is 35 percent British, 30 percent French, 15 percent "other European," 10 percent Asian, and 4 percent Aboriginal, while the rest of the population comprises at least a dozen other ethnic groups, each constituting less than 1 percent of the population. A researcher sampling for statistical representativeness would use a probabilistic sampling technique, hoping to acquire respondents in numbers consistent with their presence in the population. But while such a sample would obviously be statistically representative, 80 percent of the respondents would be of European origin. And owing to the vagaries of chance, some smaller ethnic or cultural groups might be left out of the sample entirely. In contrast, a researcher engaging in maximum variety sampling might aim to sample members of *every* ethnic and cultural group. Such a strategy would clearly be beneficial if the researcher hoped to unearth either the *variety* of human experience and perception with respect to some phenomenon or some of the

commonalities of that experience across diverse peoples.[7] The logic here is similar to the one that guides stakeholder sampling, i.e., ensuring one has heard from the full range of voices in any milieu.

◆ **Criterion sampling**: This involves searching for cases or individuals who meet a certain criterion, e.g., that they have a certain disease, meet specific age or language requirements, or have had a particular life experience. For example, the research that Chris has done with men who have been clients of sex workers would be considered criterion sampling since to have been eligible to participate in his research respondents had to have been English or French speaking, over the age of 19, currently residing in Canada, and have purchased sexual services from a sex worker on one or more occasions during the previous 12 months,

◆ **Critical case sampling**: Here the researcher might be looking for a "decisive" case that would help make a decision about which of several different explanations is most plausible, or is one that is identified by experts as being a particularly useful site because of the generalizations it allows, e.g., recent findings that life exists at the bottom of the ocean where there is no sunlight, bitter cold, and immense pressure, suggests that life can exist almost anywhere.

◆ **Disconfirming** or **negative case sampling**: With this strategy the researcher is looking to extend her/his analysis by looking for cases that will disconfirm it, both to test theory and simply because it is often from our failures that we learn the most. The general principle here is, "If you think your results are not generalizable or the existence of a particular kind of case will undermine all that you 'know' to be true about a phenomenon, then look for that kind of case." Becker (1998) sees this as a fundamental strategy for qualitative researchers; the core principle is that one should always look for the toughest test of one's developing theories because they are the ones that are most likely to cause you to rethink what you think you know and are thus by far the most interesting.

♦ **Representative sampling**: Although we have dealt separately with the issue of sampling for representativeness through probabilistic techniques, we also include it here by virtue of it being one of many purposive strategies a researcher might employ. For example, an organization that wants to determine how employees are responding to a recent structural reorganization might poll a representative sample of employees to ensure that the views of a complete cross-section of the organization are recognized.

♦ **The thoughtful respondent:** In any field-based inquiry, researchers soon realize that prospective interviewees are *not* created equal: some are incredibly informative or provocative, others are unwilling to talk, still others can talk for hours without saying anything interesting. Many researchers would trade one thoughtful, insightful and articulate respondent for a randomly chosen 50 any time.

In sum, informants who are unrepresentative of the group as a whole, statistically speaking, may still provide useful information and provocative insights that help researchers understand a group, an organization, or a situation:

> The primary feature of all these methods is that the situation of the sample is determined according to the needs of the study, and not according to external criteria, such as random selection. Participants are representative of the same experience or knowledge; they are not selected because of their demographic reflection of the general population. (Morse 1994: 229)

One danger with any purposive sampling strategy is that the way we proceed, and who we include and exclude, inevitably will reflect our understanding of the phenomenon of interest, which, because of the way that it constructs the population, may indirectly reaffirm rather than challenge existing understandings. Researchers studying illicit drug use, for example, are more likely to study people whose behaviour brings them into contact with official agencies (e.g., the police, coroners, public health nurses, treatment groups) than they are to study drug users with a productive and successful lifestyle. Researchers studying gambling are more likely to study people who frequent institutionalized gaming venues (casinos, bingo halls, racetracks) than they are to study gamblers who operate outside the law (e.g., by placing bets with "bookies") or people whose risk-taking isn't normally recognized as gambling (e.g., those who play the stock market). Researchers studying prostitution are more likely to study its more visible forms (e.g., street prostitution) than they are to study its less obvious (e.g., off-street venues such as massage parlours or escort agencies) or more subtle (e.g., prostitution of one's principles) manifestations. Certainly such choices are defensible, yet we must remain clear about the inherent limitations to understanding they entail.

Snowball Sampling

Snowball sampling, sometimes referred to as network, chain referral, respondent driven, or multiplicity sampling, takes its name from the familiar experience of starting with a small snowball and, after rolling it down a hill or around in some damp snow, ending up with a huge ball that can serve as the base for a humanoid snow figure. By starting very small, you can still end up with something very big. In the sampling realm, snowball sampling involves starting with one or two people and then using their connections, and their connections' connections, to generate a large sample. This technique is especially useful if your target population is a deviant or "closet" population, or isn't particularly well-defined or accessible.

Edna Salamon (1984) used the snowball procedure to good effect in her doctoral research on "kept women." Salamon wanted a sample of women who had received apartments, cars, trips, maintenance money, and so on in exchange for their camaraderie and involvement in an intimate relationship. But where does one acquire such a sample? There's obviously no sampling frame available. And there are no "kept woman clubs" to approach. Salamon was lamenting this problem to her hairdresser one day when he said "I know a few; I'll introduce you." He introduced her to a few kept women, each of whom introduced her to other kept women, who introduced her to others, until she had acquired a sizable sample of kept women.

The main danger in using this procedure is that one's first snowball may well influence the shape of the snow figure that results. Executives who went through Harvard Business School probably best know other executives who also went through Harvard Business School; street prostitutes are probably more likely to know other street prostitutes than they are to know call girls, who travel in more exclusive company. In general, people are more likely to know people who have similarities with them. Indeed, this social dynamic makes snowball samples possible in the first place. So one must either remain cautious in generalizing results or conscientiously try to start several different snowballs in several different niches.

Quota Sampling

A final non-probabilistic procedure is **quota sampling**, a technique that made Gallup (as in Gallup Poll) a household word after George Gallup correctly predicted the result of the 1936 U.S. presidential election. Quota sampling is still used by some pollsters, especially marketing researchers who want a heterogeneous sample but don't need

true representativeness (although quota sampling *is* formally representative to the extent that the distribution of characteristics in the sample is similar to the distribution of those characteristics in the population).

To do a quota sample, the researcher must first know something about at least the demographic characteristics of the population to be studied. Such information is usually provided by census data. Suppose that we want to ask people about child-rearing practices and that we know from earlier research that attitudes about these practices vary with the respondents' sex and educational background. The researcher would begin by acquiring census data that show how those characteristics are distributed in the population. Suppose we did so, finding the breakdown shown in Table 4.4.

For the sample to be formally representative, 30 percent of our respondents should be males who have completed high school or less, 10 percent should be females who have obtained some postsecondary education, and so on. As with stratified random sampling, quota sampling starts with a target population that has *known* characteristics. But with stratified random sampling, we'd now proceed to randomly select people from within each category: the quota sampler would merely go out and find (for a sample of 100, for example) 30 males with a high school education or less, 35 females with some postsecondary education, and so on. Since *any* 30 males with a high school education or less will do, the researcher might look for them in shopping malls, at pool halls, at union meetings, at laundromats, or just about anywhere.

Table 4.4
Hypothetical Population Breakdown by Sex and Education

	Completed High School or Less	Some Postsecondary	Completed Postsecondary
Male	30%	15%	5%
Female	35	10	5
Total	65	25	10

The quota sampling technique assumes that all people within a given stratum are equal, that for example, all males with a high school education or less will have pretty much the same attitudes regarding the phenomenon of interest. While such an assumption may not be indefensible, it's still fairly tenuous. Quote sampling's major strength is that it ensures a heterogeneous sample with respect to relevant background variables.[8]

SAMPLING CONSIDERATIONS FOR NETWORKED ENVIRONMENTS

The Internet as a Research Site

Just as the proliferation of the telephone in the 1930s and thereafter changed communication patterns and offered first minimal and then extensive new ways to conduct social research, bourgeoning use of the Internet and technological advances that make many different kinds of network-assisted research possible behoove us to give special consideration to the current status of sampling issues that are arising and being addressed in relation to such research.

Demographics of Network Connectivity

Worldwide personal computer use surpassed 1.2 billion in 2008 (Computer Industry Almanac 2009) and it is estimated that over 1.8 billion people worldwide use the Internet (Computer Industry Almanac 2010). Both the Canadian and United States governments have made strong commitments to ensuring that all citizens have access to network technology such as the Internet. The expressed goal of the Canadian government is to make Canada "the most connected country in the world" (Dryburgh 2002). Understanding who is and who isn't connected is crucial for achieving success in **computer-assisted social research** (**CASR**).

U.S. Census Bureau figures as of October 2009 showed 73.5 percent of U.S. citizens indicated that they had used Internet-connected computers from some location in the past year.[9] In comparison, Statistics Canada data for the end of 2009 indicated 80.3 percent of Canadians used Internet-networked computers.[10] Patterns within both countries are similar insofar as variation in Internet use is concerned. As you might expect, Internet connectivity and use is higher with higher income, education, and employment, and lower with increasing age, particularly beyond middle-age. When we compare usage from national surveys over time, it is clear that it is constantly rising as more and more people become connected in an ever-greater variety of ways. Although there is still at this point a "digital divide" related to the characteristics we mentioned—age, education, and income—the disparity is less and less with time, in large part because the highest user groups are close to the ceiling (91–97 percent) while the lowest user groups keep rising. That said, large portions of the North American population still do not own a personal computer (ACNeilsen 2004; Weber 2004).

Internets, Intranets, and the Wireless Globe

The statistics on computer ownership and Internet use provide powerful evidence that coverage error is an important consideration for researchers wishing to use "Internet users" as their population. Moreover, no matter how much the digital divide shrinks in the years to come, the size and fluidity of the Internet makes defining the boundaries of the population impossible.

There are many reasons to believe that Internet connectivity will continue to grow as it has until it pervades society—just as the telephone went from being an exotic tool of the wealthy to a standard appliance in virtually every home—but we also would suggest that treating "Internet connectivity" as synonymous with "opportunities for CASR" is far too narrow a way of looking at the contemporary world and the role of computers and computer-assisted research within it. There are three things we must keep in mind.

First, ownership of a computer is one thing, but access, either inside or outside the home, is quite another. It is hard to find a school, community centre, public library, corporate or commercial office, government facility, or social service agency in North America without networked computers. Second, although people often think only of the Internet when they think of "networked" computers, a sizable portion of computer networks are not connected to the Internet; instead they are connected via private institutional networks known as **intranets**. Third, while the Internet is certainly the most hyped network domain and intranets serve as the backbone for most business, health, and academic institutions, these networks are by no means the most popular or pervasive. Globally, cellphones are the largest and most utilized network technology. In 2009 more than half the world's population reported owning or using a cellphone (International Telecommunication Union 2009). In Canada nearly 75 percent of households indicated they had a cellphone in 2008, with 8 percent reporting having *only* a cellphone (Statistics Canada 2009, June 15).

Given the pervasiveness of technology in North American society it is reasonable to estimate that at least 90 percent of the North American population already has access to a network-connected device. As the cost of technology continues to drop and wireless networking becomes ubiquitous, it becomes possible for researchers to bring networked technology into the field to access the remaining 10 percent.

Sampling in Networked Environments

Perhaps the most commonly cited advantage of using networks for acquiring samples is that they offer the most effective method for soliciting larger and more demographically and geographically diverse samples (Barry 2001). Researchers have found that networked environments afford researchers a unique opportunity to access difficult, deviant, hard-to-reach, or stigmatized populations (Atchison 1996, 1998; Barry 2001;

Fox, Murray, & Warm 2003). They also have been useful for conducting research with elite groups (Bauman, Airey, & Atak 1998) and with physically handicapped, shy, and disorganized individuals (Gosling, Vazire, & Srivastava 2004) who are notoriously difficult to involve in research using other methods.

Researchers in networked environments also have utilized probability sampling methods. In the majority of studies sampling frames are created from: (1) published email addresses, (2) electronic subscription information, and (3) high-volume websites. Email addresses are frequently compiled from conventional and electronic organizational directories, newsgroups, chat rooms, or peer-to-peer chat networks that function as a type of telephone book. Researchers select a sample from these directories and treat them as analogous to probabilistic samples of networked computer users. Alternatively, electronic subscription groups can be used as sampling units of networked computer users. Various organizations compile lists of subscription groups such as Internet service providers (ISPs), Usenet newsgroups, listserv mailing lists, and Web-based discussion forum members. Rather than identifying individual users, researchers randomly sample topic-specific subgroups from these lists and then solicit subscribers of the selected groups in much the same way that stratified or cluster sampling is applied to the general population. Finally, heavily trafficked websites such as Google are often used to construct sampling frames of the general Internet-using population (Koch & Emrey 2001; Ross et al. 2003). Researchers usually begin by selecting high-traffic or topic-specific websites. After these websites have been identified, advertisements are posted that direct interested visitors to a separate research site.

SOLICITING RESPONSES AND PARTICIPATION

Regardless whether we sample participants in conventional or networked environments, once we have decided on the most appropriate sampling strategy and located prospective participants we are faced with the next challenge, which is to convince them to participate. Increasingly, it is not enough to simply approach, email, or phone a prospective participant and say "I'm a researcher from Provincial University, will you participate in my research?" The steady growth of the commercial research industry over the past 30 years and the often invasive, unethical, and/or simply annoying tactics that market researchers have used to secure participants has made many members of the general public distrustful of research in general and unwilling to contribute their time (Blumberg, Luke, & Cynamon 2006; Kaye & Johnson 1999; Sheehan & Hoy 1999). Additionally, the increasing quantity of telephone numbers reserved for fax and computer telephone lines and the growing prevalence of call-screening devices (Tuckel & O'Neill 2002) accompanied by rising cellphone use have all contributed to a steady lowering of response rates to cold contact telephone solicitation. The University of Michigan's Survey of Consumer Attitudes shows that response rates have dropped at an average of 1.5 percent per year since 1996, which is approximately double the decline of 0.75 percent per year that occurred from 1979 to 1996.

Unless we are already personally acquainted with someone from the population we are interested in sampling (e.g., insiders or informants), we most likely will have to make a direct appeal to members of the population by placing an advertisement in newspapers, magazines, radio or television programs, or by distributing flyers, poster-ads, or business cards in areas where prospective participants might see our appeal. For example, when Chris wanted to contact sex buyers he started by placing advertisements in specific adult newspapers, magazines, and trade papers that he had reason to believe were read by people who paid for sex. He also ran ads in local newspapers, magazines, and daily free papers, and distributed posters, pamphlets, and business cards to STD/STI clinics, dance clubs and bars, and novelty shops throughout Vancouver and surrounding areas. Spreading his advertisements across multiple media sources and venues allowed

him to get information about his research to a wide cross-section of the sex-buying population.

While placing ads in newspapers and magazines or on local television has been a staple of participant recruitment in the social and health sciences for many years, readership and viewership in these traditional media have been declining steadily with the continued growth of the Internet. Since 2000 newspapers in the United States have faced a cumulative 25.6 percent loss in daily circulation; magazines and local television news also have faced steep audience declines (Pew Research Centre 2010). In Canada, the drop appears to be more tempered: from 2002 through 2005, total circulation of daily newspapers declined on average by about 3 percent (Wahl 2006), although magazine sales and advertising recently have faced even steeper declines (Krashinsky 2009; Surridge 2009).

In response to this changing media landscape many researchers have begun to make greater use of network methods for contacting and soliciting research participants. Some of the most popular ways of using network technology to solicit participants include sending out bulk email, paying search providers such as Google or Bing to advertise your research website, posting notices on a social networking site such as Facebook, and placing advertisements in online discussion boards or listserves where 'communities' of people who share similar interests or experiences connect with one another. It is important to keep in mind that these are just a sample of available techniques. As networked environments continually change, there undoubtedly will be an increasing number of ways that Internets, intranets, and cellular networks can be used to contact and solicit research participants.

Finally, one of the most commonly used techniques for securing research participants is to offer them payment in the form of stipends (i.e., cash, goods) or a chance to win a larger prize. This method is so common among social and health researchers that it is often seen as the default option for getting people to participate. For example, Chris recently coordinated the Vancouver wing of a cross-Canada study looking at the positive experiences of Aboriginal people living in urban settings. Even though the study was designed in partnership with Aboriginal groups across Canada in order to provide Aboriginal people with a rather unique opportunity to challenge negative stereotypes, the group coordinating the project felt that participation rates could be improved if people were paid a small stipend for their contribution. Each participant was paid $50 in return for completing a two-hour structured interview. In the end Chris and his research team managed to secure 250 participants in just one month. Similar success was reported by the researchers who coordinated projects across nine other Canadian cities.

While paying people to participate can certainly be an effective means of securing a sample for your research there are several things we need to consider before doing this. While offering a participant money or gifts in exchange for their participation might seem like a reasonable way of expressing your appreciation for the time and energy that they contribute towards providing you with the information you need to find answers to your research questions, for some people such payment may be seen as insulting. On a somewhat related note, it is difficult to determine the relative real and symbolic value that money or gifts might have different participants. For example, offering $20 for participating in an hour-long interview is likely to mean much more to a homeless person than it would for someone who lives in a mansion and drives a Lamborghini. Furthermore, the homeless participant may be living in conditions of such desperation that the mere act of offering them money in exchange for their participation makes them feel as though they are obligated to participate in your research which, as we saw in Chapter 3, may violate their ethical right to free and informed consent. Finally, while researchers working for large corporations may find it necessary to offer gifts or money because their "research" offers little direct benefit to people or society, much of the research we do in the social and health sciences is not motivated by profit or corporate interests. Social and health researchers might be more successful in soliciting participants if we took the time to fully illustrate to participants the intrinsic and practical benefits of participating in our research and how these benefits extend far beyond those they would get from the nominal amount of money we could offer them.

One final issue to consider, especially as you read through the chapters in this book that outline the specific techniques we can employ for making observations and collecting data, is the importance of participation options in helping you convince people to participate in your research. The specific format of the research instrument greatly influences a respondent's ability to participate (Hampton & Wellman 1999). The inherent flexibility of computerized observation and data instruments offers hope in this respect. It is a relatively simple task for researchers to design shorter, simplified, and less obtrusive data collection instruments in order to improve response rates (Crawford, Couper, & Lamias 2001). Additionally, designing the instrument so that less experienced users can respond using their mouse, keyboard, touch-screen, or voice activation is an increasingly realistic option.

The plummeting cost of equipment along with improvements in portability and battery life also are making it easier to bring the computer to participants who do not have access to computers. Several years ago Chris attended the Vancouver International Jazz Festival where he participated in a computer-assisted self-administered questionnaire (CASQ) sponsored by a tobacco company. Designers had placed stand-alone terminals at strategic locations throughout the festival site, with terminals configured so that participants only needed to know how to push a button in order to participate. In the two hours that he observed three of the terminals, more than 40 people from diverse backgrounds stopped to participate.

SUMMING UP AND LOOKING AHEAD

Consistent with the theme developed elsewhere in this book, this chapter argues that there is no one "best" sampling procedure. Rather, deciding which is "best" depends once again on one's research objectives, the nature of the phenomenon being studied, and pragmatic considerations related to your choice of site and sample. And of course, sampling strategies apply both to people and any other unit of analysis that we might wish to scrutinize, including objects (e.g., the products of a particular manufacturer, types of films) or a particular type of situation (e.g., marriage proposals, casual drug use, career decisions, interactions between the police and the community).

The chapter discusses a range of probabilistic and non-probabilistic techniques, outlining their respective strengths and weaknesses (see Table 4.5). Probabilistic techniques are the techniques of choice when acquiring a representative sample is crucial; non-probabilistic purposive techniques tend to be the techniques of choice for more field-based situations where persons in the setting are not interchangeable and where position, point of view, access to particular information, and insight and ability to articulate are the more important criteria to maximize.

We've also argued here that in its broadest sense, any knowledge we generate is merely a sample of all the knowledge we theoretically *could* generate. We must therefore remain aware of how our "commonsensical" (i.e., culturally provided) understandings of the world influence our identification (and hence sampling) of target issues and groups, which in turn influences the course of future knowledge, implicitly reaffirming the status quo.

Perhaps one of the biggest developments to hit the research world in the last few decades is the parallel development of the Internet and computer (digital) technologies, and we conclude this chapter by discussing some of the unique sampling issues that arise when one considers engaging in computer-assisted social research (CASR). We review what have now become the "standard" concerns to express surrounding coverage error, representativeness, and the generalizability of findings, but suggest these problems are diminishing as the Internet and Internet accessibility become more pervasive. And while these concerns should not be dismissed by researchers wishing to make the Internet a central component in their research design, neither should their importance be overstated. Very little social research is built around questions that require perfect devotion to these requirements (Fricker & Rand 2002); concerns about the lack of universality of the Internet are well placed in a small range of research, but in many cases those concerns are overstated and esoteric. Representative samples are still possible in many intranet situations or in

Table 4.5

Examples of Probabilistic and Non-Probabilistic Sampling Procedures

Sampling Procedures	
Probabilistic	**Non-probabilistic**
Simple random sampling	Haphazard or convenience sampling
Systematic sampling with random start	Purposive sampling
Stratified random sampling	• extreme case sampling
• proportional	• intensity sampling
• disproportional	• maximum variety/diversity sampling
	• deviant case
Multistage cluster sampling	Snowball sampling
	Quota sampling

situations where finite groups of interest define themselves by subscription, and as is always true, much of the best research that is done relies on located targeted groups of persons, which the Internet and search engines facilitate tremendously.

Finally, we also suggest that the research community needs to get past the narrow view of thinking of "Internet-based research" as the only way to acquire samples for computer-assisted social research. While the Internet is certainly how many people understand networked technology, very little attention has been paid to looking at the networked environment as a means to an end rather than as an end in itself. For example, we need to move away from the assumption that in order to participate in research conducted on or through networked environments people must own a personal computer. We also need to recognize that the Internet is not the only structure linking computers to one another. To this end it is important to start looking at computers and network technology as both an observation and data-collection medium as well as a mode of contacting participants. We need to continue to develop new and efficient methods of contacting prospective participants and soliciting their participation. Network technology is pervasive in North American society; people do not need to use the Internet in order to be able to participate in social research.

With our discussion of sampling concluded, and our "getting started" and ethics chapters behind us, you now know enough to start thinking in general terms about putting a proposal together in which you set out a game plan for undertaking a piece of research. The next chapter outlines some of the issues you need to consider and articulate as you go through that process, while the rest of the book will help fill in what must for now remain blanks—the specific design and procedures you will create to answer your research questions.

STUDY QUESTIONS

1. "Any study that doesn't use a representative sample will inevitably produce findings that are not generalizable." Discuss this statement.

2. What does it mean to say that a sample is *representative* of some larger population?

3. What criteria have to be met for a sample to be considered a *random* sample? Why would you want a random sample?

4. Gwen wants to acquire a *random* sample of people who attend a very controversial film. Which of the following procedures would give her a *random* sample? (a) she rolls a dice and a "3" turns up. Gwen approaches the 3rd person in line and every 10th person thereafter; (b) Gwen goes down the line and arbitrarily picks people by whim; (c) Gwen's favourite colour is green, so she decides to interview every person who shows up wearing something green.

5. What is the relationship between *universe, population,* and *sample?*

6. Prepare a summary table of the sampling techniques discussed in this chapter. Begin by drawing four columns on a sheet of paper. Title the first column "Techniques"; in that column, list all the techniques covered in the chapter. Title the second column "Procedures"; in that column, describe in your own words the procedures involved in executing each technique. Title the third and fourth columns "Strengths" and "Weaknesses," respectively; in these columns, list situations for which each technique would be useful, along with the technique's advantages and limitations.

7. Alison wants to interview a representative sample of people who live in apartments in Vancouver's highrise haven, the West End. Unfortunately, no sampling frame is available, and it would be impossible to construct one. What sampling procedure would you recommend that she use? Why?

8. How does *quota sampling* differ from *stratified random sampling?*

9. Can an *unrepresentative* sample still be useful? If so, explain how.

10. You plan to study the department you're majoring in at your college or university. In

particular, you want to examine the undergraduate curriculum to ascertain both how it came about and how it might be improved. You want to gather data via interviews. How do you decide whom to sample? Discuss some of your alternatives, describing their respective advantages and limitations.

11. This year's student council is evenly divided on whether the student-run cafeteria should be run on a not-for-profit basis (in order to minimize the cost of meals to students) or on a for-profit basis (with all the profits going to the student society's bursary program). Riaz decides to do a survey to determine the attitudes of the current student body toward these alternatives. He goes to the cafeteria at noon on a Thursday, numbers all the tables (from 1 to 250), randomly samples 50 of the tables, and interviews all the people sitting at those tables. He finds that 57 percent of the students interviewed prefer the for-profit alternative. How confident can Riaz be that this result is representative of the opinions of the student body? Could he be more confident in the representativeness of his results if he had interviewed people from 100 randomly chosen tables?

12. Chris takes a different approach to the problem outlined in Study Question 11. She approaches the college registrar for a list of all students who are currently enrolled; using a table of random numbers, she chooses one student from that list. When interviewed, that student expresses an opinion in favour of the for-profit alternative. Is that one student's opinion theoretically representative of the opinions of the entire student body? Explain why or why not.

13. Pat wants to do an interview study of "hockey fans." Suggest two probabilistic and two non-probabilistic techniques that might, under certain conditions (which you should specify), allow her to acquire such a sample. Discuss the advantages and limitations of using each of those techniques.

14. Identify a population of people that you are interested in knowing more about and devise a way to sample and solicit them that uses computer technology. Once you have devised your strategy explain how you think your strategy is an improvement over more conventional approaches that you could have used.

15. What is the digital divide and what role does it play in computer-assisted social research?

16. Is it ever possible to obtain a representative sample of respondents on the Internet? Why or why not? What are some *advantages* to seeking Internet-based samples?

17. Devise a creative way of getting your friends to participate in a small Internet survey. Why do you think that the strategy you have come up with would be particularly successful?

NOTES

1. The figures here are derived from the Webpages of SFU political scientist Dr. Andrew Heard at http://www.sfu.ca/~aheard/elections/results.html.

2. An exception to this rule is random digit dialing (RDD), a technique developed in the context of telephone survey research, where no explicit sampling frame exists. "RDD relies ... on a procedure that, when followed properly, includes all units or elements of the target population" (Gray & Guppy 1994: 141). However, straight random sampling of telephone numbers is quickly losing favour because decades-long habits of phone use—where each household has one land line and people answer the phone when it rings—are being replaced by mixtures of land lines, cellphones, telephones no longer the exclusive responsibility of "adults," local exchanges, and area codes that are no longer predictably tied to a person's location, call display, call screening, and so on.

3. This statement assumes that the sampling procedure is probabilistic and has been executed appropriately.

4. Researchers sometimes counteract this problem by computing a "weighted" mean, a number that's adjusted to reflect what the mean (or average) would theoretically be *if* groups were represented in the sample in the same proportions as they appear in the population.

5. Although only 20 years ago, we should explain that at that time only a very small portion of the population owned cellphones (which were about the size of a brick) and while many land line phones that existed might have the touch-tone buttons we take for granted today, many still had "rotary dial" telephones, and thus could not participate in the CBS call-in poll.

6. While national polling organizations rarely go beyond a sample size of 3,000, it should be noted that Statistics Canada very often has samples 10 times that size, while the U.S. census bureau often has samples in the hundreds of thousands.

7. Is maximum variety sampling thus just another name for disproportional stratified random sampling? No. Although the maximum variety sampler in our example has essentially stratified the population on the variable of ethnicity, there's no further requirement to randomly sample within each stratum. Indeed, maximum variety sampling aims to maximize the diversity of views that are heard; thus, instead of seeking the "typical" respondent within each stratum (as is the goal of stratified random sampling), researchers following a maximum variety strategy would probably still try to sample for maximum diversity within each stratum.

8. Although George Gallup made his name with this technique in the 1936 U.S. presidential election, and successfully used it again in 1940 and 1944, he suffered huge embarrassment in 1948, when he predicted that Thomas Dewey would be the next U.S. president. The American public voted instead for Harry Truman. Gallup subsequently abandoned quota sampling techniques in favour of probabilistic procedures.

9. See http://www.census.gov/hhes/computer/publications/2009.html.

10. See http://www40.statcan.gc.ca/l01/cst01/comm35a-eng.htm.

CONSTRUCTING A RESEARCH PROPOSAL

Coming up with a good research topic and generating researchable questions is just the beginning of the research process. Making it all happen means making contacts, getting approvals, perhaps seeking funding, and convincing others that your research is well considered, ethical, and viable. It does not necessarily mean getting every last little detail settled, although that depends in part on what sort of research you are doing: straight hypothesis testing can be specified in detail; more emergent and exploratory research will be more open-ended because of the collaborative elements that need to be worked out. Nonetheless, your professors, admissions committees for graduate programs, granting agencies or the people paying you to conduct the research, university or college research ethics boards, and your prospective participants all want to know, before they say "OK" to you, that you have some understanding of what you want to do, and that your project is reasonable, ethical, and has a chance of achieving its objectives. In the social and health sciences this assurance is achieved through the writing of a research proposal.

Despite the obvious importance of writing research proposals within the social and health sciences, there are very few books available to help researchers navigate the difficult terrain of writing a coherent and convincing research proposal. Many texts on social and health research gloss over the research proposal process, leaving the impression that researchers who have specific interests or questions that they wish to pursue simply go out and start researching. The final published research papers, articles, and reports that fill the shelves of university and college libraries are often

so well polished and structured that it is difficult or impossible to piece together the underlying methodological decision-making process that produced the published results. The intent of this chapter is to help you better understand what goes into a research proposal and to provide you with some practical suggestions for developing research proposals of your own.

WHAT GOES INTO A RESEARCH PROPOSAL?

A research proposal, like every well-written academic paper, has an introduction, a body, and a conclusion. A research proposal is just like a substantive position paper in that the goal is to develop and articulate an argument supporting the thesis that the proposed study and its guiding questions are important, relevant, and interesting, and that the techniques you have selected to go about answering these questions are ethically and methodologically sound enough to allow you to successfully complete the proposed study given your resources and limitations.

Just as there are many ways one could approach writing a term paper on contemporary applications of Marxist theory, there is no single way to write a research proposal. The single most important consideration that guides how a research proposal is structured and presented is the nature of the research questions that are being asked. The research question or questions provide a general framework for the design decisions that are likely to follow, since it is toward finding the most complete answers to the research question(s) that the entire research process is directed.

While it is important to recognize that research questions, personal style, chosen research method, and audience all will influence how you go about laying out your research proposal—not to mention the requirements of whoever you are submitting your proposal to—several interrelated components are common to nearly all proposals. Within the social and health sciences research proposals contain a specific *research topic*, a critical discussion of academic *literature* relating to the research topic, a clearly stated and researchable guiding *research question*, a convincing *justification* for conducting the research; a discussion of the specific *research design* and *data analysis strategies* that will be used in order to address the research problem and answer the research question(s), and a reflexive discussion of any *research ethics* issues that pertain to your research and how you have decided to address them.

THE RESEARCH PROPOSAL WRITING PROCESS

Generating a Research Topic

The first step in writing a research proposal is to select a research topic. Often the first time a student is asked to sit down and identify a topic to research is in an introductory research methods class. Many students in that situation have a difficult time finding a research topic and generating good researchable questions.

As you saw in Chapter 2, ideas about what to research can come from many places. Research ideas that are derived through deductive approaches are guided by theory. Inductive ideas emerge from interaction with and observation of social phenomena. The research process itself gives another set of sources, and sometimes topics fall in your lap because someone presents you with one.

The biggest trick at the beginning is to care about what you are researching. In this chapter we will draw examples from several research proposals we had access to that were prepared for various purposes:

- A proposal prepared for a funding agency by Bob Menzies and Ted Palys for a project involving the history of psychiatry and the asylum as an institution of social control in British Columbia in relation to minorities
- A proposal by Tammy Dorward written as a thesis prospectus for her M.A. thesis involving the way that "community" was defined and engaged in the development of Vancouver's Aboriginal Transformative Justice Services (VATJS)
- A proposal that Chris Atchison prepared as the prospectus for his doctoral dissertation regarding prostitution and the role of the male sex buyer
- A proposal prepared by Michelle McGinn and Ted Palys designed to secure funding for research involving the views and expectations of research participants regarding various research ethics issues

Placing Your Research Topic within the Academic Literature

With topic in hand, your next step is to address how others have thought about and researched it. While it is always important to pursue new, exciting, and novel topics, ideas, and questions, quite often it is helpful to ground your study within a larger framework in order to better understand how you can best go about producing researchable questions, selecting the appropriate methods and techniques for pursuing the answers to these questions, and analyzing the information that is produced from the careful execution of these techniques. The literature review provides you with an excellent opportunity to do exactly that.

A well-written literature review situates a project and provides clear evidence that allows the audience to better assess why the topic and research questions are important and how the proposed research fits into the larger academic context. In other words, your literature review should provide a clear and concise synthesis of the major trends in theory, research, policy, and practice, and it should identify the questions or areas of concern that are considered to be the most important or relevant for the community that is currently working in the area. Recall from Chapter 2 that the point of a literature review is not to simply regurgitate what others have said about your topic but to think critically about what has been said and to identify and highlight the consistencies and disagreements in theory, research, policy, and practice that are evident. Once you have accomplished this you will be in a much better position to identify the flaws or gaps in knowledge that need to be remedied. It is by highlighting these flaws or gaps that you begin to lay the foundations for your own study.

In the case of McGinn and Palys (2005), the problem was that the existing literature featured a lot of talk and very little action when it came to understanding research participants' views of the research process and ethical issues therein:

> The Tri-Council Policy Statement on Research Ethics (TCPS), Canada's federal authority on research ethics, is not the only code of ethics to enjoin researchers and REBs to take a "subject-centered perspective" when they consider ethical issues in their research: "researchers and REBs must strive to understand the views of the potential or actual research subjects." (MRC et al 1998: i-7) Despite its centrality, a literature regarding participant perspectives on research is virtually non-existent.... The purpose of our project is both to begin and to promote research regarding participant perspectives on ethics issues.* (2)

For Menzies and Palys (1999), however, quite the opposite was the case. There was already an extensive literature around the world that had begun examining psychiatric practice from a more patient-centred viewpoint, and many historical studies. The challenge for them was thus to specify where they fit in that existing domain of inquiry, as well as to identify what new contributions their proposed research offered:

In undertaking this study, we will also be contributing to the wider historical investigation of institutional psychiatry in the province of British Columbia and Canada. In contrast to elsewhere in the country (e.g. Cellard, 1991; Dowbiggin, 1997; Mitchinson, 1991; Refvik, 1991; Shortt, 1986), a literature on the origins and development of British Columbian psychiatry and mental health has only recently begun to surface. To date, historical writing in this province has concentrated principally on criminally insane persons (Chunn & Menzies 1998), on the deportation of alien "lunatics" (Menzies, 1998), on life in the women's wards at the Provincial Hospital for the Insane (PHI) in New Westminster (Davies, 1989), and on the role of families in the involuntary commitment of women patients (Kelm, 1992). Given the immense importance of a system that has confined more than 100 000 British Columbians since its inception, and with the increasing availability to researchers of a rich historical data archive, much work remains to be done. As discussed above, in this project we propose to build on this emergent body of research by investigating one aspect of psychiatric history in the province—namely, the treatment and control of persons bearing the multiple stigma of mental disorder and racial/ethnic marginalization.[†]

There are many ways to critically address the literature relating to your topic of interest. The approach you take to structuring your review is a matter of personal style, preference, and a consideration of your audience. While different audiences are likely to be partial to a particular style of writing over another or will be sympathetic to a particular perspective on social research, it would not be unusual for a literature to address some or all of the following basic questions:

---

* M. K. McGinn & T.S. Palys (2005). *Participants' perspectives on research ethics issues: A research proposal*. Unpublished proposal prepared to seek funding from the Social Sciences and Humanities Research Council and The Research Ethics Boards at Brock University and Simon Fraser University.

† Menzies, R. & Palys, T.S. (1999). *Race, ethnicity and psychiatric regulation in British Columbia, 1875–1950*. Unpublished grant proposal prepared for the Hannah Institute for the History of Medicine Grant-in-aid program. Burnaby, B.C.: School of Criminology, Simon Fraser University.

- What have others said about this topic? Who are the major groups that have expressed an interest in the topic or issue?

- Are there particular problems or controversies surrounding the topic?

- What is the history behind these problems or controversies? How have they arisen?

- What theories have been developed around the topic and what do they say?

- What methods have been used to study the topic?

- What research has been done on the topic? What gaps are there that should be addressed?

- What policies or practices have been developed in relation to the topic?

- Are there consistencies in existing theory, methodology, research, policy, and practice relating to the topic, or is there disagreement?

- Are there flaws in the existing theory, methodology, research, policy, and practice that you feel you can remedy through your proposed research? What are these flaws and how will your research resolve them?

Stylistically, the literature review is similar to a discussion paper like the ones you would write for a theory class; the objective is to critically synthesize and assess several related academic books or articles that have been written in your area of interest. Your literature review should be a free-flowing discussion of the major themes and controversies that are highlighted among several choice books or articles that you feel are well-suited for helping you provide a solid critical overview. It is important to note that literature reviews are different from annotated bibliographies in that the latter are simply itemized summaries of articles and books while the former are critical discussions of major themes that are present within a series of articles and books.

Quite often students ask us how many pieces of literature or how many articles they need to include in the literature review of their research proposal. The answer to this question is not straightforward. The short answer is, you need enough books or articles to demonstrate that you have a good reading or understanding of the topic area. You need to show that you have given adequate attention to how others have addressed the topic within the literature. In some cases this may be eight or 10 books or articles; in other situations it might be 30, 40, or 50. The advice we generally give our students is that the more they read the better they will be at identifying potential problems, directions, important areas to concentrate on, new research questions, and alternative methodologies. Further, it is important to understand that the literature review process is ongoing throughout the design, execution, and analysis stages of a research project. Good researchers are always going back and reading more on their topic and trying to find overlaps with others.

Poor literature reviews lose the reader in details and irrelevancies, give the impression the writer is meandering, don't seem to have any particular point to them, and tempt the reader simply to skip ahead to the next section. A good literature review is just like the first chapter of a really good adventure novel: it provides the backdrop, introduces you to the main characters, and leaves you with a desire to see how the rest of the story unfolds. A core component of almost every academic article that is published is a literature review. It is a useful exercise to go and read journal articles from different disciplines to see how the literature is reviewed and presented within each of these disciplines.

Constructing Researchable Questions

In Chapter 2 you were introduced to the process of constructing researchable questions. They are clearly an important element, as developing/refining them further or actually answering them is where all of your research activities will be directed. It naturally follows that all of the research decisions that are outlined and discussed in the research proposal are contingent on whether and how they will contribute to answering your research question(s). You need to present your research question(s) in a way that helps you define the nature and scope of the research. Of course, one possible research question, particularly with more inductive/collaborative approaches, is always, "What should my research question be?" or "What other research questions should I include?" In such a case your proposal will outline what you will do and who you will talk to in order to make that happen.

Operating in relation to a well-developed literature and in the context of their own research programs that had been in place for several years, Menzies and Palys had a large and very specific list of things they wanted to know:

> During the initial stages of this project, supported by [various research grants from SSHRC and Simon Fraser University], we have generated and have begun to address a range of questions that pertain to the social and psychiatric control of racial and ethnic minority group members. These include the following: With what frequency did First Nations, Chinese, Japanese, Doukhobor and South Asian peoples enter the mental hospitals of British Columbia during the period under investigation? What were their patterns of age distribution, gender, marital status, education, occupation, and other socio-demographic attributes? What can be learned about their lives prior to therapeutic contact? Had they previous experience with mental, judicial or welfare institutions? What situations and events initiated their psychiatric confinement? What individuals and agencies were involved in the securing of their commitment to hospital? Did their racial and ethnic status contribute to prior life experiences and encounters leading to confinement? Did the reports of physicians, police and other authorities make reference to their minority identities or link these with behaviour and imputed pathologies? Once hospitalization had transpired, did racial and ethnocultural ascriptions figure into the profiles and accounts of these 200 patients? If so, how were these manifest in ward notes, official reports and correspondence? What was the apparent impact on the treatment of individual subjects? Was there evidence of differential treatment across the five minority groups comprising this study? And how did the patients respond? In their surviving notes and letters, or in the representations of their personal and legal advocates, did they articulate a sense of racial/ethnic identity or a sensitivity to partiality or prejudice in their institutional experience? Did race/ethnicity appear to impact their quality of life while under confinement, their length of hospitalization, or the conditions of release for those who were discharged? Finally, what knowledge can be garnered about the subsequent lives of those individuals who survived and returned to the outside world?*

In contrast, Tammy Dorward's master's thesis was her first significant foray into the realm of research, although she had been interested in Aboriginal justice policy issues for some time. The literature in that area identified "broad community involvement and support" as a key element in the establishment of successful Aboriginal programs, but she found that most of the literature on that topic, and most of the programs that had been developed, involved reserve-based communities where the boundaries and citizenry of the community were fairly easily defined, and where the people all shared a similar core cultural heritage. But a growing number of Aboriginal people leave the reserve to study and work. Do they still have the rights that are guaranteed to Aboriginal peoples in Canada's *Charter of Rights and Freedoms*? Do they form a "community"? How would an Aboriginal program that set out to be "community-based" identify and involve them? Dorward's thesis became a case study examination of how one program in Vancouver dealt with those very issues with respect to the creation of Vancouver's Aboriginal Transformative Justice Services (VATJS), and gave her a clear research question and focus:

---

* Menzies, R. & Palys, T.S. (1999). *Race, ethnicity and psychiatric regulation in British Columbia, 1875–1950*. Unpublished grant proposal prepared for the Hannah Institute for the History of Medicine Grant-in-aid program. Burnaby, B.C.: School of Criminology, Simon Fraser University.

Given the fundamental importance of the concept of "community" to both governance and justice, and the unique challenges that arise when that term is operationalized within the urban setting, my thesis will involve an examination of how the concept of "community" was conceptually and operationally defined in the course of developing the VATJS.*

Providing Justifications for Your Research

While having an interesting topic and solid research question is the focal starting point of any good research proposal, the research question cannot be understood apart from the deeper reason or purpose of the proposed study. The research questions do not tell people who are reading your research proposal why the study needs to be conducted; they merely tell people what will be answered. When we say that you have to justify the study, what we're really saying is you have to demonstrate to your reader why they should care. You cannot just assume that because you feel something is important, relevant, or interesting that your audience will necessarily share your beliefs or passion. If you cannot convey to readers why they should care about the particular topic, then you're unlikely to get the support, guidance, advice, or funding necessary to realize your goals.

There are several ways that you can go about justifying your study. It is often impossible to know who is going to be reading your research proposal and even more difficult to know exactly how to engage them. Fortunately, you don't need to place all of your eggs in one basket when it comes to elaborating the justifications for your particular research design, topic, and questions. You can justify your study on a number of different grounds in an effort to engage as diverse an audience and range of sensibilities possible. The easiest way to do

this is to return to the academic literature in order to draw specific connections between the proposed research and the development of a theory, method, policy, and/or practice.

MAKING A CONTRIBUTION TO THEORY DEVELOPMENT
One of the most common ways of justifying a proposed research study is to situate the research topic and questions within the theoretical literature in the area and to point to the contribution that the proposed research will make to the development of social theory. For instance, in his dissertation proposal that involved a study on prostitution and the role of the male sex buyer, Chris pointed out that by further describing, exploring, and understanding the population of men who buy sex, sociologists and criminologists would be better equipped to develop theories of masculinity and gender that were informed by specific empirical evidence rather than conjecture:

> Risk-based research authorizes researchers as expert speakers about sex buying at the same time as it de-legitimates male sex buyers as speakers and active subjects capable of framing the problems in different ways. Aside from the phenomenological investigation conducted by Holzman and Pines in the early 1980's, sociologically informed research into the nature of the socio-cultural context of sex buying has not received much attention within the theoretical or empirical literature on the client. The primary focus of [the proposed] research will be the development of a qualitatively and quantitatively informed understanding of risk decision making processes involved in the male purchase of sex. More specifically, … I hope to be able to obtain an interpretive understanding of the attitudes, behaviours and decision making practices of male sex buyers that is grounded in both an empirical investigation of self-reported attitudes and behaviours and an in-depth account of the lived experiences and varied and multiple socially and culturally informed meanings that male sex buyers attribute to the risk decisions that are pertinent to their purchase of sex.

---

* Dorward, T. (2002). *The role of "community" in the design and development of Vancouver Aboriginal Transformative Justice Services: A proposal*. Unpublished M.A. thesis proposal submitted to the School of Criminology, Simon Fraser University. Pg 8.

TAKING A DIFFERENT METHODOLOGICAL APPROACH

Another potential way to justify the pursuit of a particular topic or a research design is to point to the methodological contributions that the design will make. Perhaps the way that you have chosen to pursue your investigation is methodologically different than the approaches that other people in the field have taken. For example, if all the studies on student satisfaction with their research methods classes are based on the analysis of aggregate statistics collected from year-end surveys that ask students to rank the performance of their professors and teaching assistants using fixed-response multiple choice questions, it is safe to assume that this method will produce a limited understanding of students' experiences with those classes. Such surveys are necessarily superficial in what they ask, and rarely ask for details about the students that might be useful in understanding, for example, what sorts of professors, teaching styles, and classes appeal to what sorts of students. You could design a research project that puts a more qualitative spin on addressing student satisfaction. Instead of using an aggregate survey you could propose sampling a smaller number of students from the class and conducting more in-depth interviews with them that would cover a variety of topics and experiences. This shift in method could offer a clear contribution to our understanding of student satisfaction with their classes.

CITING IMPLICATIONS FOR POLICY OR PROGRAMME DEVELOPMENT

You can also justify a study in terms of the policy applications that could emerge as a result of the data acquired from the study: by better understanding a particular topic and answering specific research questions, social policy in relation to the topic could be developed or changed. Menzies and Palys argued in their proposal that understanding history is its own reward, in part because many of the problems of the past still exist and beg attention:

> We believe that this project will make a significant contribution to the historical understanding of

medical and social ordering in British Columbia. It will offer a unique approach to understanding the institutional treatment of racial and ethnic minorities in the province, and more generally across Canada. To the extent that problems of racialization and ethnocentrism remain entrenched in *fin-de-siècle* society, the work has both historical and contemporary relevance. It will help to expose both the manifest and implicit means by which the dimensions of race and culture get played out in the operations of our therapeutic and regulatory institutions. In addressing the practices of the past, we can learn much about the conflicts and prejudices that continue to plague British Columbian and Canadian social order as this century draws to a close.*

Tammy Dorward was more explicit in identifying her policy interests, and more succinct in her statement of it:

> My goal will be to critically analyze the concept of "community" as it was developed and implemented in the development of the VATJS and to explore the implications of that concept, and my analysis of it, for future programme development.[†]

ADDRESSING A GAP IN THE LITERATURE

For McGinn and Palys, the justification was a very basic one—that the dearth of research in the area required some basic exploratory work to identify what some important research questions in the area were:

---

* Menzies, R. & Palys, T.S. (1999). *Race, ethnicity and psychiatric regulation in British Columbia, 1875–1950.* Unpublished grant proposal prepared for the Hannah Institute for the History of Medicine Grant-in-aid program. Burnaby, B.C.: School of Criminology, Simon Fraser University.

† Dorward, T. (2002). *The role of "community" in the design and development of Vancouver Aboriginal Transformative Justice Services: A proposal.* Unpublished M.A. thesis proposal submitted to the School of Criminology, Simon Fraser University. Pg 9.

The purpose of our project is both to begin and to promote research regarding participant perspectives on ethics issues. We follow a collaborative approach and seek participant input from the outset.… Our hope is not only to provide an initial contribution to an area that begs attention, but also to help identify questions and offer interim observations that will encourage/promote others to become involved and contribute.*

As you can see, there are a variety of ways to go about justifying researching a particular topic or researching specific questions within the body of your research proposal. While the approach you take is largely a matter of personal style, preference, and a consideration of your audience, it is wise to attempt to address the following general questions:

◆ Why is the topic worth studying?

◆ Why are the research questions that have been developed worth answering?

◆ What practical significance does the proposed study have?

◆ What will be accomplished by the completion of the proposed research project?

◆ In what ways does the proposed study contribute to the general understanding of the topic or to the construction of social theories?

◆ What contribution is the research expected to make to the advancement of knowledge or to the development of new methods?

◆ What contribution is the research expected to make to wider social policy or practice?

Locating Yourself within the Study

Quite often in academic writing we're encouraged to depersonalize how we present information and arguments. Most often this depersonalization

* M. K. McGinn & T.S. Palys (2005). *Participants' perspectives on research ethics issues: A research proposal.* Unpublished proposal prepared to seek funding from the Social Sciences and Humanities Research Council and The Research Ethics Boards at Brock University and Simon Fraser University.

manifests itself in the awkward third person language that we are encouraged to use when presenting an argument, writing a research proposal, or analyzing and presenting the findings of our research. For example, instead of saying, "I believe that this design will produce the most valid and reliable results," students are often encouraged to depersonalize the claim by saying, "It is believed that this design will …" For some academic writers this depersonalization is seen as a way of ensuring that our projects remain free of bias, while others argue that by making our personal connection to the research more transparent we not only acknowledge our awareness of potential sources of bias, we avoid fraudulent disinterest and instead show how research doesn't have to be a cold and inhuman process.

Regardless of the stylistic position you adopt, or that your discipline imposes, for your own academic writing, part of designing and conducting research is being both critically aware and reflexive of your own position within that research.

When we say that you have to locate the study within your personal experience we are not saying that you have to write a tell-all autobiography confessing all your deep, dark inner secrets. We are simply suggesting that you share with the reader of your research proposal why the study is particularly important to you or how it relates to some experience you have had in your own life. There are a number of strategies that you can use to locate the study within your personal experience. One popular technique is to show how the proposed research fits into your ongoing research program or is related to experiences or insights you have gained from earlier achievements or involvement in the field under investigation. That was very much the case for Menzies and Palys in their study of asylum files:

This study comprises the second stage in a wider inquiry into the medical and legal regulation of racial and ethnic minorities in British Columbian history. Following an initial compilation, during the summer of 1999, of selected case file documents for patients admitted from the inauguration of BC's mental health system up to 1942, we now propose to expand the research to include samples of five racial/ethnic patient populations (First Nations, Doukhobor, Japanese, Chinese and South Asian) who were hospitalized through to 31 December 1950. The extension and finalization of these data sets are integral to the successful completion of this project. The work has become possible through the impending availability (as of late Fall 1999) at the BC Archives of a new data base including all public mental hospital files in the province that were closed through death or discharge between 1943 and 1969. The [proposed grant] will permit us to assemble and analyze a unique data base of clinical file records and institutional documents that will constitute the first historical study concentrating on the racial/ethnic dimensions of institutional psychiatry in Canada.*

As another example, perhaps you are planning on applying for an honours or graduate degree program; you may want to indicate how your proposed research is designed to help build your knowledge base so that you can pursue advanced studies or research. Another popular method of connecting yourself with a proposed study is to point to the ways that a particular study is motivated by events in your personal life or experiences that you have had. For example, some of our students who have undertaken research on the social challenges faced by mentally challenged youth indicated in their proposals that their research interests were motivated by their own experiences growing up with siblings who were afflicted with a particular mental disability.

While it is certainly debatable as to how much researchers should have to reveal about themselves, when it comes to putting together a solid research proposal there are considerable benefits to being reflexive and transparent about where you fit into the

* Menzies, R. & Palys, T.S. (1999). *Race, ethnicity and psychiatric regulation in British Columbia, 1875–1950*. Unpublished grant proposal prepared for the Hannah Institute for the History of Medicine Grant-in-aid program. Burnaby, B.C.: School of Criminology, Simon Fraser University.

research process. To this end we advise you to develop the style and technique that you are most comfortable with for elaborating on your own connection to the research within your research proposal. Regardless of the strategy you ultimately develop, it is important for you to remain conscious of the influences that your own experiences and position have on the research decisions that you make.

THE RESEARCH DESIGN: A ROADMAP TO SUCCESS

The Research Question

As you have seen, the research decisions that you make are influenced by a number of factors operating, sometimes silently, behind the scenes. The most important factor influencing your research decisions is your research question. After all, the whole point of conducting research is to find answers to questions we have about the world. The underlying objectives of your questions (exploration, description, understanding, explanation, or transformation) serve as signposts or route markers that guide you toward making particular design decisions. The questions will govern how complex the design has to be, including what your units of analysis will be and which sampling and recruitment strategy is best to study them, how the units should be measured or observed, and which type of analysis will produce the most valid and reliable answers.

Outlining Research Procedures: Who? What? How?

The design section of the research proposal is where the pragmatic part of your research planning begins. It is at this stage of the research proposal that you elaborate how your research strategy will unfold. A clear research design provides a roadmap for people reading your research proposal, showing them the exact route you think you will take to arrive at your empirical destination. It also lets your audience know why you think that the route you have chosen is the best one to take and should follow from your statement of research objectives and your research question. Although whatever is most important will depend on your research and the issues that are unique to it, here are some core questions that are considered in many research proposals:

- Who or what will you study in order to collect the data necessary to answer your research questions?
- Will it be appropriate to select a sample? If so,
  - What sampling strategy will you be using?
  - What processes and procedures are involved in the sampling strategy that you plan on utilizing?
  - How large will your resulting sample be?
  - How do you know that this sampling strategy and the resulting sample will be adequate to provide you with the information necessary to answer your research questions and meet your research objectives?
- If it is not appropriate to select a sample,
  - Why is a sample not appropriate?
  - What procedures will you use to select the units of analysis for your study?
  - How many observations will you be making?
  - How can you be sure that the type and number of observations that you intend to make will be enough for you to answer your research questions?

For Tammy Dorward, for example, who was interested in understanding how Vancouver's "Aboriginal community" came to be defined and involved in the process of creating the Vancouver Aboriginal justice program (VATJS), some preliminary discussions with persons who were involved in the development of the program and a perusal of some of the documentation available to her led her to identify the following as crucial to answering her research questions:

a) Examining archival data pertaining to the conception and design of the VATJS to consider how and by whom "the community" was conceptually and operationally defined.

b) Interviewing and surveying people involved in the development of VATJS to see how they believe the concept of "community" was/should be defined. In order to understand the diversity of views Aboriginal people may have regarding this topic, a wide range of people should be sampled:
   - Programme records regarding the initial Elder's Consultation lists the names of 32 participating Elders. A sample of 5-10 Elders should be interviewed.
   - Community Council members and programme personnel (3-6 interviews)
   - A survey of people attending West Coast night [a weekly gathering at Vancouver's Aboriginal Friendship Centre], which will conclude with the question of whether the respondent would be willing to discuss the topic further in an interview (10–20 from this category)
   - Students at Native Education centres (5-10 interviews)
   - Others who are identified in the course of data gathering.

For McGinn and Palys, who were very much at the beginning of what had the potential to become an extended piece of work, a more flexible, exploratory approach was warranted to identify what might be some important questions to ask, followed by an effort to cast as wide a net as possible to gain some preliminary response to those themes identified in the first phase:

In Phase I of the research, focus group interviews with purposive samples of persons who previously have participated in research will be conducted in which people are asked about their participation in and perceptions of different ethical issues in relation to the research process. We intend to use what we hear from those first targeted groups to develop more structured instruments to do the broader and more extensive web-based study described in Phase II.*

They also chose samples for the initial focus group research that were relatively easily available to them and that they also believed would be fruitful in helping them to meet their exploratory objectives:

> We believe this first foray will be most fruitful if we focus on groups who are frequently asked to participate in research and/or who live/work in a milieu in which research is common; the more experience they have, and the more different variations of approaches and procedures they have encountered, the greater the depth that will be possible in the conversation. Also, we are less interested in the facts of their participation than their perceptions of it, and use "previous participation" or "being in an environment where research is frequently conducted" as criteria for participation because we want to go beyond "research" as an abstract process to one that has some concrete meaning for the participant, at least as a referent or departure point, from which to consider why they might or might not have participated.[†]

The authors went on to outline how Palys would conduct focus groups with individuals from various niches within the criminal justice system—former prisoners, police officers, and lawyers—while McGinn would obtain various educational samples—parents of school-aged children, university students, and teachers. The benefits of visiting these particular niches are explained. In relation to the criminological samples, for example, they wrote:

Focussing on these "criminological" samples has several research benefits. Certainly criminological research has been the focus of considerable controversy for the last decade in Canada and elsewhere (e.g., see Israel 2004a; Lowman & Palys 2000; Yeager 2004), with many of the debates between researchers and REBs residing in apparently different views by criminological researchers and REB members who have no experience in researching criminological issues over the expectations that criminological samples have of researchers and the institutions who employ them. To that extent, there is an urgency to examining this domain that is duplicated by few other areas.[‡]

In Chapter 4 we talked about how one of the biggest challenges in research is determining how and where you can best approach prospective participants in your research so that they will agree to participate. Many projects that seem great on paper never get anywhere if the people are unwilling to participate and/or the data are otherwise unavailable. Indeed, the difference between "paper" research where everything always works wonderfully, and "real" research where one bumps into the vagaries of everyday life, is one of the reasons we try to have students do actual research projects rather than proposals whenever feasible. The lessons learned are invaluable for making one's next proposal better by more completely anticipating all the bases that need to be covered. Whatever your experience, one of the things you need to do in your proposal is not only to convey your plans, but to also give evidence showing they are feasible. In some instances this may be very easy—for example, you need access to a public setting and can gain that access precisely because the setting you need *is* public. But many other groups require special access, which brings in other issues—gatekeepers, greater ethical complexity regarding negotiation and consent, whether permissions have been obtained, and so on.

Sometimes, familiarity with the population that you are interested in through previous group

---

*[†‡] M. K. McGinn & T.S. Palys (2005). *Participants' perspectives on research ethics issues: A research proposal.* Unpublished proposal prepared to seek funding from the Social Sciences and Humanities Research Council and The Research Ethics Boards at Brock University and Simon Fraser University.

membership can facilitate the design process. Your "insider" status may have provided you with a working knowledge of how the group is organized, how they talk, how to gain their trust, and how to handle yourself when you are interacting with them. If you don't have this type of avenue into a group you will need to invest more time in detailing how you will get beyond your "outsider" status and encourage people to participate.

Regardless of how familiar you are with the population you wish to research, you need to convey to your audience that you have given significant thought to how you are going to "sell your project" to your prospective sample and how you will manage your research if you are not successful in making the "sale." To do this, there are several interrelated questions that are helpful to think about and address within your proposal:

◆ Who is available for your study and how will you contact them?

◆ Once you have contacted people for your study, what procedures will you use to encourage them to participate in the study?

◆ How do you know that these procedures will work?

◆ What will you do if people refuse to participate?

Identifying and Addressing Ethics Issues

Beyond knowing exactly how you are going to encourage people to participate in your research you have to remain conscious of the fact that as social and health scientists our research often involves inserting ourselves into the lives of real people. The relationships that we forge with the people who are kind enough to consent to participate in our research are not entirely neutral. As academic, social, or health researchers we have a certain degree of influence and power within the research setting, if for no other reason than the fact that it is we who ask the questions and in some cases wear the funny white lab coats. It is also important to remember, however, that the

power balance between the researcher and the participant is not one-sided. Most social research and a substantial amount of health research takes place outside the safe and secure setting of the university in environments that are more familiar to the participant than the researcher. As you saw in Chapter 3, in order to address potential abuses of the balance of power between the researcher and the participant, the academic research community has developed a variety of ethical codes of conduct by which people who conduct social and health research have agreed to abide. Relevant issues must be considered in your proposal. These may include the following:

◆ How will you obtain the free and informed consent of your participants?

◆ Are you providing any guarantees and assurances to your research participants?

◆ Might your research have a foreseeable positive or negative impact on those you study? What is the nature of that prospective impact?

◆ What procedures will you have in place to ensure that your study will not bring about harm to those involved or related to the research?

◆ What procedures will you have in place to ensure that your research participant's privacy, confidentiality, and anonymity (if applicable) are respected and protected?

For example, for McGinn and Palys there were two main ethics issues to be dealt with in each of the two phases of their research (phase I involved focus groups; phase II involved a Web-based survey): (a) consent, and (b) confidentiality, as well as recruitment issues that were relevant to the Web survey. In regard to the focus group study, they stated:

Consent

The announced intent of the discussions with participant groups will be to "have a discussion about 'research participant perspectives' in which people who have participated previously in research, or who have opinions about the research they have seen carried on in their midst, can bring and share their experiences and views." At the first opportunity prospective participants will be given an information sheet that outlines [a lengthy description follows that identifies the purpose of the research; what their participation would involve; who they should contact to find out more].

We will ensure in each case that in order to participate persons will have to make a free choice as to whether to come to the group, so that consent will be implicit in attendance at the meeting and each person's voluntary choice to participate in the conversation. A verbal explanation of the project rationale will be given that will follow the points listed in our written project description above, and a discussion begun. Michelle and Ted will lead their respective discussions, and begin by asking whether anyone present has any objection to the discussion being recorded. It will be explained that the recordings will allow a transcript to be created that maximizes accuracy of recall. In the event there is an objection, anonymized written notes will be taken instead.

Confidentiality

Participants in group discussions will be told the obvious, i.e., that there are others in the room and hence that there are limitations to how "confidential" anything might be among the persons in the room. Persons interviewed individually can be asked how confidential they would prefer the interview to be, and their wishes recognized. Our own intention is to anonymize transcripts and never use names in any presentations or reports that arise from this work because our interests are in the issues that are identified and not in the identities or personalities of those who contribute the information. Beyond that, we can only encourage group participants to be respectful of each others'

sensibilities to the extent they would like others to respect theirs.

Because participants will be talking about research in which they have participated, confidentiality issues may arise for the persons who were in charge of designing and implementing those research projects. We will never ask for the names of those persons or, if given them, will not record them, as we have no interest in pursuing that end of the experience in this project; our interest is solely in their perspective on their research experiences.*

In Chris's dissertation proposal, which outlined a project involving Web-based surveys and some subsequent interviews with men who buy sex—behaviour that may be highly stigmatized in many contexts but is not illegal—he dealt with a variety of ethics issues but identified confidentiality issues as the most significant:

Every precaution will be taken to ensure that the participants' privacy and confidentiality are protected throughout the course of the research. While knowledge of the men's identities will be requested if they are going to participate in the semi-structured interviews, it will not be a requirement for participation in the self-administered questionnaire portion of the research. There will be no way in which to identify the participants who indicate that they wish to remain anonymous, providing they do not provide any identifying information within their responses.

All men who elect to participate in the self-administered questionnaire will be given instructions and options which attempt to

---

* M. K. McGinn & T.S. Palys (2005). *Participants' perspectives on research ethics issues: A research proposal.* Unpublished proposal prepared to seek funding from the Social Sciences and Humanities Research Council and The Research Ethics Boards at Brock University and Simon Fraser University.

ensure that their responses remain protected from third party interception. The men will be specifically instructed not to give any identifying information or to mark their responses in any way which may be used to identify them at a later date by either the researchers or any third party. In addition, they will be informed of the security risks associated with transferring information via the Internet and they will be provided with alternative submission options should they feel that electronic submission is too much of a risk. Specifically, respondents will be given two options for returning responses to the researchers. Questionnaires may be filled out and returned to the researchers while on the World Wide Web via a simple HTML form and a secure socket layer connection. If the respondents have serious concerns about the interception of their responses they may download and print a PDF hard copy of the questionnaire and return it in an unmarked envelope via conventional mail to the researchers at an address at Simon Fraser University.*

MEASUREMENT AND DATA COLLECTION

With your sample and sampling strategy clearly defined and discussed, you need to turn your attention to issues of measurement and data collection. While identifying "who" or "what" you are going to study is vital to successful research, if you don't have a well-thought-out research instrument to guide or structure your observations or measurement you will not be able to answer your research questions, and all the thought and work that you put into your research plan up to this point will have been for naught.

The nature of the measures and instruments you develop in order to answer your research

questions is heavily influenced by the research perspective you use to inform your research design. While a single research question can be answered in a variety of ways, once you elect to employ a qualitative, quantitative, or mixed-methods approach the specific measurement techniques that are available to you become more narrowly defined. For example, perhaps you are interested in understanding what motivates participation in extreme sports like base jumping, rock climbing, and long-board downhill skateboarding. Answers to this question can be found using a qualitative or quantitative method or both. Perhaps you are interested in the qualitative meaning that participants attach to their extreme activities. In this case you would probably want to develop your research design around a qualitative case study of an extreme sports participant or a micro-ethnography of a particular extreme sports community. Conversely, you may think that it is more important to test a particular theory of adventure-seeking behaviour that has been developed by researchers who have looked at similar populations. In order to test this theory you may decide that a quantitative approach involving the use of a self-administered questionnaire or quasi-experimental design will provide the best answers to your question.

As you will see as you read through the remaining chapters of this book, there are many qualitative and quantitative techniques available to you for finding answers to your research questions. Your goal in the methods and data collection section of your research proposal is to provide a convincing argument for why you feel that the particular measure you have developed and the data collection technique or techniques that you have selected are the best suited for your proposed research. Again, there is no template for how you should go about doing this, but there are several key questions that you need to consider in order to present a solid argument for the decisions you have made, including the following:

---

* Atchison, C. (1998). *Men who buy sex: A Preliminary description based on the results from a survey of the Internet-using population.* M.A. thesis. Simon Fraser University

- What are the key concepts or variables in your study?

- How will you conceptually and operationally define the central concepts or variables in your study?

- In what respect do your definitions and measurement techniques duplicate, build on, or differ from those used in previous studies of this topic?

- What specific data collection technique(s) will you use to collect the data necessary to answer your research questions and address your research objectives?

- Why have you selected the data collection technique(s) that you have?

- How do you know that the observation/measurement device you plan on using for your study will give you the best information or data for answering your research questions?

- Once you have completed your observations, what procedures will you implement to store the research data?

- What procedures will you implement to ensure that the data remain secure and confidential?

Proposals will vary in the extent to which measurement instruments can be specified. In more exploratory and inductive research you may be able to do little more than list a few themes that might be addressed for starters, with everything else to be determined on a collaborative basis depending on where your conversations with research participants lead you. In other areas you may be able to specify more concretely what you will ask. For example, even though McGinn and Palys's proposed research was more exploratory in its objectives, they already knew some issues they wanted to address in the focus group portion (phase I), simply because any code of ethics lists sets of principles and so they knew what was available. The big question they were posing was whether there were *other* issues or perspectives that ethics codes had not considered that should *also* be addressed. In any event, as an example, they said the following with regard to what participation in the research would involve:

Nature of Participation

Exploratory research requires a flexible and open-ended approach that is open to new directions, observations and issues as they arise. We propose to begin with a tentative overall guiding structure and sense of purpose that can be shared and be a starting point for discussions with participants. Our focus is on ethics issues that arise in regards to research participation, and the overall guiding framework we will begin with is to follow a chronological ordering through successive phases of the research process—access and recruitment, consent processes, expectations of confidentiality and so on—along with some more overarching considerations about relations among researchers, research participants, and REBs.*

The proposal went on to list the areas McGinn and Palys knew they wanted to address, along with sample questions in each area. A requirement for participation in their research was that individuals must have had some prior research involvement they could reflect on (so that the interaction would deal with a particular research experience rather than research in the abstract), and the ordering of topics McGinn and Palys proposed to follow was created to reflect how the process would have been experienced from the research participant's point of view—starting with the way access was obtained and their participation sought, through the gathering of data and any follow-up.

ANALYSIS, EXPECTED OUTCOMES, AND BENEFITS OF THE STUDY

Once you have presented a clear and well-defended argument for what or who you will study and how you will make your observations or collect the data necessary to answer your research questions, you

---

* M. K. McGinn & T.S. Palys (2005). *Participants' perspectives on research ethics issues: A research proposal.* Unpublished proposal prepared to seek funding from the Social Sciences and Humanities Research Council and The Research Ethics Boards at Brock University and Simon Fraser University.

need to shift your attention to thinking beyond the project to envision the type of analysis you will do and what some of the expected outcomes of this analysis are likely to be. Many students find this section of the proposal very difficult to write because they find it hard to envision what the data they will be collecting will look like, and they often have not yet been exposed to the range of qualitative, quantitative, or mixed-data analysis techniques available to help researchers make sense of their research observations and data. In order to begin to think about this you will want to read through Chapters 11 and 12 to get a feel for how data are handled at the analysis stage.

By this stage in the proposal writing process you have already designed and discussed the data collection techniques that you plan on using to answer your research questions, so you should have a very clear idea of what the possible format of the information you will be collecting will look like. For instance, if you plan on using a self-administered questionnaire or quasi-experimental design in order to gather observations, you already know that the information you get back will be in a fairly structured format with many of the responses or observations already defined and ordered. Conversely, if you plan on conducting lengthy personal interviews, case studies, oral histories, or micro-ethnographies, you will most likely have to deal with large amounts of open-ended textual information and field notes.

Regardless of whether you have quantitative or qualitative data or both, making sense of it will involve a process of data reduction where you take the volumes of information that you have collected and organize and synthesize them into core components or themes that help you to best go about answering your research question(s). The point is to make the information accessible and understandable so that you can bring to light certain patterns that speak to your research questions. For the purposes of the research proposal you are generally required to provide your audience with some indication as to how you think you will go about doing this. In order to accomplish this there

are several key questions that you should address in your research proposal:

♦ How will you organize the data to make them ready for analysis (e.g., transcription, data entry, coding, cleaning [correction/synthesis/editing])?

♦ How will findings be analyzed and reported (e.g., by hand or using a data analysis program)?

♦ What specific analysis procedures are you planning on using or what kind of analysis do you plan to conduct? Are specific hypotheses being tested? How do the analyses connect back to your research question(s)?

♦ What is the purpose of the analysis?

♦ What are the projected findings, conclusions, and implications of the proposed research?

♦ How will the findings be disseminated?

♦ What effect might your analysis have on or for the population that you are studying?

ACKNOWLEDGING POTENTIAL LIMITATIONS

Far too often both novice and experienced researchers construct research proposals that promise the moon and the stars without taking into account that there are likely to be methodological and practical constraints that will prevent the delivery of such lofty promises. A well-thought-out and convincing research proposal will clearly detail the potential limitations of the project.

In the limitations section of your proposal, you acknowledge the potential weaknesses of your design that have been brought about by the compromises you have had to make in order to construct a realistic project. Limitations can include potential problems obtaining access to people or settings, possible respondent refusal, equipment failure or technological support issues, limitations on personal skills and expertise, restricted budgets and time frames, and cultural and linguistic barriers.

For example, perhaps you realize that to fully understand the effects of long-term exposure to images of gaunt and unhealthy women in fashion magazines on women's health practices a longitudinal study would be necessary. As a student who may be heavily burdened by a full course load and student loan debt you may not have the time or financial resources to conduct such a study, so instead you have opted to design your research around a more manageable qualitative cross-sectional design. It is in the limitations section of your proposal where you should acknowledge this fact but make the argument that in spite of this, the data that you will get from your study will be an acceptable first step in understanding some of the ways that these images are affecting women's health. By doing this you address potential criticisms before they are made and you lay the groundwork for future research.

SUMMING UP AND LOOKING AHEAD

Different fields of study within the social and health sciences will highlight particular aspects of the research decision-making process over others, and they will do this using their own unique language and style. In this chapter we have attempted to provide you with a general framework of questions and strategies for developing a research proposal that reflects both your own sense of style and substance while at the same time allowing you to address some of the common themes and questions that appear throughout the social sciences. Again, it is important to remember that since every research project is motivated by different topics, questions, perspectives, and techniques, there is no one-size-fits-all approach to research design.

It is important when you are writing a research proposal to recognize that you will need to remain flexible and willing to change as your design unfolds. The point is not simply to put together a proposal that looks like it might work, but rather to sketch out a well-thought-out design that demonstrates that you have given each step of the process careful thought and attention and that as a result you have produced a sound design that anticipates potential problems and incorporates methodological techniques that dramatically improve the chances

that the research will be successful. It is impossible to anticipate all the potential road closures and detours that you may confront during the journey through conception, design, implementation, and analysis. Like any cross-country road trip, the process of research is full of twists and turns, bouts of car sickness, and truly amazing and serendipitous discoveries. The point is to prepare yourself for these possibilities by familiarizing yourself with the landscape and the roadways so that you arrive at your destination safely and securely with a whole bunch of interesting stories to tell.

The remainder of this book is dedicated to introducing you to the specific methods of data collection and analysis that are contained in the toolbox of the social and health scientist. As you read on, consider the various techniques that are presented and try to relate them back to topics that you think may be interesting to investigate. While you do this, ask yourself how each of the techniques could be integrated into research on a topic that interests you. Think about the relative advantages and disadvantages that each of the techniques could offer in exploring, describing, understanding, or explaining your topic. By doing this not only will you become a more critically aware consumer of the research and conclusions that are presented to you on an ongoing basis, but you will also be able to make informed decisions about the variety of methods that are available to you in your rapidly expanding social science toolbox.

STUDY QUESTIONS

1. Select a particular research topic that interests you and develop five researchable questions to explore, describe, understand, or explain something about that topic that interests you. Once you have done this make a list of the approaches that you could use to study each of your research questions.

2. Select a research topic or question that interests you and in 250 words or less provide a convincing justification for why this topic or

question is important and why research needs to be conducted in relation to it.

3. Locate three empirical articles from refereed journals that relate to the research topic or question you have developed in Question 2 above and briefly discuss how each of these articles relates to your research topic and provide a short justification for why you selected these particular articles.

4. What is the purpose of a research design?

5. Write a paragraph detailing what makes for a researchable question.

6. Go to your favourite news website (e.g., BBC News at http://www.bbc.co.uk/news/), and identify three social or health related stories that interest you, and how each of the three stories you have identified could be made into a researchable topic.

7. Identify five social and/or health science databases (other than Google Scholar) that you could use to locate refereed journal articles and other academic literature.

8. Select three empirical articles from refereed journals in your field of study and identify at least three limitations of each study.

9. Describe the major differences between an annotated bibliography and a literature review.

10. Using the material on research design presented in this chapter, develop an outline using headings and subheadings that illustrates the basic structure of a research design.

SURVEY, INTERVIEW, AND ORAL HISTORY TECHNIQUES

Few processes are as fundamental to social and health science research as the person-to-person exchange between a researcher and a research participant. On the one hand it's so simple: you ask a question and you get an answer. On the other hand, that simple interaction has had enough written about it to fill a small library.

TYPES OF INTERACTIVE METHODS

The range of techniques that fall into the domain of "interactive methods" is incredibly large and getting larger as developing digital technologies create new opportunities for both the generation and capturing of information for research. In this chapter we start off by discussing three general classes of interactive methods, including: (1) surveys and questionnaires; (2) interviews; and (3) oral history methods. As was the case when we discussed qualitative and quantitative approaches, we'll state from the outset that a clear distinction between these sets of techniques can be a difficult one to maintain, but trust you will allow us first to emphasize the differences for the sake of highlighting each method's strengths and limitations. By the end of the chapter, however, our emphasis will be on their complementarity and symbiotic strength when combined in a multi-method approach.

We use the words "survey," "questionnaire," and "survey questionnaire" interchangeably to refer to a fairly structured set of questions or other items that are finalized ahead of time and can be either self-administered or delivered by a researcher whose role is typically to stay focused on the questions and to keep interaction to a minimum. The specific questions can be of many different types, as we outline later in this chapter, that will range from highly structured to more open-ended, but a general characteristic is that all respondents normally will receive exactly the same set of questions worded in exactly the same way. An objective of such research typically will be to amass as large a sample as possible, and for data analysis to involve any of a variety of statistical techniques ranging from simple descriptive information regarding the distribution of responses (e.g., percentage breakdowns for each item, as you often see when opinion polls are published in the newspaper) to more complex statistical techniques designed to explore the data to explain variations in responding or to compare the responses of different groups. As this description suggests, surveys and questionnaires normally are considered more "quantitative" techniques for all the reasons that you should recall from Chapter 1.

We use the word "interview" to refer to the more qualitative process of a researcher/interviewer exchanging information with a research participant in more of an ongoing conversational style. The interview may be as structured as a questionnaire to begin with–standardized questions given to each participant followed by standardized probes when the researcher wants to encourage the respondent to embellish a bit further–or completely open-ended and adapted uniquely to each interviewee. Nonetheless, for us a general characteristic of the interview is that the nature of the exchange–ongoing, "live," and interactive–allows, in theory at least, for the interaction to go to places that were not originally anticipated by the researcher, and can be adapted as it happens to whatever revelations the interviewee decides to bring forward and that the interviewer decides to pursue.

Oral histories, given our previous definitions, could, on the one hand, simply be treated as another form of interview, but are sufficiently distinctive both because of the style and extensiveness of the interaction and the sense of mission that oral historians bring to the task, that we treat them separately for reasons that will be outlined in greater detail when we get there.

Surveys and Questionnaires

At least three different types of survey questionnaires can be distinguished, on the basis of the medium through which they're administered. We will refer to these as (1) the pencil-and-paper questionnaire; (2) the telephone survey; and (3) the browser-based survey.

Before discussing their unique strengths and limitations, some comment is due regarding attributes they all share relative to interviews and oral histories. Certainly their strengths are many. One can ask questions about anything in every kind of survey, and there are many different question formats (see later in this chapter) that are all equally easy to include. Questionnaires in most cases also make it easy to gather data anonymously (other than in group situations, such as a classroom or a community meeting, where respondents are sitting shoulder-to-shoulder), which may make it easier and more likely that participants will respond to sensitive questions that might lead them to have second thoughts if they thought they could be identified. And although there are significant differences between the different media of survey administration, all three also allow one to amass a fairly substantial amount of data fairly quickly, particularly relative to the time it would take to amass a comparable number of interviews. Surveys in all their forms are also quite inexpensive relative to the costs of a comparable number of interviews.

As we noted in Chapter 2, there are also many survey data archives that can now be accessed via the Internet where any researcher, and especially beginning researchers, can see how particular issues that are often common to many surveys (e.g., the way demographic information is sought) are addressed by respected survey agencies (such as Statistics Canada in Canada or the Census Bureau in the United States). Checking these archives to see how others have asked questions in your area of interest is a good way for newer researchers to benefit from what others have done and can enhance the comparability of results across surveys. And finally, structured surveys are also highly appropriate for more deductive types of research where the phenomenon being scrutinized is already fairly well understood and/or where theoretical propositions are being tested, such that the "right" questions to ask are fairly clear.

As with any method, there are also some limitations to all forms of survey. First is that, in most cases, getting someone to complete a questionnaire requires them to be literate in the language the questionnaire is written in. The fact that most surveys are standardized instruments given to the entire sample also means that you have to make decisions about vocabulary to ensure that all questions will be understood by everyone, which may be a real challenge, particularly when the sample is highly diverse. And finally, the data you get from surveys are limited to what the respondent places on the paper or indicates on a computer screen; researchers cannot at that point ask the respondent to clarify or further embellish upon her/his response, and there are no non-verbal or contextual cues to help the researcher interpret what the respondent has stated.

THE PENCIL-AND-PAPER QUESTIONNAIRE

One way to administer a survey–and the way that was a mainstay through much of the 20th century– is to place one's questions on a piece of paper, to deliver these papers to prospective respondents by mailing them to their last known address or handing them over in person in an individual or group setting, and then simply to collect all that paper and begin processing the information the respondents have given you.

There are unique benefits to administering a survey in this way. In the case of a mail-out survey, the respondent can choose her/his own time to do the survey and return it, and if a sampling frame is available from which to randomly sample, or a multi-stage cluster sample can be identified on a geographical basis, a theoretically representative sample can be contacted. Mail-out questionnaires are also a relatively economical alternative when compared to doing interviews; the principal costs are a few cents per sheet for photocopying and the cost of an envelope and stamps, which can take your questionnaire almost anywhere in the world. Paper is also reasonably portable, can be taken anywhere (except the shower), and does not require a computer or any computer skills to read. When distributed in person in group settings, paper-and-pencil surveys allow one to amass large amounts of data very quickly, which can be very handy if the sample you are targeting is one that meets or can be brought together in a specific locale (e.g., classrooms, meeting halls, hospitals, care facilities, a prison).

But there is also a big downside to paper-and-pencil surveys, beyond the obvious one that many trees are sacrificed for their creation, which make their usefulness very limited in the 21st century. It turns out, for example, that even though a mail-out questionnaire can be done in such a way that you can identify and contact a representative sample of people, so few of them are likely to reply—somewhere between 10 and 40 percent is likely, and probably closer to the former than the latter—that the actual sample of those who participate is much less likely to be representative. Lower response rates may not be a problem if the nature of the volunteer bias can be adequately assessed and/or if the researcher wants to obtain only a heterogeneous sample rather than a formally representative sample.

The fact that respondents answer questionnaires on their own poses special constraints the researcher must consider. First, respondents must be literate in the language used in the study—and normally on paper you have to commit yourself to whatever one language the study will be in—or they won't be able to read the questionnaire. Second, even if respondents are literate, the researcher must ensure that the vocabulary used in the questions is appropriate for the entire sample group being approached; the more diverse the group, the bigger the challenge. Third, researchers designing questionnaires must successfully anticipate possible ambiguities or misunderstandings. The questions themselves and the instructions to respondents must be clear, and the design of the survey itself must be kept simple enough that anyone can follow through without getting lost. **Contingency questions**, for example—the ones that say things like, "if you answer 'yes,' proceed to question 14; if 'no' go to question 17"—must be kept to a minimum or avoided entirely.

An absent researcher cannot monitor other procedural aspects of the study. A mail-out questionnaire may be sent to a particular person, but someone other than the intended respondent may actually fill it out. Similarly, except for obvious flippancy—e.g., the respondent who answers "Mars" when asked about their place of birth—we can't know whether respondents took the task seriously and gave their most comprehensive and candid responses. Such problems are thought to be relatively uncommon, since people who aren't interested in and/or serious about the topic of study are likely to simply ignore the questionnaire and fail to return it. But to the extent that such tendencies *do* exist, they make the data less valid.

And finally, paper-and-pencil surveys end up being very inefficient when it comes to the actual processing of the data. Someone must take the checkmarks and written comments from the piles of paper they are written on and transcribe them into a computer file so that they can be analyzed. This takes time, is incredibly boring to do, and ends up being an error-prone process that is best done twice in order to catch transcription errors and ensure you end up with a clean set of data.

THE TELEPHONE SURVEY

Large-scale survey research formerly relied on face-to-face encounters with samples of people identified on a geographical basis, since this was the only way to acquire large representative samples of the general population. But from approximately the 1960s onward, those who enjoy gathering large sets of perceptual data turned more and more to telephone interview techniques. It is interesting to consider the several factors that drove that transition, both to understand something of the history of the social survey, and because of the parallels we see between the history of the telephone and its incorporation into research, and the history of the Internet and its more recent incorporation into research.

Although it was invented in the late 1800s, it was not until well into the 1900s that the telephone went from being a high-tech toy of the wealthy to an essential tool of life in the industrialized world. Concerns that were voiced in the 1930s and 1940s about the selection bias involved in contacting samples via telephone (when it was primarily wealthier and urban dwellers who had telephones) had all but vanished by the 1970s and 1980s. By the end of the 20th century, in countries such as the United States and Sweden, 94 percent to 99 percent of all households could be reached by phone. In Canada, as long ago as 1987, the Canadian Radio-television and Telecommunications Commission released data showing that "98.5 percent of Canadian households had phones, almost double the number in 1947" (see "Phone Has Become … " 1989: F6).

There were other reasons that telephone surveys appealed to researchers and became the most commonly used survey technique. The costs of administering a survey face-to-face were rising rapidly, and telephone surveys offered an inexpensive alternative with little or no loss in response rates. Personal safety was also becoming a concern, particularly in urban centres in the United States. And these concerns went both ways. Respondents were becoming increasingly reluctant to allow strange interviewers into their homes but remained willing to "let them in" by phone. For their part, interviewers were becoming increasingly worried about their own safety as they walked the streets in some neighbourhoods. Contact by telephone was safer for them, too.

The telephone was initially simply a means of contacting prospective survey participants, but ultimately what it amounted to was a survey researcher reading a paper-and-pencil questionnaire to someone over the phone and marking down their responses. There were benefits to this–a trained survey administrator was now better able to ensure that the respondent was taking the task seriously, and could clarify any ambiguities or confusion that arose, which also made more complex survey designs feasible (e.g., those involving contingency questions). The development of **computer-assisted telephone interviewing–CATI** for short–made for an even more efficient process because responses could now be entered directly into a computer file (thereby also getting rid of the transcription problem and the errors that went with it).

The centralization of telephone interviewing also meant that research directors could take greater care in monitoring "quality control." Conversations between interviewers and respondents could be taped or monitored and critically analyzed for training and "quality assurance" purposes. And instead of losing prospective respondents for whom English was not a first or preferred language, a group of interviewers could be amassed who, collectively, could handle a broad variety of language situations in one centralized location (e.g., see Gorden 1980). The development of **random digit dialing (RDD)** techniques for a time made quasi-representative sampling a real possibility.

Nowadays, however, the popularity of the telephone survey or poll is waning rapidly. RDD has become ineffective because a phone number is no longer tied to a particular family or social unit in a particular place; phone companies now let subscribers carry their phone numbers within the same area code so that the connection between localized, identifiable neighbourhoods, and phone exchanges is rapidly becoming a thing of the past. People also now have multiple phone numbers and multiple phones—cellphones, modems, faxes, the home phone—which makes sampling difficult.

In addition, far too many harassing phone calls from salespeople or market researchers phoning in the guise of a survey have made it more and more difficult for social and health researchers to distinguish themselves from entrepreneurs. Initially, survey researchers would simply set a non-respondent aside and go back and randomly sample a new individual, but how many randomly chosen individuals can you set aside before the remaining sample of randomly chosen people is hopelessly biased? Although telephone surveys are still conducted, for more serious polling purposes they are, in our view, a disaster waiting to happen. Thoughtful and forward-looking survey companies are hedging their bets and looking elsewhere.

THE BROWSER-BASED SURVEY

Prior to the popularization of the Internet, Kiesler and Sproull (1986) provided a roadmap for using networked computers to conduct social and health science research. While they were optimistic about the potential of computer technology, they felt that "until such time as computers and networks spread throughout society, the electronic survey will probably be infeasible" (p. 403). That time would seem to have arrived. The Internet is expanding at an unprecedented rate; its growth has eclipsed all other technologies preceding it (Dahlen 2002). Between 1994 and 1998, 50 million people logged on to the Internet worldwide; it took 38 years for radio and 13 years for television to acquire the same user base (United Nations 2004). It is clear that the Internet is the fastest-growing information and communications medium to date, and it will not be long before it is as common as the television or the telephone (Dahlen 2002). In December 2005 one billion people worldwide were online (United Nations 2004); by 2011, Internet usage had passed *two* billion people.[1]

Notwithstanding this tremendous growth in access and usage, browser-based survey techniques are still at an early stage of development and have much room for improvement (e.g., see Palys & Atchison 2009; in press). Most of what we have seen to date involves little more than taking a paper-and-pencil survey and placing it on a computer monitor. But the possibilities, which we have begun experimenting with both in our own research and on a consulting basis through a company known simply as SQi,[2] are far more than that.

One of the most cited practical benefits of computer-assisted survey research is the effect that implementing a computer-assisted design has on the speed and duration of the research process; computer-assisted social research (CASR) can be much faster than comparable traditional designs. In network environments the footwork of the design and administration process is done by network connections. Research teams can create, edit, and finalize the research instrument without the burden of scheduling and attending physical meetings, and the research team can administer the design without having to physically connect with the participant. Once in motion, CASR allows researchers to move from design to observation and from observation to analysis much more quickly than conventional research designs. When research is conducted over wide area networks such as the Internet, observations can be made and data collected 24 hours a day, 7 days a week.

"**Usability**" is a term employed by graphic and Web designers to refer to the importance of understanding the user interface instead of the system upon which the interface is run (Couper 2000; Fricker & Rand 2002). Computer-administered observation and data collection instruments can enhance usability in three major ways: design, control, and accessibility. Design programs such as Adobe Flash and scripting languages such as AJAX, JScript, and JAVA can be used to create attractive, interesting, and compelling research instruments (Fricker & Rand 2002; Pettit 2002; Schmidt 2002). Instead of black letters on a white screen, we often work with a graphic designer[3] to ensure the look of any survey we prepare will be appealing to the audience we seek.

Computer-assisted surveys make a whole new way of asking questions possible through the integration of pictures, audio, and video media into the research instrument. For example, researchers can include a short multimedia clip in a structured survey and ask questions related to that clip. Also, response formats can be made much more intuitive for participants. For example, instead of asking participants to rate their level of happiness using a nondescript numeric rating scale, it is possible to provide a series of detailed animations that change as the participant moves a slider up or down the scale.

The strategic use of interface design and scripting also allows researchers to incorporate **adaptive questioning** into the research instrument in a manner that is neither obvious nor disturbing to the research participant. With adaptive questioning, answers to specific questions influence which subsequent questions will be asked (Bauman, Airey, & Atak 1998; Liu, Papathanasiou, & Hao 2001). For example, an early question in a survey might ask which often different sporting activities an individual engages in on a regular basis. The responses to this question can then be used to determine which subsequent sections are asked. Someone who answers "none" will not have any further questions asked on that topic, while someone who checks off swimming, golf, and hockey will see only those subsequent questions that deal with swimming, golf, and hockey and never see the ones that deal with Ultimate Frisbee, rugby, or jogging. The obvious advantages of this design feature are that individual respondents aren't bothered with questions that are irrelevant to them, and the complexity of the overall instrument is reduced for respondents since they no longer need to read and follow skip patterns and instruction sets.

In addition to enhancing the complexity of the data collection design, a well-constructed computerized instrument can help ensure that questions are completed and completed accurately (Liu et al. 2001). Unlike a human researcher who may forget to ask a specific question, with computer or browser-based surveys all questions are asked (unless adaptively programmed not to) because the computer always follows the programmed routine (Peiris, Gregor, & Alm 2000). In less structured surveys, researchers can script in pop-up dialogue boxes that automatically ask the respondent to elaborate a bit further if a certain number of keystrokes are not present in a particular answer. Finally, computer-assisted surveys also allow researchers to build in programmed checks of the responses provided to ensure that all required questions have been answered and that the information provided corresponds to the expected format.

Perhaps one of the most promising possibilities that computerized instruments offer in the way of format and design comes in the form of improved access. Multi-modal participant input devices can be created to facilitate the participation of people who have physical disabilities, limited reading or computer skills (Black & Ponirakis 2000), and attention deficits. Additionally, instruments can be customized to adapt to language and cultural differences. For instance, participants can have the option of filling out forms in any of a number of different languages or the digital voice on a computer can be changed to one that the participant is more culturally familiar with (Black & Ponirakis 2000). It is also possible to build in instructions or construct elaborate help or frequently asked questions (FAQ) sections that can be made available to a research participant at the click of a mouse (Karr 2000). Finally, the instrument also can be set up to provide feedback or instructions to the respondent when s/he has problems navigating, filling out questions, or submitting responses (Bauman et al. 1998; Woong Yun & Trumbo 2000).

Finally, browser-based surveys allow one to control access to the survey itself–either leaving it open or creating password or other private access–and to collect precise data about the process of survey completion that can help inform better survey development. One can, for example, get information about the types of operating systems and browsers that respondents are using, and can see exactly how long it takes respondents to respond to each question, which allows the researcher to identify spots where respondents tend to slow down (perhaps indicating that the content is overly complex or confusing and thus requires simplification), and also where they stop participation before completion, if at all.

On the down side, in some cases the initial design and administration of the research can be prohibitively time-consuming. When the research team is inexperienced with the use of technology or the technological infrastructure for the research is not already in place, extra training and the installation and testing of hardware and software may be necessary. Furthermore, researchers who are new to the technology are more likely to make errors during the administration and observation stages that can result in even greater time delays in the research.

When it comes to the cost of materials and labour there are several distinct differences between CASR and conventional research methods. The hardware, software, and scripting that is required for the observation and data collection portion of a CASR project can cost researchers thousands of dollars. However, researchers can offset the software and scripting costs by using freely available open-source software and scripts instead of high-priced commercial applications. Furthermore, while equipment and design costs can be high, these costs are generally recouped through savings on paper, postage, transcription, mileage, lodging, the renting of research venues, and repeated research. While it is uncommon to find hard-to-estimate human labour costs factored into discussions of many traditional data collection methods, the introduction of computer programmers and graphic and Web designers into the CASR design process has made many social and health science researchers begin to account for the cost of labour. The rate that most programmers and designers charge can be well over $100 per hour. The result is that in some situations CASR can be quite a cost-effective solution for the North American researcher. This advantage does however depend on researchers having enough experience with technology that they can implement solutions that require specialized user and programming skills.

At present, the most significant technological limitations facing researchers wishing to use computers and network technology in the field are that secure wireless network access can be sporadic and the range of mobile research-related software applications is still limited (Greene 2001; Woong &

Trumbo 2000). Experimental researchers have found that differences among computers in graphic display (Horswill & Coster 2001; MacInnes & Taylor 2001; Schmidt 2001), data processing speed and hardware timing (Eichstaedt 2001; Finney 2001), and keyboard and mouse performance (Eichstaedt 2001) all affect the experimental data collection process. Some field researchers have expressed concerns that the use of technology in field research may influence a respondent's reactions, with a negative effect on data quality (Gravlee 2002).

It also is important to recognize that there can be considerable start-up material and personnel costs associated with CASR, but repeated research is less costly since much of the investment is saddled by the first project and the cost of upgrading vital research materials is much less than first-time creation expenditures. Moreover, some research designs are more cost-effective than others. For example, the simple email-based questionnaire, where questions are placed in the body of the email, costs almost nothing to administer, while complex computer-assisted experimental and quasi-experimental designs that require special hardware and software can cost tens of thousands of dollars.

For research designs that are not dependent upon the physical presence of a researcher, network-based CASR facilitates the solicitation and recruitment of large, geographically and demographically diverse samples (Fox, Murray, & Warm 2003; Gosling, Vazire, & Srivastava 2004). These larger samples make it possible to amass large amounts of data in a relatively short time. Additionally, with the increasing availability and affordability of handheld smartphones, tablet and laptop computers, and wireless networks, researchers are not confined to any one physical locale in order to collect and analyze data.

Interviews

Like the survey, interviews are a highly flexible method that can incorporate virtually any type of question and deal with any area of content. But interviews also avoid many of the problems that often haunt survey questionnaires. Participation rates among people approached for a face-to-face interview are typically much higher (often around 80 percent or even 90 percent) than they are for survey questionnaires, which means that volunteer bias is generally less of a problem with interviews. The interaction of interviewer and respondent also offers benefits that can enhance the quality of the data gathered. For example, the interviewer can ensure that the appropriate person completes the interview, can clarify immediately any confusion about particular questions, and can encourage verbally stingy respondents to embellish further. Also, since the interviewer asks questions and records the responses, the respondent needn't be literate, although researcher and participant do need to share a common language. And although some participants may feel less anonymity in the personalized interview setting than with the impersonal questionnaire, skilled interviewers can often build sufficient rapport to alleviate such misgivings. Finally, the rapport that's built may have longer-term benefits for researchers engaging in longitudinal research, since respondents may be more willing to participate in **panel studies**—a form of longitudinal research where a specific group of people are interviewed on several different occasions over time.

The major disadvantage to interviews historically has been the time and expense required to undertake an interview study of any proportion. However, interviews have been much more a mainstay of people doing qualitative research than of those doing quantitative research, and intensity of effort is never anything that researchers engaged in qualitative research have shied away from. The most important thing we can say about interviews relative to surveys is how well the two can complement each other as part of a multi-method strategy. While surveys are excellent at providing information about how attitudes and attributes vary within and between populations, interviews allow researchers to probe more fully into *why* people might feel

the way they do, and the broader belief system that makes those attitudes make sense. Interviews also are an excellent choice for more exploratory research in areas that are not well understood, and often can contribute knowledge that allows for the creation of better surveys than can be done by a researcher sitting behind her/his desk.

Many different types of interviews have been identified. We will discuss three: (1) the in-person individual interview, where researcher and participant sit and talk eye-to-eye, usually in some relatively private setting; (2) the focus group interview, in which the researcher acts as both moderator and interviewer for groups of respondents who articulate and discuss their views; and (3) the network administered interview, where researcher and participant meet through an intranet or the Internet. As noted earlier, a fourth type of interview–the oral history interview–will be discussed in a separate section for reasons that will become apparent at that time.

THE IN-PERSON INTERVIEW

As noted, the biggest disadvantages of face-to-face interviews were always their cost and the time required to complete a large-scale interview study. There were, first of all, all the expenses associated with transportation, whether locally or nationally and even internationally, and potentially all the expenses associated with accommodation over and above that. And then there is the time associated with the interview itself–often an hour or more per interview–with the process of interviewing so cognitively and sometimes emotionally draining that, even with efficient scheduling, it is often difficult to do any more than two or three interviews in a day. How many dozens or hundreds of surveys can be amassed in that same period?

Then there is the social dynamic of the interview process. One would sit down with the interviewee, often looking at each across a table with a digital recorder and microphone, trying to get past the initial awkwardness and make the experience as much like a conversation as possible. The more intimate connection between the researcher and respondent this face-to-face exchange allows may have many benefits associated with it, such as greater likelihood of developing rapport, but the interview's interactive nature also means that one must be more careful about **reactive bias,** also known as **reactivity**, where self-consciousness and a desire to appear "normal" leads participants to respond in a more socially desirable and "politically correct" way than they would if they were more candid and open about their views. Interviewees can be very attentive to cues that the interviewer emits, since they want to know whether they are "doing well" as participants. Thus, what you choose to write down out of their verbal responses and even your supportive and encouraging "uh-huhs" or nods of the head may be taken as cues about what the interviewee "should" be talking about. One must be careful about leading the interviewee.

Finally, although a sensitive interviewer may reassure the respondent about confidentiality, interviews clearly generate less of a feeling of anonymity than do impersonal questionnaires. Considerable effort must therefore be made to ensure that rapport is created and that the interviewee legitimately believes there is no reason to feel threatened. We say "legitimately" here on the assumption that is true. Obviously, where possibilities for repercussions exist—whether to the individual or to her/his group—because of the results of the study or the sensitivity of the information, and especially if the researcher limits her/his pledge of confidentiality in any way, ethical practice requires that respondents be informed of that possibility and that researchers build in safeguards to the extent possible.

Interviewers also must make some choices about how to retain responses, and each choice has its advantages and disadvantages. If the choice is to write down verbatim responses to questions, the process can become quite tedious and may well interrupt the flow of the interview while the respondent waits for the interviewer to finish writing down each response. The researcher may therefore choose to write down only summaries or major points from the response, but then distortion

may occur, or matters that are subsequently found to be important may be left out.

Another possibility is to record (using audio or video recording) the interview, although the permanence and unforgiving accuracy of tape may inhibit candour. Nonetheless, this approach frees the interviewer to pay attention to the interviewee and gives the most complete and accurate record of the conversation. Some would advise that the interviewer should occasionally jot down notes in any event, because doing so helps the interviewer retain the flow of the interview, most respondents expect you to write something down every so often, and notes give you a backup in case a technical foul-up renders the recording useless and you must regenerate the content of the interview from memory. On the other hand, transcribing recorded responses is time-consuming if you are the one doing the transcribing, or expensive, if you are hiring someone else to do it, as it normally takes from 4–6 hours to transcribe each hour of interview at between $30–50 per hour.

Nor does the labour intensiveness end when the interview is done. Face-to-face interviews tend to be longer and more detailed, to seek greater depth of response, and to be more open-ended in their construction to allow for phenomenological input from respondents. They're also more likely to be situated in some context (e.g., an organization, a group, a limited geographical setting such as a neighbourhood) that plays an important role in the analysis and hence must also be understood. Individual digitally recorded interviews should ideally be transcribed as soon as possible, and normally anonymized in the process. And then, instead of the nicely pre-coded and pre-categorized responses from a survey that need only be aggregated and graphed, analyzing an interview involves reading the transcript over several times, identifying and coding themes that arise–some expected, some surprising–and weaving all the material together into some valid and internally consistent story.

Of course the reward is in the richness of information one acquires in the course of a well-done interview–hearing someone tell you in their own words what their views are, what happened in a certain situation, or what they believe the key issues are facing them, their family or group. Our own interest has been in seeing how advances in digital technologies can enhance the data gathering and analyzing process, and achieve efficiencies that maintain and even enhance the validity of data (e.g., Palys & Atchison 2009; in press).

For example, the tape recorder has always been a tool *sine qua non* for researchers engaged in qualitative research, and the contemporary digital recorder is no less. However, instead of the digital recorder sitting in the middle of a table with a microphone pointing obtrusively to the participant, we have begun using two-way radio transmitter-receivers where both interviewer and interviewee are equipped with a microphone and transmitter that attaches inconspicuously to a lapel or shirt collar. Chris utilized this technique most recently in his in-person interviews with clients of sex workers, which allowed him to conduct interviews in true conversational style in pool halls, moderately busy lounges or cafes, or while walking about busy city streets. Not having the visual distraction of the recording device present and not having to worry about being restricted spatially put participants at ease, which made it much easier to establish a trust and rapport that resulted in the typical interview lasting well over two hours. Participants often commented at the end of the session how enjoyable the conversation was and how much they appreciated being able to talk so openly and freely.

The mobility associated with this approach also allows for interviews to be conducted in the field where the behaviour you are asking about usually occurs, which gives research participants visual cues they can use as they explain how particular events occurred and/or to explain their behaviour or choices, which can enhance both the comprehensiveness of recall and its validity. For example, the two of us recently advised a publishing business in the health food industry that was undertaking in-house interview research with health food retailers regarding various aspects of the industry. Our advice included the suggestion that the interviews

should be conducted in the actual store using wireless microphones while wandering about the venue. The feedback was highly positive. Retailers clearly felt more comfortable showing off and explaining "their" store, while the interviewer enjoyed having concrete referents to anchor what was being spoken about, and to be able to point to and ask about products, store features, and other issues that came to the interviewer's or retailer's attention.

As for the transcription phase, in our own work we have begun experimenting with automated transcription processes using voice recognition software. The program we use is called Dragon Naturally Speaking (DNS), which is generally recognized as one of the top voice recognition programs available at this time. Other popular commercial and open source voice recognition software applications include: IBM ViaVoice, MacSpeech, Microsoft Windows Speech Recognition, Philips SpeechMagic, Sphinx, VoxForge, and Apple's Siri. For those unfamiliar with the program, DNS, once installed, requires a brief training process in which the user reads standard passages for approximately 15 minutes. This trains both the researcher and the program—the researcher to speak in a manner that is most recognizable to the program, and the program to recognize the researcher's unique speech—and is remarkably accurate once trained. This can be supplemented with other user-generated material such as documents, which allows the researcher to introduce vocabulary that is unique to his/her interests and research. For example, Ted does face-to-face and legal research with Indigenous peoples whose traditional tribal, place, and personal names are far beyond the program's default capability, but can be produced unerringly by DNS with a few minutes of training. The same would be true of any technical vocabulary.

Our first experimentation using DNS for transcription involved simply inputting a taped interview to the program for transcription. This yielded a highly error-filled copy that required almost as much time to edit as a traditional transcription would have taken. Our next step was to exploit the fact that the program knew each of our voices by making us the medium through which the interview was taken from digitized audio file to transcript. This involved wearing headphones, slowing the tape down by 20–30 percent (using another program such as the freely available Express Scribe, the commercially available Adobe Soundbooth, or the playback provisions in NVivo), and then speaking out what we hear into DNS as the recording plays. Because this process used our own voices, which had already been trained in the program, the error rate was quite small and easily edited with only a few interviews of practice, while the total time taken dropped from 4–6 hours of transcription time for one hour of interview to about 1.5–2 hours of transcription time, i.e., a substantial time saving.

Another option would be to actually begin or end an interview by putting the respondent through the training process, the basic version of which only takes about 15 minutes. While such sessions would not be particularly useful or feasible for single-interview studies even when each interview lasts for more than an hour, they may be highly useful for something like an oral history project where a given participant is sometimes interviewed for dozens of hours. That would allow any digital recordings simply to be input into DNS and auto-transcribed. Because some training of the program will already have occurred, accuracy will be high from the start. By correcting errors from the first interview and thereby further training the program, subsequent accuracy will be even higher.

Yet another option that we have only begun to experiment with is the batch conversion of digital recordings into a single voice file for the purposes of automated transcription. In this process, sophisticated audio software such as Adobe Soundbooth is used to apply a series of specially designed sound filters to digitally recorded files. During the first stage of this process a filter is applied to remove all ambient noise that may have been present during the initial interview from the recording. In the second stage a special filter is then applied in order to change the pitch and tone of all voices present in the recording into a single voice. Once the voice is converted, a third filter is applied to the new voice

to slow down the rate of speech 20–30 percent of the original rate so that the speech is clean and methodical. The final version of the file can then be auto-transcribed using the DNS batch transcription feature.

FOCUS GROUP INTERVIEWS

The focus group interview is essentially a group version of the face-to-face interview. Focus groups have an extensive history in marketing research, but have been discovered by the broader social and health science communities only more recently (Morgan 1988; Morgan & Spanish 1984). Such groups normally involve a *target sample* or *purposive sample* of informants brought together to discuss the phenomenon in which the researcher is interested. As Fontana and Frey (1994) note, "The group interview is not meant to replace individual interviewing, but it is an option that deserves consideration because it can provide another level of data gathering or a perspective on the research problem not available through individual interviews" (364).

In marketing, a group of typical consumers might be brought together to discuss their preferences, what they value in an existing product, or what they might like to see in a developing product. General Motors, for example, might be interested in designing a new truck and would hire a research agency to bring together a group of truck owners to discuss what features they believe should be included in the design of a pick-up truck so that it would be most useful to carpenters or ranchers or whomever. Marketing researchers also use focus groups to assess other products and their packaging, such as politicians.

In the social and health sciences, however, the "product" the researcher wants to develop may be a solicitation protocol, questionnaire, or a completed study. The participants would be invited because of their relevance to the phenomenon of interest to the researcher. An early example of this would be Merton and Kendall's (1946) effort to evaluate the persuasiveness of wartime propaganda; more recently, Morgan and Spanish (1985) created focus groups to generate discussions concerning perceptions of risk factors involved in heart attacks, and Morgan (1986) brought together focus groups of widows as part of his investigation into bereavement.

Focus groups may serve several purposes for researchers. Morgan (1988) explains that focus groups can be used productively when,

> orienting oneself to a new field; generating hypotheses based on informants' insights; evaluating different research sites or study populations; developing interview schedules and questionnaires; [and] getting participants' interpretations of results from earlier studies. (11)

Focus groups also may provide provocative and/ or insightful information to the researcher who is looking for unanticipated consequences to organizational interventions; is interested in determining issues of importance to those in the research setting or in acquiring new insights about the phenomenon from those who have experienced it; and/ or is trying to develop research instruments (e.g., questionnaires, interview schedules, sampling, and solicitation strategies) that speak to the phenomenology of those under study. After a piece of research is completed and the researcher has done a preliminary analysis and interpretation of the data, these results might be imparted to additional focus groups for discussion. Such discussions may help the researcher gather alternative interpretations for further consideration and generate additional hypotheses and/or research questions on which to focus subsequent research. Indeed, it was for exactly this purpose that Merton, Fiske, and Kendall (1956) originally coined the term "focus group" (see Fontana & Frey 1994, 2003).

Although focus groups have much in common with the traditional in-person interview, Morgan (1988) argues that their inherent social dynamic gives them at least two unique advantages. First, instead of simply taking an inventory of opinion through individual interviews, the focus group setting places opinions "on the table" where differences between perspectives can be highlighted and negotiated. This process allows participants to embellish on positions, discuss related dynamics, and articulate the rationale(s) underlying their perspective. Blumer (1969) advocates identifying a small number of informed participants who are acute observers in any social setting of interest, and then states that "a small number of such individuals brought together as a discussion and resource group is more valuable many times over than any representative sample" (41). Morgan (1988) adds that a second major advantage of focus groups is the opportunity to "witness" (as opposed to "influence") extensive interaction on a topic within a relatively limited time frame.

While some advantages accrue from the social composition of focus groups, this characteristic can also pose problems. Some people will be less comfortable than others in expressing their opinions publicly; people with more extreme or unique views may be reluctant to expose them to possible ridicule; and people undoubtedly will be more concerned about maintaining their image in a public setting than in a one-to-one interview. Fontana and Frey (2003) suggest that three skills are particularly important in the group interviewer's repertoire:

> First, the interviewer must keep one person or small coalition of persons from dominating the group; second, the interviewer must encourage recalcitrant respondents to participate; and third, the interviewer must obtain responses from the entire group to ensure the fullest possible coverage of the topic. (73)

Thus, focus groups may be seen as a useful vehicle for encouraging the embellishment and negotiation of public opinion, while the traditional single-person interview or questionnaire acts as a complementary expression of privately held opinions or "secret ballots." The focus group also accords a less central but no less important role to the researcher. In an interview involving one researcher and one participant, the respondent can look only to the researcher for direction. The researcher in the focus group setting generally plays a more facilitative and less directive role. Although the researcher can set up a structured situation, s/he typically acts only to initiate, prompt, and referee the discussion. Accordingly, one might infer that the results will be influenced more by the group than by the researcher.

With respect to the role that technological aids can play in the acquisition and analysis of data, the focus group tends to be more limited in where it can occur relative to the one-on-one interview, given that the flexibility of walking with one person is unlikely to exist for a group. Controlling sound quality also can be a challenge; ensuring that everyone in the group is equally audible will certainly require more audio expertise and equipment than is required for a one-on-one interview. Assuming acceptable audio quality, transcription options would be the same as we have outlined for the one-on-one interview.

In sum, focus group interviews are compatible with an array of research objectives and are useful for answering a variety of research questions, and while they possess their own limitations, they also offer unique strengths. They thus seem a currently under-utilized addition to the social and health science researcher's procedural repertoire.

NETWORK ADMINISTERED INTERVIEWS

Network administered interviews are a relatively new phenomenon that, until now, was limited by computer infrastructure and the availability of appropriate software. The best one could do was to text back and forth via email or a chat program, which was often a long and arduous process. We were reminded of this fact recently when Chris had one interview participant in his research with the clients of prostitutes who wanted to participate, but refused to do so through any medium but instant message exchanges. In contrast to his other interviews, which typically took 1–2 hours, Chris ended up spending more than seven hours (!) with this one fellow over two evenings. The one redeeming feature of this technique was that, in the end, he

was left with a ready-made and complete transcript of the conversation.

The door opened much wider for network administered interviewing with the development (in Estonia) of Skype, and especially by Skype's introduction of video conferencing in 2006. Further development is ensured by Microsoft's acquisition of Skype in 2011. We have already seen its expansion to different operating systems (Windows, MAC, and Linux) and devices (desktop and laptop computers; tablets; smartphones). An added bonus is that Skype phone calls appear to be very secure while at the same time being easily recordable by the actual participants in each call. Because of its recency, very little has been written about network administered interviewing, although we can speculate about the possibilities.

A few researchers have found that the lack of physical presence in the research setting leaves them with less control over interactions with the participants or the setting (Epstein & Klinkenberg 2001; Pettit 2002). Accordingly, when conducting network-administered interviews or focus groups, differences among participants may be magnified and variations in the setting may be overlooked. It is also more difficult for both researcher or participant(s) to pick up on audio or visual cues that emerge during the interview or observational process, which would make it much more difficult to develop personal rapport in interview or focus group settings (Black & Ponirakis 2000). Not being able to have physical connection with the participants and the currently limited ability to pick up on context significantly limits the type and range of data that are available to researchers. However, some researchers have found that in anonymous CASR environments participants are more likely to self-disclose (Epstein et al. 2001; Gravlee 2002) and are thus more likely to take part in studies of reactive, socially taboo, or highly sensitive topics.

Oral Histories

There are two types of oral history, only one of which will be considered in detail here. Be sure you understand the difference between them. The one that receives only passing attention in this book is the type of oral history remembered and practised by Aboriginal peoples in North America.

ABORIGINAL ORAL HISTORIES

Until relatively recently, most North American Aboriginal cultures were primarily oral cultures. Consistent with this emphasis, Aboriginal peoples made extensive use of oral history, where the role of particular individuals would be to remember certain stories about their people's history, rather like walking archives.

These memories weren't merely the recollection of stories, as might have happened when your parents told you a story when you were a child, but were in fact "lived memorizations" and verbatim accounts that would be repeated in the same manner 50 years from now as they would be today. Indeed, contemporary oral histories are often found to be identical to those recorded by anthropologists at the turn of the 20th century (e.g., see Mills 1994). Part of their integrity came from the fact that one of the "jobs" of each new generation required accurately learning and remembering the stories handed down by previous generations.

Another part of their integrity came through their having survived the rigorous process of ongoing challenges to their accuracy. Among the Aboriginal peoples of the northwest coast, for example, this process occurred in the context of the feast (potlatch) system. On appropriate occasions, each speaker recounted, in this most public of settings, the history of her/his clan, the boundaries of the clan's territories, and the way its crests and songs had been acquired. Anyone at the feast could challenge this oral history; a lack of challenge signaled acceptance that the account was valid (e.g., see Gisday Wa & Delgam Uukw 1992; Mills 1994).

We make these points for two main reasons. First, we want to encourage respect for the oral histories of Aboriginal peoples. Because of Europeans' and other non-Aboriginal peoples' reliance on written documentation and reverence for materials in written archives, many Europeans and non-Aboriginals have ethnocentrically assumed that no documentary history meant "no history" (e.g., see Wolf 1982), and that oral histories are little more than some sort of quaint, ever-changing cultural fairy tale. This is far from the truth. Yet such views have been used by colonial powers to dismiss Aboriginal histories and thereby deny Aboriginal rights.[4] Second, we've made this point to put the oral histories we'll deal with in this chapter into perspective.

ORAL HISTORY IN RESEARCH

Broadly defined, "history" is everything that happened before you read this sentence. And now even that sentence has receded into history. We can never know *everything* about history, but that hasn't stopped historians and the rest of us who are interested in history from trying to understand it. In trying to do so, we realize one of the fundamental challenges of understanding history: it isn't here anymore. We thus cannot study history directly, but must do so by looking at those pieces and remnants of history that remain.

WHAT'S IN THE BOX? Now, let's imagine that the history we can study is all contained in a huge box. Of all that happened in that huge period of time we know as "history," the only things we can base our study of history on are the things inside that box, because those are the only things that remain. And while many things get inside the box, many things do not. For example, Ted's son Louis, who plays for his high school's Ultimate Frisbee team, played an absolutely great game recently against the best team in his high school league; it was the only game that the other team–a private school where every player is rumoured (by players on other teams) to have their own masseuse and personal trainer–lost all year. Louis was extremely happy about it, and Ted was glad he was there to see Louis play. It was an enjoyable moment for both of them as father and son.

But 100 years from now, when some historian sits down to write something about early 21st century humanity—even if s/he is writing about "father-son relationships in the early 21st century"—there isn't a chance in the world that this future historian will write about the day Ted's son played such a great game and Ted was there to watch. Why? Because that bit of human history, while as real as the fact that Ottawa is the capital of Canada, will never make it into the box of human events out of which future historians will manufacture history.

Or will it? Ironically, our describing that experience here makes it possible that some historian in 2113 actually *will* see some dilapidated old copy of this book and discover the fact about Louis and his dad and Louis's great day on the Ultimate Frisbee field. Because we've put it in writing, a fact that would otherwise be recalled by no one besides Louis and his dad (neither of whom will be around by then) is now part of the contents of the box of study-able human history. It's actually a very interesting example of **selective deposit**, a phenomenon we'll discuss in more detail in Chapter 8. This term reflects the recognition that some things have a higher likelihood of being put into the box than others, and that some people and groups have better access to the box than others do. It's interesting, for example, that, in Ted's role as dad, he has very little likelihood of accessing the box. No one outside his immediate family will probably ever have any sense of him as a parent. But in his roles as university professor and author, he has somewhat more access to the box, as evidenced by this book, which is now part of the historical record.

One of the tragedies of history is that so much that would be interesting to know will remain forever beyond our grasp because it was never placed inside the box. It's interesting to consider what sorts of biases have entered into that process. What people or groups have been systematically *less* likely to have had a chance to put something in the box? And what people or groups have had much *better* access to the box, allowing them to influence our sense of history by placing their experiences into the box?

Clearly, some people have had better access to the box than others. Governments, the rich, the powerful, the upper classes, and the educated all have had better access to the box than individual citizens, the poor, the vulnerable, the lower classes, and the illiterate. Similarly, it is also the case that men—because until relatively recent times, it was primarily they who formed the governments, controlled the property and wealth, and had better access to education—have had better access to the box than women. When historians open the box to try to understand history, the "facts" they look at are therefore not *all* the facts, or even a representative sample of facts, but only the facts placed there by those who had access to the box. So when we try to look at what life was like in, say, 17th-century England or 15th-century Spain, we're relying most typically on the views of the rich, the powerful, the educated, and on the views of men. Even when we find material about others whose experience we also would like to understand—the daily life of the average 15th-century Spanish peasant, say— it's rarely through *their* eyes that we see the world around them, but rather through the eyes of non-peasants who had access to the box.

RECTIFYING THE IMBALANCE OF WRITTEN HISTORY

Oral history is partly a way of trying to deal with the problems of access just outlined. It recognizes and to some extent shares the general European bias in favour of written documentation, and therefore tries to get material into the box that wouldn't otherwise be there. Oral history is consequently seen by many as "an interview technique with a mission." Fontana and Frey (2003), for example, note that "oral history differs from other unstructured interviews in purpose, but not methodologically" (79), where the purpose is to take material that otherwise might have been forgotten and make it part of the written record. Reinharz (1992) adds that "oral history … is useful for getting at *people* less likely to be engaged in creating written records and for creating historical accounts of *phenomena* less likely to have produced archival material" (131; emphasis in original). By interviewing people about their past, we "recover" parts of history that might otherwise have been lost; by interviewing people about their present, we help ensure that their record is available for future generations.

Although examples of collected oral history narratives go back to antiquity, "its modern formal organization can be traced to 1948, when Allan Nevins began the Oral History Project at Columbia University" (Starr 1984: 4, cited by Fontana & Frey 2003: 79). That quotation, of course, has a certain delicious irony, since it's another example of how people with access to the box of history (like academics at prestigious universities) are the ones whose contributions we remember and can cite because they're part of the written record.

Because of the nature of the mission associated with oral history, you shouldn't be surprised to discover that the technique has been particularly popular among people who are on the margins of society—minorities, the poor, street people, and women, for example—and those who are interested in engaging in research with such people. Oral history narratives exist *en masse* for many of the "common people" of history whose experience otherwise would be ignored or forgotten. Examples include collections in which people talk about their working lives (e.g., Terkel 1975), as well as more specific projects that focus on Pennsylvania steelworkers and their families, women working in Baltimore canneries (e.g., Olson & Shopes 1991), the experience of Blacks in the Vietnam War (Terry 1984), Palestinian women engaged in resistance activities (e.g., Gluck 1991), IRA (Irish Republican Army) and UFV (Ulster Volunteer Force) combatants during "The Troubles" in Ireland and England in the latter half of the 20th century (Moloney 2010), and a staggering array of other groups. No doubt many others haven't yet seen the light of day; as Fontana and Frey (2003) note, "often, oral history transcripts are not published but may be found in libraries, silent memoirs awaiting someone to rummage through them and bring their testimony to life" (79).

Oral history methods found particular favour among many feminist researchers, who saw oral history methods as a way to rectify the gender imbalance in the largely male-dominated documentary archives of history. Gluck and Patai (1991) note that

> The first major body of literature on women's oral history appeared in late 1977 in a special issue of *Frontiers: A Journal of Women's Studies*. This ground-breaking issue served as the key reference on women's oral history for many years, and the suggested outlines for women's oral history interviews that appeared at the back of the journal were xeroxed, dittoed, and mimeographed by women in communities and classrooms around the country. (4)

Emphasizing the gathering of women's oral histories is thus a way to include women's voices in history: "Refusing to be rendered historically voiceless any longer, women are creating a new history—using our own voices and experiences" (Gluck 1984: 222). Reinharz (1992) suggests that women's oral history actually serves a threefold function: drawing women out of obscurity, repairing the historical record, and providing stories of people with whom women readers and authors can identify.

QUESTIONS ABOUT RESEARCH RELATIONSHIPS
While feminist engagement in oral history is thus rewarding in its own right, involvement in this massive oral history project has also prompted feminists to lead the way in contemporary reconsiderations of oral history in particular, interviewing in general, and, even more broadly, the whole set of relations between respondents and researchers. The concern is not only that men's voices dominate history, since this imbalance could be addressed simply by using techniques like oral history to rectify it, but also that the methods available to us now, since they were conceived in a traditionally male-dominated social and health science, are often particularly "male" in the way they're conceived, designed, and executed. Many feminist researchers who took the plunge into oral history research found that straight application of the methods they'd been taught in graduate school needed reconsideration. Minister (1991), for example, observes that

the male subcommunication subculture is assumed to be the norm for social science interviewing.... If women aspire to become approved oral historians, they must learn to control topic selection with questions, must make certain that one person talks at a time, and must encourage narrators to "take the floor" with referential language that keeps within the boundaries of selected topics. (31)

Minister clearly doesn't intend to encourage women to aspire to those essentials. Instead, she argues that women must carve out their own version of oral history, a version that's more sensitive to, and a better reflection of, women's ways of communicating.

We will not hear what women deem essential to their lives unless we legitimate a female socio-communication context for the oral history situation. As Sue Armitage says, "We will learn what we want to know only by listening to people who are not accustomed to talking." (31–32)

Anderson and Jack (1991) agree that more female-reflective approaches are required. They believe, for example, that men tend to look at the interview purely as an information-gathering session, so that designing an interview study becomes a strategic question of how best to order and compile questions and answers. In contrast, they believe women are more attuned to relationships and process and that woman-to-woman interviews must reflect that difference:

Realizing the possibilities of the oral history interview demands a shift in methodology from information gathering, where the focus is on the right questions, to interaction, where the focus is on process, on the dynamic unfolding of the subject's viewpoint. (23)

A major problem crops up when interviewing women, according to Anderson and Jack (1991). Because men's experience has defined much of

contemporary existence, women have become used to talking in dual narratives: using concepts that reflect men's cultural domination, but focusing on their own experience, which may or may not be adequately captured by those schemas. Feminist oral history researchers must therefore be particularly sensitive to reading between the lines:

We need to hear what women implied, suggested, and started to say but didn't. We need to interpret their pauses and, when it happens, their unwillingness or inability to respond. We need to consider carefully whether our interviews create a context in which women feel comfortable exploring the subjective feelings that give meaning to actions, things, and events, whether they allow women to explore "unwomanly" feelings and behaviours, and whether they encourage women to explain what they mean in their own terms. (17)

This process is clearly an interpretive one. However understandable the position, it's also fraught with complexity and paradox. At issue here is the question of "voice" and, especially, whose voice (if either) dominates the final look of the text that's produced from the interview. An excellent self-critical analysis by Borland (1991) of an oral history interview she did with her grandmother highlights the dilemma well. The article focuses on an experience for which Borland's interpretations of "what was *really* going on" and "what was *really* being said" were completely different from her grandmother's. Rejection of the interpretation by her grandmother after reading the first draft led to further discussion, further revising, and some movement on the parts of both women as they tried to reach some jointly satisfactory resolution of the meaning of the original episode.

One of the central tenets of feminist research is that women must be able to say things in their own voice and that voice must be heard. Male-dominated science is seen as an inappropriate model to the extent that it embodies hierarchical relations between the researcher and those researched, where an "expert" researcher "extracts" data from "subjects" and then reinterprets it according to a "culturally sanitized" (i.e., male-dominated) "spin." Instead of treating each other like researcher and respondent, many feminists aim to do research in the same egalitarian and respectful manner in which one might interview one's friend or grandmother. Anderson and Jack's (1991) assertions seem to question that sort of face-value acceptance, seeing the task as one of reading between the lines and finding what the women being interviewed are "really" saying and what they "really" mean by it.

Many feminist researchers (including Borland 1991, as noted) have wrestled with these issues. Their analyses can make us all aware of how professional zeal and arrogance may lead us to usurp others' voices and take for granted some things that perhaps shouldn't be accepted. Black feminists, for example, argue that sisterhood has its limits if it means homogenizing women's experience in a way that doesn't do justice to the equally meaningful and simultaneously marginalizing experience of race (e.g., see Collins 1991; Etter-Lewis 1991; Fine et al. 2003; Olesen 1994), while others make the same point regarding Latina (e.g., Benmayor 1991), Aboriginal (e.g., Greschner 1992; Monture-Okanee 1993; Petersen 1994), and Third World women (e.g., Hale 1991; Patai 1991; Salazar 1991). All call for research considerations that acknowledge and respect cultural differences.

ASKING QUESTIONS

Once you've decided on the interactive technique(s) most appropriate for your situation, you're ready to formulate specific questions. This step involves two considerations on your part. First, you need some sense of the content you want to include or address in your questions. Second, you need to create concrete questions that will "tap into" that content; to do so, you need some sense of the different ways in which questions can be posed.

Question Content

We can't begin to count the number of times we've read undergraduate research papers that feature a good introduction that contextualizes the issues well by summarizing relevant literature and identifying a reasonable research question, followed by a reasonable "methods" section that includes a copy of the research instrument—but where the two don't match! This situation leads to some very interesting "discussion" and "conclusion" sections: students end up going through some incredible verbal acrobatics trying to actually say something about their research question from their data. Asking the wrong questions – and often being afraid to directly ask the "right" ones – are two of *the* most common mistakes novice researchers make.

An Iterative Process Starting with General Objectives

Your research questions and research objectives should come first: your subsequent decisions require a clear sense of what you're trying to accomplish. Once you know that, designing a research project becomes a matter of taking a series of steps in which you follow an iterative process and become progressively more specific in elaborating and defining the matters of interest to you. And as long as each step follows from the one before, you're assured that your final step (the questions you ask and the data you gather) will be connected to your first (your objectives). That way, when you write your final paper or report, your data will "speak" to your objectives.

Let's look at an example. Several years ago when personal computers were first appearing and various organizations were just starting to see the benefits of computerizing or implementing a computer to assist their activities, Canada's federal Department of Communications asked Ted to do a behavioural evaluation of the Mobile Radio Data System (MRDS), a computer-based communications system that the Vancouver

Police Department had installed in their cars and that was at that time state-of-the-art. The federal government had promoted its development, wanted to evaluate it, and had already undertaken an engineering evaluation and cost-benefit evaluation of the system; now they wanted to know in more behavioural terms how it was used, what people thought of it, and what impacts such a system might have on policing effectiveness and police-community relations.

But "doing an evaluation" is a rather amorphous objective. The first thing the research team had to do was to develop a clearer understanding of what "doing an evaluation" would look like in this context. Discussion among the research group, as well as with stakeholders from the funding agency (the federal government department) and at the research site (the police department), led to the identification of two key components they wanted to examine: (1) attitudes about the system; and (2) how the system was used in the process of the organization's activities.

The next step was to begin moving from abstract "issues" or "phenomena" and to start considering how exactly these abstract concepts took on life with this system in this context. Attitudes about what aspects of the system? And on what basis could you start to understand system use? The team did some exploratory research to help identify salient issues. This included reading some of the relevant "trade" literature (i.e., policing magazines and journals that included articles discussing similar information systems); going on ride-alongs with patrol officers, both to see how they used the system and to have a chance to talk with them about it away from more formal meetings at headquarters; undertaking informal target and focus interviews with different people in the police department—patrol officers, administrative staff, dispatchers—to gain insight into their opinions about the system; and some final brainstorming among the research team members to identify issues of particular interest to the group as academics. The big issue that interested the latter,

and which had captured their interest in the first place, was to try and understand the *implications* of what were then the first glimmerings of what would later become a burgeoning permeation of computerized information systems throughout society.

You can see this process beginning to unfold in Figure 6.1, which shows the beginning objective (to evaluate MRDS) followed by the various types of evaluations that were included (Engineering; Cost-Benefit; Social/Behavioural) and the first iteration of the social behavioural evaluation that identified the three main issues to be addressed in the social/behavioural evaluation—system use, satisfaction, and implications. As Figure 6.1 shows, in the end the research team was able to undertake a multi-method evaluation that would give a comprehensive view of the system and those who used it. You can read Palys, Boyanowsky, and Dutton (1983, 1984) for a description of the whole study; what we'd like to focus on here is the process they went through to generate their attitudinal survey items.

Figure 6.2 shows how the three domains of interest were taken through further iterations to get to an eventual set of items. For the first area—attitudes—the research team found several salient elements that seemed to contribute to the variety of attitudes that officers held about the system. These included effects of the system on job satisfaction (for some the system enhanced it; for others the system detracted from it); beliefs about impacts of the system on job effectiveness (some believed it helped them in their jobs; others believed it did nothing or detracted); beliefs about impact of the system on officer safety (some believed it enhanced safety; others thought it undermined it); and so on. Note, by the way, that the reason these elements were identified is because they were aspects of the system on which there was variability—people had different views about these elements—and the exploratory research had given the research team reason to believe that they were important in understanding overall views of the system.

Figure 6.1
Beginning Survey Construction Process from the VPD/MRDS Study

Evaluate MRDS	Engineering Study		
	Cost/Benefit Study		

	Social/Behavioural Study	Attitudes	• Self-administered survey
			  • 207 officers
			• Structured observation
			  • 88 ridealongs × 4 hours
			• Semi-structured interview schedule
			  • Administered on ride-alongs

		Use/Behaviour	• Archival data supplied/generated by VPD
			  • Memos from implementation
			  • System use data
			• Exploratory interviews
			  • VPD Admin
			  • VPD Patrol
			  • VPD Dispatchers
			  • VPD Technical

		Implications	• Other archival/professional literature
			  • *The Police Chief*
			  • *Sheriff's Star*
			  • *Law and Order*

Figure 6.2

Development of items in Survey Construction Process from the VPD/MRDS Study

ATTITUDES	**Job Satisfaction**	MRDS has had a positive effect on my job satisfaction.
	Effectiveness	I think MRDS helps me be a more effective officer. MRDS produces so much information it makes me a less effective officer.
	Safety	I think MRDS makes policing a lot safer. MRDS can create a false sense of security with suspects.
	(In)dependence	I find that with MRDS I end up relying on the system more and more.
	Relations with Community	I find I check out a lot more people now than I did before MRDS.
	Overall	Overall I like MRDS.
USE/BEHAVIOUR	**Ease of data access**	With MRDS I get information much more quickly than with radio only. I feel tied to my car with MRDS.
	Frequency of Access	With MRDS I probably investigate cars or people I otherwise wouldn't have bothered with.
	1-person vs. 2-person patrol	MRDS is of less use when I'm on patrol by myself than when I have a partner.
	(Non)Stressful Situations	MRDS is of less use in highly stressful situations.
	MRDS vs. Radio	I would rather work in a radio-only car. [Situational scenarios also addressed this element]
IMPLICATIONS	**Implications for officers:** • **Professionalism** • **Man/Machine** • **Autonomy/self-Def'n**	[See "attitudes" section; also arose in more depth interviews; big differences among officers in how they saw themselves and how they related to the machine; some viewed it as a duller of instincts and human connectedness, while others saw it as something that gave them autonomy, control, professionalism]
	Relations within VPD	MRDS makes me more independent of the dispatcher.
	Relations between police	Ultimately I think MRDS dehumanizes policing.

If you proceed to the next column of Figure 6.2, you'll see that the next step was simply to create items—in this case they created what are called "Likert-type" items (these are explained later in this chapter) that involve statements of belief that respondents indicate their level of agreement or disagreement with—that reflected those various elements.

When the eventual attitude scale was administered to 200 officers in the organization, the results allowed the researchers to report back to both the federal department and the local organization with answers to the question they had been posed. Why? Because each step of the iterative process was connected to the one preceding, which meant that the product at the end of this design process—the very specific and concrete items respondents reacted to—had a very clear and demonstrable connection to the objective that started it all off.

As you can see, you need to do much of your thinking *ahead of time* when it comes to designing a questionnaire or interview. That includes doing the literature review and exploratory research that will allow you to create an informed and useful research instrument. It's all time well spent because it ensures that your objectives are indeed addressed by the data you gather.

Having gone through these considerations so that we know what content we wish to include, we must next address how to ask those questions. We noted above that the items from the MRDS survey were **Likert-type items**, but there are in fact many different ways to ask questions. The following section covers some of the variety of alternatives that are available.

Question Structure

The main types of questions are open-ended and closed or structured questions. An *open-ended question* might be "What do you like most, and what do you like least, about this text?" or "What would be your overall evaluation of this course, and why?" Even more open-ended might be a simple probe like "Tell me how you feel about the course so far."

A *closed* or *structured question* on the same topic might be "Please rate the quality of the textbook on a 5-point scale running from 1 (dislike the text a lot) to 5 (like the text a lot)." As you can see, open-ended questions leave a lot up to the respondent; they really are open to a wide range of responses, depending on the respondent's own concerns. Closed or structured questions, in contrast, allow the respondent only a small range of responses (e.g., filling in a blank, checking off a point on a rating scale) and involve some *presupposition* on the researcher's part about which aspects of a given issue are important to address.

OPEN-ENDED QUESTIONS

STRENGTHS As with virtually every other method described in this text, one cannot say that either open-ended or structured questions are better on some overall basis. Each has advantages and limitations in any particular research situation. Open-ended questions are clearly superior if the researcher is interested in hearing respondents' opinions in their own words, particularly in exploratory research, where the researcher isn't entirely clear about what range of responses might be anticipated. For example, you wouldn't want to ask a question like "Which of the following attributes do you think is the *most* important for a professor to be concerned with when teaching a course on research methods: (a) punctuality; (b) wears nice clothes; (c) easy exams; or (d) other?" only to discover when you went to analyze the data that 87 percent of the respondents checked off "other."

In exploratory and pilot research, the responses to an open-ended question can be used to create the alternatives for structured questions in a later study with more focused objectives. Open-ended questions are also useful when you want to determine the salience or importance of opinions to people, since people tend to mention those matters that are most important to them first (see Kahneman, Slovic, & Tversky 1982). In this sense, open-ended questions can also operate as "indirect" measures, generating answers that are minimally affected by external influence or by suggestion emerging from the structure of the research instrument itself.

But you shouldn't feel that open-ended queries are suitable only for exploratory and small-sample research. Even in larger-scale studies, respondents enjoy being offered at least a few chances to express matters in their own words; at the very least, a space should be designated at the end for "anything else you would care to add that hasn't been adequately addressed" or "any comments you might care to add about the questionnaire." When interwoven within a structured questionnaire, open-ended items can be a rich source of illustrative vignettes that can be included in a final report and can provide material that helps the researcher interpret responses.

Finally, open-ended questions are also useful when the choice would otherwise be to offer an extremely long list. There are at least several hundred different occupations, for example; it would seem silly to try to compile a huge list of these for respondents, and then expect them to hunt through the list for theirs. A far easier alternative is simply to ask "What is your occupation?" or "How would you describe your occupation?"

LIMITATIONS Of course, open-ended questions also have disadvantages. It isn't advisable to include too many of them in a single questionnaire; after two or three, each additional question makes the respondent more likely to abandon the questionnaire without completing it. (People often get "turned off" when what's advertised as a questionnaire turns into an essay exam.) In interviews, the more open-ended the question—and the more such questions one asks—the more one requires time, a relatively private setting, and good rapport between interviewer and respondent.

The biggest drawback to open-ended questions is that the responses become incredibly cumbersome as your sample size and/or the number of questions increases. How do you *deal* with all these open-ended responses you've gathered? The uniqueness of each person's priorities, views, and means of expression can make it seem that you have as many different categories as you have respondents.

Making comparisons between different people, whether in the content or intensity or priority of the opinion they express, can become very difficult. To do it properly, content coding schemes must be developed, and coders must be trained and their inter-rater reliability assessed. Because of these difficulties, researchers, especially quantitative researchers engaged in studies with larger sample sizes, have tended to rely on more structured response alternatives that come "pre-coded." It's a much more efficient process. The major challenge is to ensure that the structured device does justice to the opinions and feelings that lie behind people's responses. Open-ended questions in smaller-sample exploratory, pilot, or field research are extremely useful for developing sensitive questionnaires.

CLOSED OR STRUCTURED QUESTIONS

Closed or structured questions have their own advantages and disadvantages. If the researcher has done a good job of considering the range of alternatives that might be considered, respondents get to consider the whole range before making their own judgments about what category to code themselves into. The fact that all responses follow a standard form (e.g., using the same set of categorical alternatives or the same rating scale) makes comparability among respondents easier, since quantification or categorization is generally inherent to the item's structure (e.g., it's both easier and clearer for us to be able to say that "64 percent of males but only 37 percent of females agreed with the proposal" or that "males gave an average rating of 3.6 while females gave an average of 5.6 on the 7-point scale" than to explain and justify verbally any differences between respondent groups). Computerized scoring and analysis of data are also made easier.

Closed questions are also particularly useful when one wants to cover a lot of ground in a questionnaire or interview, since one can ask many more structured than open questions in a given period of time. But you're obviously making a choice: do you go for *breadth* (lots of questions but relatively superficial responses) or *depth* (fewer questions but more elaborate responses)?

The Variety of Structured Questions

SINGLE-RESPONSE ITEMS

One way to present a structured question is merely to ask it, giving respondents an empty space in which to write their response. This type of question is called a **single-response item**. The following three questions are of this type:

1. In what year were you born? _____
2. What was your total family income last year (before taxes)? $_____
3. What is your official job title in this organization? _____

Each asks the respondent to supply a very specific piece of information. But there can be problems associated with this form, since people are sometimes reluctant to provide an exact number or a one-word response, especially to questions about age and income or to those that suggest more complex responses. Respondents may therefore be more likely to skip the question or to give a simplistic response that doesn't really capture their opinion on an issue. You're left with missing data in the first instance and with incomplete or invalid data in the second. Moreover, if people don't have an exact response readily available (e.g., few people know their total family income down to the last dollar), a false sense of precision may result. The answers may *appear* very precise but may really be just "ballpark" guesses. If people *are* willing and able to provide the information, *single-response* items offer both precision and great flexibility in how responses will be aggregated across participants (e.g., they can be grouped by $5,000 increments, $10,000 increments, etc.). So if you *can* ask a single-response question, do so; if you suspect that people may be unwilling to respond or unable to give precise information, choose a *categorical-response item* instead.

CATEGORICAL-RESPONSE ITEMS

Categorical-response items present categories in which respondents may place themselves. The simplest type of categorical question is the **dichotomous item**. As the prefix *di-* suggests, such questions have only two response alternatives. For example, the question "What is your sex?" has only two possible responses for most situations: you can be male or female.[5] Similarly, we might ask, "If a referendum were held tomorrow for the reinstatement of capital punishment, would you vote for or against?"

Although there are many "natural" dichotomies (e.g., sex is dichotomized into male and female), *any* continuum can be dichotomized. Attitudes about the death penalty, for example, can be seen as a continuum ranging from extreme support to complete rejection, or they might be dichotomized, as they were above, into "for" and "against." Whether you use a continuum or **dichotomy** would depend on your research purpose.

Such reduction inevitably means a loss of information, and may distort the phenomenon under consideration. For example, there was considerable discussion in Canada in the 1980s about capital punishment. Ardent supporters of the death penalty unerringly pointed to opinion polls that showed that approximately 75 percent of Canadians expressed support in answering a dichotomous question on the subject. But a more detailed analysis (Palys & Williams 1983) showed that most proponents were guarded in their enthusiasm, exhibiting considerable ambivalence about the death penalty's prospective application. The media image of Canada's collective run "back to the noose" was anything but accurate. Consistent with Palys and Williams's (1983) analysis, and quite in contrast to earlier media reports, a proposal on the issue was soundly defeated when it came before Parliament.

Other categorical items offer more than two categories. Here's an example:

What was your total family income last year (to the nearest dollar, before taxes)?

_____	less than $10,000
_____	$10,000 to $19,999
_____	$20,000 to $29,999
_____	$30,000 to $39,999
_____	$40,000 or more

Categorical items offer several advantages. First, respondents are often more willing to place themselves into categories (especially with sensitive topics like income) than they are to give exact responses. Second, accuracy is less likely to be affected by ballpark guesses, since the question itself asks people to place themselves in a ballpark. The main disadvantage with categorical items is that they are considerably less flexible than single-response items; you can always aggregate categories together, but categories can never be taken apart. This problem may not affect a given study, since you choose category intervals appropriate to your particular needs and interests, but you might find it hard to compare the results of different studies (e.g., if you used $5,000 increments to code income, and another study used $3,000 increments).

There are two characteristics of categorical items you should concern yourself with. First, the categories must always be **exhaustive**, that is, they must cover all possible alternatives. Second, for most questions, the categories should be **mutually exclusive**: there should be no overlap between categories, that is, there should be only *one* category per respondent that is appropriate. In sum, there should be an alternative, but usually only *one* alternative, for everybody. The "income" question we gave you earlier met both of these criteria: no matter what your total family income, there was a category—and only *one* category—into which you could place yourself. But consider the following question:

What was your age in years at your last birthday?

_____	less than 20
_____	20 to 30
_____	30 to 40
_____	40 to 50
_____	50 to 60

These categories are *not* mutually exclusive: they overlap. A person who is 30 years old, for example, could legitimately check either "b" or "c." Nor are the categories exhaustive. Which alternative do 65-year-olds choose, for example? There's no place for them. If you understand the notions of exclusivity and exhaustiveness, you should be able to rewrite the question above so that it meets these criteria.

Although categorical questions must always be exhaustive, one type of categorical question, the *multiple-response item*, does *not* require the respondent to choose only one alternative. For example, you might ask a question like this one:

Which of the following have you done in the last month? (check all that apply)

_____	gone out to dinner at a restaurant
_____	seen a film at a cinema
_____	seen a play at a theatre
_____	attended a professional sporting event
_____	attended a concert or dance at which live music was played
_____	read a book for pleasure
_____	gone to an art gallery or museum

As always, the choice of issues to address will reflect your research objectives and/or theoretical curiosities, as will the content and range of alternatives offered. The above example might be appropriate for a marketing questionnaire or for a study of leisure preferences among members of some identified social groups.

A limitation of the response structures described thus far is that they look no further than simple dichotomies (did/did not; true/false; yes/no; no way/way) or category memberships (e.g., is or is not described by a given category). But in most situations, we are interested in embellished *continua* that are *scaled* by gradation.

RATING SCALES

A fourth type of structured question is the *rating scale*, which is extremely pervasive in social and health science research. As its name implies, such a question asks the respondent to rate some object on some attribute. Several types of rating scales are shown in Figure 6.3. The "satisfaction" scale used by T. Atkinson (1977) shown here is probably the most commonly used; it supplies verbal labels at either end of the scale, with numbers in between that the respondent would circle depending on the *direction* (or "valence") of his or her feelings (i.e., satisfied or unsatisfied) and on the *intensity* of those feelings (i.e., the number 7 expresses more intense satisfaction than the number 5).

There are many variations on this type of scale. Figure 6.3 shows a 1-to-7 scale, but there's nothing magical about 7-point scales. It's not unheard of to see 5-point, 10-point, or even 100-point scales. Some scales leave out the numbers entirely and merely present respondents with a line, and adjectives or descriptors at the ends; the respondent puts a stroke through the line at whichever point best represents her/his opinion. "Scores" or "ratings" are produced by measuring the distance from one end of the scale to the place where the stroke intersects. As we mentioned earlier, in CASR when rating scales are administered through browser-based surveys it is possible to simply present respondents with a slide bar that allows them to use their mouse to drag the slider up and down the bar, positioning it where they feel their opinion sits along the continuum; with the aid of scripts the location where they locate the slider is assigned a precise numeric value.

Figure 6.3

Three Samples of Rating Scales

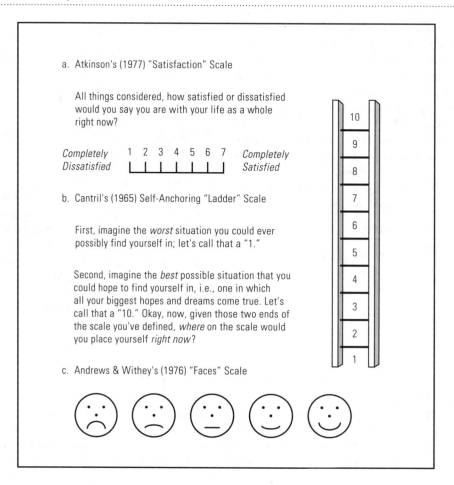

The Cantril ladder (see Figure 6.3b), another type of rating scale, was first used in an international survey conducted some years ago (see Cantril 1965). Cantril was interested in people's evaluations of their quality of life. As a respondent, you would first have been asked to imagine and describe the *worst* possible situation in which you could see yourself. That situation would be considered a "1" on the scale. Next, you'd be asked to imagine and describe the *best* possible situation in which you could see yourself, one where all your dreams and aspirations were realized. That situation would be considered a "10." With the scale's ends thus defined, the next question was "Where on the scale would you say you are *right now?*" Note that Cantril's scale is known as a **self-anchoring scale**, since the end-points are personally defined (i.e., your best aspirations and worst fears will undoubtedly be different from those of others).[6]

A final example of a rating scale is the "faces" scale (see Figure 6.3c) described by Andrews and Withey (1976). Scales like these are particularly useful when dealing with children or with others whose literacy level might be questionable. The respondent is directed to "pick the face that best illustrates how you feel" about the attitude object in question; this scale is useful when the ratings being made are on a like–dislike or happy–sad type of continuum. But note that people other than young children may find the use of such a scale somewhat condescending.

And of course all of the examples in Figure 6.3 are very static, as they would be in any paper-based survey. The same questions and scales in any digitized context can be made more colourful and dynamic, e.g., by asking the respondent to move their finger up the ladder to indicate where they are on the scale, or to adjust the smile on the faces so that it reflects their own like or dislike about whatever is being asked about.

OTHER STRUCTURED ITEMS

There are several other types of structured questionnaire items, all of which have their roots in some of the more formal attitude-assessment techniques we will discuss in the next section. We'll mention only two here.

LIKERT-TYPE ITEMS The first type of structured item is known as a "*Likert-type*" questionnaire item because its format is of the type included in an attitude scale developed originally by Rensis Likert (see Likert 1932). Two attributes distinguish a "Likert-type" item. First, the item is an *assertion* (rather than a question). Second, the respondent's task is to indicate the extent to which s/he *agrees* or *disagrees* with the assertion. Typically, if Likert-type items are used, a number of them are given in succession on a questionnaire. Once respondents get used to using the agree–disagree format, which happens very quickly, they can deal rapidly with many different issues. The following is an example of a "Likert-type" item:

All things considered, I think the death penalty should be reinstated.

_____	disagree strongly
_____	disagree somewhat
_____	neither agree nor disagree
_____	agree somewhat
_____	agree strongly

The Likert-type item is useful if, instead of being interested in hearing the respondent's position in her/his own words, you're interested in the extent to which a person agrees or disagrees with a position formulated by the researcher. For example, rather than having the respondent explain her/his views regarding capital punishment, an item like the example above might be used to give a "bottom line" position, to see whether and to what extent the respondent will agree or disagree. You might then be interested in some of the reasons behind their (dis)agreement, and hence offer a number of alternatives (e.g., an item that states a moral argument for or against capital punishment, another item that expresses a vengeance theme, and so on) to be able to identify the logic that underlies different positions, or simply to distinguish between people who hold similar positions for different reasons.

SEMANTIC DIFFERENTIAL-TYPE ITEMS Finally, another type of questionnaire item is the **semantic differential type item**. Osgood, Suci, and Tannenbaum (1957) developed an attitude scale they dubbed "the Semantic Differential." Devised to assess the *meaning* associated with particular attitude objects, it involved a set of bipolar adjectives (or dimensions) upon which any given attitude object could be described. For example, you might see the words "this textbook" (or some other object of assessment) printed at the top of the page, and your task would be to rate "this textbook" on a list of bipolar adjectives such as those shown in Figure 6.4a.

Although the original Semantic Differential still sees occasional use in attitude research, it's more typical to see its influence in the semantic differential-type response format. The respondent is asked to express her/his attitudes or feelings by providing ratings with respect to bipolar scales (i.e., opposing concepts, words, or phrases), where the two poles of the continuum are separated by some odd number of spaces (usually, but not necessarily, 5 or 7) separated by colons. For example, we might be interested in obtaining your evaluation of your local medical clinic. Instead of using the Semantic Differential (with its given adjectival pairs), we might decide to adapt the format to more relevant dimensions.

Figure 6.4a
Items from the Original Semantic Differential

Please rate *Research Decisions* on the following dimensions:

fair	__ : __ : __ : __ : __ : __ unfair
good	__ : __ : __ : __ : __ : __ bad
heavy	__ : __ : __ : __ : __ : __ light
fast	__ : __ : __ : __ : __ : __ slow
hot	__ : __ : __ : __ : __ : __ cold

We might thus ask you to rate the service provided by the medical staff at your local medical clinic on the dimensions depicted in Figure 6.4b. Note that one can use any opposing words, phrases, or other concepts that are of interest. Note also that the presentation of dimensions has been varied (i.e., the continuum's "good" end is sometimes on the left, other times on the right) in order to inhibit response sets.

COMBINING OPEN-ENDED AND STRUCTURED QUESTIONS

A useful strategy involves actually combining open-ended and structured items. When doing so, you would generally include the open-ended questions on a given topic first. Part of the rationale for using open-ended items is an interest in hearing the respondents' words and concerns in a way minimally affected by the researcher. Putting closed or structured items first can subvert this aim by focusing the respondent's attention on certain attributes of the topic.

One commonly used technique is known as **funnelling:** first asking broad, open-ended questions on a topic and following up with successively narrower, more well-defined structured questions. Successive funnels can set the pacing and break the monotony of similarly formatted questions. For example, we might begin with a very general query about your evaluation of this textbook. Then we might ask an open-ended question about the book's organization and flow and funnel down to queries about specific aspects of organization and flow. Next might follow a second funnel from an open-ended question about the clarity of explanations in the book to more specific questions about particular sections or explanations.

The alternative–asking the more structured items first and closing with the open-ended ones–is more common when the open-ended question is simply serving a "clean-up" function by asking the respondent if they have any further comments they would like to add, or whether there are any dimensions of the issue being studied that the respondent feels has been missed.

Figure 6.4b

Items in the Adapted Semantic Differential

Please evaluate the level of service you receive from the medical staff at Everyperson's Medical Clinic on the following dimensions:

friendly	__ : __ : __ : __ : __ : __ : __	unfriendly
efficient	__ : __ : __ : __ : __ : __ : __	inefficient
can never get a quick appointment for urgent matters	__ : __ : __ : __ : __ : __ : __	they always find a way to fit you in
always in too much of a rush	__ : __ : __ : __ : __ : __ : __	always have time to talk and ask questions

Question Wording

Thus far, the discussion has emphasized determining both the general content and the structure of the questions. Another important aspect of the interview or questionnaire is the actual wording of the questions (e.g., see Sudman & Bradburn 1982).

A ROSE BY ANY OTHER NAME

One famous anecdote–so famous that its origins are now unknown[7]–tells the story of two priests who argue about whether it is appropriate for someone to be smoking a cigarette and praying at the same time. No resolution is found, but the two clergymen agree that each will go and ask his respective Bishop for the "official" answer. The two go away and meet the next week and, to their surprise, find that they had received exact opposite answers from their respective Bishops. "But what did you ask?" queries each to the other. The first says, "I just asked, 'Is it acceptable to smoke while praying?' to which my Bishop said 'no' most emphatically and went on to give me a lecture about how sacrilegious it would be to sully such a sacred act with a cigarette." "Ah," said the other. "That explains it. What I asked my Bishop was, 'Is it acceptable to pray while smoking?' to which he replied, 'There is never an unacceptable time to pray.'"

The anecdote suggests that what can appear on the surface to be very minor changes in wording can have very big effects in terms of the results that are observed. But are real survey results so fragile? Researchers originally posed this question by asking another–Is there any difference to you between "forbidding" something and "not allowing" it? They went on to test this in a 1940 survey by asking the following two questions of two comparable national samples of respondents:

Do you think the United States should forbid public speeches against democracy?

Do you think the United States should allow public speeches against democracy?

The two questions seem to be addressing essentially the same thing, but one is positively worded and the other negatively worded. The percentage of people who *agree* with one item ought to be roughly equal to the number who *dis*agree with the other. That is, if 30 percent of the people say "yes" to the first item (that the United States should *forbid* such speeches), a similar percentage should say "no" to the second item (that the United States should *not allow* them).

But in fact, while only 54 percent said that the United States should *forbid* such speeches, a full 75 percent said that they should *not be allowed*. In hindsight, perhaps we can think about the two words and make some distinction between them, but who could have predicted such huge variation on the basis of what still seems little more than a difference of nuance? A swing of 21 percent on the basis of a small shift in wording makes any statements about the sampling error's being "plus or minus 2.5 percent, 19 times out of 20" seem downright trivial. If such enormous swings can occur because of relatively small wording changes, then perhaps *wording* is the more important issue to attend to.

One of the few studies to directly and comprehensively do so was by Schuman and Presser (1981), who went beyond single examples like "forbid versus allow" to ask broader questions about general types of wording shifts. For example, the forbid/allow variant is subsumed under the general category "changes in the tone of the wording." Their general finding, consistent with the forbid/allow example, is that small differences in wording can produce substantial swings in results. Ironically, however, and contrary to the common wisdom, the most blatant examples of biased wording were the *least* effective in influencing results. Schuman and Presser explain that "respondents seem to recognize and discount the more obvious instances of bias."

The authors note that one implication of this finding is that when researchers want to examine changes in attitudes over time by comparing newly acquired data to old, it's very important to replicate the original wording exactly. For example, when they replicated the forbid/allow experiment in the 1970s, they found the same 20 percent difference between the two wordings. But when they compared the results of the two *matched* sets of wordings (i.e., comparing the 1940 "forbid" data to the 1970s "forbid" data, and the 1940 "allow" data to the 1970s "allow" data), each matched set revealed about a 30 percent change in the direction of a more tolerant response. The importance of keeping wording constant is made clear, though, when one considers what conclusions would have resulted had *mismatched* wordings been used:

> The two possible *mismatched* replications of the question (comparing 1940 data from the "forbid" version to mid-1970s data from the "allow" version, and vice-versa) would yield two very different results: evidence of either a slight (less than 10 percent) increase in tolerance, or a whopping increase of 50 percent. (2)

Clearly, then, question wording must be kept identical if a researcher wants to compare the results of two or more surveys. If a change of wording is necessary for some reason, the researcher should include both wordings on at least one occasion, so that an explicit comparison can be made that will allow an assessment of the effect of the wording change.

OTHER ADMONITIONS

A number of sources are available that do a good job of explaining other considerations that should be kept in mind when wording questions (e.g., see Gray & Guppy 1994; Schuman & Presser 1981; Sudman & Bradburn 1982).

CONTEXT-APPROPRIATE WORDING When choosing the wording for questions, keep the age and education level of your target population in mind. A certain vocabulary may be appropriate for your university endeavours but may not be a language that your respondents understand. Still, the fact that most people haven't had your educational opportunities doesn't mean they're stupid. The challenge to communicate effectively is yours.

You should be sensitive to local jargon and be able to use terms that have well-defined local meanings. For example, if doing research in a prison, instead of referring to "a prisoner who shares information with prison authorities," it would probably be appropriate simply to use the term "rat." Another technique involves first asking the people you interview what word *they* prefer to use for a given thing or behaviour. In a survey on sexual behaviour, for example, you might begin by asking respondents what words they use to refer to two people engaging in sexual intercourse. If a respondent says "make love" (or whatever), you would then use that phrase in any question about that behaviour, for example, "Do you think it is acceptable for two people to make love on their first date together?"

This is a place where the adaptive questioning that is possible in browser-based research can be very helpful. To continue the above example regarding sexual behaviour, if the person responds that "make love" is the phrase they use to describe sexual intercourse, then that phrase can be used for the remainder of the survey whenever a question includes reference to that behaviour.

MINIMIZING BIAS In most cases, and especially in survey research where one is creating a standardized set of questions that will be administered to a diverse array of people who likely hold a diverse array of views, question wording should be kept neutral in order to avoid biasing responses. Do not use loaded terms. Referring, for example, to "dangerous" drugs, "disgusting" pornography, "hard-working" students, or "sensitive" erotica is tantamount to telling participants how you expect them to respond.

An interviewer's manner is also important for avoiding bias. The clichéd description of the ideal interviewer as tolerant, friendly, interested, supportive, detached, professional, and neutral is really quite accurate. The idea is to provide an environment that facilitates rapport and imposes as little as possible on respondents' views. To do this, you must be sincerely interested in understanding the interviewee's perspective and be able to consider the expression of your own views irrelevant.

This is particularly so when asking "threatening" questions, such as those involving illegal or socially stigmatized behaviours. Rather than asking respondents whether they have ever *used* illegal drugs like cocaine, for example, you might ask whether the person has ever *experimented* with the drug. And instead of asking "*Did you vote* in the last election?" you might ask "*Were you able to vote* in the last election?" Applying a more neutralizing and non-judgmental spin in a question's preamble may also facilitate the reporting of undesirable behaviour.

AVOIDING AMBIGUITY Watch for ambiguities in the terms you use. Even though *you* may know what you mean, you must ensure that you and the respondent are talking about the same thing. Many of the descriptions we ask people to offer of themselves contain inherently ambiguous labels. If we ask people whether they go skiing or have a drink "often," for example, "often" may well

have different meanings for different people, or even for the same people for different behaviours. There are many other examples of ambiguous concepts. A question about "drug use," for example, is highly ambiguous. Do you mean Aspirin? Alcohol? Prescription drugs? Marijuana? Heroin? You must be very specific, or at least ensure that you and the respondent are on the same wavelength by, perhaps, describing what you are trying to find out about in a preamble. With browser-based surveys it is possible to indicate what a specific word or phrase means by highlighting the word as a link so that when the respondent rolls their mouse pointer over the word a pop-up dialogue box appears displaying the full definition. But note that these issues are more problematic in a questionnaire than in an interview, since interviews allow for some clarification of ambiguities (assuming you catch them); in a questionnaire, they simply produce unreliability and inconsistency in responses.

MEANINGLESS RESPONSES Avoid questions that can be answered by the respondent without any knowledge about the topic, for example, "Do you agree with the prime minister's new foreign policy initiatives?" This question could be answered by someone who doesn't know who the prime minister is, let alone anything about her/his foreign policy initiatives. Rubenstein (1995) reports that when surveys include questions that ask respondents to express their opinion on nonexistent laws (e.g., a nonexistent *Public Affairs Act*), 25 percent to 35 percent express an opinion anyway, while the rest (65 percent to 75 percent) will volunteer that they have never heard of the Act or say they have no opinion on it. A good way to minimize the chances that a respondent answers a question on a topic they have no knowledge about is to simply include a preliminary question asking them if they are aware of the prime minister's new foreign policy initiative. If they are you can then ask them how they feel about it; if they are not, you can have them skip to the next question. Of course in browser-based surveys the skipping is done for the respondent and they will never see questions that do not apply to them.

DOUBLE-BARRELLED ITEMS Avoid **double-barrelled items**, that is, two questions in one. For example, the question "Would you be upset if you found out that your 18-year-old son or daughter was smoking and selling marijuana?" is really asking about four things: smoking and selling and sons and daughters. The respondent might not feel the same way about all parts of the question.

ACRONYMS Don't assume that people know acronyms, unless you're dealing with a very specialized audience and have done the preliminary exploratory work that allows you to feel confident that "everyone" in the setting is familiar with them. In other words, you should generally avoid questions like "What's your SIN?" or "Do you know anyone at VPD?" or "Would you rather be a PO, a PC, or work at the AG's office?" But if you're engaged in research with civil servants in Ottawa, they may well find it condescending if you don't use terms like PMO, DM or ADM, and DND.[8] In any event, watch what you take for granted.

ALWAYS DO A PILOT STUDY You should always do a brief **pilot study** or trial run before going out and administering your research instrument "for real." There are always things you take for granted without recognizing, and there are always surprises you never even considered when constructing the questionnaire. The time to catch these difficulties is before you commit major resources to duplicating the questionnaire or to time spent interviewing. Focus groups can be ideal venues for piloting a questionnaire.

STRATEGY AND PROCESS

The most frequent situation in survey and interview research involves a researcher approaching a respondent that s/he has never met before. Respondents know nothing about you or your study's purpose other than what you tell them, and their participation is a fragile gift that can be withdrawn at any time.

So far, we've concentrated on the discrete elements of questionnaires and interview schedules: choosing content, considering different ways to word and structure individual questions. Now it's time to consider the research instrument as a whole. How do you put a sizable number of these individual questions together in a way that will make the experience of completing the survey or interview as enjoyable and free of frustration as possible for respondents, while ensuring that your own objectives as a researcher—to maximize response rates, minimize error, and obtain candid responses—are also met?

General Organizational Issues

For the most part, general matters of organization are similar in the preparation of both questionnaires and interviews, but some elements are also clearly unique. For the questionnaire, because respondents must complete the document on their own, aesthetic concerns like the questionnaire's "look" and apparent ease of completion play an important role. For the interview, because the interviewer is present and there's a constant interchange back and forth between the interviewer and respondent, the choices the interviewer makes—whether and when to probe, how to rephrase a question, when to hold back and when to go ahead with a more intimate question—will have a big impact. In the discussion below, we will deal with general questions of organization that are applicable for both interviews and questionnaires but will also occasionally pursue matters that are applicable only to one or the other.

AESTHETIC APPEAL

Many texts, particularly those that deal with more quantitatively oriented survey research, emphasize the creation of a questionnaire that is aesthetically inviting and easy to follow (e.g., see Gray & Guppy 1994). The general impression given by this literature is that if a questionnaire looks pretty and professional, is well laid out and easy to follow, doesn't include too many open-ended questions, and doesn't seem too big, you'll increase the likelihood of snagging a respondent. This view may be overly simplistic, but certainly if the converse is true—if your questionnaire is *not* well laid out, seems difficult to follow, has too many open-ended questions, and is big enough that it looks like it will take a sizable chunk of time to complete—only the most motivated of respondents will complete the questionnaire, and your response rates will suffer.

ANTICIPATING A CONVERSATION

Beyond the first impression, your next challenge is to organize the questionnaire or interview and its constituent parts so that it follows a logical sequence and, ideally, reflects and anticipates a social conversation. Numerous principles can be used to guide the sequencing of questions. If a chronological sequence is involved in the phenomenon being addressed (e.g., the way information is processed in an organization, the development of a romantic relationship from first date to some state of mutual commitment, questions on child rearing that ask about the different stages of child development), the questionnaire's sections can merely follow that chronology. Alternatively, questions can be arranged by topic, grouping together the ones that are thematically related, from general to specific, from most important to least important, and/or from least threatening to most threatening (Gray & Guppy 1994).

The big trick with creating a questionnaire is to try to organize it in a way that mirrors a conversation you might have with a respondent. The same is true of the interview, of course, but the very nature of the interview means that you can adapt somewhat to the unique social dynamic that arises with each respondent; in contrast, once the questionnaire is photocopied, you're stuck with the standardized setup you've created. Browser-based surveys allow more opportunity to change after the fact, but any time a change occurs any earlier responses to what has now been identified as a flawed document are lost. Preliminary exploratory work, through exploratory interviews, focus group discussions, and/or participant observation, can play a crucial role in helping us know how best to

organize our research instruments, and a pilot study that includes pre-testing of the research instrument on a sample similar to the one that will be involved in the research is invaluable.

THE RESPONDENT'S PERSPECTIVE

It is that actual or imaginary *conversation*, preferably with an emphasis on the way the *respondent* would probably organize things, which should guide the structure of the interview or questionnaire, and *not* your anticipated analysis. Data can always be reorganized when you start your analysis. Too many novice researchers let *their* perspective and interests dominate the interview or questionnaire, instead of putting their own structures "on hold" and letting the respondent's schema organize the show. Of course, you'll want to ensure that all the questions that are important to you are addressed. But the order in which they are addressed should be governed by the respondent's convenience, not yours.

SOCIAL CIVILITY: UNWRITTEN RULES

Perhaps the place to begin is by discussing briefly some of the unwritten "rules" of conversation, so that we can then consider how they'd apply to the questionnaire or interview setting. Imagine that you're at a party or some other social gathering. Somewhere between the chip dip and the *petit fours* you find yourself standing next to someone you've never met, and the two of you begin a conversation. Such conversations never begin with requests for intimate details. ("Hi. Did you ever consider suicide during your adolescence?") Instead, they usually start with an exchange of pleasantries and chitchat that does little more than serve as a warm-up and allow time to determine whether you'll pursue the conversation further. These beginning portions of the conversation typically deal with basic, superficial details of our lives that we're prepared to share with anyone. ("So what do you do?" or "So are you here because you know the host or the hostess?") As long as the person you're chatting with isn't completely weird (in which case the exit/escape sequence is enacted), these initial moments often involve a search for common interests that can provide the basis for further conversation.

COMMON GROUND

Once the first "real" basis of conversation is tacitly agreed on (e.g., you find that you both like outdoor activities such as hiking and camping), the two of you will typically "go with it" for a while, perhaps comparing notes on favoured hiking trails or outfitters and/or trading stories. This sort of conversation can consume the whole evening if you find an intense compatibility of interest. More often, though, the first topic soon becomes exhausted; the conversation then either terminates or moves into another phase.

Phase 2 may simply be another topic, related to the first (e.g., you move on to canoeing) or not (e.g., you find that you also have a common interest in impressionist painters). But now that you've "checked each other out" and decided that you share some things in common and that you each seem like a reasonable human being, the exchange often moves to a more intimate level. Rather than dealing only with activities and interests, you start to ask about and share more in the way of feelings and opinions. Two people who hadn't met half an hour earlier are suddenly trading information about some frustrating aspect of child rearing, comparing their fears about having vasectomies, or talking about what dipsticks men (or women) sometimes can be.

OVERSTEPPING BOUNDARIES

Of course, few conversations ever go completely smoothly. At times, one person may feel comfortable enough to stretch the bounds to a more intimate topic or level: "So, I hear you and Kim separated recently; how's that going for you?" If such an attempt is made prematurely, the other person is caught off guard. Perhaps you've touched a nerve. Perhaps your motives are unclear: are you asking to be caring, because you want to ask the other person for a date, or because you're about to disclose your own experiences (which the other person isn't yet ready to hear)? Whatever the reason, an avoidance ritual begins. Sensitive listeners notice these things—the slight blush, the superficial response, the subtle change of topic—and, respecting

that they've crossed an inappropriate boundary, back off a bit. Later, when the other person understands our motives better or simply feels more comfortable with us, we or the other person may return to that issue, and this time the conversation will continue to flow. But for now, the matter is put on hold and another topic is addressed.

WITHDRAWAL

When conversations turn intense, we rarely terminate them abruptly. Instead, a "shutdown" sequence is often enacted: we withdraw gradually, often by returning to a more superficial level of conversation that reconnects us with what's happening around us. ("Oh … I see some people are starting to dance; do you like to dance?") Sometimes this process marks the beginning of a new friendship or romance. Other times we merely go our separate ways and, despite having enjoyed the interaction, may never see the other person again.

Additional Considerations Unique to Research

A FORMAL INTRODUCTION

Many of these same "rules" are followed in organizing a questionnaire. Your first task in a questionnaire or interview should always be to introduce yourself with a brief statement about who you are and the purpose of your study. Any promises you're prepared to make, for example, that a brief summary of results will be sent to participants following completion of the study if they're interested, also should be made here. In the case of a questionnaire, respondents should be told whether they should write their names down or complete it anonymously; for interviews, or when respondents' names are obtained on a questionnaire, you should specify clearly what steps you will take to safeguard their confidentiality. This all can be accomplished in a few sentences or a short paragraph, for example,

My name is Pat Wallace, and I'm a graduate student in sociology at Provincial University. This questionnaire is part of my master's thesis, which deals with how different parents teach "appropriate behaviour" to their children, so it includes a number of questions that ask about your parenting practices. The whole thing should take no more than about 20 minutes to complete. I hope you'll answer all the questions, but feel free to leave out any that you feel uncomfortable about. Finally, please note that responses to this questionnaire are intended to be anonymous. If you'd like to receive a brief summary of the results of the study after it is completed, please fill out the small card at the end of the questionnaire and submit it separately from your completed questionnaire. Thank you very much for agreeing to participate.

GETTING TO KNOW YOU

After the basic introduction, the first topic that's asked about is often relatively trite and superficial, devoted to acquiring preliminary information, for example, to ensure that the respondent is an eligible participant in the study and perhaps to ask about a few demographic details (although one generally avoids such "threatening" demographics as income and education at this point). Because respondents are often looking for cues, we give them signposts that tell them what we are doing (e.g., "First I need to ask just a few general questions so that we have a record of how many kids you have and how long you've been a parent"). The first section also sets the pace for the interview or questionnaire, establishing a rhythm of query and response, query and response.

TRANSITIONS

After passing this "getting to know you" phase, the interview or questionnaire bridges to the first set of questions about the main phenomenon of interest. Again, some sort of signpost is often given, both to keep the respondent informed and to provide a bit of a mental break before digging into the next section. For example, a transition might be "Okay, that completes the first section regarding some of your early experiences as a parent; now I'd like to ask a few questions on how you handle different kinds of situations that can arise with young children."

If only one set of questions deals with the main phenomenon of interest, the questions in the set would normally be ordered from least to most threatening; if there are several *sets* of questions, then the *sets* would also be ordered from least to most threatening. Each time there's a change of theme, another signpost should be offered to help make the transition.

LOOSE ENDS AND THE FINAL WORD

The final section of the interview or questionnaire should tie up loose ends and leave some positive resolution. For example, a final section often includes some "basic" demographic items that will help you describe the sample and perhaps engage in subgroup analyses. An additional benefit of including such items is that when dealing with populations with known characteristics, one can use responses to these questions to assess the sample's representativeness. In any event, the final section should leave respondents with a good taste in their mouths. Conclude with a thank-you, asking respondents (in interviews) whether they have any questions they'd like to ask and (for both interview and questionnaire respondents) whether they have anything they wish to add or further comments to make.

Perspectives on the Research Interview

Although the above discussion pretty much covers the "general organization" issues that pertain to the more structured survey methods, interview researchers, particularly those who engage in semi-structured or unstructured interviews, have gone much further in analyzing the process of interaction in the interview setting. Some apparently hope merely to make prospective interviewers aware of the various cues respondents can give (e.g., nonverbal cues) as to whether they're feeling comfortable, becoming defensive, or whatever (e.g., Gorden 1980; Gray & Guppy 1994). Other texts are written more along the lines of a strategic manual, where the name of the game is to control the setting in such a way that the respondent tells all and feels comfortable about doing so.

A DRAMATURGICAL PERSPECTIVE

Berg (2001), for example, offers what he refers to as a "dramaturgical analysis of the interview," analyzing in detail the different roles that interviewer and respondent occupy and the expectations that each commonly has of the other. He also discusses how the researcher can get maximal information with minimal defensiveness through sensitive attention to both verbal and nonverbal cues. Resistance in the respondent is thus a challenge to be overcome. For example, Berg spends considerable time discussing the "evasion tactics" enacted when we step over the line and ask about things that are too personal or painful.

> Such evasion tactics may involve a word, phrase, or gesture that expresses to another participant that no further discussion of a particular issue (or in a particular area) is desired. Conversely, people also usually acquire the ability to recognize these evasion tactics and, in a natural conversational exchange, to respect them. (84)

But the interview isn't a "natural" encounter, and deferring to people's evasion tactics all the time would mean that much data of interest would be lost. Berg makes no bones about the mission:

> This sort of deference [ceremony] simply cannot be permitted during the course of a research interview. In fact, the emergence of evasion tactics during the course of an interview is among the most serious obstacles to overcome—but overcome them you must! … The interviewer must maneuver around a subject's avoidance rituals in a manner that neither overtly violates social norms associated with communication exchanges nor causes the subject to lie. (84)

For Berg (2001), the interviewer's role is a complex one; he argues that besides being an actor in the setting, the interviewer must also serve as director and choreographer. With respect to evasion tactics, for example, Berg advises that the interviewer must recognize them as they occur and should respond to them with deference, but must also look for a chance to return to that sensitive area. The strategy being advocated thus mixes sensitivity with persistence. By deferring to the evasion tactic, the interviewer shows that s/he is not insensitive to the respondent's feelings, earning "rapport points" by doing so. Berg suggests that the respondent will now be more likely to reply because the interviewer has shown that s/he knows when to back off.

FEMINIST VIEWS: A MORE EGALITARIAN EXCHANGE?

Such analyses, however insightful they may be about the subtle dynamics that pervade the interview setting, also can sound incredibly manipulative and exploitative. Particularly lamentable are the sorts of "strategic" analyses that treat the prospective respondent as a fish to be reeled in or a conquest to be mounted. Many feminist researchers have been particularly assertive about this issue, pointing out how often relations between interviewer and respondent are construed in a way that merely recreates the inequity, hierarchy, manipulation, and exploitation that exist in the world (e.g., Fonow & Cook 1991; Reinharz 1992). Thus, although the interview is seen as a very appropriate research tool—and, some would argue, a particularly *female* type of research tool because of the value it attaches to sensitivity, empathy, good listening skills, and the ability to deal with and talk about feelings (e.g., see Gluck & Patai 1991; Reinharz 1992)—the belief is that the whole interaction needs to be reconstrued.

Many feminist methodologists concur that the interview should be a more egalitarian exchange, guided by principles of mutual respect and collaboration. But feminist researchers differ considerably in how far they'd go in asserting that principle. Oakley (1981), for example, maintains that feminist interviewing should be characterized by openness, engagement, intimacy, self-disclosure, and the potential for developing a long-lasting relationship. Making friends with everybody would seem a formidable task, though, and could also limit the range of research one could conduct.

Others assert that an egalitarian exchange does not require promises of friendship or mutual self-disclosure as either conditions or preconditions for conducting a mutually respectful, mutually beneficial interview. Indeed, many argue that one reason people open up and "tell their stories" is precisely because the researchers *are* strangers and *won't* be seen again. Zimmerman (1977) makes this point in her interview study of women who had undergone abortions:

> The interviewer was a stranger—not a part of the woman's world and someone she would not likely see again. The interviewer was also a professional who would not discuss the interview with anyone else. For these reasons, the women may have felt they could talk about their most private lives and feelings relatively freely. (210)

After summarizing some of the diverse opinions that exist on this issue, Reinharz (1992) concludes that "clearly, there is no single feminist perspective on researcher–interviewee relations and self-disclosure" (34). Yet the fact that such questions are being posed at all must be seen as a most healthy sign for social and health science. As Reinharz notes, these "ethical questions are heightened in feminist interview research because feminists try hard to avoid perpetuating the exploitation of women" (27).

THE MEANING OF SELF-REPORTS

The techniques described in this chapter reflect social and health scientists' desires to systematically unearth people's perceptions via self-report. Whether we use an interview or questionnaire, and whether our items are open-ended or structured, at the heart of our efforts is the goal of acquiring whatever information people will tell us about their thoughts, feelings, beliefs, attitudes, opinions, or behaviours. Once we have our data the temptation is to feel that we have unearthed some inherent truth(s). And perhaps we have.

Still, self-report techniques are but one method and represent but one way of engaging truth(s). We must therefore try to contextualize these truths as we would any others. What exactly do we have when a respondent places a checkmark on a rating scale, answers "yes" to item 16, or embellishes in great detail when we ask an open-ended query? Although many different issues apply to self-report measures as a class, two will be considered here: the dangers of literalist fallacies and the relationship between self-reported attitudes and related behaviours.

The Naiveté of Literalism

As the preceding paragraph implies, we commit a major interpretive error when we give self-reports (or any other type of data) the status of *prima facie*, or literal truth. Questions and rating scales are perhaps best seen as vehicles we create through which respondents can express their thoughts, feelings, and so on, making them visible to the researcher in the same way that smoke is used in wind tunnels to afford visibility to the air currents that exist but would otherwise go unseen. Two questions plague the researcher: what do those utterings and checkmarks mean, and how useful are the individual and/or aggregate ratings for the research objectives at hand?

This is not to say that we cannot believe what people say, even though we must sometimes be cautious about that, too. As Kelly (1955) suggests, "If you want to know something about someone, *ask them*—they might just tell you." And as Kidder and Campbell (1970) have found, measures of reliability and validity are maximized when questioning is direct. By and large, our own experience tells us that people who participate in research generally don't set out to deceive you. They may package their information to show their best side, but in general, people seem motivated to put forth their views "truthfully" within the constraints you provide for their responses. Those who are not, assuming they have free choice about whether to participate, simply will choose not to take part.

Most respondents in social and health science research, particularly the typical university student or average member of the North American population, appear to understand the tasks we give them. They understand order and magnitude (i.e., that 2 is larger than 1 but not as large as 6) and appear able to deal with rating scales.

But a problem arises when we try to make comparisons among individuals. Does the fact that one person checked 5 while another checked 6 mean that one person's attitude is stronger or more extreme than the other's? Not necessarily. Researchers using quantitative techniques frequently assume that people's ratings really take on meaning only when they're aggregated (i.e., when we compile the responses of many different people together). The belief is that our various individual propensities—to avoid extreme categories or rely on them heavily, to be cautious or audacious in our responses, to underestimate or overestimate our perceptions—will cancel one another out overall in the population, or will be equivalent overall in different groups we might wish to compare. This is the main reason that reliability and validity assessment almost uniformly relies on groups of individuals to assess or demonstrate their strengths; it is at that level that such power can be shown. Interpolating or extrapolating from aggregate to individual behaviour is courting trouble.

Attitudes and Behaviour

The question of meaning is not bypassed by focusing at the group level. Even when the attitudes or opinions of groups of individuals are assessed by interview or questionnaire methods, one must still consider what relation these measures, and people's responses, have to other indicators or measures of interest. One issue that has plagued researchers for years is the question of the relationship between what people *say* about their beliefs, attitudes, and/or opinions when you ask them and what they actually *do* when faced with real or simulated behavioural choices.

This area of inquiry was given a provocative initiation by LaPiere (1934), who performed a study in racist, ethnocentric middle America during the Depression years. LaPiere was interested in studying prejudicial behaviour toward minorities

in real-world settings. Anticipating that there'd be a lot of it, he travelled around the United States with a young, foreign-born Chinese couple, carefully recording the number and nature of their interactions with the owners and employees of the hotels, auto camps, and restaurants they visited. He also varied the conditions of their approach (i.e., sometimes he did the talking, sometimes one of the couple did; sometimes he went in with them, sometimes they entered alone). In all, the trio travelled more than 15,000 kilometres, stopping at 250 different establishments, and during all that time, they were refused service *once*.

That original finding would have been heartening, given their expectations, were it not for the follow-up study LaPiere undertook once he and the couple returned home. Six months after completing his original study, LaPiere created questionnaires, which he sent to each of the 250 establishments they'd visited on their trip. Recall that when they actually visited the places, LaPiere found that 249 out of 250 places (or 99.6 percent) welcomed them, while 1 (or 0.4 percent) did not. The 128 replies he received in response to his questionnaire from those same establishments revealed a very different story.

His questionnaire asked "Will you accept members of the Chinese race as guests in your establishment?" In response, 118 (or 92.2 percent) said "no," while 9 (or 7.0 percent) said "it depends," and only 1 (or 0.8 percent) said "yes." Rather surprised by these results, since they were so opposite to the trio's experience, LaPiere wondered whether their own visits to those establishments might have affected the responses. Accordingly, LaPiere then sent the same questionnaire to 128 similar places they had *not* visited—but the results were the same.

LaPiere felt that his study revealed severe limitations to questionnaire responses. He did see some utility to them (e.g., in asking about beliefs), but the huge inconsistency he observed between the questionnaire and behavioural data led him to distrust self-reports:

The questionnaire is cheap, easy, and mechanical. The study of human behaviour is time-consuming, intellectually fatiguing, and depends for its success upon the ability of the investigator. The former method gives quantitative results, the latter mainly qualitative. Quantitative judgments are quantitatively accurate; qualitative evaluations are always subject to the errors of human judgment. Yet it would seem far more worthwhile to make a shrewd guess regarding that which is essential than to accurately measure that which is likely to prove quite irrelevant. (LaPiere 1934: 237)

CONSIDERING (IN)CONSISTENCY

Although we agree with LaPiere's assertion that it's advisable to tackle what is most important rather than what is easiest, we question, as have others (e.g., see Oskamp 1977), whether or in what ways LaPiere was justified in calling the results of his behavioural and questionnaire studies "inconsistent." Certainly, we assess people's attitudes not only because we're interested in their attitudes per se, but also because we believe that knowing people's attitudes will help us understand and/or predict their behaviour (e.g., see Fishbein 1967; Oskamp 1977; Zimbardo, Ebbesen, & Maslach 1977). The relationship between the two is thus of interest to us and has been investigated extensively. For this text, the question becomes how we might gather attitudinal data so that attitude–behaviour links can be addressed. The literature on this topic notes five considerations to keep in mind when assessing the correspondence between attitudinal and behavioural data, considerations that indirectly offer advice on how to assess attitudes.

SITUATIONAL THRESHOLDS Consider the following scenario. You approach a woman at your local library as part of a study on attitudes about environmental issues and ask her first to rate her concern about the environment (i.e., an attitudinal measure) and then to tell you whether she attended last Saturday's "Walk for the Environment" (i.e., a behavioural measure). She indicates that she's "strongly" concerned about the environment but did *not* attend last Saturday's event. Is this an example of attitude–behaviour inconsistency?

Campbell (e.g., 1963) is among those who have suggested that situations like the above don't necessarily reflect inconsistency but, rather, may just indicate differences in situational thresholds. Expressing an attitude is much easier than doing a behaviour (which invariably requires some level of time, effort, money, etc.). If people do the easier thing but not the harder thing, their apparent "inconsistency" in behaviour may merely reflect the fact that they're prepared to go only so far; they surpass the first situational threshold but not the second. True inconsistency, according to Campbell, is evident only when a person exhibits the harder behaviour (i.e., goes on the "Walk for the Environment"), but fails to exhibit the easier one (i.e., does not express support for environmental issues). The literature reveals that such inconsistencies rarely occur (see Oskamp 1977).

DIFFERENT STIMULI Returning to LaPiere's (1934) study, consider the two stimuli with which the hotel and restaurant managers were presented. The attitudinal measure asked whether they would allow "members of the Chinese race" as guests. In contrast, the behavioural measure, in effect, asked whether they would allow as guests the two specific people with whom LaPiere showed up. Were the attitudinal and behavioural responses made to the same stimulus? If not, then it hardly seems fair to draw a conclusion of inconsistency.

And evidence certainly suggests that the two stimuli were indeed *not* the same. LaPiere notes the stereotypical and prejudicial attitudes of Americans at that time to many ethnicities, including Chinese, and these are clearly reaffirmed in studies done during the same period by Bogardus (1925) and Katz and Braly (1933). But LaPiere's two Chinese travelling companions were "a young Chinese student and his wife," who were both "personable, charming, and quick to win the admiration and respect of those they had the opportunity to become intimate with." Further, although both were foreign-born, they spoke "unaccented English" (LaPiere 1934). Researchers who wish to predict reactions to a particular behavioural criterion should ask about that criterion in their attitudinal measure.

COMPETING MOTIVES Questionnaire items often query attitudes in the abstract: respondents are asked how they feel, in general, toward environmental issues, tax increases, or Latvians. In contrast, behaviours usually take place in the context of everyday life, where we face many situational contingencies and choose among alternative actions. The question "To what extent are you concerned with environmental issues?" asks in general terms for an expression of concern for the environment. In contrast, the behavioural criterion of, say, whether the respondent attends a meeting that evening concerning a local development project involves many situational contingencies (e.g., free time, the availability of transportation to the meeting) and competing motives (e.g., concern with environment balanced against interest in development; time at the meeting balanced against desire to go bowling or spend time with family).

AVAILABILITY OF ALTERNATIVES Questions asked in the abstract also ignore the fact that the lack of behavioural alternatives may foster what would seem to be inconsistent behaviour. You may not be particularly enamoured of your local morning newspaper, for example, but may buy it anyway because it is the only morning paper available. Similarly, some persons watch television programs they don't like only because they have nothing better to do or because they find it a non-medicinal way to relax and fall asleep at the end of a busy day.

"NORMATIVE" PRESCRIPTIONS OF BEHAVIOUR Many social situations prescribe particular ways of behaving as "appropriate"; individuals may suppress the expression of some attitudes in certain contexts. We're taught, for example, to be polite to people even if we do not particularly like them; and, in Canada in the 21st century, expressions of racism or chauvinism are seen as offensive and tasteless. In 1930s America, however, the situation

was quite the reverse; white hegemony dominated, and few thought it inappropriate to express racist and prejudicial attitudes as the questionnaire respondents did to LaPiere (1934). But when faced with a particular stimulus (like the couple LaPiere travelled with), people felt similarly free to "make exceptions" if they chose to, perhaps depending on such considerations as how "white" and counter-stereotypical the couple appeared to be.

AVOIDING THE PITFALLS

These five considerations suggest that overall, in the aggregate, there are many reasons *not* to expect a one-to-one correspondence between attitudinal measures and behavioural criteria, even if both are valid. At the same time, the existence of such pitfalls indirectly suggests precautions the attentive researcher can follow to avoid them.

GENERAL INTERESTS? GENERAL QUESTIONS! First, the evidence (see Fishbein & Azjen 1975) suggests that correspondence between attitudinal and behavioural measures is generally weakest when a single-item attitudinal measure (e.g., "To what extent are you concerned with environmental issues?") is correlated with a single behaviour (e.g., "Do you plan to attend Friday's meeting on environmental issues?"). Why? Partly because there's room for error in both. Psychometric studies show that the more times and the more different ways you express a question, the more reliable will be your characterization of the person on the issue at hand. The same is true in the behavioural domain.

Note that in each case we're looking at a general *domain* of interest to us (i.e., attitudes about the environment, behavioural manifestations of environmental concern), but sampling only one element of each. There are many different components to environmental attitudes, and there are many different ways to express one's environmental concern (or lack thereof) behaviourally. Just as we should be reluctant to generalize more broadly on the basis of a survey that samples only one person, we also should be reluctant to generalize about a person's attitudinal or behavioural leanings on the basis of one question or one behaviour. To assess general proclivities, one must sample more broadly across both the attitudinal and behavioural domains.

SPECIFIC INTERESTS? SPECIFIC QUESTIONS! If a researcher is interested in predicting a very specific behaviour, the situation warrants a very pointed question that simulates the criterion setting as closely as possible, either by varying the actual setting or by describing a specific hypothetical scenario in a preamble. Some of the most successful efforts at predicting actual behaviour on the basis of attitude measures are pollsters' astoundingly accurate election predictions. Part of their success is attributable to appropriate sampling for such a research objective, that is, by obtaining a representative sample of voters. But another factor is that respondents are asked a very specific question about their intentions about the behaviour in question (i.e., "How would you vote if the election were held today?"). Further, efforts are often made to simulate actual voting conditions as much as possible (e.g., by providing respondents with some way to cast a "secret ballot" where only aggregate results can be known).

CONSIDERING STEREOTYPING/PROTOTYPICALITY Researchers should consider that people may hold many opinions about things with which they've had little experience. People do not refrain from having opinions about Morocco even though they have never been there, have never met anyone who lives there, and know little about the country and its history. The stereotypes people hold about other social groups (or social objects or social policies) may or may not be accurate in general and are always inaccurate when they deny the possibility of exception. Yet people often use stereotypes as a departure point when we ask them about some social category "in general."

So researchers should consider the relationship between the stimulus they provide and the particular behavioural criterion they have in mind. For example, Ted's research experience regarding "pornography" shows that survey questions must be very carefully worded because of variation in what "pornography" means to different people. Asking whether "pornography" should be censored, classified, or left unregulated, for example, leads to trouble. Some respondents think the question refers to material that has some sexual content, whereas others assume the researcher is referring to sexual material that depicts violence, particularly toward women (see Palys, Olver, & Banks 1983). The solution here is to (1) ask respondents to articulate their definition or sense of the term; (2) provide a definition for respondents; or (3) not even use the term but, rather, describe the scenario/stimulus you have in mind (e.g., video scenes involving female nudity; videos showing explicit sexual activity involving gay couples), since you're the one doing the research and hence have some objective in mind.

ASSESSING CONTINGENCIES Finally, researchers can surmount the difficulties associated with "contextualizing" questionnaire responses by asking about the contingencies and competing motives that might intercede between attitude and behaviour. Fishbein and Azjen (1975) show strong correspondence between the two with only three intervening variables considered.

SUMMING UP AND LOOKING AHEAD

This chapter reviews techniques that involve interaction—sometimes immediate (as with an interview) and sometimes delayed (as with a survey questionnaire)—between researcher and participant. The advantages and disadvantages of each are discussed, and some of their similarities and differences noted. Considerable time is also spent outlining the various ways that questions can be phrased, some of the strategies and techniques used in the overall organization and implementation of a questionnaire or interview, and some of the obligations and responsibilities entailed in dealing with a respondent on a human-to-human basis.

The chapter places the techniques into three main groupings: *surveys* (which include the various types of questionnaire plus telephone surveys), *interviews* (including the face-to-face individual and focus group interviews), and *oral history methods*.

Survey techniques have been the favourite of researchers asking more quantitative questions, largely because such methods embody many of the criteria that those holding strict realist beliefs feel are characteristic of "good science": a researcher-centred deductive approach, analytical distance from one's "subjects," a way to amass large quantitative data sets in order to identify patterns of relationships that hold across many individuals regardless of their circumstances, and so on. But ironically, what has been called "good science" by *strict positivist* researchers has been considered "poor science" by many *interpretivist* researchers. Similarly, much of what has been "good science" to interpretivist researchers has been seen as inefficient and misguided by many strict positivist ones.

There's probably a useful distinction to be made between a technique *itself* and how that technique has been used *in practice*. Once that distinction is made, it becomes clearer that the various clusters of researchers don't have big problems with the variety of methods represented in this chapter; rather, they differ in terms of how those methods have been designed and put into play. Many feminist and indigenous researchers, for example, criticize the quantitative survey for being little more than a recreation of the non-egalitarian problematic that exists in the world (e.g., see Reinharz 1992; Smith 1999), while many others point out the crucial role that quantitative surveys have played in making people aware of the pervasiveness of such phenomena as sexual harassment and other violence against women).

The broader theme of this chapter, then, isn't that you must declare allegiance to one method (and the associated cluster of researchers) or another. Instead, look at the different methods as different ways of compiling and understanding people's views. As you engage a research area, different methods will be useful to you at different times, depending on your objectives in a given project. Nor do we want to leave you with the impression that the various methods are discrete entities that, like dinner entrées, must be chosen one at a time. It would be far better to approach them as a smorgasbord in which the particular combination of methods you use is up to you.

For example, in the police study described in this chapter (Palys, Boyanowsky, & Dutton 1983, 1984), the researchers used both interview and questionnaire techniques, knowing that they'd complement each other in supplying the information sought. Because the researchers came in after the system had already been in operation for more than a year, and the archival record on the system's development and implementation was at best sporadic, oral histories helped fill in the gaps, giving a more human face to the multiplicity of meanings that people place on a new technology. By doing target interviews with people throughout the organization, Ted and his colleagues were able to get a good handle on the perceived positives and negatives of the data system they were evaluating. But because of the limitations of target interviewing, they weren't sure whether the views they were picking up were held broadly or just by a few vocal people. Accordingly, they used the results of the interviews to design a questionnaire that was meaningful to the people involved, both in how it was worded and in the issues it addressed.

The questionnaire's great strength was that it allowed the research team to gather a large amount of data to see how broadly certain feelings and views were held among patrol officers who used the system. But the limitations of self-administered questionnaires (where you can't ask many open-ended questions) meant that, while they could get a good sense of *what* people's attitudes were, they were limited in their ability to understand *why* the respondents felt that way. Another round of interviews with a cross section of the patrol officers allowed the researchers to ask for officers' interpretations of why those attitudes were expressed, and at least get a sense of why *some* people might feel that way. The study's strength was thus that it effectively combined *both* quantitative *and* qualitative methods, benefiting from their respective strengths and offsetting their respective limitations.

And, finally, some time was spent in this chapter introducing network technology as an increasingly important means of conducting primary social and health research. We shouldn't look at computer-assisted social research (CASR) as a replacement for existing methods; instead we should see it as another tool in the proverbial toolbox that the 21st-century methodologist can utilize in order to better understand our social world. With the recognition that CASR is likely to continue to grow in popularity as a mechanism for collecting social and health science data, it is vital that serious academic efforts be made to assess the methods we use to acquire our data in this information age. To this end critical discussion of the use of computer technology in social and health science research needs to be expanded beyond the confines of specialized academic publications to the pages of books and journals with a broader readership. Furthermore, greater emphasis must be placed on educating the research community about computer technology in general and CASR in particular. With very few exceptions, most popular research methods textbooks in the social and health sciences pay only scant attention to computer technology and CASR, and quite often the discussions found in these books only illustrates the utility of CASR as a form of secondary data collection.

When it comes to the design and development of CASR, it is apparent that the most significant technical issue confronting the social and health science research community is the lack of standardization across hardware and software applications (Ranchhod & Zhou 2001; Smith 1997; Wolfe & Reyna 2002). The most significant practical issue relates to the underdevelopment of research-specific software (Tse 1999). Until operating systems, hardware, and software are standardized and made more accessible, cost-effective, reliable, and functional it may be necessary for the social and health research community to establish partnerships with software developers, network administrators, computer programmers, and graphic and Web designers.

Similar issues will arise in subsequent chapters. Whether the topic is observational methods (Chapter 7), archival techniques (Chapter 8), or the variety of experimentalist approaches (Chapters 9 and 10), we'll see that different clusters of researchers have tended to construe each set of methods in different ways, using them to largely different ends and eschewing the way others have used them. Our approach throughout will be to articulate their diversity in a way that will, we hope, help us understand how we can all benefit from it.

STUDY QUESTIONS

1. The president of your university is interested in assessing the attitudes of people in this province or state regarding postsecondary education. Unsure whether to do the study using a telephone interview or a browser-based survey, s/he comes to you for advice. What advantages and limitations do you see to each approach in this situation? How about if s/he wanted to do the survey with students and faculty at the university? Would the advantages and disadvantages be the same?

2. Compare the following in terms of their relative strengths and limitations: (a) in-person interviews and focus group interviews; (b) in-person interviews and telephone interviews; (c) a browser-based survey and in-person interviews; (d) in-person interviews and in-person survey questionnaires.

3. What does CASR stand for and what advantages and difficulties does it bring to the research process?

4. What advantages does the Internet offer as a place to conduct social and health research? What are some of its limitations?

5. Indicate the role that question wording and question context can play in the results obtained in a large-scale telephone survey. What is the magnitude of their effects, relative to the degree of sampling error that usually

exists in most large-scale studies (which often have sampling error in the range of plus or minus 2.5 percent or 3 percent, 19 times out of 20)?

6. Chris is conducting oral history interviews with women who worked in munitions factories in World War II. What are the relative advantages and disadvantages in this case of (a) taking general written notes during the interview and trying to write any "juicy" quotes down verbatim; (b) using a tape recorder to tape the interviews; (c) taping the interview and writing down key points as the interview proceeds?

7. What unique advantages do focus group interviews have to offer? What limitations do you have to be aware of? What can you do to try to minimize those limitations?

8. What is "selective deposit," and how is it related to the study of history? In what sense do oral history methods address some of the problems of selective deposit?

9. Look again at the section "Question Content" to see the steps involved in translating a general set of objectives into an inventory of concepts, and then into specific questions that ask about those concepts. Form a study group with other people in your class and consider how you might follow through those steps if you wanted to put together a questionnaire that could be used at the end of any course offered in your department to evaluate student satisfaction with the course and with the effectiveness of its instructor.

10. The president of your university wants to include both open-ended and structured items in the study described in Study Question 1. Which ones should be placed first? Why?

11. Create a small questionnaire on a topic of interest to you that includes one open-ended question and one of each of the types of structured items discussed in this chapter (i.e., a

dichotomous item, a single-response item, etc.).

12. Jeff wants to include a question on income in his questionnaire. What are the relative merits of using a single-response item or a categorical-response item to get this information?

13. Indicate what is obviously wrong with the wording of each of the following questions, and then rewrite each question in an appropriate manner.
    a. How many times would you say you have purchased drugs within the last six months?
    b. Do you feel that pliobenthamiacine (PBM) should be made legal for over-the-counter purchase?
       _____ Yes
       _____ No
    c. Do you feel that the use of marijuana and cocaine should be decriminalized?
    d. How do you feel about the depraved individuals who use a dangerous drug like heroin?
    e. Finally, please indicate your age in years at your last birthday:
       _____ 20 years or less
       _____ 20 to 30 years
       _____ 30 to 40 years
       _____ 40 to 50 years

14. The discussion in this chapter about the research interview encouraged you to consider the relationship between researcher and researched. At one end of this continuum, we can consider our scientific aspirations, where part of learning the "tricks of the trade" involves knowing how to use what you know about the interview situation to get the most out of every interview, for example, by the way you design the situation, ask the questions, build rapport, and so on. At the other end, we've seen a view that the interview should be an egalitarian exchange of information between "friends." In a study group or in an essay, discuss the strengths and limitations

of each of those views. Consider, for example, how these decisions relate to the qualitative–quantitative distinction and to your own view of research. Consider also the implications for knowledge that would arise if each view were "the" dominant mode of interviewing in your particular area of interest.

15. Compare and contrast the feminist and dramaturgical views of the interview that were discussed in this chapter.

16. When asked what political party she prefers in the next election, a respondent replies "the Green Party." But she doesn't make a financial contribution to the party when asked to do so. Is this an example of attitude–behaviour inconsistency? Suggest alternative interpretations.

NOTES

1. See Internet usage statistics at http://www.internetworldstats.com/stats.htm.

2. SQi comes from surveys, questionnaires, and interviews. See http://www.sqi.ca.

3. We thank Jodi Atchison of One Smart Chick designs for her work. Ms. Atchison also designed the cover for this edition of *Research Decisions*.

4. For a dismissive and self-serving treatment of oral history evidence in the Canadian legal system, see the original B.C. Supreme Court Decision of Chief Justice McEachern in *Delgamuukw* v. *British Columbia* [1991] B.C.J. No. 525 and its analysis by Cassidy (1992) and Culhane (1998). For a termination of that policy by the Supreme Court of Canada and more respectful consideration of Indigenous oral history, see their decision in *Delgamuukw* v. *British Columbia* [1997] 3 S.C.R. 1010. For a paper that argues there is still a long way to go see Napolean (2005).

5. One can imagine situations where this question could get much more complex, such as when hermaphrodites, transsexuals, or people undergoing sex changes are explicitly made a focus of study, but these situations are fairly rare and hence are ignored here.

6. Cantril also content-analyzed the descriptions people gave of their best and worst situations, comparing them across the 16 countries in the study. Cantril's (1965) book *The Pattern of Human Concerns* is an interesting blend of qualitative and quantitative analysis that offers a textured portrait of the varying contexts in which many of us live.

7. Any reader who feels they know the original source for this story is welcome to let us know; we would be happy to acknowledge their contribution in any future edition.

8. For the uninitiated, your SIN is your social insurance number; VPD is the Vancouver Police Department; and PO, PC, and AG refer to being a probation officer, police officer (or police constable), or working in the attorney general's office. As for the Ottawa-speak, the PMO is the Prime Minister's Office; DMs and ADMs are deputy ministers and assistant deputy ministers; and DND is the Department of National Defence.

OBSERVATION AND ETHNOGRAPHY

Because observation is something that all of us do all the time, we begin by dispelling the idea that observation as a research method involves no more than "just looking." Observation as a research strategy involves *looking in a planned and strategic way with a purpose:*

> As members of society, we also make observations of the everyday world. These guide us in forging paths of action and interpreting the actions and reactions of others ... What differentiates the observations of social scientists from those of everyday-life actors is the former's systematic and purposive nature. Social science researchers study their surroundings regularly and repeatedly, with a curiosity spurred by theoretical questions about the nature of human action, interaction, and society. (Adler & Adler 1994: 377)

One fairly typical and concise definition of observation offered by Weick (1968) describes it as *"the selection, provocation, recording and encoding of that set of behaviours and organisms in situ which is consistent with empirical aims"* (360; italics in original). To aid digestion of that mouthful, let's break the definition into its component parts.

Selection reminds researchers that "observation" is *not* a process whereby everything that happens is somehow visually recorded by the researcher. Try as we might, in most cases we cannot be everywhere watching and listening to everything at the same time; we must always choose a focus for our gaze. But recall that in more quantitative/deductive traditions, researchers are more commonly testing specific hypotheses borne from theory and thus go

into or create situations with a particular focus in mind. For that reason, the "blinders" that focused observation involves may be less of a problem, and may even be an advantage because of the singular and focused preparation to observe it allows. Nonetheless, it still means that anything outside one's field of vision cannot be seen. Among more qualitative/inductive traditions, however, where the whole idea is to try and take in "everything" while deciding where to focus one's attention, the selection that is inevitably involved may be more of a problem, and the biggest challenge is to ensure that one does not do so prematurely without good reason. Despite their differences in how they get there, in the end both traditions eventually seek focus, which makes it incumbent upon us to be self-conscious of how we do so and of the limitations it imposes.

Provocation is an optional element. Observation may be done obtrusively or unobtrusively, and may involve a more passive approach that emphasizes accurate description of what is going on, or may involve some manipulation of the setting as is done in lab or field experiments. Observational techniques thus can be employed within a wide range of research contexts, since they're consistent with all research objectives; indeed, observation is in many ways the foundational research method.

Recording or *encoding* refers to the fact that we gather data for analysis. This can involve a broad range of alternatives from keeping ongoing field notes—an open-ended and less structured approach more commonly used in qualitative field research— to employing more structured observational coding schemes to categorize or count behaviours, as is more typical of quantitative research. This may be done "live" as events are occurring, or may involve video or photographic recording for subsequent analysis. Either way, "encoding" necessarily involves *simplifying* what we observe, and the challenge is to ensure that the encoding process doesn't do an injustice to the process we're attempting to describe or understand.

The reference to "that set of behaviours and organisms" points to the desirability of observing *multiple behaviours* and *different measures of the same behaviour* in any given context.

Including *in situ* (a Latin phrase meaning "situated" or "in context") in the definition underscores how our observations always occur *in context* and hence that we should make an effort to understand the role that the context has on whatever we are observing. Important factors here will include such elements as where it occurs (e.g., in a place that is familiar or strange to the person(s) being observed), the explanation that is given (if any) for the observation, the nature of the relationship between observer and observed, and so on.

Leaving the term *empirical aims* intentionally open-ended, Weick acknowledges that observation may serve many functions, from straight *in vivo* (a Latin phrase meaning "in life") description to the formal testing of hypotheses. Observation is consistent with many research traditions, and if one had to boil it down to a word, is almost synonymous with "empiricism"; it is what researchers do.

In the field research context, the most highly touted advantage of observation is that we can see things unfold in the setting in which they usually unfold. Instead of hearing in a survey what people *say* they do, we have an opportunity to actually witness the choices people make in a context in which all of the contingencies that normally affect their behaviour are operative. Just as legal cases place high priority on eye-witness testimony, there is a high degree of credibility attached to observational data, particularly given that, unlike most eye witnesses in criminal cases whose accounts often arise in adrenaline-filled situations that just happened to occur when they were present and come and go in a flash, the observational researcher *chooses* to be in

that situation and is *prepared* to observe with note book and/or video camera in hand.

Our objective in this chapter is to acquaint you with the range of observational methods at your disposal, and the general principles that one is expected to consider when employing these techniques. As with previous chapters, we will begin by warning you that although we will occasionally make sharp distinctions between methods for pedagogical reasons, in practice these are often very difficult to sustain, and the "ideal" strategy is very often one that combines different approaches to best exploit their respective advantages and overcome their respective limitations.

THE RELATIONSHIP BETWEEN OBSERVER AND OBSERVED

Weick (1968) and other sources in both qualitative and quantitative traditions (e.g., Adler & Adler 1994; Angrosino & Mays de Pérez 2003; Babbie 1989; Judd, Smith, & Kidder 1991) suggest that a major element differentiating observational studies is the nature of the relationship between the observer and the observed. The traditional continuum of roles that many researchers envision (see Gold 1958) can range from the **complete participant** to the **complete observer**, as depicted in Figure 7.1. Although the continuum is not as widely held as before for reasons that will become apparent below, it is a helpful place to start because it sensitizes us to the variety of relationships that might exist between observer and observed, each of which has its own advantages and limitations. We'll examine the two extremes of the continuum first, and then try to make some sense of the middle ground.

The Complete Participant

With the "complete participant" role, the observer does not reveal himself or herself as a researcher. From the perspective of those being observed, the researcher *is* a participant. There are two ways this might occur.

Figure 7.1

The Tradtional Observational Continuum: "Complete Participant" to "Complete Observer"

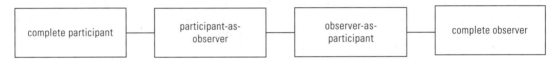

THE *POST HOC* OBSERVER

In the first, the observer *really is* a participant, with any efforts at "observation," in its empirical sense, done on a *post hoc* (a Latin phrase meaning "after the fact") basis. That is, someone who has been a participant in some social situation decides to write about it after his or her participation ends. Examples would include a politician who decides to write his or her memoirs after retirement; anyone sitting down at the end of the day to make a diary entry; or someone who has been a prisoner, a sex worker, or the head of a major corporation writing after the fact about her/his experiences. The defining aspect here is that as the process occurs, the person *is* a participant; only after the fact does s/he decide to reflect on her/his experiences and write an analytical account based on earlier observations.

This *post hoc* development of accounts has both advantages and limitations. Accounts produced by former participants can be very analytical and insightful; the information they provide often has all the immediacy, intimacy, and insight that can come only from direct involvement. Besides the interesting perspective these accounts represent in their own right, the heuristic benefit of providing them as raw data for subsequent analysis also should not be overlooked.

But the limitations to the "*post hoc* observer" role are several. First, ethical issues are raised by a transition from "complete participant" to later "writer/ analyst," since the "informed consent" provisions of ethical guidelines are clearly violated. Second, it's virtually a research truism that to minimize reporting bias and distortion in data gathering, the researcher should be prepared to systematically gather relevant evidence while the observation is

in process. Observation as a social and health science research method requires preparation, attention to detail, and the systematic retention of notes. Because of the *post hoc* observer's after-the-fact change in role, his or her accounts are more likely to be subject to errors of memory or selective recollection of events (since s/he was busy participating at the time). Exceptions here might include people whose role involves an ongoing archiving or logging of activity, such as politicians, where a good proportion of their activity is scheduled and recorded, their correspondence archived, and their policies and the motives behind them often the subject of analysis and speculation in news media. In any event, "complete participants" who wish to make the transition to "writer/analyst" should be particularly sensitive to the need for independent corroboration of their accounts (e.g., by compiling memos, recordings, or other documentation; interviewing other participants; compiling media accounts); such evidence may also help to jog one's memory or fill in gaps.

One also must consider the motives of those who adopt an observer role after the fact. Do they have a particular axe to grind or image to convey? This surely will be reflected in their accounts. Politicians, for example, although they may well be in the position of having some of the most complete personal archives, often also are interested in cementing their place in history as one of the great leaders of their time (if only they were better understood). For this reason, their memoirs are often more usefully treated as raw data—their explanation from their perspective of their career or of some particular episode in which they were involved—as part of a broader social record and more comprehensive historical analysis.

THE SURREPTITIOUS OBSERVER

The second way to adopt the "complete participant" role involves the researcher entering a situation fully intending to engage in observational research, but doing so without ever telling those being observed what s/he is doing. Laud Humphreys's (1970) *Tearoom Trade* (noted in Chapter 3) would fall into this group. Another example is a classic study entitled *When Prophecy Fails*, by Festinger, Riecken, and Schachter (1956), in which several graduate students joined a doomsday group that had made a very specific prediction about when the world would end in order to see what would happen within the group when it didn't. Yet another is the pseudo-patient role that David Rosenhan (1973) and some of his graduate students played at different mental hospitals—each was to arrive at the admissions office and complain about "hearing voices" and otherwise to act as their normal selves—in order to better understand the processes by which labels of mental illness are conferred and maintained.

But as with the *post hoc* observer, the lack of informed consent and the presence of deception should wave red flags for you in the realm of ethical concerns. Key factors to consider here are (a) whether the situation is "public" or not; (b) whether the data that are gathered involve identifiable persons; and (c) whether publication of one's observations can be done without violating confidentiality to ensure that those who unknowingly participated in the research are nonetheless protected from harm.

Few people have any problem with the idea of doing observational research on the way that people use public spaces such as waiting rooms, elevators, shopping malls, and parking lots. Lyn Lofland (e.g., 1973), for example, has spent a considerable amount of time sitting in bus depots and other public places observing the way strangers use space in public settings. And John Lowman (1989), as part of his study evaluating the effects of changes in the "communicating" laws regarding prostitution, included simply mapping the location and counting the numbers of prostitutes who could be observed working the streets both before and after the change in the law. One can easily imagine other examples: examining crowd behaviour while attending a sporting event or music concert; spending time in the emergency room of a hospital watching interactions among paramedics, police, nurses, and doctors. In each case, the researcher participates as just another member of the crowd; the process of observing such behaviour doesn't seem like a violation of privacy, since one is examining only those actions people reveal in public anyway. Further, because there's rarely any attempt to acquire people's names in this sort of setting, anonymity is preserved. In most such cases the people are not identified and cannot be after the study is over.

But what if the researcher wants to video record the way people spontaneously order themselves as they enter buses or get on escalators? For some researchers, public behaviour is public behaviour and possible identifiability is not a concern. Others would be concerned about consent issues while still others would have no problem with it as long as individual identities are camouflaged or the only people who see the recordings are members of the research team so that confidentiality is preserved. All of these approaches are potentially valid; no doubt the particular behaviour(s) being observed would play a role in determining which course would be most appropriate.

Also, we have glossed over any difficulties with separating "public" from "private" spaces, but is the line always so easily drawn? What about meetings of Alcoholics Anonymous (AA)? They are open to anyone who wants to attend, or is the "open" invitation implicitly limited to those with a drinking problem who want to seek help? Can the "open" invitation also be exploited by researchers, journalists, and so on? Lofland and Lejeune (1960) did exactly that in their study of AA and were chastised by some and praised by others when they published their work.

Similar questions are asked about cyber opportunities such as discussion boards, some of which are completely open; others require "memberships" that are simply a matter of registering, while others are more surreptitious and closed (see Atchison 1999 and Kitchin 2002 for discussions about these issues as they pertain to cyber-research). Is it acceptable for researchers to "lurk" in such cyber-settings in order to observe the interaction and then to write about it without the consent of those involved? For example, in a recent study of clients of prostitutes, Chris became a member of several listservs that were created by clients where they discussed and rated different services and exchanged information about different sex practices and where to find them. Doing this gave Chris important insights into how at least this one part of the community of sex buyers was organized, which helped him understand how and where to best approach them for possible participation in the survey and interview portions of his research. In his case, he felt this was all simply part of the "exploration" that any good researcher must do in order to understand the perspective of those one is researching, and that his commitment to ensuring their identities remained confidential made surreptitious observation acceptable.[1]

Social and health scientists continue to be divided about the wisdom of doing surreptitious research, as they have been for years. Some maintain that a lack of informed consent is never acceptable. Others argue that such an approach is reasonable as long as (1) the research question is of sufficient merit; (2) those being observed are not adversely affected or diverted by one's presence; and (3) appropriate precautions are taken to ensure confidentiality. Still others suggest that even those restrictions are too cumbersome and that when observational research is designed to expose and analyze abuses of power and other corruptive practices, anything goes (e.g., see Punch 1994 for a discussion of that perspective and Miller & Tewksbury 2001 for a broader discussion about the utility and ethics of covert methods). Perhaps intending to steer a midcourse, others have gathered data as "complete participants" but have then sought "informed consent" after the fact by informing those involved of their motives and asking whether they might be permitted to use the data (e.g., Alfred 1976).

Finally, it has also been argued that from a purely scientific perspective, the "surreptitious observer" role cannot be dismissed, since it combines the dual advantages of being an observer (and hence being prepared, systematic, etc.) while also minimizing the reactivity of participants through the shared participant role.

When a decision is made to engage in surreptitious observation, other issues arise. For example, assuming a strictly participatory identity in the setting, while still maintaining your observational motives, requires you to assume multiple roles, a situation that can create role conflict (e.g., see Cicourel 1964; Marquart 2001; Riecken 1969). The problems are twofold. First, because (by definition) the "real" participants can't know that you're an observer, you can't take notes while observing. As a result, you must either make numerous trips to the bathroom in order to jot down notes or write down a choice quotation, or wait until the end of the day to write daily synopses. In the former case, if not perceived as having a bladder problem, you may be viewed suspiciously. In the latter case, the longer the delay between when you make your observations and when you actually write them down, the greater heed you must pay to distortions of recall or the bias of selective memory. Cicourel (1964) argues that such distortions represent one of the biggest problems in research involving the complete participant.

A second problem arises from the fact that, in order to continue the participant guise, you must *participate*. But by doing so, you potentially alter the very process you are trying to observe. When Festinger's graduate students joined a doomsday group in order to study them, did the mere act of their joining and participating in the group's activities help convince the original group members of the veracity of their vision? And once you've joined, what do you do when someone turns to you during discussion and asks, "So what do *you* think?" If you say something and people follow your suggestion, you may have influenced the group to go in a direction it might not otherwise have gone. If you say something and your suggestion is *not* followed, this sequence of events might be the beginning of disharmony or factionalism within the group. But if you *don't* say anything, you may engender suspicion about your presence, or contribute to feelings of indecisiveness or ambiguity among members of the group. The challenge is to participate while still remaining a neutral influence; this is one instance where politicians, many of whom seem quite expert at sounding like they're responding to a question while really saying nothing, may provide a useful model.

The Complete Observer

At the other extreme of the continuum is the "complete observer" role. This position is epitomized by the researcher who identifies himself or herself as being engaged in observational research, and who either sets up a study in his or her own setting (such as a laboratory or clinic) or gains access to another setting (such as an organization or group) by seeking and obtaining the permission of someone appropriate. Once in the setting, the complete observer typically does his or her best to remain relatively inconspicuous, doing nothing other than observe with the full knowledge of all who are present that that's why the researcher is there.

CONSIDERING REACTIVITY

One of researchers' biggest worries is whether their presence and the mere act of observation will somehow "change" the behaviour of those being observed. This is an issue of reactivity; that is, whether and how the researcher's presence causes research participants to change from their "usual" or "normal" behaviour patterns because they know they're being watched.

It's certainly easy to think of many situations where this might occur, particularly when the behaviour being observed is a socially undesirable one that would not reflect well on the research participant. Parents whose child-rearing styles are being observed, for example, are probably less likely to engage in abusive behaviour when they're being observed; teachers are probably less likely to yell at

their pupils; police officers are probably less likely to engage in civil rights violations, at least in the short term.

Several factors, some of which the researcher has some control over, can minimize reactivity in most observational settings. An obvious one is the *conspicuousness of the observer*. All else being equal, a researcher who's in the middle of the action will be more conspicuous than one who stands discreetly at the edge of activity. Related to this are the *characteristics of the observer*, particularly the *similarity* of characteristics between the observer and observed. In general, the greater the similarity between observer and observed (in age, dress, race, for example), the less conspicuous the observer will be and, hence, the less reactivity will be generated.

The *characteristics of the participants* also affect reactivity. Children, for example, seem to forget about an observer's presence a lot more quickly than adults do, although the novelty of being observed wears off fairly quickly for both groups. Indeed, another important principle is that *the longer the observational period*, the more reactivity is reduced. This is so for several reasons: (1) novel stimuli in a person's environment (such as an observer) dominate the person's attention initially but soon fade into the background; (2) rapport is often established between the observer and those being observed, so that the observer becomes a less threatening presence; and (3) although it's easy to construct and maintain an image for a short time, most people find it very hard to keep up a false front over a longer period.

The *rationale for observing* given to participants also plays a role in the defensiveness they exhibit. For example, in an evaluation concerning the Vancouver Police Department's Mobile Radio Data System (which gave officers access to various data banks from a computer terminal located in patrol cars), Palys, Boyanowsky, and Dutton (1984) went out of their way to assure officers that it was the *system* rather than *them* that was being evaluated (although it took some time before patrol officers actually became convinced that this was the case). As well, the fact that several of the observers had prior policing interests and/or experience seems to have minimized reactivity (note that the factor used to their benefit was one of trying to maximize the similarity between observer and observed).

Palys and his colleagues also were fortunate in that study to have a way of assessing the extent to which the presence of observers generated reactivity, since they were able to scrutinize computerized archival records of system use, thereby comparing in some ways how officers used the system when observers were present versus how they used it when observers were not. The differences turned out to be quite trivial, although officers had clearly minimized their frivolous use of the system (e.g., to send riddles and jokes to one another; to make arrangements for lunch) in the presence of the observers.

As this example suggests, *the nature of the phenomenon the researcher is observing* also will influence reactivity. The more deviant or stigmatized the activity being scrutinized, the more reactive the situation, and the longer it will take to build appropriate rapport.

OBSERVING ON HOME TURF

There's an extensive tradition of observational research in the laboratory, particularly among experimental social psychologists and those who study child development. Such studies typically involve setting up a particular situation, with the observer then retreating behind a one-way glass to make notes or systematically code the behaviours that emerge. This method was particularly popular in the "group dynamics" domain, for example, where researchers would test theories about the dynamics of groups under varying conditions. There are two great advantages to this approach. First, it's ethically non-problematic (assuming participants aren't misled about the purpose of the research), because participants are informed from the start that they're participating in an observational study. Second, because it happens on the researcher's own turf in a predetermined manner, s/he is ready to observe, using checklists or other coding schemes that have been prepared ahead of time.

The biggest *dis*advantages associated with such research are the often artificial nature of the setting and the reactivity that can occur when research participants know they're being observed. The artificial nature of such settings means that while they may be reasonable research sites for testing theoretical propositions (i.e., hypothesis testing)—since such testing requires only a setting in which the scope conditions designated by the theory are met—one must be cautious about generalizing one's results to other settings where different contextual conditions hold. Reactivity remains a problem no matter what one's research objectives are.

THE COMPLETE OBSERVER IN THE FIELD

Besides considerations of reactivity, the complete observer in the field must first deal with problems of access. You must address the question of why any group or organization should let you—a stranger—observe its behaviour. Although we might like or hope for the prospective participants to trust us immediately because we are affiliated with a university and/or have a project due next month and/or are basically honest and well-meaning, reality is rarely so benevolent. Instead, the complete observer often must be prepared to deal with a gatekeeper (Broadhead & Rist 1976) and talk his or her way into the group. Lofland and Lofland (1984) suggest that you'll be most effective in doing so if you come armed with connections, accounts, knowledge, and courtesy.

With respect to *connections*, Lofland and Lofland (1984) suggest that, if you're not connected with the target group or organization already, you'd do well to cast about among your friends and acquaintances to find someone who is and who would be willing to provide an introduction. They recount the experiences of Joan Hoffman (1980), who was herself a member of an elite family and who had attempted to talk to community elites who were serving on hospital boards:

Introducing myself as a sociology graduate student, I had very limited success in getting by the gatekeepers of the executive world. Telephone follow-ups to letters sent requesting an interview repeatedly found Mr. X "tied up" or "in conference." When I did manage to get my foot in the door, interviews rarely exceeded a half hour, were continuously interrupted by phone calls ... and elicited only "front work" ... the public version of what hospital boards were all about ... By chance during [one] interview, my respondent discovered that he knew a member of my family. "Why didn't you say so?" The rest of the interview was dramatically different than all my previous data. (Hoffman 1980: 46; cited in Lofland & Lofland 1984: 25)

Even when you know no one in the setting, connecting with one person who can act as an "in" and/or "key informant" can make all the difference between getting a project off the ground and not. For Whyte (1943), in his classic *Street Corner Society*, for example, the person who made all the difference was "Doc." For Duneier (1999) in his study of sidewalk entrepreneurs in *Sidewalk*, it was seller of "black books" Hakim Hasan, with whom he struck up a conversation when he noticed Hasan was selling a book Duneier had written previously. For Horowitz (1983), the beginning came with a mixture of persistence and luck:

I chose to sit on a park bench where many youths gathered from noon until midnight. On the third afternoon of sitting on the bench, as I dropped a softball that had rolled toward me, a young man came over and said "You can't catch" (which I acknowledged) and "You're not from the hood [neighbourhood], are you?" This was a statement, not a question. He was Gilberto, the Lions' President. When I told him I wanted to write a book on Chicano youth, he said I should meet the other young men and took me over to shake hands with eight members of the Lions. (7; cited in Berg 2001: 146)

Once a preliminary connection is made, Lofland et al. (2006) argue that you also should be prepared with *accounts*, by which they mean "a careful explanation or account of the proposed research" (43). Use words and concepts that are meaningful to the prospective sample, and while you should be prepared to offer an academic justification for your project, that's probably not what's being sought here. Instead, you should be ready to offer a simple, straightforward, and honest explanation that addresses the question "Why are you interested in us?"

Ironically, Lofland et al. introduce "being knowledgeable" as a liability, though at times it can also be an asset, depending on the situation. A commonly used strategy is to represent yourself as a "learner," which indeed you are (otherwise, there'd be no need to engage in the research). The advantages of taking that approach are twofold. First, it reduces the extent to which you might be perceived as threatening. Second, the process of "teaching" reveals much about a person's understandings.

Difficulties can arise when you are already an insider and are essentially asking people to ignore that fact so that you can hear their views in relation to the study topic. For example, Angrosino and Mays de Pérez (2003) recount Angrosino's experiences in conducting oral histories with members of the Southern Anthropological Society on the occasion of its 30th anniversary. He had long-term ties with many of the members he was to interview, and it was clear they felt very awkward when he would ask them to comment on an event in SAS's history when they knew he knew what had happened and why:

It was very difficult for professional anthropologists to act as informants, particularly when the interviewer was already assumed to be in the know. Some others decided to short-circuit an uncomfortable situation and, in effect, to hijack the interview, carrying on in lecture/monologue fashion without paying attention to the interviewer's questions. Still others demanded to be interviewed by one of the graduate assistants; "I can't talk to you with a straight face," one of them told Angrosino. (125)

There are other ways the role of "naive observer" can end up interfering with the acquisition of rich data. In some situations being perceived as unknow-ledgeable may lead to you receiving little more than what Hoffman (1980) referred to above as "front work," that is, superficial information of the type that usually appears in brochures or on guided tours. Particularly when people are very busy and/or are more senior members of the organization, you must demonstrate that you're worth their time and that they, in particular, are the only appropriate sources for what you need to know. Showing that you've done your homework, that you don't ask the same simple questions that everyone else asks, that you can speak "the language" of that profession, and that you know something about the phenomenon you wish to observe (but do not have too many preconceived notions and are willing to watch and listen) is a good recipe for being treated seriously.

Finally, Lofland et al. (2006) emphasize that you must show *courtesy* and respect in negotiating for entry. This means phoning ahead to make appointments at a time convenient to your guide(s); taking the time to tell everyone who's interested a little bit about your research, even if a given person isn't directly involved; and ensuring that you also get permission from dependent or subordinate populations as well as from those who act as gatekeepers (e.g., asking the kids for their permission and not just their parents and the daycare person).

Mixing Participation and Observation

The two middle roles in the observational con-tinuum are labelled **participant-as-observer** and **observer-as-participant**. As their titles sug-gest, both involve a mixing of the participatory and observational roles, with the difference based on which of the two predominates. This in itself may not be particularly clear-cut, and participant observers often float back and forth between the two, depending on the particular situation.

One perfect example of a mixture of roles was chosen by Muzafer Sherif in his famous "Robber's Cave" studies (see Sherif et al. 1961). Sherif was interested in studying group dynamics, particu-larly with respect to group formation, cohesiveness,

and conflict, and used a boys' summer camp as the context in which to perform his research. As far as the boys were concerned, it was summer camp and nothing more. But for Sherif, it was also an opportunity to manipulate different aspects of the situation (e.g., setting up teams, facilitating the development of rivalries, setting up a situation where an obstacle could be overcome only through cooperation) to systematically investigate their effects. Everything that happened involved typical summer camp experiences; Sherif's interest was in making things happen at particular times rather than leaving them to chance.

The ideal from Sherif's perspective was to be a participant—to avoid reactivity effects and to be close to the centre of the action—while at the same time remaining detached from the action so that he didn't inadvertently influence it. If you were Muzafer Sherif, what role would *you* occupy in order to ensure that you didn't interfere uninten-tionally in the course of events? He obviously couldn't pretend to be one of the boys. He might have chosen to be a camp counsellor, but then might have become a special focus of attention for the kids. The brilliance of Muzafer Sherif is revealed in that, even if you were at the camp, you prob-ably wouldn't have given him a second glance. He was the janitor and part-time maintenance person, one of those invisible service people who are always there but in some way socially nonexistent or out-side the action, perhaps raking leaves, picking up litter, or fixing a faucet. His presence likely would go unnoticed.

Of course, the Sherif example comes close to being surreptitious observation insofar as the chil-dren who attended the camp knew little or nothing about the field experiments and observational research they were a part of. Most participant obser-vation and ethnographic research is more trans-parent than that to those involved, and involves a more cooperative relationship between researcher and participants. In such cases, participant observers look for ways to be helpful while at the same time doing their best to avoid directing the action. For example, Lofland et al. (2006) describe how

Pierette Hondagneu-Sotelo (1994), during her year-and-a-half study of a Mexican immigrant barrio in San Fransico, offered assistance ... by becoming a community activist and personal helper, providing transportation, assisting immigrants in collecting paperwork and preparing their cases for legal migrant status under new legislation, and helping them in their pursuit of employment, as well as being a sympathetic confidante for their personal and familial problems. (71)

Many other examples appear in the literature of researchers finding a way to be useful by helping to carry in groceries, being a general "gofer," serving as a volunteer in a community centre, teaching reading to the illiterate, helping the innumerate fill out tax forms, and so on. The main challenges arise when one is asked to do things that beg the question of where one will draw the line. For example, William Foote Whyte, in the years he spent in "Cornerville" at one point helped out his group by voting four times in a municipal election—once in his own name and three other times under an assumed name. Years later he expressed regret for this action:

> I had to learn that, in order to be accepted by the people in a district, you do not have to do everything just as they do it. In fact, in a district where there are different groupings with different standards of behavior, it may be a matter of very serious consequence to conform to the standards of one particular group.
>
> I also had to learn that the field worker cannot afford to think only of learning to live with others in the field. He has to continue living with himself. If the participant observer finds himself engaging in behavior that he has learned to think of as immoral, then he is likely to begin to wonder what sort of a person he is after all. (Whyte 1993: 317)

In many ways, mixing the participant and observer roles surmounts the problems of each

role in isolation. To the extent that the researcher's status as an observer is honestly presented, ethical concerns about deception or lack of informed consent are minimized. And to the extent that the researcher acts as a participant in the setting, reactivity is often reduced because, as a participant, he or she more quickly fades into the group.

The Participant–Observer Continuum Reconsidered

We mentioned earlier that not all researchers subscribe to the "traditional" continuum of roles from "complete participant" to "complete observer" that we have outlined in this section. Many ethnographic researchers, in particular, began to express reservations with the role continuum to the extent it implies that one *can* be a "complete observer" devoid of any preconceived notions of what one is observing. But as Atkinson and Hammersley (1994) point out,

> although it is important to recognize the variation to be found in the roles adopted by observers, this simple dichotomy is not very useful, not least because it seems to imply that the nonparticipant observer plays no recognized role at all ... In a sense *all* social research is a form of participant observation, because we cannot study the social world without being part of it. (248–49; see also Hammersley & Atkinson 1983)

This statement reflects the growing recognition that we cannot study the world without acknowledging the "we" that is doing the studying. As Denzin and Lincoln (1994) remind us, "any gaze is always filtered through the lenses of language, gender, social class, race, and ethnicity. There are no objective observations, only observations socially situated in the worlds of the observer and the observed" (12). Our collective and individual biographies—whether because of the experience or the *lack* of experience (and hence perspective) they entail—cannot help but enter into and influence our work. Left at that, the challenge becomes one of trying to understand the role that biography might play in our work, and either make an effort to counteract it or simply be forthright about its existence and let the reader decide what to make of it.

But the problem becomes magnified when we consider the power relations that have traditionally existed whenever we carry out a piece of research. We may try to be thoughtful about how we consider the research participant(s) we're observing and may do our best to listen to them carefully as they tell us about their world; at the end of the day, though, it's typically we alone who take the data home and "make sense" of it. The power of the text is ours:

> Many voices clamor for expression. Poly-vocality was orchestrated and restrained in traditional ethnographies by giving to one voice [that of the researcher] a pervasive authorial function and to others the role of sources, "informants" to be quoted or paraphrased. (Clifford 1986: 15)

Much attention has been paid in the ethnographic literature to this relationship between "self" (the observer) and "other" (the observed). bell hooks (1989) captures the attitude well:

> Often this speech about the "Other" annihilates, erases: "no need to hear your voice when I can talk about you better than you can speak about yourself. No need to hear your voice. Only tell me … your story. And then I will tell it back to you in a new way. Tell it back to you in such a way that it has become mine, my own. Re-writing you, I write myself anew. I am still the colonizer, the speak subject, and you are now at the center of my talk." Stop. (70)

The concept around which much of the debate has centred is that of "privilege," a term that refers in this context to the control that being the researcher gives over the content and form of the final text (for example, the book or article that emerges from a piece of research).[2] The very nature of the research and publication process gives us the last word. Recognizing that fact reminds us of the weighty responsibility and ethical obligations that being a researcher entails. People entrust their views to us, and part of our moral obligation is to ensure that they are treated with respect, fairness, and a sense of justice. Indeed, many would argue that part of the academic mission is to facilitate our own obsolescence by helping create the social conditions in which people generally, and the disadvantaged in particular, can speak for themselves.

Whatever role the researcher takes in relation to his or her participants, a question to consider is always how the character of that relationship influences for better or worse, or neither or both, what the researcher is allowed to discover.

STRUCTURED OBSERVATION

Within the quantitative tradition of observation in particular, the preference has been for more structured observation used in concert with a deductive approach that relegates the act of observation to the testing of hypotheses or the gathering of data that are defined by the researcher as important. Walking this path inevitably involves attaching high priority to generating demonstrably reliable and valid data, so it is important we discuss how to develop, assess, and implement a reliable and valid **coding scheme**.

Checklists and Coding Schemes

Researchers engaged in quantitative observation are expected to begin with a clear sense of purpose and a well-developed coding scheme that will result in the accumulation of reliable and valid data. These criteria are met through use of standardized checklists and coding schemes. Deductive research involves constructing such tools on the basis of theory and the literature, whereas inductive research involves incorporating issues and indicators that emerge from preliminary exploration. This section describes some of the types of coding schemes that have been constructed and briefly discusses the assessment of reliability and validity.

As a first dimension to consider, coding schemes might be conceived of as either *static*, where particular attributes of the setting are noted (e.g., age and sex of participant, public or private setting) or *dynamic* (i.e., focusing on behaviour and its unfolding). Dynamic coding schemes may include simple categorizations (e.g., whether someone gives change to a busker) or more complex ones (e.g., whether eye contact is made, how the initial verbal appeal is delivered, whether there is a movement to check for funds).

There are two main types of observational coding schemes: **sign systems** and **category systems**. With *sign* systems, the researcher essentially waits, noting each time a predetermined criterion behaviour occurs. For example, a researcher investigating the incidence of prosocial behaviour among children in a play-school setting might observe the children over the course of a day and (after having taken care to develop an operational definition of what kinds of acts will be considered "prosocial") note each time a prosocial act occurs. In contrast, *category* systems attempt to create a set of mutually exclusive, and exhaustive, categories into which any given behaviour might be classified. Thus, rather than checking off each prosocial act, the researcher might code on a minute-by-minute basis and, within each minute, code (at its simplest) whether the behaviours the children are exhibiting are prosocial or non-prosocial or (in a more complex coding scheme) whether the dominant behaviour was prosocial, affectionate, communicative, aggressive, or whatever.

A sign system would give a better indication of *how many* prosocial acts were witnessed (since every act is counted), whereas a category system would give a better indication of the *temporal flow* of the prosocial acts during the day (e.g., Was the amount of prosocial behaviour greater in the morning, when the children were fresh, or in the

Figure 7.2

Bales's (1970) Interaction Analysis: A Category System for Observing Interaction in Groups

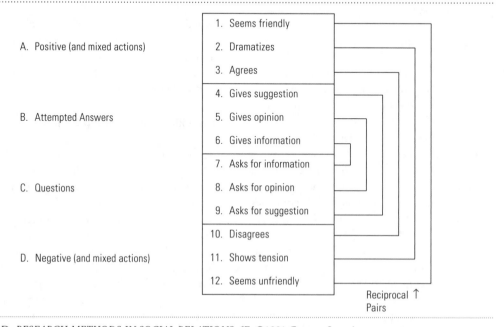

A. Positive (and mixed actions)
1. Seems friendly
2. Dramatizes
3. Agrees

B. Attempted Answers
4. Gives suggestion
5. Gives opinion
6. Gives information

C. Questions
7. Asks for information
8. Asks for opinion
9. Asks for suggestion

D. Negative (and mixed actions)
10. Disagrees
11. Shows tension
12. Seems unfriendly

Reciprocal ↑ Pairs

From JUDD, *RESEARCH METHODS IN SOCIAL RELATIONS*, 6E. ©1991 Cengage Learning afternoon, when they were more tired? Was there more prosocial behaviour before they watched *Transformers* or after?).

One classic example of a coding system used in structured observational research is a category system developed by Bales (1970) known as Interactional Analysis. Figure 7.2 shows the 12 categories it includes: they're intended to be mutually exclusive and exhaustive of all that might happen, in general terms, in a group. When engaged in discussion or a problem-solving task, each person who contributes to the group dynamic (whether verbally or nonverbally) has his or her verbal contribution coded according to one of the 12 categories. As a general framework, it offers a way to investigate such phenomena as differences between group members in participation styles, for example, or a way to look at changes in the group dynamic as a function of variation in the composition of the group, the nature of the problem, and/or the nature of the instructions. Bales's system has been one of the more popular coding systems for studying group dynamics and has been in use for more than 35 years. There are many such systems that can be used *in toto* or adapted. In another domain, for example, Judd, Smith, and Kidder (1991) noted that "at least 73 systems for observing young children are available in the literature" (283).

Assessing Reliability

Whichever alternative is chosen, researchers are obliged to consider the reliability with which their coding scheme can be implemented. If the coding scheme is sufficiently well defined, different individuals should be able to code the same material or events independently and come to the same conclusions. Thus, if we're using a sign system to code incidents of violence in a mixed martial arts (MMA) event we're in big trouble if you count 30 incidents and another researcher counts 700 when we watch the same fight. Clearly, the researcher should assess the reliability with which a coding scheme can be applied *before* doing the actual study, since doing the study is a waste of time if one cannot have any

confidence in the reliability of the observational scheme.

In general, this is done by having different individuals code the same material independently. The reliability of the category coding scheme is the extent of inter-rater agreement. For example, in a one-hour observational period where two raters were using a category system to code the "types of fight moves" in each one-minute period, what percentage of the time did the two raters make the same categorizations, and what percentage of the time did they differ? If the inter-rater agreement is above 80 percent, and especially if it's above 90 percent, then you're doing pretty well and can feel comfortable going ahead and coding "for real." If it's lower than that, a better coding manual and/or more training might be required. In either case, the data should be examined carefully to determine exactly where the disagreements are occurring; this approach will help highlight what aspects of the coding scheme or training program need to be rectified.

A number of factors are known to influence the reliability of coding schemes:

- The more *clearly defined* and *non-overlapping* the coding system, the higher the reliability.

- The shorter the period of time between the event and the coding of it, the greater the reliability of the recording; coding while observing is obviously optimal here.

- Reliability is lower when inference is required: observers can agree more easily whether people are "walking" or "running" (two overt behaviours) than on whether people are "happy" or "sad" (two emotional states or feelings that involve more inference) about heading to their destination.

- Reliability is higher when the number of categories is small. A larger number of categories generally requires finer, more difficult distinctions.

- Coder training will affect reliability. The researcher must determine just how much training is required in order to maximize the reliability of the observational scheme.

Reliability is particularly enhanced by a careful articulation of your nominal definition of the construct(s) under consideration. For example, in one graduate-level methods class he taught, Ted informed students that they were going to study coding schemes the next week. In preparation, they were each to watch the first period of a hockey game that was to be broadcast that weekend, and were to come to class the next week ready to state how many violent acts occurred during that first period. When the students returned and gave their counts, the numbers ranged from zero to 140!

Clearly, "violent" meant different things to different people, so Ted asked the students to explain what the term had meant to them. The person who counted "zero" considered "violent" to be synonymous with "fights," and noted that there were none during the period that was observed. For the person who counted 140, "violent" meant any non-accidental physical contact between players, and there were many incidents of bumping, boarding, and such during the period. Others argued for definitions that recognized professional hockey as a contact sport and hence focused on "gratuitous" contact as the defining aspect of "violence." Still others felt that, to meet their definition, the contact had to be gratuitous *and* outside the rules; these people focused on penalties emerging from contact (e.g., "tripping" would be a violent rule violation, but "delay of game" would not). They spent much of the class discussing which definition was "best" for their purposes. Once they agreed on what definition to employ, each of the students independently counted incidents of violence in a videotaped period of hockey. This time, there was very little variation in their counts. In other words, their coding was now *reliable;* independent observers could code the same material and come up with essentially the same results.

There are several other comments to make about this example. First, recall the distinction between reliability and validity. Although the students had become *reliable* in their coding, the *validity* issue still remained. In one sense, all four of the definitions supplied were "valid." All you can do is choose

definitions consistent with your research objectives and theoretical approach, and then articulate these choices for scrutiny by other researchers. The "best" choice will vary depending on the theory and objectives that guide you, as well as the context. If one player intentionally bumps another during a football game, we may consider it "nonviolent" because it is "within the rules" and "part of the game." But the same behaviour on an escalator at Sears might be considered "violent" because it's gratuitous in that setting. The challenge is to derive a definition that is useful in your research context and to articulate your choices so that others can judge the utility of your definition to them.

ETHNOGRAPHY/PARTICIPANT OBSERVATION/FIELD RESEARCH

Researchers engaged in more qualitative modes of observation have tended to favour less structured and more flexible observational methods. Known variously as "participant observation" (in sociology), "ethnography" (in anthropology), or simply as "field research" (in various other disciplines), such methods have been the favoured ones for trying to gain understanding into the phenomenological world of the "other," that is, coming to *know* people who are different from one's "self." John Lofland (1971) suggests that it's more characteristic in modern life for us to *know about* people and things than to *know* them:

> A significant feature of being a modern person— of living in what we call the modern world—is to *know about* a wide variety of other human beings but not to *know* them. To know about a category of human beings is to have it represented by second parties that such a category exists. We can know about Hottentots, Russians, presidents, delinquents, hippies, or whatever through newspapers, television, face-to-face reports, and other *mediated* means. (1)

But, adds Lofland (1971), "to know about— to know through stereotype and typification—is not enough. We want a more direct sense of what other people are about and what their lives are like than that provided by casual and unexamined typifications" (2).

The difference between "knowing about" and "knowing" is the difference between casual curiosity and the more systematic, strategic interest of social scientists. By arguing for direct contact, Lofland reaffirms that part of being a social scientist is to *interact* with the phenomena we wish to understand; as Morgan (1983) phrased it, we "engage" them. We seek *direct* evidence from the world that bears on the theoretical issues that we deem—or that emerge as—important, and observation is a way to gather such data.

Lofland (1971) suggests that *knowing* requires the social scientist to be close to the people being studied in four respects:

> (a) He should have been close in the physical sense of conducting his own life in face-to-face proximity to the persons he tells about; (b) This physical proximity should have extended over some significant period of time and variety of circumstances; (c) The [researcher][3] should have developed closeness in the social sense of intimacy and confidentiality. He should have developed relationships that provided him reasonable access to the activities of a set of people through their entire round of life; (d) He should have conducted his recording activities in such a way that his reportage can give close and searching attention to … the minutiae of daily life. (3)

Not all researchers would agree with Lofland. While Lofland's distinction between *knowing about* and *knowing* may be useful in reminding us of the limitations of what we think we know, many would question whether it's ever *really* possible to know (in the most profound sense) without having lived the life one aspires to understand. Can a non-Aboriginal person ever *really* understand what it's like to grow up as an Aboriginal person in Canada? Can a physically healthy person ever *fully* appreciate the

life of the physically challenged? Certainly there are aspects of the experience about which we can gather information, but perceptions and understandings founded on a lifetime of experience are very hard to capture in even the most extensive research program. But to the extent that we *can* understand those others, Lofland's admonitions seem a reasonable set of criteria to adhere to, and they can be well met with participant observational and ethnographic methods.

Both participant observation and ethnography refer to methods whereby the researcher spends extensive time (e.g., months or years) in a setting trying to understand some aspect(s) of the setting from the perspective of those in it, often using a combination of methods (e.g., observation would typically be the core of a multi-method approach that would be supplemented with interviews and archival analysis). But at another level, ethnography is so completely different in its history and in the way it's construed that it merits separate attention for the issues that have arisen in its development. By way of background, Vidich and Lyman (1994) explain that

> *ethnos*, a Greek term, denotes a people, a race or cultural group … When *ethnos* as a prefix is combined with *graphic* to form the term *ethnographic*, the reference is to the subdiscipline known as descriptive anthropology—in its broadest sense, the science devoted to describing ways of life of humankind. *Ethnography*, then, refers to a social scientific description of a people and the cultural basis of their peoplehood. (25; italics in original)

Understanding the Culture of the "Other"

The history of ethnography conveys much about the history of social science and its attempts to grapple with the understanding of an "other," that is, someone other than ourselves. Vidich and Lyman (1994, 2003) suggest that ethnography grew out of Europeans' interest in understanding the "primitive" cultures they encountered when Columbus stumbled across the "New World."[4] Trying to understand someone so completely different from oneself poses a very big problem. As Vidich and Lyman (1994) phrased it,

> in practice, it becomes this question: By which values are observations to be guided? The choices seem to be either the values of the ethnographer or the values of the observed—that is, in modern parlance, either the *etic* or the *emic* ... Herein lies a deeper and more fundamental problem: How is it possible to understand the other when the other's values are not one's own? (26)

THE EARLY ETHNOGRAPHER

Good question! Early cultural ethnographies (in the 15th and 16th centuries) by Europeans were done from a clearly European perspective, and evaluated indigenous practices and beliefs using a European yardstick. Most of these written accounts were produced by explorers, missionaries, and colonial administrators. Not surprisingly, when the implicit question was "how European" indigenous cultures were, the answer was "not very." Since the Europeans of that time saw themselves and their Christian religions as the epitome of "civilization," indigenous peoples were regarded as inferior, thereby giving justification to the incredible greed and horrific treatment many of these "civilized" visitors exhibited toward their hosts (e.g., see Berger 1992; Churchill 1994; Wright 1992).

The beginnings of "modern" ethnography are typically said to have emerged in the late 19th and early 20th centuries, when anthropologists like Bronislaw Malinowski (e.g., 1922) and Margaret Mead (e.g., 1928/1960) actually left their homes and went travelling to see firsthand how these "others" lived.

> The field-worker, during this period, was lionized, made into a larger-than-life figure who went into and then returned from the field with stories about strange people. Rosaldo (1989, p. 30) describes this as the period of the Lone Ethnographer, the

story of the man-scientist who went off in search of his native in a distant land ... Returning home with his data, the Lone Ethnographer wrote up an objective account of the culture he studied. (Denzin & Lincoln 2003: 20)

Once again, the criteria for analysis were clear. The application of Darwinian evolutionary theory to social matters—an approach that placed humans at the top of the natural order and was conveniently adapted by Social Darwinists to place Caucasians at the top of the human order—allowed any concerns about social relativism to be easily placed aside. If "we" were the top of the human heap, then surely "ours" were the most appropriate criteria to be used in understanding and evaluating other cultures. Thus, "objectivity" meant employing European standards and imposing a European point of view. The scholar's challenge was to translate indigenous beliefs and practices into terms that Europeans could understand.[5] But when taken out of context that way, practices that might have played an important social role in indigenous cultures for thousands of years could appear quaint, trivial, and trite, if not completely beyond "rational" belief. The result made some people wonder how contemporary North Americans might appear if they were studied and written about in the same manner (e.g., see Miner 1956).

DISCOVERING THE "OTHER" AMONG US

The next "moment" of ethnographic history (to use Denzin & Lincoln's [1994] term) featured a number of American sociologists who began to practise a similar method to understand the "other" that existed at home. Although there were other isolated examples of this "urban ethnography," it was at the University of Chicago's sociology department in the 1920s through the 1940s (the "Chicago School") where this approach was practised with zeal. The names Robert Park, Ernest Burgess, W. I. Thomas, and Louis Wirth are prominent in such accounts. Central to their approach was the idea that American cities are brimming with heterogeneous people of differing lifestyles and worldviews, and that an understanding of American culture requires some understanding of that diversity. Park was the one to conceive of the "natural area" as the appropriate unit to be studied:

> Every American city has its slums; its ghettos; its immigrant colonies, regions which maintain more or less alien and exotic cultures. Nearly every city has its bohemias and hobohemias, where life is freer, more adventurous and lonely than it is elsewhere. These are called natural areas of the city. (Park 1952: 196; cited in Vidich & Lyman 1994: 33)

Park encouraged sociologists to undertake case studies of these natural areas. And he, along with his colleagues and students, did so *en masse* for more than three decades. Studies were undertaken of "the Jewish ghetto, Polonia, Little Italy, Little Germany, Chinatown, Bronzeville and Harlem, the gold coast and the slum, hobo jungles, single-room occupants of furnished rooms, enclaves of cultural and social dissidents, the urban ecology of gangdom, and the urban areas that housed the suicidal, the drug addicted and the mentally disabled, and on the social and economic dynamics of real estate transactions," to name only a few areas (Vidich & Lyman 1994: 33).[6] It was in keeping with this tradition that William Foote Whyte actually moved into an Italian-American neighbourhood to engage in research he called "participant observation" (see 1943/1993).

Despite the differences between these two earlier moments of ethnographic history, they also shared a certain similarity. Underlying both was a sense of social scientific mission born from a kind of Euro-American imperialism that romanticized the "others" they scrutinized, while at the same time seeing their eventual passing as tragic, but inevitable, in the march of "progress" and assimilation. For anthropologists like Malinowski, the study of indigenous peoples was important primarily because it was a way to have a last brief glimpse of prehistory before it became ensnared by the inevitable onslaught of "progress" and "civilization" and faded into oblivion. For sociologists like Park,

however much hobos or immigrants were lauded and romanticized, one senses the belief that the urban ethnographers' texts would ultimately stand as museum pieces once all lost their uniqueness in the "melting pot" that was America.

But assimilation, it turned out, was not at all inevitable. Although challenges to theories that touted its inevitability were first raised in the 1930s (even by Park himself), a third moment of ethnographic history laid these views to rest. Vidich and Lyman (1994) describe the process: "During the two decades after 1970, ethnological studies of African-American, Amerindian, Mexican-American, and Asian peoples also cast considerable doubt on whether, when, and to whose benefit the much-vaunted process of ethnocultural meltdown in America would occur" (37). Other studies would attempt to give a voice to other of society's underclasses, while also attempting to bring new levels of rigour to the process of qualitative analysis (e.g., see Becker 1958, 1963, 1979; Becker, Geer, Hughes, & Strauss 1961; see also Kidder 1981a; Smith & Manning 1982).

Participatory Action Research: A New Relationship?

Much of the early history of ethnography (in anthropology) and participant observation (in sociology) involved the educated westerner wandering off into some foreign land or urban enclave to understand some "other" culture, which often meant translating those others into terms that were meaningful for the folks at home without due consideration for the meanings or implications they would hold for those being researched. Researchers were the ones who posed the important questions; research participants were simply supposed to go ahead with their lives and let us observe and then write about them. As Chambers (2003) outlines, very often the purpose of these early anthropological studies was to help colonial administrators deal with the populations they sought to control.

But the world and ethical sensibilities have changed. Among Indigenous peoples, for example, the favourite of anthropologists, we see more and more works by Indigenous authors extolling both the desirability and necessity of research with Indigenous peoples being done by Indigenous researchers incorporating Indigenous methods and epistemologies (e.g., Deloria 1991; Duran & Duran 2000; Hoare, Levy, & Robinson 1993; Smith 2001; Wilson 2008).[7] As Wolf (1992) reminds us,

> We can no longer assume that an isolated village will not within an amazingly short period of time move into the circuit of rapid social and economic change. A barefoot village kid who used to trail along after you *will* one day show up on your doorstep with an Oxford degree and your book in hand (137).

Increasingly one sees encouragement of what has come to be known as participatory action research (or PAR), which can be thought of as a more collaborative model of ethnography that is both participatory (i.e., there is an ongoing collaboration between researcher and community or group or organization or whatever) in the identification of the definition of the research question, and action-oriented (i.e., there is an overall objective not only of understanding something better, but also to do so in a way that advances the interests of the participants).

An excellent example of this more collaborative approach is a piece of video ethnography conducted by Margolis (1994) in coal mining communities in Colorado that had seen better days. The process began with Margolis contacting the communities and beginning to identify purposive samples of individuals who could be interviewed on video about different periods in the communities' history. By involving the community in telling their own story, the study soon became a victim of its own success. Participants started lining up to be interviewed and began bringing out supplementary materials—old newspapers, photographs, family albums, documents—that gave an even more comprehensive community record. The product that Margolis was seeking to

produce was a documentary, and the collaborative nature of his process continued into the analysis and editing stage. A first "draft" of the film was shown to those in the community who were given an opportunity to comment on its strengths and weaknesses before Margolis went back and re-edited a final product. Margolis (1994) recounts the process:

> I intended to use the editing process to produce "documents" rather than documentaries. My role as editor was not that of providing the sociologist's standard of objective truth, but rather to arrange an order that reflected the living relation between biography and history. I wanted to capture the emphasis of knowledge held in common by communicating people's analysis in their own words. As much as possible I wanted to avoid relying on a narrator or expert commentator to impose an overview or legislate meaning. The process was designed to avoid forcing a preconceived analysis on the material. Ethnographic editing techniques allowed the raw materials to inspire both form and content. Certain topics brought up in almost every interview suggested scenes: immigration, ethnic relations, changing techniques and technology of mining, exploitation in the company town, the struggle to organize, the Ludlow strike, the IWW Strike, disasters, etc. Each individual biography lent unique content even as people recounted history that they made in common. Historical categories were not imposed by the editor but were nominated by coal people out of their own experience.

Ted was recently involved in a similarly motivated project with an Aboriginal justice program in Vancouver known as Vancouver Aboriginal Transformative Justice Services (VATJS). He had been involved as an observer in the late 1990s when discussions were ongoing between members of an Aboriginal caucus that included representatives from many Aboriginal organizations that offered services to Aboriginal offenders and a Steering

Committee that was comprised of many of the Aboriginal representatives as well as representatives from various Canadian justice agencies (e.g., offices of the BC Solicitor General; BC Attorney General; federal Department of Justice; Vancouver Police Department; and so on) who were either funders or who would be involved in developing protocol agreements with VATJS. Generally speaking, the program involved diverting certain categories of offenders to VATJS, where they would be subject to procedures formulated by the Aboriginal community on the basis of traditional justice processes.

All had proceeded well for more than a decade when the number of referrals to the program from the Canadian courts began to slow to a trickle. Because of his history with the program, Ted arranged for a small study to be conducted by Jana Nuszdorfer and Richelle Isaac, two graduate students who were interested in the relationship between Canadian and Aboriginal justice programs. They interviewed persons who were part of the Canadian system and VATJS in order to determine what the source of these problems were and how they might be addressed. Because it addressed both the history of the development of VATJS and the aspirations that both members of the Canadian justice system and VATJS expressed for their future relationship, the final report (Palys, Isaac, & Nuszdorfer 2012) provided a foundation for the development of an updated protocol agreement between VATJS and the Regional Crown.

HOW AND WHAT DO YOU OBSERVE?

The sections above on more- and less-structured approaches to observation research urge us to consider both the research role we occupy and the nature of the relationship that exists—or that we create—both between us as researchers and those we observe. Unless we do only the more contrived form of observation, the kind that occurs in situations that we construct and that occur on our own turf (which nonetheless has its own advantages and uses), both forms of observation must consider

problems of access and/or the ethical issues that can be associated with observing others surreptitiously.

But assuming that we *do* get access to the setting or group that we wish to observe, the researcher's next challenge is to make specific decisions about what, and then how, to observe. A detailed inventory of all the various techniques and alternatives is beyond the scope of this text, but various sources offer us a few basic points to consider.

Options Regarding Structure

We mentioned at the beginning of this chapter that we would be making distinctions between different approaches for pedagogical reasons that might be difficult to sustain, and the one we made between structured and "unstructured" approaches to observation is one of them. This is so for two main reasons. The first is that it is becoming more and more commonplace to combine observational techniques, and indeed to combine observation itself with other methods to gain the benefits that arise from multi-method inquiry.

The second is that, particularly with more qualitative approaches, very often the general strategy is not to have a singular plan and follow it rigidly, but to start off with broader observational coverage and gradually develop a focus after spending some time in the field. Ted recalls his time during a previous sabbatical when he had the opportunity to spend time with Howard Becker when he was at the University of Washington and join him in a graduate class on field research that Becker offered each week. Students were continually frustrated when they would ask him what sorts of things they should write down in their field notes and he would always respond by saying "everything." His admonition was another way of saying that one should write down as much as possible because one never knows what will turn out to be important later and be an eventual focus of the study.

During the preliminary phases, one tries to contextualize the phenomenon of interest, gathering basic descriptive information that will inform subsequent analysis (e.g., How frequently does the phenomenon occur? Who's involved in the process? What other aspects of the process warrant scrutiny?). This is also a time to sharpen research questions, to consult with people who are knowledgeable in the field along with those who are most likely to be affected, and to decide what particular types of data will be used as indicators for the key concepts of interest.

A primary hazard to avoid here is in *not* making the transition to more focused observation. Certainly a more focused research question facilitates this transition, as does the imposition or generation of theory. The danger, as Cicourel (1964) notes, is that without theory or a clearly focused research question, the researcher has no guide for his or her activity, in which case the method may amount to little more than a never-ending "pilot study" that accomplishes little or nothing.

Some Places to Start

CHARACTERISTICS, CAUSES, CONSEQUENCES

Obviously, what you look for will depend on your particular research question(s) and objectives and understanding of the phenomenon of interest. Nonetheless, an inventory of some "basic" attributes may be considered. Most generally, John Lofland (1971) argues that, when you boil it all down, everything we call "social science" can be said to address one or more of the following three questions:

◆ What are the *characteristics* of a social phenomenon, the forms it assumes, the variations it displays?

◆ What are the *causes* of a social phenomenon, the forms it assumes, the variations it displays?

◆ What are the *consequences* of a social phenomenon, the forms it assumes, the variations it displays? (13)

As one might expect when all of social science is summarized in three sentences, Lofland's synopsis subsumes considerable complexity. Consider how time is represented in these questions. In pointing

to *characteristics* or attributes of the phenomenon under study, Lofland is talking about *now*, the present. Implicit is a detailed description of the phenomenon as it is. Questions about *causes* direct our attention to the *past*. What are the antecedents of the phenomenon? Which of these are noteworthy in the generation or emergence or shaping of the phenomenon? Finally, questions about *consequences* direct us to the *future*. In what sense is the phenomenon itself an initiator or cause of subsequent events? How does variation in the phenomenon relate to subsequent variation in other phenomena of interest?

Lofland (1971) considers the delineation of *characteristics* to be qualitative analysis and the articulation of *causes* and *consequences* to be quantitative analysis. But what characteristics are of interest to us?

PARTICIPANTS

Since social and health science most often focuses on human behaviour, it seems reasonable to focus on the humans who inhabit our chosen milieu. Thus, as a minimum, you should describe participants in terms of demographics (e.g., age, sex), as well as other variables of interest that you note when observing, that appear in the literature as identified correlates, or that your particular theoretical dispositions dictate. *Who are these people?*

ACTS AND ACTIVITIES

What people *do* is clearly of interest to social and health scientists; their behaviour in the setting of interest will be one component of any complete observational account. Such behaviour may include anything from relatively brief, situationally constrained acts to elaborate activities that occur over more extended periods of time. What is happening? Involving whom? What aspects of the behaviour are of particular interest to you (e.g., the way strangers are socialized into the setting; the way friendships form; the informal social rules that guide action)? Observation that extends over time helps researchers identify regularities and idiosyncrasies in behaviour patterns that will in turn help focus subsequent research.

WORDS AND MEANINGS

Related to but not necessarily synonymous with what people do is what they *say*. This element of the observational process can obviously include a lot: for example, the attitudes and beliefs that are espoused during ongoing activity, the explanations and accounts that people offer for what they do and how they do it, and the personal and social meaning that people see in and derive from what they do.

There are many decisions to be made about how to capture speech. One choice will pertain to how passive or provocative the researcher chooses to be in relation to the participants. Will you listen to ongoing and spontaneous conversation, or will you actively question and unearth information of interest to you? These two stances should not be seen as mutually exclusive. You might, for example, wish to be more passive during the initial, exploratory phases of the research, in order to acquire information about spontaneous activities and utterings, but later take a more provocative role in asking questions or seeking explanations/accounts. Often these will occur "offstage" in debriefing sessions with a key contact with whom you have rapport and to whom you can say, "What just happened there?"

RELATIONSHIPS/NETWORKS

The elements listed above focus on individuals, but people exist—both implicitly and explicitly— in relations with other people in the production of phenomena of interest. Many aspects of relationships might therefore be of interest to us in an observational setting. You'll want to know, for example, who's a "regular" in the setting and who's more transient or tangential. You also may wish to ascertain the formal and informal roles different people occupy in the setting, and what these roles mean to them. And of course, all of social psychology opens up to you when you begin focusing on relationships: Who talks to whom? How and with whom is information shared? How are individuals recruited or screened for participation in the setting? What power relations exist? How do friendships and animosities evolve? How is status reaffirmed? What brings these people together?

THE SETTING OR ENVIRONMENT

Action must happen somewhere, and the "somewhere" will tell you something about the individuals or group in question and potentially influence the action. What is the setting, and how is it perceived by both participants and the broader society? How do participants personalize and utilize the setting? To whom is the setting open, and to whom is it closed? How is accessibility conveyed? What objects are present, and what do their nature and position convey about the group or individuals being observed?

HISTORY

Social scientists rarely study situations that just appear. Our presence on-site often in itself signifies that the group or setting we're observing has been around at least long enough to have caught our attention. Many observers in the social and health sciences view a knowledge of the history of any setting or group as an integral part of understanding its current complexities.

Any study of history will be partly *descriptive* (e.g., certain persons or groups participated; certain events occurred on particular dates) and partly *interpretive* (e.g., we make inferences about why certain people were involved and the role they played, or we articulate what we feel is the broader significance of the processes we observed). Thus, historical accounts are themselves worthy of study *as* accounts, since they reflect the perspective of the person or group offering the account. It's no accident, for example, that the Euro-dominated societies of Canada, the United States, and Australia typically trace their histories to their "discovery" by, respectively, John Cabot (in 1497, although French Canadians more typically ignore Cabot and begin with Jacques Cartier in 1534), Christopher Columbus (in 1492), and Arthur Phillip (in 1788), as if no other cultures had ever visited these places before (although in fact that wasn't so; see Wolf 1982) and as if the land the European explorers found had been barren of any human population at the time (which it certainly was not). Who the heroes and heroines are, what events are identified as "important," and the nature of myths and legends all tell something about the individual, group, or setting under study.

At the same time, you should always be aware of history as a social construction, and its openness to revision. We have always been struck by the profundity of the statement "History is a justification of the present."[8] History is, virtually by definition, always written from the writer's vantage point. And since those in power are the ones who write mainstream histories, their samplings of past events comprise all those things that were "important" (from that perspective) in getting to where we are today. To the extent that certain events are impossible to ignore (such as world wars or changes of government), the "spin" placed on them typically makes "our" people the heroes and heroines, while others are ignored or their contributions minimized, and the vanquished are deemed unworthy of mention.[9] Current events and characteristics are assumed to be "natural" or "inevitable," and history is the name given to accounts of the glories and errors we encountered en route to the enlightened present. Still, as Yogi Berra is reputed to have said, "It ain't over 'til it's over"[10]—that is, no history can ever hope to be "complete" until there's nobody left on earth to write it. In the interim, social scientists should be as interested in and as cautious about historical accounts as they are concerning other data sources.

COMBINING ELEMENTS

The components listed above shouldn't be seen as an inventory of things to include or as a rigid outline for your ultimate report. To quote Lofland (1971), "what have been outlined … [are nothing more than] … *elements* with which to sort and classify observations and to build some *other kind* of analytic scheme for one's observational materials" (54; italics in original). The researcher's task is to ascertain what is important and what isn't, and then to build or test a theory or account of how the relevant elements interact over time to produce the phenomenon of interest.

This is not to minimize the importance of a clearly defined research question and set of research objectives. Indeed, the components discussed tie in with Becker's (1958) delineation of the phases of observational research. Two of the phases he notes are (1) selecting problems to study, concepts to employ, and indicators through which to operationalize the phenomenon and its attendant explanatory concepts; and (2) gathering descriptive and relational information concerning the frequency and distribution of the phenomenon under study. A central aim is the contextualization of the phenomenon under study, that is, determining where and how the phenomenon of interest fits into the process being observed. This leads us to Becker's (1958) third phase, which involves (3) articulating individual findings *along with* a model of the organization (or group or process) under investigation.[11]

In sum, Becker (1958) exhorts us to articulate our understanding of the process that the phenomenon under study is part of, since doing so will help organize our findings and indicate something of their meaning to both the participants and the researchers.

Field Notes

Many novice researchers, as suggested at the beginning of this chapter, fail to distinguish "observation" from "just looking." "Just looking" is something we all do whenever we enter a setting. "Observation" is an empirical technique that involves looking for a purpose—one has an analytical interest and is prepared to gather "relevant" data, however those terms are defined.

In more formal/structured settings, the researcher's role is clear; you will arrive with clipboard or tablet computer and coding scheme in hand, and there will be predetermined rules you will have established (when you decided how to operationalize your variables of interest) that specify whom to observe and at what times. But even when all your formal data coding is done on prescribed sheets, we strongly advise that you either include a space for "comments" at the bottom of your coding scheme or have a digital recorder or small pad of paper at the ready. In some settings, a video recording may be made of the activity for future analysis. And in even less structured situations, the researcher who doesn't have easy access to paper and pen is a fool.

Even for structured observation methods, but especially for less structured ones like participant observation and ethnography, field notes are integral to observation. *No* observational session is complete until those notes have been done. The notes should specify the time and place of observation, the people present and their spatial distribution and interaction, and any other details the observer deems of interest. Field notes are normally very personal documents, and they have a crucial role, particularly in less structured observational research, because they're the raw data on which your analysis will be based. They are rarely shown to anyone but members of one's research group and would virtually never be published as is (see Malinowski 1967 for an exception). So feel free to insert comments, make queries to yourself, and speculate about what might be occurring.

Richardson (1994), for example, advises that when taking field notes, she distinguishes between several different types of notes via a shorthand she has developed for herself:

Observation notes (ON): These are as concrete and detailed as I am able to make them. I want to think of them as fairly accurate renditions of what I see, hear, feel, taste, and so on.

Methodological notes (MN): These are messages to myself regarding how to collect "data"—who to talk to, what to wear, when to phone, and so on. I write a lot of these because I like methods, and I like to keep a process diary of my work.

Theoretical notes (TN): These are hunches, hypotheses, poststructuralist connections, critiques of what I am doing/thinking/seeing. I like writing these because they open up my text— my field note text—to alternative interpretations and a critical epistemological stance. It is a way of keeping me from being hooked on my "take" on reality.

Personal notes (PN): These are feelings statements about the research, the people I am talking to, myself doing the process, my doubts, my anxieties, my pleasures. I do no censoring here at all. I want all my feelings out on paper because I like them and because I know they are there anyway, affecting what/how I lay claim to knowing. Writing personal notes is a way for me to know myself better, a way of using writing as a method of inquiry into the self. (526)

Our systems aren't so differentiated, although we try to include the same variety of notes that Richardson (1994) reports. Ted simply distinguishes between things he's describing (on the basis of observing, hearing, etc.) and remarks he makes to himself that bear on personal feelings, tentative interpretations, questions to consider, future information to acquire, and so on. He just writes the former directly, enclosing the latter in square brackets to set them off as notes to himself. [For example, at this point in the reading, you might be remarking to yourself that you would benefit from borrowing one of the classic ethnographies referred to in this chapter from the library to see firsthand how the process of ethnography is often described.]

Regardless of the particular style you develop, such notes are important. Because they create an ongoing record or personal archive over the course of your study, they act as a diary of the process you've gone through. You can look back over them to see how your knowledge and understandings of the situation have changed over time, to check whether all your ongoing speculations have been tested, or to discover any discrepancies or inconsistencies that might have become evident over time.

Of course, it may not always be comfortable or feasible to actually take notes in the setting itself, although it's always advisable to at least jot down very brief notes or key words that will help you remember the chronology of the session. Whatever the case, always leave time at the end of each observational session to retire to a private location as soon as possible, *before* engaging in any other activities, to flesh out and organize the notes you've taken, which often are written all over the paper, in the margins, and with circles and arrows and perhaps little maps all around. And don't underestimate the length of time it'll take you to do so; many experienced observers suggest that you can expect to spend four hours formalizing your notes for every hour of observation (e.g., see Adler & Adler 1994; Berg 2007; Lofland et al. 2006). The longer you wait, the poorer the record.

If you make note-taking a habit, your skills will improve substantially with experience. For example, Ted now finds that as long as he's able to jot down a few notes and key words that reflect the overall chronology of a session, he can use them to generate an astonishingly detailed description of events that can leave people wondering whether the session was actually digitally recorded. A good place to practise such note-taking is in your classes. You probably take notes on lectures. If you do not already do so, try sitting down as soon as possible after each class and rewriting your notes, embellishing important points. With practice, you should soon be able to virtually recreate the whole lecture, and you'll find your later notes far better organized and thoughtful than the ones made during class, where the lecture's pace can cause you to leave points out. The worst thing you can do (besides taking no lecture notes at all) is take your lecture notes and then not look at them again until it's time to study for your exams. By that time, the train of thought will have been lost, the squiggles and arrows that seemed so meaningful at the time will appear completely unfathomable, and you may have trouble following your notes, although they seemed perfectly logical when you first wrote them.

And finally, note that this practice of generating "notes to self" that begins in field notes does not end when the data gathering is finished. Qualitative data analysis programs such as NVivo, for example, which we will describe in greater detail in Chapter 11 allow you to create memos to yourself as you go through the process of listening to interviews, watching video, or reading transcripts or other text and begin the process of coding your data and develop that more in-depth understanding that will end up in written reports and accounts.

SUMMING UP AND LOOKING AHEAD

This chapter gives preliminary consideration to the extensive range of activities subsumed under the notion of observational research. We've seen that observational strategies are very flexible techniques that can be used in a broad variety of research settings. Indeed, "observation" is a highly generic term that can describe activities ranging from casual to formal and from structured to unstructured—activities that may or may not involve interaction between researcher and participants, and that may or may not be mixed with other methods as part of a multi-method strategy. The chapter emphasizes some of the many issues that weigh on the researcher up through and including the process of gathering data. Little is said, however, about how to make sense of those data, which is addressed in subsequent chapters.

We've seen in this chapter that an observational approach offers several advantages, not the least of which is that it often (although not necessarily) involves behaviour in its real-world context. But observation is rarely used alone. Instead, it is either a precursor to more intimate research, where the researcher starts by checking out the scene, or an important element in a comprehensive participant–observation or ethnographic situational analysis in which observation of behaviour *in situ* is combined with supplementary strategies (e.g., interviews, questionnaires, archival analysis).

The importance of supplementing observation with other techniques (especially self-report) cannot be overemphasized. Most obviously, it allows you to compare what people *say* with what they *do*. Sensitive observational study may greatly assist in the generation of new interpretive information that may didactically inform the overall analysis, which in turn may suggest further elements of the setting to observe in greater detail.

Finally, both more and less structured approaches to observation are discussed. Besides differing in degree of structure, the two approaches also are shown to differ significantly in the way they conceive of the observational setting itself. Researchers engaged in quantitative research, particularly those rooted in positivist traditions, are more likely to engage in structured observational strategies and to see themselves as separable from the act of observation, i.e., that it is possible to be an aloof, detached, and totally objective observer. In contrast, researchers conducting more qualitative and field-based research are more likely to see such divisions as artificial, and question whether the act of observation can ever be separated from the issue of who does the observing. Related to this are questions concerning the standards or criteria used to make judgments based on observational data. Recent trends challenge us to consider the implications of trying to understand the "other" without autocratically presuming that our particular way of knowing is necessarily "privileged" or "authoritative." Even more common these days is a form of ethnography and observation that goes under the name of participatory action research where researcher and participants engage each other collaboratively to produce something that enhances the researcher's understanding of the group or site under study while simultaneously helping to advance the participants' interests.

STUDY QUESTIONS

1. Louise wants to do an observational study of cocaine use among Toronto's upper class. But she's unsure about what role to adopt on the continuum from "complete participant" to "complete observer." (a) Discuss each of the possible roles in terms of the ethical issues and reactivity involved. (b) What other advantages and disadvantages do you see to the various roles in this situation? (c) Indicate how you might approach this situation, and what you might look for at your first cocktail party.

2. Anne-Marie is designing a study of how Vancouver's major newspapers go about investigating, defining, and portraying "crime news." The study will involve an observational component, and Anne-Marie recognizes that her study may induce some degree of reactivity among the sample group. She comes to you for advice. Explain what reactivity is and give two suggestions about what Anne-Marie might do to minimize reactivity in her study. In each case, explain why you believe the suggestion you make will lead to a decrease in reactivity.

3. What is the difference between a *sign system* and a *category system* in observational research? Show that you understand the difference by indicating how each would be used in coding a children's cartoon show for its violent content.

4. Several years ago, a study was conducted regarding the social content of video pornography. The study incorporated scene-by-scene coding of video content in terms of sex, aggression, and sexual aggression. Each scene was viewed and coded as to whether it included sex and/or aggression and/or sexual aggression, or none of these. (a) Did the video study utilize a *sign* system or a *category* system when coding scene content? Show that you understand the difference between these two by explaining your choice. (b) Describe one way you could assess the reliability of the coding scheme.

5. Pick a social setting of interest to you (e.g., your classroom, a video arcade, a bowling alley, a bus, an elevator), and approach it as an observer engaged in preliminary exploratory analysis. Keep field notes, and speculate on the "rules" that govern behaviour in that setting. Also consider the ethical issues involved in observing in such a manner.

6. Differentiating possible observer roles on a continuum ranging from *complete participant* to *complete observer* was standard for many years. Why is that continuum now seen by many researchers as problematic?

7. What is *reactivity* and why is it a concern for observational researchers? What factors affect reactivity? What constructive suggestions would you offer to another researcher who asks what s/he can do to help reduce reactivity when she goes out to do field research? If your answer is "it depends," what would it depend on?

8. Jamal wants to do research on how people adapt to catastrophic news in relation to their health and finds that there are several listservs on the Internet where people recently diagnosed with cancer exchange information about how this diagnosis is affecting the lives of them and their families. It is not a completely open listserv—you have to be a member to participate and see what others are saying—but anyone can join. Jamal himself is not in that position now, although something like that happened to him years ago when his mother was diagnosed with cancer and passed away shortly thereafter. Discuss whether you agree with Jamal's decision to join the group and "lurk" there as a passive observer of the group's discussions.

9. When engaged in participant observation/ ethnographic research, researchers often try and be helpful as part of a respectful exchange—they help you by allowing you access; you help them in whatever small way makes you useful to them—but the issue often arises as to where you will draw the line. For example, if you are studying people who engage in illicit drug use, should you feel obliged to participate if they offer you some? Or let's say you are doing research in a hospital and a nurse asks you to hold a patient down for the nurse to administer a drug that the patient clearly does not consent to. Would you do it? Discuss some scenarios that might arise in research areas that you are interested in to see what range of opinion exists among you and your peers on where that line should be drawn.

10. *Can* men do research about women? *Should* men do research about women? Discuss this issue in a study group or in an essay.

11. In what way does participatory action research overcome some of the problems associated with earlier approaches to ethnography?

12. Why is it important to allow time immediately after any observational session to sit down alone and flesh out your field notes?

NOTES

1. When doing such online research, researchers have to be careful when we quote someone "anonymously" because powerful search engines such as Google now make it quite plausible that today's "anonymous" quote can and perhaps will be attached to a person via some cyber-group's electronic archive.

2. We say "for example" here because there are many kinds of "texts" other than written ones. We may produce a film, for instance, or begin to represent ourselves as "experts" on a certain group (in conferences, workshops, or policy-making sessions) because of the access we have had to their lives. There may be good reasons to do so, but part of our interest as researcher/ citizens should be in trying to find ways to enhance opportunities for people—especially those who are disadvantaged and who lack access to media—to speak for themselves.

3. Lofland actually uses the term "reporter" here, since this quotation is excerpted from a broader discussion about individuals who report in one way or another about life (e.g., social scientists, reporters, novelists, filmmakers).

4. We have some concerns regarding Vidich and Lyman's (1994) historical account, largely because it's both Eurocentric (i.e., conveying the idea that nobody but Europeans were ever interested in understanding the different cultures they encountered in their travels)

and Americentric (i.e., adopting the perspective that anything important in history must somehow have involved the United States of America). Those who attempt to avoid the mistake of citing an overly recent past have returned to the "classics" and traced the beginnings of ethnography to the ancient Greeks (e.g., see Atkinson & Hammersley 1994), who are often recognized as having offered the beginnings of Western European thought. But all the peoples of the world have been encountering other cultures for millennia (e.g., see Wolf 1982), and no doubt all have had curious individuals among them who were interested in learning the other's language and "making sense" of how other people in other cultures live. The attributions Vidich and Lyman make thus should be viewed critically as embodying the perspective of two American researchers who implicitly accept the primacy of document-based European history. These limitations notwithstanding, Eurocentric views *have* dominated "the academy" for the last several hundred years and hence deserve consideration for the changes of method and sensitivity that have been evident over the years.

5. Although we continually refer to "Europeans" here, the term is actually shorthand for Western Europeans—or, more specifically, to Western European thought. The latter is generally considered to have originated in ancient Greece and refers to an epistemology that continues to dominate what we now know as the "Western," "industrialized" world, that is, Europe, North America, Australia, and New Zealand.

6. The authors note references in their article for each of these areas of study. We have omitted them here in the interests of continuity and space, and because our intention is merely to convey the intensity and diversity of the collective research effort.

7. For a great video consideration of these issues, see a clip of Maori scholar Moanna Jackson talking about the way his people have been portrayed by Western science. He suggests Western speculation about a Maori "warrior gene" was little more than a Western fantasy, and that a better understanding of Maori life might well have concluded that Maori had a "gardening gene." See http://www.youtube.com/watch?v=HfAe3Zvgui4.

8. In an earlier edition of *Research Decisions*, Ted asked for help in locating the source of this quote. University of Toronto sociology major Maria Nunes suggests it comes from Herbert Butterfield's (1931) *The Whig Interpretation of History*, which he criticized as little more than a "justification of the present." See, for example, http://news.bbc.co.uk/2/hi/programmes/the_westminster_hour/4258793.stm.

9. For example, many American histories of World War II depict Americans doing all the important things while the Canadians, French, British, and Russians contribute valiantly in their shadows. (When of course *we* all know that the *Canadians* were the centre of everything!) And imagine how different the history you learn in school would be if the Nazis had won WWII. Of course, control over history goes two ways. On the one hand, those in power can look back and write history in a manner that justifies their existence, so that their being in power is clearly "natural" and "inevitable." On the other hand, those who successfully argue for a different history may well succeed in changing the future, to the extent that they may bring to light events that question the legitimacy of those in control to remain so. The success of the feminist critique of male-dominated history, for example, while it has produced "better" history (because of filling in gaps that were previously ignored), has also reaffirmed women's growing social empowerment to those who might otherwise have been resistant to it.

10. Yogi Berra is a former player for the New York Yankees and former coach/manager of

the New York Mets, two professional baseball teams in the United States. Berra's quotation is commonly used in sportscasts these days whenever a team makes a dramatic comeback, emerging victorious at the last possible moment. Each mention reaffirms the qualities of tenacity and persistence and their value in sport.

11. Becker (1958) goes on to describe a fourth phase, in which the problems of inference and proof are addressed. This issue has broad applicability and is discussed in Chapters 9 and 10.

UNOBTRUSIVE AND ARCHIVAL METHODS

Chapter 6 included a discussion of numerous inter-active methods, while Chapter 7 focused on a broad range of observational techniques, varying from simple observation of ongoing social processes to detailed participant observation and ethnographic studies that involve extensive contact in getting to know an "other."

This chapter extends the notion of observa-tion to understanding people and culture through the things we produce. Since producing things is part of what we do, studying the things we pro-duce is another way to learn about us (and others) as people. By examining things people produced long ago, we can also understand something about our past, the "we" who lived before. Such materials include archival data (e.g., police and government statistical reports and secondary data archives), contemporary products (e.g., newspapers, tele-vision, magazines, Webpages), and a wide variety of historical material (e.g., old newspaper reports, books, historical documents). Again, while we dis-cuss specific qualitative and quantitative approaches to unobtrusive and archival data collection, it is important to keep in mind that the technique(s) you employ will be determined by your research question(s) and objectives.

UNOBTRUSIVE MEASURES

In 1966, a rather significant monograph titled *Unobtrusive Measures* (Webb et al. 1966) was pub-lished. In it, and in a subsequent edition (Webb et al. 1981), the authors argued that the choice of oper-ationalizations/indicators for attitudinal and behav-ioural variables of interest had, by and large, tended to emphasize self-report and straight observational methods (e.g., attitude scales, interviews, question-naires, and observation of ongoing behaviour in the lab or field). Although not disparaging of these techniques, the authors pointed out that all of these "direct contact" techniques share the problem of "reactivity" or "centre of attention" effects, because the respondent or participant in such research is typically aware of being observed. Even a multi-method approach is limited if all the methods used are subject to reactivity. Consequently, the authors argued, we should expand the scope of our choice of indicators to include what they called "**unobtrusive measures**." Aptly enough, the subtitle of their book is *Non-reactive Research in the Social Sciences*.

Unobtrusive Measures offered a compendium of techniques and measures that are less influenced by the intrusion of the researcher. These techniques are non-reactive because (1) the "data" are typically produced without thought that the "evidence" might someday be scrutinized by social scientists; and (2) generally, the researcher arrives on the scene after, and sometimes *long* after, the "participants" have left. They cast the researcher in the role of a detective perusing a scene and attempting to infer individual and collective attitudes and behaviours on the basis of the evidence that has disappeared or remains.

Unobtrusive measures are generally divided into two categories: **physical trace** and **archival measures**, although it might be argued that the latter are merely a special case of the former. The next section gives a brief overview of the physical trace and archival measures described most compre-hensively by Webb and colleagues (1981), and then examines in greater detail an archival measure found throughout the Western world: the crime statistic.

PHYSICAL TRACE MEASURES

When people engage in virtually any kind of behaviour, they generally leave behind some sort of evidence of that behaviour. The evidence may be that something is *missing* from the scene that was there before or that something is *present* in the scene that was not there before. These two states of affairs correspond to the two general classes of physical trace measures delineated by Webb and colleagues (1966, 1981). **Erosion** refers to some sort of wearing away or removal of products or materials because of our physical presence or activity, while **accretion** refers to some sort of addition to or building up of products or materials because of our physical presence or activity.

To illustrate the two, one can do no better than observe the master of inference at work. In "The Red-Headed League," Sherlock Holmes observes a man who has walked into his office. Within seconds, Holmes turns to Dr. Watson and comments that his "only" deductions prior to hearing the man speak are that "he has at some time done manual labour … that he is a Freemason, that he has been in China, and that he has done a considerable amount of writing lately" (Doyle in Dougle 1892/1980). Both Dr. Watson and the stranger are astonished by these statements—all of which turn out, of course, to be correct—until Holmes explains the basis of his inferences. The statements regarding manual labour, Freemasonry, and China were based on what Webb and colleagues (1966) would call accretion measures, since in each case Holmes observed instances of materials being present that spoke of prior activity. The inference that the stranger had done manual labour was based on the observation that the muscles of one hand were significantly more developed than those of the other, while the conclusion that the fellow was a Freemason came from observing a particular pin he was wearing. As for the statement about visiting China, Holmes had done prior research on tattoos and knew that the design and coloration of the stranger's tattoo could only have been created in China.

In contrast, the inference that the man had done a considerable amount of writing recently was based on an erosion measure. Specifically, Holmes observed that one cuff and elbow of the stranger's suit were worn to the point of being shiny, and that the worn spots coincided with the spots where one's clothing would make contact with a desk.

Of course, physical trace measures can offer information about more than a particular individual. Webb and colleagues (1981) discuss a variety of erosion measures that have been used in social science and applied settings. Examples include

- using the rate of tile replacement in a museum as an index of exhibit popularity;
- assessing the wear on library books as an index of reading consumption (since just looking at loan records can't tell you whether the book was read or used as a doorstop); and
- using naturally eroded paths between apartment buildings as an index of interaction among apartment dwellers.

An even greater variety of accretion measures has been reported. Particularly pervasive is the graffiti seen on exterior walls and in washrooms around the world, which has been analyzed for what it reveals about our social attitudes (e.g., see Webb et al. 1981, as well as Mockridge's *The Scrawl of the Wild* 1968). Other examples include:

- using the setting of buttons on car radios as an indicator of listening preferences;
- looking at smudge, fingerprint, and dirt accretion on books as an indicator of reading consumption;
- analyzing the imagery presented on vases, paintings, and other objects of art (e.g., murals) as an index of cultural attitudes and character; and
- scrutinizing garbage to reveal consumption practices, as well as to reveal activity described in memos, notes, and early drafts of written material.

Certainly Webb and colleagues' (1981) motives are provocative. Their stated overall aim is "to inspire researchers to get out of the rut of routinized research measures, [and] to brainstorm a wide range of possibilities before narrowing down on the feasible few for the actual research" (12).

The primary advantages of physical trace measures are their inconspicuousness and their anonymity. Traces are generally not produced with the idea that, at some future point, they will be analyzed in some way by a social or health scientist. Often they are clearly anonymous; for example, worn-out paths may reveal aggregate patterns of activity without the possibility of identifying particular footprints.

But for certain indicators in this category, invasions of privacy and issues of confidentiality and lack of informed consent must in fact be considered; after all, many people would be offended if they found that someone was going through their garbage. Another disadvantage of physical trace measures centres on the sometimes unknown representativeness of the information that survives. The problems here are twofold: **selective deposit** and **selective survival**.

To fully understand these terms, you must begin by appreciating the difference between two kinds of history. On the one hand, there are all the events of our collective history, that is, everything that has ever happened up until the very moment that you read this sentence. The second kind of history is the history we create, that is, the sort of material you read in history books. One might hope that the latter would be a representative sample of the former, but it isn't. This is so for several reasons, not the least of which is that all the "facts" of history are not equally accessible to us. People who are interested in writing histories are constrained by the nature of the evidence that remains.[1] It thus behooves us as social and health scientists to consider the relationship between what was and what remains, so that we can better appreciate the limitations to our understanding that are engendered by the gaps between the two.

We introduced the notion of selective deposit in Chapter 6 to explain the appeal of oral history methods. Recall that it attunes us to one source of bias in the historical record on which our analysis of history is based, i.e., the fact that, of all the individuals and societies that inhabit "history," some individuals and some societies are more likely than others to have placed their beliefs and experience into the historical record on which our study of history is based. If we want to have some picture of how people lived and what they looked like during the Renaissance, for example, we are likely to be looking primarily at the experience of the wealthy: there were no cameras at the time, and the wealthy are more likely to have commissioned art in their likeness. Similarly, while royalty and others who held power would have been able to express their opinions and worldview through official proclamations and documents, the lower classes probably didn't have the same opportunity to make their positions heard.

While the notion of selective deposit reminds us that some people are better able to place things in the historical record to begin with, it's also the case that, among those things that *are* initially put into the historical record, some have a better chance of surviving the ravages of time than others. This process is referred to as selective survival. Once again, it is the wealthy and powerful who seem to have the advantage.

For example, suppose we want to gather data about life expectancies in 14th-century France. While it may be the case that virtually everyone who was buried there at that time was provided with some sort of grave marker showing her/his name and years of birth and death (i.e., selective deposit was equal), the marble and brass tombstones and sarcophagi of the wealthy would have survived longer than the wooden crosses of the poor.[2] Similarly, since more aggressive peoples often destroy as many cultural remnants as possible of those they conquer, historical evidence of the victors frequently survives while that of the vanquished does not. For example, evidence of the Spanish in the post-Columbian Caribbean survives, while much of the historical evidence of the Carib people—who inhabited what is now known as the Dominican Republic and other Caribbean islands (e.g., Cuba) until they were virtually annihilated by the Spanish—does not.

At the same time, it would be shortsighted of us to think of "archives" in nothing more than historical terms. One of the things that the joy of finding some old treasure trove of artifacts (or some empty space where they might have been but were lost) should sensitize us to is what we can be doing right now to preserve artifacts that have great social value, as the information we are producing now is the history of the future.

Reading through old documents that were produced more than a century ago is quite an incredible experience. Ted did just that with colleague Bob Menzies in a study of asylum files that went back to 1879 (see Menzies & Palys 2006). The candidness of the file reports was striking, and the opportunity they had to look at them in the aggregate—allowing them to see how minority patients were dealt with relative to "white" ones, how women were dealt with and discussed as opposed to men, and how the files reflected changing mores and other societal changes that had implications regarding insanity and its treatment. Such files are more than simply "data"; they are a part of our cultural heritage and experience from which we can learn about ourselves.

In that regard we have to comment on a truly regrettable tendency that is having and will have a profound effect on possibilities for future analysis. This involves the notion of selective survival, and is reflected in our shortsightedness with respect to the retention of archives. An excellent example of this was brought to our attention by criminologist Ron Melchers of the University of Ottawa, who noted that the City of Ottawa was considering destroying a century's worth of records regarding juvenile fire setters. A concerned archivist who had recommended they be permanently archived had brought them to Melchers's attention when his recommendation met with resistance from the Fire Department—which saw them as having no value and was not legally required to consider any broader social concerns—as well as the city's Access to Information and Privacy Office, which apparently saw them as easier to dispose of than to consider how the rights of the individuals in the files and the greater social interest served by social

research might be reconciled. It is fascinating also that Professor Melchers received no help from his Research Ethics Board—they simply said that privacy law in Ontario would never allow the use of these files for research without the consent of the persons named in the files, which shows an astonishing trivialization of the value of research and unwillingness to find ways to reconcile these considerations.

The general impression one gets from such cases is that rather than being seen as a social resource that has value as both a historical artifact and potential research resource, archives are seen as complicating and a problem—complicated rights claims to deal with, complicated ethical issues to consider and resolve, and retention of a history that can come back to haunt you if and when someone were to sue or make other claims against an organization. One sees this even with research ethics boards at universities, who one would think would have some larger perspective about the historical value of retaining documents. Far more attention is paid to how long one "must" keep records until one can dispose of them than is paid to their long-term value as a social archive. If academic institutions are so shortsighted about such issues, small wonder that others whose mandates do not involve a research component care even less. Fortunately there are persons like Professor Melchers and the City of Ottawa archivists who are sensitive to these issues and ready to speak up. In the end the two of them orchestrated a very hopeful resolution to this: the City of Ottawa is now in the process of establishing a permanent mechanism—the *City of Ottawa Archives Ethics and Advisory Circle*—for better involving the research community in discussion and advice regarding the appraisal of collections for their research and historical value and the reconciliation of the ethical issues involved in prospectively making available those collections that are retained.

ARCHIVAL SOURCES

Archival measures comprise any information that is contained in "hard copy" or digital records or documents.[3] And while they may include such materials as written or taped records of speeches, photographs, newspapers, books, magazines, or private materials such as diaries and letters, probably the biggest class of archival materials available is the Internet, which contains billions of Webpages, documents, images, videos, and audio files created by governments, corporations, academics, and the general public. One could argue that archival measures are nothing more than a particular type of accretion measure, since the documents referred to are indeed products of human activity, but they are sufficiently different and voluminous to be treated as entities worthy of consideration on their own.

Numerous advantages accrue from studying archival materials, not the least of which is that an inspection of historical evidence encourages us to think in terms of social *process*, reminding us that things were not always as they are now and suggesting, therefore, that this is also not how they always must be. Many archives also allow longitudinal analysis, and because they already exist and may cover an extensive time span, allow longitudinal analysis to be done *now;* that is, one needn't wait for 20, 40, or 100 years for the process to unfold.

Further, archival sources *exist;* they are a concrete artifact that was prepared in some bygone time. That assertion may sound obvious, but it implies that we and others *can* go back to a given document or archive again and again to subject it to greater or different scrutiny, unlike the oral history of the Beothuk people (the original inhabitants of Newfoundland), for example, which died with the last of the Beothuk in 1829 (see Upton 1988). We may disagree on our interpretation of what a document means, but at least we are working with the same document. While mass death from plagues or diseases brought by colonists wrought havoc with oral cultures, document-based cultures have their own sources of disaster—more than one archive has burned in a fire, been destroyed in an earthquake, or been scattered to the wind by a tornado or hurricane. These days we also hear of files lost to viruses and frozen hard drives that have not been backed up.

An advantage of archival study is that conducting such research typically costs much less than many other research methods. And as with other unobtrusive measures, archival data are generally less influenced by reactivity than interactive techniques. But one should always consider the reactivity of one's archival source rather than merely assuming that reactivity is absent. *Hansard* (in Canada) and *The Congressional Record* (in the United States) contain speeches that may not have been prepared with the knowledge that a social or health scientist might peruse them, but that *were* prepared (and, in the case of *The Congressional Record,* were also later edited) for public consumption in a political context. The same is true of political memoirs and of many institutional records, where contemporary standards of "political correctness" and risk management undoubtedly influence what is committed to paper.[4] Personal diaries and letters, in contrast, may have been prepared for a limited audience or with the thought that no other person would ever read them. Minutes of meetings for some organizations will be complete and thorough; others may worry about the role such documentation can have in law suits.

Archival sources are subject to the vagaries of selective deposit and selective survival. The researcher's task is always to consider how such availability will influence the conclusions. Some examples of selection are fairly blatant: government archives are more likely to be available than those of smaller groups or individuals. But others are more subtle. Cook and Campbell (1979), for example, point out the bias toward "outcome" rather than "process" data in many series put together for monitoring purposes. The existence of such tendencies in historical sources reaffirms the value of having one's research question *guide* the research, lest one be seduced into believing that the *available* data are necessarily the most *important* or *relevant* data. Researchers must be sensitive to the ways in which data availability constrains their conclusions and the range of theory that can be developed, while also recognizing the value in the treasure they have found.

Finally, researchers who delve into the archives should be on the lookout for possible shifts in how particular data series are defined and in the procedures for recording or saving material. If the series is local enough to have been prepared by a single person, then one must consider that any changes following her/his retirement might reflect little more than the presence of a different recorder, rather than changes in the phenomenon of interest. Similarly, policy shifts in recording practices, or computerization of a previously manual system, may produce differences in what otherwise look like continuous and comparable time-series data.

In sum, archival data can be treasure troves of information that tell about society. They are necessarily secondary data that are unlikely to have been prepared for research purposes. This is both their limitation and strength; the information was prepared by someone else, and for some other purpose than for supplying evidence that might be useful to a researcher. The influence of the data's *context of production* must be considered (although this is no less true of any other data-gathering technique). The intermediary process between event and datum, or between having the thought and putting it to paper, must be considered and articulated.

This chapter scrutinizes examples of research that use several different kinds of data archives. First, we'll consider one you've probably seen on the TV news or read about in newspapers or magazines. This topic has also received attention in one way or another from researchers in sociology, criminology, psychology, anthropology, economics, and education, to name but a few of the fields. The data series we refer to are crime statistics.

An Example: Constructing Crime Statistics

Although several varieties of crime statistics are produced by criminal justice agencies, "crimes known to the police" typically receive the greatest attention from academics, the media, and the general public. Every month, in every jurisdiction in North America (in fact, in most of the industrialized world), the police compile and send off their statistics to their respective federal governments, who dutifully publish these figures, along with computed crime rates. Periodically, articles appear in the media about how the crime rate is up or down, along with various pet theories to account for this change. Many sociologists, criminologists, and others analyze these statistics to try to find out whether crime is up or down, and why; comparisons are made between various cities and countries. Crime statistics undoubtedly rank with the consumer price index and unemployment rates as one of the primary indicators of our quality of life. But what do they mean? And how are they compiled?

Perhaps the best way to begin answering these questions is to introduce the notion from test theory that every observed score (O) is a function of a "true" score (T) plus some degree of error[5] (e), that is,

$$O = T + e$$

Ideally, we attempt to reduce error to zero so that $O = T$. That is, we want our observed scores (i.e., the crime rates published by the federal government) to reflect nothing but the "true" situation (i.e., the actual amount of crime that exists in society). The problem, of course, is that we can never know reality directly; if we could, we wouldn't need crime statistics. Still, that should not stop us from considering the possible strengths and weaknesses of the measures we *do* choose. Thus, in assessing any measure, from crime statistics to survey results, we need to consider how systematic error might have been introduced in our measurements.

One way to do so is to look at how a given statistic is constructed. A simplified model of how crime statistics are constructed is shown in Figure 8.1 (adapted from Skogan 1975). The process begins with the generation of a "true score," that is, the occurrence of a "criminal event," a behaviour contrary to the laws of Canada.

Even in making that opening statement we're already in hot water, since the more we emphasize a country's laws as the defining measure of "real" crime, the more guilty we are of subscribing to

Figure 8.1

The Process by Which a Crime Statistic is "Constructed"

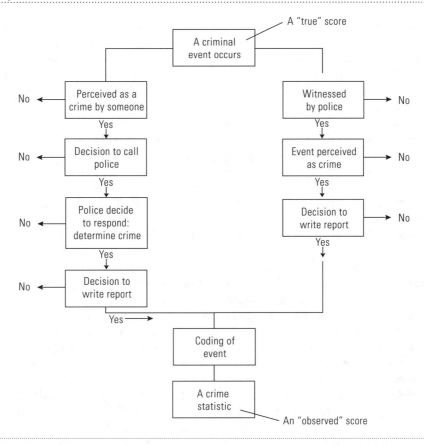

SOURCE: Adapted from *Journal of Criminal, Statistics*, 3, W.G. Skogan, Measurement Problems in Official and Survey Crime Rates, pp. 17-32.(1975), with permission from Elsevier.

status quo definitions of good and bad. There will no doubt be good reason for our choice, but we have to understand that along with acceptance of this definition comes an *ideological* choice. Many would argue, for example, that certain behaviours we now define as "crimes" (e.g., drug possession, illegal acts committed by the police when trying to catch elusive criminals) should not be so defined or that many behaviours we do *not* currently define as crimes (e.g., violations of worker safety regulations, some "civil" matters) *should* be so defined. The law is a human creation and thus reflects

society, culture, and values. An extensive discussion of such issues is beyond the scope of this book (but see Lowman & Palys 1991). What's important for now is that you appreciate the connection between theory and method, ideology and data.

WE START WITH A "TRUE" SCORE

For exposition's sake, let's accept "contemporary Canadian law" as our referent for "reality." We begin with an act, a "true" score, to see what filters it must pass through before it becomes a "statistic" (i.e., an "observed" score).

Basically, this process begins in one of two ways. Either the "crime" is perceived as such by a private citizen or it is noted in some other way by the police. Let's deal with those two separately.

WAS THE EVENT PERCEIVED AS A CRIME?

Going down the left-hand side of Figure 8.1, we see that the first step in the process lies with the community: someone must first perceive the event as a crime. If no crime is perceived, nothing is likely to be done. Some reasons that the citizen might not perceive an act to be "criminal" could be that they may not have been aware that the act occurred or they might not know the act was illegal.

People's tendencies to perceive a given event as a crime also may vary depending on cultural factors (e.g., among different ethnic groups), as well as spatially and over time. For example, one study (Dutton et al. 1982) involved visits to communities ranging from extremely remote to highly urban in eight different provinces where policing was provided by the RCMP. The concept of "assault" clearly varied considerably by place; a certain amount of "roughness" was tolerated in a mining town like Flin Flon, Manitoba, for example, that would likely have been treated as "assaultive" in a suburb like Burnaby, British Columbia. The upshot is that comparability of data regarding criminal and/or deviant behaviour across time, space, and cultures can be extremely problematic.

WERE THE POLICE CONTACTED?

If an act *is* perceived as criminal, the next step in its becoming a statistic is that the police must be contacted. It's obviously difficult to ascertain from police records why people *don't* phone the police. But some hints have been forthcoming from victim surveys, where individuals who report having been victimized to the interviewer are then asked whether they contacted the police—and if not, why not. The results from such surveys indicate that people might not report victimization to the police for a variety of reasons including: they feel nothing will be done about it; they think that the incident is not serious enough to involve the police; they feel

that reporting will be time consuming or inconvenient; or they have decided to report the incident to someone else.

In sum, not all crimes are enumerated in crime statistics reports because, for varying reasons, the crime may not have been reported in the first place. It's usually these unreported crimes that are referred to as the "dark figure" of crime (e.g., see Skogan 1975).

DID THE POLICE RESPOND?

When a crime *is* reported, the ball is in the police's court. The first decision they make is whether to respond to your call. They must decide whether they agree that the matter is one for the police, and then whether it's possible or worthwhile to send someone out to the scene. In many instances, the police won't respond at all.

WAS A REPORT WRITTEN?

If police *do* respond, one of the things they determine is whether or not a crime has been committed. But even if they agree that one has, officers have considerable discretion in deciding whether to write a report and whether to recommend the laying of charges.[6]

Research by Black (1970) and by Black and Reiss (1970) shows that a variety of extralegal factors influence officers' decisions about whether to write a report. The officers in those studies were *less* likely to do a report when the relationship between perpetrator and victim was close, since they believed that such cases would less frequently make it to court.[7] Officers were *more* likely to write a report when the victim was deferential or of high status.

THE POLICE AND POLICY OF CRIME DATA

Crime reporting and hence crime rates are sensitive to policy shifts, some of which can be self-serving. Seidman and Couzens (1974) examined reports for the Washington, D.C., police, concluding that a decrease in crime rate that city had appeared to enjoy was primarily a product of the police chief's orders to get the crime rate down, a task that was most easily accomplished by underreporting and downgrading crimes. Skogan (1975) notes that these tactics are particularly prevalent in those urban centres where police chiefs are evaluated by their ability to reduce the crime rate.

Policy changes may occur for other reasons as well. Priorities may change because of both political pressures and pragmatics (e.g., courts getting full). In British Columbia, for example, it is not unusual for the Crown to issue informal policy directives (e.g., don't bother me with charges for marijuana possession where the amounts are small; report *all* wife assaults) that police are expected to honour. As a result, some authors (e.g., Ditton 1979) argue that crime statistics have *nothing* to do with the amount of crime that "really" exists, instead reflecting little more than shifting foci of social control. Certainly police efforts in the area of victimless crimes bear only a tangential relationship to the amount of that crime that exists; a case can be made that this statement is also true of some crimes involving victims (e.g., wife assaults).

Crime statistics also change when record-keeping practices change. In London, England, for example, "robbery" statistics formerly included only those cases where the robbery was certain or probable; "suspected" robberies were written in a separate book. But then a policy change called for *all* robberies, whether suspected or certain, to be recorded; a 220 percent increase in the "crime rate" was subsequently observed (Skogan 1975). Similarly, a shift in recording policies in New York City helped the robbery rate the next year go up 400 percent, while assaults with a weapon rose 200 percent, larcenies went up 700 percent, and burglaries rose by 1300 percent.

And of course, a big policy change occurs when the law changes. Resulting shifts in the crime rate may thus not reflect any change in behaviour; rather, they may merely reflect a change in the breadth or existence of a criminal designation or in the evidentiary rules that make cases more or less likely to be investigated and prosecuted.

Although this discussion has so far focused primarily on the left-hand side of Figure 8.1, many of the same arguments hold with respect to the

right side of the figure, which refers to proactive efforts by the police to control crime. Suffice it to say that there will be much crime that the police will not witness and that much of the crime that *is* witnessed will be either ignored or not formally reported.

HOW DO WE COUNT?

Whether the reporting source is a police officer or a citizen, some events will pass through the various filters noted above and be considered worth recording as an official crime statistic. Here we come to a bit of a problem: coding the event. Remember that we want to enumerate the amount of crime that exists in our society. To do so, we must agree on how to count, and such agreement is a lot harder to reach than one might expect. Brantingham and Brantingham (1984) offer the following example to illustrate the complexities involved:

> Two men go on a crime spree. They enter a convenience store, rob the proprietor and three customers, shoot a police officer who attempts to apprehend them, knock cans and bottles off the shelves, and set the store on fire as they leave. (51)

How many crimes are involved here? An ambitious Crown attorney might find 16: (1 murder + 4 robberies + 1 vandalism + 1 arson + 1 weapons charge) x 2 defendants = 16 crimes. At the other extreme, one might argue that because there was only a single event, there must be a single crime—or perhaps two crimes, because there were two perpetrators. But if we decide to call it only one crime, what do we call it? The first one (i.e., robbery)? The last one (i.e., arson)? The most frequent one (i.e., robbery)? The most serious one (i.e., murder)? Another possibility is that we could count the number of victims (one proprietor, three customers, one police officer), and hence count five. So which is it? One? Two? Five? Sixteen? Something else?

Since 1962, Canada has joined the United States and much of the rest of the industrialized world in adopting Uniform Crime Reporting (UCR) procedures in an effort to standardize (or make more reliable) reporting across jurisdictions and police forces. The general rules are as follows: for crimes of violence, one counts the number of victims; for crimes of property, one counts the number of events; and for multiple offences, only the most serious offence is recorded. In our example, therefore, the local police would tell Statistics Canada that one murder had been committed.[8]

The use of this scoring system has several implications. First, since Canada did not use UCR procedures until 1962, you're courting difficulty if you compare pre-1962 and post-1962 crime figures, and potentially also those before and after 1990 (see note 8). It also suggests that crime rates overstate the relative frequency of violent crimes relative to property crimes, and that crime rates are an understatement of the number of offences reported to the police.

As Skogan (1975) suggested, the advent of UCR brought greater reliability but sacrificed an already tenuous validity in the process. On the other hand, there is evidence that we should *also* be concerned with the reliability of UCR reporting. The British Columbia Police Commission audited UCR in 1979 among different police forces in the province and found reasonable comparability on homicide, sex offences, robbery, breaking and entering, and *nothing* else.

FINAL COMMENTS ON CRIME STATISTICS

Crime statistics released by a government agency look terrifically official and precise. They're frequently perceived as "objective" indicators of crime. By now you should realize that this is *not* exactly the case: crime statistics (like any other statistics) are the result of a human process. As Skogan (1975) states,

> *Every statistic … is shaped by the process which operationally defines it, the procedures which capture it, and the organization which interprets it.* (17; italics in original)

In other words, every statistic, regardless of whether it is the crime index published by Statistics Canada or a self-report to a survey, is in some sense a *social construction* that comes into being as a function of various psychological, sociological, and organizational processes. One of the big difficulties with archival statistics is that because of their assumed/perceived "objectivity," their reliability and validity often have been subjected to less scrutiny than is the case with perceptually oriented survey measures.[9] To the extent that they have been assessed in this way, their validity and reliability appear questionable. More to the point, we must consider what they mean, as we must do for any data.

Those who frequently use crime statistics argue that even though crime statistics are invalid, they're nonetheless useful. Brantingham and Brantingham (1984), for example, compare them to a bathroom weigh scale that's miscalibrated and always reads 10 kilograms too light. The weight readings are incorrect (i.e., invalid), they say, but could still be used to measure *changes* in weight or to compare different people, since the error is constant. However, the errors in crime statistics do *not* appear to be constant. The various "scales" in North America are miscalibrated to varying unknown degrees; even given scales in given locations change their degree of miscalibration over time. Comparisons are still possible, but they must be done with some sensitivity to the changing context(s) in which crime statistics have been produced and with some understanding of how far any comparisons can be stretched (e.g., see Brantingham 1991).

But to the extent that crime statistics *don't* show the amount of crime in an area, what *do* they show? Various arguments have been put forth. Some authors (e.g., Ditton 1979) argue that crime statistics show little more than social control policies; that is, crime statistics are an indicator of police priorities and activity more than of crime per se. Certainly this argument is easy to support when considering victimless crimes, and there's evidence that the same is true to varying degrees with respect to certain crimes involving victims (e.g., assaults, wife assaults). But such an argument becomes more difficult to make with other crime categories, such as murder, where the proportion of "social control" versus "real crime" probably tips in favour of the latter.

Crime statistics also reflect public confidence in and expectations about police performance. Some events are so trivial they'd probably *never* be reported, while some events are so serious that they'd virtually *always* be reported. But there's a big grey area between those two extremes, where "confidence in the police" can play a significant role in whether the police are informed. Evaluations of a crime prevention program known as Operation Identification (OI),[10] for example, often find an *increase* in the crime rate after OI is introduced to an area. Apparently people are more likely to call the police, since they've been told that the probability of recovering stolen goods is enhanced (Lowman 1983).

This is not to say that all official crime statistics produced to date should be scrapped or that people who produce them should be looking for other jobs. Instead, crime statistics should be treated the way we treat all other data we gather: as a social product that is related to, but is only an imperfectly mirrored reflection of, the phenomenon it aims to describe. Indeed, the trick is to understand the crime statistic (or whatever other data you gather or produce) as a part of the phenomenon you're scrutinizing.

A splendid example is provided by Lowman (e.g., 1984, 1989; Lowman & Fraser 1995), whose research on the prostitution issue has focused on time-series data concerning charges and convictions, but treats those data as a subset of a larger information pool that includes interviews with women who work as prostitutes and with criminal justice personnel, longitudinal observation of the solicitation and control processes, content analysis of media attention to the issue, and other archival analysis. The result not only contributes to the academic theoretical literature but also informs relevant policy matters.

WORKING WITH ARCHIVAL VISUAL DATA

While many social and health scientists study the content of written archival documents such as crime or health statistics, there is a wealth of knowledge to be gained by looking at non-textual sources of archival data such as images and video. Over the years several of our students have been very interested in describing, understanding, and explaining various social and health related phenomena that have been visually documented. The research questions they have built their proposals and subsequent investigations around have been motivated by inductive and deductive interests and, as a result, their projects have scrutinized visual media in both qualitative and quantitative ways. We will address some of the specific analytical techniques available for making sense of visual media in Chapter 11; in the current chapter we discuss ways that visual methods may be used to answer a broad array of research questions and address issues researchers must consider when employing archival visual methods.

Archival visual data are everywhere: images in print media such as magazines, pamphlets or posters; television programs, films, cinema verité and documentaries; video sharing websites such as YouTube; photographic images that appear in family albums, social networking sites such as Facebook, Pinterest, and Tumblr as well as in public and private archives; the art that adorns the walls and halls of museums such as the Louvre; and the graffiti one finds on subway and bathroom walls. While students of cultural and media studies, communications, and visual anthropology will know the utility of using visual media as a rich source of data for answering a range of research questions, these sources also can be very useful for people working in a range of other social and health science disciplines for obtaining critical insights into social life.

It is often said that a picture is worth a thousand words. It is certainly true that images and video are capable of providing rich data to answer research questions that conventional observations and data collection techniques simply would not be able to accurately and comprehensively record. Visual data offer social and health researchers a way of actually *seeing* aspects of phenomena that we would otherwise only be able to hear or read about through second hand accounts obtained through the range of more obtrusive methods we have discussed in previous chapters. Photo and video allows us to access basic information such as the number of people attending a particular event or complex social interactions and narratives such as the movements, activities, and conflicts of those individuals who participated in the riot in Vancouver after the Canucks lost the final game of the Stanley Cup finals to the Boston Bruins in 2011.

Photographs and videos are historical documents. As representations of often complex historical activity, visual data are incredibly useful for documenting historical change in a way that is generally possible only through expensive and time consuming longitudinal studies. For example, recently Kimberly Neuendorf and her colleagues (Neuendorf et al. 2010) were interested in determining whether prevailing societal norms about women and female sexuality have changed over time. While there are many ways that Neuendorf et al. could have addressed this question, they did so by studying the idealized portrayals of female beauty that are perpetuated through films (2010). Out of countless television programs and movies they could have selected, they decided that the long-running and popular James Bond movie franchise with its infamous "Bond girls" was particularly well suited for achieving their research objective. The researchers carefully coded and analyzed 20 Bond films beginning with 1962's *Dr. No* and ending with 2002's *Die Another Day*. Their results indicated that "despite social progression of feminist ideology, the women of Bond continue to be portrayed in rather limited sex-stereotypical manner" (Neuendorf et al. 2010: 758). While the number of female characters represented has increased over time and the roles of women in the franchise have expanded with women becoming more autonomous, the characters have become more sexually attractive and are more likely to be the recipients of physical harm. While the researchers acknowledge that visual data alone do not provide insights into how these changes are internalized by the viewing audience, they speculate that the exposure to

stereotypical portrayals likely finds its way into the minds and lived relations of at least some members of the viewing audience.

Just as the information contained in photographs and videos offers researchers rich opportunities for finding answers to a diverse array of research questions we also should acknowledge that the people, places or events that *do not* appear in visual images also offer important information for answering a range of research questions. For example, while Chris was studying at the University of Toronto he would routinely walk the halls of King's College, Hart House and Simcoe Hall where the pictures of graduating classes from as far back as 1870 were displayed. While the images of these early alumni revealed much about the dress and decorum of the time with each photo displaying mostly wealthy Caucasian men wearing double breasted waistcoats with pocket watches, Chris was more fascinated by what was *not* present in picture after picture, year after year. Very few of the pictures were of women and racial minorities, a condition that did not appear to change dramatically until the 1950s. The photographic images of graduating classes that are displayed in every university contain valuable information for researchers posing questions about gender, race, and class.

It is important to remember that just as official crime statistics are imperfect reflections of the 'reality' we wish to explore, describe, understand, explain, or transform, there are several important caveats that researchers working with visual data need to keep in mind.

Perhaps the most significant challenge facing researchers wishing to use visual data relates to the fact that it is sometimes difficult to ascertain the authenticity and credibility of images or video since such medium can easily be forged or manipulated. For example, it is quite common to hear people say "before I put that picture up on Facebook I'll have to 'Photoshop it'." All computers and now even many smartphones come pre-packaged with basic image and video editing software, allowing anyone to edit the 'reality' that is present in the video and digital images that they preserve. Individuals and groups with access to greater resources will find it even easier to edit visual materials. This manipulation can be as simple as removing the red eye from a photograph or as complex as removing full segments of time from a video. Just as elements of the 'reality' captured in an image or video can easily be removed they also can be added. Such additions or removals can be almost impossible for the untrained eye to detect. So while image and video offer researchers the opportunity to observe aspects of a phenomenon, in a digital age we need to be increasingly aware of the possibility that the 'reality' that we think is being represented in a picture or video is nothing more than a clever re-crafting of a particular event. How closely to you think the images of the celebrities that don the covers of many of the magazines we see in the check-out isle of our local supermarket are the way these people really look?

Even when an image or video remains unaltered, we need to keep in mind that visual representations are merely snapshots or clips of selected aspects of social reality and these clips reflect the gender, class, and racial position of the person who took the photo or created the video (see also Becker 1979). Historically cameras and video-capture devices were available only to those who could afford such technologies, as a result much of the visual data that is preserved in physical and virtual archives represents another example of selective deposit that will over-represent particular class interests and perspectives. With the increasing availability of cheap and often disposable cameras and cellphones with built in high resolution cameras, this situation may be changing. An example of an attempt to move beyond the typical privileged representations of social life is the "Hope in the Shadows" project run by a charitable organization in Vancouver's Downtown Eastside (DTES). This project involves distributing disposable cameras to people living in one of Canada's poorest communities and asking them to photograph the images that depict the story of the community through their eyes and not those of privileged outsiders or mainstream media outlets. The result is an archive of nine years of images that depict a very different story of Vancouver's DTES than one normally sees and that researchers could use to address a range of research questions.[11]

It is also important to keep in mind that photographs and videos frequently contain a performative element. When individuals or groups are the subject of a photograph or video they frequently 'perform' or pose for the camera consciously representing themselves in a particular light thereby distorting 'reality.' Somewhat related to the performative aspect of visual media is the fact that the content that people choose to capture in pictures and video frequently is that which has particular significance or tells a particular story as they see it. It is exceedingly rare to see people taking pictures or video of mundane events. More frequently photos and video either depict the best or worst of the human condition or the specific story that the person creating the visual wants to relay. As a result, visual records often do not tell us much about the typical conditions underlying a phenomenon of interest.

Visual records also more commonly deal with *anticipated* events owing to the more cumbersome weight that bringing along a video camera would involve. This is rapidly changing with the newest generations of smartphones; now huge numbers of people are carrying photo- and video-capable phones in their pockets, creating situations where, at the Vancouver riots following the 2011 Stanley Cup playoffs, for example, there were literally thousands of video clips of rioters taken by individuals who had never anticipated such an event, but had the technology to produce video footage of the event when it happened. We see the same happening at "Occupy" events around the world and during protests and state repression in what came to be called the "Arab Spring;" YouTube, Facebook, and Twitter ensured that messages and images about these events were being beamed to the world within moments of their occurrence.

The quality of the images and video can greatly impact the 'reality' that is captured and a researcher's ability to extract the information from the visual data. While it is increasingly common for images and video to be captured with high resolution digital cameras or high definition digital recorders, much of the visual data contained in public and private archives that is available to social and health researchers is stored on microfilm, microfiche, 16mm or 8mm film reels, beta or VHS tapes, computer disks, or in the pages of dusty old books or photo albums. The detail that is captured by these media vary dramatically. Microfilm and microfiche often store only low resolution black and white images of original photographs that may themselves have been in a heightened state of erosion at the time they were archived. While 16mm and 8mm film format store both video and audio tracks, the resolution of the film and the accuracy of the colour is inferior to that of even the most basic modern day cellphone. The relative disparities in the quality of the visual content of differing media dramatically impact the depth and breadth of data that researchers can extract, which in turn impacts the reliability and validity of their results and conclusions.

In addition to dramatic differences in the quality of the original recording media, the temperature and relative humidity as well as the lighting and air conditions of the public and private archives where visual media are stored dramatically impacts the quality of the archived material over time. It is not uncommon for photographs or video to become faded or yellowed over time or for microfiche and 8mm film to dry and crack. As a result of the ravages of time librarians, archivists, and private collectors are often faced with difficult decisions about what data they are able to continue to preserve and what format they should preserve it in. There is currently much debate among archivists about whether it would be more effective to preserve text and images contained in old books on microfiche or as digital PDF files. While only time will tell what preservation format will be selected, with new technologies emerging at such a rapid rate it is only a matter of time before these preferred archival formats once again become obsolete and another collection of valuable visual archive material is lost.

SUMMING UP AND LOOKING AHEAD

This chapter focuses on data sources that are growing in importance to many social and health scientists as they broaden their investigative strategies beyond interviewing or direct observation to include a historical dimension in their research and/ or to take advantage of existing archival sources. After first differentiating between "physical trace" and "archival" evidence, the chapter details some of the data available to researchers who seek to employ archival methods as a way of finding answers to their research questions.

The first type of data considered in detail are "official crime statistics," which are analytically deconstructed in an effort to show how a statistic of this sort is produced and to show the many qualitative elements contained in its construction. The reason for doing so is not to cast any sort of pejorative light on crime statistics per se, but rather to make the point that the same range of considerations should be implemented when one considers *any* set of archival statistics, no matter what government, agency, organization, or institution produced them. At the root of this view is the idea that we must always be prepared to ask questions about what the numbers *mean,* an approach that requires understanding something about the procedures and perspectives that combined to produce them.

The second class of archival data that we considered was the rich array of visual data found in print, television and film media, Internet image and video sharing sites, family albums, and various public and private archives. In detailing specific examples of the range of visual data that are available to social and health researchers we began to see how the inclusion of images and video offer unique opportunities for *seeing* social and historical aspects of phenomenon we are interested in that would have otherwise been hidden if we were to employ more reactive methods. While visual data possess many uniquely advantageous characteristics it is important to acknowledge that images and video are socially constructed artifacts that both reflect and are reflections of particular relations of power and privilege. As such, the images and video we draw upon to answer our research questions need to be carefully scrutinized for authenticity, credibility, and representation.

Just as we saw in earlier chapters that questioning (in Chapter 6) and observation (in Chapter 7) give one a "take" on reality (rather than "truth" itself), unobtrusive and archival measures must also be considered in the light of the methodological and organizational procedures and assumptions by which they were produced. Each technique and each data source offers only a slice of truth—using a certain implement to reveal a certain perspective. Ultimately, the researcher's task is not only to uncover these truths but also to articulate the perspectives that gave rise to them.

Of course, gathering data is not an end in itself, nor can it ever occur in a vacuum. Inductive perspectives notwithstanding, one never "just" gathers data in the hope that some self-evident truth will emerge. Even inductivists begin with an orienting strategy (see Wagner 1984) or some preliminary "commonsensical" understanding that leads them to focus on certain bits of information to the exclusion of others (e.g., see Campbell 1978). At the other extreme, deductivists are guided to particular variables by whatever theory they attempt to test or impose.

In both cases, the data that *are* gathered will be influenced by considerations of ethics and by situational constraints. No researcher can research everything, nor can one avoid pragmatic considerations in a world where research funding and data accessibility are limited. Researchers must decide what data to use; those who await "perfect" data are in for a very long wait, and will probably never do any research at all. It's no sin to use "imperfect" data; the sins arise when one begins to assume that the *available* data are necessarily the most *important* data and/or fails to continue asking about the meaning of the data and about the organizational, cultural, and/or methodological context in which they were produced.

Data are gathered for some purpose. Whether for theory generation (inductive research) or for theory probing and testing (deductive research), the business end of the research process generally involves gathering information about "what is happening" and, perhaps more important, about why or how it's happening that way. Generating and testing such explanations or theories involve not only gathering data, but gathering them in a context and according to a plan, a plan that helps researchers choose among rival plausible explanations concerning what, how, and why. Doing so involves considerations of *research design,* a topic to which we will now turn in greater detail.

A certain logic underlies matters of research design, a logic that applies broadly to both quantitative and qualitative techniques and perspectives. This logic is best appreciated in highly structured situations where social and health scientists are given complete licence to create a situation that meets their inferential needs. Accordingly, we'll begin our discussion with a detailed examination of the logic underlying the highly structured laboratory experiment. As you read Chapter 9, pay particular attention to the *logic* that underlies how inferences are made in the different settings.

STUDY QUESTIONS

1. Differentiate between *erosion measures* and *accretion measures,* and give an example of each.

2. Explain what *selective deposit* and *selective survival* are, and what implications each of these has for our ability to analyze history.

3. Monty's sister has been accepted to medical school at McGill University. He goes to visit her during the holiday break. As she gives him a tour of the buildings where her classes are held, he notices that there are pictures of every graduating class from the McGill medical school from the previous year all the way back to 1875. What are two research questions you could pose that could be addressed by an analysis of those pictures?

4. How did Vancouver's Stanley Cup riot of 2011 and the "Arab Spring" of 2011 exemplify the impact that smartphones have had on the kinds of historical archives that can be produced?

5. Skogan (1975) states that *"every statistic … is shaped by the process which operationally defines it, the procedures which capture it, and the organization which interprets it"* (17; italics in original). In what sense is this claim true of the crime rate estimates produced by the police for Statistics Canada? In what sense is it true of the crime rate estimates that are produced by victimization surveys?

6. Some criminologists (e.g., Ditton 1979) argue that crime rates based on police data have nothing to do with crime and everything to do with police involvement in social control activities. To what extent do you agree or disagree with that perspective?

7. In what ways do crime statistics exemplify the advantages and limitations of archival data cited in this chapter?

8. Three people go on a crime spree. They break into a sporting-goods store and steal several shotguns, shoot and kill the store's owner, steal a nearby car, drive the wrong way down a one-way street to make their getaway, and then speed off down the highway. How would these activities be coded using the UCR system of crime-counting?

9. A researcher wants to evaluate the impact of a Canadian law that changed in 1962, and decides to use a time-series design. What difficulties do you see immediately with a study of that type?

10. This chapter has subjected crime statistics to considerable scrutiny aimed at demonstrating the relationship between particular events and our archival record of them. Try to apply the same type of scrutiny to any other archival statistic(s) of interest to you (e.g., suicide rates, unemployment rates, hospitalization rates, abortion rates, or rates of adolescent drug use).

11. You are approached by another student who has been assigned an archival research project that looks at the portrayal of people who used marijuana during the late 1800s. They have been instructed that possible sources of data include records of parliamentary debates, pamphlets produced by local church groups, and personal correspondence between local politicians. (a) What cautionary note would you give this student regarding the pitfalls associated with selective deposit/survival? (b) How could they overcome these pitfalls/weaknesses?

12. Find out which newspapers your college, university, or municipal (public) library keeps and how many years' worth of issues they've retained. Design a quantitative and/or qualitative study that compares the way newspaper reports from different time periods treat an issue of interest to you. For example, you might look at (a) how women are portrayed in articles from the 1960s, 1970s, 1980s, 1990s and 2000s; (b) how environmental issues and/or environmental activists are portrayed in the 1960s and in the early 2000s; or (c) whether the composition of the newspaper's front page is different now than it was at the turn of the 20th century.

NOTES

1. There are, of course, other limitations that we have alluded to elsewhere in this text. For example, one limitation comes from the social position of those who write histories; in this regard, it is often the case that "history is a justification of the present," in that the elements of our collective history that we look at are those that speak to how we got where we are today. That is, historians write about those aspects of history that are relevant to *them*. Another factor, in many ways related to the first, concerns the beliefs that historians have about the "usefulness" or "preferredness" of certain forms of evidence over others. For example, European traditions place great

emphasis on documentary (written) evidence, which, coincidentally, benefits their own views of history and disadvantages other, more oral, cultures (e.g., see Wolf 1982).

2. Actually, we don't have a clue about burial practices in 14th-century France. We created this example simply for purposes of illustration. An alternative possibility is that the wealthy (who were more likely to be literate at that time) may have written their years of birth and death on their tombstones, while the poor (who were less likely to be literate) did not. If that were the case, then it would be an instance of selective deposit rather than selective survival.

3. In keeping with the issues of selective deposit and survival addressed in the previous paragraphs, remember the limitations that arise from focusing only on written materials here. Oral histories are an equally important source of historical information, as discussed in Chapter 6.

4. This example should sensitize us to the need for understanding the context in which different documents are created. Novice archival researchers are often astonished at the sorts of negative views of different groups that exist in official documents from earlier in the 20th century and before, when imperialism and colonialism were at their heights and when ethnocentric and arrogant views of "others" could be expressed with the "certainty" that no one of "their" ilk would ever read the documents. While some people may hold similar views today—and evidence of racism and intolerance is certainly everywhere—such views are much less likely, given the advent of "freedom of information" legislation and the like, to be expressed in institutional materials. Thus, even a given type of archival material, institutional records, for example, may suffer differing degrees of reactivity at different times.

5. The error that is "added" may be positive or negative; that is, error can sometimes reduce and sometimes inflate scores from their "true" value.

6. This practice varies from province to province. In some provinces, police decide whether a charge should be laid; in others, police can recommend a charge should be laid but the choice of whether to actually lay one is made by the Crown prosecutor.

7. A study by Rigakos (1994, 1995) in a Vancouver suburb is of interest here. He interviewed members of that suburb's primarily male police force and found that they, too, expressed the common belief that women "typically" would not show up in court or would refuse to testify about assault or violations of court injunctions. But when queried in detail, the officers in this study revealed that such cases were in fact quite rare, with the few that did occur having taken on a sort of "legendary" status. Rigakos (1994, 1995) interprets these data as evidence of male officers' insensitivity to the plight of women in abusive relationships and the justification that these "legends" give for their continuing inaction.

8. Note that counting procedures changed again, with the current move being toward a more incident-based approach (see Lowman & Palys 1991).

9. This has not been the case with crime statistics, however. As this chapter shows, such statistics have been subjected to considerable theoretical and empirical scrutiny (see Lowman & Palys 1991 for a more extensive review).

10. Operation Identification, a police program for preventing burglaries, operates on the assumption that clearly recognizable goods are less desirable for thieves because such goods can more easily be traced as stolen and hence are "hotter." Residents are encouraged to borrow an engraver from the police and to engrave an identifying number (e.g., their social insurance number or driver's licence number) on their valuable goods.

11. See http://www.hopeinshadows.com.

ELIMINATING RIVAL PLAUSIBLE EXPLANATIONS: THE EXPERIMENT

Thus far in this book, we've discussed general approaches to science, some of the ideals cherished by members of the scientific community, and some of the variety of ways in which information about humans is gathered. But having such data in and of themselves is not enough. The bigger question involves how we can either structure or take advantage of the existing structure of these data so that our inferences about "what's going on" are both reasonable and justifiable. These issues of inference are addressed in a group of research approaches that includes the classic experiment, quasi-experimentation, and case study analysis. In this chapter we explain how the three share a common underlying logic that involves eliminating *rival plausible explanations* to make reasonable inferences about "causes" and other processes, but vary in the degree of pre-determined structure each involves and the degree to which they emphasize either **manipulative control** or **analytic control** they employ on the road to inference.

ISOLATING CAUSES: THE CONTROLLED EXPERIMENT

It seems we are always making attributions about causes and effects in the world around us, sometimes with good reasoning and sometimes with bad. We attribute the gulf that has been developing in the relationship with our partner to the fact that they are spending too much time with their friends, or have lost interest, or are going through one of "those" times, or are simply no longer the person we thought them to be. Much superstitious behaviour comes

from causal attributions we make that may make us feel better but are unlikely to have any real causal effect: we wear a certain hat to our final exam and do well, and from then on we "always" wear our "lucky hat" to exams. But as fallible as we are, it is probably a good thing, and perhaps even a uniquely human thing that we can problem solve at a high level of abstraction and broad scope—and thereby were able to figure out where babies came from, learned which plants would poison us and which made good eating, and discovered that leaving a plot of ground fallow every once in a while would help future harvests.

But how can we ensure we do it well? Methodologists and philosophers have given considerable thought to the way we draw inferences from what we observe. Historically in the social and health sciences, experimentation, and laboratory experimentation in particular, has been seen by many as *the* route to the generation of reliable and dependable knowledge. Although research embodying experimentalist principles was being conducted long before our current canons of research were formulated (e.g., see Cook & Campbell 1979), our major contemporary debt in this realm is to John Stuart Mill, who said that, before we could say that one event or person "caused" some other effect, we had to demonstrate that three criteria held:

1. **Temporal precedence**, i.e., because we believe that causes always come *before* effects, the first criterion requires us to show that the thing we think is a cause occurred *prior* to any changes or differences that we think might have been produced by it. If a light goes on, and *then* we flip a light switch, in other words, our

flipping of the switch cannot be the reason the light went on. Only if we flip the switch and *then* the light goes on can we continue to believe that the flipping of the switch *might* be the cause of the light going on.

2. **Association** or relationship, i.e., if the alleged cause does indeed act to produce a given effect, then the second criterion we must meet is to show that changes in the putative cause co-varies in some reliable way with its alleged effect. To continue the light switch example, we would have to show that whenever we flip the switch, the light goes on, and conversely, whenever we don't flip the switch, the light does not go on. Of course the light switch is a very physical and deterministic example. In the social sciences, where causes and effects usually are not so mechanistic and many other variables can intervene, we do not expect a certain cause will necessarily happen *every* time the alleged effect is present, but we do expect it to happen "often," where "often" is typically defined as "more frequently than you would expect on the basis of chance or coincidence alone."

3. **Elimination of rival plausible explanations**, i.e., we are obliged to demonstrate that it is the putative cause per se that is responsible for changes in the dependent measure, rather than related variables, nuisance variables, artifacts, or any of myriad other potential causal agents that might have been present.

Part of the reason that the contemporary laboratory experiment is so revered is because it does such a splendid job of addressing these criteria.

THE TERMINOLOGY AND LOGIC OF EXPERIMENTATION

Experimentation begins when we recognize or create a situation that includes the phenomenon of interest to us and embodies parameters suggested by theory, or includes the intervention whose impact we wish to address. The situation or intervention does not need to exist in the real world; the lab affords us the ability to deal not only with realities that exist, but also to consider *possible* realities that *might* exist if our particular technology or organizational structures were implemented, or if the world were arranged in the manner imagined by us or our theories.

You should see how the experiment makes it possible to meet Mills's first two criteria. Because the laboratory experiment is conducted on our turf, as we arrange it, and when we want it to happen, we have the luxury of causing the cause to occur at our convenience, enabling us to be there with measurement instruments in hand (whether that be an observational schedule, or interview, or questionnaire), waiting to catch the anticipated effects when and if they occur. The *temporal precedence* criterion is met because of the manipulative control that the researcher imposes on the timing of events. The *association* or *relationship* criterion is met by seeing the extent to which change has occurred, and using statistics to assess whether the change observed is no more than you would expect on the basis of chance variation alone, or is more than that and hence worth getting excited about.

The trick is the third criterion (see Palys 1989). The problem is two-fold. First is the truism that you probably have already heard about, which is that "correlation does not necessarily equal causation." Just because two things happen to go together does not mean that one is necessarily the cause of the other. A famous example concerns fire trucks and fire damage: the more fire trucks there are at a fire, the more likely it is that the buildings they are trying to save will burn to the ground, but that does not mean that the fire trucks are causing the damage.

Second, isolating causes can be a tricky process because so many different variables intervene between cause and effect, and so many others are often occurring at the same time. We may isolate one variable as a cause—and are often encouraged to do so because of our other beliefs and philosophies—but that may say more about us than it does about the world we are trying to understand. What is the source of Canada's financial troubles? For Conservatives the "causes" are a government that has grown too large and is paying for too many services for too many Canadians who do not really need it. For Liberals it is because the government is spending too much money on fighter jets, submarines, policing, and prisons instead of social programs that will build community and prevent crime. For New Democrats the cause is the great divide in wealth that sees the rich get richer while the middle class and poor pay taxes, waiting for the "trickle-down" benefits that somehow never quite arrive. And none of them knows for sure because the Canadian economy is far too complex, driven by far too many factors, and subject to far too many external influences to isolate any particular cause.

But now let's move to a more social science type of example; we'll start with a very simple design and build from there. Suppose we want to know whether watching a series of films about immigrants' contributions to Canadian culture will influence people's attitude toward immigration policies and current immigration levels. Assuming that we've followed the procedures described earlier in this text and have constructed a reliable and valid measure of this attitude, one way to assess the impact of exposure to the films would be to measure the preliminary attitudes of a group of individuals regarding current immigration levels; show this group of people the series of films; and measure the group's attitudes once again afterward, in order to see whether any change in attitude had occurred. This process is illustrated in Figure 9.1.

Independent and Dependent Variables

Our hypothetical study has two key variables. The first variable is the one whose impact we want to assess, namely, the exposure to a series of films.

Figure 9.1

Diagram of One Way to Assess Change in Attitudes (One-Group Pretest/Posttest Design)

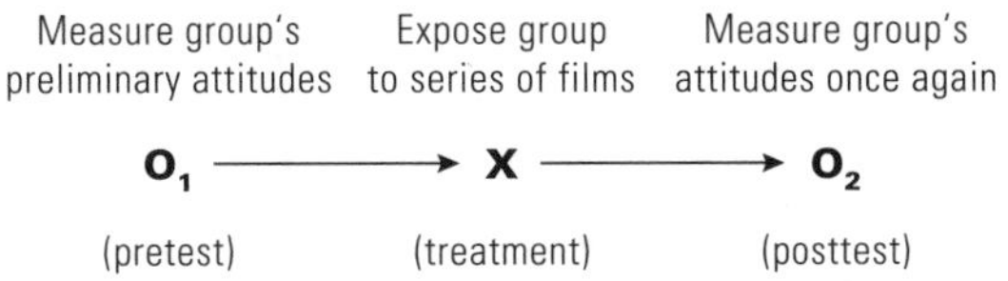

Measure group's preliminary attitudes	Expose group to series of films	Measure group's attitudes once again
O_1	⟶ X ⟶	O_2
(pretest)	(treatment)	(posttest)

The second is the one we measure in order to see whether any effect has indeed occurred, namely, attitudes toward current immigration levels. Note that the choice of which variable to impose or manipulate (i.e., exposure to the films) represents a decision we make *independently* of the actual execution of our study. This variable whose impact we are trying to assess is known appropriately enough as the **independent variable** or the **treatment variable**.

How about the other variable in our study, i.e., the attitudes that we are attempting to measure? What level or values will they take on in the actual study? We can't really answer that question until we actually do the study, since the values that variable takes on will *depend* on who is in our subject sample, what their attitudes are, and how potent or effective the independent variable actually is in causing change. Rather than being independent of the actual execution of the study (as was the case with the films), the values that the attitude variable takes on are very much *dependent* on what happens during the actual execution of the study. This variable is known as the **dependent variable** or **outcome variable**.

Internal Validity

Suppose that we do the study and find that, following exposure to the films, there *is* a change in our dependent measure. What can we conclude from that observation? We might *like* to conclude that the change we observed was attributable to the independent variable of interest (i.e., the film series). But how confident can we be in drawing that inference?

It's time to introduce a major concept: the **internal validity** of a study. This term, coined by Campbell and Stanley (1963), refers to *the extent to which differences observed in the study can be* unambiguously *attributed to the experimental treatment itself, rather than to other factors.* In other words, to what extent can we be confident that the differences we observe are caused by the independent variable per se, rather than by other, rival plausible explanations? In the current example, how confident can we be that it was the film series that caused the change? Or could it have been something else?

But what else could it have been? After defining the term, Campbell and Stanley (1963) delineate a number of classes of "threats" (i.e., concerns or rival plausible explanations) that one should keep in mind when assessing internal validity. A number of these are relevant to our hypothetical research design.

POSSIBLE THREATS TO INTERNAL VALIDITY

HISTORY The first potential threat to internal validity is **history**, which refers in pretest/posttest designs to the *specific events occurring between the first and second measurement in addition to the independent variable.* In other words, what other events might have occurred between the pretest and posttest that might also account for the results that we observed? In our hypothetical study, *many* events other than the film series might have occurred that could also have led our respondents to change their attitudes. They might have seen newspaper articles or TV shows about immigration successes or have been exposed to classroom materials dealing with immigration policies. How do we know it wasn't one of those *other* factors or variables that caused a change in attitude, rather than the films we showed? In the research design we have right now, there's no way we can tell for sure.

MATURATION Another type of threat to internal validity noted by Campbell and Stanley (1963) is **maturation**, defined as *processes within the research participants themselves that change as a function of time* per se (i.e., not specific to particular events), such as growing older, more tired, more hungry, and so on. This threat draws our attention to the fact that sometimes changes occur merely because of biological processes that happen over time, and we must be careful to recognize those processes and their effects when we're assessing the effects of other independent variables.

For example, suppose we come to you with a pill and suggest it will help children learn to walk. In order to demonstrate the effectiveness of this pill, we first acquire a sample of six-month old children, none of whom can walk. We give each of the children (or their parents) a box of the pills, with the instruction that the children are to take one pill a month for a year. One year later, we come back and find that every single one of the children (now one-and-a-half years old) knows how to walk. The design would be like that depicted in Figure 9.2. Were the pills effective? Maybe. But a rather compelling rival plausible explanation would be that it wasn't the *pills* that caused the change, but rather maturational change within the children (i.e., physical processes like bone development, physical competence, coordination) that now allowed them to walk. In other words, they probably would have learned to walk anyway, with or without the pills.[1]

The above example may seem fairly obvious, but it shows how maturational processes can threaten internal validity. Sometimes, though, the effects of maturational processes are more subtle and, consequently, ignored. Returning to our immigration example, suppose we start by giving a questionnaire in the morning about immigration policies (i.e., our pretest), spend a solid eight hours showing various films to our research participants, and end the day by again giving the questionnaire on current immigration policies (the posttest). In the end, we find that our participants show more hostile attitudes and appear to be more critical of immigrants. Can we conclude that exposure to the films caused the change in attitude?

The films *may* have caused the change. And historical factors wouldn't be a threat to that conclusion, since our participants have been insulated

Figure 9.2
A Pretest/Posttest-Only Design Showing Effects Pertaining to Maturational Processes

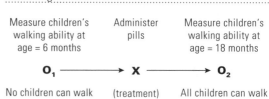

from other events (e.g., news media reports). But look what we've done. We've required our participants to put in a long day, given them no opportunity to have lunch, and kept them busy doing our questionnaire and viewing our films. What happens to people in that type of situation? Many people get tired and hungry; over the course of a long, demanding day, they may also become more impatient, terse, and grumpy. Because of these physiologically based "maturational" changes, in other words, we might expect that by the time of the posttest, participants will have become slightly more hostile in their responses to our questions. Can we therefore conclude that the *films* caused the change to more critical attitudes? Although we might like to do so (given our interests), we would also have to consider (as a rival plausible explanation) that maturational changes may have caused the change.

TESTING A third threat to internal validity is **testing**, specifically, *the effects of taking a test on scores in the second testing*. Such effects can operate in several different ways. Having taken a test, you may become sensitized to the issue involved in a way that you wouldn't have been otherwise. Suppose somebody gives you a questionnaire regarding your attitudes about current immigration levels. The mere fact that you were administered the questionnaire may lead you to be more sensitive to, or more likely to pay attention to, related material that's presented in the press, on TV, on the radio, or in your classes. When you then receive the posttest after the administration of the independent variable, and it turns out your attitudes have changed, researchers can't be sure whether the change was produced by the independent variable or by the greater sensitization to issues induced by the pretest. Consequently, this phenomenon, known as **pretest sensitization**, is a threat to internal validity. Why? Because it offers a rival plausible explanation for the source of change.

Another way in which testing can threaten internal validity is through *practice effects*. If we

were trying to assess your abilities, for example, it would be difficult to know in the posttest situation whether you had improved purely because of the practice the pretest gave you or because of the independent variable we had imposed on you.

REGRESSION TOWARD THE MEAN

A related yet very different threat to internal validity is known as **statistical regression** or **regression toward the mean**. Recall that, with testing, we were talking about *real* change occurring between pretest and posttest (e.g., because of practice, sensitization to issues, or greater motivation); in such a situation, the threat to internal validity relates to uncertainty about whether the independent variable or the testing effect was the source of the change.

With statistical regression, we also observe a change, but in this instance, the change is more illusory than real. We know that any measuring we do is subject to a certain amount of random error, no matter how many precautions we take to minimize it. Many (if not most) times, these positive and negative chance influences will be distributed equally across a group, or across time for a particular individual, so that in the long run, the *average* score of a particular individual or group will be a good indication of their "true" score. But on any given occasion, chance events may "stack up" in a positive or negative direction. Also known as regression toward the mean, statistical regression refers to *the propensity of extreme scorers on the first testing to score closer to the mean (average) of the group on the second testing*. This phenomenon occurs because chance events are unlikely ever to stack up to precisely the same degree on two successive occasions.

Let's take LeBron James as an example. In case you haven't heard of him, LeBron James plays for the Miami Heat, a National Basketball Association (NBA) team. An astoundingly good basketball player, he dominates a game in the manner of a Michael Jordan or a Magic Johnson, averaging roughly 30 points a game. But even LeBron James has good games and bad games. Basketball fans know that James is a great basketball player because they observe his performance over the course of a whole season year after year. But in the social and health sciences, we rarely have the luxury of such extended observation. Instead, our situation is often more like that of the person who goes to only one basketball game in which LeBron James happens to be playing.

Suppose this person goes to a basketball game to assess how good a basketball player LeBron James is. And suppose James has a great night: he can't do anything wrong, and he ends up scoring 50 points. If, on the basis of that single assessment, our observer concludes that "LeBron James is amazing; he gets 50 points a game," basketball fans know that the observer is *overestimating* James's "true" ability. But (and here's the important part) what if the same observer goes to see LeBron James play in a *second* basketball game later in the same season? The last time s/he saw James, the basketball player scored 50 points, but his *average* is about 30 points a game. Now, if you were a betting person, would you bet that on this second occasion LeBron James will (1) do even better than he did last time and score more than 50 points this time, (2) do the same as he did last time and score exactly 50 points, or (3) do more poorly than he did last time and score fewer than 50 points?

If you picked (1) or (2), please send us your name and address: we could use the money. James *may* get 50 points or more in this second game, but the likelihood is much higher that he will perform more in keeping with his average or typical performance and get something closer to 30 points. This is true *not* because James has changed or because of anything special that might have happened between the two games, but purely because the first performance was atypically high due to chance factors. This phenomenon—the tendency of extreme scores to move ("regress" is the technical term) closer to the mean on a subsequent testing—is known as *statistical regression* or *regression toward the mean*. The more extreme the first score, the greater this propensity.[2]

Regression toward the mean threatens internal validity whenever a group is picked *because* of the extremity of their scores on a pretest. For example, suppose that in the study concerning attitudes about current immigration levels, we decide to administer our immigration questionnaire to 100 people and then pick the 20 people from that group who were apparently *least* in favour of current immigration levels (i.e., the 20 people with the lowest scores on the pretest) to see whether exposing them to our film series will lead them to temper their attitudes somewhat. Although we're confident about the reliability and validity of our scale, there will *always* be *some* degree of error in the scores. And as argued above, the odds are high that to the extent that we've erred in assessing our group's attitudes toward current immigration levels, the errors among the *lowest* scorers will likely be errors of *under*estimation (e.g., see Figure 9.3). Since on a second testing, the *chance* errors that contributed to the extremity of those low scores are unlikely to stack up to the same degree as before, the scores on the second testing will be less extreme (i.e., closer to the mean of the group). Thus, it will *look* as though there's been attitude change (because the average score changes), but all we've *really* witnessed is that phenomenon known as regression toward the mean. And we'll be uncertain as to what extent the change we observe is attributable to the independent variable (i.e., the film series) or to the regression artifact. As Cook and Campbell (1979) say,

> statistical regression (1) operates to increase obtained pretest-posttest gain scores among low pretest scores, since this group's pretest scores are more likely to have been depressed by error; (2) operates to decrease obtained change scores among persons with high pretest scores since their pretest scores are likely to have been inflated by error; and (3) does not affect obtained change scores among scorers at the center of the pretest distribution since the group is likely to contain as many units whose pretest scores are inflated by error as units whose pretest scores are deflated by it. (52–53)

History, maturation, testing, and statistical regression are the only threats to internal validity we will deal with at this time. But keep in mind that

Figure 9.3

The Different Propensity of Scores from Three Areas of the Normal Distribution for Regression toward the Mean

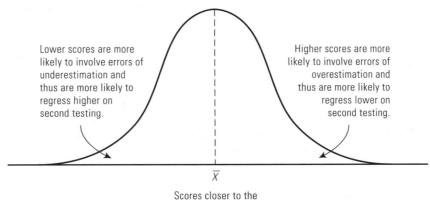

Lower scores are more likely to involve errors of underestimation and thus are more likely to regress higher on second testing.

Higher scores are more likely to involve errors of overestimation and thus are more likely to regress lower on second testing.

$\overline{X}$

Scores closer to the mean are equally likely to involve errors of overestimation as underestimation and thus, overall, will not change on second testing.

selection biases (see Chapter 4's discussion of sampling) and **instrumentation** changes (see Chapter 8's discussion of archival methods) may also threaten internal validity. Those interested in further reading should consult Campbell and Stanley (1963), or Shadish, Cook, and Campbell (2001).

The main point here is that, in any study, one should always ask *why* a particular result was observed. Did the independent variable produce the result, or could it have been produced by something else, i.e., some rival plausible explanation? In our hypothetical study, how confident are we that the changes in attitudes regarding current immigration levels were produced (caused) by the film series and not by something else? Given the *one-group pretest/ posttest design* we have so far, we can't be very confident at all that the film series caused the change; in other words, we have low internal validity. Somehow we have to overcome that problem.

Controlling for Rival Plausible Explanations

While the one group pretest-posttest design did an admirable job of addressing the first two of Mills's

criteria—we saw that a change happened and that it came after the putative cause we were testing—it failed miserably on the third. There were just too many *rival plausible explanations* that might also account for the observed result. The most common way to deal with that problem is to incorporate a second group into our design—known as a **control group** or **comparison group**. The control group starts off the same as our first group (the experimental group) and is treated identically to the experimental group in *all* respects *except* the control group *doesn't* receive the independent variable. This gives us the design shown in Figure 9.4: the *pretest/posttest control group design*. In our hypothetical study, our control group would receive the pretest and the posttest at the same times as the experimental group, but *wouldn't* be exposed to the film series. Instead, the control group might quietly sit and wait, watch a travelogue about a surfing contest in Waikiki, or do something else that kept them busy for the same amount of time and at the same type of activity as the experimental group but that wasn't directly related to attitudes regarding immigrants or immigration policies.

Figure 9.4

A Pretest/Posttest Control Group Design

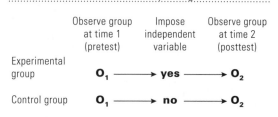

Suppose we do this study and obtain the results shown in Table 9.1. The control group's scores have changed slightly, but nowhere near as much as those of the experimental group. Now can we confidently assert that the changes in attitudes in the experimental group were a function of the film series rather than of rival plausible explanations?

Our internal validity in this case is actually fairly high. The best way to see this is to *try out* some rival plausible explanations to see what happens. Could the experimental group's attitudes have changed because of *history*? Maybe, but probably not. Why? Because the control group (as a group) was subject to those same historical factors, and their scores didn't change much at all. Could *maturation* have entered in? Maybe, but the control group had the same time delay between pretest and posttest, and it didn't cause them to change. Well, how about the effects of *testing?* Once again, pretest sensitization can't account for the results, because it would have had an equivalent effect on the control group, and they didn't change at all. So why did the experimental group change their attitudes? Given that the experimental and control groups were equal to begin with (as shown by their similar pretest scores), and given that they were treated alike in every respect except for the imposition of

the independent variable, the most likely explanation is that any change in the experimental group that wasn't observed in the control group must have been a function of the one element on which they differed: the film series.

The control group doesn't always have to be a "do nothing" group. *Control* groups are simply *comparison* groups that help us isolate and assess the impact or influence of particular variables. Accordingly, the nature of a control group will depend on what you're trying to assess, within the constraint of ethical considerations. Let's take two examples.

In the first example, imagine that you want to assess the effects that viewing explicitly sexual films has on those who view them. Your experimental group will thus comprise people to whom you show a sexually explicit film. In order to assess the effects of the film *per se*, you must choose an appropriate comparison group, a group that's similar to the experimental group in all respects, except that this group doesn't view a film with sexually explicit content. Let's say that the sexually explicit film you're showing is 30 minutes long. The procedures require that you welcome your experimental group to the lab, explain the nature of their participation, answer any questions, take them to the viewing room, and then give them a posttest measure. What would be an appropriate control group?

One possibility is simply to have a control group of people who come in, complete a pretest, sit around for 30 minutes, and then complete a posttest. But such an approach creates more differences between the experimental and control groups than mere exposure to a sexually explicit film. Those who watch the sexual film have a whole range of experiences besides watching the film itself; for example,

Table 9.1

Hypothetical Results for the Pretest/Posttest Control Group Design in Figure 9.4

	Pretest Scores	Impose Independent Variable	Posttest Scores
Experimental group	Average score = 43.6	yes	Average score = 58.6
Control group	Average score = 44.1	no	Average score = 46.8

they receive the degree of attention (including instructions and explanations) accorded to people who are central to the research, and their attention is focused by a TV or film screen that they've been asked to watch.

A control group that comes in and does nothing, therefore, not only doesn't see the sexually explicit material, but also doesn't receive the same degree of attention from the experimenter and doesn't have their attention monopolized by a screen. Thus, when you come to the end of the study and want to evaluate internal validity, you can't tell for sure whether any differences between the two groups are due to the film, the attention paid to people, or to diverting their attention to a screen. A better procedure would involve giving everyone in the control group the same attention you give those in the experimental group, and showing them a film, too, but ensuring that it contains absolutely no sexual content. In that way, you duplicate all aspects of the experimental group's experience except for the one element whose effects you wish to test: that is, the effects of viewing a sexually explicit film.

For the second example, consider someone who has developed a new drug, treatment program, or counselling approach that is used for people in need (e.g., for depressed patients). At the moment, suppose that these people receive "Don't Worry, Be Happy" (DWBH) counselling that focuses on the counter-productiveness of compulsive worrying. People who use that method have a decent success rate, but you think that your program may be better, so you set out to evaluate its effectiveness. Your experimental group thus will comprise people who receive your new program. But what is an appropriate control group here?

A "do nothing" control group would be problematic in two ways. First, it would be a problem for the same reason noted in the preceding paragraph regarding the assessment of the effects of the sexually explicit film, that is, "attending a counselling program" and "doing nothing" differ on many more variables than just the content of the therapy. To counteract that, you might have the control group come in for equal periods of time and engage in some other form of interactive activity (e.g., playing table tennis for an equivalent time period).

But ethical issues arise whenever you engage in research with people in need. "Doing nothing" may be a violation of your ethical obligation to ensure, to the best of your ability, the well-being of people under your care. Because of this, researchers in this situation will often use the "best known treatment" or "usual treatment" (the DWBH counselling, in this instance) as their basis of comparison.

The research question then changes from "Does the new program *work?*" (a question that implies a comparison between giving the program and doing nothing) to "Does the new program work *any better* than what we do already?" (a question that implies a comparison between giving the new program and giving the old one). Often in such instances, the evaluation will measure many more variables than simple "treatment success," thereby allowing comparisons between treatments on other dimensions. It might be found, for example, that the new treatment is no different from the existing treatment in terms of success of treatment, but that it achieves that success at significant cost savings, allows clients to go home more quickly, has fewer side effects, or is less intrusive.

As the above discussion reveals, the logic of experimental design goes like this: *if* you have two (or more) groups who are equal to begin with and if you treat them equally in all respects *except* one (that being exposure versus non-exposure to the independent variable), any subsequent differences between the groups must be attributable to the one variable on which the groups differed. *Control* and *comparison groups* play a valuable function in empirical research by allowing one to isolate a particular reason behind any change that is observed. They're called "control" groups because they help control for rival plausible explanations.

ENSURING INITIAL GROUP EQUIVALENCE

One point was glossed over in the preceding discussion. Thus far, we've said that *if we can assume our experimental and control groups were equal to begin with* and if we use appropriate controls, high internal validity will result. The italicized phrase refers to the **assumption of pretest equivalence**. But it includes a very big "if." How reasonable is the assumption that our groups are, in fact, equal to begin with?

In some instances, the assumption of pretest equivalence can't be made at all. This is typically the case in many *existing groups* situations. For example, suppose we want to evaluate whether jail or the imposition of a fine is more effective in reducing the likelihood that people will re-offend. To do this, we get a sample of 1,000 people who have been sentenced to jail and 1,000 people who have been fined, and then see how many in each group commit another offence during a two-year follow-up period. Would comparing these two rates tell us the relative effectiveness of the two sanctions in reducing recidivism? No. Why not? Because the two groups likely differed on many attributes other than type of sanction; that is, they probably also differed in terms of offence committed, prior record, or other variables that are also plausible alternative influences on our dependent variable.

The same is true whenever groups are formed on something other than a chance basis. Allowing *self-selection* or *volunteer selection* (i.e., letting people choose the groups in which they want to be), for example, can be problematic. Suppose we want to evaluate the effectiveness of a "defensive driving" course. We offer such a course to 16-year-olds at a local high school; some students sign up for it, whereas others do not. Two years after the course is completed we compare accident records for all those students who received a licence and find that those who took the course have been involved in significantly fewer accidents than those who didn't. Was the course effective? Well, maybe. But it's also possible that the two groups were not equal to begin with. Those who "self-selected" themselves into the course may have done so because of a greater concern over safe driving and, hence, might have been expected to have fewer accidents whether or not they took the course.

The opposite might happen when membership in the experimental group is *mandatory*, for example, where people charged with impaired or dangerous driving are sentenced by the courts to take a safe-driving course. In this instance, we might well find that the "experimental" group does more *poorly* than a control group of other drivers picked at random—not because the course is poor, but because the process of group assignment created an experimental group that included those with poorer driving records and less skill and/or less motivation to drive carefully.

In either case, differences in motivation or concern may "cause" any subsequent differences in accident rates, rather than the driving course per se. Selection biases threaten internal validity by making the source of the observed change more ambiguous (i.e., increasing rather than reducing the number of rival plausible explanations).

In sum, selection biases form another possible threat to the internal validity of experimental research. So how can we ensure that our assumption of pretest equivalence is tenable, thereby enhancing internal validity? There are two major ways to do so: *random assignment* and *matching*.

RANDOM ASSIGNMENT Given that you have a group of people ready to participate in your research, **random assignment** is achieved by letting "chance" be the *sole* determinant of which group (i.e., experimental or control) any given person is a member of. You might, for example, cut a deck of cards before each person comes to see you, with a red card indicating that the next person will go into the control group and a black card meaning he or she will go into the experimental group. Or you might flip a coin or use a table of random numbers. *Any* purely chance process is fine. Any procedure that's *not* a chance process (e.g., using existing groups, letting participants choose the group in which they want to be, putting the neediest or the first to arrive in the experimental group) is inferentially problematic.

Random assignment, coupled with adequate group sizes (e.g., at least 30 per group), allows you to assume, with a reasonable degree of confidence, that the two (or more) groups, on average, are fairly equal on all pre-experimental variables everything from their "average" attitude about nuclear disarmament to their average shoe size. Another way of looking at it is to assert that you have no reason *not* to assume that the groups are equal to begin with. And if they're similar overall in all respects, those variables have been equalized (or "held constant across groups") and hence can't threaten internal validity.

We have found that there is a common misunderstanding that novice researchers have about threats to internal validity that warrants explanation here. Let's take the example we used earlier that involved seeing whether exposure to a certain film series might change people's attitudes about appropriate levels of immigration. To do so, we randomly assign a large number of people to one of two groups: the experimental group views a film series that shows some of the many immigration successes we see in Canada; a control group, in contrast, sees a film series dealing with traffic safety (i.e., a topic that has nothing to do with immigration issues). In the end, we find that the group who viewed the immigration film series expresses significantly more positive attitudes toward Canada's immigration policies than the group who watched the unrelated films. When we use this example in our classes, we invite criticism of the design; more than one student has said, "But what if there are a few recent immigrants in the experimental group; wouldn't they be more positively disposed to immigration anyway?" or "What if there's someone in there who had a recent negative experience with an immigrant; wouldn't that bias the results?"

While such people certainly exist, and may well find their way into our study, random assignment allows you to assume that these people will be *equally distributed* across all the groups in the study. Thus, while the experimental group may have some relatively recent immigrants in it, random assignment allows you to assume that there are probably just as many recent immigrants in the control group. Similarly, the two groups also will be equal, on average, in terms of the overall positivity or negativity of their experiences with immigrants.

Thus, even though we can think of lots of possible "contaminants" that might threaten the internal validity of our design, the question is always whether, overall, we have any reason to expect that such people will be *differentially* assigned to either of the two groups. No matter how many such "contaminants" we can think of, as long as the two (or more) groups are equally affected by their presence, then the two groups remain "equal overall to begin with," and internal validity is not threatened.

Note that the power of random assignment allows an alternative to the pretest/posttest control group design. This new design, which is called the *posttest-only control group design*, is illustrated in Figure 9.5. The pretest is considered redundant in this design, since one can *assume* that the groups are equal to begin with; thus, this design circumvents the problems associated with pretest sensitization (which cannot occur if there is no pretest).

In sum, random assignment is a very powerful research procedure that directly addresses the crucial experimental assumption that your experimental and control groups are equal in all respects *before* you impose or administer your independent variable—the assumption of pretest equivalence. But random assignment has some limitations. Chance does occasionally play little tricks on us. Even though you flip a "fair" coin 10 times, and it *should* come down heads about half the time, and it usually does follow that pattern (or close to it), it may well happen that heads comes up every time— or never. Similarly, if we randomly assign people to groups, we assume that the groups are equal in all respects, but occasionally it might not work out

Figure 9.5

The Posttest-Only Control Group Design

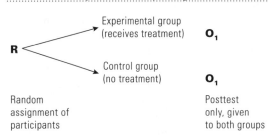

that way. Thus, if we rely on random assignment, we'll generally be in fine shape but may occasionally be surprised.

The likelihood of being surprised in that way, however, is strongly related to group size. If our group size is small (i.e., fewer than 30 per group, and especially 10 or fewer per group), the chances rise of our getting an uneven distribution of characteristics between groups. Thus, researchers who rely on random assignment to create equivalent groups with small sample sizes are playing with fire, although even in that case it is noteworthy that the researcher is letting nothing other than chance influence assignment to groups and thereby creating a "fair" test and avoiding "stacking the deck" in one direction or the other. But what can you do if you have no choice but to use small samples and/or if you're unwilling to put your faith in chance? A second technique for ensuring group equivalence is known as *matching*.

MATCHING While random assignment allows you to *assume* pretest equivalence, the **matching** process intentionally *creates* equivalence. In our study regarding attitudes toward immigration policies, for example, we may choose to match the groups on their pretest scores *or* (more typically) on some variable(s) we know to be related to attitudes regarding immigration policies (e.g., political conservatism, attitudes toward minority groups, authoritarianism). To show you how this would be done, let's use the example of matching groups on political affiliation.

To begin with, we have a bit of a procedural problem, because we obviously first need to know all our research participants' expressed political preferences. If we can get this information, we can look for matched pairs of individuals (e.g., two New Democrats, two supporters of the Bloc Québecois, two Liberals, two Conservatives, another two New Democrats, two Green Party members, etc.). For each pair, we might flip a coin to assign one individual to the experimental group and the other to the control group. In this way, we'd be guaranteed groups that are constituted equally with respect to political affiliation, and hence (since political affiliation is related to views regarding immigration

policies) on pretest attitudes regarding immigration policies as well.

While the strength of matching lies in the fact that using this technique *ensures* pretest equivalence, its main weakness lies in the pragmatics of using it. Good matching technique requires that we identify "good" variables on which to match and that the information on which we're basing our matching is available. Achieving both of these conditions is often easier said than done.

In addition, matching very quickly gets out of hand if you try to match participants on more than one variable. For example, suppose we want to match respondents on sex, education, religion, political preference, and income. In order to create matched pairs on all five variables, we might have to find two "male Protestants with less than grade 10 education who vote Conservative and make between $20,000 and $30,000 per year," two "female Catholics with some university education who vote NDP and made more than $30,000 last year," and so on, depending on the particular people in our sample. Needless to say, this becomes a very complex and difficult task.

Random assignment, in contrast, is easy. Theoretically, one can use random assignment to create groups whose average units are essentially equivalent with respect to sex, age, political affiliation, attitudes regarding immigration policies, how they feel about their mothers, authoritarianism, height, how long it has been since their last bath, and all other variables, both interesting and mundane. In sum, matching (at least within the controlled experiment) hardly seems worth the effort, and might be justified only when sample sizes are too small for random assignment.

EXTERNAL VALIDITY Our focus so far has been entirely on *internal validity*: the extent to which *differences between groups* can be unambiguously attributed to the experimental treatment. But there are three other types of validity on which any given study can be evaluated: **external validity**, **ecological validity**, and **statistical conclusion validity**. (Note that there are numerous other types of validity we haven't yet considered; some will be addressed later in this book, whereas others are included in more specialized texts.)

External validity refers to the *generalizability of results beyond the specifics of the study*. As you now know, doing research involves applying relatively abstract, theoretical concerns to very concrete situations. Suppose our theoretical interest is in assessing the relationship between "anxiety" and "performance." Following the literature in this area, we might say that there is a curvilinear relationship between these two concepts (see Figure 9.6): performance is optimal when anxiety is at a moderate level and poorest when anxiety is either very high *or* very low.

Our *theoretical* interest lies in the relationship between *all* types of anxiety and *all* types of performance in *all* situations and across *all* people. But we obviously can't be everywhere and do everything at once. Rather, we must become very concrete in how we assess these variables. For "anxiety," we might choose to focus on the anxiety that some students feel when they write exams, and we might operationalize "anxiety" as the response people give when asked "Please rate how anxious you feel right now, on a 10-point scale," as they sit down to write their final exam in this research methods course. For "performance," we might decide to look at the grade the students receive on that final exam. Our sample of research participants might include all

Figure 9.6

The Theoretical relationship between Anxiety and Performance, According to the Yerkes-Dodson (1908) Law

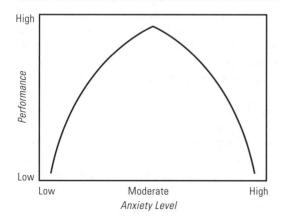

students taking your research methods course this semester.

Suppose that, having done the study just described, we do indeed find the curvilinear relationship between "anxiety" and "performance" we hypothesized. What have we found? In a literal sense, all we have found is that when one class of this semester's research methods students sat down to write the final exam, their self-reported levels of anxiety were curvilinearly related to their grades on the exam. But, ultimately (theoretically), that's not what we're interested in; our study was just one of many possible studies we could have done to assess the *theoretical* anxiety–performance relationship in which we're interested. Thus, we'd want to know whether the results we observed were obtained merely because of the specifics of our study or whether they reflect the more general relationship between anxiety and performance.

In sum, we are interested in the *generalizability* of our results to other people, situations, and times. Would we have obtained the same results if we'd done the study with other students? In other courses? In other semesters? If we'd taken physiological rather than self-report measures of anxiety? If we'd looked at anxiety in a job interview or before giving a speech rather than in an exam situation? Or if we'd used a measure of performance other than grades? These are obviously all empirical questions that could eventually be addressed in other research. In the interim, they suggest that we'd be wise to consider the limitations of what we've achieved and to be cautious in how far we extrapolate.

Before concluding this discussion, let us reaffirm that *external validity* refers to the extent to which one's results are generalizable beyond the specifics of the current research project. It *doesn't necessarily* have anything to do with how *representative* one's sample is. Suppose we acquire a sample of male first-year university students who play on the football team. We prick each one with a needle on the baby finger of his right hand. Each time we do this, the finger bleeds. Now, male first-year university student football players probably aren't representative of anyone other than male first-year university student football players, but the *result* that we observe here (i.e., they bleed when we prick their fingers) is probably *generalizable* to many other kinds of people as well; hence, we could say that the result or finding has high external validity. But if we ask all these football players how they feel about Canadian foreign policy regarding Libya, the results we obtain will probably *not* be generalizable to other groups; hence, external validity on that question would be low. External validity doesn't *necessarily* depend on the representativeness of the sample per se; rather, it depends on the nature of the phenomenon with which one is dealing and on one's research objectives.

ECOLOGICAL VALIDITY As we've seen, the question of *external validity* is both a statistical and a theoretical one. Our particular experiment is basically a sample of all the experiments that could have been done to assess the theoretical relationship under investigation, so the issue that concerns us is the representativeness of our particular experiment with respect to that theoretical universe. But there's another type of validity—*ecological validity*—that's a little more pragmatic in its sensitivities and that's especially relevant when there's a particular kind of situation to which we are interested in generalizing. It can be considered a type of external validity, since it also addresses issues of representativeness and generalizability, although it does so in a slightly different way.

The term *ecological validity*, first used by Brunswik (1955), refers to the representativeness of the treatments and measures you use in relation to the particular milieu to which you wish to generalize. For example, let's return to the anxiety-performance study described above. In the earlier example, we were interested in the *theoretical* connection between anxiety and performance: the particular experiment we did was therefore one of many studies that could have been done that embodied the key constructs specified by the theory.

But suppose we now want to take a more *applied* approach and are interested in studying anxiety and performance in the classroom. We might very well

end up designing the very same study—one that looks at the relationship between pre-exam anxiety and exam performance—but our analysis of it would be quite different. Here, instead of asking how well the experiment's conditions represent the theoretical universe, our question becomes how well the situation represents the kinds of situations to which we're interested in generalizing, that is, how well does the experiment represent the social *ecology* of our situation of interest?

In this example, ecological validity would be fairly high, since we're using real students who are experiencing real anxiety of a type that commonly occurs in classrooms and who are engaged in an ecologically relevant task (the exam) with real consequences (their final grade) on the line. But it's easy to imagine other studies that aren't so clearly connected to their real-world counterparts.

For example, consider one line of research in which researchers were interested in learning about how we form our impressions of people. Typical studies in that area investigate how we combine information about people, how we resolve conflicting information about people, and how different aspects of our history or character affect the impressions people have of us. One series of studies investigated the way that wearing glasses can affect impressions. In study after study, the experiments demonstrated that if you show photos of people either wearing glasses or not wearing glasses to the typical sample of volunteer undergraduate research participants and ask them to rate the people in the pictures on myriad different dimensions (like intelligence, sincerity, and honesty), participants will quite reliably rate people with glasses on more highly on those dimensions than people who aren't wearing them.

The nice thing about using an experiment to test this effect is that taking that approach offers tremendous control over the situation: you can actually have participants rate the *same people* with and without glasses, thus controlling for other differences, such as attractiveness. Now, if you wear glasses as well as contact lenses, does this mean you should wear your glasses to job interviews to get an edge over all those people with 20:20 eyesight?

At first glance it would seem so. The results of those studies, in addition to being *internally* valid, were also very high in *external* validity: different researchers in different settings at different times using different subject groups have produced the same result again and again and again. However, the experiment isn't particularly *ecologically* valid. Recall that we're trying to learn about how people really form impressions about others. But there are actually very few situations in which people are required to form impressions based on a single variable alone. Even if we must generate an impression from just looking at a photo of someone, we instantly see not only whether s/he wears glasses, but also her/his attactiveness, approximate age, style (e.g., hair, clothing, jewellery, tattoos, etc.), demeanour, and other factors, any or all of which might also influence the impression we form. And how often do we really make judgments on the basis of just a picture alone? When we meet people at parties, are introduced by good friends, or learn about them in job interviews, we also can talk to the person; hear about her/his attitudes and values; glean more information from the way s/he dresses, acts, and talks about himself or herself; and so on.

Thus, while the "glasses" experiments may have high *internal* validity, and their results may have fairly good *external* validity, they may well have poor *ecological* validity, because the experiments fail to simulate the kinds of situations we're most interested in understanding. That state of affairs creates a certain irony: it becomes possible to create knowledge that's true in *theory* but misleading in *practice*. The results of the glasses experiment show that glasses *can* make a difference, but whether they *do* make a difference in a real-world evaluative situation is another issue entirely.

Indeed, some years later Michael Argyle of Oxford University—a primarily laboratory-based experimental social psychologist who was beginning to consider the role of context in experimentation—extended the basic "glasses effect" research in an interesting way. Instead of making "glasses versus no glasses" the *only* piece of information that raters knew about a person, Argyle *began* by gathering the "first impression" data (showing that he could replicate the well-known "glasses effect"), but then simply let the scene run further: the people in the pictures started talking about their interests, values, and experiences. The end result? Not surprisingly, under those conditions there was *no* "glasses effect."

In sum, the "glasses effect" is "true" in the sense that it can be reliably replicated by any experimenter who wants to perform the study, but it's true *only in particular circumstances* within the strict confines of the laboratory, that is, when "glasses versus no glasses" is the *only* information people have on which to base their judgments. As soon as they have access to other information they can use, the "glasses effect" no longer occurs; what previously seemed like such an important variable (when it was the only variable under consideration) faded into nothing. Because of this, many authors (e.g., Manicas & Secord 1983; Palys & Lowman 1984) suggest that while the purely theoretical "can" questions are eminently suitable to experimental analysis, an experiment may *not* be a particularly useful launching point for the "does" questions unless ecological validity—how well our research conditions represent the important elements of the context to which we wish to generalize (e.g., see Palys 1978; Palys & Lowman 1984)—is explicitly considered.

Statistical Conclusion Validity

Suppose you watch someone who has a $1 coin. He flips it once and get tails. He flips it again … and get tails. Once again … and it's tails. Another flip … another tail. Another flip … another tail. If he continues flipping the coin and continues getting tails, at some point you'd probably begin to suspect that the coin is rigged, that he's not reporting truthfully, or that he's not flipping correctly. Ted has in fact done just this in his undergraduate research methods classes on a few occasions. Students usually start voicing suspicions after the fourth or fifth tail in a row. Why do you think that happens?

From experience, we "know" that there are two possible outcomes when we flip a coin: heads or tails. The probability of getting tails on any given flip of the coin is 1 out of 2. The joint probability of getting tails twice in a row is 1 out of 4. For three in a row, it's 1 in 8. The event "four tails in a row" has a joint probability of 1 in 16. And the joint probability of getting five tails in a row is 1 out of 32.

When Ted starts flipping a $1 coin in his class, people seem to assume that he's flipping a "fair" coin and that he's accurately reporting what he sees. There's nothing unusual about a coin coming up tails when you flip it. Nor is there anything especially atypical about getting two tails in a row. Three in a row might be worth a chuckle, but still represent no particular problem. But four in a row? Suddenly people start to wonder. That *is* a fair coin, isn't it? Five in a row? What's going on? Note that we *start* by supposing that "nothing special" is going on, that chance alone is operating, and that the rules of probability theory apply. When what we see deviates only slightly from what we'd expect by chance alone, we might find the oddity interesting or cute, but strange things do sometimes happen, so we likely don't question our assumptions. There comes a point, though, when what we observe is a little *too* atypical; that's when we start to question whether it's really chance alone that's operating or whether something else is going on.

Researchers in the social and health sciences go through much the same sort of process when they come to the end of a piece of research. Suppose we did the "attitudes about immigration policies" study described earlier; suppose further that at the end of the research, we want to compare the attitudes of those who were exposed to the film series to the attitudes of those who were not. What are the alternatives? One alternative is that there's no difference between the experimental and control groups. If that happens, we'd probably say that there was no evidence that the film series had any effect.

But we shouldn't be too surprised if the mean scores of the two groups aren't *exactly* the same, since we might expect a certain amount of variation just by chance alone. In other words, the average scores in the two groups might not be 4.64 and 4.64, but they might be 4.64 and 4.65. That does not

seem like much. How about 4.64 and 4.70? 4.64 and 4.90? 4.64 and 5.34? At what point are we no longer prepared to write off the difference as mere chance variation? At what point, in other words, do we decide that the difference is sufficiently large that chance variation *alone* can't account for it and that something else must therefore be going on? Where do we draw the line?

Social and health scientists rely on elementary probability theory to help them make this decision. Many statistical tests (e.g., *t*-tests, chi-square, analysis of variance) are designed to tell us the exact probability of obtaining the results we observe *if* chance alone is operating. For social and health scientists, this information is crucial, since the central issue is not the mere magnitude of differences between groups but the probability of observing that magnitude of difference *if* chance alone is what's operating.

Recall that the students in Ted's classes tend to get suspicious about his coin flipping when the probabilities reach in the neighbourhood of 1 in 16 (.06) or 1 in 32 (.03). In the social and health sciences, researchers agree that the odds must be at least 1 in 20 (i.e., .05) or *less* (i.e., .02, .01) before we can say that something other than chance must have been operating to produce the observed results. Only at that point, in other words, are researchers prepared to say that a difference they've observed is **statistically significant**.

Why .05? Why not .10 or .01 or some other level? Although Sir Ronald Fisher (1925) is generally credited with fixing .05 as the required probability for considering a difference statistically significant, Cowles and Davis (1982) identify Karl Pearson as having played an important role with his development of the chi-square "goodness of fit" test in the 1890s, since this test was the first to allow the computation of the exact probability that observed deviations from expected (theoretical) distributions could be attributed to chance variation. Pearson and his contemporaries exchanged views concerning which value to use as a cutoff for statistical significance. Articles by various authors in the first two decades of the 20th century gradually homed in on .05 as the consensus choice.

Fisher (1925), whose contributions in research design and in developing the analysis of variance earned him senior academic status, may thus be seen as having given his blessing to a well-established tradition. Ultimately, the choice of .05 was relatively arbitrary; it simply represents the consensus of turn-of-the-20th-century academics.

The subjective appeal for this choice is certainly reaffirmed in Ted's experiences with the coin-flipping exercise. Students quite reliably get suspicious after about four or five successive "tails" flips—the probabilities of which are .06 and .03, respectively—suggesting that the .05 level *does* correspond reasonably well to people's intuitive sense of when a given observation is sufficiently "special" or "atypical" or "unique" to get excited about. And while the choice of .05 per se is merely a tradition or convention, its value rests in the very fact that it *is* a tradition, generally considered to be beyond the control of the experimenter/researcher. As such, .05 is an independent arbiter that impartially distinguishes between observations that are statistically significant (and hence deserve further scrutiny) and those that aren't (and hence can be written off to chance variation).

In this sense, statistical significance is an all-or-none event; either a result *is* statistically significant or it *isn't*. Hockey provides a useful analogy here: when Jonathan Toews of the Chicago Blackhawks skates down the ice, "success" is defined as shooting the puck into the opposing team's net. Either Toews scores a goal or he doesn't; if he *doesn't*, it doesn't particularly matter whether his shot hits the goal post or misses the net by a metre (although our hearts may flutter a bit more in the former instance). Similarly, observations that have a probability of occurrence of .05 or less are considered statistically significant; if the probability level is any higher (regardless of whether the observed probability level "hits the goal post" at $p = .06$ or "misses by a metre" at $p = .20$), the results are still considered within the range of what could be expected on the basis of chance variation alone.

What, then, does it mean to say that your data are statistically significant? All it means is that if

chance alone was operating, the probability of obtaining the results you did is equal to or less than 5 in 100 (i.e., $p \leq .05$). In other words, your results are sufficiently unique to suggest that chance alone cannot account for them. And if chance alone cannot account for the results, something else must be going on. Statistical significance does *not* imply that what you've found is important. Nor does it imply that your study is internally valid, since the statistics are blind to the adequacy of your design (at least in terms of its internal validity). Importance and internal validity are both separate issues; neither is indicated by statistical significance alone.

AN EXAMPLE: ASSESSING THE EFFECTS OF VIOLENT PORNOGRAPHY

In order to see how the concepts we've talked about "work," we'll now take a step back and take a close look at one particular study from a highly controversial program of primarily experimental research that sought to assess the effects of viewing violent pornography. We've picked this experiment for several reasons. First, the issue of violence against women is very important, and violent pornography has been cited by various theorists as one of many factors that exacerbate that phenomenon. Second, the experimental research that's been done in this area, primarily by Ed Donnerstein of the University of Arizona and Neil Malamuth of the University of California at Los Angeles (UCLA), adheres particularly well to experimental principles. Third, these researchers and their research became quite influential in the social policy arena. Donnerstein and Malamuth have served as expert witnesses in courts, testifying about the effects of viewing violent pornography, and both have also testified before federal commissions in Canada and the United States that looked into whether and to what extent pornographic materials should be the subject of legal censure.

In 1994, Malamuth gave evidence in *Little Sister's* v. *The Queen*, a case heard in the British Columbia Supreme Court. From the start there was every indication that, no matter what the outcome in the provincial Supreme Court, the case would eventually proceed to the Supreme Court of Canada, which it did. The case concerned Little Sister's Book and Art Emporium, a retail establishment in downtown Vancouver that sells primarily sexually oriented material (mostly books and magazines) to a largely homosexual (both gay and lesbian) clientele. The case arose because materials destined for Little Sister's from other countries were often impounded at the border by Canada Customs officials, who would then notify Little Sister's, who then had to go through an extensive legal and bureaucratic process in an attempt to have the material released. Indeed, such seizures happened so often, and so much *more* often than they happened to bookstores and video outlets that deal primarily in heterosexual sexual material, that Little Sister's decided to take Canada Customs (and the federal government) to court, alleging that the store was a victim of homophobic harassment and that this process of prior restraint was inexcusably contrary to the Canadian Charter of Rights and Freedoms. The federal government acknowledged that its procedures *were* contrary to the Charter, but argued that such procedures were necessary to prevent the harms that would result from the proliferation of such material.

This large, complex case occupied considerable court time. One issue that had to be considered centred on the question of whether exposure to gay sexual material, especially violent gay sexual material, creates harms, in particular, by somehow promoting sexual violence. The federal government hired Malamuth, one of the foremost experimental researchers in the field, to make its case, a task that he tackled by relying almost exclusively on the experimental evidence that he and his colleagues had generated over the previous decade or so. Ted offered to help Little Sister's (which had a shoestring budget and relied extensively on volunteer help) by writing an opinion on Malamuth's opinion (see Palys 1994).

The way Ted approached that task was *not* to question Malamuth's qualifications or the quality of the research that he and his colleagues had done. Malamuth is clearly well-respected in the field of experimental social psychology, and his research is exemplary within that tradition. Indeed, a large part of Ted's written opinion involved showing how carefully constructed the research was. At the same time, Ted expressed concerns about how Malamuth and his colleagues interpreted the results of their research. Ted reexamined their research using the various concepts we've discussed in the chapter (although so far at a largely theoretical level), as well as posing questions about the meanings we attribute to our research.

Isolating and Operationalizing the Variables

The laboratory experimenter's challenge is to contrive a situation where the effects of a single variable can be isolated and observed without changing the very nature of what is being looked at. As we've seen, experimental social psychologists approach this problem in much the same way that physicists or chemists might seek to observe a single electron or observe a chemical reaction in a contrived situation ostensibly free of worldly contaminants. Implicit in this view is the idea that the thing being observed may be changed in *magnitude* by its removal and relocation into the laboratory, but not in *character*.

People who want to ban (or strictly regulate the distribution of) violent video pornography argue that allowing it to be available creates social harms, primarily by increasing the likelihood that those who are exposed to it will themselves engage in sexually violent behaviour, for example, pedophilia and rape. Looking at such behaviour directly, either in the lab or anywhere else, would clearly be unethical. Researchers who wanted to test this hypothesis thus had to look at other kinds of aggressive behaviour, with the understanding that the behaviour investigated in the lab, the act of giving small electric shocks to a stranger, although clearly far removed from the brutality of a sexual assault, is nonetheless comparable to such an assault in essence: both behaviours are manifestations of the concept "aggression"; and the two behaviours differ only in magnitude, not in kind. The primary *dependent variable* in the "effects" research area is thus the average level of electric shock that one person is prepared to deliver to another person.

The key "causal" variable (or *independent variable*) of interest in the effects literature is exposure to pornography, especially violent pornography. In order to assess pornography's effects on the *dependent variable* (the level of aggression exhibited against a stranger), the logic of the experiment requires the researcher to create two conditions (in the simplest case) that are identical in all respects except one: the presence or absence of the variable whose effects one wishes to test. Most of the effects literature involves more complicated designs, but the fundamental principle that drives such studies involves comparing two or more groups that are equivalent in all respects, on average, on every variable except one.

A Paradigmatic Effects Study

A "typical" design in the effects area is offered by Donnerstein and Berkowitz (1981). That study is paradigmatic insofar as its operational choices have been replicated dozens of times in subsequent research; it provides the standard against which subsequent research is often judged. Malamuth cites the study frequently and favourably.

THE SAMPLE

The research participants in Donnerstein and Berkowitz (1981) were all male, undergraduate, introductory psychology student volunteers, as is true of most studies in this area. Eighty males took part in this study. When each participant showed up for his appointment at the lab, he was told that another person (always a woman) also had an appointment and that the two of them would be participating in the study together.

PROCEDURES AND DESIGN

Following introductions, the experimenter turned on a tape recorder. The taped instructions revealed that one of the two participants would be a "learner," whose job would be to try to remember certain word pairs; the job of the other would be to assist the experimenter. An allegedly random draw was then held to determine who would play each role. But unbeknownst to the male participant, the draw was actually rigged: the woman always became the learner, while the man always became the experimenter's assistant. The woman, as you may suspect, was actually an employee or a confederate of the experimenter's. She was trained to respond in the same preprogrammed manner each time the experiment was run.

With the pair's roles determined, the experimenter next stated that the woman would be given some time to study the word pairs before a "test" was given. The man, in the interim, was to spend his time writing a brief essay about the possible legalization of marijuana. When he finished, the woman was brought back into the setting, where she was supposed to evaluate the essay. She remained on the other side of a partition, though, and wasn't supposed to communicate directly with the man. Instead, she communicated *in*directly, by written note and through the delivery of some electric shocks via finger electrodes placed on the man's hand. Her evaluation of the essay was unambiguous; her written evaluation stated that the essay was terrible, and when faced with the choice of how many electric shocks to deliver to the man, she delivered 9 out of a possible maximum of 10.

This little interchange served two experimental goals. First, it helped reaffirm the "reality" of the electric shocks to the male participant. This was important, because the man would soon have an opportunity to deliver electric shocks to the woman, and the experimenter needed the man to believe that any shocks he delivered were real. Second, this interchange—known among effects researchers as the *anger manipulation*—has become a virtual requirement of effects testing, since it seems that unless the woman first angers the man, no effects of exposure to violent pornography are observed.[3]

After the anger manipulation is performed, the woman is allowed further time to study. Noting that this studying will take some time and that the male participant now has nothing to do, the experimenter says something along the lines of "By the way, a friend of mine down the hall is preparing some film clips for another experiment, and he needs people to make some ratings of them. Since we have some time to kill, would you be interested in going down the hall and helping him out for a few minutes?" Virtually all participants agree to do so.

At this point the manipulation of the independent variable occurs. Participants are *randomly assigned* to one of four experimental conditions; the only difference between the conditions is the type of film clip to which participants are exposed. In Donnerstein and Berkowitz (1981), two of these clips portrayed (1) a *nonsexual and nonviolent* clip of a talk show, and (2) a *sexually explicit but nonviolent* depiction of a man and a woman engaging in mutually consenting intercourse. Each video segment was about five minutes long. The other two clips were of similar length; both involved a scene in which three people—a woman and two men—are studying together when the men begin to make sexual advances toward the woman. She resists but is raped. The difference between the third and fourth films was not in their visual content (which was identical), but in the voice soundtrack: in one version (3), the woman protests at first, but soon begins to enjoy the process (a rape myth depiction; the "*sexually violent/positive outcome*" condition); in the other (4), the woman resists at first and throughout the process, experiencing all the horror of a sexual assault she is powerless to stop (the "*sexually violent/negative outcome*" condition).

Thus, the *independent variable* in the study was the "exposure to a film" at one of four "levels," one corresponding to each of the four conditions above. The *dependent variable* was the average level of shock delivered by participants from each of the four groups. Technically speaking, this design is a *randomized non-pretested comparison group design*, as is represented in Figure 9.7.

After viewing one of the four film clips and completing a few rating scales (consistent with the cover story that was offered), the male participant returns to the first experimenter, who is now ready

Figure 9.7

The Randomized Non-pretested Comparison Group Design Used in Donnerstein and Berkowitz (1981)

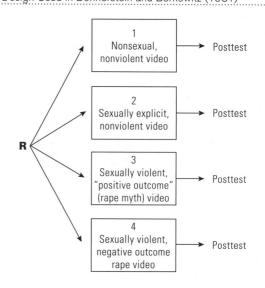

to receive him. By this time, the woman has completed her studying and has had some electrodes attached to her fingers. The man, adopting his assigned role of assistant to the experimenter, begins assessing whether the woman remembers the word pairs she has been studying. Whenever she makes a mistake, the male participant's job is to determine how many electric shocks she should receive and then to deliver them. Of particular interest to the experimenters was the average number of electric shocks that the male participants would deliver (i.e., the *dependent variable*) and how (if at all) that number would vary depending on the type of film clip the participant had viewed.

WERE THE DIFFERENCES SIGNIFICANT?

Recall the basic logic of experimentation: *if the groups are all equal to begin with*, any subsequent differences in the dependent variable (here, the average shock level) among the groups must be due to the one variable on which their experience varied (here, the type of film to which they were exposed). We must first, therefore, try to find out whether there are in fact any "differences" to worry about.

If there are no differences among the groups, then there's nothing further to explain.

Donnerstein and Berkowitz (1981) found that after being exposed to the anger manipulation, the two groups who viewed the sexually violent film clip (whether it was accompanied by a "positive outcome" or by a "negative outcome" soundtrack) administered a significantly higher average level of shock than did either the group of participants who viewed the sexually explicit but nonviolent depiction or the group who viewed the nonsexual and nonviolent talk show clip (see the graph of these results in Figure 9.8).

ASSESSING INTERNAL VALIDITY

Remember that a result's statistical significance does not imply anything about that result's importance. Nor does it necessarily imply that the independent variable had an effect. It means only that the degree of difference between the two groups is greater than one would expect on the basis of chance variation alone. If chance alone cannot fully account for the difference, clearly something else must be going on. But what might the "something else" be?

After reading Donnerstein and Berkowitz (1981), we might like to suggest that the differences between the groups are a reflection of the effects of viewing the films. But we must assess the study's internal validity before taking our best guess in that regard. Let's consider the various threats to internal validity that were explained earlier in the chapter to see how well Donnerstein and Berkowitz (1981) controlled for them.

IF THE TWO GROUPS ARE EQUAL TO BEGIN WITH...

A first possible threat is *selection*. This threat would strike right at the heart of the design, since it undermines a fundamental element of experimental logic: the assumption that the two groups are equal to begin with. If the groups are not equal to begin with, any after-the-fact differences may merely reflect the before-the-fact differences.

We can indeed assume that the four groups in Donnerstein and Berkowitz (1981) were identical to begin with. Why? Since participants were

Figure 9.8

Graphed Results from Donnerstein and Berkowitz (1981) Showing Mean Shock Level Administered by Each Group

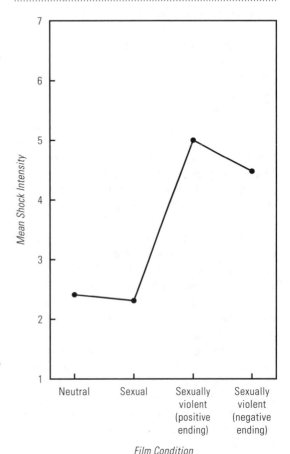

Film Condition

assigned on a purely *random* basis to one of the four conditions, we have no reason to believe that, before viewing the videos, one group (overall) was any different from any other group (overall). People who have more or less proclivity to violence, more or less experience with having viewed video pornography, more negative or more positive attitudes toward sexual material, or whatever other individual difference variable that we can think of all will have been equally distributed across the groups. We might feel more comfortable if the researchers had assigned

30 or more participants per group rather than 20, but there's still no reason to assume that the deck has been stacked in favour of one group any more than any other. So selection doesn't seem to be a threat to the internal validity of this design.

... AND ARE TREATED IDENTICALLY IN ALL RESPECTS...

Several other threats can also be ruled out. *History* cannot be a threat, because every effort was made to treat everyone identically in all respects except for the level of the independent variable they received. They all came to the same lab, met the same female confederate and the same experimenter, heard exactly the same tape-recorded instructions, and received the same evaluation of their essay by the confederate, all according to the script laid out by the researchers. Even the four levels of the independent variable were administered in similar ways: all four groups were asked to do "a favour," all four groups had to go down the hall to meet another experimenter in another room, all four groups saw a video of similar length (with only the content varying), and all four groups completed a series of rating scales after they saw the film.

The whole experience occurred within an hour for each participant, so *maturation* seems unlikely to have entered in as a threat. In any event, to the extent that there *were* any maturational influences, such as the participants' getting more tired as the experiment progressed, these would have been equal, overall, across all groups.

Testing couldn't have been a threat, because there was no pretest. Similarly, *statistical regression (regression toward the mean)* couldn't have been a threat, because neither group was selected on the basis of any sort of extreme score.

Taken together, the preceding paragraphs suggest that the internal validity of the Donnerstein and Berkowitz (1981) study is quite high. Although we cannot be positive, because there might have been some threats we haven't considered, it seems that the only difference between the four groups was in the content of the film they viewed. And if that's so, it must be because of the content of the films that they reacted differently to the confederate when given an opportunity to administer electric shocks.

EXTERNAL VALIDITY

Although their theoretical interests are in the effects of exposure to violent pornography on "people," Donnerstein and Berkowitz (1981) conducted this study, as is the case with most of the experimental research in this area, using a specific type of research participant: male, undergraduate, introductory psychology students who volunteered to take part in the study. Because such a group is obviously anything but a "representative sample" of the general population, many critics of the effects literature (e.g., see Byrne & Kelley 1989; Fisher 1986) question the *external validity* (generalizability) of the research results. Can *any* result obtained with such a sample be generalized to the broader population of interest (i.e., all people, or even all males)?

We do *not* see that criticism as particularly relevant here. Even if we acknowledge that male introductory psychology students are *not* typical of all people, so that the question of who is sampled becomes an important one, a criticism based on their being "unrepresentative" is empty unless we identify the nature of the sampling bias that exists and then consider the possible implications of that bias for the results the researchers obtained.

In that regard, we can expect several differences between male, undergraduate, introductory psychology students and the general male population. Not only have such students received more extensive formal education than the average population member, but we might also speculate that they might be less likely to use "physical" means to solve conflicts or achieve goals, and perhaps be more introspective about their behaviour and the motives underlying it, for example. But if that's so, it might be argued that these people may be even *less* likely than the general population to engage in aggressive and assaultive behaviour. Indeed, the upshot of the sample's "unrepresentativeness" is that if it can be demonstrated that even such a relatively well-educated and literate group can be affected by exposure to violent pornography, then this study's results may well be, if anything, a *conservative* estimate of the extent to which such effects will exist in the population as a whole. [Malamuth (1989: 183) makes a similar argument.] In sum, although external validity is ultimately an empirical question worth considering, no immediate issues of external validity seem inherently problematic to this study's conclusions.

ECOLOGICAL VALIDITY

The laboratory experiment involves creating a contrived setting designed to provide a "pure" test of a theoretical proposition among a designated sample of research participants. This contrived setting can pose a problem when researchers engage in experimental research that is later used to influence social policy. The problem arises when, in the interests of experimental purity, researchers (1) create situations that are related only obliquely to situations in the world that the researchers are ostensibly trying to help us understand, and (2) create misleading results because of the way in which they virtually *create* the very effects they're allegedly trying to *test*. These considerations have been embellished in greater detail elsewhere (see Palys 1989; Palys & Lowman 1984), but also deserve some attention here.

Laboratory experimentalists are taught several basic principles for use in designing an experiment. Two of these, both rooted in the F-ratio[4] (the statistic typically used to compare groups), are (1) the principle of *maximizing between-groups variation* (i.e., the degree of difference between experimental and control groups), to make as clear a differentiation between conditions as possible; and (2) the principle of *minimizing within-groups variation* (i.e., the degree of "natural" and "random" variation that exists within the groups being tested), to make as "sensitive" a test of the hypothesis as possible.

In studies like the one being considered here, researchers accomplish the former goal by choosing the most gruesome "violent pornography" they can find, choosing sexually explicit material that is extremely explicit and not at all violent, and making

the "neutral" material as devoid of sexual and violent content as they can. They accomplish the latter goal by using relatively homogeneous populations of respondents (e.g., male, undergraduate, introductory psychology student volunteers) and by attempting to exert experimenter control over the situation to standardize conditions as much as possible (e.g., by using tape-recorded instructions to minimize any variations in the reading of the instructions, variations of the sort that would otherwise happen over time if the experimenter were to read the same instructions again and again; and by having the woman confederate send her insulting statement about the male participant's essay via written note so that the message remains exactly constant across all tested groups).

A third principle of experimentation advises experimenters to *control all available response alternatives* so that any impetus to behaviour that is created by the conditions of the experiment is harnessed in the service of the dependent variable. Underlying this view is something of a "hydraulic" model of human behaviour: the belief is that if a stimulus can effectively energize a behavioural response, the astute experimenter will "dam up" all behavioural alternatives but one, so that the magnitude of all behavioural impulses will be visible in the chosen place. In the context of the effects literature, where the interest has been in determining aggressive impulses, this has meant that participants have been given only one way to express themselves: by delivering electric shocks to the woman on the other side of the partition.

All of these principles have been employed in the studies described in the effects literature produced by Donnerstein, Berkowitz, Malamuth, and their colleagues. Indeed, they are widely represented as principles of "good experimentation" (e.g., Aronson & Carlsmith 1968; Festinger & Katz 1953; Kerlinger 1973; Rosenthal & Rosnow 1984), and they do make great sense *if* one is addressing a purely theoretical question of interest, where the central issue for the researcher is whether a theoretically hypothesized relationship *can* be given empirical life.

But when we make decisions about cases in court or try to develop social policy, we're interested not *solely* in questions of theory, but also in their implications for practice. The interest of the court, for example, in *Little Sister's* v. *The Queen*, as Ted understood it, was not in the answer to the question "*Can* exposure to aggressive pornography increase the likelihood of subsequent harm?" but rather in the answer to the question "*Does* it do so?"

Those are two very different questions. The first is more purely theoretical. To ask whether something *can* happen is to ask simply whether a particular phenomenon can be generated, that is, whether there is any evidence that a specified theoretical linkage can occur. The second is a more contextualized and applied question; it asks whether, in the real world, the conditions exist in which the phenomenon of interest occurs. Think back to the studies reviewed earlier in this chapter about the effects of wearing glasses. The early experimental research showed that wearing glasses *can* affect the impressions that other people derive of you. But later research showed that it generally *doesn't*, unless that's the only piece of information that people have of you, a condition that rarely applies outside laboratory experiments. In sum, it's not inconsistent or implausible for the answers to those two questions to be "Yes, it *can*" but "No, it *doesn't*."

Donnerstein and Berkowitz (1981) clearly show that, under certain conditions, viewing violent pornography *can* affect the likelihood that people will engage in aggressive behaviour. But in order to address the question of whether it *does* have such an effect, we must consider the study's ecological validity, asking how well the experiment's conditions approximate or represent the actual conditions in the world in which pornography is consumed. Stated another way, we must ask whether, in the interest of living up to experimentalist ideals, Donnerstein and Berkowitz have made the situation into something *other than* that which they set out to investigate. For example,

1. While the aggressive behaviour that's of interest to us is *severe* (e.g., violence in the form of sexual assault and other sexual abuses), ethical requirements constrain laboratory investigation to behaviour that's relatively *trivial* (small electric shocks that cause minimal pain and no long-term trauma or damage) and hence probably result in an overestimate of the extent to which people are prepared to engage in the more severe forms of such behaviour.

2. While aggressive behaviour is *discouraged* in society (e.g., one is subject to arrest and imprisonment for behaviour such as sexual assault), the experiment requires it to be *encouraged* in the experimental setting by an experimenter who, as an authority figure, represents the interests of legitimate science.

3. While in the real world we have many *alternatives* about how to respond when we're angered (e.g., by withdrawing from the situation, by talking to the person who has angered us), the effects researchers offer their research participants *only one way* to communicate any displeasure they may feel: by imposing an electric shock to the fingertips of the woman on the other side of the partition.

At least two studies have investigated the impact of some of the above factors. Regarding caveat 3, for example, Fisher and Grenier (1994) wondered what would happen if research participants were given a broader array of response alternatives than just delivering shocks. They discovered that when response alternatives were given, the vast majority of respondents—no matter which film they'd been exposed to—chose to *talk* to the woman who'd angered them, rather than to deliver electric shocks.

Regarding caveat 2, relevant evidence has been supplied by Malamuth (1978). He describes this research in a later publication (1984) as follows:

Following exposure to these [visual] stimuli, all subjects were insulted by a female confederate and then were placed in a situation where they could aggress against her via the ostensible delivery of electric shocks under one of two assessment conditions. Half of the subjects were assigned to read a communication that suggested it was "permissible" to behave as aggressively as they wished (disinhibitory communication); the other half were given a communication designed to make them somewhat self-conscious about aggressing (inhibitory communication) … The results revealed no significant differences in aggression following the inhibitory communication. (35)

In sum, as soon as conditions in the experiment start to better approximate those in the real world, that is, when people have alternative ways of responding and when aggressive responses are discouraged, the findings of the laboratory-based research appear to vanish, and no effects are found.

At the same time, by creating a set of conditions under which effects of viewing violent pornography *were* observed, Donnerstein and Berkowitz (1981) *have* helped to show some of the parameters that might affect the likelihood of aggressive behaviour in the world, for example:

1. One element of their research was that students were, by the nature of the situation, actually *encouraged* to aggress. This should attune us to the need to ensure that people are discouraged from believing that aggression is a legitimate way to respond to angers and frustrations in the world.

2. Similarly, Donnerstein and Berkowitz's (1981) study involved a situation where respondents experienced *no consequences* for their aggression, either to themselves (in the form of punishment) or to their victims (in the form of pain and trauma). This suggests that those who see sexual assault and violence against women as behaviours they can engage in with impunity may be more likely to engage in such behaviour. And this in turn should sensitize us to the need for competent investigation and prosecution of assaultive behaviour, so as to maximize deterrence.

Similarly, it suggests that greater emphasis should be placed on educating people about the experience of assault victims, particularly in terms of the pain and suffering that they have had to endure.

3. Further, the Donnerstein and Berkowitz (1981) study, coupled with Fisher and Grenier (1994), shows that aggression is more likely to occur when there are no behavioural alternatives available or when none are *perceived* to be available. This should sensitize us to the need to encourage people to recognize that there are a variety of ways to deal with frustration and anger other than through aggression; people who know no other way of responding may well continue to aggress.

In sum, this analysis suggests that looking for effects of certain images per se is probably a fruitless task. Instead, we've suggested that any effects are mitigated by other variables, such as the meanings that are attached to our behaviours and the context in which those behaviours occur.

THE FRAGILITY OF MEDIA INFLUENCE EFFECTS

It seems fairly clear from the literature that any "media effects" that can be attributed to the message or content of violent pornography per se are, in the grander scheme of things, a fairly trivial influence. Even Malamuth (1989), who built much of his reputation on demonstrating these effects, recognized that the media may not even be a particularly important element in the behavioural equation:

As with many behaviours, it is apparent that antisocial behaviour against women is a function of many interacting causal factors. It is very difficult to gauge the relative influence, if any, of media exposure alone. However, by itself, it is likely to exert a small influence, if any. (198)

CONTEXT, MEANINGS, AND BEHAVIOUR

The experimental paradigm is typically silent with respect to variables of the sort that people doing qualitative social and health research cherish most dearly, for example, the *meaning* of images to people and the role that culture and individual differences can play in the generation and interpretation of images.

In this regard, Abramson and Hayashi (1984) offer a comparative analysis of Japanese and American pornography, attitudes about sex, the role of sex in the media, and so forth. They note, for example, that Japanese laws and mores completely prohibit images that many North Americans would find relatively tame (e.g., neither pubic hair nor adult genitalia may be shown), while at the same time allowing a variety of images that many North Americans would find horrendous (e.g., the admonition against showing pubic hair has resulted in the proliferation of sexualized images of pre-pubescent girls):

> Of particular note in Japanese pornography (film and novel) is the recurring theme of bondage and rape. Although movies are much less explicit than their American and European counterparts, the plot often involves the rape of a high school girl ... In fact, one of the best ways to ensure the success of a Japanese adult film is to include the bondage and rape of a young woman. This juxta-position of sexuality and aggression is evident in almost all forms of Japanese sexual material, including cartoons, films, and sexological museums. (178)

Given these differences, if it were in fact the case that sexually violent themes and images in and of themselves somehow "cause" greater aggressiveness, sexual aggression would be rampant in Japan—and at higher levels than in the United States. But despite the pervasiveness of such material, rates of sexual assault and other forms of sexual abuse in Japan appear to be far lower than those in Western countries.

> In comparison to Western nations, Japan has a substantially lower incidence of rape: in the United States there are 34.5 reported rapes per 100,000 population; in England, 10.1; in West Germany, 10.7; in France, 3.2; and, in Japan, 2.4 ... The discrepancy in the incidence between the United States and Japan cannot be attributed to variance in the laws because the laws are basically the same (although prosecution rates may vary).

> If there is a direct connection between the prevalence of rape imagery and rape behaviour, Japan should have an overwhelming occurrence of rape. As indicated in the preceding paragraph's rape statistics, it does not. Consequently, it is our suggestion that mediating circumstances are involved, especially in the form of internal constraints to maladaptive behaviour. (181)

These observations about the importance of culture in the rules of sexual practice and the interpretation of sexual and sexually violent images are particularly germane to the court case involving Little Sister's Book and Art Emporium. Since Little Sister's caters primarily to the homosexual community, another question of interest in considering this case concerns whether—and if so, to what extent—any of the findings reported in the effects literature are applicable to that community.

EXTERNAL VALIDITY REVISITED: GENERALIZING TO WRITTEN MATERIALS AND THE GAY COMMUNITY

All the experimental effects research has involved video materials and mixed-sex dyads. Can the results of that research be generalized to exposure to written materials? And would the effects observed among mixed-sex dyads also be seen if same-sex dyads were involved? These questions clearly concern the *external validity* of the research. Malamuth was asked by the Department of Justice to comment on that issue with respect to the Little Sister's trial.

GENERALIZING TO WRITTEN MATERIALS Malamuth begins by acknowledging that no available data reflect directly on the issue of whether the results from video research can be generalized to exposure to books and magazines. But he then speculates that the potential harms he discusses may occur just from exposure to the written word. He predicates this suggestion on his belief that the important element is the *message communicated*, rather than the medium of communication.

The type of analysis being offered here is certainly consistent with Malamuth's more quantitative approach. Just as he refrains from looking into the meaning of sexual/pornographic stimuli to the consumers of such materials, so also does Malamuth emphasize the concrete, externally visible stimulus (the overt message), apparently assuming that the message itself has some objective meaning that is uniform to all. Stating that the important element is the *message communicated* downplays any consideration of the person who receives the message, any attribution of meaning to its content, and any situational and/or cultural factors that might enter into its interpretation.

Our own sense is that several differences between written and oral media may be recognized. First, while video pornography is often consumed in social settings (see Palys 1984), written pornography (books and magazines) is more likely to be consumed by one individual at a time. Second, one needn't be literate to watch a video, but literacy is required for reading a book. In both cases, one could envision that these variables (i.e., solo versus social consumption; literacy requirements and the propensity to read books, especially as related to educational attainment and cultural differences) might make a difference in who seeks out each type of pornographic material and also in the range of interpretations that are made by that selection of people.

GENERALIZING TO THE GAY COMMUNITY Regarding whether the results of the effects research can be generalized to the gay community, Malamuth suggests that any effects that are observed for heterosexual pornography among members of the heterosexual community will in all likelihood be the same for homosexual pornography among members of the homosexual community. Although he acknowledges having no data that bear directly on this issue, he bases his speculation on the answers

to three questions: (1) Are the messages in homosexual pornography basically the same as those in heterosexual pornography? (2) Are the minds of homosexuals basically the same as the minds of heterosexuals? (3) Are there problems of sexual conflict within the homosexual community? In all three cases he answers yes and, hence, concludes that the same processes prevail among the homosexual community as among the heterosexual one.

Although Malamuth is correct in saying that no existing data bear directly on this issue, the most closely related finding we know of (concerning male–male aggression following exposure to violent pornography) would urge more caution in reaching such a conclusion. Summarizing the findings from his and Donnerstein's (1984) laboratory research, Malamuth notes that "the data show that exposure of male subjects to aggressive pornography increases aggressive behaviour against *female* but not male targets" (35).

Besides that result, the problem with Malamuth's responses is his tenacious belief in the objective qualities of messages. When he asks whether homosexual pornography and heterosexual pornography are basically the same, Malamuth is led by his belief in the "objective," observable content of messages to answer yes. To Malamuth, the question "Are homosexual minds and heterosexual minds basically the same?" involves only knowing whether the basic physiological material and information-processing capacities of homosexuals and heterosexuals are the same; he concludes that, at that level, there are no differences between the homosexual mind and the heterosexual mind. And, of course, he's right.

But Malamuth misses the point. Although the superficial content that appears in some heterosexual pornography and some homosexual pornography may be similar, the *meanings* associated with those images, and hence their relationship with behaviour, may well be considerably different. In this regard, we must remember that the historical experience of homosexuals and heterosexuals has been very different. While heterosexuals have enjoyed feeling "normal" about their sexuality, the gay community has endured many years of being considered "deviant" and/or "unnatural," and it is not even that long ago that it was actually illegal. Because being homosexual has been an unwarranted source of stigma for many years, many gay people still feel reluctant to "come out of the closet." Given homosexuality's historical status as an oppressed lifestyle (e.g., through institutional harassment and "gay-bashing"), one might anticipate that gays' marginalized status would have left a greater sense of shared community and interdependence among homosexuals than among heterosexuals. Some authors have also argued that, when it comes to matters of sexual violence, the situation in homosexual relations is unique in the sense that it might be more inherently egalitarian because of the gender similarity of the two people involved (e.g., see Brock & Kinsman 1986).

Taken together, all these differences between homosexuals' and heterosexuals' life experience would leave us surprised if the two communities did *not* attach different meanings to sexual practices and sexual images. There's clearly a need for more research in that area, particularly by gay researchers, to articulate these issues. In the interim, the safer course would be to assume, on the basis of gays' significantly different social history, that differences in meaning do exist.

A third element considered by Malamuth was whether there is any evidence of violence in the gay community; to this question he also answers yes. And indeed, the gay community, like any other community, is not immune to sexual violence. But to assume that the same dynamics must therefore characterize both homosexual violence and heterosexual violence seems inconsistent with the feminist literature that Malamuth suggests informs his analysis. For example, to the extent that sexual violence between men and women involves not only violence but *gender* violence, embedded in a history of patriarchal relations, how could patterns of sexual violence among same-sex partners (who are equal in overt gender status) be a product of the same dynamic? Overall, the biggest threats to homosexuals involving violence probably involve people from *outside* the gay community (harassment—and

worse—from the intolerant and from gay-bashers) more than people from *inside* it.

Final Comments on the Effects Research

In offering the preceding detailed analysis of the Donnerstein and Berkowitz (1981) study, we have several aims: we hope we've shown how analyzing and critiquing a piece of research involves considering it in the light of the concepts (e.g., statistical conclusion validity, internal validity, external validity, ecological validity) introduced in more abstract form in the earlier part of this chapter. You should now be able to go through any example of experimental research and do the same.

You also should consider experimental research in the terms introduced much earlier in the text, particularly in terms of notions of engagement. As we've noted several times before, doing a piece of research involves *engaging* a phenomenon of interest, and the results that one acquires will bear the imprint of the tools we use to engage them. We are reminded of the analogy that Morgan (1983) offered regarding the various ways one can engage an apple: by looking at it, touching it, eating it, comparing it to other fruits, and so on. Each is simply a different way of engaging an apple, and the "truth" that emerges from each method of engagement is no more and no less true than any other; each just gives its unique glimpse into the apple's qualities.

Similarly, we can engage phenomena by observing them, interviewing people about them, gathering archival information about them, or experimenting with them. Seen in this way, the experiment, as a way of understanding, is no more right or wrong than any other means of gathering data; it has unique strengths and weaknesses, and the thoughtful researcher must consider these when interpreting an experiment's results.

THE EXPERIMENT IN PERSPECTIVE

The experiment represents a powerful venue in which to develop a certain kind of dependable knowledge. The lab offers maximal manipulative control over the experimental situation and is ideally suited to situations where creating or simulating the phenomenon of interest is conceptually defensible and causal inference and precision are the highest priorities. In the lab, we can randomly assign our participants to the various experimental and control groups and hence ensure that the crucial experimental assumption of pre-experimental equivalence is met. Since we create these groups, we can construct situations ideally suited to the research questions we wish to pose. And of course, because these experiments occur on our own turf, when we want them to, we are best prepared to measure the dependent variable with instruments of demonstrated reliability and validity.

This creative power has other benefits as well. In the laboratory, situations can be created that do not yet exist in the world, as can situations that we hope will not exist. As an example of the former, we might use the lab to do preliminary testing of emergent technologies or different organizational structures before they're foisted on users in the field. As for the latter, we wouldn't intentionally make a real airplane carrying real people crash, but we can use lab simulations to assess and/or train those who might have to deal with such events (e.g., see Palys 1978).

Finally, it could probably also be stated that the laboratory experiment is ideally suited in many ways for addressing strictly theoretical questions, perhaps more so than practical or applied research questions. Given that various authors (e.g., Kerlinger 1973) have affirmed that theory is *the* goal of science (as opposed to "truth" or "knowledge" or "facts" per se), this suggests that the lab plays an important role in social and health science. Note also that much theorizing is of the *ceteris paribus* variety (implying that theories assert the relationships among variables of interest, all else being equal), and laboratory experimentation is one manifestation of that logic. If a theory suggests that variable *A* should or might have a certain effect on variable *B*, for example, then one could observe variable *B* in a lab situation where all variables except variable *A* are held constant or otherwise equalized across groups (e.g., by random assignment to groups). Variable *A*, of course, would be present in one group (the experimental group) but not the other (the control group). By doing so, we would have investigated the effects of variable *A* on variable *B, ceteris paribus.*

As long as our interests are purely theoretical, and as long as we limit our interpretation to this generic *ceteris paribus* situation, the laboratory can serve a useful role. But if we're more interested in contextualized behaviour in that open system we call the world, the lab's role may be more limited (e.g., see Manicas & Secord 1983). Researchers who extrapolate answers to applied questions from their theory-based lab research may be on tenuous ground, since all else is never equal in the real world; every setting embodies its own unique context (e.g., see Palys & Lowman 1984).

Until relatively recently, many social and health scientists believed that the controlled lab situation allowed a "pure" test of the relationships among variables in a vacuous, context-free situation (e.g., see Festinger 1953). But in the early 1970s, various European authors began to challenge this view (e.g., see Israel & Tajfel 1972). They asserted that since all behaviour occurs within a context and since "laboratory behaviour" is still "behaviour," attention is warranted to the context within which lab behaviour occurs and to the relationship between the lab context and the context of the "real world" (see especially Tajfel 1972).

Argyris (1975) and Brandt (1975) were among those to agree that the laboratory does indeed embody a social context, but both authors suggest that in many ways that context is the "wrong" one. They depict the experiment as embodying the most imperialist of tendencies—a centralized authority (the experimenter) defines the game and decides the rules, participants are often kept in the dark as to the experimenter's full motives and methods, the role of "subject" is to accept the experimenter's definition of the situation and respond within those constraints, and the preferred epistemology underlying the experiment is one that embraces the utility of manipulative control. Too centralized; too controlling; too hierarchical; too secretive; too minimizing of participants' views and interpretations. The authors remind us of our social responsibilities and suggest that such control-oriented methods encourage control-oriented policy (see also Latour 1987); instead of empowering, such methods and policies are arguably exploitative.

More recently, Manicas and Secord (1983) took up the torch in their articulation of the contemporary critical realist perspective in social science. They agree with those who assert that the laboratory is a place to test theory (e.g., Kerlinger 1973; Mook 1983), since it's a closed system in which basic structures of individual human behaviour (e.g., competencies, abilities, powers) can be investigated. But there's a bigger question: Do our interests lie exclusively with the concoction of theories of lab behaviour per se, or are we also interested in theorizing about life in its broader context? If the latter, then Manicas and Secord (1983) assert that it's a whole new ball game. In sum, they argue that traditional experimentalists are accurate in their analysis (as it pertains to lab behaviour), but myopic (because the conditions they study exist only in the lab).

As this summary suggests, some of the major questions about laboratory research revolve around the notion of exactly what lab behaviour means. But the lab has even more clear-cut limitations. Not the least of these is that there are many phenomena that we would prefer to attend to *in vivo* (a Latin phrase meaning, literally, "in life"). Not all phenomena can be transported into the lab, nor can all be scrutinized conveniently in the typical hour-long laboratory session (e.g., the aging process, the development of criminal careers, observations of social change, the impact of deinstitutionalization, etc.). And when the mountain can't come to us, then we must go to the mountain.

SUMMING UP AND LOOKING AHEAD

When people construct an experiment, they're usually doing so because they're interested in assessing the *causal* impact of one variable (the *independent* or *treatment* variable) on another variable (the *dependent* or *outcome* variable). Philosophically, the criteria governing when you can legitimately infer that a causal relationship has occurred are delineated by John Stuart Mill (1843/1965). Mill states that one must meet three criteria:

1. *temporal precedence* (i.e., since we believe that causes come before effects, we must demonstrate that change in the variable we think is a cause did indeed come before its alleged effect);

2. existence of *a relationship* (i.e., if the alleged cause really *is* a cause, changes in it should be associated with subsequent changes in its alleged effect); and

3. *elimination of rival plausible explanations* (i.e., one must rule out the influence of all possible variables *other than* the one being considered as a source of causal influence).

The traditional experiment elegantly addresses these three criteria. Inherent in the traditional conception of the experiment is the idea that the experiment happens *because* and *when* you want it to happen. Thus, you are able to prepare suitably *reliable* and *valid* measures of your *dependent variable*, and can measure it at appropriate times. In the same vein, you *make* the experiment happen by manipulating the *independent* variable and assessing its effects. Thus, the *temporal precedence* criterion is addressed: because you "cause" the cause to occur, you are able to assess whether the level of the dependent (effect) measure is different only *after* the imposition of the independent variable.

Of course, we'd expect to observe a certain amount of variation (i.e., change) in the dependent variable over time purely as a function of chance. The first question of interest to us after completing a study, therefore, is whether any change we observed is greater than we would have expected on the basis of chance alone. This question concerns the *statistical significance* of the results. If the change we observe is statistically significant, we will have demonstrated the *relationship* criterion that Mill espoused: we will have demonstrated that a change in the independent variable *is* associated with a change in the dependent variable and that the latter change is greater than might be anticipated on the basis of chance variation alone.

Remember, though, that finding statistical significance in our results *doesn't* immediately allow us to say that the *independent variable* caused the change. All we know at this point is that chance alone wasn't the cause of the change. But what was? That's an *internal validity* question. We must consider rival plausible explanations as well, such as history, maturation, testing, and other threats to internal validity. According to the logic of experimentation, if two groups are equal to begin with and if they are treated identically in all respects *except* for the presence or absence of the independent variable, any subsequent differences between those groups can be accounted for only by the influence of the independent variable. And while *control groups* exist to ensure that the groups are "treated identically" in all respects, recall that either *random assignment* or *matching* allows us to ensure that the groups were indeed equal to begin with.

Even if we can meet Mill's criteria, we face the question of whether the results we've observed are *generalizable* beyond the specifics of the study. Can the results be generalized across *time, people*, and *settings?* This, of course, is a question of *external validity*.

And finally, the concept of *ecological validity* raises questions about how well an experiment captures or represents the setting to which we wish to generalize. It's an important element for considering whether theoretical processes that *can* happen actually *do*.

The last part of this chapter analyzed a particular example of experimental research—Donnerstein and Berkowitz's (1981) experiment to assess the effects of viewing violent pornography on its viewers—in order to show how the abstract concepts described earlier in the chapter can be used to design, analyze, and critique a particular piece of research. The case is also made that, far from being a "privileged" mode of creating knowledge, the experiment, like any other method, is a tool that engages phenomena in a particular manner, with unique strengths and weaknesses in the way that it does so.

STUDY QUESTIONS

1. Yasmin feels she has developed a cure for the common cold and wants to test it out. Fifty cold sufferers come to her office one Monday; each receives her treatment. A week later, they all come back, and Yasmin finds that 44 of them (88 percent) no longer have colds. She concludes that her cure is indeed very effective and cites an 88 percent cure rate. Would you agree with her conclusion? What *rival plausible explanations* would you entertain? How might you *control* for these?

2. Bill is a cautious fellow who wants to buy a safe car. He reads some published statistics that compare all the various models of cars in terms of the frequency with which they are involved in accidents. On learning that the BMW 735i sedan (a very expensive car) has the lowest number of accidents and the lowest number of fatalities, he goes out and buys one, believing that he will be safer. From an empirical perspective, would you agree with the logic underlying his decision? Why or why not?

3. Students who take our undergraduate research methods courses receive tutorials (small group "help" sessions where attendance is optional) in addition to the weekly lecture. Since we've often wondered how helpful the tutorials are to students, we've constructed an evaluation to find out. All semester long, attendance is taken at the tutorials. At the end of the semester, we use the attendance reports to construct three groups: those who always or almost always came to tutorial (e.g., missed no more than two tutorials over the semester); those who never or almost never came to tutorials (e.g., came to two or fewer tutorials over

the semester); and those who fell in between (i.e., came sometimes). We then compare the average final grades in the course for the three groups. Suppose that this semester, we find that those who always or almost always came to the tutorials had the highest average grade, those who came part of the time had the next-highest average grade, and those who never or almost never came received the lowest average grade. Suppose further that the differences between the groups are statistically significant.

a. Name the *independent variable* in this study.

b. Name the *dependent variable* in this study.

c. What does it mean to say that the differences between groups are *statistically significant?*

d. Evaluate the study's *internal validity*, identify what threat(s) to internal validity you believe might be present, and state how you might redesign the study to control for those threats.

e. Show that you understand the concept of *external validity* by identifying our external validity concerns in this study.

f. Evaluate the study's *ecological validity*.

4. Jill intends to perform an experiment in which she'll compare whether "factual" appeals or "emotional" appeals are more effective in changing people's attitudes regarding nuclear disarmament. About 100 people have volunteered to participate in her study, and she wonders whether *random assignment* or *matching* would be the better procedure to use in assigning participants to groups. Compare the relative advantages of these techniques in Jill's situation, state which you would recommend, and explain how you would do it.

5. Why are control groups called *control* groups, that is, what do they *control for?*

6. People are different from one another. In what sense, then, can random assignment or matching be said to *equalize* groups?

7. Jerry reads the Donnerstein and Berkowitz (1981) study regarding the effects of viewing pornography on aggression, and says, "Yeah, but I'll bet some of the people in the control group were consumers of pornography *before* they participated in the study. Wouldn't that undermine differences between the groups and mess up their conclusions?" How would you respond?

8. Bob, the head coach for Little League, has developed a series of clinics to teach the kids the essentials of base running. A total of 60 kids end up playing on league teams. Always seeking a challenge, Bob identifies the 20 kids who had the slowest times during the tryouts and makes them the "experimental" group, which is then exposed to his base-running expertise. Another 20 kids are randomly chosen to be the "control" group, that is, they are not given any particular instruction in base running. In order to equalize the amount of attention the two groups receive, however, the control group is given extra practice at bunting, a skill that has no relation to base-running speed.

After two weeks, the kids are assessed again. Bob finds that the base-running times of those in the experimental group have improved significantly, while times of the control group have remained unchanged. He concludes that the techniques utilized in his base-running clinics are indeed effective.

a. Name the *independent variable* in Bob's study.

b. Name the *dependent variable* in Bob's study.

c. Indicate what *threat(s) to internal validity* Bob should be concerned with here.

d. Indicate what Bob's *external validity* concerns might be in this situation.

9. Differentiate between *random selection* and *random assignment*. Which is more relevant to internal validity and which to external validity? Explain.

10. Just because an experiment shows that a phenomenon *can* occur in the lab does not mean that it *does* occur in the world. Would you agree or disagree with that statement? Explain.

11. What are some of the strengths of experimentation as a method? What are some of its limitations?

12. Although the initial conceptualization of the experiment was something along the lines of what a test tube is in chemistry or a vacuum in physics—a clean and "pure" setting apart from the rest of life that allows testing under controlled conditions—some researchers disagreed. They argued that all behaviour occurs in context, and that the laboratory was no exception. So how would you characterize the context in which experimental behaviour occurs?

NOTES

1. We also cannot say for sure that the pills *weren't* effective. They may actually have been helpful, but the research design described here doesn't allow us to assess that. This design produces low internal validity because it leaves us with ambiguity over whether the change was due to the pills, maturational factors, the two combined, or something else.

2. Note that statistical regression does not necessarily imply a drop in performance on the second occasion. We would have expected an increase in James's scoring if the first time we had seen James play he had had a very poor night and only scored 12 points. Because 12 is less than his average of 30 points per night, we would expect on the second night that he would likely get more than 12 points.

3. It was in Donnerstein and Berkowitz (1981) that the anger manipulation was tested for the first time. We've left out that half of the experiment in our description here in order to simplify the discussion.

4. Because we haven't yet discussed much in the way of statistics, we keep our treatment at a relatively conceptual level here. The analysis of variance and the *F*-test are discussed in greater detail in Chapter 12.

FROM MANIPULATIVE TO ANALYTIC CONTROL: QUASI-EXPERIMENTATION AND CASE STUDY ANALYSIS

Discussing the logic of experimentation was a convenient way to introduce and apply some very basic empirical concepts (e.g., operationalization, internal validity, external validity, statistical significance) that are relevant to all experimental and experimental*ist* inferential research. But not all interesting phenomena can be recreated and/or observed in the laboratory. Nor would we necessarily *want* to spend all our time in the lab. But is it possible to maintain the intellectual and inferential rigour of the experiment in the field? And would we want to if we could?

DONALD T. CAMPBELL AND QUASI-EXPERIMENTATION

Not even 40 years ago, most researchers in the social and health sciences felt that leaving the lab and entering the real world meant that one had to throw principles of experimentation, and opportunities for causal inference, out the window. Only in the lab could one gather "clean" data in well-controlled situations created at the whim of the experimenter; the field necessarily involved "dirty" data subject to too many uncontrolled influences. Aspects of the experimental method that were seen as integral to experimentation—random assignment to groups, for example—were seen as impossible to duplicate to any significant degree outside the lab. Hence, the notion of "field experimentation" was seen as a virtual contradiction in terms, and "evaluation research" (e.g., studies that attempt to assess the effects of a particular program or legislative changes) was seen as a necessarily subjective,

qualitative, and error-prone task. There was a clear hierarchy of methods, with the experiment at the top and case study methods at the bottom.

The individual who played the most significant role in encouraging us to reconsider that view was the late Donald T. Campbell, formerly of Northwestern University just outside Chicago.[1] His classic article "Reforms as Experiments" (1969b) was the one to break the ice, although its themes had been the subject of discussion for some years before it was published (e.g., see Campbell 1957; Campbell & Stanley 1963). Campbell's contributions were twofold. First, he supplied a vocabulary and a set of dimensions on which research might be evaluated (e.g., the terms "internal validity" and "external validity" are due to him). Second, he argued that researchers should not confuse the trappings of experimentation with its underlying logic.

Recall the three criteria of causality that John Stuart Mill (1843/1965) said must be satisfied in order to identify a "causal" relationship:

1. Temporal precedence: the presumed cause (X) must come *before* (i.e., is "temporally precedent" to) the effect (Y);

2. Relationship: the presumed cause and effect are indeed related to each other (i.e., the presence or absence of X is associated with an increased likelihood of the presence or absence of Y); and

3. Elimination of rival plausible explanations: the relationship between X and Y is not explained by the presence of other plausible causal agents.

We saw in Chapter 9 how these criteria are addressed in traditional experimental design. The temporal precedence criterion is met by the fact that one manipulates the presumed causal variable (i.e., the researcher "causes" the presumed "cause" to occur) and is there waiting to measure changes that occur afterward in the dependent (or "effect" or "outcome") variable. The existence of a relationship is demonstrated by an observed difference between the "experimental" or "treatment" group and the "control" group beyond what would be expected on the basis of chance variation alone. The final criterion—the absence of rival plausible explanations—is addressed by the concept of internal validity which, in the context of the traditional experiment, was accomplished by (1) manipulation of the independent variable; (2) the creation of experimental and control groups; and (3) random assignment to groups. These directly and elegantly addressed Mill's criteria. Surely proceeding without them would be like trying to fly without wings.

But Campbell (1969b) encouraged us to take experimentalist logic a step further. He recognized the importance of being able to do research in the "real world," arguing that we'd all be a lot better off if we could somehow evaluate the effects of legal reforms and other social changes—that is, become more of an "experimenting society" rather than operating chiefly on the basis of intuition and subjective self-interest (see Campbell 1991). To do so, he suggested, we would first have to stop confusing the *trappings* of experimentation with its *logic*. To quote one of his former colleagues at Northwestern:

> the assumption of [quasi-experimental design] is that the experimental method has much broader application than its laboratory version suggests.... What is important is *not* [the] ability to manipulate and assign randomly, but the *ends* these procedures serve ... The problem then becomes one of providing the proper translation rules to get the social scientist out of the lab and into the "real world," while retaining some of the strong inference characteristic of

the laboratory setting. (Caporaso 1973: 6–7; our emphasis)

In other words, if manipulation of the independent variable and random assignment to groups become difficult to accomplish in field settings, we should not resign ourselves to the feeling that causal inference is thus impossible, but rather should look to the underlying logic of experimentation for alternative procedures that will fulfill these same experimental objectives. According to Campbell (e.g., 1969b), the temporal precedence criterion of causality (i.e., cause before effect) is relatively easily dealt with in many field situations by the acquisition of time-series data. With respect to the inability to randomly assign participants to groups, Campbell (1969b) notes that

> the advocated strategy in quasi-experimentation is not to throw up one's hands and refuse to use the evidence because of this lack of control, but rather to generate by informed criticism as many appropriate rival hypotheses as possible, and then to do the supplementary research ... which would reflect on these rival hypotheses. (413)

The Logic of Quasi-Experimentation

One of the first places that Campbell demonstrated the logic he was advocating in quasi-experimentation was in his analysis of the effects of a crackdown on speeding that occurred in the state of Connecticut in the 1950s. The crackdown was implemented following a year in which a record number of people died on Connecticut highways. Like many others, Connecticut Governor Abraham Ribicoff believed that excess speed was a major cause of traffic fatalities and that the point system that had been in effect in Connecticut until that time was ineffective in keeping speeders in check. In its place, Governor Ribicoff announced that henceforth, all people convicted of speeding on the highways would have their licences suspended. There would be a 30-day suspension for the first offence, a 60-day suspension for a second offence, and an indefinite suspension, the exact duration of which would be the subject of a hearing after 90 days, for a third.

There were, in fact, fewer deaths on the highways of Connecticut the following year: 284 persons died, which was 40 fewer than had been killed on the highways in the previous year. Ribicoff was most pleased with this decrease, arguing that the saving of 40 lives was well worth the inconvenience to individuals who had been guilty of speeding. The Connecticut crackdown was the subject of considerable national attention because of its apparent success, and Governor Ribicoff proudly accepted awards from agencies such as the National Safety Council for his efforts.

Campbell and Ross (1968) did not question Governor Ribicoff's statements that the saving of 40 lives was "worth it," since the relative worth of 40 lives versus inconvenience to speeders is obviously not an empirical question, but rather one of value and philosophy. Instead, the two researchers addressed the question of whether Ribicoff was correct in identifying the crackdown per se as the causal agent in the change that was observed, or whether some other rival plausible explanation(s) might have accounted for the results.

WAS THERE A CHANGE IN THE DEPENDENT VARIABLE?

Campbell suggested that the place to start with such an evaluation is to determine whether there is any evidence at *all* that the crackdown was effective. The answer to that one is fairly obvious, since we've already noted there were 40 fewer deaths after the change than in the year before. So change did occur, and it was in the predicted direction (i.e., fewer rather than more deaths). This is immediately evident in the simple before–after "gee whiz" graph[2] shown in Figure 10.1.

WAS THE INDEPENDENT VARIABLE REALLY MANIPULATED?

The second thing you'd want to establish is whether a speeding crackdown really did occur, as Governor Ribicoff said it did; that is, is there evidence that the independent variable of interest really *was* manipulated? If it *wasn't*, then one could hardly argue that *that* was the variable causing the change. This may sound somewhat obvious, but much of politics is theatre, and it's not uncommon for politicians to say something will happen when in fact it doesn't. On some occasions this failure occurs at the political level, for example, when the proposed change does not make it to or survive the legislative process. On other occasions, the institutions or bureaucracies that are *supposed* to carry out the change in policy can be quite inventive in finding ways *not* to do so (e.g., by finding loopholes in the policy, giving the matter low priority, or moving discretion to another bureaucratic level).

The evidence generally supports the notion that a crackdown really did occur, just as Governor Ribicoff had said it would. To ensure compliance among judges, Ribicoff went on public record to state that judges who did not follow his directive of suspending speeders would find that they wouldn't be reappointed next time their positions came up for renewal. The most direct evidence on this point would be an increase in the number of licence suspensions, and Campbell found that in the first six months of the year the number of suspensions did indeed increase dramatically, from 231 in 1955 to 5,398 in 1956 (an increase of more than 2,000 percent).

So what do we know at this point? First, we know that there really was a change in procedures. The independent variable really was manipulated. Second, we know an attendant change in the dependent variable occurred *after* the independent variable was manipulated; that is, a decrease in deaths was observed *after* the speeding crackdown came into effect. In investigating the assertion that "the Connecticut speeding crackdown caused a substantial decrease in the highway death toll," two of Mill's criteria have thus been established: (1) the presumed "cause" *was* temporally precedent to the alleged "effect"; and (2) the cause and effect *did* covary in time. It is Mill's *third* criterion that's missing at this point: we haven't yet demonstrated that

Figure 10.1

Traffic Fatalities in Connecticut Before and After the Crackdown

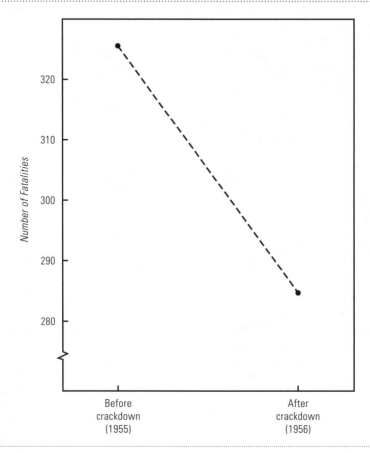

SOURCE: D.T. Campbell and L.H. Ross (1968), "The Connecticut Crackdown on Speeding: Time-Series Data in Quasi-Experimental Analysis," *Law and Society Review*, 3, p. 38. Reproduced with permission of Blackwell Publishing Ltd.

the observed change in the dependent variable was not caused by some plausible factor(s) *other than* the crackdown. And of course *that's* the tough part!

In traditional laboratory experimentation, we simultaneously eliminate numerous rival plausible explanations by randomly assigning participants to groups (thereby ensuring pretest equivalence) and by creating a control group that is equivalent to the experimental group in all respects except for the independent variable. But that luxury obviously isn't available to us here; you can't randomly assign

laws to some states and not others, or randomly assign some drivers to be suspended while others are not. So what can we do?

ELIMINATING RIVAL PLAUSIBLE EXPLANATIONS

At this point, Campbell (1969b) encourages us to make a cognitive shift in our approach to experimentation. What is our objective in this situation? We want to rule out rival plausible explanations. But how do we do that here? By starting off with the *assumption*, on the basis of the data shown in

Figure 10.1, that the prevailing evidence suggests the crackdown *was* effective, and then systematically *deriving*, and then *testing, all* the plausible rival hypotheses we can think of.

In other words, Figure 10.1 can be viewed as the result of a one-group pretest/posttest research design that shows that there was an effect associated with the change in the independent variable. But what might have caused that change? The independent variable, that is, the crackdown, may have caused it. But what *else* might have caused the change? This is where our list of potential threats to internal validity comes into play. The advocated strategy is not to be an armchair quarterback and say, "Oh, too bad there's such poor internal validity because this or that threat was not controlled" and leave it at that, but to say "Let's try and figure out what threats might actually be plausible in this situation, and see whether we can find the data we need to address each one."

At the top of the list is *history*. What events might have occurred between the pretest and the posttest other than the speed crackdown that might have caused the decrease in deaths? Well, we know that weather conditions can make a difference to accident rates, so one possibility is that the year before the crackdown was particularly wet or snow-filled and/or that the year after the crackdown was particularly dry and/or snow-free. Meteorological records speak to this issue, so Campbell and Ross tracked down the appropriate records, and it turned out that in neither year was the amount of rainfall or snowfall exceptional in any way. One rival plausible explanation shot down.

What other possibilities are there? Well, road quality could make a difference. Did Connecticut make any significant improvements in the roads before and after the crackdown? Road improvement budgets speak to that possibility, so Campbell and Ross went to check them, and it turned out there were no unusual expenditures for roads before and after the crackdown. Another rival plausible explanation eliminated.

Car safety perhaps? Did car manufacturers come up with some new technological development that would make new cars safer? Or were seatbelt laws or some other law changed that could also be expected to reduce the number of highway deaths? Once again the answers were "no" and "no." Two more rival plausible explanations go down in flames.

Another class of rival plausible explanations that deserves special note here is *statistical regression*, or *regression toward the mean*. Remember how we said in the previous chapter that the situation in which you most need to worry about regression artifacts is when the members of your "treatment" group are chosen *because of* the extremity of their scores? The political climate that contributes to many programs coming into existence in the first place makes statistical regression a threat you must always worry about when evaluating the effects of social programs. Campbell (1969b) makes the point well in his facetious advice to "trapped" administrators: to look good, all you have to do is pick the worst administrative unit under your control as the target for your "experimental" program, and then wait for a year; there's a high probability that your performance will improve just because of regression toward the mean (but you, of course, take all the credit).

Even when such an approach isn't being taken by administrators for self-serving reasons, "extreme circumstances" often give birth to programs at short notice. When the media headlines scream "Worst Crime Wave Ever" or "Unprecedented Slaughter on the Highways," politicians and civil servants may use their discretionary funding to show that they're doing something and to reassure the public that everything's under control. Of course, it's exactly such circumstances that are most often associated with regression artifacts, in which case the situation will in all likelihood improve by next year, whether or not anything is done.

So one of our concerns with the Connecticut speeding crackdown data should be the question "How typical was 1955?" A "treatment" as severe as the Connecticut speeding crackdown would most likely arise in the kind of extreme conditions most conducive to regression artifacts, and we were told that 1955 involved a "record high" number of highway traffic deaths. How can we address that threat to internal validity? The answer: by gathering time-series data that *show* the maturational trend of the data. These are shown in Figure 10.2. You can see where the 1955–56 pre–post comparison graph (Figure 10.1) fits into the picture. Figure 10.2 suggests that regression to the mean is indeed a plausible concern; 1955 *was* an atypically high year, and so it should be no surprise that there would be a decrease in the next year. We won't go into all the details here (but see Campbell & Ross 1968 or an earlier edition of *Research Decisions* if you are interested), but suffice it to say that, in the end, Campbell and Ross concluded that some portion of the decrease was probably due to a regression artifact, but that the change was so substantial and long-lasting (note in Figure 10.2 how the change in direction in 1956 is followed by further decreases in

subsequent years) that it was likely the speed crackdown was producing a good part of the decrease as well.

You've probably caught the general drift by now. The emphasis is on *informed critique* as a source for generating rival *plausible* explanations; your job is to be your own best critic, to anticipate as many rival plausible explanations as possible, and then to test systematically the plausibility of each one by gathering whatever data are appropriate. This places considerable onus on the researcher both to recognize potential rival explanations that are actually plausible and to identify the sorts of data that will address those possibilities—one probably wouldn't want to put too much trust in Ray, the character depicted in Figure 10.3—which makes both quasi-experimentation and qualitative case study analysis

Figure 10.2

Single Time-Series Data on Fatality Rates

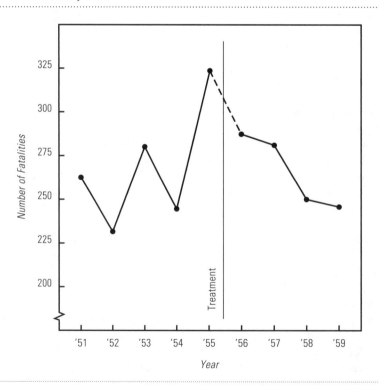

SOURCE: D.T. Campbell and L.H. Ross (1968), "The Connecticut Crackdown on Speeding: Time-Series Data in Quasi-Experimental Analysis," *Law and Society Review*, 3, p. 42. Reproduced with permission of Blackwell Publishing Ltd.

challenging to do well. The resulting analysis will leave you with either (1) *no* rival plausible explanations remaining, in which case we conclude that the crackdown itself is the most compelling explanation we are left with, or (2) *some* (or many) rival plausible explanations remaining, in which case we can do no more than list what these might be. The researcher's task is to make a comprehensive inventory of these and to test them out as thoroughly as possible.

and randomly assign people to this or that group—was not the be all and end all of experimentalist research, and that *analytic control*—using our heads to anticipate and address all rival plausible explanations—could accomplish the same ends. Part of the trick then is to understand the kinds of rival plausible explanations that should be considered. Campbell had supplied a number of categories in relation to laboratory experimentation

Appreciating the Social Dynamics of Field Settings

The **time-series design** that the analysis of the Connecticut speed crackdown is based on is not the only way to proceed in the field. Campbell and his colleagues have come up with many different types of quasi-experimental designs, far more than we can cover in this book. Those interested in more advanced treatment of the topic should consult the classic reference by Cook and Campbell (1979) or its newer incarnation as Shadish, Cook, & Campbell (2001).

New Threats to Internal Validity

The important turn that Campbell took us through was the idea that *manipulative control*—the ability to create situations at whim

Figure 10.3: Techniques involving analytic as opposed to manipulative control—such as quasi-experimentation and qualitative case study analysis—are a challenge to do well.

that we considered in Chapter 9—history, selection, statistical regression and so on. While these threats should still be considered in quasi-experimental research, several other classes of threats to internal validity become particularly relevant to the evaluative setting in the field. We will discuss five of these: diffusion of treatment, compensatory equalization, compensatory rivalry, resentful demoralization, and mortality.

DIFFUSION OR IMITATION OF TREATMENTS

Within the confines of the laboratory, it's generally fairly easy to isolate experimental and control groups from each other. Even when participants know that there are other groups, they probably won't know much, if anything, about how their own experience differs from what's being experienced by others. Their participation is usually short-lived, and lines of communication between participants in different groups are rare or nonexistent. From the experimental perspective, this is as it should be, since clear inference benefits from clear isolation of groups.

In the field, however, it's not unusual to be faced with intact groups that can't be isolated from one another. Instead of having two (or more) comparison groups that are clearly different on the independent variable being considered, we may find that the boundaries between the groups are or become somewhat blurred. For example, if the groups are differentiated by their access to varying sets of information, any communication between groups about the nature of this information will make each group a little more like the other(s). This **diffusion of treatment** (sometimes called **imitation of treatment**) will act to minimize the groups' separation and heighten their similarity. The independent variable, in other words, doesn't have a real opportunity to "work." If this occurs, you might be left concluding— perhaps erroneously—that the treatment variable is ineffective, when in fact it might have been quite effective had it just been given a reasonable opportunity and if the difference between groups was more clearly defined.

COMPENSATORY EQUALIZATION

Similarly, **compensatory equalization of treatments** may act to obscure differences between groups, leading to an erroneous finding of "no difference." Cook and Campbell (1979) explain that this problem arises when the treatment being evaluated involves goods and/or services deemed desirable, and where there is a large disparity between groups. Administrators, those charged with implementing the treatment, or some of the recipients may reroute some goods or provide access to services among some or all members of the disadvantaged group in an effort to alleviate disparity. This in most cases will be well-meaning and well-intended by those involved—they see their colleagues disadvantaged and want to slide some resources under the table to reduce some of the inequity—but this plays havoc with one's ability to evaluate a program. The more compensatory equalization occurs, the less likely one is to find a difference between treatment and comparison groups because the boundary between them has become less and less clear.

COMPENSATORY RIVALRY

New programs and legislative changes are often much more public than experiments occurring in laboratories. If it's known that an evaluation is in progress, one may see **compensatory rivalry** by those who are receiving the less desirable treatment(s). Knowing that one is in the disadvantaged group may spur a competitive spirit to overcome adversity and perform well. This is particularly likely to be the case in situations where the group already perceives itself as a group (e.g., work teams, crews, classes) and has a lot to lose if a difference is revealed.

This threat to internal validity has also been dubbed the **John Henry effect** (see Cook & Campbell 1979), after the legendary individual who, when he learned that his performance was to be compared to that of a steam drill, worked so hard that he outperformed the drill but died in the process. As a threat to internal validity, compensatory rivalry obscures "real" differences between groups, potentially leading you to conclude "no difference" when, under more normal circumstances, there would be.

RESENTFUL DEMORALIZATION

In contrast, if it's known that an evaluation is in progress, individuals who are in the disadvantaged group may respond with **resentful demoralization** if they perceive the result as adverse and inevitable. They may not even try to compete, and they may even intentionally reduce their performance. In this instance, the researcher may *overestimate* the actual potency of a treatment.

MORTALITY

Although mortality is a threat to be considered in laboratory research and was featured even in earlier treatments of internal validity (e.g., Campbell & Stanley 1963), we left it for this chapter as it is a threat more likely to occur in field research. **Mortality**, in the present context, refers to a situation in which some individuals drop out of the research before it's completed. Single-session, short-term laboratory experimentation virtually precludes mortality as a problem. But in the field, where time-series data and a succession of follow-ups are more likely, the mortality problem increases in relevance. Some individuals who are recorded as participants at the beginning of the study do not return to receive the dependent measure at follow-up; for example, they drop out of therapy, choose to resign from the group, move to another jurisdiction, are released on parole, join another club, get lost, or die.

To illustrate the problem with one type of example, let's say that a "March for Millions" is being held in your city—a walk or run in which people register to walk for 40 kilometres for a particular charity and the farther they walk, the more money that is raised. We won't get into the details of it, but a theory such as cognitive dissonance theory would suggest that the farther you walk, the more you will believe in the legitimacy of the cause you are walking for. The prediction arises from your alleged need to rationalize to yourself why you are expending so much energy: the longer you walk,

and the more energy you expend, the stronger your need to rationalize, and hence the more fervent you will become about the cause in order to justify to yourself why you didn't stop 10 kilometres ago when the blisters started appearing on your feet.

In order to test the theory, a researcher goes to each 10-km marker along the route and asks people to provide a number of ratings about how important they think the cause is that they are walking for. The findings are as predicted: at the 10-km mark, the average rating is that the cause is "pretty important;" by the 20-km mark the average rating is that the cause is "very important;" and by the end of the walk, the average rating is that the cause is "extremely important." The researcher concludes that the theory is supported. Would you accept that conclusion?

The problem, as we hope you can see, is one of the *selection bias* that creeps in because of participant mortality. To the extent that there are differences between those who depart and those who remain, it spoils our ability to conclude that it is the independent variable per se (the walk in this instance) that is causing a change in attitude. The problem arises because each group at each 10-km marker is comprised of a different subset of people from the one preceding it, and the group that finishes is not the same as the group that began. Consequently we do not know whether the people who continue walking are becoming more and more enthusiastic about the cause, as the theory would predict, or whether attitudes are not changing at all, but it only looks that way because the people who care less about the cause are dropping out along the way.

This threat is particularly problematic when there is differential mortality between groups, a situation that happens often, since those in the control group have the least reason to return and are often participating only as a favour. Whenever mortality occurs, one must question not only the representativeness of those who remain, but also people's reasons for leaving. The questions to address are (1) Who are those that drop out? (2) In what ways, if any, do they differ from the remaining individuals in the group? (3) What is the relationship between

(a) the variables on which those who drop out and those who remain differ and (b) the dependent measure? The trick in this situation is to anticipate this possibility and gather sufficient pretest information to deal with this eventuality. Can you think of a way that you could deal with these issues in the "March for Millions" example?[3]

As the above discussion suggests, many new problems await one in the field. But why do these things happen? Some are simply the product of the social interaction that is a part of everyday life that experimenters work so hard to control and preclude in the lab. On some occasions, the vagaries of chance just seem to stack up against you, and Murphy's law[4] rules the day. But much also happens because of the human motives and emotions that are awakened by the particular topic of study. Welcome to the politics of evaluation research.

The Politics of Evaluation Research

Field research is more blatantly a part of the phenomenon it investigates than laboratory-based research. Certainly, the negotiation of design and measurement techniques for evaluation research is an interpersonal as well as a cognitive process, and the consequences of one's decisions and findings may be more visible. For these and other reasons, field research is a different kind of animal.

In Chapter 3 we discussed some of the ethical and moral decisions that researchers face when negotiating the terms under which a study will be conducted. Here, we'll discuss evaluative research within a political context, attempting to make explicit some of the roles researchers play within that process. In keeping with this book's general theme, the emphasis is less on telling prospective researchers what to do than on articulating the decisions researchers must make; these decisions should most certainly be made as a result of conscious choice rather than out of habit or naiveté.

PROGRAMS ARE POLITICAL CREATURES

In an article that has become a classic in the evaluation research literature, Weiss (1975) identifies three major areas in which evaluation researchers should be aware of political considerations. The first she notes is that programs aren't the result of some anonymous individual exclaiming, "Gee, why don't we give *this* a try?" Quite the contrary: "they [have typically] emerged from the rough-and-tumble world of political support, opposition and bargaining; and attached to them are the reputations of legislative sponsors, the careers of administrators, the jobs of program staff, and the expectations of clients" (14). In sum, many, if not all, *programs are political creatures.*

This reality has several implications. First, researchers should realize that the program's official goals are not necessarily a reasonable statement of its initiators' actual goals. In an effort to appease various interest groups and to sell the desirability of program implementation, legislators and policymakers often make inflated and even grandiose claims that go beyond the capacity of any given program. A basic goal of public housing, for example, is to provide decent accommodation to those who might otherwise be disenfranchised. Yet what one hears in the news is that "public housing will not only provide decent living space; it will also improve health, reduce crime, and lead to improved school performance" (Weiss 1975: 16).

At the same time, public articulation of goals and objectives may also *omit* mention of many other goals that were considered when the program was formulated. These might include the desire to avoid layoffs of bureaucratic personnel, a desire to extend political power and influence, and/or the need to be perceived by the public as *doing something* about some area of social concern. Researchers also must realize that the perception of project goals will not necessarily be consistent throughout all levels of program implementation. As Weiss (1975) notes, "what the [government] writes into legislation as programme objectives are not necessarily what the secretary's office or the director of the programme see as their mission, nor what the state or local project managers or the operating staff actually try to accomplish" (16).

Thus, evaluation researchers must appreciate that there *are* political dynamics to the process of program development and implementation, and they must make sure that their evaluations and reports *speak* to the various constituencies. This is not to say that researchers should become co-opted by political considerations, whether by coercion (e.g., you will only be given the opportunity if you show that you will deliver a positive evaluation) or voluntary zeal (e.g., the researcher takes an advocacy role and is willfully blind to potential problems). In our view the best evaluator is one who respects the objectives of the program, understands that different factions will view it differently, and seeks to be an *independent* evaluator who *realistically* examines the program or phenomenon from the perspective of multiple constituencies.

We also encourage you to consider *science* as one of your constituencies; that is, you should not forget your academic heritage. Indeed, for us, the opportunity for academic benefits is a prerequisite for involvement in evaluative research. Thus, an evaluation of a police department's computerized database system not only produced information that was useful to the police department and federal Department of Communications (Palys, Boyanowsky, & Dutton 1983), but also provided the basis for a broader discussion on the implications of computer technology for decision making (Palys, Boyanowsky, & Dutton 1984). Similarly, Chris's participation in a national study of Aboriginal people living in urban centres not only provided information of use to Aboriginal leaders looking to develop educational and program opportunities in their communities, but also allowed him the opportunity to test out ways of incorporating digital technologies for inter-communication and the overall management of researchers and data in a multi-site study (Palys & Atchison in press).

THE POLITICS OF THE DECISION-MAKING PROCESS

A second way that Weiss (1975) notes that politics enter the evaluation research process requires an appreciation for the *politics of higher-echelon decision making*. To begin with, the funds that pay for evaluation research rarely come from the particular program being evaluated. More frequently, these funds originate from more senior bureaucratic levels, which are less concerned with program and organizational survival than those on the front lines. In this sense, one might think that senior decision makers might be more likely to consider the research evidence more dispassionately. But they have their own constituencies with whom they must deal and to whom they're accountable.

In sum, the decisions of senior decision makers ostensibly go beyond considerations of program effectiveness per se:

> Their decisions are rooted in all the complexities of the democratic decision-making process, the allocation of power and authority, the development of coalitions, the trade-offs with interest groups, professional guilds, and salient publics … [The research evidence] will not be the sole basis for a decision, and legitimately so: other information and other values inevitably enter a democratic policy process.* (Weiss 1975: 17)

The researcher, in other words, *can* make some reasonable statements about how things *are*, but affirmations about how things *should be* enter moral and ideological rather than empirical grounds. Researchers *can* expose fallacious belief, and they *can* unearth some historical or contemporary consequences of particular strategies of action. But in arguing over the desirability of different social futures, they are just one of many voices in the democratic decision-making process.

THE POLITICAL STANCE OF THE EVALUATION ITSELF

As Weiss (1975) points out, the third major way politics intrudes into evaluation research is in the stance of the evaluation itself:

---

* Weiss, C.H. (1975). Evaluation research in the political context. In E.L. Streuning and M. Guttentag (Eds.) *Handbook of Evaluation Research* (Vol. 1. pp. 13-26) Beverly Hills, CA: Sage

Social scientists tend to see evaluation research, like all research, as objective, unbiased, nonpolitical, a corrective for the special pleading and selfish interests of program operators and policy-makers alike. Evaluation produces hard evidence of actual outcomes, but it incorporates as well a series of assumptions; and many researchers are unaware of the political nature of the assumptions they make and the role they play.* (19)

As noted earlier, one of the differences between the laboratory and the field is that the latter is a more interpersonal and visibly consequential process. Although one rarely sees evaluation research on the evening news, it *is* a matter of some significance in the milieu under consideration. The researcher is a professional, but often an outsider, brought in to evaluate. His or her mere presence on the scene has several implications: it suggests that the researcher accepts the legitimacy of the goals and objectives being pursued. It also implies that the rationale underlying the program is a reasonable one. If it wasn't, why bother to evaluate the program? The researcher's presence alone gives an aura of legitimacy. All the above suggest a status quo orientation. Furthermore, the money to do the evaluation will probably have come from an "establishment" source, and those to whom the researcher will have access and who will read the report are most likely to be members of that group.

Typical design considerations also often promote a status quo view. Researchers should be aware that, when they limit their selection of independent variables to a particular set, they're implicitly stating that other variables are irrelevant or unchangeable. It's no accident that biogeneticists offer genetic solutions, economists see economic solutions, and lawyers offer legal solutions. Obviously, one must limit one's choice of variables in order to actually *do* a finite piece of research. But most evaluations limit their comparisons to those who receive the program

and those who don't, ignoring (both in the design and in the final report) the social-structural conditions within which the program operates—and thus implying that these conditions are a constant.

Researchers also have been employed as the heavy; they were particularly useful (and used) in the conservative climate of recessionist restraint and fiscal retrenchment in the late 1970s and early 1980s. Most programs that have been evaluated show little or no direct effect in the social areas they have been designed to address (Weiss 1975). For example, consider a study like Campbell and Ross's (1968) classic evaluation of the Connecticut speeding crackdown. Campbell clearly selected that program as the one to write about because it allowed him to illustrate principles of quasi-experimental design. Governor Ribicoff conveniently made his pronouncement at the end of the calendar year, thus affording an easier year-to-year comparison. The change he introduced was implemented swiftly, intensely, and pervasively. And even in that situation, the picture *could* have been more clear-cut, since regression artifacts were never completely dispensed with as a rival plausible explanation.

So how much *can* be expected of any more modest program? One more hour of counselling isn't going to eliminate crime, and one more housing development is not going to eliminate poverty. Nor is one more program of any kind going to alleviate all our social ills. So why are some programs picked for evaluation and others not? "The evaluation researcher—now that somebody was paying attention to findings—was cast in the role of political hatchet man" (Weiss 1975: 23). Evaluations of particular programs have often been treated as synonymous with evaluations of the *objectives* that underlie them. Rather than leading us to seek alternative ways of pursuing worthy social goals, evaluations often lead decision makers to cut funding for certain programs as a class and hence for the goals that those aim to reach. The political dilemma has been a real one for many researchers, who feel uncomfortable seeing programs that address important social objectives being terminated without replacement.

---

* Weiss, C.H. (1975). Evaluation research in the political context. In E.L. Streuning and M. Guttentag (Eds.) *Handbook of Evaluation Research* (Vol. 1. pp. 13-26) Beverly Hills, CA: Sage

SO WHAT CAN A PERSON DO?

Weiss (1975) offers three pieces of advice for dealing with this array of potential pitfalls and complexities. First, she suggests that program goals be put "in sensible perspective," a task that requires attention to the plurality of goals represented by multiple constituencies. If one is going to believe in the virtues of heterogeneity and tolerance, then one must tolerate heterogeneity of perspectives and address these in the context of one's research design. Certainly one must consider alternative models of social justice to the utilitarian one that so pervasively guides evaluation research (e.g., see House 1976; Pepinsky 1987; Rawls 1971).

Weiss's (1975) second piece of advice is "to evaluate a particularly strong version of the program before, or along with, the evaluation of the ordinary levels at which it functions" (23). Clearly, such an approach would represent a fairer test of the efficacy of any given piece of social tinkering at its best. It is also consistent with Campbell's (1969b) notion of the "experimenting society," where we essentially adopt a local "pilot policy" approach to assess the prospective large-scale effect of policy alternatives. The articulation (and hence greater accountability) of social objectives that such a society would require might promote a welcome dialogue. But in practice, this advice brings us back to the status quo orientation inherent in the evaluation process when researchers limit themselves to the perspective of the funding agency. As Henry (1987) argues, even when one is critical of or attempts to set oneself apart from some other group, any discussion in that group's terms serves only to reaffirm its perspective—and hence its power.

This brings us to Weiss's (1975) third admonition, which is to do something *other than* evaluation research. She may be overly narrow in her implied definition of evaluation research as in-house evaluation bound by the perspective of the funding agency. But we concur with her statement that too often

we concentrate attention on changing the attitudes and behaviour of target groups without

concomitant attention to the institutional structures and social arrangements that tend to keep them "target groups." ... There may be greater potential in doing research on the processes that give rise to social problems, the institutional structures that contribute to their origin and persistence, the social arrangements that overwhelm efforts to eradicate them, and the points at which they are vulnerable to societal intervention.* (24)

More recently, Weiss (1993) has written a reflective article that she describes as "mellower" than the statement she wrote in the 1970s. Although she reaffirms her belief in the need to understand the political climate in which evaluations are conducted, she also believes that evaluation itself has matured in the intervening years and, as a result, has become both more useful and more credible. In particular, she notes that,

> In part, the successes are the result of using more realistic standards for evaluating success. Evaluations are generally not holding programs up to the inflated and unreasonable expectations that prevailed in the past. In part, too, the happier messages have come through because evaluation has widened its purview. Instead of concentrating solely on the outcomes of programs, evaluations now examine the whole context in which programs operate: from the initial definition of problems, through the development of program models, to the operation of programs in their settings. With this broader orientation, evaluations learn much that enriches our understanding of social needs, interventions, implementation, and community response.
>
> Evaluations are also making effective use of a wider array of methods and techniques. Perhaps the most notable difference from earlier days is

---

* Weiss, C.H. (1975). Evaluation research in the political context. In E.L. Streuning and M. Guttentag (Eds.) *Handbook of Evaluation Research* (Vol. 1. pp. 13-26) Beverly Hills, CA: Sage.

the more frequent use of qualitative methods of study. Evaluators today engage in intensive interviewing, observation, review of documents, and other such techniques. They often spend enough time on site to observe changes in environment, program, and participants and to develop insights about conditions associated with beneficial change. They have more to say about the "how" of programs and the "why" of consequences.* (108)

We agree. While evaluation began as a very centrally controlled enterprise dominated by funding agency definitions and seeking to impose the desiderata of experimental and quasi-experimental design on "bottom line" evaluations of effectiveness, the biggest developments in evaluation research in the last two decades have been in (a) the broader range of perspectives that are recognized as requiring inclusion in any comprehensive evaluation; (b) the growth in respect for the unique contributions that qualitative approaches bring to evaluation and the greater light they shed on process as opposed to a more simple bottom line; and (c) the wisdom of utilizing more collaborative approaches, such as those integral to participatory action research, that make for more culturally sensitive and more inclusive designs (see Samuels & Ryan 2011) that "speak" to those most directly affected. In order to more fully appreciate these developments we need to extend our articulation of experimentalist logic by taking the next step to qualitative case study analysis.

QUALITATIVE CASE STUDY ANALYSIS

Several methodological features of qualitative approaches have been outlined so far in this book: we've noted that qualitative research is typically inductive and places a high value on preliminary exploration that benefits from the insights of local sources in the process of finding a research focus and

---

* Weiss, C.H. (1993). Politics and evaluation: A reprise with mellower overtones. *American Journal of Evaluation Research*, 14(1): 107-109. Sage Publications

establishing operational definitions (Chapter 2), extols the virtues of target or purposive sampling (Chapter 4), and emphasizes that one should maintain flexibility and reap the advantages of more open-ended research instruments (see, for example, Chapters 6, 7, and 8).

Researchers engaged in qualitative research also were described as particularly interested in the *processes* through which phenomena are produced. Phenomena are scrutinized by these researchers with an eye toward how they "unfold" and "evolve," and this view is reflected again in the belief that sensitive inductive research should similarly "unfold" and "evolve" as more and more is understood about the phenomenon or research site under consideration.

That is actually quite an incredible array of skills to bring to the evaluation research table—being used to adapting oneself to circumstances in the field; having experience at gaining access and establishing rapport with individuals in real social settings who are often different from oneself; familiarity with purposive sampling strategies and the skills it requires to identify appropriate participants who will represent the range of relevant stakeholders and can bring a diversity of perspectives to the data; being able to gather, manage and analyze a range of data including interviews, observation, and archival materials. And what is evaluation research but a case study of one or more of a particular kind of agency or organization or program? Qualitative approaches were a natural for incorporation into evaluation research and the biggest surprise is how long it took more quantitatively inclined evaluation researchers to discover and embrace them.

Analytic Control in the Case Study Context

Certainly there was a time that skepticism about qualitative case study approaches ruled. Donald T. Campbell in his earlier writings even referred to case studies as "pre-scientific" and "of little inferential value." For example, in his influential monograph with Julian Stanley (Campbell & Stanley 1963), Campbell caustically noted that as has been pointed out, such [case] studies have such a total absence of control as to be of almost no scientific value. . . . Such studies often involve tedious collection of specific detail, careful observation, testing, and the like, and in such instances involve the error of *misplaced precision.* ... It seems well-nigh unethical at the present time to allow, as theses or dissertations ... case studies of this nature. (6–7)

The main problem Campbell saw with such studies was that there were too many possible explanations and too few observations against which to assess the veracity of those explanations. We heard the classic example of this problem on a recent radio news program, which contained a story about a British gentleman who was celebrating his 111th birthday. As is usual in such interviews, the man was asked to what he attributed his longevity. Such a situation is problematic to the social and health scientist, in that it presents only one observation (i.e., the man is 111) and a lifetime full of explanatory variables that could potentially account for that outcome. As Campbell (1979) later explained:

> The caricature of the single case study approach which I have had in mind consists of an observer who notes a single striking characteristic of a culture, and then has available all of the other differences on all other variables to search through in finding an explanation. . . . That he will find an "explanation" that seems to fit perfectly is inevitable, through his total lack of "degrees of freedom." (It is as though he were trying to fit two points of observation with a formula including a thousand adjustable terms, whereas in good science, we must have fewer terms in our formula than our data points). (54)

Much to his credit for the open-mindedness that it showed, Campbell later understood this to be an undeserved stereotype and acknowledged his shortsightedness:

> In past writings ... I have spoken harshly of the single-occasion, single-setting (one shot) case study, not on the ground of its qualitative nature, but because it combined such a fewness of points of observation, and such a plethora of available causal concepts, that a spuriously perfect fit was almost certain. Recently, in a quixotic and ambivalent article (1975), I have recanted, reminding myself that such studies regularly contradict the prior expectations of the authors, and are convincing and informative to sceptics like me to a degree which my simple-minded rejection [did] not allow for. (Campbell 1978: 201)

The turning point for Campbell was this: if case studies are so easily supportive of whatever explanation the researcher brings to the situation, why do so many qualitative researchers report being surprised, changing their beliefs, and revising their theories (see, for example, Becker 1970; Campbell 1978, 1979)? Part of the reason for Campbell's change of heart was that he reconstrued case studies. He *had* seen the case study as *one* (collective) observation, as one would from the perspective of aggregate statistics. Later, he acknowledged that *myriad* observations are possible within the context of a given case study:

> While it is probable that many case studies professing or implying interpretation or explanation, or relating the case to theory, are guilty of [the faults he had outlined], it now seems to me clear that not all are, or need be, and that I have overlooked a major source of discipline. . . . In a case study done by an alert social scientist who has thorough location acquaintance, the theory he uses to explain the focal difference also generates predictions or expectations on dozens of other aspects of the culture, and he does not retain the theory unless most of these are also confirmed. In some sense, he has tested the theory with degrees of freedom coming from the multiple implications of any one theory. The process is a kind of pattern matching ... in which there are

many aspects of the pattern demanded by theory that are available for matching with his observations on the local setting. (Campbell 1978: 57)

In sum, just about *any* theory can account for a *single* observation. The trick is to evaluate and develop the theory by looking at the *multiple* observations it implies and by constantly considering rival, plausible explanations that might account equally well for some or all of these observations.

The generic research process Campbell envisions is one in which a rigorous and self-critical scholar can use *any* source of information as a vehicle for generating or evaluating the multiple implications of theory.[5] To the extent that the scientist is attuned to such multiple implications, and systematic and forthright in evaluating the consistency of any given theory, "science is much better than ignorance and, on many topics, better than traditional wisdom. Our problem as methodologists is to define our course between the extremes of inert skepticism and naive credulity. *When a scientist argues that a given body of data corroborate a theory, invalidation of that claim comes in fact only from equally plausible or better explanations of those data*" (Campbell 1978, p. 185; emphasis in original). We are led to the picture of science as a community of disputatious, questioning truth-seekers, whose role is to marry a critical approach with an anticipation of rival plausible explanations.

Campbell is arguing for "the quasi-experimentation of everyday life," and suggesting that "good" case studies are those that expend the effort to achieve thorough local knowledge, draw inferences through the process of offering explanations to account for observations, and eliminate rival, plausible explanations. This process has been articulated by two former students of Campbell's—Louise Kidder (e.g., see 1981a) and Paul Rosenblatt (e.g., see 1981)—who studied both with Campbell (a more quantitatively oriented psychologist) and Howard Becker (a more qualitatively oriented sociologist) at Northwestern University. Kidder (1981a), for example, offers an integration of the quasi-experimentational framework with three different qualitative case

studies, including Becker's (1963) classic study on "becoming a marihuana user." Becker (1979) offers a similarly qualitative account that is clearly framed within a "rival plausible explanations" perspective, which Rosenblatt (1981) argues has utility in ethnographic research.

By emphasizing a potential reconciliation of case study methods with experimentalist principles, a unification might be forged between the logical/rational discipline of the best of social and health science analysis and the phenomenological integrity of what have been considered more "qualitative" modes of research. We have distinguished for too long between the "subjective" understanding of participants and the "objective" aspirations of social and health scientists. Those who cling to this dichotomy are urged to reconsider, as Campbell (1979) did.

> Too often quantitative social scientists, under the influence of missionaries from logical positivism, presume that in true science, quantitative knowing replaces qualitative, common-sense knowing. The situation is in fact quite different. Rather, science depends upon qualitative common sense knowing even though at its best it goes beyond it. Science in the end contradicts some items of common sense, but it only does so by trusting the great bulk of the rest of common-sense knowledge. Such revision of common sense by science is akin to the revision of common sense by common sense which, paradoxically, can only be done by trusting more common-sense. (50–51)

This is *not* an invitation to indulge in naive credulity or gullibility. One can see the knowledge of science as "special" if for no other reason than that it emerges from a community of disputatious, quarrelsome truth-seekers who make the acquisition of such knowledge their business, and who believe in a constant interplay between theory and data. At the same time, our inquiry (in both laboratory and field) would be better informed by more extensive interaction with our milieu of interest, and by an appreciation of the phenomenology of those who lie within.

When we get down to our own practical work, a plausible-rival-hypothesis approach is absolutely essential, and must for the most part be implemented by common-sense, humanistic, qualitative approaches. In programme evaluation, the details of programme implementation history, the site-specific wisdom, and the gossip about where the bodies are buried are all essential to interpreting the *quantitative* data.

Qualitative knowing is absolutely essential as a prerequisite foundation for quantification in science. Without competence at the qualitative level, one's computer printout is misleading or meaningless.

To rule out plausible rival hypotheses we need situation-specific wisdom. The lack of this knowledge (whether it be called ethnography, or programme history, or gossip) makes us incompetent estimators of programme impacts, turning out conclusions that are not only wrong, but are often wrong in socially destructive ways. (Campbell 1984, pp. 30–34)

Instead of the traditional hierarchy of empirical "goodness" that tautologically reaffirms the desirability of manipulative control, the argument here puts the continuum on its side, and acknowledges that each of the alternatives listed employs some mixture of manipulative and analytic control in seeking possibilities for inference. It suggests that case studies that violate all the desiderata of experimental practice may nonetheless afford considerable inference capability *if* sufficient care has been taken to gain local knowledge and gather data that anticipate rival plausible explanations and conclusions.

The trick, of course, is to ensure that we have the analytic acumen to do that job well. Unlike the classic experiment, where rival plausible explanations are addressed by creating and manipulating the situation using such techniques as random assignment and equivalent control groups, quasi-experimentation and qualitative case study analysis move us into the realm of analytic control where the researcher has to understand the logic of experimentalist inquiry and the phenomenon under study so well that a reasonable inventory of rival plausible explanations can be generated and the data that will address those rival plausible explanations are sought.

Life as a Case Study

An interesting implication of Campbell's preliminary analysis would be that much of what we experience in life can *never* be analyzed "scientifically" (Campbell & Stanley 1963); after all, what is life but a never-ending case study? But if it is so impossible, why do so many individuals do it so well every day? For example:

+ The historian attempts to explain why King John signed the *Magna Carta* at Runnymede in 1215.
+ The coroner must ascertain the cause of death for each individual corpse.
+ The physician, in order to prescribe an effective treatment, must diagnose why that rash appeared on your forearm.
+ A plane crashes and all on board are killed. The Federal Aviation Board investigates to determine its cause.
+ An engineering troubleshooter is brought in to determine why a certain bridge fell down during a recent flood.
+ A young adult is arrested at a public park for having an open can of beer. He is taken back to the station. Three hours later he is dead from a gunshot wound and the police interrogator claims he shot the man in self-defence. An inquest is called to determine whether that is really what happened.
+ The mechanic must figure out why your car doesn't start.
+ The detective seeks to determine "whodunit."
+ The transit investigator must determine why one subway train crashed into another.

If "scientific" case study analysis were impossible, how could these people make sense out of these case study situations? And why are some people better at it than others?

Causal Checklists and the Modus Operandi Method

As Scriven (1976) describes it, common to all these occupations is an underlying logic to their inquiry, which he refers to as a **modus operandi method**. The analytical challenge common to all the examples noted above is to identify a cause or a set of causes for a given phenomenon. But where and how do we begin?

Invariably, we begin by relying heavily on existing knowledge, whether derived from the more formal literature or from our "common sense." We never enter a situation devoid of theoretical constructs: there's no such thing as "immaculate perception." Campbell (1969b) metaphorically describes knowledge as a ship rotting at sea—we know the ship is rotten, but we can't merely take it apart and reconstruct it or we'd sink! Thus we're left to change the ship one plank at a time, relying on all those other old planks (some rotten and some not) to keep the structure together and afloat as we replace its parts, eventually creating a whole new ship. New knowledge can't be created unless we trust a good portion of the knowledge we already have.

The "knowledge" we do have may vary from scientific to intuitive, but whatever its nature, Scriven (1976) says that we'll use it in "problem" situations as a source for generating "causal checklists." For example, suppose your car doesn't start and your mechanic now has the task of fixing it. Fixing the car requires first diagnosing why it does not start. The mechanic approaches your car knowing that numerous factors must combine in order for a car to start: among other things, there must be gas in it (assuming you have an internal combustion engine), the key must be turned, the ignition system must function properly, the battery must not be dead, spark plugs and points must be clean and properly set, and so on. In order to determine why your car doesn't start, the mechanic begins with what Scriven calls a "presence or absence check" to see whether each of the causal requirements is met.

In research jargon, the mechanic seeks to generate and consider *rival plausible explanations* that might account for the phenomenon of interest. Is there gas in the car? Are the plugs and points okay? Is the battery charged? If all but one of the causal requirements are met (e.g., the battery is dead, but there's gas in the car, the points and plugs look fine, etc.), then *that* is the probable cause. If *none* of the causal requirements appears to be absent (i.e., everything in the initial checklist seems fine), we may try to expand the list of possibilities by considering more remote alternatives, by applying causal lists from analogous phenomena, or by asking other knowledgeable people to suggest further possibilities.

In the event that *more than one* plausible factor emerges, Scriven (1976) suggests that we look for a modus operandi (MO) to help identify the actual cause, just as a detective might identify a criminal by the characteristic manner in which a crime is executed. Scriven (1976) goes on to explain that "the MO of a particular cause is an associated configuration of events, processes, or properties, usually in time sequence, which can often be described as the characteristic causal chain ... connecting the cause with the effect" (105).

Of course, one must have—through prior research or experience—a reasonable understanding of particular MOs and a decent list of rival plausible causes. Given that one has such a list, Scriven says, the following procedures apply: first, check for the presence or absence of each plausible cause in this situation. If only one plausible cause is present (or, in some cases, if only one is absent), the factor that's present (or absent) is the most likely cause; if more than one plausible cause is present, check for the presence of complete MOs. If only one MO is present, the cause associated with that MO is the cause in this case. If no recognizable MOs are present, none of the factors in the preliminary causal list is the cause; look for others. If more than one MO is evident, the causes that produce those MOs are likely co-causes.

Although the above account may be helpful the next time you try to figure out why your toaster isn't popping, the important point for the purposes of this book is that the logic Scriven (1976) espouses is not particularly distant from the experimentalist logic of inference we have already discussed. Once again, the technique involves systematically generating and considering rival plausible explanations, looking for relevant data that will help you compare their relative plausibility, and trying to isolate the most likely causal factor(s). The name of the game is to achieve control over rival plausible explanations. But instead of using *manipulative control* as one might do in an experiment, you exercise *analytic control* to achieve the same effect (see Palys 1989).

As Campbell (e.g., 1979b) came to recognize and as these examples show, case study analysis involves more than merely explaining *one datum*. Although the physician begins with one phenomenon to be explained (e.g., the fact that you have a pain in your stomach), a "good" explanation and effective treatment require that a *whole set of related data also* be considered (e.g., exactly where the pain is located, whether the pains are acute or chronic, your eating habits, how much stress you've been under, and so on) and that any explanation you offer must be consistent with the *complete web* of evidence. Taken together, these examples leave us to conclude that rigorous case study analysis does seem to be possible.

At the same time, two aspects of the above examples must be noted. First, the "causes" being assessed address only the most mechanistic meanings of that term. Second, the operating principles of toasters and cars are well known, so that "searching through rival plausible explanations" may be less clear-cut in the social sciences. How well Scriven's (1976) modus operandi method can translate to the social sciences—where the challenge is to understand the dynamics of a *human* milieu and where, in any event, most social scientists consider "cause" in a much less determinative fashion—needs to be considered.

RIVAL PLAUSIBLE EXPLANATIONS IN THE CASE STUDY CONTEXT

In a particular social and health science research situation, a specific list of rival plausible explanations to consider may or may not exist; if it

does exist, it may or may not be well developed. We've already reviewed Campbell's (e.g., 1957; Campbell & Stanley 1963) efforts to articulate general classes of threats to internal validity in quantitative experimental research (e.g., selection, history, regression toward the mean) as well as those others that are uniquely problematic in field settings (e.g., compensatory equalization and compensatory rivalry).

In the qualitative case study realm, rival plausible explanations also must be considered, and the challenge to researchers is to take the general classes of threats Campbell identified and figure out how they might manifest themselves in whatever context you find yourself in. To date, however, little effort has been devoted to systematically articulating threats in the manner of Campbell. A creative example to the contrary, however, comes from Howard Becker. Besides his other talents, Becker is also a photographer. He became curious about photo archives as a source of historical data, which in turn led to his writing an essay that considers the "truth value" of photographs, "Do Photographs Tell the Truth?" (Becker 1979).

At one level, Becker (1979) argues, *every* photograph is "true," insofar as any picture results from a purely mechanical/chemical process that occurs when rays of light reflect off the object in front of the camera and strike the film, thereby recording an image of the object. But, Becker notes, one could equally well assert that every photograph is to some degree "false," since one could easily have taken a very different photograph of exactly the same scene, a photo that might have resulted in a totally different set of inferences being made. How can we decide which of those two characterizations is more appropriate for any given photograph?

Becker's (1979) discussion focuses chiefly on an explicit consideration of reasons why a particular photo might be *false*: (1) the photo was faked (e.g., retouched, contrived); (2) the photographer was more interested in esthetic concerns (e.g., impact, genre) than in creating a historical record; (3) the photo inadequately samples events (e.g., focusing on unrepresentative parts of the action); and/or

(4) censorship, whether externally or internally imposed, was involved. Each of these threats to the validity of an image has a parallel in interactive research: (1) data might be "fraudulent" in the sense that respondents may distort the representation of their beliefs or behaviour; (2) researchers may give an unrepresentative edge to their work by limiting it to a particular ideological genre; (3) data may be sampled inadequately; and/or (4) censorship, whether self-imposed or externally imposed, may influence the range of inferences.

In telling you about Becker (1979), we are not aiming to encourage you to consider the truth value of photographs per se; rather, we hope to draw your attention to the *process* he followed, exactly the process that any researcher should follow when examining her/his data. More specifically, the researcher is compelled not only to try to create an account that "explains" the data, but also to try to consider all the various reasons why that account might *not* be true. In qualitative data analysis, these requirements appear not only when considering the "truth value" to ascribe to any particular datum, but also when engaged in negative case analysis in the context of **analytic induction**.

Analytic Induction

Although notions of inductive analysis have a lengthier history in philosophy, analytic induction was first described as a social science technique by Znaniecki (1934) and is now a standard inclusion when qualitative techniques are outlined (e.g., Denzin 1989; Manning 1991; Preissle 2008; Silverman 1985; Strauss 1987; Vidich & Lyman 1994). Denzin (1989) describes analytic induction as a procedural analogue to experimentation that borrows the notion of experimental and control groups to direct attention not only to instances of the phenomenon under study, but also to non-instances, that is, occasions when the phenomenon does not occur. Vidich and Lyman (1994) explain further that

> distinguishable from deductive, historical-documentary, and statistical approaches, analytic induction [is] a "non-experimental sociological method that employs an exhaustive examination of cases in order to prove universal, causal, generalizations." The case method was to be the critical foundation of a revitalized qualitative sociology. (39)

In the context of inductive research, the process begins when the researcher attempts to formulate some generalization or theory to capture the data that were observed (recall Wallace's wheel from Chapter 2). Having formulated a theory, the investigator turns it back on the data in order to systematically test how well the theory actually accounts for the data. Contrary to the character portrayed in Figure 10.4,

Figure 10.4: Unlike the characters depicted here, good researchers are always on the lookout for evidence that will disprove their beliefs.

researchers engaged in qualitative case study analysis need to remain particularly open to and even go out of their way to search for negative evidence, since the times you're wrong can provide particularly rewarding information about how to improve your theory. Lindesmith (1952) describes this process:

> the principle which governs the selection of cases to test a theory is that the chances of discovering a negative case should be maximized. The investigator who has a working hypothesis concerning his data becomes aware of certain areas of critical importance. If his theory is false or inadequate, he knows that its weaknesses will be more clearly and quickly exposed if he proceeds to the investigation of those critical areas. This involves going out of one's way to look for negative evidence. (492)

Kidder (1981a) offers a most explicit articulation of analytic induction in terms of the underlying logic it shares with experimental and particularly quasi-experimental approaches.[6] Her article "Qualitative Research and Quasi-Experimental Frameworks" reviews several classic studies from the qualitative archives, illuminating how the qualitative procedures may be translated in terms of an underlying quasi-experimental framework and vice versa. Our discussions of Becker (1963) and Cressey (1953) below rely heavily on her analysis.

The basic challenge to the inductive analyst is to offer a general account, or theory, that accurately describes all known instances and non-instances of the phenomenon under study. Becker (1963), for example, in his study of marijuana users, ultimately concluded that there were three prior conditions that all had to be present before an individual would become a regular marijuana user: (1) the person must learn the "proper" smoking techniques that allow an effect to be produced; (2) the person must learn to identify the relatively subtle effects that the drug produces; and (3) the individual must come to define those effects as enjoyable. As Kidder (1981a) describes it, the adequacy of that explanation was tested by assessing the extent to which all known

Table 10.1

Depiction of Classification of a "Successful" Analytic Induction

		Phenomenon	
		Present	Absent
Prior Conditions	Present	100%	0%
	Absent	0%	100%

SOURCE: Adapted from L.H. Kidder (1981a), Qualitative Research and Quasi-Experimental Frameworks. In M.B. Brewer and B.E.Collins (Eds.), *Scientific Inquiry and the Social Sciences: A Volume in Honor of David T. Campbell* (pp. 226-256). San Francisco: Jossey-Boss. Used with permission of Louise Kidder.

cases (of regular marijuana use, and of non-interest in its use) could be fit into a cross-tabulation like that shown in Table 10.1.

Becker's (1963) analysis can be restated as a formula, where PC stands for "Prior Condition": PC1 + PC2 + PC3 = Regular User. Thus, in all cases where Becker found that a person was a regular marijuana user (i.e., phenomenon present), all three of those prior conditions were present (i.e., upper left-hand quadrant of Table 10.1). And in any case where a person was *not* a regular marijuana user (i.e., phenomenon absent), at least one of those prior conditions was missing (i.e., bottom right-hand quadrant of Table 10.1).

Also deserving of consideration are the remaining two cells of Table 10.1, both of which would be examples of *negative cases*, that is, where Becker's account didn't hold. The bottom left-hand corner would include instances of users (i.e., phenomenon present) who had *not* gone through all three phases specified by Becker. The top right-hand corner would include individuals who *had* gone through all three phases, but even so did not become regular marijuana users.[7] Cases in these two cells would clearly show the analysis to be inadequate or incomplete, since they'd reflect instances in which the theory was "wrong." The analyst's task is thus to formulate progressively better explanations that will empty the cells of negative cases and fill the cells that are consistent with the theory. The final score, in other words, must be 100 to nothing, or the researcher must go back to the drawing board and try again.

The actual process of offering, testing, and revising one's analysis is splendidly demonstrated in Cressey's (1953) study of embezzlers: as Kidder (1981a) notes, Cressey expressly articulates the four successive explanations he tried en route to arriving at a fifth explanation he found satisfactory.[8] On the basis of prior literature and research dealing with white-collar crime, Cressey (1953) relates that he began his investigation thus:

> The first hypothesis ... was that positions of financial trust are violated when the incumbent has learned in connection with the business or profession in which he is employed that some forms of trust violation are merely technical violations and are not really "illegal" or "wrong," and, on the negative side, that they are not violated if this kind of definition of behaviour has not been learned. (27)

But it took only a few interviews with inmates (convicted embezzlers) for Cressey to realize that the initial hypothesis was inadequate. In terms of Table 10.1, he came across *negative cases* where the phenomenon was present (i.e., the person had embezzled), but the prior conditions specified by the preliminary working hypothesis were absent. Many interviewees indicated that they'd known full well at the time of the embezzlement that their behaviour was wrong and illegal (instances reflected in the lower left-hand quadrant of Table 10.1).

Cressey (1953) went back to the drawing board, returning with Hypothesis 2: "Positions of [financial] trust are violated when the incumbent defines a need for extra funds or extended use of property as an 'emergency' which cannot be met by legal means" (27). Subsequent interviews with embezzlers showed that many of them were well described by the second working hypothesis, since there were many examples of such "triggering" incidents

(i.e., hypothesized prior conditions present, phenomenon present). But negative cases were also revealed. Some embezzlers admitted taking funds even when no "emergency" situation existed (i.e., phenomenon present, but hypothesized prior conditions absent). Others indicated that there were occasions where emergencies arose when they did not embezzle (i.e., hypothesized prior conditions present, but phenomenon absent).

Accordingly, a third hypothesis/explanation was formulated: "It shifted the emphasis from emergency to psychological isolation, stating that persons become trust violators when they conceive of themselves as having incurred financial obligations which are ... nonsocially sanctionable and which ... must be satisfied by a private means" (Cressey 1953: 28). An example of this situation might involve an individual who accumulates large gambling debts with a bookie; because such financial obligations are "nonsocially sanctionable," the person might find it difficult to approach a bank manager for a loan.

The revised hypothesis was checked against all cases to date, as well as new ones; once again, Cressey (1953) discovered that it fell short. Negative cases came to light where the situation that triggered the embezzlement couldn't really be considered a "financial obligation" (i.e., phenomenon present, but hypothesized prior conditions absent) or where the existence of "nonsocially sanctionable" financial obligations wasn't fulfilled by means of embezzlement (i.e., hypothesized prior conditions present, but phenomenon absent). A new explanation was required.

Cressey's (1953) fourth hypothesis differed from the previous one by "emphasizing this time not financial obligations ... but nonshareable *problems*[,] ... that is, ... the subject could be in financial difficulty not only because of an acknowledged responsibility for past debts, but because of present discordance between his income and expenditures as well" (29). Although more successful than all prior attempts, the fourth explanation also revealed negative cases. Cressey (1953) then came to his final revision:

Trusted persons become trust violators when they conceive of themselves as having a financial problem which is nonshareable, are aware that this problem can be secretly resolved by violation of the position of financial trust, and are able to apply to their own conduct in that situation verbalizations which enable them to adjust their conception of themselves as users of the entrusted funds or property. (30)

The adequacy of this final explanation was tested against all cases for which he had gathered information, and no negative cases were found. The explanation also held when he tested it with 200 other cases compiled by another researcher, and again with another sample of embezzlers interviewed by Cressey himself in a different penitentiary.

In sum, by paying particular attention to negative case analysis in the context of analytic induction, Cressey (1953) was able to formulate an explanation that accounted for all cases, thereby promoting theory development in the area of white-collar crime. Note also that the power of Cressey's analysis was enhanced by the fact that he didn't just content himself with having "explained" the data from his own study, but also tried to use the explanation on *new* cases. Analytic induction is done poorly when one fails to include all relevant cases (e.g., one notices only data that support one's contentions) and one makes no effort to apply the explanatory scheme to information beyond the data used to generate the theory.

Although Cressey (1953) is presented here as an analytic "success," he can be faulted on at least two points: his successive revisions to the theory represented the mere addition of caveats rather than true revision, and his theoretical conclusions are overly limited by the fact that only *convicted* embezzlers were included in his samples. We don't know whether people who get away with embezzling differ in some way from Cressey's samples. It may be, for example, that our "commonsensical" conception of embezzlement as a financially motivated activity makes it more likely that individuals who embezzle for those reasons will get caught. If

so, empirical scrutiny of only those who have been caught would simply reaffirm our original understanding about the phenomenon. People who embezzle for completely different reasons may be less likely to get caught because we don't treat them seriously as suspects; hence, they wouldn't end up in prison samples like Cressey's, posing a challenge to his theoretical formulations.

Finally, although analytic induction clearly declares itself to be an inductive technique, more recent formulations have tended to place greater emphasis on the inevitable interplay between induction and deduction, as well as that between theory and data. Strauss (1987), for example, reflects on that in an allusion to his earlier monograph with Glaser on the discovery of "grounded theory" (Glaser & Strauss 1967). He notes: "Because of our earlier writing in *Discovery* (1967) where we attacked speculative theory—quite ungrounded in bodies of data—many people mistakenly refer to grounded theory as 'inductive theory'… But as we have indicated, all three aspects of inquiry (induction, deduction, and verification) are absolutely essential" (12).

AN EXAMPLE: SHERLOCK HOLMES AND "THE ADVENTURE OF SILVER BLAZE"

It's hard to convey the richness of analytic induction in the context of qualitative research, if for no other reason than that the space-saving figures and tables of aggregated quantitative data must be replaced by verbose descriptions of the rationale by which conclusions are generated. Studies that appear in journal article format must fit within the 30- to 35-page limit most journals impose. Many of the classic examples such as Cressey (1953) therefore appear in book-length form, making them tough to summarize in a section of a chapter.

We therefore needed a briefer example of an analysis that illustrates something of the ongoing interaction between theory and data, and induction and deduction, required for a comprehensive analysis. Fortunately, such analyses are prevalent in fiction, where, for example, sleuths sometimes show admirable methodological acumen. In this realm, one can do no better than to look at that master of sleuths, Sherlock Holmes. From Conan Doyle's many suitable stories, we've chosen to focus on "The Adventure of Silver Blaze."[9]

The Phenomena: A Disappearance and a Murder

Silver Blaze is a racehorse, a particularly excellent one who has won many races and prizes for his owner, Colonel Ross. The adventure begins when we find that Silver Blaze has disappeared from his stables and that his trainer, John Straker, has been murdered. Although such a disappearance and murder likely would have been newsworthy in any event, they are particularly so for having occurred within a week of the running of the Wessex Cup, for which Silver Blaze was the favourite until his disappearance.

Holmes, along with many other Britons, has been reading about the case with interest in some of the daily papers. The story begins with his realizing that his preliminary working hypothesis has been refuted. As Holmes describes it,

> "I made a blunder, my dear Watson—which is, I am afraid, a more common occurrence than anyone would think who only knew me through your memoirs. The fact is that I could not believe it possible that the most remarkable horse in England could long remain concealed, especially in so sparsely inhabited a place as the north of Dartmoor. From hour to hour yesterday I expected to hear that he had been found, and that his abductor was the murderer of John Straker." (Doyle, in Dougle 1987: 185–86)

With two days having passed since the horse's abduction and Straker's murder, Holmes thus realizes that the case isn't as straightforward as it first appeared and, hence, that immediate closer attention is warranted. The disappearance and the murder are thus the phenomena that await explanation, and Sherlock Holmes applies his investigative techniques to that end. Will he be successful in time for Silver Blaze to run in the Wessex Cup?

Gathering Preliminary Data

Holmes is often regarded as the master of *de*duction, but it's noteworthy that he begins his efforts at explanation in this case by following the *in*ductive practice of gathering data first. His preliminary information regarding Silver Blaze has been based largely on archival sources, primarily the treatment of the case appearing in the daily newspapers. While such sources can be important, Holmes also recognizes their shortcomings:

> "The tragedy has been so uncommon and so complete, and of such personal importance to so many people that we are suffering from a plethora of surmise, conjecture and hypothesis. The difficulty is to detach the framework of fact—of absolute, undeniable fact—from the embellishments of theorists and reporters. Then, having established ourselves upon this sound basis, it is our duty to see what inferences may be drawn, and which are the special points upon which the whole mystery turns." (Doyle, in Dougle 1987: 185)

Accordingly, Holmes also supplements his examination of newspaper accounts with direct communication with Colonel Ross, who has invited his involvement in the case, and Inspector Gregory, the member of the local constabulary to whom the case has been assigned.

Two stables are approximately two miles (three kilometres) apart in the otherwise minimally populated moor around Tavistock. Silver Blaze had been housed at King's Pyland; Desborough, his primary rival in the Wessex Cup, is kept at Mapleton Stables under the management of Silas Brown. Silver Blaze had clearly been the early betting favourite. Besides horse and trainer, Straker's wife, a maid, three stable boys, three other horses, and a dog all make their home at King's Pyland.

Security precautions had been taken as the race approached, with the three stable boys rotating through successive eight-hour shifts in the locked barn: while one was on duty, the other two slept in the loft above. The maid brought meals to the stable for the lads. On the night in question, she was carrying a dinner of curried mutton to the barn when a stranger, later identified as Fitzroy Simpson, suddenly emerged from the darkness. He offered a bribe to the maid and to Ned Hunter, the on-shift stable boy, apparently wishing to obtain inside information concerning Silver Blaze's fitness for the upcoming race, but fled when the two refused his money and Hunter set the dog on him. A note of clarification to Holmes from the inspector reveals that Hunter had locked the stable door behind him before giving chase and that the open window isn't large enough for a person to pass through.

John Straker, the trainer, seemed rather excited when told about these events, and must subsequently have had trouble sleeping: his wife saw him getting dressed and heading out to the barn at 1:00 a.m., despite the rain. Mrs. Straker awoke at 7:00 a.m. to find that her husband had not returned. On going outside, she and the maid found the barn door open, Hunter in a drug-induced stupor, the other two boys still soundly asleep in the loft, and Silver Blaze gone. About a quarter of a mile (half a kilometre) away from the stables, John Straker's coat was found hanging from a tree branch, flapping in the breeze. Close to it lay the trainer's body.

> "His head had been shattered by a savage blow from some heavy weapon, and he was wounded in the thigh, where there was a long, clean cut, inflicted evidently by some very sharp instrument … In his right hand he held a small knife, which was clotted with blood up to the handle, while in his left he grasped a red and black silk cravat, which was recognized by the maid as having been worn on the preceding evening by the stranger who had visited the stables." (Doyle, in Dougle 1987: 189)

When he regained his senses, Hunter agreed with the maid that the cravat was indeed the one worn by Simpson the night before. He also believed that the stranger must have drugged his food while distracting him with questions about Silver Blaze

and the race. Analysis later revealed that his curried mutton was indeed laced with powdered opium, although the people in the house ate the same dish with no apparent effect. A check around the Tavistock area, including an examination of Mapleton Stables, showed Silver Blaze nowhere to be found. But some gypsies who had been seen camping in the area had apparently vanished the day after the crime became news.

Preliminary Induction

The gathering of preliminary data, as Scriven (1976) reminds us, is never done with "immaculate perception." The person who goes about gathering data will bring "commonsensical" or "informed" understandings to the situation, no doubt influenced by ideological and/or theoretical leanings. The data that are gathered, and the interpretations as to what those data mean, influence the range of alternative explanations considered. Preliminary induction involves drawing inferences from one's data to create a plausible account of the causal agent(s) or sequence of events that "produce" the phenomenon.

For Inspector Gregory, suspicion fell immediately on Fitzroy Simpson, the stranger who had appeared on the night of the murder. Witnesses (the maid and stable boy) placed him at the scene of the crime, and his intentions appeared to be less than honourable. Hunter indicated that Simpson had had an opportunity to drug his curried mutton, and John Straker was found with Simpson's cravat in his hand.

Simpson was easily found in one of the villas near Tavistock the day after the crime, and new evidence seemed consistent with the idea that he might have committed the crimes. Apparently Simpson is "a man of excellent birth and education, who had squandered a fortune upon the turf, and lived now by doing a little quiet and genteel bookmaking in the sporting clubs of London. An examination of his betting book shows that bets to the amount of five thousand pounds had been registered by him against the favourite" (Doyle, in Dougle 1987: 189). Further, his clothes were wet from being in the rain the night before, his red and black cravat was indeed missing, and he was in possession of a lead-weighted walking stick, which might conceivably have caused the head injuries from which the trainer died.

Analytic Induction: A Dialectic of Theory and Data

Preliminary induction from the above data might be sufficient to generate the theory that Fitzroy Simpson was the murderer of John Straker and the abductor of Silver Blaze; however, the process of analytic induction requires that the investigator or researcher pay attention to *all* relevant data, particularly to *negative* evidence that could serve to disconfirm one's theory.

The inspector was sufficiently confident in his theory to arrest Fitzroy Simpson, but Sherlock Holmes's attention to the case brings with it a healthy air of skepticism over whether the theory has yet been exposed to adequate scrutiny. In explaining his thoughts on the matter to his colleague and biographer, Dr. Watson, Holmes states,

> "I am afraid that whatever theory we state has very grave objections to it … The police imagine, I take it, that this Fitzroy Simpson, having drugged the lad, and having in some way obtained a duplicate key, opened the stable door, and took out the horse, with the intention, apparently, of kidnapping him altogether. His bridle is missing, so that Simpson must have put this on. Then, having left the door open behind him, he was leading the horse away over the moor, when he was either met or overtaken by the trainer. A row naturally ensued, Simpson beat out the trainer's brains with his heavy stick without receiving any injury from the small knife which Straker used in self-defense, and then the thief either led the horse on to some secret hiding place, or else it may have bolted during the struggle, and be now wandering out on the moors. That is the case as it appears to the police, and improbable as it is, all other explanations are more improbable still." (Doyle, in Dougle 1987: 189–90)

Holmes begins by questioning whether all evidence to date is indeed consistent with the theory, a reflection of proper negative case analysis. He wonders first why Straker's body was covered with considerable blood and bore a knife cut, suggesting a struggle, while Simpson's clothes had no bloodstains and showed no signs of struggle. But Dr. Watson notes that the blows to the head might have caused involuntary convulsions, which in turn may have led Straker to have cut himself with his own knife. Holmes next notes that Silver Blaze is still missing; he asks how a stranger from London could know enough about the local area to keep a horse hidden on an apparently barren moor. The Inspector suggests that Simpson might have passed the horse over to the gypsies, who have now vanished, adding that Simpson was *not* a stranger to the area, having stayed there for significant periods during two prior summers.

But Holmes isn't convinced. He suggests that the Inspector's case is still circumstantial, at best:

> "A clever counsel would tear it all to rags … Why should he take the horse out of the stable? If he wished to injure it, why could he not do it there? Has a duplicate key been found in his possession? What chemist sold him the powdered opium?" (Doyle, in Dougle 1987: 191)

The inspector responds to each query, but the responses are weak insofar as none has any sort of concrete manifestation. Perhaps he took the horse out so no one would hear the creature when the injury was done, or perhaps the motive was indeed abduction rather than injury. As for the key, perhaps it was acquired during one of his previous summer visits, and he probably threw it away once the crime was committed. The opium was probably bought in London, making it difficult to trace.

Holmes becomes more skeptical than ever at this "shadow" evidence. He gives the coup de grâce by noting two events that, to him, make the current theory untenable and direct attention elsewhere. First, Holmes knows that opium powder has a very distinctive flavour, and he considers it too large a coincidence that the maid just happens to have served a curried mutton that night, a dish that would conveniently hide the taste of the opium. Clearly, Simpson could not have caused the particular choice of dinner that night; the perpetrator must therefore be a person in the house who could make such a choice. Further, Holmes notes that although the dog barked loudly when Simpson paid his evening visit to the maid and the stable boy, it did *not* do so when the murderer/abductor arrived at the stable later that night. This fact suggests that the dog must have known the intruder, again focusing attention back on the members of the Straker household.

Another theory is clearly required, and with his attention now directed toward the Strakers, it's time for Holmes to gather more evidence. Holmes first turns his eye to the murder victim, John Straker, asking what objects were in his pockets on the night of the murder. These include numerous items, the most noteworthy of which are a candle, some papers, and the knife that had apparently caused Straker's leg wound. Curiously, the papers include a bill for a very expensive dress from a London milliner; the invoice is made out to a Mr. William Darbyshire. Holmes is informed that Darbyshire is apparently a friend of Straker's and that letters to him are occasionally received at the Straker home. As for the knife, closer inspection by Watson reveals that it is a very small, delicate, razor-sharp knife of a type used for cataract operations, leaving Holmes curious as to why Straker would have possessed such a knife and why he would have taken such a thing along as a weapon against an intruder, when larger kitchen knives were just as easily available.

Because the data that Holmes uncovers suggest that the murder/abduction was an "inside job," Holmes's attention clearly turns to the Strakers, for only they could have chosen the menu that allowed the stable boy to be drugged. Although both may have been involved, only John Straker meets all the criteria of being able to determine the meal to disguise the opium, clearly having a key to the stable,

being able to handle the horse he trained, and being known to the dog so that it would not bark and wake the sleeping stable boys when he arrived to do something to the horse. But what was he intending to do? How? Why?

After identifying John Straker as having had less than honourable intentions, Holmes wonders whether Mrs. Straker was also involved; he looks for a motive for the crime. His inductive leap emerges from examining the invoice to William Darbyshire that is among Straker's personal effects. Why would Mr. Darbyshire have millinery bills delivered to the house of John Straker? Could John Straker and William Darbyshire have been the same person? Perhaps Mr. and Mrs. Straker have been living beyond their means, using double identities, and were led to the crime by a need to meet debts created by an extravagant lifestyle.

To pursue this lead, Holmes employs a technique of indirect questioning to discover whether the dress billed to William Darbyshire had indeed been intended for Mrs. Straker:

> "Surely I met you in Plymouth, at a garden party, some little time ago, Mrs. Straker," said Holmes.
> "No, sir; you are mistaken."
> "Dear me; why I could have sworn to it. You wore a costume of dove-coloured silk, with ostrich feather trimming."
> "I never had such a dress, sir," answered the lady.
> "Ah; that quite settles it," said Holmes. (Doyle, in Dougle 1987: 192)

And indeed it did. But if Mrs. Straker isn't the woman for whom the dress was intended, then who is? If William Darbyshire was indeed John Straker, is there *another* Mrs. Darbyshire/Straker? Or a mistress, perhaps?

The Master of Deduction

Holmes has arrived at a theory that offers some consistency with the evidence gathered to date. Certainly none of the evidence has yet been demonstrated to be *inconsistent* with the theory that John Straker, due to financial pressures from some possible parallel life he was leading, was involved in some despicable plot to abduct or injure Silver Blaze in order to gain funds, whether through bets or through bribery. But at this point Holmes goes beyond the domain of analytic induction alone: he now also starts including the deductive mode that so characteristically distinguishes him from most other fictional sleuths. More specifically, Holmes begins to hypothesize about data that *should* exist *if* his theory is true.

Straker's possession of a surgical knife leads Holmes to speculate that Straker may have been intending to somehow surreptitiously injure Silver Blaze temporarily so that the horse wouldn't be able to race. If that was so, Straker probably led Silver Blaze to the depression on the moor where the murder subsequently took place in order to ensure that any cries from Silver Blaze wouldn't wake the stable boys who were asleep in the loft and to ensure that he wouldn't be seen perpetrating this deed. And if that was so, other evidence of that action should be found. Straker's coat, presumably removed in order to better perform the "operation," and an abundance of hoof and footprints in the vicinity of the body were certainly consistent with Holmes's theory, although not definitive. Recalling that candles were found in Straker's pocket, and surmising that he would have required a light of some sort in order to undertake an operation, Holmes hypothesizes that *if* his theory is correct, other evidence of candles or matches should be present at the scene. But neither Watson nor the inspector is aware of Holmes's deductions as Holmes begins to closely scrutinize the area where the body was found:

> Stretching himself upon his face and leaning his chin upon his hands, [Holmes] made a careful study of the trampled mud in front of him.
>
> "Halloa!" said he, suddenly, "what's this?"
>
> It was a wax vesta, half burned, which was so coated with mud that it looked at first like a little chip of wood.

> "I cannot think how I came to overlook it," said the Inspector, with an expression of annoyance.
>
> "It was invisible, buried in the mud. I only saw it because I was looking for it."
>
> "What! You expected to find it?"
>
> "I thought it not unlikely." (Doyle, in Dougle 1987: 193)

Holmes next turns his attention to Silver Blaze. If Straker abducted him but was then killed, Silver Blaze must have run off somewhere. But if so, why hasn't he been found? Holmes heard the inspector express the belief that the gypsies might have found and taken him, but views this idea as being based on a convenient but inaccurate stereotype. And even if they had done so, surely it's absurd to believe that gypsies could have walked off with and sold the most famous and sought-after horse in England without anyone's noticing. On the basis of his knowledge of horses, Holmes speculates with Watson on Silver Blaze's location:

> "The horse is a very gregarious creature. If left to himself his instincts would have been either to return to King's Pyland, or go over to Mapleton. Why should he run wild on the moor? He would surely have been seen by now …"
>
> "Where is he, then?"
>
> "I have already said that he must have gone to King's Pyland or to Mapleton. He is not at King's Pyland, therefore he is at Mapleton. Let us take that as a working hypothesis and see what it leads us to." (193)

But the inspector had already stated that he checked for 100 metres in all directions from the crime scene and was unable to find any further tracks. Still, acting on his theory and looking for indicators that could further test that theory, Holmes continues:

> "This part of the moor, as the Inspector remarked, is very hard and dry. But it falls away toward Mapleton, and you can see from here

that there is a long hollow over yonder, which must have been very wet on Monday night. If our supposition is correct, then the horse must have crossed that, and there is the point where we should look for his tracks." (193)

Holmes brings along one of Silver Blaze's horse-shoes, and evidence soon turns up that provides some support for Holmes's theory. Hoofprints are indeed found, indicating that Silver Blaze did walk in the direction of Mapleton. In the process of following them, Watson chances on a second pair of prints—from a human's square-toed boots—that are seen to come from Mapleton and to intersect with the horse's hoofprints; horse and human travel in parallel toward King's Pyland for a short while, after which they reverse ground in tandem and head back to Mapleton.

On the basis of these new observations, found serendipitously while following through with an investigation of implications (i.e., hypotheses) that flowed from his theory, Holmes induces that someone from Mapleton must have come on Silver Blaze as he wandered on the moor after running from Straker and, having begun to return Silver Blaze to King's Pyland, suddenly had a change of heart, succumbing to the temptation to take advantage of the act of fate that had brought Mapleton's main rival to its doorstep and taking the opportunity to hide the horse in the Mapleton stables until after the Wessex Cup. The most likely candidate is Silas Brown, the trainer of Desborough and the manager of Mapleton Stables; only he would have known how to disguise or hide a horse, and only he would have the authority to bring a new horse in to the stables unchallenged.

If that theory is true, Brown would have to have been the first to rise that day. When they arrive at Mapleton, Holmes checks his reasoning indirectly, by querying a groom who, seeing Holmes and Watson coming, has directed them to be gone:

"I only wished to ask a question," said Holmes, with his finger and thumb in his waistcoat pocket. "Should I be too early to see your master,

Mr. Silas Brown, if I were to call at five o'clock tomorrow morning?"

"Bless you, sir, if anyone is about he will be, for he is always the first stirring. But here he is, sir, to answer your questions for himself." (194)

Holmes's first hypothesis is thus supported, and a second is as well when Silas Brown strides toward him wearing square-toed boots that match the unique footprints Holmes and Watson observed on the moor.

Resistant at first, Brown admits to having hidden Silver Blaze after Holmes describes the events in such detail that Brown believes Holmes must have witnessed the entire scene. Empathizing with Brown's having succumbed to serendipitous temptation without original criminal intent, Holmes provides Brown with a way to show his remorse: by promising to care for the horse and to ensure that the animal appears at the Wessex Cup on racing day.

Back at King's Pyland, feeling confident that his theory is most plausible but still wanting to ensure that all loose ends are covered, Holmes generates two further hypotheses that suggest two final tests of the theory. First, if Straker had been intending to administer a delicate but impairing incision to Silver Blaze, Holmes speculates that Straker would probably have practised on other animals at the stables, and his eyes "[fall] upon the sheep." Accordingly, he questions one of the stable boys:

"You have a few sheep in the paddock," he said.

"Who attends to them?"

"I do, sir."

"Have you noticed anything amiss with them of late?"

"Well, sir, not of much account; but three of them have gone lame, sir."

I could see that Holmes was extremely pleased, for he chuckled and rubbed his hands together.

"A long shot, Watson; a very long shot!" said he, pinching my arm. "[Inspector] Gregory, let me recommend to your attention this singular epidemic among the sheep. Drive on, coachman!" (196)

With all but Holmes baffled at the meaning of that interchange, Holmes and Watson leave to test a further hypothesis. Promising Silver Blaze's owner that they'll see him and the horse on racing day, Holmes takes a photo of Straker along to London.

The one portion of the theory that Holmes has not yet tested involves the question of motive. We do not yet know whether John Straker and William Darbyshire were indeed the same person, and whether Straker's extravagant lifestyle led him to attempt to solve his financial problems by fixing the Wessex Cup against Silver Blaze. Taking Straker's photograph to the milliner at the address on William Darbyshire's invoice confirms Holmes's suspicions.

A Satisfying Resolution

On the day of the Wessex Cup, Silver Blaze does indeed appear; moreover, he wins the race. But with Silver Blaze safely found and returned, all of those present are still at a loss as to the identity of Straker's murderer. It is thus with no small sense of satisfaction that Holmes fills in the last piece of the puzzle: the murderer was none other than Silver Blaze!

> "The horse!" cried both the Colonel and [Dr. Watson].
>
> "Yes, the horse. And it may lessen his guilt if I say that it was done in self-defense, and that John Straker was a man who was entirely unworthy of your confidence." (198)

Holmes continues with his litany, which is consistent with all the evidence, both inductively and deductively gathered. He recounts the evidence concerning Straker's double identity and the extravagance of his lifestyle. The choice of curried mutton to drug Hunter, the dog that didn't bark, and Straker's possession of the cataract knife are all explained. As for the trainer's death, Holmes describes the chain of events:

> "Straker had led the horse to a hollow where his light would be invisible. Simpson, in his flight,

had dropped his cravat, and Straker had picked it up with some idea, perhaps, that he might use it in securing the horse's leg. Once in the hollow he had got behind the horse, and had struck a light, but the creature, frightened at the glare, and with the strange instinct of animals feeling that some mischief was intended, had lashed out, and the steel shoe had struck Straker full on the forehead. He had already, in spite of the rain, taken off his overcoat in order to do his delicate task, and so, as he fell, his knife gashed his thigh. Do I make it clear?"
>
> "Wonderful!" cried the Colonel. "Wonderful! You might have been there." (200)

Dénouement

Sherlock Holmes's approach in this tale provides a splendid example of qualitative case study analysis, even though the flow of the reasoning is more characteristic of the realm of fiction than of the realm of social and health science research, where "truths" are neither so singular nor so straightforwardly amenable to analysis. "The Adventure of Silver Blaze" illustrates the issue of access, which in Holmes's case is facilitated by his considerable reputation and by the invitation he receives from Colonel Ross to participate in the investigation. Although Holmes's initial information comes from the newspaper, he is clearly aware of the strengths and limitations of such data, and he uses this appreciation to whittle down the set of data that are "relevant" and that call for explanation. Further evidence is gained by visiting the actual scene of the events and by supplementing the archival data with interview data from a purposive sample of respondents who are identified as the investigation evolved.

The gathering of preliminary data is followed by attempts at induction, with inferences regarding particular data combining to generate a preliminary theory. Unlike Inspector Gregory, Holmes doesn't fall into the trap of prematurely accepting an induced theory, but continues to engage in a dialectic of theory and data that specifically includes generating plausible explanations and seeking out evidence that would either disconfirm them or support their plausibility. The process of analytic induction leads to the generation of a theory that is consistent, or at least not *inconsistent*, with all available evidence. Holmes then deduces the evidence that *should* exist *if* the theory is true, so that actual observation of concrete evidence (as opposed to the "shadow" evidence accepted by Inspector Gregory) will allow him to test the adequacy of his evolving theory.

In the process of undertaking these hypotheses and gathering relevant data to support or refute them, Holmes evinces a splendid understanding of how unobtrusive measures can be used to illuminate human (and equine) behaviour. His speculation regarding Silver Blaze's whereabouts is a beautiful example of how one must look in "visible" places for relevant data; while the inspector was unable to find hoofprints on the hard ground for 100 metres in all directions around the crime scene, Holmes speculates on *one* direction—toward Mapleton—and identifies a distant low-lying area between the crime scene and Mapleton as the likely location (because of its softness) for finding hoofprints *if* his theory is true. Besides thus providing a test of his speculations, Holmes is also rewarded with the serendipitous discovery of Silas Brown's boot prints, which help round out the sleuth's theoretical descriptions of the events of that fateful day.

SUMMING UP AND LOOKING AHEAD

The previous chapter showed the logic underlying traditional laboratory experimentation; the current chapter encourages you to consider the principles underlying the inference process and to translate those to the investigation of behaviour in the world in quasi-experimentation and qualitative case study analysis. In each case the challenge is in how best to eliminate rival plausible explanations, with the difference between them residing in the extent to which each uses manipulative and/or analytic control to accomplish that.

In contrast to laboratory experimentation where the researcher creates the situation and uses techniques such as random assignment to exert manipulative control for the elimination of rival plausible explanations, quasi-experimentation and case study analysis utilize analytic control for those same ends. Doing so involves being one's own best critic and brainstorming with those who have strong local knowledge about what those rival plausible explanations might be, and then gathering the data that allow one to address those possibilities. The social dynamic attendant to many field situations led us to discuss some of the unique categories of rival plausible explanations that can arise there and hence must be addressed. Ideally, one will be able to eliminate all but one of the rival possibilities, in which case the one remaining is the most plausible explanation.

Quasi-experimentation was developed in part because of Donald T. Campbell's dream of us becoming an "experimenting society" where researchers did not make societal decisions, but instead used systematic field-based methods to inform political leaders and the citizenry about how well socially important goals were being met, and what strategies worked best in achieving them. The major limitation of using quasi-experimental methods is that they work best when asked to inform about whether the bottom line is being met, i.e., purely outcome-oriented.

While qualitative case study approaches have much broader utility than evaluation research per se, one of their great advantages in the evaluation research context is the extent to which they help shed light on *process*—all those things that happen between inputs and outputs—and bring skill sets that have been found to be highly important in doing effective evaluation: adapting to emergent situations; establishing rapport with those in the setting being evaluated; familiarity in dealing with multiple sources of data; understanding the logic underlying purposive sampling; and so on.

Our description of Sherlock Holmes's methods in the adventure of Silver Blaze offered a way to outline the type of problem-solving approach that researchers bring to field research, and to illustrate the way that researchers bounce back and forth between induction and deduction, search for information that allow one to test out developing theories, and to choose between emerging rival plausible explanations that account for the full range of data one has gathered.

The strong logical ties underlying the whole continuum from quantitative experimental study to qualitative case study analysis are also clearly revealed. Particular data are gathered from the literature, from an experiment, from a case study, or from our personal life experience in order to generate a theory or theories that offer a plausible explanation for the occurrence and/or non-occurrence of the phenomena under study. Negative cases are particularly sought; more data are gathered, and their (in)consistency with the theory is scrutinized. Ultimately, the research task, whatever form it takes, is a dialectic process involving theory and data, where the goal is to generate and decide on the relative plausibility of prospective competing explanations.

In the next chapter we discuss in greater detail some of the different ways one can take advantage of the strengths of more qualitative and quantitative approaches in the context of multi-method or mixed-method approaches.

STUDY QUESTIONS

1. What are some advantages and disadvantages of laboratory experimentation?

2. State John Stuart Mill's three criteria for inferring the existence of a "causal" relationship, and explain how these criteria are met by the traditional experiment.

3. In traditional laboratory experimentation, internal validity is maximized by randomly assigning participants to groups and by creating control groups that are equivalent to the experimental group(s) in all respects *except* for the independent variable. But those luxuries are frequently not available in field

settings. What substitutes for them in quasi-experimental research, and how do those alternatives address the elimination of rival plausible explanations?

4. What is the difference between *manipulative* control and *analytic* control? What are their similarities?

5. According to Donald T. Campbell, why must researchers always be *particularly* vigilant about checking for *regression toward the mean* (otherwise known as *statistical regression*) when evaluating the effectiveness of social programs?

6. Field researchers often face evaluation research situations in which they must deal with intact groups who know about and can share information regarding the evaluation. What new threats to internal validity arise from this state of affairs? Explain how these *are* threats to internal validity, and in each case suggest how the researcher can prepare for or deal with those problems.

7. Your provincial government decides to introduce photo radar in order to control speeding, which your provincial premier believes is getting out of hand. They do so in July. In the first month after it is introduced more than 49,000 speeding tickets are sent out to speeders caught by photo radar. Danielle and Sanjeeta undertook a study to determine whether the advent of photo radar was indeed effective in reducing the number of accidents on provincial roads as the police suggested. They approach the provincial government for relevant accident data and are given accident records for August of the previous and current year for 10 regions of the province (areas around the province's 10 largest business centres) in which photo radar was used in the first month of operation. These data revealed that, in every one of the 10 jurisdictions, there were fewer accidents after the introduction of photo radar than in the same month the previous yea. Danielle and Sanjeeta did

the appropriate statistical test on the data and found that, overall, the reduction in accidents was statistically significant.

a. What is the *independent variable* in Danielle and Sanjeeta's research?

b. What is the *dependent variable?*

c. What are two *rival plausible explanations* (RPEs) that you believe may threaten the internal validity of their research? What data you would ask for/obtain to address those RPEs?

d. What is *external validity?* Give two specific concerns Danielle and Sanjeeta might have regarding the external validity of their study.

e. Would *time-series data* be useful for Danielle and Sanjeeta? What advantages might if offer them?

8. In what sense is evaluation research part of a political process? What can the researcher do to avoid being or becoming a mere pawn in that process?

9. Explain what is meant by an *iterative* process. Give an example of an iterative process beyond those given in this text.

10. What are some of the "insidious biases" that Huberman and Miles (1994) suggest must be avoided in qualitative analysis? What are some of the things you can do to try to avoid each one?

11. Explain the process of *analytic induction* in your own words, using Wallace's wheel of science (from Chapter 2) to organize your explanation.

12. Why did Donald T. Campbell think, in his earlier articles on experimentation (e.g., Campbell & Stanley 1963), that "rigorous" case study analysis was impossible? How might Michael Scriven (1976) and Louise Kidder (1981a) have tried to change his mind?

13. If you like to read novels, check out Robert Pirsig's *Zen and the Art of Motorcycle Maintenance* (New York: Morrow, 1979). In the context of an absorbing tale about someone who's trying to find himself, it also includes a splendid running commentary on case study methods.

14. Experiments emphasize manipulative control; case study analysis emphasizes analytic control. Discuss the relative merits and demerits of the two approaches as routes to understanding.

15. Choose any of the Sherlock Holmes stories other than the one featured in this chapter, and consider Holmes's investigative process from the perspective of qualitative case study designs.

16. We offered several examples of professionals who are required to engage in case study analysis (i.e., physicians, mechanics, coroners, engineering troubleshooters). Can you think of other occupations that make the same demand? If you know someone in any of those occupations, interview her/him about the way s/he tries to isolate causes. Does s/he follow the logic outlined in this chapter? Explain.

17. Select an article from a recent issue of a newsmagazine that purports to be "analytical" about current events (e.g., *Maclean's, Time, Newsweek*), and consider the way the article's author develops her/his analysis. Is the logic of the analysis evident? Does the writer follow the steps required for rigorous case study analysis?

NOTES

1. After a lengthy and illustrious career at Northwestern, Professor Campbell moved to Lehigh University in Bethlehem, Pennsylvania. He was a great man who was very generous with his time to younger scholars like Ted, who had the honour of spending part of his first sabbatical with him. Campbell passed away in the spring of 1996, at the age of 81.

2. The "gee whiz" graph is a mainstay of many advertising campaigns because the existence of change is so obvious and convincing (Huff 1954). Of course, as researchers we need to go beyond such hype and consider the evidence for change and its causes.

3. One possibility—not the only one—would be to ask a few questions of every participant when they register for the walk, including some measure about how important they believe the cause to be. That way, when we ask those questions of the people who show up at each 10-km mark, we can determine where those who drop out and those who keep walking fit in the group as a whole.

4. Murphy's law, a rule originated by engineers, states that if something *can* go wrong, it will. It explains, for example, why your peanut-butter-on-toast will always fall peanut-butter side down, and why anything you buy will work perfectly until just after the warranty expires.

5. We hasten to add that Campbell is not suggesting that "anything goes," nor would he refrain from arguing that some situations or sources of information are "better" than others in terms of the confidence or inference they allow. But we believe he would also assert that no particular situation or type of situation is more inherently connected to "Truth," and that we should not avoid information purely because it is not packaged in the manner we might like. Whatever the situation, he would admonish us to self-consciously consider the inferences we wish to make in terms of all the rival plausible explanations that are available or that we can generate. As an aside, he would also encourage each new generation of researchers to realize its obligation to generate a whole new set of rival plausible explanations, and to argue vehemently about "Truth."

6. Kidder's academic pedigree is noteworthy, since she was a student of both Donald T. Campbell and Howard Becker while completing her doctorate at Northwestern University.

7. Consider who such negative cases might be. The bottom left-hand corner seems particularly unlikely to have anyone in it, since if a person couldn't smoke "correctly," was unable to perceive the effects, or didn't see the effects as enjoyable, one wonders why that person would continue using the drug. For the top right-hand corner, one could imagine that a person may have met all three prior conditions but be deterred from using the drug on a regular basis due to other factors (e.g., perception of personal weakness, worry about the illegality of the behaviour and/or possible criminal sanctions involved). When considering Becker's results, one should appreciate that at the time the study was done (i.e., the 1960s), marijuana use was perceived somewhat differently than it is now in the "Just Say No" generation. Becker's findings may thus have been coloured by the relative ignorance that existed about marijuana in the late 1950s and early 1960s, prior to its broader acceptance and use in the mid- to late 1960s and in the 1970s. Whatever the influence, the central point here is that external validity concerns are as relevant to qualitative data analysis as they are to quantitative data analysis.

8. Although the references we cite in this section will be to Cressey (1953), we are relying heavily on Kidder's (1981a) analysis (see particularly pages 241–44).

9. We'll try to provide enough information from the story to allow you to follow the gist of this mystery and Holmes's resolution of it; however, we strongly advise that you secure a copy of the story and read it before reading the analysis that appears here. A video of the story is also available, in a series produced for the British Broadcasting Corporation (BBC) by Granada television in Great Britain; these star Jeremy Brett, who, in our opinion, gives a terrific portrayal of Holmes.

11

TEXT, IMAGE, AUDIO, AND VIDEO: MAKING SENSE OF NON-NUMERIC DATA

Once a researcher has completed the process of observation and/or data collection the next task is to make sense of the information they have collected. Making sense of the data usually involves taking it apart, understanding its components, and coming to some determination of the underlying patterns and meanings. One important thing to keep in mind is that it does not matter what form of observation or data collection a researcher selects in order to acquire the data or observations necessary to answer their research questions; the underlying goal of all analyses is the reduction of data into a form we can use to answer our research question(s) and/or make particular arguments. As this suggests, the researcher who is trying to make sense of responses to thousands of questionnaires is trying to accomplish the same thing as the researcher who is sorting through hundreds of pages of interview transcripts or looking at hours of video footage.

MAKING SENSE OF NON-NUMERIC DATA

When a researcher sits down and is confronted with hundreds of pages of transcribed interview text, thousands of image files, or hours of video footage it is not uncommon for them to feel overwhelmed at the task of trying to make sense of this wealth of rich data. This situation is worsened by the fact that many researchers have never been exposed to formal techniques for making sense of data that emerge from interviews, focus groups, newspapers, magazines, institutional/agency files, textbooks, speeches, photographs, films or videos, television programs, diaries, and letters. Making sense of non-numeric

data is often presented as the product of some form of mystical revelation as opposed to the learning of a particular set of analytical techniques. Furthermore, published qualitative analyses are often criticized for lacking transparency with authors rarely making the data analysis process explicit or systematic (Miles & Huberman 1994; Ragin 1987). Perhaps the most negative effect of the mystic quality of the analysis of talk, text, images, and video is that it can serve to de-legitimate these types of data and the resulting analyses in the minds of individuals who hold more naive realist positions on social and health research.

Admittedly, the 'unstructured' nature of non-numeric data presents a challenge when it comes to detailing techniques of analysis. Unlike its numeric counterpart, there are few well-established and accepted rules for analyzing text, images, audio, and video. In this chapter we try to demystify the processes involved in analyzing and interpreting non-numeric data by introducing you to a few of the possibilities available to you. We begin with an overview of a range of inductive and deductive strategies, followed by consideration of some of the advantages, disadvantages, and applications of computer-assisted qualitative data analysis software (CAQDA).

THEORETICAL AND DISCIPLINARY PERSPECTIVES

The way that data are understood varies depending on the disciplinary interests and theoretical perspective of the researcher. For example, researchers working from within more sociologically informed traditions maintain that non-numeric data offer special insights into the "reality" of the human condition. In contrast, those operating from within more linguistic traditions (e.g., in disciplines and traditions such as linguistics, communications, critical media studies, cognitive science, post-structuralism, and semiotics) are more likely to see the "text" as a unit of analysis unto itself for which there are multiple possible interpretations. The meanings derived from the analysis of a particular text are always at best partial and contentious since every text can be both produced and interpreted from a variety of different subject positions (e.g., Ryan & Bernard 2003). While a discussion of these varying approaches is beyond the scope of this chapter, we mention this variation here simply to point out the connection that often exists between theory and method, as each of these approaches has implications for what sorts of data one might look at, the particular approach that one will take, and the range of meanings one might draw from them.

Coding and Memoing

Regardless of the particular technique one chooses almost all analytical techniques that focus on non-numeric data involve coding and memoing.

CODING

Coding helps achieve the goal of data management and data reduction; that is, when a researcher codes the volumes of data they have collected they are in essence organizing and reducing the data into smaller more manageable segments that can be retrieved easily and compared with other coded segments of data. A coded segment might represent or illustrate a specific theoretical or analytic concept, or it can simply reflect elements of the data that we want to highlight or think about further, just as we might use a yellow highlighter to draw our attention back to a specific quote or idea that we see in a book. Applying a coding scheme might be as simple as deciding whether, in a given passage, a certain word or type of behaviour or theme is present or absent, or may involve more complex judgments about the thematic content of a paragraph or scene or segment of the source material.

DEDUCTIVE AND INDUCTIVE APPROACHES

Codes may be generated and assigned to research data in either a deductive or inductive fashion, although there is nothing stopping researchers from incorporating some of both. **Deductive coding** sees the analyst coming to the data with a well-specified or predefined set of interests. For example, when Ted was doing research on the social content of video pornography for the Fraser Committee on Pornography and Prostitution, there was a clear interest from the outset to focus specifically on sexual, violent, and sexually violent behaviour (Palys 1986). Similarly, when Neuendorf et al. (2010) set out to content code all of the James Bond films, their interest from the outset was to focus on relations between men and women in the films—and especially those between Bond and the "Bond girls"—and how those had changed, if at all, over time.

Generally speaking, the process of deductive coding involves beginning with a specific set of interests and using that to identify a "relevant" set of passages, quotes, images, scenes, and so on (often referred to at this basic level as **descriptive coding**), and then further elaborating on those preliminary codes by making finer distinctions within each coding category (known as **interpretive coding**). For example, in Ted's study of video pornography, a first step involved viewing each scene to determine whether sex and/or violent and/or sexually violent behaviour was occurring; for scenes where one or more was present, a second step involved coding other aspects of the scene such as who was involved, who initiated the interaction, and so on. In Chris's recent study of clients of sex workers, one general category that Chris was looking at was "risk behaviour," which he would later differentiate more specifically in terms of the kinds of risks that were engaged—sexual (e.g., the possibility of acquiring a sexually transmitted disease), physical (e.g., the possibility of being threatened or beaten), and economic (e.g., the possibility of being robbed). Yet another step might see the researcher engaging in **pattern coding** as different associations became evident, e.g., when it became evident that various risk behaviours took on different characteristics and meanings depending on the social context in which they occurred, such as work, family, and social environments.

In contrast, **inductive coding** generally begins with the identification of general themes and ideas that emerge from a very literal reading of the data (often referred to as **open coding**) and can proceed in either direction, i.e., sometimes elaborating a category by making finer and finer distinctions, and sometimes beginning with very specific descriptive coding categories that are subsequently combined to create more general categories that bring disparate events or descriptions under the same conceptual umbrella.

For example, in Chris's research on sex buyers he began his analysis of his in-depth interviews by reading through each transcribed interview and highlighting passages that appeared to stand out, such as where his participants talked about why visiting sex workers appealed to them, how prices for services were determined and paid for, and how they described their interactions with sex workers. This initial stage of reading and coding allowed him to begin to identify some of the themes that emerged from within interviews and then to create some broader categories by combining more specific categories (e.g., aspects of the solicitation, negotiation over price, and the service sought and delivered were all seen as part of "relationship with sex seller") as well as finding it useful to distinguish within categories (e.g., distinguishing between different participants—such as heterosexuals, bisexuals, and homosexuals—who seemed to approach the exchange in different ways for different reasons.

Ted was in a similar situation when he was serving on the Social Science and Humanities Working Committee on Research Ethics (SSHWC), a federal committee mandated to look at the impact that the federal government's ethics policy—the *Tri-Council Policy Statement* (CIHR et al. 1998) on research with human participants—was having on social science and humanities research. A first task of the committee was to find out just what Canada's social science and humanities research communities felt the problems with the initial policy statement were. An open solicitation brought scores of replies

from researchers and research groups across the country, and the first analytic task involved going through the responses, coding each one in terms of the ethics and research issues that were being identified, using the results to help establish priorities, and reporting back to the research community what had been found and the plan of action the committee envisioned to address those difficulties (see SSHWC 2004).

In both cases, the development and elaboration of the coding scheme arose out of the material that was being scrutinized. While deductive approaches to coding see the researcher begin with an identified focus, the two more inductively guided projects described above began with open coding and gradually moved to more **focused** or **axial coding** as the analysis became elaborated and more refined.

MEMOING

While the processes of open and focused coding involve attaching theoretically relevant labels to segments of our non-numeric data, **memoing** allows us to record and reflect upon the observations and insights accrued through the research and coding process. A memo is in essence a note that we write to ourselves where we elaborate upon the categories of meaning that are beginning to emerge from the research or coding process, just as we might write margin notes in a book we are reading, or include thoughts and other "notes to self" in our field notes as we think of them.

The two are not independent processes; we constantly move back and forth between coding and memoing. The memoing process allows us to clearly and concisely explain—to ourselves and any others involved in the project—the meanings we have attributed to particular codes that we have assigned to elements of our data. Over time, our series of memos will show the development and elaboration of our coding scheme. Memos also allow us to reference or link to other data or observations that help us demonstrate the validity and reliability of our coding. We often memo by placing annotations, in the form of margin or sticky notes, on or near coded content where we will comment on our general feelings about what the content means (i.e., conceptual definitions), possible links to literature, or other locations in his data where similar or different themes are present (e.g., other interviews, images, or news media reports). We use these annotations during subsequent analysis to help us start to make sense of the relationships among and between our data and to help us craft the resulting story that emerges from it.

TYPOLOGICAL AND OTHER MORE COMPLEX ANALYSES

In many cases, coding involves either highlighting and labelling segments of interest and/or the straightforward application of coding rules to talk, text, images, and/or video. The coding itself may be more fluid and evolving or more highly structured and rigidly imposed. Coding may also be a stepping stone toward examining more complex concepts and relations within the data. **Typological analysis**, for example, sometimes referred to as **cluster analysis**, is a method of organizing coded material that involves placing similarly thematically coded information (e.g., people, places, events, or social artifacts that share common characteristics) into relational categories that allow the analyst to make distinctions among groupings or clusters of people, places, and so on that are meaningful to the researcher and/or participants. This process is similar to the creation of a contingency table in quantitative analysis, with the entries in the table this time being actual content—quotes from an interview; segments of a video; quotes from a newspaper article or from a Twitter comment—rather than numerical frequencies.

For example, a researcher interested in understanding the potential links between sexual safety behaviour and drug use among teens might begin by classifying coded passages from interviews with teenagers that pertain to sexual safety behaviour (e.g., condom use during differing types of sexual activities) and types of drug use (e.g., consumption of various types of legal and illegal drugs). Once the researcher decides what it is that they want to classify, the next step in typological analysis is to

map the relationships among and between similarly coded content.

The researcher studying drug use and sexual safety among teenagers might begin by building a typology of drug users, organizing participants' accounts about their drug use according to the class and 'severity' of the drugs they use [e.g., differentiating between (1) opiates such as heroin, crack or powder cocaine, methamphetamines, ecstasy or MDMA, gamma-hydroxybutyrate or GHB; (2) hallucinogens such as LSD; and (3) anaesthetics such as Ketamine, anabolic steroids, hashish, cannabis, tobacco, and alcohol]. Organizing coded material according to such groupings would allow the analyst to start to look at differences and similarities among participants' accounts of sexual safety behaviour on the basis of the type or severity of the drugs they indicated using.

Typologies are very useful ways of classifying and organizing similarly coded material and, as is the case with coding more generally, can be done deductively or inductively. More deductive approaches will see researchers arrive with particular categories of theoretical interest in mind; more inductively minded researchers will want to ensure that the typologies they create reflect groupings that are meaningful for those they are investigating instead of merely reflecting their own preconceived notions of what is important. In our example of teenage drug use, for example, a more medically minded researcher might be tempted to identify drug clusters based on their pharmacological similarity, while a criminologist might be tempted to identify drug clusters based on the way the various drugs are treated (or not) within the Criminal Code. The teenagers involved, on the other hand, might be more likely to cluster the drugs on the basis of the social context in which they are consumed, such that ecstasy, Ketamine, methamphetamine, LSD, and GHB might be strongly associated with raves; alcohol, hashish, and cannabis with recreation; and steroids and some forms of methamphetamine such as diet pills with 'health,' 'fitness,' or 'body image.'

In order to guard against developing typologies that do not reflect 'real' aspects of the phenomenon under investigation it is important that the analyst establish a clear and concise reasoning for the typologies s/he develops. In order to do this s/he should consider the nature of the categorical membership by asking the following types of questions:

- Is the coded content a type of a larger class of things? (e.g., is the drug part of a larger class of drugs? Adderall, Dexedrine, and Benzedrine, for example, are all part of a larger class of drugs called amphetamines)
- Is the coded content part of some other phenomenon? (e.g., is drug use part of some other phenomenon such as crime, social activity, health, and fitness regimes?)
- What conditions precede the occurrence of the coded content? (e.g., what activities or mental states do participants identify as occurring before they use drugs?)
- What conditions follow the occurrence of the coded content? (e.g., what happens to participants after they use drugs?)
- What factors are responsible for the coded content occurring? (e.g., what reasons do participants provide for using drugs? What is the particular drug generally used for?)
- Where does the coded content occur? (e.g., are there any particular locations where people use different types of drugs?)

Asking questions such as these that are relevant to the phenomenon under investigation and the unit of analysis selected helps the researcher avoid developing meaningless typologies that hinder their ability to reveal valid and reliable patterns underlying coded content.

Once the researcher has coded content into meaningful and relevant categories the next step is to begin the process of identifying the spaces where overlap exists between the categories in relation to the phenomenon under investigation. In our example of sexual safety behaviour and drug use, once we developed categories of drug use based on social behaviours such as going to raves, general

recreational activities and 'health, fitness, and body image,' we would next want to determine if teens who engage in risky sexual activities (e.g., vaginal or anal sex without a condom) do so across social contexts or vary their behaviour depending on context (e.g., do teens who use drugs at raves report similar or different sexual safety routines than those who use drugs as part of a 'health' and 'fitness' regime or those who use then purely for recreational purposes?).

This process of comparison continues until we have exhausted all of the coded categories of drug users and sexual safety behaviour and we are able to then create meaningful labels for the various unique categories of the phenomenon under investigation (e.g., "high risk drug users," "medium risk drug users," and "low risk drug users"). We might visually display our typology in a Venn diagram, network map, or flowchart.

CONTENT ANALYTIC APPROACHES

While the richness of the information that talk, text, image, and video contain lends itself to more inductive analytical strategies that emphasize the identification and elaboration of themes that appear in the subject material, some research questions are better approached through techniques that allow the analyst to focus his or her attention on locating specific content in a more structured, deductive manner. Social and health scientists have developed several analytic techniques that use static and clearly identifiable elements of the data as starting points for identifying important concepts and themes. These approaches include **word count analysis**, **key-word-in-context (KWIC) analysis**, and **classic content analysis**.

WORD COUNTS AND KEY-WORD-IN-CONTEXT (KWIC) ANALYSIS

Word count analysis is a rather simple yet useful technique for identifying themes that are present within a particular body of text. This technique assumes that the words that most frequently occur within speech or writing are the ones that represent the concepts or concerns that are most prominent or important to the speaker or author. Identifying the most frequently occurring words allows analysts to identify cognitive-, structural-, and process-related components of talk and text that can be used to gain valuable insights into a variety of social and health related attitudes, beliefs, and behaviours.

When the frequency and type of word use is sub-divided along another axis of analytical interest analysts are able to locate themes in the data that may not have been immediately obvious. For example, let's say we conducted a word count analysis of online dating profiles and found that the words most frequently used by people when describing their interests were sports, football, music, movies, fishing, friends, laughing, dancing, shopping, cooking, camping, beach, outdoors, reading, family, golf, concerts, travelling, fun, and tattoos. On its own this analysis tells us quite a bit about the general interests most people looking online for a mate have. We can clearly see, for example, that physical activities are quite popular.

But suppose we wanted to know if the interests differed for men and women. By placing our word counts into a matrix that separated the responses of males and females we would see that the interests most often listed by women are music, movies, friends, dancing, beach, reading, family, concerts, travelling, shopping, laughing, fun, and tattoos while males indicate they are interested in sports, music, movies, fishing, camping, cooking, outdoors, golf, football, beach, and travel. From this we can see that women tend to indicate they are interested in activities that involve social bonding and entertainment while men appear to be more interested in outdoor activities. We can also see that both men and women share interests in music and movies.

While word count analysis is useful for identifying patterns in word use it does not provide any information on the context within which the words are used. KWIC analysis involves locating all the places in a textual document where a particular word or phrase appears and then analyzing the context that the word or phrase appears in. To do this we generally begin by selecting a word or phrase

we are interested in and what range of words surrounding it we will look at in order to determine context. Most analyses of this type select 20–30 words that come before and after the appearance of the selected word.

The purpose of this type of analysis is to generate a listing of the words that are most often associated with the selected word or phrase—this is called a **concordance distribution**. This technique is particularly useful in the analysis of mainstream print media coverage where the researcher is interested in seeing what terminology is often used alongside the mention of a particular word or phrase. For example, a researcher interested in studying the way that Aboriginality is presented in mainstream media might conduct a KWIC analysis of all of the articles appearing in major Canadian news media between 2000 and 2012 by searching for any mention of the word Aboriginal. Generating a concordance distribution would allow the researcher to determine the adjectives that are most frequently used by journalists in conjunction with their use of the word Aboriginal. They could further analyze these adjectives to determine if Aboriginals were being presented in a positive, negative, or neutral light.

CONTENT ANALYSIS

While some approaches to analyzing non-numeric data are designed to provide a pure descriptive account of the frequency of the appearance of a particular element—such as a word or bodily display—in the text or image, more complex analyses can be designed to provide empirical evidence of differences between different depictions or changes that have occurred over time.

Content analysis is a method of data analysis that allows an analyst to present an 'objective' description of key features of non-numeric data. Demonstrations that the content analytic scheme can be applied reliably and validly are paramount. A central objective of classical content analysis is to present a precise numeric account of the frequency, type and features of words, ideas, actions, depictions, or other elements of interest present in textual or visual data. A related objective is to also present a thorough analysis of the themes and valuations that are present within the text or images being scrutinized.

A THEMATIC EXAMPLE

An excellent example of a more inductively oriented or 'qualitative' analysis of non-numeric data is offered by Trigger (1988), who examined the portrayal of Aboriginal peoples in histories of Canada. The study is an important one for understanding the relationship between Indigenous and non-Indigenous peoples not only because most Canadians know very little about the history of those relations, but also because it shows how what we understand as "history" changes depending on the particular lens through which we view it. In addition to offering an important perspective on historical study and Canada's Aboriginal peoples, Trigger's study serves as an example of a relatively unstructured qualitative thematic analysis of this unique archival material.

Trigger's data included every written history of Canada he could find from as far back as he could find them. The earliest written history he found was authored in 1744 by Pierre-François-Xavier de Charlevoix, a French Jesuit priest. Charlevoix lived extensively among different First Nations during a four-year stay in Quebec and on a two-year trip from Quebec to New Orleans and back. His descriptions of the Aboriginal peoples he encountered are by and large very positive. He considered the continent's natives to be every bit as rational as the Europeans, perceiving them as skilled traders and valuable military allies who did especially well when dealing with Europeans who underestimated them (Trigger 1988).

Charlevoix's accounts were an influential source for later histories in English, such as those written by George Heriot in 1804 and William Smith in 1815, that continued to portray Aboriginal peoples in a positive fashion. This was particularly so after the Iroquois were instrumental in defeating the French—a defeat that ensured the British would

remain the dominant European power in North America—and during the American Revolution, when the Iroquois again fought beside the British against the upstart Americans.

At least that was true of *English* histories; the depiction of Aboriginal peoples in *French* histories changed dramatically after France's 1759 defeat on the Plains of Abraham: "The image of native people in contemporary French-Canadian folklore … kept alive the memory of Iroquois attacks against missionaries and European settlers during the seventeenth century" (Trigger 1988: 21).

One highly influential history was written by François-Xavier Garneau in 1845. "This book was written explicitly to be a history of the French-Canadian nation and sought to glorify the struggle of a people to survive and maintain their cultural identity in the face of the British threat" (Trigger 1988: 21–22). The Indians,[1] and particularly the Iroquois, whose alliance with the British helped bring about the fall of New France, were clearly among the enemy.

Trigger notes that, unlike Charlevoix, Garneau had little experience with Aboriginal peoples, so there was little to inhibit him in developing his accounts of French valour in the face of tremendous adversity. He depicted Aboriginal peoples as savage and backward; described them as constantly engaging in scalping, torture, and massacres; and charged them with sexual promiscuity, mistreating their children, and enslaving their women.

Garneau's history in turn influenced subsequent generations of French-Canadian historians, such as Jean-Baptiste Ferland, Etienne-Michel Faillon, and Henri-Raymond Casgrain (who were all priests, and hence added a more embellished role for the church in bringing "civilization" to the New World). "This gave them an additional motive to stress the vices of native people, whom they generally portrayed as dirty, immoral, cruel, and animal-like prior to their conversion to Christianity" (Trigger 1988: 22).

The latter part of the 19th century saw publication of Darwin's (1859) *On the Origin of Species*; evolutionary theory was subsequently applied to Aboriginal/non-Aboriginal differences, with French historians Benjamin Sulte and Lio-Adolphe Groulx asserting the biological superiority of the French over the Indians and Métis, an assertion that was used to further justify their oppression.

Although the British histories took longer to arrive at a similarly negative tone, they soon did so nonetheless. As long as the Indians were of use to the British—as trading partners, guides, hunters and fishers, and military allies—the depictions of Aboriginal peoples in written Canadian histories remained positive. But after the War of 1812, there was no longer any military threat, and the Europeans' interests in the fur trade waned. At that point the Indian became of little use to the British, who now saw Aboriginal peoples as little more than an impediment to the acquisition of land for settlement and cultivation. By 1855, John McMullen's *History of Canada* showed that the British had quickly and conveniently forgotten how instrumental the Iroquois were in the establishment of British North America; their role in those struggles was now depicted as marginal. In the words of Trigger (1988), McMullen went out of his way to depict Aboriginal peoples

> … as primitive and animal-like. Particular emphasis was placed on their cruelty, dirtiness, laziness, and lack of religion, while their love of freedom, which Heriot and Smith had praised, was now dismissed as being wild and primeval in nature. Indians were frequently asserted to be incapable of becoming civilized and hence doomed to perish with the spread of European civilization.* (Trigger 1988: 23)

Such portrayals further "legitimized" the minimization of the important role that Aboriginal

peoples had played in the history of the country—how could peoples so "backward" and "uncivilized" ever have been involved in nation-building?

At the same time that Canadian colonials were relegating Aboriginal peoples to the broom closet of history, exploiting their lands, and creating treaties only to violate them, Canadian historians were writing self-adulatory accounts of how well we were treating our "native wards." John Castell Hopkins's 1901 *Story of the Dominion* "informed readers that in Canada, Indians had never suffered from racial antagonism, treaty breaking, removal from their reserves, abuse by greedy Europeans, or failure to receive legal justice" (Trigger 1988: 23):

> These interpretations of Canadian history required great self-deception, or hypocrisy, on the part of writers whose governments were treating their former allies with much the same mixture of repression and economic neglect as American governments were treating defeated enemies.† (24)

Trigger notes that English-Canadian histories written in the first decades after 1900 all but abandoned the Indian, apparently accepting the view that they were "a primitive and static people who were doomed to disappear" (24). French-Canadian histories, on the other hand, continued to lament the losses of the past, with Aboriginals simultaneously and contradictingly being portrayed as lazy, immoral, unorganized, and uncivilized until "saved" by the Jesuits and Christianity, and among the primary architects of France's military misfortune.[2]

More recently, Trigger (1988) suggests that Canadian and Native histories seem to have fallen into one or the other of two camps. The first continues the tradition of the past 100 years but with a somewhat less overtly racist edge:

> Although the more obviously pejorative stereotypes have largely been excised from historical works … the neglect of native peoples has persisted in mainstream Canadian historical

---

*† Trigger, B. G. (1988). The historians' Indian: Native Americans in Canadian historical writing from Charlevoix to the present. In R. Fisher & K. Coates (Eds.), *Out of the background: Readings on Canadian Native history* (pp. 19–44). Reprinted with permission from University of Toronto Press (www.utpjournals.com)

studies, French and English. In most works, it has become fashionable to point out that European settlers learned how to use canoes, snowshoes, local foods, and herbal medicines from the Indians and that the Indians had a religion adequate to their needs and were often better nourished than were European settlers. Such observations, for all their good intentions, leave native people far from centre stage; indeed, they continue to treat them more like props than like actors.* (24–25)

The other view of history that is now being seen is one that avoids sole reliance on the self-serving accounts of missionaries and colonists, instead subjecting such accounts to critical analysis through the use of a broader array of sources. Interestingly,

> … this renewed interest in the role of native people in North American history corresponded with their growing importance in modern society. After World War II native populations, which had continued to decline into the 1920s, began to increase rapidly both on reserves and in the cities. In the 1960s native groups became politically active and started to demand the right once more to control the resources necessary to shape their own lives. Their struggle against poverty and government tutelage was accompanied by a cultural renaissance that witnessed native painters, singers, and actors gaining worldwide recognition.[†] (Trigger 1988: 36)

These factors—coupled with the need to deal with growing Aboriginal social problems and political unrest and with advances Aboriginal peoples were making through the courts, in international forums, and in government circles, as well as with the growing numbers of Aboriginal academics and Native leaders who have captured Canadian attention—have all rekindled an interest in Native history that is not based solely on documents created by missionaries and colonial agents.

But while much is changing, much remains to be done. As Trigger (1988) reminds us,

> … only as these studies progress will we be able to distinguish systematically between the manner in which previous generations of Euro-Canadians treated native peoples and the false consciousness that justified their actions and coloured the historical records they produced. This in turn is a necessary preliminary to a deeper and more genuine understanding of native history. In spite of the progress that has been made so far, there are strong reasons to believe that entrenched European stereotypes continue to distort our understanding of native peoples and their history.[‡] (40)

LESSONS FROM TRIGGER

It would have been difficult if not impossible for Trigger (1988) to generate a more concrete coding scheme that could transcend the wide range of sources and time periods he was scrutinizing. His study represents a way of analyzing non-numeric data that relies on a well-defined research question and a thematic reading of his sample materials.

Recall Skogan's (1975) admonition from Chapter 8 that *"Every statistic … is shaped by the process which operationally defines it, the procedures which capture it, and the organization which interprets it"* (17; italics in original). Although initially asserted in an article on police crime statistics, Skogan's comment is equally applicable to historical accounts—just replace the word "statistic" with "historical account"—reminding us that researchers must always be critically aware of the processes and perspective embodied in

---

*[†][‡] Trigger, B. G. (1988). The historians' Indian: Native Americans in Canadian historical writing from Charlevoix to the present. In R. Fisher & K. Coates (Eds.), *Out of the background: Readings on Canadian Native history* (pp. 19–44). Reprinted with permission from University of Toronto Press (www.utpjournals.com)

their sources and of the contexts in which those accounts were produced.

To his credit, Trigger did exactly that. He notes that missionaries believed in the divine inspiration of their activity, had a strong need to justify its rightness and success, and often overestimated their success at conversion. Further, he discovers that most of the documents available for analysis were prepared by missionaries "for publication in tracts designed to encourage European donors to support their work; hence, few failures [or doubts] are discussed at length" (Trigger 1988: 32), and negative portrayals of the Indians would help underline the magnitude of the challenge facing them. Trigger advises that one should always be on the lookout for independent sources for corroboration, and concludes that "it appears that what historians … have concluded about missionary successes in New France is largely a reflection of the hopes and fears of the missionary chroniclers and of what modern scholars wish to have been the case" (32).

Regarding the accounts of colonial writers, Trigger is no more flattering. He approvingly cites Jennings's (1975) work, which

> forced American historians to recognize that those settlers who initially recorded relations between native people and Europeans often either did not understand why Indians acted as they did or else had vested interests in misrepresenting their behaviour in order to portray self-seeking and exploitation by Europeans in a benevolent or at least an innocent fashion. Historians since the seventeenth century, especially those who were naturally predisposed to idealize Euro-American history, have tended to accept these accounts at face value. One role of

[current historical research] is therefore to free mainstream North American history from its legacy as a colonial ideology.* (Trigger 1988: 36)

Trigger's advice is "to learn to combine the study of written documents more effectively with data provided by ethnology, historical linguistics, ethnosemantics, archaeology, and oral traditions, as well as with the analytical perspectives of economics and ecology" (35).

This is good advice, with applicability beyond the restricted range of Aboriginal history per se. Indeed, it is advice that has already been offered in this text in another form: the need for multi-method inquiry, as well as the need for listening to a range of "voices" when constructing analytical accounts. Certainly the most biting aspect of Trigger's historical critique is the extent to which, except for the earliest histories and some of the most recent ones, Aboriginal "voices" have been completely missing from historical accounts.

A MORE STRUCTURED CONTENT ANALYTIC EXAMPLE

Content analysis requires the researcher to have some clear idea of what he or she is after. However the focus is derived—from the researcher's personal interests, from theory, or from exploratory study—the researcher must begin with a clear specification of his or her research question(s) and objectives. Simon Davis's content analysis of media portrayals offers us a good extended example of how non-numeric data can be analyzed in this deductive manner.

Defining the Focus

For Simon Davis (1990), the interest was in looking at mate selection. Previous research had indicated that the selection of opposite-sex partners often follows traditional sex-stereotyped roles. In Davis's terms, stereotypical media portrayals have a long history of emphasizing women as "sex objects" (preferably attractive, alluring, seductive), while for

---

* Trigger, B. G. (1988). The historians' Indian: Native Americans in Canadian historical writing from Charlevoix to the present. In R. Fisher & K. Coates (Eds.), *Out of the background: Readings on Canadian Native history* (pp. 19–44). Reprinted with permission from University of Toronto Press (www.utpjournals.com)

men, the emphasis has been on portraying them as "success objects" (preferably intelligent, wealthy, professional). In keeping with this pattern, the evidence on mate-selection practices had found that men emphasized physical appearance more than women as a factor in mate selection, while women emphasized personality, commitment, and financial security. However, much of the research that showed those tendencies was dated, which left Davis (1990) wondering whether it was still the case in the more progressive 1990s: "Were traditional stereotypes still in operation, that is, [were] women being viewed as sex objects and men as success objects?" (45).

The Research Site

Davis's research question could have been addressed in many ways. He could have created a survey or interview study in which he asked people to indicate the characteristics they were looking for in the "ideal mate," or he could have approached married or cohabiting couples and asked them to explain what it was about the other person they had found so appealing. But if men were most interested in ensuring that they coupled with a woman who looked good on their arm, would they admit it? And if women most valued someone who was smart and successful, thereby providing social status and financial security, would they confide that to him? Davis was worried about the "social desirability" bias that might permeate these methods. Accordingly, he looked for a research venue where social desirability influences would be minimized.

The location he decided on was the newspaper, specifically, the "personals" columns, where many people advertise for a prospective partner or mate. It seemed to meet the criteria: here, men and women seek mates; in the process, they must decide which aspects of themselves they think are most "relevant" to specify, as well as which aspects of the prospective mate they feel are most important. Even better, they're doing so because they really do want to find a partner, and reactivity would be negligible because they are

unlikely to be thinking about the possibility that some social or health scientist might ever read their ad as part of an analysis of factors involved in mate selection.

Of course, many different kinds of newspapers, magazines, and online sites include such "personals" in their classified advertising. Many cater to specific audiences, such as lesbians, gays, executives, or people who seek sexual kinkiness. Although the mate-selection practices shown by such groups may be of interest, Davis chose to start with more "mainstream" ads, particularly those that involved prospective heterosexual relationships. Accordingly, the newspaper he scrutinized was his city's main daily newspaper, which in Davis's words is perceived as a "conservative, respectable journal" (1990: 45), rather like the Victoria *Times Colonist*, *Winnipeg Free Press*, *Toronto Star*, or Montreal's *La Presse*.

Many city libraries keep old copies of the local newspaper as part of their document archive, and it was to the city library that Davis went to check for old editions of his local paper, the *Vancouver Sun*.[3] A preliminary examination of these papers revealed that, although one can place a personals ad on any day of the week, Saturday was clearly the "big" day for such ads: 40 to 60 ads appeared every Saturday, as opposed to between two and four ads per day during the week. So he decided to focus only on Saturday editions. Of the 52 Saturday editions in the year before he started the study, Davis chose to randomly sample six from throughout the year, subjecting *every* ad in each of those editions to analysis. The random sampling would ensure that the editions he analyzed could be considered theoretically representative of the issues published during that year;[4] at 40 to 60 ads per weekend edition, he could expect to end up with 200 or 300 ads, which seemed a reasonable number to analyze. But how to analyze them?

Operationalizing the Variables of Interest

Davis had stated that he was interested in this notion of women (in men's eyes) as "sex objects" and men (in women's eyes) as "success objects." But how do you analyze the typical personals ad for those elements? That is, how do you determine whether any given ad is or is not an example of those phenomena?

Davis approached this question by looking for particular words that could be taken as indicative of the concepts of interest to him. First, he decided to analyze only that part of the ad in which the ad's writer specified what attributes he or she sought in a prospective mate. Within that portion, he decided (after reading many ads to see what kinds of words and phrases were typically used) on the codes shown in Table 11.1.

Three other attributes the ads were coded for included the sex of the ad's author; the age of the

Table 11.1

Coding Scheme Used by Davis (1990) for an Analysis of Mate-Selection Patterns Evident in Personal Newspaper Advertisements

#	Code	Explanation
1	Attractiveness	Coded when the author of the ad indicates that he or she seeks someone who is *pretty, attractive, handsome,* or *good-looking.*
2	Physique	Similar to category 1, but focused more on the body than on the face; relevant key words here would include *muscular, fit, and trim, good figure,* or *well-built.*
3	Sex	Used when reference is made in the ad to desirability of *high sex drive, sensuous, erotic;* or where there is a clear message that author wants to find someone interested in engaging in sexual activity (i.e., *lunchtime liaisons–discretion required*).
4	Picture	Some ads request that respondents send along a photo of themselves, while others do not. Davis (1990) assumes that if a picture is requested, appearance is important.
5	Profession	Used when the author indicates that prospective partner should be a *professional* person.
6	Employed	Coded when the ad specifies that the person should have a steady *job* or *steady income.*
7	Financial	Used whenever the ad indicates that the person sought should be *wealthy, financially stable,* or *financially secure.*
8	Education	Coded whenever an indication is given that the prospective mate should be *well read, college educated,* or simply *well educated.*
9	Intelligence	Key words for this category include a request for someone who is *intelligent, bright,* or *intellectual.*
10	Honest	Coded when the ad requests someone honest or states that respondent should have *integrity.*
11	Humour	Coded when reference is made to the desire for the prospective mate to have a sense of *humour,* to be *cheerful,* or to enjoy a good laugh.
12	Commitment	Used when author explicitly indicates that he or she seeks a liaison that would be *long-term, might lead to marriage,* or similar phrasing.
13	Emotion	Used when there are indications of the desirability of emotional expressiveness, such as *romantic, expressive, sensitive,* or *responsive.*

Source: Based on S. Davis (1990), "Men as Success Objects and Women as Sex Objects: A Study of Personal Advertisements," Sex Roles: *A Journal of Research,* 23, pp. 45–46. Springer New York LLC.

ad's author, but only if a *specific* age was indicated; and the ad's length (expressed as the number of lines).

Note, by the way, that the first nine codes fall neatly into the general categories Davis had been talking about with respect to his primary study objectives. The notion of the "sex object" is reflected by the first four categories—words or phrases that mention "physical attractiveness," "physique," or "sex" or that request a "picture." The notion of the "success object" is addressed by the "employment" cluster contained in the next three categories—"profession," "employed," and "financial"—as well as the "intellectual" cluster represented by the categories "education" and "intelligence."

The remaining four categories—"honest," "humour," "commitment," and "emotion"—all related to a "personality" cluster that had been found in the literature to be more commonly concerns of women; hence, although they were of interest to gather data about, they didn't explicitly relate to the focal concepts of "sex object" and/or "success object."

Davis's elaboration of categories took what had been a very ephemeral idea—the notions of "sex object" and "success object"—and began translating them into fairly concrete, operational terms. Certainly one positive outcome of doing so would be that the coding could probably be done with a high degree of reliability, since such categories reduce the amount of inference required of the coder.[5] Note also how his study design involved a step-by-step approach, in which each step builds on the one preceding; as a result, the data address his objectives adequately and clearly.

You should see, for example, that if we were to now go ahead and code the various ads to ascertain how often ad authors of each sex used terms like "attractive," "professional," and "well educated," we should have a fairly clear answer as to whether men are indeed more interested in meeting "sex objects" as defined in this study and whether women are more interested in meeting "success objects" as defined in this study. And that's exactly what Davis went on to do.

While Davis might have been able to get away without undertaking a reliability assessment because his coding essentially involved little more than looking for specific key words and thus would be expected to be quite reliable, normally content analysis would require the researcher to demonstrate that the coding scheme that has been developed can be implemented reliably. This is most commonly done by having two or more coders sit down and independently code the same material. Several different statistics can be used to compute an inter-rater reliability coefficient, depending on the type of data one has. When Ted did his content analysis of video pornography, for example, five different coders were involved and inter-rater reliability was established by having all five independently code the same film; elaboration of the coding manual and discussion of what the various categories meant continued until all five coders agreed more than 80 percent of the time (see Palys 1986). Similarly, when Neuendorf et al. (2010) did the content analysis of the James Bond films that we noted in Chapter 8, an integral part of their process involved creating a content coding manual, testing inter-rater reliability across the eight coders who were involved, and further developing the coding manual until an acceptable standard of reliability was met.

Aggregating and Coding the Data

With his 13 coding categories in hand, Davis could use them to code the various ads. One problem he anticipated was that a few particularly zealous "sex object" seekers or "success object" seekers could really throw off the data if they said the same thing a dozen different ways; that is, if each of the 13 phrases were counted as an instance of the phenomenon of interest, the total number would inflate the average for their group (i.e., for men or for women). Accordingly, Davis decided to code each of the categories as either "present" or "absent." Operationally, this meant that he would sit down with each ad, ask whether each of the 13 categories was evident, and then code it on a purely yes-or-no basis.

Thus, if an ad said that its author was looking for someone "with a great body," that ad would be coded as a "yes" for the "physique" category. If another ad expressed its author's interest in someone who was "muscular, fit, with great body tone, and curves and bulges in all the right places," that ad, too, would be coded as a "yes" for the "physique" category, even though its author repeated essentially the same thing four times in succession.

Davis then went through each of the randomly sampled Saturday editions, finding a total of 329 ads. He decided to omit one of them from the analysis (appropriately noting the decision in his article) because it involved a gay relationship rather than the heterosexual relationships on which he had decided to focus. Of the 328 remaining ads,

215 (or 65.5 percent) were placed by men, while 113 (or 34.5 percent) were authored by women.

Because he had coded for the age of the person in each ad, he also was able to tell us a bit about who these people were: the average age of those who reported it was 40.4 years, with very similar average ages for the men (40.7 years) and the women (39.4 years) who had included that information. The biggest problem here was that a full half of the women (50.4 percent) and almost a third of the men (32.6 percent) did not report their *exact* age.

Once all the ads were coded, Davis had only to begin making the appropriate comparisons. His first analysis scrutinized the differences between men and women in each of the 13 categories. These data are reported in Table 11.2: where Davis

Table 11.2

Gender Comparison for Attributes Desired in Partner

Variable	Gender		Chi-Square
	Desired by Men($n = 215$)	Desired by Women($n = 113$)	
Attractiveness	76 (35.3%)	20 (17.7%)	11.13(*)
Physique	81 (37.7%)	27 (23.9%)	6.37(*)
Sex	25 (11.6%)	4 (3.5%)	6.03(*)
Picture	74 (34.4%)	24 (21.2%)	6.18(*)
Profession	6 (2.8%)	19 (16.8%)	20.74(*)
Employed	8 (3.7%)	12 (10.6%)	6.12(*)
Financial	7 (3.2%)	22 (19.5%)	24.26(*)
Education	8 (3.7%)	8 (7.1%)	1.79(ns)
Intelligence	22 (10.2%)	24 (21.2%)	7.46(*)
Honest	20 (9.3%)	17 (15.0%)	2.44(ns)
Humour	36 (16.7%)	26 (23.0%)	1.89(ns)
Commitment	38 (17.6%)	31 (27.4%)	4.25(*)
Emotion	44 (20.5%)	35 (31.0%)	4.36(*)

NOTE: (*) means that the difference between the male- and female-authored ads was statistically significant at the p < .05 level; (ns) means that the comparison was non-significant, that is, the difference observed was no greater than what you would expect on the basis of chance variation alone.

Source: S. Davis (1990), "Men as Success Objects and Women as Sex Objects: A Study of Personal Advertisements," Sex Roles: *A Journal of Research*, 23, p. 47. Springer New York LLC.

found significant differences, we've shaded the side with the significantly higher percentage. Most (10 out of 13) of the individual comparisons were statistically significant (i.e., the differences were found to be larger than would be expected on the basis of chance variation alone; see Chapters 9 and 12 for discussions of statistical significance); all the differences, significant or not, were in the anticipated direction. Thus, for the "sex object" cluster, men were more likely than women to specify that they were seeking someone who was attractive, had a nice physique, and/or was interested in sex, and were more likely to request a picture of the respondent.

For the "success object" cluster, women were more likely than men to express a preference for someone who was a professional, employed, and/or financially secure. The data on the "intellectual" cluster were a little less clear: there were no statistically significant differences between the sexes in the extent to which they mentioned the desirability of "education" (although women had the higher percentage again), yet the category "intelligent" was noted significantly more often by women than men.

As for the "personality" cluster, women were more likely than men to specify attributes that fell into all four of these categories. But the size of the difference was statistically significant only for "commitment" and "emotion," and not for "honesty" and "humour."

Another way to look at these data is to group them into the overall categories of interest, for example, to aggregate all the "sex object" categories—appearance, physique, sex, picture—to create one overall index. This is shown in Table 11.3, which reaffirms the overall differences between male-authored and female-authored ads that were already evident when we scrutinized the individual categories. Men are shown to be more likely than women to state in an ad that they're seeking someone who's physically attractive; women are more likely than men to say that they're seeking someone who's financially stable and well-educated.

Alas, despite all the gains that have been made in the realm of sexual equality, Davis's (1990) data seem to show that many men and women—at least in the early 1990s—still follow very traditional patterns when seeking a mate.

Table 11.3

Gender Comparison for Physical, Employment, and Intellectual Attributes Desired in a Prospective Partner

Variable	Gender		Chi-Square
	Desired by Men ($n = 215$)	**Desired by Women** ($n = 113$)	
Physical (aggregating variables 1–4)	143 (66.5%)	60 (44.2%)	15.13(*)
Employment (aggregating variables 5–7)	17 (7.9%)	47 (41.6%)	51.36(*)
Intellectual (aggregating variables 8–9)	29 (13.5%)	31 (27.4%)	9.65(*)

Note: (*) means that the difference between the male- and female-authored ads was statistically significant at the p < .05 level.

Source: S. Davis (1990), "Men as Success Objects and Women as Sex Objects: A Study of Personal Advertisements," Sex Roles: *A Journal of Research*, 23, p. 48. Springer New York LLC.

Caveat and Critique

Or do they? Probably the most positive element of Davis's analysis is the use it makes of an unobtrusive archival measure to scrutinize "real" processes involved in searching for a mate (i.e., the people who placed the newspaper ads were in fact searching for partners) and the avoidance of reactivity that this approach allows. But we should still be careful about how much confidence we place in the conclusions.

Davis expresses caution related to the apparent age of his sample. Having determined that the average age of those ad authors who cited their exact age was around 40, he suggests that the results may merely reflect the particular age cohort represented in the ads. Just because the 40-ish people who placed these ads seem to follow very traditional patterns of mate selection does not mean that people of other cohorts—those in their teens and 20s, for example—also do so.

One also must question the selection bias associated with those who use ads as a way of selecting mates, rather than more conventional means such as introductions through friends, meeting at social events such as parties, and/or meeting at venues of common interest such as the gym, library, or opera. Indeed, the fact that those who placed ads were in their 40s and were still (or newly) unattached may suggest that ads are a venue for mate selection largely for those who are unable or unwilling to meet people through conventional means and/or for those who may still be unattached precisely *because* they had a rigidly sex-typed and traditional conception of roles and desirable attributes.[6] People who are more socially egalitarian may have met someone already, and hence do not need to place an ad.

As this implies, those who chose mates *not* because they sought someone with a great body or a large bank account, but because they sought a well-rounded person who combined many positive attributes, may well be sitting out there happily ensconced in and enjoying their relationships, and may never even have considered placing a personals ad. Thus, although Davis's findings are indeed consistent with his hypothesis regarding differential bases for mate selection, they may well have emerged precisely because people who seek mates for the attributes he hypothesized are the people who end up placing personals ads and not because they reflect the way men and women in general seek and select mates.

AN INTRODUCTION TO COMPUTER-ASSISTED QUALITATIVE DATA ANALYSIS SOFTWARE

While the studies by Trigger (1988) and Davis (1990) exemplify the sorts of procedures that are involved in more thematic/qualitative and more structured/quantitative analysis of media, both studies were done at a time when there was no such thing as software for the analysis of non-numeric data. It was a time when researchers began the process by typing up their handwritten field notes or tape recorded interviews, photocopied their visual data, and plopped themselves down on a wide open floor. Once situated in their space they would organize the mountain of paper into smaller hills and begin the time-honoured tradition of slowly and methodically weighing through the data, highlighting transcripts and photos with markers, scribbling annotations in the margins, and recording memos on sticky notes and index cards. This inevitably would lead to countless attempts at restacking and reorganizing the data into progressively smaller piles that at times might resemble typologies, taxonomies, or mental maps. This painstaking ritual would proceed *ad nauseam* until the analyst emerged from the ruins with her/his finely crafted typed analysis.

While this image of the procedure for analyzing non-numeric data might conjure up feelings of nostalgia for people born long before the advent and mass marketing of the personal computer in the early 1980s, many social and health researchers who work with non-numeric data now use technology to assist in various aspects of the research and analyses process. Instead of recording interviews on analogue tape we now digitally record interviews, field notes, and memos so that we can listen to them on our MP3 players or desktop or laptop computers and transcribe the recordings using software such as Express Scribe or Dragon Naturally Speaking. We use word processing software such as Microsoft Word or Open Office Writer to create transcripts of our field notes, memos, or interviews. We store research data on flash or hard drives or DVDs rather than on paper in filing cabinets. We use electronic file and referencing software such as Windows Explorer, RefWorks, or Zotero to organize and link our literature and research data files. We use electronic search tools built into operating systems or word processing software to locate details or perform word counts within literature, textual, or visual data. We highlight key words, phrases, or ideas in text using the text formatting or review options in our word processing software and we use audio, image, and video editing programs such as Adobe Photoshop, Gimp, Adobe Soundbooth, Audacity, or Adobe Premiere to edit our rich media data and field notes. Finally, we use programs such as Microsoft Publisher, Microsoft Visio, Scribus, or Dia to develop visual displays or models of our thinking about the relationships in our data. In the remainder of this chapter we discuss how to use some of these technologies in order to analyze non-numeric data, note what new possibilities arise because of the efficiencies that these developments— and particularly the development of qualitative data analysis (QDA) software—represent, and consider some of the implications of doing so.

Technological Options

While the contribution that developments in digital and computer hardware and software have made toward improving the efficiency of the data collection and analysis process are undeniable, many of the applications we highlight above were not developed specifically to aid social and health researchers in the analysis process. While there is clearly a dizzying array of software that we can employ to meet our needs, it can be rather daunting for any one researcher or research team to have to

acquire (sometimes at considerable cost) and master such a large number of programs. This can leave those of us who are faced with having to make sense of mountains of non-numeric data with the sinking feeling that we are going to have to "go old school" whether we like it or not.

Fortunately for us, an increasing number of specialized software applications for making sense of both numeric and non-numeric data have emerged in the mainstream market place over the past 30 years. While we will discuss applications created for numeric data in the next chapter, the most popular applications for working with non-numeric data include QSR NVivo, ATLAS.ti, MAXqda, HyperRESEARCH, QDA Miner, and The Ethnograph.

Selecting a Software Package

Although no single program is superior in all respects to all others at present, each of the packages listed above provides an excellent range of features for the analysis of non-numeric data. When selecting a QDA package, there are several things you should keep in mind. First is the amount and type of data you are going to be working with, as each of the programs has particular strengths and weaknesses. Some deal with text files only while others allow you to work with images, video, audio, hypertext, posts on social networking sites (e.g., Twitter feeds), GeoData (e.g., Google Maps), or structured questionnaires. Further, some programs are limited in the amount of data they can handle; some place a physical cap on the number of objects (i.e., interview transcripts or images) you can analyze while others simply become unstable and crash when you attempt to bring in too many files.

What you wish to describe, understand, or explain through your analysis and your approach to analysis is also an important consideration when selecting a program. While all the software applications we've named will provide you with the tools to conduct a basic search, code and retrieve style of analysis, if you want to conduct a more sophisticated analysis involving linking data elements, complex visual displays or models, or integrative analyses of mixed data you need to take a careful look at what different software can do before you invest the time and money to adopt one.

While open source and freeware QDA programs are available (e.g., Weft QDA, RQDA), they tend to offer a very limited range of features and little to no user support. The more sophisticated programs such as NVivo, AtlasTi, and MaxQDA offer educational and student pricing, although even these are not cheap, with educational licences ranging from \$500–\$700 and student licences ranging from \$99–\$199.[7] All are relatively easy to learn as they are all built upon the menu-tool bar-based user interface that is standard in the word processing software we all use on a daily basis. That said, as with any program there is a learning curve that will be steeper for inexperienced users than for technophiles. Fortunately, the popular commercial applications offer very good learning resources in the form of instruction manuals and online tutorials and community forums.

As we have mentioned throughout the book, both of us do research in a wide variety of academic, government, non-profit, and commercial settings where we sometimes work alone and sometimes work with large teams of researchers from different disciplinary backgrounds. The projects we are involved in can range in size from a few focus groups or in-person interviews to large-scale mixed methods investigations that involve hundreds of in-depth interviews, dozens of focus groups, community and research meetings, and seemingly limitless numbers of PDF documents, image, and video files. Because we are involved in such a wide range of projects with a diverse array of researchers our research questions fall all along the inductive-deductive/constructionist-realist continuum so the types of analyses we are called upon to perform can range from discourse analysis to classical content analysis and beyond. When we were trying to decide on what QDA program to use we needed to find one that was adaptable to the widest range of conditions possible. While programs such as Atlas Ti and Max QDA both offer an excellent range

of features and are certainly ones you should consider when making your own choice, we ultimately decided that QSR's NVivo was best suited for our needs.

USING NVIVO FOR SOCIAL AND HEALTH RESEARCH

The utility of NVivo begins with the manner in which it duplicates digitally what qualitative researchers and students have been doing manually for years. Instead of using your yellow highlighter to emphasize a certain passage, NVivo does so digitally. Instead of writing little notes to yourself in page margins or on yellow stickies, NVivo allows you to create digital memos that accomplish the same thing. Even on these simple tasks, however, there are benefits to working with software like NVivo instead of manually. An analogy would be to say that word processing is to writing on a piece of paper what NVivo is to the manual coding of non-numeric data. In each case one is doing the same activity—writing with ink on a pad of paper or writing with keystrokes on a computer using word processing software are two means to accomplish "writing" and neither medium guarantees or precludes you winning the Nobel Prize for literature—but the flexibility and possibilities that the word processor brings to the activity of writing are far richer than the possibilities that come with ink on paper.

NVivo does all of the things that you might do with a yellow highlighter and a pencil, but does so digitally in a way that maximizes the amount of information that you can deal with, and the number of different ways you can conceptualize and re-conceptualize your "data,"[8] whatever that data happens to be. It is as if you have an infinite number of highlighters in every conceivable colour for each one of the categories of information you want to highlight and can call up any single colour or set of colours you want at any time. There also is no more worry about "now where did I see that quote?" because any quotes we've coded are immediately retrievable, and even if we didn't code it, the program's search capabilities mean that we should be able to locate the quote with a few well-chosen search terms.

We also appreciate the range of material NVivo allows us to work with. While our yellow highlighter works well with text, we are at a loss of how to code when we want to include a video or picture or radio interview or piece of music in our project. NVivo allows all those types of sources to be coded using what is essentially a digital highlighter, which makes them all retrievable as well whenever we want it. Because we also have been known to change our minds from time to time as our familiarity with and understanding of our data develops, we also like the flexibility that NVivo offers us to change our coding labels, disaggregate or aggregate coding categories, or do the work for us in finding all references to a certain kind of content that we have an interest in.

Just these basic features make us wonder why anyone out there still uses yellow highlighters and stickies in any research project, but there is far more that the program can do. While providing step-by-step "how to use NVivo" is beyond the scope of this book, we will outline some of the basic features and functions of the program and how we have used them in various social and health research contexts to give you a better idea about some of the possibilities that QDA software holds.[9]

Project Planning and Organization

Part of the appeal of NVivo for us is that we see it as more than just a QDA application. The program can deal with virtually any kind of content—text, images, video, audio files—and, as such, does double duty as a central file management facility where we can store: (1) digital copies of relevant literature; (2) project organizational material such as meeting notes, research instruments, and spreadsheets; (3) research data and observations such as field notes, memos and annotations, digital recordings and transcripts of interviews, and images and video files (see Palys & Atchison 2009, in press). Having all the material relating to a particular research project in one central location, called a project file in NVivo, allows us to work more efficiently and effectively both alone and in team environments. One of the first things we do when we are starting a new project is create an NVivo **project file** so that we can import or link to all relevant materials that we produce as the research takes place, in this sense the project file is an organic entity that grows with the project.

Working with Data

NVivo allows us to import a wide range of data and file formats directly into our project. The data and file formats supported by the program include: text files (doc, docx, rtf, txt), image files (bmp, jpg, tif, gif), mixed text and image portable document format (PDF) files, audio files (mp3, wma, wav), and video files (mpg, wmv, avi, mov, qt, mp4). In addition to allowing us to work with a wide range of text, image, audio, and video data directly within the program, we can work with websites and peripheral digital files either by way of external links that open Web browsers or other programs or by directly importing the content of the sites using a feature of the program called NCapture. This feature is particularly useful when conducting research with online communities or social network sites (e.g., Facebook or Twitter) or when working on mixed or multi-methods projects where we have collected numeric data that we analyze in spreadsheet or quantitative data analysis programs such as Microsoft Excel or SPSS.

In addition to being able to import a wide variety of digital material directly into NVivo as well as being able to link up to external material, the program also allows us to create and edit text-based documents with its built in word processor. A built in word processor and audio-player allows us to transcribe digitally recorded data and observations such as interviews and field notes right in the program. We also use it to create memos to assist us in our research and analysis as it progresses.

Since an increasing number of books and articles are available digitally as PDF files we get digital copies of textual materials whenever possible and treat these sources as "data" that we read and code as part of the research process. In fact, since a large part of our research begins with our reading of the available literature relating to the topic we are investigating, we generally begin most of our projects by importing all of the relevant journal articles, policy papers, book chapters, and print media into our project file where we can easily read and code it for use during the design, collection and analysis stages of our research (see Palys & Atchison 2009, in press). A great advantage of having all these materials under an NVivo project umbrella is that all of the text contents are searchable—rather like having your own personal search engine that is specific to your project.

Coding Non-Numeric Data Through Nodes

NVivo offers a variety of ways to code any piece of information that you feel is relevant to your project including literature, memos, interview audio files or transcripts, or image and video from the field or the archives. The basic coding unit that the program uses is referred to as a **node**. A node is quite simply a short label representing an idea, theme, persona, place, interest, or concept. In NVivo nodes are used to store all of the references from the data (e.g., segments of text, image, video, or audio material) that correspond to a particular theme, topic, idea, or concept we identify. Nodes can be created in several different ways within the program including: (1) *a priori* based on our identification of factual, thematic, or theoretically relevant ideas; (2) *in process* on the basis of our reading of the data; (3) *in vivo* using the exact phrasing of our participants; or, (4) *automatically* on the basis of the formatting of our data or using a text or word search to identify the most commonly occurring words or concordances of words in your data. As this makes clear, use of the program is equally compatible with inductive, deductive, and mixed approaches.

One advantage of the digital highlighting NVivo allows is that any given segment of data can be assigned a unique code or be assigned to any number of different nodes, unlike your yellow highlighter, which gets confusing if you try to code any given section using more than one colour of highlighter. Furthermore, as the coding progresses and we begin to develop more specific ideas about the data and the relationships among and between coded content, nodes can be grouped together by merging them or dragging and dropping them into folders, sets, or models where they can be organized into hierarchies (e.g., taxonomies) or visual displays (e.g., typologies or mental maps).

For example, if we are reading through the medical records of people diagnosed and treated for attention hyperactivity deficit disorder (ADHD) in order to answer research questions about the different treatment options that have been utilized by doctors and psychologists, we might create a node labelled "treatment options." Once created, any time we come across information in the patient files that refers to ways that ADHD is treated we can simply highlight the material and assign it to the "treatment options" node. As we read through more and more of the medical records files we could continue to identify examples of treatment that we can add to the "treatment options" node. At any time, the program can be asked to produce a report that compiles and shows all of the sections that have been highlighted with a given code.

Nodes can be disaggregated as well. For example, the 'treatment options' node might be further subdivided into therapeutic, education or training, and pharmaceutical by creating three new 'child' or branch nodes under our main 'treatment options' node and then rereading the content we have coded at 'treatment options' and reassigning or recoding each entry into the new treatment categories. Passages where multiple treatment options are used can be coded in multiple overlapping nodal categories.

Being able to rapidly compile every time a particular concept is illustrated, or every time a quote includes reference to or illustrates a particular position or point of view is incredibly helpful in several respects. Analytically, it allows us to see all instances of a particular concept, which allows us to reflect on the concept itself and perhaps also to ask what elements are missing that have not yet been sampled. It also provides a basis for more systematic comparative analysis by allowing the researcher to, for example, subdivide the quotes one has for different subgroups. At the writing stage, it becomes easy to compile all quotes about a particular topic in one place, thereby facilitating one's choice of what quotes to include to ensure that the range of ways the topic is discussed is illustrated.

Coding Static Attributes Through Classifications

While the majority of the coding of non-numeric data is accomplished through the use of nodes, we are also frequently interested in coding more static elements such as the demographic characteristics of a particular participant, the publication and content information of a book chapter or journal article, or the geographic coordinates where a photograph or video was created. This type of information might be referred to as the "quantitative" content in qualitative data.

The classification facility of NVivo is an ideal place to catalogue the static attributes of non-numeric data. There are two main types of classifications—*source* and *node*—with each serving different purposes. We use source classifications to record information about the static and comparable details of the literature we include in our project file. For example, Ted is currently working on an article related to a confidentiality case that has arisen out of Boston College in Massachusetts. More than 400 sources have been compiled in the year the case has been in process—including newspaper articles, legal submissions, affidavits, radio interviews, videos, blogs, letters, and so forth—and one issue of interest to Ted is how the different sources compare in their coverage. NVivo allows each source to be coded as to the type of source, which in turn will allow him to generate a report that includes all of the entries that address a particular issue, or to subdivide them by type of source, which will allow him to inspect whether the type of source is associated with different views about the

case. Alternatively, node classifications can be used to code demographic information about our units of analysis (individuals, locations, photographs, or videos). In Ted's case, for example, he could code whether particular comments about the case are uttered by a researcher, university administrator, journalist, or politician, which again allows him to either look at comments about a particular issue (i.e., node) as a whole, or to subdivide the report so that the different commentators are separated, thereby making it easier to inspect the entries to compare the views of these different groups.

Readers of this book who are familiar with programs such as Microsoft Excel, Open Office Calc, or SPSS will already be familiar with ways of storing information in tabular form. For those who are not, spreadsheets, data files, and classification sheets all store and display information in columns and rows. Generally, each column represents the attribute or variable (e.g., sex, age, data collection technique, publication type, year of publication, file type) you are classifying and each row represents the individual case or unit of analysis (interview participant, audio recording, photograph, or video file). Each case or unit can be classified in terms of the value they possess for a particular attribute. For example, if we decide to code participants on the attributes of age, sex, sexual preference, and racial background, we can then create categories within that attribute that will allow us to code our next respondent as male, 18 years old, bisexual, and Caucasian while the one after that might be female, 26 years old, heterosexual, and Asian. Classification sheets, like spreadsheets and data files, allow us to record, code, and analyze the static attributes of our research data. When retrieved, attributes are displayed in the form of a spreadsheet that can be used to perform advanced queries and analyses within NVivo—for example, we might want to compare how men and women talked about the risks and benefits associated with condom use— or can be exported to quantitative data analysis programs such as SPSS for more sophisticated quantitative analysis.

Recording Observations Using Memos and Annotations

The most basic way we can record our ideas, insights, interpretations and understandings of our research throughout the process is through the use of **memos**. In addition to acting as catalogues of our thinking process, in NVivo memos are codable pieces of data that we can link to other elements of our research data such as research participants, segments of image or rich media, or attributes in a classification. While memos can take the form of standalone documents that we create inside the program they also can take the form of an **annotation**—a virtual sticky note—that we attach to a particular element (section of text or area of image, video or audio) of any project document.

Memos and annotations serve a variety of functions during the project design and data collection stages. We use theoretical memos and annotations as a way of cataloguing the theoretical insights that we have as the research and analysis progresses. For example, in the early stages of research design we might come across a particular passage in an article or book we are reading discussing a certain theory that we think might be useful at some point in the research. We might create a memo we call "theoretical note" that briefly details the theory and provides a couple of key references to the people responsible for creating the theory or we might create an annotation that records our immediate thoughts or insights about the specific passage where the theory is mentioned.

Methodological memos we create in our project are often based on our thoughts and reflections on particular aspects of our research such as the sampling or solicitation approaches we are using or ideas on how to better record interviews or notes when we are in the field. Project memos are similar to methodological memos but we use these to record our thoughts and observations on key details, goals, assumptions, and decisions we make during the research that may impact the information we gather and our subsequent analyses. Similarly, we use case or field memos to record our observations about a particular interview participant, research setting, or other unit of analysis. These memos are great for summarizing our thoughts about an interview or our impressions of a particular participant. They are also very useful for highlighting some of our initial ideas about what is going on in our research that frequently find their way into our coding of the research data.

In addition to being superb ways of recording insights regarding theory and methodology as well as ongoing observations about your research, memos and annotations are helpful for tracking our developing analysis and help ensure that we are being as transparent as possible in making sense of the data.

Analyzing Data

While we see NVivo as an excellent tool for file and data management and project organization that provides a great space for recording and cataloguing our thoughts and observations and coding our research data and field notes, one of the program's greatest strengths lies in the range of options it provides for the analysis of coded material. Analysis in NVivo can take a wide variety of forms, allowing analysts to employ any or all of the analytic techniques we highlighted earlier in this chapter. The technical procedures for analyzing data within the program include simple point and click retrieval of coded content, retrieval and display through framework matrices and advanced queries (searches), and retrieval and display through advanced visualizations and modelling.

Retrieving Coding Using Point and Click

One of the most useful and basic ways to quickly retrieve and display all the material that we have coded under a specific node within NVivo so that we can analyze it is simply to ask the program to retrieve and display the contents of the node we are interested in. This allows us to see all the locations in the data where a particular theme or concept is present as well as allowing us to look more closely at the coded content to make sure that it has been consistently and accurately coded.

When we conduct simple thematic analyses we often code our data in nodes over successive readings and then retrieve the content of each node when we are ready to sit down and begin writing. Quite frequently we organize our nodes thematically as typologies, taxonomies, or mental maps using features of the program that allow us to group content into sets (folders for elements with equal or shared features), nodal hierarchies, or models (a chart-creating feature that allows us to visualize the relationships among and between nodes or cases). We often find that this code and retrieve style of analysis is more than suitable for the identification of the key themes that we piece together as we write since specific references can be quoted, summarized, synthesized, compared, and contrasted further during the writing process. This approach to analysis is particularly well suited for the thematic analyses that students writing extensive literature reviews, substantive papers, or comprehensive exams are often required to do; demonstrating once again that NVivo has uses far beyond formal research environments.

Queries and Word Frequency Analysis

While the simple code retrieval functions of NVivo are far more efficient than conventional non-computer assisted approaches for analyzing data, the techniques we've described are just the tip of the iceberg in terms of what NVivo offers when it comes to analyzing coded data. The program also offers a range of sophisticated query (e.g., search, organize, and retrieve) options that support a wide variety of analytical approaches. The analytical tools available include simple and advanced searches, compound queries, framework matrix and coding analyses, and coding queries, just to name a few! We'll describe just two of those in the introductory treatment we intend here.

The *text search* facilities that are built into the program allow you to quickly find and retrieve all the places in your data (including our memos and annotations) where particular words, phrases, concepts, ideas, or themes are present or intersect with one another. It can be used to perform a range of analytic searches from basic identification of every instance where an exact word appears in the research data to complex queries involving wildcards, conditional statements, and proximity specifications such as those we would use for KWIC (key-word-in-context) analyses. Moving from a text search to a KWIC analysis is quite simple since results of text searches are presented in a way that we can ascertain the number of times a particular word appears in each piece of our data (e.g., in each interview), can see the exact points in the text where the word appears, or can view the word context visually in the form of a customizable word tree that allows us to see a branching display of a specified number of words appearing before and after our key word across all or part of our data. A simple text search can be extended using the compound query option to combine two separate text search terms, which allows us to locate spaces in our data where they occur together in the same sentence or passage.

The program also has a sophisticated *word frequency query* that allows us to determine which words or concepts appear most often in any textual data we have in our project. In addition to being able to specify the minimum size of the words we wish to include in our search, the program also allows us to specify how close of a match (e.g., an exact word through to synonyms and words sharing generally the same meaning) common words should be located on. The program displays the results in the form of numeric summaries showing the frequency and percentage of the appearance of words in the data or visually in the form of a word cloud, tree map, or cluster analysis. While we rarely use word frequency alone to analyze our data we find that it is an excellent tool for quickly identifying potential themes or frequently occurring concepts in our data or to get a deeper understanding of the language that participants use to describe certain concepts or phenomenon.

Analysis Through Visualizations and Models

For many, visually displaying relationships between people, places, things, themes, codes, and concepts is the most efficient way to make sense of non-numeric data. Accordingly, the final set of NVivo facilities for analyzing coded content that we will highlight are those relating to visualization and modelling of coded data.

Charts in NVivo are particularly useful for identifying how frequently a particular node is coded across cases or for determining if a particular node is more or less likely to be associated with specific case attributes. For example, if we are interested in visually displaying which interview participants discuss 'recurrent thoughts of death or suicide' and how frequently each participant mentions this in their interviews we could generate a chart that summarizes our coding for the node 'recurrent thoughts of death or suicide' for all of our participants. The result would be a chart that would not only show us differences in frequencies of experiences but one in which each of the bars representing these frequencies could be clicked on to retrieve the actual text where we have coded participants 'recurrent thoughts of death or suicide.'

A more intricate way of visualizing the patterns in our coding of people, places, things, or themes in our data is through cluster analysis. This technique allows us to visually display the grouping (clustering) of sources or nodes that share similar wording, attribute values, or coding. Cluster analyses are incredibly useful for identifying patterns in data since they graphically display relationships between elements of our data; the closer clusters of elements are to each other in the visual display the more similar they are to each other. So if we were interested in seeing how similar the wording that various women who have experienced postpartum depression use to describe their experiences is, we could accomplish this through a cluster analysis.

Tree maps are another useful way to visualize patterns in our data. A tree map is a diagram that displays the hierarchical relationships among coded content. Tree maps display coding frequency in the form of a series of nested rectangles presented horizontally from left to right with the largest rectangle on the left-hand side of the display representing the node with the greatest amount of coded content and nested rectangles becoming increasingly smaller in size as one looks to the right-hand side of the display.

Finally, models are probably the most sophisticated way to use NVivo to visually explore and display coded elements of our research. Models can be either dynamic or static. A static model is simply a point-in-time snapshot of a dynamic model that we often find useful as a way of cataloguing our thinking as our analysis unfolds. Dynamic models are organic representations of the connections between virtually any aspect of your research data (e.g., internal and external text and rich media documents or links, memos, nodes, attributes, sets, or annotations). What makes these models dynamic is that as our projects develop and we code more information, create new memos that we link to aspects of our data, and specify relationships between different elements of our project the models are automatically updated by the program to reflect these changes. We find this particularly useful when we are developing and testing theories as the models provide us with immediate visual feedback on the presence of confirmatory or contradictory evidence from within our data of specific aspects of the theory that we are developing.

Pros and Cons: The Debate Over Using Computers to Analyze Non-Numeric Data

Despite the growing availability of specialized software packages designed to improve the speed and efficiency of coding and analyzing the diverse forms of non-numeric data that social and health researchers are likely to collect, there are still some people who object to using computers to code and analyze rich textual, audio. and visual data. Many social and health researchers who were born before the Internet or who were taught how to analyze this type of data by someone who refused to accept and/or learn new technologies and techniques still prefer going "old school" and analyzing talk, text, image, and video using highlighters, sticky notes or index cards, and scribbling in the margins of printed paper. Some argue that using a computer removes the analyst from the analytical process and from the research data itself, blunting our senses and removing us from the data in ways that dramatically and negatively impact the depth and breadth of the resulting analyses. Still others accuse programs such as NVivo of being nothing more than an attempt to 'quantify' qualitative data, a process that could very well result in increasing demands that the data meet solely quantitative criteria for rigour, thereby undermining the way data integrity is defined in the more qualitative context.

On the other side of the fence, proponents of QDA software maintain that these programs make it easier for us to create, store, organize, edit, correct, and locate an increasingly diverse and expansive array of research data. It also provides us with a range of efficient ways to code multiple forms of data and to record, access, and link our thoughts (e.g., our memos and annotations) about our project and data to other aspects of our emergent analysis. It gives us the ability to quickly search volumes of coded and uncoded material so we can easily extract relevant bits as we pursue ideas, clarify concepts, and develop models and theories. It allows us to quickly and easily apply a variety of content analytic strategies ranging from simple word counts to KWIC to more complex matrix-based analyses. It enables us to retrieve and display thematically coded material in a variety of visual formats including typologies, taxonomies, mental maps, flow charts, and matrices. Finally, it facilitates both individual and collaborative writing of the analyses that form the basis of our research reports, articles, and books.

The two of us see QDA software as simply another tool in our research tool belt. Software programs such as NVivo can be used to help us make sense of our data; they cannot do our analysis for us. No matter how sophisticated the software becomes, strong analyses will always require the researcher to painstakingly and meticulously code the material, thinking through the meanings and various possible interpretations and returning to the data to test their assumptions in an effort to develop both nuanced and comprehensive explanations and theory.

SUMMING UP AND LOOKING AHEAD

One of the great benefits of more qualitative approaches—their ability to produce reams of rich data—is also in some ways their greatest liability. What is a researcher to do when s/he sits down at the end of the day with hundreds of pages of interview transcripts, thousands of words of information in his or her field notes, and/or computer directories full of audio and video files? Unlike more quantitative research, where the researcher can take stacks of numbers and incorporate them into well-defined statistical techniques to summarize and focus the analysis in the form of a few tables, charts and graphs, the procedures involved in managing more qualitative data are rarely discussed. And yet never has the need for such a discussion been greater given the virtual explosion of text, image, audio, and video data that we can create and/or download thanks to the digital revolution we are experiencing. Indeed, one can argue that the biggest challenge facing analysts of any stripe these days is the simple question of how to manage all the data that is out there. The current chapter attempts to redress that inattention by outlining some of the issues and strategies involved in the collection and analysis of non-numeric data.

The two main processes involved in analyzing text, images, audio, and/or video data are coding and memoing. In both cases the objective is to take the piles of data we have accumulated and find ways to present them in a manner that reduces the volume of information we are working with, effectively and transparently summarizes the patterns that exist in the data, and helps us to achieve our empirical objectives without doing any injustice to the data.

Coding can be deductive or inductive. Deductive coding occurs when your research focus and interest are well-defined from the start so that decisions about what to code are made independent of the data in front of you. Common practices with the more deductive coding techniques include word counts and key-word-in-context analysis, as well as classic content analysis. Notwithstanding a clear focus from the outset, the deductive coding still often involves initial categories being finetuned and elaborated in contact with the data. More inductive approaches to coding are more squarely rooted in the data themselves, often beginning with a process known as open coding, where researchers begin simply by noting thematic elements of the data that are of interest. Subsequent coding then often involves aggregating specific segments together as common processes and related events are brought together and identified as theoretically interesting.

Memoing refers to the common practice in more qualitative research to write analytical notes to oneself in field notes as the data are being gathered, but also extends to the coding process as categories are gradually defined and embellished and one's memos to self become an archive of the development of one's understanding and the coding categories that go with it. Coding and memoing are not independent processes; researchers typically go back and forth between the two as they expose themselves to and begin to try to understand their data.

Two examples of research where coding was involved appear in the chapter. Bruce Trigger's analysis of the portrayals of Aboriginal people at different stages in Canada's history was offered as an example of a more thematic, qualitative form of analysis in which the researcher is *not* armed with checklists and coding schemes, but begins with a well-defined question that is used to focus analysis of a sample of material defined by the research question as relevant. Although not in itself directly concerned with inquiring about the "facts" of Canadian history, Trigger's research sensitizes us to the way in which historical accounts can be self-serving accounts that do little more than justify the context in which they are produced. The raw data of history are yet another archive that deserves exploration, and part of the researcher's task must involve an effort of deconstruction as part of exploring what those data mean, that is, considering the processes and perspectives embodied in their construction.

Simon Davis's (1990) coding of personals ads as a vehicle for understanding male and female priorities in mate selection exemplified more structured content analysis. Attention is also drawn to the broad range of materials that can be subjected to this more quantitative form of analysis, including virtually everything from antique vases to bumper stickers and T-shirts. The dénouement of his (and our) analysis again involves taking a step back and asking just what the numbers mean, thereby reinforcing the point again that one should never simply take one's numbers at face value. Any data series is partly descriptive and partly interpretive; the thoughtful researcher pays heed to both aspects.

The chapter concludes with a discussion of qualitative data analysis (QDA) software. We describe the variety of these that are available, indicate some of the considerations to keep in mind when deciding which QDA software is right for you, and follow this with a discussion of some of the possibilities that arise in NVivo, which we rely on because it offers the most flexibility for the kind of work we do. The discussion makes clear that QDA tools such as NVivo are useful for more than simply data analysis, and that it also serves as a general information management tool in the context of a project that allows you to input text, audio, video, images, code them, write memos, and where all the text is searchable. For example, this makes it an ideal program for managing all of the literature that you accumulate in digital files (which are increasingly becoming the way we store all sorts of data). The program also allows both thematic and attribute coding, with the latter allowing for separate retrieval for different groups, thereby enabling comparative analysis [see also Palys & Atchison (in press) on these points].

Notwithstanding our own interest in and affection for the data management and analytic power that QDA software like NVivo allows, we also note the resistance in some quarters to the use of computers for qualitative data analysis, and some of the reasons we have heard that lay behind that resistance (see also Palys & Atchison 2009, in press). In our view QDA software is simply another analytical tool that is rooted in qualitative analytical practices of yesteryear—coding, memoing, highlighting, reflecting, searching—and that creates certain efficiencies, but does not do the work for you and still requires an engaged analyst to use effectively.

Our biggest disappointment at the moment is that we know of few universities and colleges to date who have embraced and made available QDA software such as NVivo to the same extent that quantitative statistical packages such as SPSS or SAS are routinely available on campuses, even though one does not have to be a qualitative researcher to benefit from NVivo's information/data management capabilities. Although we hope the situation will have changed when and if a sixth edition of *Research Decisions* comes into existence a few years down the road, we have kept our discussion of the software more conceptual and introductory here in order simply to whet your appetite, knowing that opportunities to use the program at your university or college for free may be limited in the near future. However, we strongly encourage more adventurous faculty members and students who pride themselves in being "first adopters" to go to the QSR website and download a free 30-day trial version of the program. The downloadable tutorials that have been prepared will get even the most timid user up and running very quickly; QSR also often holds Webinars to explain the program and answer questions from newbie and veteran users alike.

Having focused in this chapter on analytic techniques that can be employed in the analysis of more qualitative, non-numeric data, in the next chapter we examine the other end of the continuum, i.e., some foundational techniques for summarizing, representing, and analyzing more structured, quantitative data.

STUDY QUESTIONS

1. Discuss the main differences between numeric and non-numeric data and briefly describe the major challenges that are associated with analyzing non-numeric data. What similarities do the coding of numeric and non-numeric data share?

2. Distinguish between deductive and inductive coding. Do you have to choose between one or the other in any given project?

3. Explain what memoing involves and indicate some of the ways that memoing is useful in the process of coding non-numeric data.

4. The section of this chapter entitled "Typological and Other More Complex Analyses" offers three different ways of creating a drug typology—by pharmacological similarity; by their categorization within the Criminal Code; and user-generated typologies based on where and how the various drugs are consumed. Imagine now that you are conducting a study on how drug use finds its way into a particular school subculture. What do you think would be the advantages and disadvantages of incorporating each of the three types of typologies into your analysis?

5. Why do simple word counts make sense to include as part of your analysis of non-numeric data? What do they offer you? What extra information does KWIC (keyword in context) analysis give you?

6. Find out which newspapers your college, university, or municipal (public) library keeps and how many years' worth of issues they've retained. Design a quantitative and/or qualitative study that compares the way newspaper reports from different time periods treat an issue of interest to you. For example, you might look at (a) how women are portrayed in articles from the 1960s, 1970s, 1980s, 1990s, and 2000s; (b) how environmental issues and/or environmental activists are portrayed in the 1960s and in the 2000s; or (c) whether the composition of the newspaper's front page is different now than it was at the turn of the 20th century.

7. Choose your five favourite songs, obtain the lyrics from the Internet, and develop a coding scheme that you could use to identify and code words or actions that reflect themes of gender, race, or class.

8. Crime statistics suggest that about 90 percent of the crimes that are committed in Canada each year are nonviolent, while about 10 percent are violent. Does the coverage of crime news in your local newspaper reflect that state of affairs? Using Davis's (1990) study, reported in this chapter, as a guide, design a content-analytic study to answer that question.

9. Pick some textual source of data that exists at your college or university and design a study to systematically compile and content code that data. The examples we have in mind would include projects such as (a) analyzing washroom graffiti to see whether there are any differences between the arts and sciences or between men and women in what is written; (b) analyzing the messages and images on people's T-shirts; or (c) analyzing the messages on bumper stickers displayed in your university or college's parking lots.

10. Develop a taxonomy of the course offerings of one of the departments in your college/university.

11. What are some of the advantages and disadvantages of using qualitative data analysis software such as NVivo to analyze text, images, audio, and/or video non-numeric data?

NOTES

1. As Kline (1994) and Palys (1996b) have shown, part of European ideology has involved depicting North America's diverse Aboriginal peoples as a singular, homogeneous "other," known collectively as "Indians." When we use the term "Indians" in this section, it's only because we're recounting a source that saw Aboriginal peoples in that way—an erroneous and self-serving European construction. When using our own voices, we use terms like "Aboriginal peoples," "indigenous peoples," or simply "First Nations," since these are more consistent with Aboriginal peoples' understandings of themselves.

2. It doesn't say much for the French, of course, if so "inferior" a people did such a good job of facilitating the demise of the French colonies in North America.

3. Note that Davis's study was done before there was such a thing as the Internet. It might be interesting to replicate his research now that almost 20 years have passed; something like the Craigslist personals would be a very appropriate and easily accessible source. An additional positive quality of Craigslist is that one can easily access sites from all over the world, which allows the possibility of a comparative dimension as well.

4. Six is a relatively small number that could be ripe for sampling error; a better way to express his choice would be to say that, by randomly choosing dates, he would be avoiding any obvious sampling bias.

5. Although the coding method was concretized to the extent that reliability should be high, it's unfortunate that Davis didn't take the extra step of undertaking a reliability analysis. What might this have involved had he done so?

6. We don't mean to suggest this as a characterization of *all* people who place personals ads, since many reasons might drive one to try using this method of meeting a potential mate. But it seems plausible that such people are *among* those who place ads and that there may be enough of them to produce the results Davis (1990) observed.

7. We encourage those of you wishing to take a firsthand look at these programs to download the fully functioning free 30-day trial versions of the software that are available online through each company's website.

8. We put "data" in quotes here because we are using the term in its broadest way to refer not only to formal data that is gathered in a research context, but also include any other information—journal articles, books, field notes, pictures—that you want to retain and manage.

9. There are several very good introductory instruction manuals available and we predict (hope) that in the years to come a greater variety of courses on the analysis of non-numeric data will be offered in colleges and universities to complement the already dense array of courses offered on the analysis of numeric data. Excellent how-to guides for NVivo available now include Patricia Bazeley's (2007) *Qualitative Data Analysis with NVivo* and Lyn Richards's (1999) *Using NVivo in Qualitative Research*. NVivo also comes with an excellent online help section and user tutorial that, when used in combination, can get even the most technologically timid user working with the program within a matter of hours.

A CONCEPTUAL INTRODUCTION TO QUANTITATIVE DATA ANALYSIS

Our lives are full of numbers. The moment we're born, the person attending measures our height and weight. We count our teeth as they start to grow, and every child must be asked her/his age a million times. Soon, we move on to grade 1, then 2, then 3, and our efforts are evaluated with numerical grades or As, Bs, and Cs. Our education includes knowing various units of measurement (e.g., cups or litres, pounds or kilograms, dollars, miles or kilometres, hours). As we grow up, we become more interested in the world around us. We turn on the nightly news and discover that the Dow Jones Index went up 14 points, only 32 percent of the national voting population supports the current government and its policies, the rate of violent crime has dropped 3 percent since last year, the median housing price went up by $4,000 in the past 12 months, and the Vancouver Canucks defeated the Detroit Red Wings 7–4.

Numbers are a fact of life. They are also a tool of social and health science in the same way that they are a tool of everyday life: they help us describe, make comparisons, and express relationships. Of course, they can also be used to distort, mislead, and stonewall. Indeed, one of the implications of entering the information age seems to be that *everybody* can now point to *some* data *somewhere* that "proves" the correctness of her/his view of the world. So it makes sense to try to understand data and how they're used.

Data needn't be intimidating, although many people seem to find them so. Indeed, some people assert—sometimes even with a sense of self-righteous pride—that they aren't "numbers" people. As Toronto statistician Chuck Chakrapani commented in a CBC-TV report, it's interesting how many would never boast about being *illiterate* brag about being *innumerate.*[1] Don't get us wrong. You can do perfectly good, interesting, and valuable research *without* getting into razzle-dazzle multivariate statistics, as we hope the earlier chapters in this book have shown. But any researcher who skips through the data section of an article or a report and takes the writer's conclusions at face value, and any citizen who uncritically accepts the reportage offered in contemporary news media, is doing himself or herself a disservice. Any competent researcher and citizen needs to understand some statistical basics, and that's what this chapter will attempt to offer at a conceptual level.

This chapter will address the sort of data that are characteristic of quantitative research, that is, structured, systematically derived data amenable to aggregation and statistical analysis.[2] We'll consider two ways to represent and examine those data: through **descriptive statistics**, which present the data in summary form, and through **inferential statistics**, which analyze sample data to reveal relationships among variables and to make inferences about populations. You'll see that the latter may be used inductively, to suggest possible relationships, or deductively, to test hypotheses. This chapter will emphasize the conceptual underpinnings of numbers and some of the statistical procedures to which they might be subjected. The aim is not to turn you into a statistician, but to discuss some statistical fundamentals in a way that will help you understand the statistics you will likely be getting either in lab periods or some other course.

VARIABLES AND CONSTANTS

In order to discern what it is about numbers that might interest us, we must take a step back and talk about the concept of variables. Stated simply, a variable is anything that varies. The opposite is a **constant**, which is something that *does not* vary. In your research methods class, for example, most likely all of you sitting in the chairs are students; that is, the social status of "student" is a constant in your class. Presumably all class members are also human beings, so we might say that "species" is also a constant in your class. But there are many *variables* in your class as well. The sex of your colleagues is a variable, for example (unless you attend an all-male or all-female educational institution), because your class includes both male and female students. Other variables might include students' declared majors, whether they are enrolled part-time or full-time, their ages, their ethnicities, their vocational aspirations, their attitudes on social issues, and so forth. The whole task of social and health science is to *explain* variations (e.g., why are the proportions of males and females so different in computing science compared to sociology?) in relation to other variations (e.g., variation in life history, competencies, aptitudes, interests).

As soon as you begin attaching numbers to things, several other processes are automatically activated. Numbers imply classification, for example, since the simple counting of objects implies that the objects are part of the category whose frequency you are counting. This is sometimes a relatively simple process, for example, your fingers and toes or the numbers of males and females in your class. But on other occasions, the boundaries that define a category may be rather more blurred; one must decide, for example, whether a death was an "accident" or a "suicide" or whether the punishment a parent delivers is "a spanking" or "physical abuse."

This chapter won't discuss the constructionist aspects of how social categories are derived, why some areas of life are more or less fully enumerated than others, or the social and political dynamics by which particular categories are negotiated (but see,

for example, Lakoff 1987). But don't forget that such issues permeate this chapter. Numbers always have an aura of precision about them; behind every number is a social process that has caused that number to exist (e.g., see Chapter 8's section on crime statistics). Maintain the same healthy skepticism about numbers that you do about any other information you might be presented with.

LEVELS OF MEASUREMENT

The types of descriptive and inferential statistics to use in any situation depend to some degree on the types of variables with which you are dealing, which in turn depends on how you've gone about measuring them. Remember that social and health science research involves a continuing interplay between theory and data. The variables that interest us are theoretical constructions—abstractions we draw from our experience—that we feel are useful in describing and interpreting human activity. But empirical research cannot be done in the abstract.[3] We must give our variables empirical meaning by operationalizing them for a given research context. The correspondence rules by which those operationalizations are imposed (i.e., the way we take observations and change them into variables for analysis) define the type of measurement taken.

Nominal or Categorical Measures

The simplest way to measure an object is simply to categorize it, that is, say what it is and what it is not. Examples of **categorical variables** include sex (male or female), whether one owns or rents one's abode, a student's choice of academic major, and whether a person is in a treatment group or a control group. In each case, any assigning of numbers to those categories would be completely arbitrary. We can code oranges as "1" and apples as "2," but that makes no more or less sense than coding apples as "1" and oranges as "2." The different values the variable can take on (e.g., apples or oranges, for the variable "fruits found in lunchboxes") are merely different from one another; one value doesn't embody or possess *more* or *less* of the variable under consideration. Apples and oranges, for example, are just different fruits, with neither being any more or less of a fruit than the other.

Ordinal Measures

A second level of measurement we can impose is called **ordinal measurement** because the numbers ascribed to our classification possess order. That is, not only are the values *different* from one another (as was the case with categorical variables), they also embody differences of *magnitude* with respect to the variable under consideration. For example, full-time faculty members in North American universities are classified into three categories: (a) assistant professors, (b) associate professors, and (c) full professors. There's an underlying sense of *order* to these categories; each successive category is "higher" in the academic hierarchy than the previous one. Numbers imposed in order to code and analyze the distribution of "academic rank" are somewhat arbitrary—we could equally legitimately call the categories 1, 2, and 3; or 3, 2, and 1; or 5, 10, and 15—but they aren't *totally* arbitrary, since using 1, 3, and 2 would destroy the underlying order we see.

At the same time, the limits of ordinal measures also are evident. In the real number system, the distance or interval between 1 and 2 is equal to the distance between 2 and 3, but that property does not hold for an ordinal variable like academic rank. The numbers are merely rankings; the order is important, but the distance between ranks is not constant. Another example might be "order of finish" at a track meet. Runners come in first, second, third, and so on; the order is important, but the distance between the first and second runners may not be the same as the distance between the second and third.

Interval-Level Measurement

When the property of equal distance *is* met, **interval-level measurement** is said to exist. In the monograph that originally differentiated these measurement types, Stevens (1951) gave

thermometer readings as an example. Note that a temperature of 30° Celsius is *different* from a temperature of 20° Celsius (i.e., it meets the requirement of categorical measurement). It's also *higher* than 20° (i.e., there are magnitude relations, as in ordinal measurement). But a new criterion applies: one can also say that the *interval* between 20° and 30° is equal to the interval between 10° and 20°, or that 1° is of equal magnitude at any point in the scale. On the other hand, certain limits are imposed because the scale does not have a "true" zero point.

In the social world, suppose we ask a university's faculty members to indicate which they value more highly: the research or the teaching component of their jobs. To express their answers, we give them a five-point scale with the following verbal designations: (1) research is much more valued than teaching, (2) research is somewhat more valued than teaching, (3) research and teaching are about equally valued, (4) teaching is somewhat more valued than research, and (5) teaching is much more valued than research. Psychometric research (e.g., see Altemeyer 1970; Dawes 1972) has shown that people can use such scales quite easily and that unless the verbal designations are very poorly chosen, we use such scales in a manner consistent with at least interval-level properties.[4]

Ratio Measurement

The final level of measurement noted by Stevens (1951) is called **ratio-level measurement**, and the prototypical example is that of a ruler measuring distance or length. Ratio measurement embodies all three previous levels of measurement. A distance of 3 centimetres is *different* from a distance of 2 centimetres. We can also say that it's *longer* than 2 centimetres. Further, the differences between the points are meaningful: the interval between 1 centimetre and 2 centimetres is the same as the interval between 8 centimetres and 9 centimetres.

A notable new property of ratio-level measurement is that the scale has a true zero point; in other words, the number zero *means* something: namely, that there's none of the quality being measured.

This property allows us to say, for example, that 2 centimetres is twice as long as 1 centimetre, or that the ratio of 2 centimetres to 1 centimetre is the same as the ratio of 8 centimetres to 4 centimetres (i.e., both are 2:1). Note that this situation differs from that in the thermometer example. The zero point on most thermometers is arbitrary: zero degrees, whether on the Celsius scale or the Fahrenheit scale, doesn't mean a total absence of heat or molecular activity. So one cannot say, for example, that 80° Fahrenheit is twice as hot as 40°, or that the ratio of 80° to 40° is the same as the ratio of 30° to 15°.[5] Other examples of ratio scales include measures of time, mass, and volume.

Levels of Measurement and Statistical Analysis

Stevens (1951) argues that it's important to differentiate between these levels of measurement because the range of mathematical operations one can legitimately perform on one's data is limited by the level of measurement. With nominal/categorical data, for example, it's reasonable to create frequency distributions and to indicate the most frequently occurring (or modal) categories, but it makes no sense to compute an "average" when the numerical coding of categories is completely arbitrary to start with (e.g., an "average" sex of 1.2). At the other extreme, with ratio-level data, one can meaningfully employ a wide range of mathematical operations.

There was a time when social and health science researchers bowed to Stevens's (1951) typology with the reverence otherwise reserved for works of scripture. But much has changed in the decades since that article was written. The onslaught began with a humorous article by Lord (1953) that focused on the relative merit of performing various statistical analyses with the numbers on football jerseys.

The numbers on football jerseys are obviously categorical: the fact that a quarterback wears number 12 while a halfback might wear 33 conveys no information at all about who is the better player. Computing average jersey numbers or comparing the average jersey number of one team to that of another would

be a mathematical absurdity, according to Stevens (1951). But the central character of Lord's (1953) fictitious story—a certain mathematics professor at an unnamed university—does exactly that (in secret, of course) when the players on the university team complain that the other teams laugh at them because their numbers are "too low."

To address this question, Lord's hypothetical professor does what to Stevens (1951) would have been unpardonable: he compares the mean (average) football number on his team to those of other teams and finds that his team's numbers are indeed significantly lower than those of their opponents. But given the particular question being posed, comparing the "average" jersey numbers actually made reasonable sense. The moral of Lord's (1953) story? One can do anything one wants with numbers, since the numbers themselves haven't a clue what's "being done" to them, but it's up to the researcher to make decisions about the range of operations that are meaningful to perform on given data in a given context. If the question (to continue Lord's example) is whether one team's numbers are significantly lower or higher than another team's numbers, computing the mean (average) numbers and comparing them is a meaningful and reasonable thing to do. But if the question were something like "Which team is 'better'?" then comparing the average number on football jerseys would be meaningless and absurd, since football numbers bear no relation at all to the underlying variable "athletic skill."

One can indeed fault Stevens's (1951) scheme for the qualities ascribed to various measures, since the level of measurement is *not* inherent in the data itself; rather, one must always consider the use to which the data are being put. For example, Stevens argues that the ruler is a perfect example of a measurement scale (for distance or length) with ratio properties. In social and health science, though, our interests are *not* with the empirical variables per se, but with the underlying *theoretical* variables they're thought to represent.

As long as distance per se is all that interests us, in other words, the measures do have ratio-level properties. But rarely are we interested in distance per se in social and health research; instead, we're interested in distance as an operationalization or indicator of some theoretical variable of interest (e.g., social distance or interpersonal closeness). And it's the range of operations we feel comfortable using *when the measure is used as an indicator for the underlying theoretical variable of interest* that will influence the range of mathematical operations we can legitimately perform on the data.

Thus, using a ruler to measure height is one thing, but using the same ruler to measure the distance between two people as a measure of how much they like each other is something else. The first has ratio properties; the second may or may not. As this example reaffirms, the property lies not in the measure itself, but in how the measure is used.

This isn't the place to get into a lengthy review of statistical debates on the range of statistics that might legitimately be employed with any given type of data. Suffice it to say that numerous **"Monte Carlo" computer simulations** have shown that many statistical techniques, and certainly the ones in this chapter, can be quite robust to violations of the theoretical assumptions underlying them. One needn't, therefore, be as rigid as Stevens proposes, although one also shouldn't jump to the opposite conclusion, that "anything goes." Your research questions should guide your data analysis, with the caveat that the researcher must consider how meaningful the analysis is, given the type of data and the theoretical use to which they are being put.[6] The question for us, then, is what those uses might be.

DESCRIPTIVE STATISTICS

A very basic use of statistics is to summarize one's data. Instead of saying that we have this marble, and this marble, and this marble, and so on, we can much more succinctly say that we have 10 red marbles and 12 blue ones. Such brevity is admired in the social sciences, where the nature of the scientific task requires us to *describe,* in conceptual terms, the nature of our social universe.[7] Descriptive techniques fall into three general categories: depictions of the *distributions* of each variable, statistics that convey the *central tendency*

of each distribution, and statistics that convey the *variability* or *dispersion* that exists in each distribution. Within each of these three categories various techniques may be most useful, depending on such considerations as level of measurement.

Depicting Distributions

The first and most straightforward step we can take toward summarizing our data is to create frequency distributions to summarize the number and percentage of persons occupying each of our analytical categories. Indeed, whenever you finish gathering and coding your data, the first thing you should do is prepare frequency tables for each of your variables, to better visualize how they are distributed. To illustrate the various types of descriptive techniques available to you, we'll continue the example of the faculty members at a fictitious university, which we will call Provincial University (or PU). Tables 12.1 to 12.4 show frequency distributions summarizing the number of male and female faculty members (Table 12.1), the number of faculty members at each rank (Table 12.2), responses to a question about the relative value faculty members ascribe to the teaching and

Table 12.1

Distribution of University Faculty by Sex

Sex	Frequency	%
Male	240	60
Female	160	40
All faculty	400	100

Table 12.2

Distribution of University Faculty by Rank

Rank	Frequency	%
Assistant professor	170	42.5
Associate professor	130	32.5
Full professor	100	25.0
All faculty	400	100.0

Table 12.3

Distribution of Responses to Question Regarding Relative Priority of Teaching as Compared to Research

Response	Frequency	%
Research valued much more highly	50	12.5
Research valued somewhat more highly	75	18.8
Research and teaching equally valued	150	37.5
Teaching valued somewhat more highly	75	18.8
Teaching valued much more highly	50	12.5
All responses	400	100.1

Note: Total percentage deviates from 100.0 as a result of rounding.

research components of their job (Table 12.3), and the numbers of years faculty members have been employed (Table 12.4).

These four tables collectively demonstrate a number of different aspects of frequency distributions. Note that frequency distributions are appropriate for data at all levels of measurement: sex (Table 12.1) is a categorical variable, academic rank (Table 12.2) is an ordinal variable, responses to the query about research and teaching priorities (Table 12.3) may be treated as an interval-level variable, and number of years of employment (Table 12.4) represents a ratio-level variable. Because each of the tables shows the distribution for one variable at a time, they're called *univariate frequency distributions* (*uni* = one; *variate* = variable).

A second thing to consider about Tables 12.1 to 12.4 is how they are presented. Each table has a number to identify it and a title that describes its contents. Each table also has clearly labelled columns, the first naming the category being described (under Sex, Rank, Response, and Years Employed). Also included in each of the tables is a column titled *Frequency* that indicates the number of observations that fall into each of the categories listed, and another indicating the percentage (%) of the total sample that is described by those categories. The bottom row of each table shows totals for each of the columns.

You can see from the bottom line on Tables 12.1 to 12.4 that 400 faculty members were involved in

this fictitious sample and that complete information was obtained on all four variables for all 400 faculty. If data are missing for any of the variables, you'd normally include a category called "Missing" to show the completeness of your information. If total percentages deviate from 100 (as occurs in Table 12.3), you'd also note the reason why (e.g., because of rounding errors or because respondents were allowed to check more than one category).

The differences between the tables are also noteworthy. Table 12.4 is the only table to give *cumulative frequency* and *cumulative percentage* (*cumulative %*) across categories. These are included for Table 12.4 because it summarizes a sufficiently large number of categories and because there's a clear ordering on the "years employed" variable, from lowest to highest. Thus, it can be seen that approximately one-eighth (12.0 percent; $N = 48$) of the faculty have been employed at the university for four years or less; or it can be computed that approximately half the faculty (49.25 percent; $N = 197$) have been employed at the university for 15 years or more.

But using year-by-year categories in Table 12.4 leaves us with 25 different categories! Such a detailed inventory may be of interest in some situations, but hardly serves the purpose of data summary. Thus, you'd normally collapse so many categories into perhaps five to eight *aggregated categories* or *class intervals*, as has been done in Table 12.5.

Table 12.4

Distribution of Number of Years Employed at Provincial University

Years Employed	Frequency	Cumulative Frequency	%	Cumulative %
1	13	13	3.25	3.25
2	12	25	3.00	6.25
3	12	37	3.00	9.25
4	11	48	2.75	12.00
5	11	59	2.75	14.75
6	9	68	2.25	17.00
7	9	77	2.25	19.25
8	8	85	2.00	21.25
9	12	97	3.00	24.25
10	13	110	3.25	27.50
11	16	126	4.00	31.50
12	17	143	4.25	35.75
13	19	162	4.75	40.50
14	20	182	5.00	45.50
15	21	203	5.25	50.75
16	23	226	5.75	56.50
17	23	249	5.75	62.25
18	25	274	6.25	68.50
19	25	299	6.25	74.75
20	23	322	5.75	80.50
21	19	341	4.75	85.25
22	18	359	4.50	89.75
23	16	375	4.00	93.75
24	13	388	3.25	97.00
25	12	400	3.00	100.00
All faculty	400		100.00	

Table 12.5

Distribution of Years Employed at Provincial University, Using Five-Year Intervals

Years Employed	f	Cumulative Frequency	%	Cumulative %
1–5 years	59	59	14.75	14.75
6–10 years	51	110	12.75	27.50
11–15 years	93	203	23.25	50.75
16–20 years	119	322	29.75	80.50
21–25 years	78	400	19.50	100.00
All faculty	400		100.00	

Category ranges should be of equal size (those in Table 12.5 all involve a 5-year range), should be based on an easily comprehended unit (e.g., 5 categories of 5 years each, rather than 7 categories of 3.57 years each), and should represent the full range of data. But note that such aggregation is achieved only at a cost; we've lost information on exact years of employment.

A second way to depict a frequency distribution is to graph it. Figure 12.1, which shows the distribution of the sex of the faculty members, is a simple *pie chart.* Such charts are best suited to situations in which a small number of categories are distributed reasonably equally (to avoid having many "slivers" of pie that are too small to be easily labelled) or for displaying how some entire entity (100 percent) is divided by category frequency.

Figure 12.2 uses a *bar graph* to show the distribution of academic ranks among the faculty in Provincial University (or PU), whereas Figure 12.3 shows a *histogram* of responses to the query regarding the relative value attached to teaching or research. Note that all three figures are numbered, and each has a title that identifies the variable being shown. Each segment of the pie, and each bar of the bar graph and the histogram, is also clearly labelled.

Figure 12.1

Faculty Membership by Sex

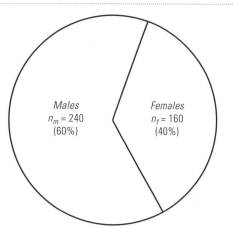

Figure 12.2

Faculty Membership by Academic Rank

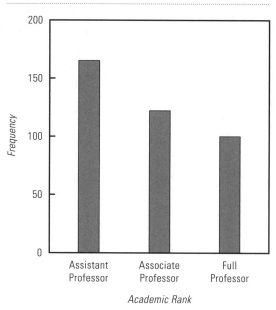

A fourth form of graph, known as a *frequency polygon* or *line graph,* is particularly useful when there's a relatively large number of categories. Figure 12.4 shows the distribution of the numbers of years of employment among university faculty members (using the data supplied in Table 12.4), while Figure 12.5 depicts a bar graph of the categorized years-of-employment variable (using the data supplied in Table 12.5). Once again, note that all figures are clearly numbered, titled, and labelled.

Measures of Central Tendency

After depicting the distribution of each variable, whether through frequency tables such as Tables 12.1 to 12.5 or graphically as in Figures 12.1 to 12.5, the researcher is then ready to begin describing the distributions statistically. First to be considered are measures of *central tendency,* or the "typical" datum for each variable. The three available to you are the mode, the median, and the mean.

Figure 12.3

Response to Query Regarding Relative Priority Attached to Teaching as Compared to Research

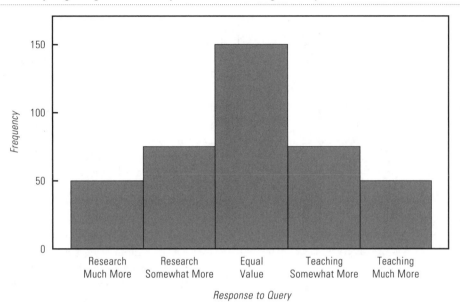

Figure 12.4

Distribution of Number of Years Employed

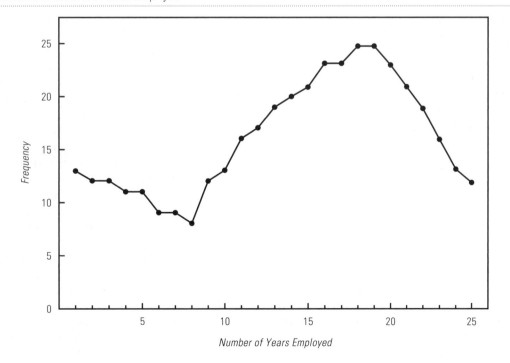

Figure 12.5

Bar Graph of Years of Employment in Five-Year Intervals

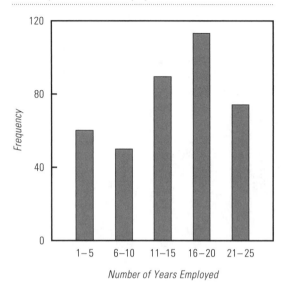

Number of Years Employed

THE MODE

The **mode** identifies the score or scores that are "typical" in the sense that they represent "the most frequently occurring category." Thus, at PU, the modal faculty member with respect to the sex variable is a male, and the modal academic rank is that of assistant professor. As for the query about the relative value attached to research and teaching, the modal response was that the two are valued equally. And finally, more of the current faculty were hired 18 or 19 years ago than at any other time. As these examples suggest, the mode can be used to describe data at any level of measurement.

THE MEDIAN

The second statistic for revealing central tendency is the **median**. This statistic identifies the "typical" datum as that which splits the distribution in half: 50 percent of the sample data lie above it, and 50 percent lie below it. The median is thus the middle score, rather like the median on a highway that separates the two halves of the road. But note that the median is not always a meaningful statistic; the idea of a "median" sex, for example, seems absurd, since the "typical" case cannot even exist. Indeed, the median is useless with nominal-level variables, because the order that is required to have a midpoint is absent. Medians can thus be used only with ordinal-, interval-, or ratio-level data. Returning to the data presented in Tables 12.2 to 12.4, you should see that the median academic rank at PU is a relatively junior associate professor (since the middle case is only 7.5 percent beyond the assistant professor category), the median opinion on the attitude item is one of valuing research and teaching about equally, and the median number of years employed at PU is 15.

THE MEAN

The final measure of central tendency to consider is the **mean**, or what you may know as the arithmetic average. It is computed by simply taking the sum of the values and dividing by the total number of scores. Thus, for example, if your midterm marks in the five courses you're taking were 76, 79, 82, 93, and 81, the mean would be the sum of those marks (76 + 79 + 82 + 93 + 81 = 411) divided by the number of courses ($N = 5$), or 411/5 = 82.2.

Since a mean is computed by adding and then dividing numbers, it has little meaning if the numbers are assigned arbitrarily. Thus, the mean has even more limited utility than the median when it comes to the kinds of variables for which it may be meaningful. Certainly it would be meaningless for nominal variables (e.g., a mean sex?), and it should be used cautiously or not at all with ordinal data (depending on the degree of arbitrariness of the coding scheme). Problems are fewer with interval data and nonexistent with ratio-level data. Thus, if the five responses to the attitude item (Table 12.3) were coded 1 through 5, we could say with little discomfort that the mean response is 3.0 (research and teaching equally valued). And you should be able to calculate (from Table 12.4) that the mean length of employment at PU is 14.3 years.

In sum, the mode, the median, and the mean are three descriptive statistics; each gives a picture of the "central tendency" of the distribution of scores you've obtained. Each expresses an "average" or "typical" score in its own way: for the mode, central tendency is identified as the most frequently occurring score; for the median, the typical score is the one that lies on the 50th percentile, splitting the distribution in half; for the mean, central tendency is defined as the arithmetic average. Let's review the results we obtained with the variables we observed at PU.

Sex is a *categorical* variable, so the only measure of central tendency that seems appropriate to use is the mode. The modal faculty member at PU is a male.

Our attention then turns to academic rank. Using the mode, we find that the most frequently occurring academic rank is that of assistant professor. The *ordinal* nature of the academic-rank data also leads us to use the median. But the median gives us a different indication of central tendency—that of junior associate professor—than does the mode.

Since responses to the query concerning the relative value associated with research and teaching represent an *interval*-level variable, mode, median, and mean are all appropriate statistics. Here, all three statistics point in the same direction: "equal value associated with research and teaching."

The last variable on which we have information is "years of employment at PU." Because this is a *ratio*-level variable, mode, median, and mean are all appropriate statistics. But here they give three different answers regarding the "typical" faculty member. The *modal* faculty member was hired 18 or 19 years ago (see Table 12.4); the *median* faculty member was hired 15 years ago; and the *mean* faculty member was hired 14.3 years ago.

Why do the mode, the median, and the mean point sometimes in the same and sometimes in different directions?

CENTRAL TENDENCY, SYMMETRY, AND SKEW

In order to answer that question, we have to consider one more characteristic of distributions: *symmetry* versus *skew*. A symmetrical distribution is any distribution in which the two sides are essentially mirror images. Thus, the three distributions shown

in Figure 12.6(a), Figure 12.6(b), and Figure 12.6(c) are all symmetrical, even though their shapes are otherwise very different.[8] Whenever we have a symmetrical distribution (as was the case in Table 12.3 and its counterpart, Figure 12.3, with respect to the

Figure 12.6

Three Examples of Symmetrical Distributions

(a)
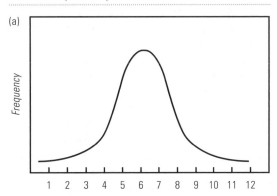

(b)
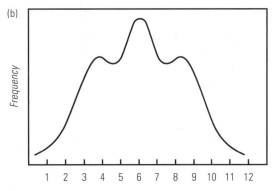

(c)
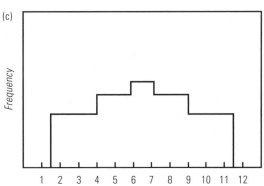

attitude variable), the mode, the median, and the mean will all lie in exactly the same place. When our distributions are *asymmetrical*, or "skewed," the situation changes.

Look at the three graphs included in Figure 12.7. You should recognize immediately that Figure 12.7(b) shows a symmetrical distribution, while Figures 12.7(a) and 12.7(c) show skewed distributions. In order to distinguish between the two kinds of asymmetrical distributions, mathematicians use the convention of describing the direction of the skew based on where the distribution's thinner end, or "tail," is. Thus, Figure 12.7(a) is referred to as a "positively skewed" distribution, since its tail is at the positive end of the number line; Figure 12.7(c) is referred to as a "negatively skewed" distribution, since its tail is at the negative end of the number line.[9]

As noted above, when distributions are symmetrical, the mode, median, and mean will all lie in the same place; Figure 12.7(b) illustrates this situation. But when distributions are asymmetrical, or skewed, the situation changes. Since the mode is by definition the most frequently occurring score, it remains at the highest "bump" in the distribution. The mean and the median, though, will be differentially affected by the extreme scores that lie at the distribution's "skew" or "tail" end. The mean, which is particularly affected by that tendency, will be "pulled" farthest away from the modal value. The median also will be affected but less so; it normally will lie between the mean and the mode.

HOW TO LIE WITH STATISTICS
While the statistics we have been dealing with thus far have been extremely "simple," they're also extremely important. *Any* data analysis should begin with an inspection of raw univariate distributions so that you can see how the variables are distributed and choose accordingly the type of statistics you report. In general, the more the better. Modes can be reported for any type of data. Medians are appropriate when the data have at least ordinal qualities; they are also the "better" statistic with interval- and ratio-level data when the distribution is skewed, especially when there are a few

Figure 12.7
Examples of (a) a Positively Skewed Distribution, (b) a Normal Distribution, and (c) a Negatively Skewed Distribution

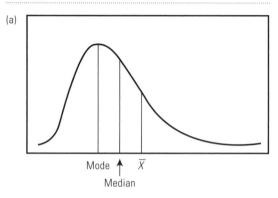
(a)

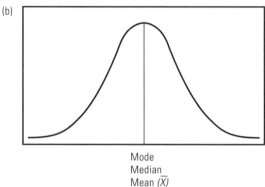
(b)

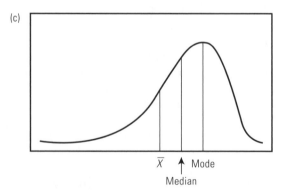
(c)

extreme scores. Means always should be cited for interval- and ratio-level data, but should be used more cautiously with ordinal-level data and with highly skewed distributions.

Not showing univariate frequency distributions and being selective in the statistic to report are favourite techniques of those propagandists who use statistics to provide distorted images. The whole idea of using statistics is to concisely summarize a set of data; implicit are the ideas that such summarization is a relatively neutral process and that summary statistics give a representative picture of the data as a whole. People's general faith in those suppositions allows the unscrupulous to manipulate statistics to their own ends. For example, tourist or investment brochures may extol how splendid an area Upper Oceana is, noting that tourism and property costs are very reasonable despite the fact that most Upper Oceanans live in comparative opulence—the average annual income is in fact a fairly comfortable $95,455 per year! Sounds great, eh? If only the rest of us were so well off! The impression we get is that the average Upper Oceanan is doing very well financially; perhaps some are doing better or worse, but the average standard of living, at least as measured in economic terms, seems quite high.

But examining the entire distribution of incomes leaves us with a rather different impression. It seems that for every Upper Oceanan who has an annual income of $1,000,000, there are 10 others who earn a measly $5,000 a year. Thus, it turns out that the "average" (i.e., the mean) masks a situation where a few individuals live in wealth, while the majority live in poverty. Generally speaking, the median should be reported along with the mean, since the median is less distorted by deviations from symmetry. Examining the univariate distributions is always a wise move, as is presenting them in a research report.

Examples of individuals and groups using statistics to mislead and distort are so numerous that they could easily fill a book. Indeed, readers interested in an enjoyable and thoughtful book on that topic should have a look at Darrell Huff's *How to Lie with Statistics* (1954; reissued in 1982 and 1993). In very readable fashion, Huff does an excellent job of explaining basic descriptive statistics and showing how they're often misused to distort and mislead. An awareness of such tricks

should be part of everyone's education as a citizen and consumer. As a social and health scientist, your job is to appreciate such techniques as things to *avoid;* as a prospective member of the social and health science community, your task is to be open and complete in your descriptions and analysis of data.

Measures of Variability

Measures of central tendency convey one aspect of the nature of the distribution: the "typical" or "average" score. But distributions also can differ in their *variability*.

While measures of central tendency attempt to describe a distribution in terms of *similarities* (by focusing on a "most common" or "typical" score), measures of variability focus on *differences* among the scores (by attempting to generate measures of *dispersion*). So variability represents a key stepping stone in our analytic venture, since it's the basic "stuff" that social and health science is trying to explain.

THE RANGE

The most basic expression of the degree of dispersion that exists is given by the **range**. When dealing with categorical or ordinal variables, where any numerical coding that's involved is relatively arbitrary, providing the range involves giving a full enumeration of all the categories in which observations were obtained. This allows critical readers to inspect your categories to see what range of categories has been included. You also can articulate the range of frequencies that exist in your categories: this will tell your reader whether there is an approximately equal distribution of people across categories or whether they are more prevalent in one than another. Of course, such information can also be made available in tables or graphs of univariate frequency distributions.

With interval-level data, where the numbers begin to have some intrinsic meaning, the range is expressed as the difference between the maximum and minimum values. Thus, the range of responses on the "years employed" variable (see Table 12.4) was 24 years—from the most recent hiring, 1 year ago, to the earliest, 25 years ago.(i.e., 25 – 1 = 24).

Although the range is an important statistic to report, it's not sufficiently definitive. The difficulty is revealed by inspection of Figure 12.8, which shows two different distributions superimposed on each other. The distributions are symmetrical, have the same mode, median, and mean; and have exactly the same range, but only a cursory visual inspection is needed to see that they're still very different. One of the distributions is very dispersed, with scores spread across the whole range. The other is much more compressed, with a huge majority of scores squished in very close to the distribution's mean, a pattern that reflects very little variation.

Another problem with the range as a descriptive statistic is that it only takes one weird/extreme score to change it dramatically and thereby give an unrepresentative impression of the degree of variation that exists. For this reason, many researchers prefer to use a measure known as the **interquartile range (IQR)**.

Figure 12.8

Two Distributions with Identical Ranges but Different Degrees of Dispersion

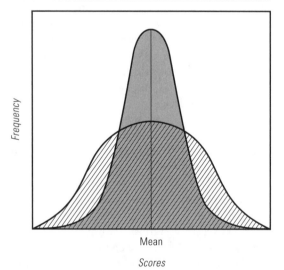

Mean

Scores

The "quartile" part comes from the fact you begin by dividing the distribution into quarters. If we look at the distribution of scores in Table 12.4 regarding "years of employment," for example, we can see that the 25 percent point (marking the "1st quartile") comes in the category of people who have been at PU for "10 years"[10]; the 50 percent point (marking the "2nd quartile" or median) comes in the category "14 years"; and that the 75 percent point (marking the "3rd quartile") comes in the category "20 years."

The "inter" part of the term comes from our desire to look at the distance between the first and third quartile points, that is, we want to lop off the extreme scorers in the top 25 percent and bottom 25 percent of the distribution and then look at the range that describes that middle 50 percent.

The IQR for the data in Table 12.4, therefore, is 20 – 10 = 10 years. In and of itself, this statistic is not particularly meaningful, but it would be, for example, if we wanted to compare the distribution of years of employment at PU to that at other universities. This brings us to yet another limitation of both the range and the interquartile range as descriptive statistics: although they are useful for comparing relatively similar types of distributions using similar units and similar categories, they are relatively meaningless in and of themselves and cannot be used to compare different distributions.

STANDARD DEVIATIONS AND VARIANCES

The challenge, therefore, is to develop a statistic that not only can convey differences in variability between similar-based distributions such as the two superimposed in Figure 12.8, but also has broader utility across a wider range of distributions.

The place mathematicians began to look for this statistic was at the concept of deviations from the mean, which seems reasonable enough, given that the variability we are trying to get a handle on involves variability around that central point. We can follow through the logic of it by starting with a distribution of scores, computing its mean, checking out how much each score we have deviates from the mean, and then maybe finding an "average" deviation around the mean.

Table 12.6 shows two distributions of scores,[11] under the left-hand columns "Thin" and "Dispersed." Both columns have the same range (i.e., in each the lowest score is 1, and the highest score is 9), and the mode for each distribution is 5. We'll leave it to you to do the computations that show that they also have the same median and mode (5.0 in each case). The table's third and fourth columns show how much each of the scores deviates from the mean of its group; at the bottom of each of those columns you can see the sum of the deviations about the mean. Funny thing—the total works out to zero in both cases!

Indeed, it turns out that this will always be the case, since the mean is in fact the numerical value for which the sum of deviations is zero: all the pluses and minuses will inevitably cancel one another out, and they'll always add up to zero. Just adding up deviations from the mean would thus seem to be a dead end; they don't do the job we require of them.

Not being the sort of folk who give up quickly, however, and always ready with a handy technique to take care of inconvenient things like pluses and minuses that cancel one another out, mathematicians next looked at the possibility of taking the absolute magnitudes of the deviations (i.e., ignoring the sign of the difference), but that didn't work out very well in more complex algebraic calculations. Then they came up with the possibility of *squaring* all the deviations about the mean. The nice thing about squaring each deviation is that it makes every number a positive number (i.e., −5 squared and +5 squared both equal 25); it also gives greater weight to deviations the farther they are away from the mean (i.e., a 1-unit distance, whether plus or minus, when squared, gives 1; 5 points of distance, whether plus or minus, when squared, gives 25). Columns 5 and 6 of Table 12.6 show what happens when we begin looking at the squared deviations; the sum of the squared deviations is given at the bottom of each column for the respective distributions. Do we have success?

The sum of the squared deviations about the mean is indeed greater for the dispersed distribution than it is for the thinner one. But our success is more apparent than real. Although the sum of the squared deviations about the mean is indeed successful at differentiating between the two distributions shown in Table 12.6, it turns out that other examples can easily be invented that make our success short-lived. More specifically, note that the dispersed distribution and the thin distribution in Table 12.6 have exactly the same number of people in them. What would happen if we took the thin distribution and simply doubled the number of scores we have? The range would be the same; the mean, median, and mode would all be the same; and the form of the distribution would be the same, but suddenly our sum of the squared deviations would be twice as large, suggesting that the thin distribution is even *more* variable than the dispersed one! That's a problem.

Fortunately, the problem is short-lived as well. The hint for a solution comes from the fact that our problem seems to be related to the number of observations. The solution comes when, instead of merely summing all the squared deviations about the mean, we then proceed to divide that sum by the number of observations, thereby giving us the *average* squared deviation about the mean. Once we do that, everything in the hypothetical examples works out splendidly. We see that the average squared deviation about the mean is substantially larger for the dispersed distribution in Table 12.6 than it is for the thin one (4.17 versus 3.08, respectively)— just as, logically, we feel it should be. And if you take the thin distribution and double the number of observations we made, it turns out that, when we divide that doubly large sum of squared deviations by the doubled number of observations, we still end up with exactly the same average squared deviation. Once again, this is consistent with the logical notion that indicators of the form of a distribution, in terms of its variability, should not be influenced by other considerations such as sample size.

If you follow the reasoning above, you now understand the basis of two incredibly important statistics that form the basis of analysis for a wide array of statistical techniques. The summary statistic we ended up with above—the average of the

Table 12.6

Describing Thin and Dispersed Distributions

Scores		Deviations from Mean		Squared Deviations	
Thin	Dispersed	Thin	Dispersed	Thin	Dispersed
1	1	−4	−4	16	16
2	2	−3	−3	9	9
3	2	−2	−3	4	9
3	3	−2	−2	4	4
4	3	−1	−2	1	4
4	3	−1	−2	1	4
4	4	−1	−1	1	1
4	4	−1	−1	1	1
5	4	0	−1	0	1
5	4	0	−1	0	1
5	5	0	0	0	0
5	5	0	0	0	0
5	5	0	0	0	0
5	5	0	0	0	0
5	6	0	+1	0	1
5	6	0	+1	0	1
6	6	+1	+1	1	1
6	6	+1	+1	1	1
6	7	+1	+2	1	4
6	7	+1	+2	1	4
7	7	+2	+2	4	4
7	8	+2	+3	4	9
8	8	+3	+3	9	9
9	9	+5	+4	16	16
Sum = 120	Sum = 120	Sum = 0	Sum = 0	Sum = 74	Sum = 100
$N = 24$	$N = 24$			Mean = 3.08	Mean = 4.17
Mean = 5.0	Mean = 5.0			$\sqrt{3.08} = 1.75$	$\sqrt{4.17} = 2.04$
				S.D. = 1.75	S.D. = 2.04

squared deviations—is known in statistical parlance as the **variance** of a distribution.

As for the second statistic of importance, the one weakness of the variance as a measure of dispersion is that it's expressed in *squared* units rather than in our original scale of measurement. To make our statistic more meaningful in our original context, recall that we originally squared all the scores to get around the problem of having the pluses and minuses cancel each other out. Thus, to get back to our original units of measurement, all we need do is take the *square root* of the variance statistic. Given that we originally squared the deviations and, after finding their average deviation from the mean, are now taking the square root, our new statistic simply reflects the average deviation about the mean that is present in our distribution. That statistic is called the **standard deviation**. We will hear of it again.

INFERENTIAL STATISTICS

As the previous section stated, the notion of variability is a crucial one in social and health science. It's the variance in life that we spend the most time trying to explain: Why are things one way one time and a different way another time? To use the example of the faculty at Provincial University once again, it's all well and good to say that the largest number of faculty members are assistant professors, but an *understanding* of university life requires that we explain why some people are assistant professors, others are associates, and still others are full professors. And while it's nice to know the distribution of length of employment, things become even more interesting when we start asking why members of some social groups seem more or less likely to get hired than others, why and how these propensities might change over time, why more or fewer people are hired in one year than in another.

The rest of this chapter discusses two general classes of statistics that examine such relationships: *measures of association* (i.e., where the question of interest is in how two or more variables "go together" or are associated with one another) and *measures of difference* (i.e., where the general question of interest is typically whether the means of

two or more groups differ). This distinction is to some degree contrived, but as you'll discover near the end of the chapter, it's a useful pedagogical distinction to make at this time.

Examining Relationships Among Categorical Variables

CROSS-TABULATION AND CONTINGENCY TABLES

The researcher who's interested in examining the relationship between two nominal or categorical variables will normally begin by cross-tabulating them, that is, creating a celled matrix or contingency table where the joint (or bivariate) frequencies are shown. For example, the Provincial University (PU) scenario involves two categorical variables: sex (male or female) and academic rank (assistant, associate, or full professor). The *univariate* frequency distributions for those two variables were depicted in Tables 12.1 and 12.2; their *bivariate* frequency is illustrated in Table 12.7. Such bivariate tables are a purely descriptive technique but are an important prerequisite for *inferential* analysis.

Like other tables, this one has an identifying number, a title that denotes its contents, and clearly labelled variable names and attendant levels. Across the table are three columns, each signifying an academic rank. At the bottom of each column are the (univariate) column *marginals* (i.e., totals): 170, 130, and 100 for the three ranks, as in Table 12.2.

Table 12.7

The Cross-tabulation of Sex by Academic Rank for Provincial University Data

		Academic Rank			
		Assistant professor	Associate professor	Full professor	Row marginals
Sex	Female	90	50	20	160
		Ex = 52	Ex = 52	Ex = 52	
	Male	80	80	80	240
		Ex = 102	Ex = 78	Ex = 60	
	Column marginals	170	130	100	Total = 400

The two rows, labelled on the left side of the table, signify sex. On the table's right-hand side are the (univariate) row marginals: 160 females and 240 males, as in Table 12.1. The total number of faculty members, 400, is shown at the bottom right-hand corner of Table 12.7; there, we crosscheck to ensure that the total number of faculty members by rank (170 + 130 + 100) is the same as the total number by sex (160 + 240).

Within each cell of the table are the bivariate frequencies; that is, the number of people who manifest the joint characteristics of a given sex at a given rank. The number 90 in the top left-hand corner, for example, shows that there were 90 female assistant professors on the faculty at PU. You can see that the number of female faculty members decreases as you go up the ranks (90 assistants, 50 associates, 20 full professors), while male faculty members are spread evenly across the ranks (80/80/80). It's also easy to compute that while roughly 53 percent of all assistant professors are female (i.e., 90/170 × 100), only 38 percent of associate professors and 20 percent of full professors are females; conversely, 47 percent of assistants, 62 percent of associates, and 80 percent of full professors are males.

Inclusion of a bivariate frequency distribution (also called a **contingency table**) is a very helpful way to summarize and represent your data. In this case, we immediately get the impression that sex and rank are associated at PU: female faculty members seem especially underrepresented at the senior levels of the academic hierarchy.

Another appropriate way to represent the data would be to use a grouped or clustered bar graph. Figure 12.9 shows such a graph for the "Rank by Sex" data of Table 12.7.

THE CHI-SQUARE DISTRIBUTION

But a social and health scientist researching this situation would not stop there. He or she would first want to know whether the joint variation of sex and rank we observe is still within the realm of what we might expect from mere chance variation or whether it exceeds those bounds. This is a question

Figure 12.9
Sex and Academic Rank of Faculty at PU

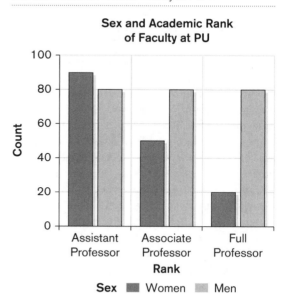

of the *statistical significance* of the results. In order to determine it, we need some sort of measure by which we can decide how likely or unlikely we are to obtain the particular distribution we observe. This is given by a statistic known as **chi-square**, which allows us to assess whether two categorical variables are associated beyond what would be expected on the basis of chance variation alone. Doing so requires us to first compute a chi-square statistic to describe the particular pattern of frequencies and then compare our chi-square statistic to the chi-square distributions to see how likely that particular chi-square value is to be observed.

The chi-square statistic describes deviations between what we'd *expect* (on the basis of chance, i.e., if the two variables were indeed independent) and what we actually *observe*. To compute the expected values, we take the univariate marginals (i.e., row and column totals) as givens. An *expected frequency* is then computed for each of the cells, depending on the relevant column and row marginal for each cell. In essence, we thus say, "Given that there are more male (240) than female

(160) faculty members, and given that there are more assistants (170) than associates (130), and more of both than full professors (100),[12] how many female assistant professors would we expect there to be if there were no association between rank and sex?"[13] We do that by taking the column marginal for assistant professors (170), multiplying that by the row marginal for females (160), and dividing by the total number of observations (400) to get the expected frequency of 68 that you see in Table 12.7 in the "female/ assistant professor" cell. Thus, if there were *no* association between sex and rank, we'd *expect* there to be 68 female assistant professors; in fact, we observe many more ($n = 90$).

The same procedure is followed for each and every cell. To obtain the number of expected female full professors, for example, you'd take the row marginal for females (160), multiply by the column marginal for full professors (100), divide by the total number of observations (400), and get 40— many more than the 20 female full professors we actually observe. We'll leave it to you to check our calculations on the other four cells; just follow the same rules noted above (i.e., relevant column marginal, multiplied by relevant row marginal, divided by total number of observations). You can check your calculations by summing your expected frequencies for each row and column; they should add up to the actual marginal totals (since the marginals are treated as givens). For example, note that the expected frequencies for males in each of the cells in that row (102, 78, 60) add up to 240, which is indeed the total number of males we have; similarly, the expected values for the associate professor column (52, 78) add up to 130, which is indeed the total number of associate professors among the faculty at PU.

We now have *two* different bivariate frequency distributions: one of *observed* frequencies and another of *expected* frequencies. The chi-square statistic involves a comparison between the two. To compute it, we first take the *difference* between what we expected and what we observed for each cell. For example, in the "male/assistant professor"

cell, we observed 80, but would have expected 102 if there were no relationship between sex and rank and if nothing other than chance had been operating—a deviation of $80 - 102 = -22$. But note that if we observed 22 *fewer* male/assistant professors than expected, then, given the marginal, we must have had 22 *more* female/assistant professors than expected; indeed, that is the case (i.e., $90 - 68 = 22$). We once again have the problem that a simple summation of all the deviations will add to zero; the mathematical solution, as with the variance statistic, is to square those deviations to get rid of the pluses and minuses. Thus, for the "male/ assistant professor" cell, our squared deviation statistic is $(-22)^2$, or 484.

At the same time, we must also acknowledge that a deviation of 22 will be differentially "surprising," depending on the number we expected in the cell. If we had expected 500 people in the cell, for example, a deviation of 22 people might not seem especially large; if we had expected 50, on the other hand, a deviation of 22 is quite substantial. To take into account the relative magnitude of the deviation, we take the squared deviation statistic we computed above (484) and divide it by the expected value for that cell (102), to come up with 4.7.

The final step is to *sum* these individual cell statistics across all six cells, in order to create our final chi-square statistic for our contingency table. You should compute these values and the total for yourself, but the values we obtained (running from left to right across successive rows of Table 12.7) are 7.1, 0.1, 10.0, 4.7, 0.1, and 6.7, which sum to 28.7.

But what exactly does 28.7 mean? Is that big? Small? Surprising? Expected? We must take our sample statistic and compare it to the appropriate chi-square distribution in order to answer those questions. Appendix A shows a listing of critical values for different probability levels; pay particular attention to the .05 and .01 levels. These are values that our sample's chi-square statistic must *meet* or *exceed* before we're prepared to say, with 95 percent or 99 percent confidence, that the deviation between expected and observed values in our distribution was *statistically significant* (i.e., greater than one would expect on the basis of chance variation alone). But Appendix A gives a lengthy list of such criterion values. Which ones are "ours"?

DEGREES OF FREEDOM Note the column at the left of Appendix A, the one titled *df* (*degrees of freedom*). The reason we need that column recalls the problem we faced in calculating deviation statistics. The magnitude of a chi-square statistic will be sensitive to the number of cells included in the analysis. Our example table had two rows and three columns (or six cells), and we derived a chi-square value of 28.7. Would a table with three rows and four columns (i.e., 12 cells) have resulted in a higher chi-square value merely because of a greater number of cells? The answer, all else being equal, is yes. Thus, we must take the *size* of the contingency table into account, and we do so by considering the number of degrees of freedom it possesses.

Degrees of freedom (*df*) is a very hard concept to nail down, although you see it whenever an inferential statistic is being discussed. At its core is the notion that the theoretical distribution will vary in form depending on the number of parameters that are free to vary. With contingency tables, where the distribution of data is framed in terms of certain numbers of *rows* and *columns,* the *df* we have are constrained by the fact there are two rows and three columns in our table; the number of cell values free to vary, given the marginal values, is relatively small.

The process might be illustrated by telling you how we went about creating that contingency table, in order to have an example that we could use as an illustration. Our earlier presentation of the univariate frequency distributions at PU (Tables 12.1 and 12.2) had established our givens (i.e., the observed univariate marginals). Because we wanted to create a situation where sex *is* related to rank, we first decided that we'd put most of the "female" observations into the "female assistant professors" category. We could have chosen any number from 0 to 160 to put in that cell, but we chose 90.

Then we went to the next cell. What limitations did we have? We know (from the given marginals)

that there are 160 females, and now we also "know" from our choice above that 90 of them are assistant professors; thus, when we went to create a number for the "female/*associate* professors" cell, we could choose any number from 0 to 70 (since 160 – 90 = 70) as the number for the cell. Like the first (female/assistant) cell, it had constraints but was still *free to vary.* We chose to put the number 50 in that cell.

The process continued: we went to the third cell—female full professors. But here our choices are no longer free to vary. Given the female row marginal of 160, and given our two choices in the female/assistant (90) and female/associate (50) cells, the number in the third cell *must* be 20—the *only* number that can go there if the marginal is to remain as set.

And the same is now true of all the other cells. There were 90 female assistant professors; if the column marginal for assistants (*n* = 170) is to remain, there *must* be 80 male assistant professors. Given there are 130 associate professors, and 50 of them are female, then there *must* be 80 male associate professors. Similarly, the number of male full professors *must* be 80.

In sum, as we went through the process of creating the above example, there really were only two cell values where we could make choices when setting the observed cell values. Mathematically, one says that in this 2 × 3 contingency table, despite the fact that there were six cells, we "really" had only two *degrees of freedom* that we could vary. After those two, *every* choice was "determined," *given* the marginals.

A formula has been derived that allows you to easily determine the degrees of freedom for a contingency table. Take the number of rows (2 in our case) and the number of columns (3 in our case), subtract 1 from each (i.e., 2 – 1 = 1; 3 – 1 = 2), and then multiply those two numbers together (i.e., 1 × 2 = 2). Mathematically, the formula is $df = (R - 1)(C - 1)$, where R is the number of rows, and C is the number of columns.

Thus, we now know that the particular values that are "ours" in Appendix A are the ones associated with 2*df;* our chi-square value must meet or exceed 5.99 in order to be considered "statistically significant" at the 95 percent level of confidence (i.e., because the probability of observing our results on the basis of chance alone is less than 5 percent, or $p < .05$) and must exceed 9.21 in order to be considered statistically significant at the 99 percent level of confidence (i.e., $p < .01$). Both of these values are in fact handily exceeded by our chi-square statistic of 28.7. Thus, we can say with 99 percent confidence that the suggestion that rank and sex are *not* associated at PU is probably false. The likelihood of our observing these results by chance variation alone is so improbable that we reject the "null" hypothesis—that rank and sex are *not* related—and infer that sex and rank probably *are* related.

INTERPRETING THE RESULT So what does our finding really mean? No matter how we slice it, males appear more likely to have been promoted up the ranks than females. Is this indicative of biased promotional practices at PU? Is this yet another social example of how an "old boys' network" can make it hard for women to succeed? Certainly the data presented are consistent with that explanation; this is exactly the sort of bivariate distribution one would expect if discriminatory promotional policies were in place. But are there rival plausible explanations to consider?

One such explanation might assert that the significant association between sex and rank we observe is in fact not a result of discriminatory *promotional* policies, but rather the legacy of discriminatory *hiring* practices that acted to keep women out of university and graduate schools, and hence out of the academy, for many years. Thus, since women at PU may not have been adequately represented on the faculty until recently, perhaps those who are at PU are still at too junior a stage of their careers to have accumulated the sort of scholarly record that should lead to promotion.

If that were the case, then we'd expect to see it in our data. For example, we'd expect there to be a significant association between sex and length of employment, such as seems apparent in Table 12.8. We can see that the propensity to hire female faculty members has changed considerably over time. Of those still remaining from the hirings of 21 to 25 years ago, only 21.8 percent of the faculty hired were female,[14] while in succeeding five-year categories, the hiring rate for females went up to 34.5 percent, then 47.3 percent, then 50.9 percent, and finally to 54.2 percent. We'll leave it to you to work out whether the chi-square value for that contingency table is indeed significant. If it is, any interpretation must still consider the impact of *mortality* on the results.[15]

Table 12.8

The Cross-tabulation of Sex by Length of Employment at Provincial University

		Length of Employment					
		1–5 yrs.	6–10 yrs.	11–15 yrs.	16–20 yrs.	21–55 yrs.	
	Female	32	26	44	41	17	160
		Ex = 23.6	Ex = 20.4	Ex = 37.2	Ex = 47.6	Ex = 31.2	
Sex	Male	27	25	49	78	61	240
		Ex = 35.4	Ex = 30.6	Ex = 55.8	Ex = 71.4	Ex = 46.8	
		59	51	93	119	78	Total = 400

Even if we could take the bivariate frequencies of Table 12.8 at face value, the hypothesis that *promotional* practices are discriminatory has not necessarily been negated. We cannot simply ignore the earlier finding, which revealed proportionately fewer women appearing in the higher ranks. With this additional finding of differential likelihood of hiring females over time, several rival explanations remain plausible: (1) promotional practices favour males, (2) former discriminatory hiring practices mean that few women have been on faculty long enough to warrant promotion, (3) both of the above statements are true to some extent, or (4) neither of the above statements is true, and some other variable(s) account for the result. For example, it may be that promotional and hiring policies have always been equitable,[16] but the problem may lie elsewhere, for example, not enough women had access to university, entered graduate school, graduated with doctoral degrees, or whatever.

The next step in any comprehensive analysis would be to seek out data that bear on those various explanations. You might, for example, attempt to gather archival data on the comparative success ratios of male and female applicants for promotion, or the comparative research and teaching records of male and female faculty members at the time they were considered for promotion, to check for any evidence that more stringent criteria were imposed on female candidates than on males. Or you might want to consider whether the criteria themselves favour males over females, given existing social structures and vocational constraints. Alternatively, you might turn your attention to graduate-school admissions records or to proportions of male and female job applicants over time. Each set of data would shed further light on the dynamics of this microcosm of society and how it has changed (or not) over time. The only constraints will be the availability of data and the analytical intelligence of the researcher.

OTHER MEASURES OF RELATIONSHIPS FOR CATEGORICAL DATA

Many other statistics can also be computed for cross-tabulation; Norusis (1993) provides a full list of them. She also explains why some might be desirable by describing the limitations of the chi-square statistic:

> The chi-square test is a test of independence; it provides little information about the strength or the form of the association between two variables. The magnitude of the observed chi-square depends not only on the goodness of fit of the independence model but also on the sample size. If the sample size for a particular table increases *n*-fold, so does the chi-square value. Thus, large chi-square values can arise in applications where residuals are small relative to expected frequencies but where sample sizes are large. (208)

In sum, while the chi-square test may allow you to reject the null hypothesis of independence, it does not in itself do a particularly good job of informing you about the degree of association that exists between two variables. The chi-square is also very *n*-sensitive; the larger your sample size, the more "easily" you'll be able to obtain statistical significance, even when the degree of association between the variables is actually rather small.

But what other kinds of statistics are there for this situation? Norusis's (1993) inventory includes examples that range from measures of the degree of association between two categorical variables all the way up to interval data. These latter inclusions stray a bit too far for us at this point in the discussion, so we'll limit the following discussion to a few statistics that we see as more likely to be of interest with categorical data.

Your choice in what further statistics you might look at should be governed by the kind of information that's most suitable for your situation. Norusis (1993) explains why:

> Indexes that attempt to quantify the relationship between variables in a cross-classification are called *measures of association*. No single measure adequately summarizes all possible types of association. Measures vary in their interpretation

and in the way they define perfect and inter-mediate association …

A particular measure may have a low value for a given table, not because the two variables are not related but because they are not related in the way to which the measure is sensitive. No single measure is best for all situations. (209)

STRENGTH OF ASSOCIATION There are two general classes of statistics that address the degree of association in cross-tabulations. The first has paid homage to the widespread use of the chi-square statistic by attempting to modify the statistic in a manner that will be less influenced by sample size and more reflective of association.

One of these, the **phi-coefficient**, takes the chi-square statistic, divides it by *N,* and then takes the square root of that quotient. By doing so, it attempts to take sample size into account and establishes a statistic that can range from zero to approximately 1.0. The **coefficient of contingency** and **Cramer's V** do essentially the same but use slight modifications of the sample size element of the computational equation. In the case of a 2 × 2 table, all these statistics are pretty well equal in magnitude to the **Pearson's *r*** (correlation coefficient) that would be computed on the same data. For our rank/gender cross-tabulation (which of course is *not* a 2 × 2 table), the three statistics are 0.267, 0.259, and 0.268, respectively, all of which were statistically significant ($p < .05$), as was the case with the chi-square statistic.

REDUCTION OF ERROR The second type of test statistics are those based on the concept of "proportional reduction of error" (PRE).

These measures are all essentially ratios of a measure of error in predicting the values of one variable on knowledge of that variable alone and the same measure of error applied to predictions based on knowledge of an additional variable. (Norusis 1993: 211)

To take our rank/gender example again, you start by saying, "If I don't know what sex a particular faculty member is, and I want to predict what rank s/he holds, what prediction would I make, and how often will I be incorrect in my prediction?" Then you continue: "Okay, now what prediction would I make if I *am* told the *sex* of the person whose rank I am trying to predict, and what is the likelihood of me being wrong now?" And finally, "To what extent (if at all) will my predictions in the second case be better than my predictions in the first case?"

The first statistic considered is Goodman and Kruskal's lambda statistic. In answer to the first question, Goodman and Kruskal assert that the logical prediction to make is whatever category is the modal one. In our rank/gender data, for example, the largest number of people in the sample were assistant professors (170 out of 400 faculty members), that is, 42.5 percent of all faculty members, or 0.425 of the sample. If we were to just guess "assistant professor" every time we were asked to guess an individual's rank without knowing what sex s/he is, we thus would be "correct" 42.5 percent or 0.425 of the time. The probability of being wrong is then given as $1 - 0.425 = 0.575$. File that number in your head as p_1.

The next question is what prediction we'd make if we *knew* the sex of the person. Answering it requires us to identify the modal category within each sex and to make that prediction for that sex. The situation is a bit odd for the males in our fictitious example, given that we have exactly the same number of men (80) at each rank, which means that any one of the three ranks could be used as our basis of prediction. Regardless of which category we decided to guess, we would end up being right about a third of the time, that is, 33.3 percent, or 0.333 of the time for *all the males,* or 0.200 of the *sample as a whole* (because the 80 men who comprise any one category represent 20.0 percent of the entire sample of 400 faculty members). For women, the modal category is "assistant professor," so if we predicted that category for every woman we would be correct 56.25 percent, or 0.5625 of the time among all females, or 0.225 of the sample as a whole. In combination, our "correct" guesses for the men and women faculty members, respectively, would cover $0.200 + 0.225 = 0.425$ of the sample as a whole; conversely, this means we will still be wrong in our prediction $1 - 0.425 = 0.575$ of the time. File that number in your head as p_2.

If you compare p_1 (0.575) to p_2 (0.575), you can see immediately that, although the chi-square and other measures of association were statistically significant, in fact our ability to predict rank from sex has not been enhanced at all. When we ignored the sex of the faculty member, we were wrong in our prediction 0.575 (or 57.5 percent) of the time. Now that we have taken sex into account, we are still wrong 0.575 (or 57.5 percent) of the time. Because the numbers are identical, it's fairly obvious the lambda statistic will be non-significant, but just for the record we'll note that the way you compute the lambda statistic is to calculate the degree of improvement in prediction:

$$\frac{p_1 - p_2}{p_1} = \frac{0.575 - 0.575}{0.575} = \frac{0.000}{0.575} = 0$$

That is, our predictive ability has improved by 0.0 percent, and that value, 0.000, is our lambda statistic. The statistics can range from 0 (where taking one variable into account offers zero improvement in prediction, as was the case in our example) to 1 (where taking the independent variable into account allows perfect prediction).

Finally, note that the extent to which your predictability will be enhanced will vary depending on which variable you are predicting from and which you are predicting to. In the example above, we tried to predict the rank of the person in two situations: where we did not know the sex and where we did. Our predictability did not improve at all, in part because so many of the faculty members at PU are assistant professors. What would happen if we went the other way and asked whether knowing the rank of a faculty member would help us predict gender?

Remember the place to start is by asking what prediction we would make knowing nothing about the faculty member. At PU, the largest number of

faculty members are men, who comprise 240 out of 400, or 60.0 percent of all faculty members. Thus, if we know nothing about the faculty member, we should guess "man," and we will be right 60 percent (or 0.600) of the time. Conversely, we will be wrong $1 - 0.600 = 0.400$ of the time. That is p_1.

What do we predict if we know the rank of the person? For assistant professors, the modal category is "woman" (90 out of 170, or 0.529). If we guess "woman" for all assistant professors, we thus will be correct 52.9 percent of the time across all assistant professors, or 22.5 percent across the sample as a whole (90 out of 400). For associate professors the modal category is "man" (80 out of 130 or 0.615), so that if we guess "man" for every associate professor we will be correct 61.6 percent of the time across all associate professors, or (80 out of 400 = 0.200) for 20.0 percent across the sample as a whole. Finally, for full professors the modal category is "man" (80 out of 100, or 80 percent). If we always guess "man" when we know the person is a full professor, then we will be right 80 percent of the time across all full professors, or (80 out of 400 = 0.200) for 20 percent of the sample as a whole. In combination, our "correct" guesses across the three ranks will be $0.225 + 0.200 + 0.200 = 0.625$ for the sample as a whole; the flip side is that we will still be wrong $1 - 0.625 = 0.375$ of the time. That number is p_2.

Now if you compare p_1 (0.400) to p_2 (0.375), you can see our predictability is something other than zero (as we computed above), although it is still quite small. When we compute the lambda statistic this time we get

$$\frac{p_1 - p_2}{p_1} = \frac{0.400 - 0.375}{0.400} = \frac{0.025}{0.400} = 0.0625$$

That is, our lambda statistic is 0.0625, which means that our predictive ability has improved by 6.25 percent. However, the probability of this occurring if nothing other than chance alone were operating is 0.443,[17] which means that the enhancement in predictability is no greater than one would expect from chance variation alone (i.e., $p > .05$).

Examining Relationships among Continuous Variables

THE LIMITS OF CONTINGENCY TABLES

The chi-square statistic discussed above is a useful measure of association when dealing with two categorical variables where each has relatively few levels. Although it's possible to use this type of statistic with larger numbers of categories, you need reasonably large expected cell frequencies in order to do the analysis with some degree of mathematical integrity; thus, sample size requirements rapidly become prohibitive as the size of the contingency table increases. For example, the contingency table involving sex and rank was a 2 × 3 table with 6 cells; with a minimal requirement of 5 to 10 expected observations per cell (or 30 to 60 observations in total), the 400 observations we had were clearly adequate to perform the analysis.

But suppose we want to look at the relationship between the length of time faculty members have been employed at PU (originally reported in Table 12.4, these data range from 1 to 25 years and thus have 25 levels) and their opinions on the relative value of teaching and research (see Table 12.3; the scale has 5 points and thus 5 levels). We *could* cross-tabulate those two variables, but the contingency table would be 5 rows deep by 25 columns wide—125 cells! With the requirement for minimal expected frequencies of 5 to 10 per cell, we'd need somewhere in the order of 600 to 1,200 observations before the statistical analysis became meaningful. Suddenly, our 400 observations look very puny.

Of course, we could always collapse cells in order to help our data fit the statistical requirements. Instead of the 5 levels on the opinion item, we could collapse down to 3: (a) research valued more than teaching (i.e., categories 1 and 2), (b) research and teaching equally valued (category 3), and (c) teaching valued more than research (categories 4 and 5). Similarly, we could group "years of employment" data into 5 levels of 5 years each (as was done in Table 12.5). These two steps would reduce our 5 × 25 (or 125-cell) table down to a 3 × 5 (or 15-cell) table, which would clearly be more reasonable, given our total number of observations.

But while we *can* do that, most researchers would be reluctant to do so, other than for simplifying, illustrative purposes. We'd lose too much information. Another alternative would be preferred: the **scatter-plot diagram**. Then we could go further, assessing whether the relationship between variables is linear by using the **Pearson product–moment correlation coefficient** (otherwise known as Pearson's *r*).

SCATTER-PLOT DIAGRAMS

A scatter-plot diagram is a graph that depicts the status of each respondent on the two variables whose association we're interested in assessing. It offers the great advantage of allowing us to "see" the nature of the relationship that exists between the two variables. Scatter-plot diagrams are a useful way to see what *kinds* of relationships might exist between your variables. Figures 12.10(a) through 12.10(h) show some of the variation we might see; for discussion purposes, note that for each of the diagrams we've created a "best" regression line or have placed a "balloon" around the entire set of data points in order to visually illustrate the amount of variation in scores that exists around the regression line.

The first dimension to consider is whether the relationship appears to be *linear* or *curvilinear,* or whether there is no apparent association at all. Figure 12.10(h) shows a curvilinear, inverted-U-shaped relationship. As an example of this sort of relationship, consider the data from the PU faculty members. It's conceivable that a curvilinear relationship exists between academic rank and the relative importance attached to the teaching and research aspects of the job. Assistant professors may value research more highly because they see it as an important element in tenure and promotion considerations. Associate professors may then pay greater heed to their teaching role, but full professors will undoubtedly include those whose research interest has won them international recognition for their work (since this is a prerequisite for promotion to full professor). We don't know how widely that pattern actually occurs, but it seems a plausible curvilinear relationship.

Other sorts of curvilinear relationships are also possible: U-shaped, circular, or any of myriad others. A consideration of those relationships is clearly important, since they're orderly and no less meaningful than linear relationships, although a detailed consideration of how to investigate them is beyond the scope of this chapter.

Figure 12.10(d) shows no relationship between the two variables at all. Points are strewn all over the scatter plot. These are of no great interest to us here, either.

The remaining scatter plots *do* concern us here. All depict *linear* relationships, albeit with varying strengths of association.

In distinguishing between those scatter plots, the first dimension to consider is that of the *direction* of the relationship: Are increases in one variable associated with increases or decreases in the second variable? The relationship is considered *positive* or *direct* if *in*creases in one variable are associated with *in*creases in the other; the relationship is considered *negative* or *inverse* when *in*creases in one variable are associated with *de*creases in the other. Figures 12.10(a), 12.10(b), and 12.10(c) represent positive or direct relationships, whereas Figures 12.10(e), 12.10(f), and 12.10(g) represent negative or inverse relationships.

The second dimension of interest is the *magnitude* of the relationship. The highest-magnitude relationships are depicted in Figures 12.10(a) and 12.10(g), where all points fall along the same straight line (known as the *regression line*). Next are the relationships evident in Figures 12.10(b) and 12.10(f), where there's a little dispersion around the line, but where the "balloon" fits quite tightly. Figures 12.10(c) and 12.10(e) are still lower in magnitude; there's still a definite direction to the mass of points—positive in Figure 12.10(c); negative in Figure 12.10(e)—but there's also considerable dispersion around the regression line.

QUANTIFYING THE RELATIONSHIP: PEARSON'S *r*

Not surprisingly, mathematicians have sought ways to quantify the direction and strength of the relationship between two quantitative variables. Karl Pearson's work around the turn of the 20th century resulted in the development of a statistic known as the Pearson product–moment correlation coefficient, or, more briefly, as Pearson's r.[18] Note that Pearson's r describes only linear relationships.

There are two components to any correlation coefficient: a sign and a number. The *sign* indicates the *direction* of the relationship: a plus (+) sign indicates a **positive or direct relationship**, and a minus (–) sign indicates a **negative or inverse relationship**. The *number* component is defined so that its range is between zero and one.[19] Zero is used when there is *no* linear relationship; 1.0 describes a *perfect* linear relationship, where every data point lies on the same straight line.

Figures 12.10(a) to 12.10(g) have been labelled with rough approximations of the Pearson correlation coefficients that might describe those data. You can see that Figures 12.10(a) to 12.10(c) differ from Figures 12.10(e) to 12.10(g) insofar as r values for the former all show a "+" while all the latter begin with a "–". Note also that the magnitude of the relationship decreases as one goes from the perfect relationship in Figure 12.10(a) ($r = +1.0$) to that in Figure 12.10(b) ($r = +0.80$) to that in Figure 12.10(c) ($r = +0.50$), and similarly as one goes from Figure 12.10(g) ($r = -1.0$) to Figure 12.10(f) ($r = -0.80$) to Figure 12.10(e) ($r = -0.50$).

The sign and numerical components together allow us to make immediate comparisons between relationships in terms of both their direction and their strength. For example, the relationships depicted in Figures 12.10(e), 12.10(f), and 12.10(g) are all similar in direction but different in magnitude; those in Figures 12.10(b) and 12.10(f) are identical in the strength of the relationships but opposite in direction.

A COMPUTATIONAL EXAMPLE It's fairly easy to compute a correlation coefficient for any given set of paired observations. We won't show the formula's derivation here, but conceptually, it can be understood as a weighted count of how often data

Figure 12.10

Scatter-plot Diagrams of Eight Different Relationships between Two Variables

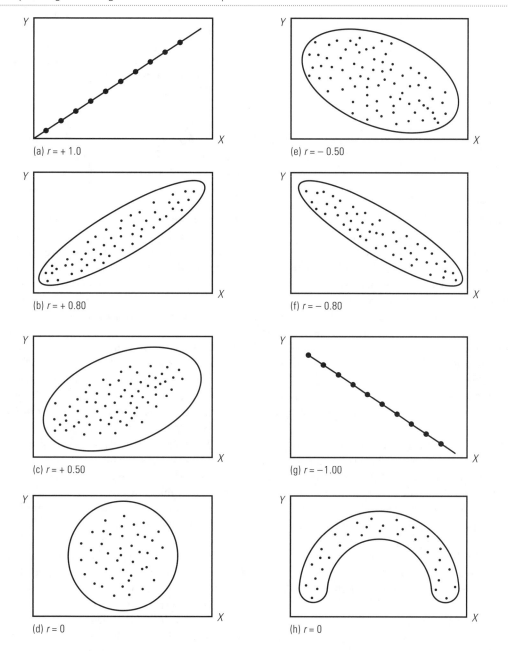

Figure 12.11

Four Quadrants of a Scatter-plot Diagram

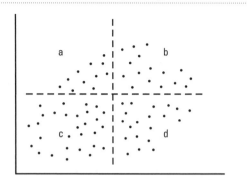

points fall in quadrants "b" and "c" versus quadrants "a" and "d" of Figure 12.11.

Table 12.9 shows the computational sequence for a set of data involving the midterm and final exam grades for eight students taking a course in research methods. As you can see, the formula requires you to compute a number of different terms along the way. Generally speaking, the formula takes the scores on each variable, transforms them into "standardized" scores (so that the variables don't have to be on the same scale or expressed in the same units), and then compares how variation in one variable coincides (or does not) with variation on the other.

The correlation coefficient of $r = +0.85$ derived in Table 12.9 indicates a strong relationship between performance on the midterm and performance on the final: those who do well on the midterm generally do well on the final, while those who perform poorly on the midterm tend also to do less well on the final. But the relationship isn't perfect, suggesting also that some changes take place: some students who do well on the midterm are perhaps overconfident, don't study as much for the final, and therefore blow it; others take their poor midterm performance to heart, work harder, and improve on the final; or illness that affects some students during one exam is not a factor during the other. Measurement error also occurs: tests are imperfect, thus allowing regression toward the mean to occur.

The next question is whether the correlation we observe is greater than what we would have expected on the basis of chance variation alone. Once again (as with chi-square), this is a question of the *statistical significance* of the results.

We use r distributions in the same way as chi-square distributions. Appendix B shows a listing of criterion values for r, the Pearson correlation coefficient.

Once again, the criterion value depends on *degrees of freedom*. For correlations, the number of degrees of freedom is equal to the number of *paired observations* minus two. Thus, for our data, we have $8 - 2 = 6df$. Appendix B shows that for $6df$ we require a computed correlation of $r = 0.7067$ or higher in order for our relationship to be considered significant at the .05 level, or $r = 0.8343$ for the .01 probability level.[20] Our obtained correlation of $r = +0.85$ exceeds both those criterion values: we can therefore say with 99 percent confidence that the two sets of scores are related beyond the level one would expect on the basis of chance alone.

THE PROPORTION OF VARIANCE ACCOUNTED FOR: r^2

While the correlation coefficient (r) conveys the magnitude and direction of a relationship between two variables, we'll also note here (but won't go into the proof) that the proportion of variance that's shared by two variables is equal to the square of their correlation coefficient. Thus, if we determine that the correlation between two variables is $r = 0.90$, then we also immediately know that $r^2 = (0.90)^2 = 0.81$ (i.e., that 81 percent of the variance in one variable is shared by the other).

Besides understanding the inherent relation that r and r^2 have with each other, a consideration of *how* they're related may give you a slightly different take on correlation coefficients. Figure 12.12 plots the relationship between r and r^2. You can see that correlations in the neighbourhood of 0.10 to 0.30 look fairly puny in this light, since even a 0.30 correlation between two variables means that they share only a paltry 9 percent of their variances in common (since $0.30^2 = 0.09$). Even

Table 12.9

Computing a Correlation Coefficient

Student	Mid-Term Score (X)	Final Exam Score (Y)	X^2	Y^2	XY
Wenona	18	18	324	324	324
Abby	19	23	361	529	437
Rajesh	30	25	900	625	750
Ali	33	28	1089	784	924
Sakura	27	34	729	1156	918
Chris	32	38	1024	1444	1216
Shihong	41	37	1681	1369	1517
Alexis	47	42	2209	1764	1974
$N = 8$	$\sum X = 247$	$\sum Y = 245$	$\sum X^2 = 8317$	$\sum Y^2 = 7995$	$\sum XY = 8060$

Computation

1. Take the sum ($\sum$) of the X scores: $\sum X = 247$
2. Square the sum of X: $(\sum X)^2 = (247)^2 = 61\ 009$
3. Square each X score. Take the sum of those squared X scores: $\sum X^2 = 8317$
4. Take the sum of the Y scores: $\sum Y = 245$
5. Square the sum of Y: $(\sum Y)^2 = (245)^2 = 60\ 025$
6. Square each Y score. Take the sum of those squared Y scores: $\sum Y^2 = 7995$
7. Compute cross-products by multiplying each X score by its associated Y score. Take the sum of those cross-products: $\sum XY = 8060$
8. Note the number of paired observations: $N = 8$
9. Insert the computed figures into the following formula to compute r, the correlation coefficient:

$$r = \frac{N \sum XY - (\sum X)(\sum Y)}{\sqrt{[N \sum X^2 - (\sum X)^2][N \sum Y^2 - (\sum Y)^2]}}$$

$$= \frac{8(8060) - (247)(245)}{\sqrt{[8(8317) - 61\ 009][8(7995) - 60\ 025]}}$$

$$= \frac{64\ 480 - 60\ 515}{\sqrt{[66\ 536 - 61\ 009][63\ 960 - 60\ 025]}}$$

$$= \frac{3965}{\sqrt{(5527)(3935)}} \quad \frac{3965}{\sqrt{21\ 748\ 745}}$$

$$= \frac{3965}{4663.6} = +0.850$$

10. Compute the degrees of freedom, which is given by the number of paired observations minus 2, that is, $df = N - 2 = 8 - 2 = 6$.
11. Determine whether the observed correlation is statistically significant by inspecting the critical values listed in Appendix B, for the appropriate degrees of freedom. You should see that for $6df$, the critical values that must be exceeded are $r = 0.7067$ and $r = 0.8343$ for $p < .05$ and $p < .01$, respectively. In our example, where $r = 0.850$, we would conclude that our correlation is indeed statistically significant at $p < .01$; that is, the correlation is greater than we would expect on the basis of chance alone, suggesting that the two variables are indeed associated.

Figure 12.12

An Illustration of the Relation between r and r^2

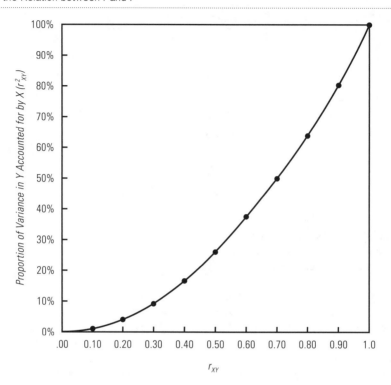

a correlation between X and Y of $r = 0.50$, which many researchers would normally get very excited about, means that X accounts for no more than a quarter (25 percent) of the variance in Y; this still leaves another 75 percent of the variance in Y that is *not* yet accounted for. Not until correlations get into the 0.71 ballpark do you begin to account for even half of the variance in Y. Thus, while the unsquared correlation coefficient (r) may be useful in indicating direction, it may well give an impression of a stronger relationship than would be the case if you were to pay greater heed to r^2 and its proportion of variance interpretation.

WHAT CORRELATION COEFFICIENTS DO NOT TELL YOU

You've computed a correlation between two variables and found it to be significant. What does this mean? Literally, it means that the two sets of data you've correlated are associated more closely than you would expect on a purely chance basis. But before you jump to the conclusion that you've unearthed some immutable truth, look at some of the reasons you might have obtained the correlation coefficient you did. Consider the following:

1. *Whether the theoretical variables are related.* The discovery of a significant correlation is an *empirical* finding, which you may or may not be able to generalize to the theoretical domain. First, there's a question of the relationship between your theoretical variable and your operational one; that is, the epistemic relationship between the two. Second, as is true of any empirical finding, its *external validity* (or generalizability) must be considered; this is a separate sampling issue.

2. *Whether the association is a causal one.* Every methods textbook will tell you that *correlation does not mean causation.* The fact that two variables happen to "go together" doesn't in any way mean that there's necessarily a causal connection between the two of them. It *may* be that the first variable causes the second; it *may* be that the second variable causes the first; or it *may* be that both variables are influenced by some third variable that you haven't yet recognized. Other variables may "share variance" with both sets of scores, such that the correlation you observe may not reflect a "real" association between the two variables you are investigating, but merely the variance they share with that third variable. There's undoubtedly a correlation between the number of fire trucks that appear at a fire and the amount of damage done, for example, but this doesn't mean that the fire trucks cause the damage or that the damage causes the trucks. It's more likely that a third variable (the size of the fire) influences both.

A similar situation might be evident in the example of midterm and final exam scores. The correlation *may* reflect consistency in the evaluation of "competence in research methods" (as we hope), but it may also just reflect similarities in test-taking behaviour (which is independent of research methods competence per se). Many social beliefs are clearly supported by people's erroneous belief that correlation implies causation. For example, the occasional covariation of visible-minority status and "low levels of social achievement," however selectively that observation is obtained in the first place, is often used to try to justify the racist belief that visible minorities in some way "cause" their "inferiority," when instead social structures, racism, and institutionalized poverty are often causes of both. The tendency to blame the victim is another manifestation of confusing correlation with cause. Victims might in some cases be the architects of their own misfortune, but just as clearly might not.

The example above urges you to be cautious about jumping to conclusions when you find a significant correlation. Similar caution is warranted when you *don't* find a significant correlation. Pearson's *r* is designed to test for a very particular type of relationship between variables—a linear one. Just because a correlation is not significant does not necessarily mean that a patterned, orderly relationship does not exist. When looking at correlations, you should always look at scatter plots to avoid indulging in interpretations that may turn out to be nonsensical.

Examining Differences between Categories

A SLIGHTLY DIFFERENT WAY OF MAKING COMPARISONS

Thus far in our look at inferential statistics, we've emphasized techniques for measuring association. Let us now introduce another set of techniques that tackle another very basic task one is often faced with in the social and health sciences, that is, making comparisons.

To explain how that is done in different situations, consider a situation in which you, as a student, might often find yourself. Suppose you complete two midterm exams, later finding that you scored 22 out of 27 on the Anthropology 101 midterm and 41 out of 55 on your Philosophy 330 exam. Did you do better in anthropology or philosophy? To answer that question, you might look for some common ground on which to compare the two scores, perhaps by translating your scores into percentages. On doing so, you find that your anthropology grade was actually 81.5 percent, while your philosophy score was 74.5 percent. Comparing the two, you conclude that your performance was better in anthropology than in philosophy.

Social and health scientists who analyze such data would actually take the analysis a step or two further, as we'll soon see. But first we'd like to draw your attention to exactly what you did when you tried to compare your midterm exam grades in that way. You created an abstract, hypothetical situation in which a crucial element that made the two grades incomparable in the first place—the fact that one exam was marked out of 27 while the other was marked out of 55—was negated by looking at a theoretical distribution of numbers (who said you had no understanding of statistical concepts?) called percentages. Neither of the exams was actually marked out of 100. But you took the 22 out of 27 in anthropology and said, "Well, *if* this exam had been marked out of 100 points, and my performance and the marking remained constant, what would I have received as a grade?" And you came up with 81.5 percent. The same process with the philosophy grade led you to conclude you would have received a grade of 74.5 percent on that hypothetical exam. By establishing a common ground, you made the two grades comparable.

When we describe percentages as "theoretical," it isn't because percentages are unreal or completely abstract. Rather, the term implies that there's no particularly good reason, other than as a completely arbitrary standard of judgment on which people have agreed, to look at percentages or to have defined percentages as necessarily being a score out of 100. There's no law of mathematics stopping us all from deciding tomorrow that percentages will henceforth be computed with a base of 1000 rather than 100 (although a desire for linguistic integrity might lead us to call them "permillages" rather than "percentages") or even with a base of 472, if we so please. Percentages (or other such standardized ratios) may be arbitrarily defined, but given that we have defined them that way, the results we garner through them are anything but arbitrary.

Members of the social and health sciences go through a somewhat similar process, but they take a few more details into account. Since you've already learned the hard part—characteristics of distributions, and particularly the concepts of standard deviations and variance—the rest will be easy.

Z-SCORES AND THE NORMAL DISTRIBUTION

In the same way that percentages provide a common ground for comparing grades, social and health scientists have looked for a common ground on which to compare different distributions of scores. The creation they came up with is known as the **normal distribution**. It's "normal" in the sense that it's typical of many distributions we come across in everyday research; indeed, after more than a decade of gathering all sorts of data—from exam grades to attitude scores to aptitude measures to behavioural indices—we never cease to be amazed at how often one encounters distributions that are roughly normal in their form. There's a central tendency where scores cluster more closely together than anywhere else along the frequency distribution; as one moves farther and farther away from that mean/median/modal point, one sees fewer and fewer scores, until they disappear into infinity. Figure 12.13 depicts a standard normal distribution.

In the same way that "percentages" were arbitrarily defined as being out of 100, the standard normal distribution was also given some characteristics on a relatively arbitrary basis. The distribution's mean was set at zero, while the standard deviation was set at 1.0.[21] Of course, no such choice is *completely* arbitrary. Making percentages out of 100 rather than of 472 certainly makes computation easier, as does setting the normal distribution with a central tendency (i.e., mean) of zero and with variability (i.e., standard deviation and variance) of 1.0.

Once the normal distribution is defined, it becomes possible to calculate, for a particular observation at a given distance from the mean, the probability of getting an observation at least that far from the mean. This requires first that we have some measure of deviation from the mean. Since we've already discussed the notion of a standard deviation, it should come as no surprise that social and health scientists seized on the "standard deviation unit" as the ruler to use for any given distribution of scores. They could have called these "standard deviation units" or "SDUs" (or maybe BENDERs or LEELAs). But being the conservative lot that they are, mathematicians decided to call deviations computed in terms of standard deviation units "**z-scores**."

Figure 12.13

A Standard Normal Distribution, Showing Proportions of Cases Falling at Different Distances from the Mean

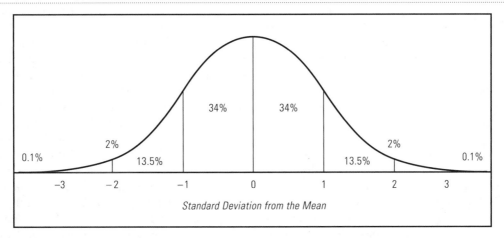

Let's return to the example of your midterm exam grades. A social or health scientist wouldn't be content with merely using percentages as a common ground of comparison. Treating those percentages as comparable assumes that both exams were equally difficult and that both professors (or their teaching assistants) marked with equal stringency. But as you may well have found in your own courses, that may be a tenuous assumption. So a social or health scientist would be interested in knowing whether the scores on that anthropology midterm are approximately normally distributed—and, if so, what the mean and standard deviation of the distribution are.

Suppose it was a particularly difficult exam, so hard that the mean score among your classmates was 15 out of 27, with a standard deviation of 10. That means that your score of 22 was actually 7 points above the mean, or $7/10 = 0.700$ standard deviation units above the mean. In other words, your z-score on that exam would have been $+0.7$ (the "$+$" signifies your score was above the mean; recall that the mean of the distribution is zero, and that deviations from it can be in a positive or negative direction).

Next we'd want to gain the same information for your philosophy midterm. Suppose that it, too, was a fairly difficult exam. Most of your classmates managed to pass, since the mean and median were both 30 out of 55, but very few of them did either very poorly or very well: the standard deviation was a mere 8.0. With a mean of 30 and a standard deviation of 8.0, your score of 41 was, in fact, $11/8 = 1.375$ standard deviation units above the mean; in other words, you achieved a z-score of $+1.375$. Thus, when we compare your performance to that of your classmates, we find that you actually scored somewhat better in philosophy (with a z-score of $+1.375$) than you did in anthropology (where your z-score was $+0.700$), even though your percentage grade in philosophy (74.5) was lower than the one you received in anthropology (81.5).

The process is similar in many ways to what you did in translating your two grades into percentages. In looking for a common ground, you chose percentages, which are arbitrarily established to be expressed out of 100. The logic was essentially to say, "*If* both exams had actually been based out of 100, what would my two scores have been?"

The social or health scientist, however, says, "*If* the scores on both these exams were drawn from normal distributions, then what is their comparative likelihood of being drawn?" By referring your grades to the normal distribution, we could compute exact probabilities for obtaining at least any given score, or we could give percentile estimates of where you (or any other person) stack up in the distribution. But we'll leave that technique for your course professor to cover if s/he thinks it is useful. We now turn to a situation where we have two variables of interest—one categorical and one continuous—and we seek to determine whether the categories differ in their status on the continuous variable.

COMPARING MEANS THROUGH THE *t*-STATISTIC

In looking at your score on the anthropology exam, we tried to understand it by placing it in its distributional context. But social and health scientists, and particularly quantitatively oriented ones, aren't often interested in single scores. Scores are interesting only in the context of distributions. Similarly, samples are interesting only when they're linked to the populations from which they were drawn.

In comparing distributions, we're usually interested in whether the means differ: the **t-statistic** is the measure that mathematicians have invented for us to use in this instance. People seem to rest so much easier when abstract concepts are reified—we relate so much better to Santa Claus than to the abstract ideals of harmony and sharing. Perhaps the *t*-test is little more than a tentative concrete response to the question "How big is big?"

One person who tried to answer that question was W. S. Gossett, who worked as a chemist at the Guinness Brewery in Dublin, Ireland, in the late 1800s. Apparently company policy forbade the publication of research, so Gossett published under the pseudonym "Student," which is why the *t*-distribution is known as Student's *t*-distribution and its descriptive statistic as Student's *t* (e.g., see McGhee 1985). The story begins where the standard deviation left off.[22]

When the question under consideration was the extremity of your anthropology exam score, we first found out where your score stood relative to the mean of the distribution of scores (i.e., we took the difference between score and mean). We

then determined what the standard deviation of the distribution was, using that as a kind of ruler with which to measure your score in standard deviation (or *z*-score) units.

When a social or health scientist wants to know whether any two groups differ, the question is phrased in terms of whether there's a difference between the two group means. Not surprisingly, therefore, step 1 in computing a *t*-statistic involves finding the difference between the two means. But once we know the difference, how do we know whether it's a "big" difference or whether it might be expected to occur through chance variation alone?

Gossett grappled with that question by asking us to assume the null hypothesis, that is, that the two groups we're dealing with are actually just samples from the same population. Suppose we have a distribution that is normally distributed and that comprises an infinite number of observations. We randomly sample one group of five observations and compute their mean score, sample another group of five observations and compute *their* group mean, and then compare the two means to see how close they are to each other. Then we take another two samples of five observations each, computing and comparing their group means, then another two samples, and another two, until we've made an infinite number of comparisons. If we looked at those comparisons, we'd see that purely on the basis of chance variation, group 1 sometimes scored higher than group 2—sometimes by a little, sometimes by a lot—while other times group 2 scored higher than group 1. We could begin creating a frequency distribution of all of those differences.

Because the two samples were always drawn from the same population with the same population mean, we'd expect that over the long run the most frequent difference we'd observe would be zero and that frequencies would diminish as one moved away from that central tendency. Indeed, with extensive repeated sampling (as is done in Monte Carlo simulations), it can be demonstrated that a frequency distribution of differences between two sample means will be normally distributed, with a mean around zero, regardless of whether the population from which the observations are drawn is normal. If that's the case, it should be possible to determine the probability of *any* given difference, as long as we take into account the particular distributional characteristics we're working with. The *t*-statistic that Gossett developed was intended to provide us with exactly that information.

But how extreme is any given *t*-score? Not surprisingly (we hope), we determine that fact by checking our *t*-score against the Student's *t*-distributions, the critical values of which are reproduced in Appendix C. Just to put some flesh on this search, let's return to the example of the faculty members at PU.

Suppose we're interested in comparing 10 male and 10 female faculty members in terms of the relative value they attach to the research and teaching aspects of their job. Table 12.10 shows these hypothetical data; the females have a mean of 2.3 on the 5-point scale, whereas the males have a mean of 3.4. As this suggests, the female faculty members have a mean opinion that's on the "teaching valued more highly" end of the scale, whereas the male faculty members have a mean that's closer to the "research valued more highly" end of the scale (recall Table 12.3). The difference between them is thus 3.4 − 2.3 = 1.1 scale points. But is that difference "significant," or is it within the realm one might expect on the basis of chance variation alone? The computations necessary for deriving a *t*-statistic are shown in Table 12.10; we compare that *t*-value to the critical values summarized in Appendix C.

As with chi-square and *r*-values, critical *t*-values take into account degrees of freedom, which, in this case, are determined by sample size. This is because, all else being equal, two samples of 5 people each are much more likely to have divergent group means than are two samples of 100 people each. The various *t*-distributions reflect this, as do the critical values listed in Appendix C.

Thus, we first compute degrees of freedom, which, for the *t*-test, are given by the formula $df = N_x + N_y - 2$, where N_x is the total number of observations in one group, and N_y is the total number in the other. When the sample sizes of the two groups are equal, the formula is more simply stated as $df = N - 2$, where N is the total number of observations in the two groups taken together. Since we sampled 10 female and 10 male faculty members, for a total $N = 20$, our degrees of freedom equals 20 − 2 = 18. Accordingly, we must look at the line for 18*df* in the list of critical values given in Appendix C; there, we see that the critical value for *t* to be significant at the .05 level is 2.101, while the critical value at the .01 level is 2.878. Thus, the difference between male and female faculty members on the attitude variable, which resulted in a *t*-score of 2.31, exceeds the criterion for $p < .05$ but doesn't exceed the criterion for $p < .01$.

Limits of Two-Variable Analyses

ERROR RATES WHEN UNDERTAKING MULTIPLE ANALYSES

Researchers rarely do studies that involve only two or three variables. It's far more common to have several independent variables, several dependent variables, or a dozen or more questionnaire or observational variables. As the size and complexity of your data collection increase, one possibility is to do more two-group comparisons via the *t*-test or more bivariate (i.e., two-variable) correlations to take the additional variables into account.

But as the number of variables increases, the number of possible comparisons that can be computed increases dramatically. With two groups, for example, only *one* possible comparison (i.e., group 1 versus group 2) can be made. With three groups, there are *three* comparisons possible (1 versus 2; 1 versus 3; 2 versus 3). But with four groups, there are suddenly *six* comparisons possible (1 versus 2; 1 versus 3; 1 versus 4; 2 versus 3; 2 versus 4; 3 versus 4). And by the time we reach 10 groups, there are *45* different two-group comparisons that can be made! Substitute "variables" for "groups" and "correlations" for "comparisons" and you can see that the same is true for correlation coefficients.

You could always just go ahead and do each of those individual comparisons or correlations. But statistically that approach poses a problem. To

Table 12.10

Computing the t-Statistic

The distribution below shows responses for 10 male and 10 female faculty members to the query whether they value the research or teaching aspects of their role more highly; possible responses were were (1) teaching much more highly valued; (2) teaching somewhat more highly valued; (3) teaching and research equally valued; (4) research somewhat more highly valued; (5) research much more highly valued.

Males (X)	Females (Y)	X^2	Y^2
2	1	4	1
2	1	4	1
3	1	9	1
3	2	9	4
3	2	9	4
4	2	16	4
4	3	16	9
4	3	16	9
4	4	16	16
5	4	25	16
$\Sigma X = 34$	$\Sigma Y = 23$	$\Sigma X^2 = 124$	$\Sigma Y^2 = 65$
$N = 10$	$N = 10$		
Mean $= 3.4$	Mean $= 2.3$		

Computation

1. Take the sum of the scores in group 1 (males): $\Sigma X = 34$
2. Square the sum of group 1 scores: $(\Sigma X)^2 = 1156$
3. Square *each score* in group 1, and take the sum of those squared scores: $\Sigma X^2 = 124$
4. Note the number of scores in group 1: $N_x = 10$
5. Compute the mean score for group 1: $\bar{X}_w = 3.4$
6. Take the sum of the scores in group 2 (females): $\Sigma Y = 23$
7. Square the sum of group 2 scores: $(\Sigma Y)^2 = 529$
8. Square *each score* in group 2, and take the sum of those squared scores: $\Sigma Y^2 = 65$
9. Note the number of scores in group 2: $N_y = 10$
10. Compute the mean score for group 2: $\bar{Y}_w = 2.3$
11. Enter the appropriate figures into the following formula for the computation of t:

$$t = \sqrt{\frac{\left[\left(\Sigma X^2 - \frac{(\Sigma X^2)}{N_X}\right) + \left(\Sigma Y^2 - \frac{(\Sigma Y^2)}{N_Y}\right)\right]}{N_X + N_Y - 2} \times \left[\frac{1}{N_X} + \frac{1}{N_Y}\right]}$$

$$= \sqrt{\frac{\left[\left(124 - \frac{1156}{10}\right) + \left(65 - \frac{529}{10}\right)\right]}{10 + 10 - 2} \times \left[\frac{1}{10} + \frac{1}{10}\right]}$$

Table 12.10

(continued)

$$= \frac{1.1}{\sqrt{\left[\frac{(8.4)+(12.1)}{18}\right] \times \left[\frac{2}{10}\right]}}$$

$$= \frac{1.1}{\sqrt{(1.14)(0.2)}} = \frac{1.1}{\sqrt{0.228}} = \frac{1.1}{0.477} = 2.31$$

12. Compute the degrees of freedom by taking the number of observations in group 1, plus the number of observations in group 2, minus 2, i.e., $df = N_x + N_y - 2 = 10 + 10 - 2 = 18$.

13. Determine whether the observed correlation is statistically significant by inspecting the critical values listed in Appendix C, for the appropriate degrees of freedom. You should see that for 18df, the critical values that must be met or exceeded are $t = 2.101$ and $t = 2.878$ for $p < .05$ and $p < .01$, respectively. Thus, our observed difference in the current example would be considered statistically significant at $p < .05$, but not at $p < .01$.

understand why, recall that the notion of "statistical significance" suggests that we find a point on the distribution under consideration (i.e., chi-square, t, r) where we can feel confident that a difference is "real" or "reliable." We can never be certain that a difference is real; we can only be confident to varying degrees. Traditionally, the social sciences have adopted $p < .05$ as the default criterion, that is, the criterion to use unless there's some reason, articulated beforehand, to do otherwise. We choose that level because 95 percent confidence (i.e., in all likelihood being "right" 95 out of 100, or 19 out of 20, times) represents "good odds" that our decision to treat a difference (or correlation) as real is appropriate.

The other side of that figure, however, is that on approximately 5 out of 100 occasions, or in 1 out of 20 situations, we'll be *wrong*—we'll proclaim a result to be reliable when in fact it is not. If we're making only one comparison or a few comparisons, we're prepared to live with that uncertainty. But if 20 or 50 or 100 comparisons are made, the odds are high that some of the comparisons we observe to be "statistically significant" will in fact be spurious. If only a few of those comparisons are significant, we probably shouldn't be terribly excited by them; they're probably mere ephemeral shadows that will disappear next time we look at them. If you compute 100 correlation coefficients, for example,

the odds are that around 5 of them will emerge as statistically significant purely on the basis of chance variation alone. Accordingly, researchers must be particularly cautious when interpreting the results of numerous tests on the same set of data.

There are at least three ways around this problem, however. The **Bonferroni technique** involves splitting the adopted probability required for significance across the entire range of comparisons to be made (e.g., see Kirk 1968; Pedhazur 1982). For example, if you're adopting a significance level of $p < .05$ and plan to undertake 10 separate t-tests (or chi-squares or Pearson correlations), the Bonferroni procedure involves merely spreading the .05 (known as the *experiment-wise error rate*) across the 10 comparisons, with the result that a .05/10 = .005 significance level would have to be achieved on any given comparison before you'd be prepared to consider it "reliable." This approach makes for rather conservative testing (since a .005, or 5/1000, criterion is a very stringent one), but this is considered preferable to engaging in "much ado about nothing."

Alternatively, if you're in the luxurious situation of having a very large number of cases (e.g., 10 times as many cases as you have variables), your data are amenable to a procedure known as **jackknifing**. There are several ways to do this, but the simplest is to randomly split your sample of cases into *two* samples, do the analyses you want to do separately in the two samples, and then focus only on those results that emerge as statistically significant in *both* data sets.

The logic of this approach is that while some correlations or comparisons may well turn out to be statistically significant on the basis of chance error when one is doing a large number of these calculations in one sample, it's highly unlikely that specific chance occurrences will replicate on a second occasion. Only those with some substance to them will do so, and hence only those that can pass the significance hurdle *twice* are thought to warrant further consideration and discussion.

The third alternative is to learn some more techniques that have been developed precisely in order to overcome that error rate problem. The **analysis of variance (ANOVA)**, for example, is conceptually akin to doing multiple *t*-tests on a given set of data, but controls for error rate in the process. Similarly, **multiple regression analysis** has been developed to deal with situations in which one is attempting to correlate many variables with some criterion (dependent) measure. But these techniques are beyond the scope of this book, so you'll have to await further courses in statistics to see how they work.

SUMMING UP AND LOOKING AHEAD

This chapter has been one of the more difficult ones in this book to write, in large part because keeping it true to the book's themes has involved an articulation of the logic underlying selected quantitative techniques, more so than describing how to do them. As the book's title suggests, the overall emphasis is on looking at research as a *decision-making* process, and it's impossible to make decisions unless you know what conceptual issues lie underneath. Accordingly, we've tried to explain the various formulas in terms of the logic through which they were derived.

The chapter begins with a discussion of *variables* and *constants* and then introduces the notion of *levels of measurement,* explaining the differences between

nominal, ordinal, interval, and ratio scales. One's level of measurement influences, to some degree, the range of statistics with which a variable may be analyzed. At the same time, it is not the empirical variable per se, but the underlying *theoretical* variable that's most important to consider when identifying our level of measurement—and hence which particular statistical operations are appropriate.

A number of *descriptive techniques*—frequency distributions, pie charts, bar charts, histograms, frequency polygons—are then discussed as ways of presenting distributions of obtained data. The task is to explain how one describes those distributions statistically. Indicators of *central tendency* include the mode, the median, and the mean; each is an appropriate summary statistic in some situations, but each can also be misused. Also included is a discussion of descriptors of distributional *variability,* including the range, the standard deviation, and the variance.

The focus then turns to *inferential statistics* that can be used to examine the relationships among variables. A distinction is made between those statistics that focus on the degree of *association* among variables (e.g., chi-square, correlation) and those that focus on examining the *differences* between groups (e.g., *z*-scores, *t*-tests). These tests are called inferential statistics because we're ultimately less interested in the sample per se than in using the sample as a vehicle through which to make inferences about populations.

First, the section on inferential statistics looks at examining relationships among categorical variables. The *cross-tabulation* or *contingency table* is a way to represent such *bivariate* relationships, while the *chi-square* statistic is the appropriate measure of the extent to which observed cell frequencies deviate from those expected on a purely chance basis. Comparing a computed chi-square statistic to its chi-square distribution gives the probability that the deviations we observe would occur on the basis of chance alone. Using the concept of *degrees of freedom* and Appendix A, you can determine the criterion value your chi-square statistic must meet or exceed in order to be proclaimed significant. A "statistically significant" result implies 95 percent or 99 percent confidence in stating that the distribution was unlikely to have been obtained by chance variation alone, suggesting that the two categorical variables are indeed associated with one another.

The chapter then scrutinizes ways to examine the relationship between two continuous variables. The *scatter-plot diagram* can be used to illustrate such bivariate distributions, and the *Pearson product–moment correlation coefficient* describes the direction and magnitude of a linear relationship. The critical values in Appendix B, along with the degrees of freedom, determine the particular criterion value that must be matched or exceeded in order for the correlation to be declared significantly greater than zero.

But a significant correlation coefficient does *not* tell us whether the underlying theoretical variables are, in fact, related or whether the association, however strong, is a causal one. A nonsignificant *r*-value doesn't necessarily mean that there's *no* relationship between the variables. Pearson's *r* tells you only about significant *linear* relationships; other curvilinear relationships may or may not exist and must be tested for separately.

Attention then turns to techniques that emphasize the assessment of difference; these normally involve looking at differences between groups (a categorical variable) on some continuous variable, that is, a comparison of group means. The *t*-statistic and *t*-distribution are useful in comparing two group means. But while a significant *t*-score leads us to conclude that the two groups do indeed differ, discerning the reasons *why* they differ remains an analytical (rather than purely statistical) task. Rival plausible explanations must be considered.

With the analysis of your data behind you, it's time to start writing it all up in a final research report. The next chapter looks at how to do that.

STUDY QUESTIONS

1. Distinguish between *variables* and *constants*. Show that you understand the difference between them by identifying three variables and three constants that might be used to describe the people in your research methods class.

2. Give examples of one variable at each of the four levels of measurement, and explain in your own words why that is the correct label for each.

3. "Measures of length and distance are ratio-level variables no matter what theoretical variable they are being used as operationalizations for." Would you agree or disagree? Explain.

4. Prepare a brief questionnaire that includes variables at all four levels of measurement. Designate your variable names, and state explicitly what level of measurement you feel each is being measured at. Invent responses; then prepare frequency distributions and compute summary statistics for each.

5. Perform appropriate bivariate analyses on the data gathered for Study Question 4.

6. For what kinds of variables (or levels of measurement) are the mean, median, and mode considered appropriate descriptors of central tendency?

7. In a recent edition of your local newspaper, look for an article that offers statistical information. Would you consider the data well presented? Why or why not?

8. Why is the standard deviation a "better" indicator of dispersion than the range, for interval-, and ratio-level variables?

9. Acquire data from the relevant person at your educational institution (e.g., office of analytical studies, personnel office, faculty association, or union) regarding your university or college faculty (e.g., information concerning distributions of sex, visible-minority status, rank, salary levels, years employed, etc.), and undertake an analysis of those data. Are they consistent with the view that you're attending an egalitarian educational institution? Offer rival plausible explanations, and indicate the sorts of data you might seek or generate to look into the matter further.

10. Encourage the professor in your research methods class (if s/he does not do so already) to tell you not only the class mean on your most recent or next quiz or exam, but also the standard deviation. What was your grade on that exam? What z-score would that be?

11. Hollie gets 87 percent on her final exam in Syrian Epistemology, where the mean of the class was 80 percent with a standard deviation of 5 percent; she manages to get 93 percent in Neo-Gregorian Chants, where the mean of the class was also 80 percent with a standard deviation of 15 percent. In sum, she scored above the mean in both cases. Compared to her respective classmates, however, did she do better at Syrian Epistemology or at Neo-Gregorian Chants?

12. Why do we need to know the degrees of freedom in our data before checking whether the chi-square or r- or t-value we have is significant?

13. Why is a high, statistically significant r-value not necessarily indicative of a causal relationship between the two variables being correlated?

14. A researcher computes bivariate correlations between pairs of variables by hand and ends up with correlation coefficients of –0.46, +0.52, +0.83, –1.04, and –0.87.
    a. Which of those r-values *must* be incorrect? Why?
    b. Of the remaining values, which represents the strongest association between two variables?
    c. For the correlation coefficient you chose in 14(b), what proportion of variance do the two variables share?

15. A researcher asks a sample of 47 males and 52 females whether they support the idea of censorship for sexually violent films. Among the females, 37 say yes, 11 say no, and 4 are uncertain. In contrast, 22 of the males say yes, 19 say no, and 6 are uncertain. Create a contingency table to depict these data. Do

the necessary computations to learn whether there's a significant association between sex and opinions regarding censorship in that sample.

16. A graduate student wants to test out the notion that there is an inverted-U-shaped relationship between anxiety and performance (i.e., whether performance is lowest with either very low or very high levels of anxiety, and highest with moderate levels of anxiety). Given that the relevant data are gathered, would the Pearson correlation coefficient offer a useful way of testing whether the hypothesized relationship is indeed found? Why or why not?

17. A student gathers data on 15 variables from a sample of 100 shoppers at a local mall and proceeds to intercorrelate all the variables, resulting in a total of 105 different correlation coefficients having been computed. Although disappointed at the fact that not many of the relationships prove to be statistically significant, he's pleased to see that seven of them are, and he writes up an analysis that focuses on those seven. Is that a reasonable thing for him to do? What if he increases his sample size to include 200 shoppers?

18. What is the *Bonferroni procedure,* and when might you use it?

NOTES

1. Dr. Chakrapani is currently president of Leger Marketing, an independent research firm, and distinguished visiting professor at Ted Rogers School of Management at Ryerson University in Toronto, Ontario.

2. Although such data may also appear in qualitative research, people conducting qualitative research typically place greater emphasis on target sampling and flexibility in data collection, rather than on standardizing data collection and the opportunities for aggregation and comparison that such standardization allows.

3. You may well quibble about that statement, since there are many instances of legitimate scientific research that has taken place nowhere but in the mind of a scientist. Albert Einstein, for example, was well known for his reporting of the thought experiments that culminated in the development of the general theory of relativity. But this shouldn't detract from the general applicability of the assertion we're footnoting: the social sciences have taken great pride in their emphasis on the need to engage the world and gather data.

4. Altemeyer's (1970) research was done with adult university students; some authors therefore suggest that greater skepticism is warranted (i.e., not assuming greater than ordinal-level measurement on such scales) when dealing with samples of young children, the cognitively challenged, or dyslexic or innumerate people.

5. The Kelvin scale, in contrast, *is* an example of ratio-level measurement, since its zero point represents absolute zero or a total absence of molecular motion.

6. This is not to say that "anything goes"; students are advised to follow the general principles of analysis stated here until they know enough about statistical and measurement issues to know when deviations from the "rules" are permissible.

7. This brings us back to the whole question of *categories,* discussed earlier in this chapter, and to the philosophical issues that underlie the choice of one summarizing/categorizing scheme over another, for example, Why are marbles worth describing? And why is describing marbles by their colour any more or less meaningful than describing them in terms of size, hardness, or whatever?

8. Figure 12.6(a) shows what's known as a "normal" distribution. Such distributions are of considerable theoretical importance, since most of the inferential statistics we'll discuss are based on the assumption that the scores

for any variable are normally distributed in the population. We'll consider the normal distribution in more detail shortly.

9. Another mathematical convention is that smaller or negative numbers go to the left end of any graph, and positive and larger numbers go to the right. When discussing theoretical distributions, mathematicians generally assume that values can range from negative infinity (at the left end of the x-axis, or abscissa) through zero (in the middle) to positive infinity (at the right end of the x-axis).

10. Just in case it is not immediately evident what we are doing, note from the "Cumulative %" column of Table 12.4 that 24.25 percent of the sample has "9 years" of experience or less. By the time we get to the end of the group that has "10 years" of experience, we have included 27.50 percent of the sample. Thus, the 25 percent point comes among those people who are in the "10 years" category.

11. The technique we're using here is to take a situation where we "know" what the answer "should" be—because we start with a situation that has been constructed to deal with a certain type of problem—in order to try out different possibilities to see what will give us an acceptable answer. In this case, we've created the example in Table 12.6 to show how misleading the range can be and to pose the problem of how we can differentiate between two distributions that have identical characteristics in many respects (e.g., same range; same mean, median, and mode; same number of observations), but that are so clearly different in their dispersion.

12. This in itself should give us pause, since rather than taking them as givens, one might wish to pay separate scrutiny to why the male:female ratio deviates from 50:50 and why the rank structure is the way it is.

13. The chi-square statistic, like all the others we'll be discussing in this chapter, requires that we express our hypotheses (e.g., that

there is a significant relationship between sex and rank) as *null hypotheses* (i.e., that there is *no* relationship between sex and rank). The reasons for this will be explained shortly.

14. The figure 21.8 percent is not in the table. We computed it by noting that in the column "21–25 Yes," there was a total of 78 hirings, 17 of which were women. This works out to (17/78) × 100 = 21.8 percent. We'll leave it to you to check whether the percentages we've shown for the remaining four columns are correct.

15. Recall from Chapter 10 that *mortality* refers to people who drop out of the sample and, hence, out of the analysis. All we have to go on here is the hiring history of those men and women who are here today. It may be that there were many more women (and/or men) who were hired but who died, moved to other universities, or entered other professions. A more complete analysis would thus require going back over archival hiring records to see to what extent "mortality" existed, and particularly whether rates of mortality were essentially similar or significantly different for the men and women who were hired.

16. Our definition of equity here assumes that in an egalitarian setting, the characteristics of the sample (e.g., faculty members) will be representative of the distribution of those characteristics in the broader society. For example, if 50 percent of the people in Canada are female, then, if this were a completely egalitarian society, one would expect that approximately 50 percent of the university faculty would be female, 50 percent of the engineers would be women, and so on.

17. We derived this number from an SPSS printout we undertook to doublecheck all our calculations.

18. Our understanding is that the letter *r* was chosen because it is the first letter in the word *relationship.*

19. This is arbitrarily done, in the same way that we arbitrarily set percentages to be based out of 100, or the way we set probabilities to run from zero to one.

20. Criterion values are expressed only in terms of the *magnitude* of the relationship; the direction doesn't matter.

21. Incidentally, this implies that the variance is also 1.0, since the variance is the square of the standard deviation.

22. Budding historians are asked in advance to forgive us for the story that follows, which is best described as an academic "docudrama" rather than a historically accurate rendition of discovery. Our interest was in articulating a logical progression of thoughts that would help illuminate the nature of the statistic being discussed. Our description may or may not actually represent the flow of Gossett's thinking when he developed the *t*-statistic.

WRITING YOUR RESEARCH REPORT

You're in the home stretch now. You worked out your research question, you designed the research and made a proposal that satisfied you and others in your attention to ethics issues, you gathered all the quantitative and/or qualitative data, you did some preliminary analyses that led you to believe you have some understanding of your data, and now you're ready to start writing it all up.

There are many splendid books and chapters within books that offer advice about how to write research reports. For example, Howard Becker's *Writing for Sociologists* (1986) is a great one that continues to be used widely. Another is Harry Wolcott's (1992) *Writing Up Qualitative Research*. Psychologists can consult the *Publication Manual* published by the American Psychological Association (1994). *The Elements of Style* (1999), by William Strunk Jr. is another classic. In chapters, Lofland and colleagues (2006) offer useful advice on writing in *Analyzing Social Settings*, as does Berg (2007) in *Qualitative Research Methods for the Social Sciences*. And of course, more and more resources appear every year on the Internet.[1]

Although we will duplicate some of their coverage, our emphasis is on suggesting general organizational considerations that you should keep in mind when writing. These considerations apply to your final research report, whether it's a term research project for a course, an article for publication, or a report you're writing as a consultant or agency researcher. We'll begin with some very general observations about the process of writing—and some of the problems people have with it—and conclude with more specific considerations that should be kept in mind for the various sections of your report and the linkages between them.

SOME GENERAL THOUGHTS ABOUT WRITING

Get Comfortable

One of the fascinating things we have found (that will someday be the focus of a research project) is that everyone has certain habits—one might even call them rituals or compulsions—that go along with feeling comfortable and able to write. These are highly personal practices that make little or no rational sense and serve no apparent purpose other than allowing you to feel like you can sit down and write. Some people need to clean the house first. Some need to sharpen pencils. Some like to have music playing while others require complete silence. Some prefer to write on a computer; others would rather write on paper and transcribe to a computer later.

Nor are the two of us immune to these nesting behaviours. Ted needs to play one game of Sudoku before he starts to write each day, prefers silence and darkness, and is most happy writing on his home desktop computer with its three monitors that allow electronic documents and whatever else to be posted on the sides while focusing on the document he is writing in the middle. This is actually a big change from when he was in graduate school, at which point writing simply did not feel right unless he was doing it on yellow lined pads with a Mont Blanc fountain pen using chocolate brown ink. Chris has a multi-monitor desktop setup similar to Ted's but prefers to work in the middle of what Ted would find multimedia chaos: lots of visual stimuli outside his third storey window; movies and/or

TV programs and/or music (often more than one at a time) playing in the background.

Get to know what your rituals are and give in to them. While at one level they make "no rational sense," we view them like the sleeping rituals that people go through that are part of having a good night's sleep. In many cases they often are the transition time in which you get rid of other mental clutter and get your thinking focused on this task, and this paper, and what you want to say.

Spew It Out

If there is one thing common to professional life in all sorts of disciplinary domains it is writing. We know that academics are supposed to write articles and books, but academics are not the only people who are expected to write on an ongoing basis. Most professions require you to have the skills to write reports, or memos, or letters, or report cards, or briefing notes, or press releases, or case summaries, or policy recommendations, and on and on. It is fascinating, therefore, that whenever the discussion in our classes turns to writing, one of the first things we find out is how few people there are who enjoy writing. Most reactions seem to range from "can do it if I have to" to a kind of paralytic fear that leaves people staring at a blank page or computer monitor waiting for that magical opening sentence they hope will open the floodgates, and waiting, and waiting.

Becker (1986) suggests the biggest cause of this deer-in-the-headlights paralysis is the mistaken belief that one draft and perhaps at most a mini-edit are all it should take to produce a decent paper. This creates huge pressure, unrealistic expectations, and a sense of failure when students try and do their first college or university research paper in one late-night marathon and come up short. Step One is thus to get real and understand, first of all, that the typical university or college paper is more complex in terms of the ideas being knocked around than was the case in high school. Step Two is to realize that there is a sampling problem here—all you ever see that anyone else has written is their final product; what you typically don't see is what it took to get there.

Writing is a bit like driving to a place you've never visited before. Some general principles and a roadmap will help get you there, but it's not until you've arrived and have a clear sense of your destination that you can begin to determine the "best" route and where you can flatly and easily reject some possibilities as "dead ends" or "the wrong direction." However, that is sometimes easier said than done when it comes to writing, where we often discover new things as we try explaining to someone else what we think we know. Gaps in our understanding begin to appear. We realize that the flow of logic we thought was so impervious to criticism is more porous than we imagined. Or we find the order in which we decided to tell the story turns out not to work that well after all. Discovering any of these is not a bad thing. These unanticipated problems are actually one reason we enjoy writing—not *really* knowing what we think about something until we have written it down and worked through all the details (e.g., see also Richardson 2003).

The main implication is that we need to think of writing from the very start as something other than a one-shot deal. To use the driving analogy again, think of your task as one of describing the best route to this new destination. The major accomplishment of your first draft is simply that it's done—and "getting there" is in itself no small feat—but that first draft still contains all the wrong turns, misreading of maps, traffic jams, dead ends, and so on. It's a route that got you there but is by no means the most direct route. Now, there *are* times when you might actually want to describe that *whole* journey, for example, when you're 80 and explaining in your memoirs all the trials and tribulations you faced *en route* to those great ideas that brought you the Nobel Prize, but in most cases the rest of the world just wants to know what your point is, how you came to that conclusion, and what it means for them. To do that, we need to take our first draft and start whittling it down to the essentials, the basic information the reader needs to know to understand and travel the route.

The message here is that good writing is a *process* that will always take more than one draft, and this is true regardless of how good and experienced a writer you are. It normally takes no less than five, and often more than 10, drafts before we think of our work as done; Ted has the record between us with 26 drafts of a report that he and a colleague prepared regarding confidentiality issues. First drafts stick out like a sore thumb: they wander all over the place; they sound like you are making it up as you go along; and they're generally pretty boring because it's never really that clear where you're taking the reader. How many drafts do you need to do? As many as it takes. There *does* come a point of diminishing returns, where you're better off getting the paper out there to have other people read it, but a big part of good writing is being super-compulsive about wanting to get it right.

Generally speaking, the idea is to say what you need with as much economy as possible, but doing so—making every word count—is a very time-consuming process. It reminds us of a quotation from Pascal, who wrote a long letter to his friend and concluded by saying, "I have only made this [letter] longer because I did not have the leisure time to make it shorter."[2] Being concise takes time; allow for at least one more draft than you do now.

Understanding that the first is no more than that—the first draft—should take the pressure off you to feel that the world will end if your first draft is not perfect. Like Becker (1986), if you are sitting there looking at an empty monitor, we encourage you to make your first draft nothing more than a "spew" draft where you simply spit out your story, saying everything you feel you might want to say as quickly as you can type or write it down without recourse to notes. Spewing it out gets it down so that you can work on it. By promising yourself that you will not look at any notes you give yourself permission to make mistakes because, after all, who can simply write a first draft off the top of their heads? After the spew draft comes reflection: Is the story complete? Or are there parts of the story that have not yet been told that need to be included? Are *all* the parts currently there necessary for the story? Are there "extra" parts that are not crucial to your story that can be discarded? Going through this exercise is helpful because it helps you identify all the essential pieces of the puzzle, helps you get rid of extra fluff, and shows you what work needs to be done in the second and subsequent drafts. And in the end, the only draft that matters is the last one; no one will see the others, so say whatever you want in them because they are only a way of getting to the one that counts.

Speak to Your Audience

There is no One Right Way to do a paper. Any given story can be told equally well in several different ways, with the final look of it depending on what works for you in allowing you to tell the story you wish to tell, in the style that you are comfortable telling it, *and* that speaks to the audience to whom you are telling that story.

Knowing your audience helps you with two crucial elements—assumptions and vocabulary. "Assumptions" are important because what you can assume will vary from audience to audience. For example, if you are writing to a highly specialized audience who shares your exact research interests, you will already share understandings such as what the "classics" in the area are; what issues are current; and what methods are normally used to study your problem or question. In that case you can be very direct, use specialized vocabulary that you can assume people in the area will know, and will probably spend most of your time outlining your analysis, the elements that lead to your conclusions, and their implications for other researchers in the area.

Knowing your audience also means that you take into account what their expectations will be, i.e., what elements must be there before they accept your story as both solid and complete. With a professional but more general-interest audience you will have to take the time to contextualize your problem or question a bit, but can probably still assume a fair amount in terms of shared understandings about methods and sampling, for example. Non-professional audiences will need more in the way of contextualization, and you will probably end up spending less time on the actual analysis other than to perhaps give an illustration or two. The papers you write for your professors represent a situation where it is probably best to assume a certain degree of ignorance because part of what you are trying to do is to show that you understand your course material sufficiently well enough to apply it. Even though your research methods professor will no doubt know what "internal validity" is, for example, you will want to explain it and show how it applies in your research as a way of showing you understand. But no matter who your audience is, we have to disagree with the sentiment that Calvin and Hobbes express in Figure 13.1; there is no reason whatsoever for academic writing to be a boring, impenetrable fog.

Your medium of writing may vary depending on your audience as well. One of the big mistakes many people make when giving oral presentations is that they write down speaking notes as if they were writing a paper, and then use those notes for their presentation, often reading them in painstakingly boring detail. We speak differently than we write: the cadence is different; there is more room for informality; and we typically need to speak more directly and less complexly so that people can follow our thoughts with fewer visual cues than exist on paper. After we *read* a sentence, it is easy to go back over it again to ensure we understand it; after we *hear* a sentence, it is gone, and so it is more incumbent on us to ensure we are not leaving any listeners behind. One way to deal with this is to actually "write" your paper by dictating it into a speech recognition program such as Dragon Naturally Speaking, which will leave you with a transcript that you can then use as the first draft of your presentation. Another trick is to make sure that you read each draft out loud—and not just in your head —to hear what the words will sound like when you actually say them. Do they come out of your mouth naturally? Or do they sound too pompous, technical, and awkward? Even better, have a friend read your draft to you so you can hear what you are saying sounds like to your audience. If you don't have any friends available you can use the built in text-to-speech option that almost every word processor and operating system has and you can have the computer read your paper to you.

Pass It Around

Once you have a draft that you feel does the job, get someone else to read it. Faculty members who write alone are always looking to circulate papers among knowledgeable colleagues looking for critical feedback. Those who write collaboratively have each other as drafts go back and forth, but they, too, come to a point where another set of eyes is needed. This may come from simply passing the draft over to another colleague you know will be interested in the topic, by submitting the article to a journal so that it can undergo peer review, or, as is the case with this book, by involving a professional copy editor who goes through what we have written

Figure 13.1: Academic writing doesn't have to be esoteric and boring

word-by-word and line-by-line to rein in our verbal excesses, ensure our language is consistent, and make suggestions about wording that makes our point more directly and efficiently.

Of course one thing that faculty members often have are the luxuries of choice and time. We are the ones who decide that it is time for an article or book to be written, and although we often have deadlines to deal with, especially when we have agreed to write a chapter for a book or have signed a book contract, the choice of whether to commit to any of those projects in the first place is ours. In contrast, your deadlines are imposed by your professors and are typically within a single semester course, which means that being well-organized, getting an early start, and ensuring that you leave yourself enough time at the end for redrafting and perhaps exchanging drafts with a friend should be a high priority. Another function this serves is that it gives you time to think about other things during the time your friend is reading your work, which allows you to take a fresh look at what you have done when you read it again. As Howie Becker once told Ted, we learn far more from rewriting than from writing.

The main trick here is to understand that criticism is good—not something to shelter yourself from—because it can improve your final product and make you a better writer. The two of us really learned to write when faculty members we respected spent the hours it took to make line-by-line and word-by-word commentary on our work. Although a sea of red ink on a hard copy or dozens of "track changes" in a document file may be momentarily disappointing, the better way to see these responses is that they have been written by someone who cared enough about you and saw enough value in your work to take the time to give detailed commentary and encourage you along. Ted will always feel indebted to Bob Altemeyer at the University of Manitoba for the care he took in commenting on Ted's early papers, while Chris acknowledges the similar role played by John Lowman and Dalia Vukmirovich at Simon Fraser University in that regard.

TELLING YOUR STORY

We title this section "Telling Your Story" because there are many parallels between writing a research report and writing a story or screenplay. Novelists, playwrights, and screenwriters will all tell you that every story has three parts to it: a beginning, a middle, and an end. Those same parts exist in every research report as well. Let's wander through each of those sections and discuss the kinds of considerations that are involved.

Beginning

The *Introduction* is where the characters are introduced and the stage is set; your "characters" will be things like articles from the literature or perspectives on a problem (which typically are tied to sources in the literature). Which characters are appropriate for you to introduce will depend on the research questions that guided your research and what you want your report to focus on now that you're finished.

We make a distinction here between "your research" and "your report" because the two are not the same. During the research design and data-gathering process there's always a tendency to gather more data than you will actually use. The common view is "better too much data than too little," so we always stretch a little further than we originally intended to ensure we've covered all our bases and have some sense of the broader context in which our core research fits. Because of this, it is typical that you do *not* describe all of your research or detail all of your findings in a single report, in the same manner you will not cite everything you read or discuss everything you thought while you were doing the research. The journey that research involves can be a lengthy one with assorted side trips and dead ends, but the objective of your final written report is to tell a focused, concise story. The only things that appear on paper are elements that help that story get told. Get to the point.

If you are writing a relatively short research report, like a journal article or term project (i.e., anything up to about 25 double-spaced pages), then your cast of characters will be lean; no one should be introduced who does not have an important role to play. Longer projects, such as honours or graduate theses, which can be anywhere from 50 to hundreds of pages long and allow commensurately more room for character introduction, in part because you are allowed in those contexts to tell a more elaborate and complicated story. However, you should still be judicious about what is included, and everything that appears in your final draft should be there for a purpose. This requires having a preliminary sense of what your paper is about because that is a prerequisite to being able to decide what is "relevant" and "necessary" to include.

PROVIDING AN "INTERESTING" FRAME

Speaking to your audience means making it "interesting" for them, so one thing you want to do right at the start is to whet that interest by explaining why reading your paper is the most important thing a member of your intended audience can do. But what makes a paper "interesting"? Murray Davis (1971) asked a similar question when he decided to try and figure out what makes different *theories* "interesting." To address the topic he first determined which theories were most frequently represented in sociology textbooks—and took these as his sample of theories that were considered "interesting" enough to write about—and then considered whether there were any discernible differences between the theories that appeared frequently in texts and others that covered similar ground but did not garner the same attention.

Davis opened his article by suggesting we need to reconsider theoretical/methodological lore, which tells us the theories that get the most attention are those that best explain data. In fact, the truth is much more "interesting" than that:

> It has long been thought that a theorist is considered great because his theories are true, but this is false. A theorist is considered great, not because his theories are true, but because they are interesting. (309)

Davis's introduction is actually itself an example of a principle he explains in the article, which is that one way to catch readers' attention is to challenge what they believe to be true, or what the literature believes to be true. The general form would be along the lines of, "One state of affairs *seems* to be the case, or is *believed* to be the case, but in fact *something else* is true." Much of his article involves the elaboration of that basic principle in a variety of different scenarios, e.g., what seems stable is actually changing; what seems disorganized and chaotic is actually highly structured and predictable; phenomena that seem very diverse are in fact all essentially similar. And this holds for their opposites as well, that is, something that always seems to be changing is in fact very stable, what seems structured and predictable is actually highly chaotic and disorganized, and some things that seem very similar need to be distinguished.

If there is a general message here about what makes something interesting, it is that readers are captivated when we challenge what they know, when we give information that encourages a new way of thinking about an issue, or when we inform them on a topic they know little about. The question for you as an author therefore becomes how best to present your research so that readers immediately see the value it might have for them. Some of the specific ways these justifications play out include the following:

1. "The common wisdom says" or "Everyone knows" X is true. But is it?

   So much of what we "know" is based on "the common wisdom" or what "everyone knows," which often turns out not to be true at all. If your research was designed to shed light on such a state of affairs, and particularly if your findings *do* challenge people's assumptions, then inform readers of that right from the start.

2. Some people think X is true. Some people think Y. What is going on?

   Controversy is interesting. If you've been doing research in an area where there has been considerable debate about what is "true" and/or where there has been disagreement over the "appropriate" thing to do, then offering your report as an effort to better understand and perhaps resolve the controversy is another way of capturing your reader's attention.

3. Our policies (and/or procedures) about X assume that Y is the case. But is it?

Policies and procedures always involve understandings or assumptions about (1) the nature of the problem the policy was designed to address, (2) the people for whom the policy is intended, (3) those who will be responsible for implementing the policy, and (4) what options led this particular policy initiative to be considered the "best" way for dealing with the situation at hand. If our research was designed to address these assumptions, then one way to frame our research is to identify the assumption and assert our interest in testing it out, for example, by seeing whether the people who apply for a program really are of a certain type or whether the treatment (or supplement or method) really is the best one available, and so on.

4. X is a phenomenon we know little about. It is interesting because …

There are many things in the world that catch our interest but that we don't know much about. It may be a relatively new phenomenon or a bourgeoning phenomenon that is only now starting to appear on our radar screen. If your research pertains to such a phenomenon, then your introduction should describe what we know about it and supply any information about the pervasiveness of the phenomenon and/or the attention the issue has been receiving.

5. A theory suggests a certain phenomenon is interesting.

Those taking a more deductive approach may be engaged in explicit theory testing and may well have decided to investigate a particular

phenomenon because it so clearly embodies the conditions addressed by the theory and, hence, is conducive to testing hypotheses derived from the theory. If that is the case, then your introduction should explain the theory and articulate the connection you see between the theory and the research setting or phenomenon.

HOOKS

Remember that the primary purpose of your introduction is simply to introduce the research that you've done, but recall also how we said that part of the trick of writing well is to identify all of the pieces of the puzzle that you are trying to put together. It is for this reason that some people suggest that you should actually leave the writing of your introduction to the end. Becker (1986), for example, recalls how one of his mentors, Everett Hughes, would tell him, "Introductions are supposed to introduce. How can you introduce something you haven't written yet? You don't know what it is. Get it written and then you can introduce it" (80).

While there is a lot to be said for writing the introduction last, we personally do not do it that way, preferring instead to take a shot at an introduction even though we know it is no more than a preliminary statement of what we think the paper will be about, and thus knowing that one of our future editing tasks will be to figure out what parts of our first draft still belong, what in the end was irrelevant, and what is missing that needs to be included. But lying behind these statements is another lesson about writing your papers—the various parts of it must interconnect, be consistent, and lead from one to the next.

For example, Patricia Ratel (2008) focused on single-parent mothers who were trying to balance the demands of single parenthood with those of being a student trying to complete a degree. In her introduction, Ratel cited several key findings from the literature that deals with women who balance parenting with other life demands (usually work), including noting that (1) most single-parents are women; (2) women in that situation are often in poverty and/or living on social assistance; (3) balancing the demands of single parenthood with other responsibilities has impacts for the mother such as sleeplessness, poor nutrition, high stress, and an inadequate social life; (4) social resources one can rely on to share the burden of responsibility are important; and (5) impacts on the children include their becoming "latchkey" children and having more than the usual level of responsibility placed on them at a young age.

We call these elements "hooks" because they are the themes on which the rest of the paper will hang. What you talk about in the introduction should be what you will have included in your research, which is what you should talk about in your results, which is what you should highlight in your conclusions. And indeed, after noting in her introduction that most single-parents are women, we are not surprised to hear in a later section that her own research focuses on women.[3] When she tells us about her interviews, we are not surprised to hear that she will ask about finances, social resources, impacts on the women, and impacts on their children. This in turn sets up the conclusion that connects back to those themes she introduced at the beginning.

You should be able to see more clearly now what we mean when we say that the biggest challenge in writing a tight paper is in determining what puzzle pieces you have to work with, and ensuring that you keep that consistency throughout the paper. Similarly, when we say that you should expect to do multiple drafts, it is because part of your job will be to ensure that each of the sections "speaks to" and sets up the next, which will give your paper continuity and flow.

Middle

The middle of the paper is normally the largest part—as in any film or novel—because it is the place where the plot thickens as we articulate all the specifics of our research. This includes a *Methods* section, where we describe *what we did* (our

procedures, including any research instruments) and *with whom or with what we did it* (our research sample), and a *Results* section, which outlines *what we found* (the data). Let's consider each in turn.

METHODS

There are a number of elements that need to be included in any methods section. One would be to describe your sampling and solicitation procedures and the sample that resulted: who or what were your basic units of analysis? where did you find them? how did you gain access? how did you get people to participate? and what makes your research site and sample an appropriate venue/sample in/with which to have done your research? An important point to make here will be in how your sampling is related to your research objectives. For example, were you trying to describe a particular group and sought to identify a representative sample? or were you more interested in exploring the variety of perspectives that exist within an organization on some issue and thus sought to identify more of a stakeholder sample? Recall that one of the main themes in the chapter on sampling (Chapter 4) is that there is no one "best" sampling technique; the appropriateness of any choice is a function of several factors, not the least of which is how well it matches your research questions and objectives. The methods section is where you explain how that connection plays out in your particular project.

It is also important in the methods section to show that you understand enough about the validity issues that will concern your reader to provide information about your sample that bears on these issues. For example, was there a prior relationship between the researcher and the participants that might have affected the completeness and authenticity of responses to interviews? In Ratel's (2008) study of single-parent mothers, for example, Ratel felt that her preexisting knowledge of and friendship with the women, as well as the fact that she, too, was both a student and a single-parent mother, likely enhanced their trust in her and led to open reporting and valid data. In contrast, when Zellerer (1996) interviewed Inuit women in a remote northern community about their experiences with sexual violence, she believed that being a woman and a *stranger* to the community helped because the women knew they could share their stories without having to worry about the repercussions that might arise if they were to speak with people from within their community.

At the same time, just because a researcher says everything went wonderfully does not make it so. Ideally you also will be able to point to other evidence that is consistent with the idea of full and accurate reporting. This might take the form of noting the length of time that was spent in the community or simply the length of the interviews— a two-hour interview presumably shows greater commitment than a more superficial half-hour interview, for example. Alternatively, the kind of information that was shared might be an indication of the degree of rapport that existed; the more important, sensitive, and detailed the information, the more we are prepared to believe in its comprehensiveness and truthfulness.

Also useful in your methods section is an overall description of your participants. In Ratel's case, the emphasis was placed on showing how her small sample of single-parent mothers (n = 9) was nonetheless quite diverse with respect to such variables as their academic major, how many children each woman had, how long each had been a single-parent and the age(s) of their child(ren). In many survey-based studies a portion of the survey will ask for demographic information not only because of its usefulness for analysis, but also because it allows the researcher to describe who the participants are. Also to be noted here as appropriate would be such facts as your response rate, whether any participants were not included in the analysis, and why (e.g., flippant responses; combative attitude; too much missing data).

The methods section will also give a concrete and detailed description of how the data were generated, and the implications of these choices for validity of the information should be explained. Was there a structured survey or interview schedule or observational protocol, or was a less-structured

approach such as a guided interview taken? Why? Copies of any research instruments used would be included in an appendix to a thesis or report from a course project; journals and books rarely publish such items but should be made available to anyone who asks for a copy. Also to be noted are how the data were recorded. For example, were the responses to a survey recorded automatically through on online form and database or with a data capture program? Or did respondents write responses down on paper, which required subsequent transcription? In the case of interviews, did they occur in a private or public location? Was confidentiality promised? In the case of interviews, did the interviewer record the conversation? or did s/he take notes? In the case of observation, how were notes recorded and what procedures were implemented to ensure reliability and validity of encoding?

Generally speaking, this is the section where you outline what you did and why. The emphasis at this point should be on the positives, i.e., why you made the choices that you did and what advantages you gained by doing so. The possible limitations of your choices normally will be considered in a later section when you reflect on the strengths and limitations of what you have done.

RESULTS

You always gather more data than you end up writing about in a report. Frequency distributions, cross-tabulations, correlations, and measures of difference in many quantitative studies can go on for dozens and dozens of pages of printout. Transcriptions of field notes and interviews from more qualitative studies can quickly run into hundreds of pages. There is no way you can report all that data. Your challenge is to prepare a summary of the data that is concise and informs your audience of the main themes or patterns that emerge from your analysis.

There are at least three basic principles that can guide the writing of a good *Results* section. First, the organization of the results section as a whole, and every table and statement within it, should be connected explicitly to whichever research question or other methodological matter the data address.[4] Second, you should present data summaries concisely; don't use three tables if you can collapse them into one. Third, avoid redundancy. For example, if something is already in a table, then do not also describe it in the text; stick to pointing out individual highlights that speak to specific issues you want to address or patterns in the data to which you want to draw the reader's attention.

To return to Ratel's (2008) study of single-parent mothers in academe, recall how we talked about the "hooks" she included in her introduction. These included mentioning several key variables that were important in understanding the single-parenting experience, such as women's financial situation; the physical and emotional stress of trying to keep up with responsibilities by oneself in multiple, and often competing, domains; impacts on the children; the mitigating role of social support mechanisms; and the unique interest that Ratel brought forth in wanting to examine how single-parent women fared in the academic context. It thus should come as no surprise that her interviews, which she outlined in her methods section, focused on those very issues. Nor will it be surprising that the themes around which she organizes her results include headings such as "Financial Circumstances," "Physical and Emotional Stress," "The Children," "Social Support," and "Academics."

By organizing her results section using themes first identified in the introduction, Ratel is making it easier for the reader to make connections with that material. Within each of the themes identified, the results will again be organized in a manner that best explains to the reader what was found by connecting back to thematic hooks that were included earlier and forward to issues you want to address in the discussion section, which will conclude your report.

The way you present data will depend in part on the type of data you gathered. For quantitative data, you should follow the principles discussed in Chapter 12 regarding the proper formatting of tables. For more qualitative data, the presentation is handled in a somewhat different way, although

once again the type of data you have and the analytical strategy you employ will make a difference. In some projects the data may involve describing how some phenomenon occurs, or how a particular organization or other group works. It will be up to you to determine how best to present that data—if it is a process you are focusing on, then the data might be presented chronologically, organized around how the process or narrative develops; if an organization, your data might be organized by the different clusters of people who work there, the various roles they fill, and how the various clusters interact with each other. In more structured interview-based studies like Ratel's, the presentation could be by theme, as we described. Whichever you choose, the basic process involved in the presentation of more qualitative data involves going back and forth between the researcher's interpretation of what went on, and the evidence that bears on that interpretation.

We see the presentation of qualitative data as very much a credibility-building exercise that plays out between the researcher who writes the report and her/his reader. The job of the researcher is to present their interpretation of what is going on, and then to present illustrative evidence that the researcher sees as supportive of that interpretation. For example, consider the following paragraph from Ratel's discussion of "Physical and Emotional Stress" as it plays out in the mothers' lives:

All the women interviewed stated emphatically that they were physically exhausted. The multi-faceted nature of their lives, the adoption of three separate and distinct roles (i.e., wage earner, student, and mother) created demands on their time and energy that were difficult to manage. Inevitably, the women sacrificed their own well-being to meet these demands. Collectively, they reported that they are in poor physical health and pointed to lack of sleep, lack of exercise, and inadequate diet as the key contributing factors. The women contend with some anxiety because of their financial situations, but also must face the pressures associated with the academic environment, as well as meeting the challenge of raising their children alone. There is a distinct cyclical element to this situation in which the inability to cope with the physical demands manifests itself in an inability to deal with the emotional stresses. This in turn takes a toll on their physical well-being. As Karen stated:

I was on anti-depressants for the first year I was in school. I came very close to having a nervous breakdown, twice actually. I have a prescription for Valium but I'm trying not to rely on the drugs any more. I live on coffee and cigarettes; I'm always exhausted. After I deal with the kids at night, cook and clean, read bedtime stories, you know … I have to work until two or three in the morning because it's the only time I have to study. I get up at 5:30 in the morning so I can have a half an hour to myself before the kids get up and I start all over again. Occasionally, I force myself to back off and get some sleep. As soon as the semester starts, I'm counting down the weeks hoping I can make it through to the break. People tell me I don't deal with the stress appropriately, that I should get some exercise and get some more sleep. I know they're right but I have to laugh. Who's got the time? They just don't have a clue what I'm dealing with here.*

Note that Ratel presents data in two ways: (1) by offering her statement about one of the themes that emerged from her interviews; and (2) by including a quotation from one particular interview that illustrates the theme. We can compare the two. In the first paragraph, Ratel describes how the women are exhausted, they burn the candle at both ends, they don't sleep or eat well, and it all takes a toll on their health. The quotation that follows gives the words of a particular respondent ("Karen"), and what is she saying? That she's exhausted, burns the candle at both ends, doesn't sleep much, and that it all

---

* From Patricia Ratel, One Day at a Time: Single Parent Mothers in Academe, in T.S. Palys, ed., *Starting from Where You Are* (Burnaby, BC: School of Criminology, Simon Fraser University, 1989). Reprinted with permission from Patricia Ratel

takes a toll on her health—a perfect illustration of exactly what Ratel had said was going on. This is of course only one quote, and ideally one would have two or three brief ones to include just to show that one was not making a big deal about something that only one respondent had said, but the general form here is exactly what the reader is looking for. We get to the end of it and think, "Yup. Sounds like stress to me. And poor nutrition, lack of sleep … all those contributing things that Ratel said were there." Ratel thereby earns some credibility points and we continue on from there, and each successive round of concept/evidence establishes more and more credibility for Ratel as an insightful observer.

But now read the following example, which we made up:

The women all relied heavily on superstition and saw conspiracies everywhere. With all of life's forces beyond their control, the end result, not surprisingly, was a sense of abandonment and alienation that manifest itself in apathy toward the other women whom they previously thought of as sisters. For example, one woman stated:

My mother always told me that "what goes around comes around," so I guess I've always tried to go out of my way to treat others how I would like them to treat me. I know some of the others view it differently, and they have every right to, but that's just how I always thought of it, I suppose.

If we were to read a paper that included something like the above, our reaction would be "Huh? Are you kidding?" Is it reasonable to see a phrase such as "what goes around comes around" as evidence of "superstition"? Or to pull the phrase "I know some of the others view it differently" out of context and infer that the woman was seeing "conspiracies"? Or to see the source's acknowledgment that women all have a right to their own opinions as "apathy"? We think not. And on the assumption that the kinds of examples a researcher will give are in all likelihood the *best* examples from the interviews that *most clearly* illustrate the concept offered by the researcher, then our fictitious researcher is on truly thin ice. There are just too many other ways to look at that quotation, and we begin to have doubts about everything else the researcher claims. If we can't agree with the researcher on the matters for which evidence is put forward, how can we ever trust her/his claims on other summary statements where we don't have direct access to the data to know what misinterpretations may be operating? We can't. Contrast this with Ratel's clear connections between conceptual assertions and data. You believe Ratel because she demonstrates to you that her observations are credible and the inferences she draws reasonable.

Another notable aspect of Ratel's results section is the manner in which she identifies her respondents, where each quote is attributed to a particular person. The names are, of course, fictitious, as she makes clear in a footnote, consistent with her pledge to maintain confidentiality. However, use of a name does two things. First, it maintains a human touch; the respondent is "Karen" rather than "Subject 28" or "Respondent A." Second, with respect to our methodological concerns, it helps us to keep track of who is being quoted throughout the paper.

To appreciate this point, you should consider the presentation of results from a sampling perspective. With quantitative data presented in tabular form, for example, survey data showing the distribution of responses or the mean or median response to a particular questionnaire item, the summary data that appear in the table "represent" the sample in the sense that everyone who is part of the sample is contained in the distribution and have had their data included in the computation of the mean. We paid a certain price for that. Everyone accepted that their views would only be expressed as a checkmark indicating a preference between predetermined categories, and we lost all the texture and nuance that comes when we hear people speak in their own words. What we gain in return is the ability to make charts and graphs that can easily and succinctly summarize people's views.

When we stay with qualitative data, as Ratel did, we have the great advantage of getting all that texture as we read the words of the women, but,

because we cannot quote everything every woman said, we present only "illustrative" quotations where Karen (in this instance) presents a view that "stands for" the sample. The thing you have to demonstrate when you present data of that sort is that you are not simply selectively presenting one individual's opinions that you happen to like and that you are sampling more than one point of view.

One way to do this is to provide a source for each quotation. Citing pseudonyms allows us to see in the paper as a whole who is being quoted at different times, without violating any confidences. Another problem with our fictitious quotation, therefore, is that we simply attributed it to "a woman" but did not attribute a particular source. How can you tell whether the next quotation comes from the same woman, who we may be quoting again and again, or someone different? In our case you can't, but you could if, like Ratel, we attributed every quote to a particular source, which would allow the reader to see that we are offering quotations from various participants and not simply quoting the same one again and again.

End

DISCUSSION AND CONCLUSIONS

Remember the image of the hourglass that we mentioned earlier? In the introduction, you started off broadly at the top end of the hourglass by connecting with the literature and noting the big social issues and concerns that got you interested in the subject matter. Also in the introduction, you started getting more and more specific about your interests. In that section you ended by outlining the more concrete and narrow focus of your particular research project.

The methods and results sections represent the middle portion of the hourglass, where all you're writing about is what you encountered in your research. Your challenge is to do as good a job as possible with your research participants on the topic you have chosen to study. It's not that we don't care about the bigger issues at that point; it's just not the time to be discussing them.

That time comes in the discussion and conclusion sections, which sometimes are combined, depending on the preference of the author and the dictates of the situation. You have several loose ends remaining to be tied in these sections: (1) giving a brief final statement of how your results "speak" to your research questions; (2) what the implications of these results are for the bigger issues that made this research "interesting" for you in the first place; (3) tempering your inferences with critical reflection on the strengths and weaknesses of the research; and (4) any final statements you want to make about your research and its implications. All four are expected to be done in a straightforward manner with a minimum of flourish or hype.

If the results of your research are *at odds with* the research literature, then your next task would be to consider what differences between your research/sample/context and that other research might account for any differences in findings. That will have implications for the kinds of research you might do next to see whether your speculations about the basis of those differences have any merit. However, if your research is more *consistent with* the extant literature, then your research adds evidence that speaks to the generalizability of those original findings. In that case, you might speculate on what sorts of research might be done next to further extend the generalizability of the findings, e.g., to other groups of people, or perhaps to other kinds of processes or research sites. We join Becker (e.g., 1998) in suggesting that the best place to go to next is to the place or group of people from whom you can learn the most, which often means looking for the situation that has the greatest potential to shoot down your developing views.

Tracking

You would be amazed at how often we go to read research reports that have been prepared by students and find that the introduction looks reasonable, and the methods section on its own sounds good, and the discussion and conclusions

are alright, but where the three sections have no connection to one another! The introduction may raise some interesting issues, but if these issues do not find their way into the research, then why raise them in the first place? Most painful of all is when students seem afraid for one reason or another to bluntly ask the question they want to know the answer to, and instead dance all around it and end up not being able to offer any direct answer to the question they posed! It is for this reason that we have emphasized how any research report should exhibit continuity from one section to the next:

- The introduction should lead us to the research question, lay the groundwork for the methods section, interest us in the outcomes of certain data, and provide the thematic framework that we will want to return to in the discussion and conclusion section.

- The methods section is connected to the introduction insofar as it addresses the research question(s) introduced there and tells us how they will be answered, thereby providing fodder and direction for the results and discussions sections that follow.

- The discussion and conclusions section connects back to the introduction by offering answers for the research issues introduced there, being integrated with the literature cited there, and commenting on the bigger context first considered there. It connects back to the methods and results sections because it arises from and incorporates the data and data-gathering procedures outlined there.

A colleague of ours—John Lowman—uses the word "tracking" to describe this aspect of the rewriting process. He is referring to that one aspect of redrafting: ensuring that what you have written "tracks" correctly, so that all the essential elements of your paper follow from each other and speak to each other following a logical flow. No information is missing that is required to maintain the flow; nor is there any superfluous information since these are tangents and distractions.

Figure 13.2

Components of a Standard Research Report

ABSTRACT

♦ Offers an overview of the research in no more than 150 words.

♦ Usually written last to ensure it reflects the content of the final research report.

♦ Should include an overview of your study's objectives, sample, research site, method(s), main finding(s), and, if appropriate, a statement of its implications for policy or practice.

♦ Must stand alone sufficiently well that readers can look at it and determine whether it speaks to issues of interest to them.

INTRODUCTION

♦ Provides the overall context for the research and describes why it might be "interesting" to persons who engage in research and/or develop policy and/or develop theory.

♦ Presents a clear statement of the problem motivating the research.

♦ Moves from more general to more specific and provides a justification for the research.

♦ Includes a focused and critical review of the literature that "sets up" the research by identifying themes that will be addressed in the research and considered in the discussion/conclusion - no more and no less.

♦ Concludes with a specific statement of the purpose of the research and any specific research questions being posed.

METHODS

♦ Offers an overall description of the research procedures.

♦ Outlines and justifies choices made with respect to sampling of research participants and setting.

♦ May include copy of research instrument if a standardized protocol is being followed or may simply include it as an appendix.

♦ Provides a clear statement of the research question(s) that the research has been designed to answer.

RESULTS

♦ Clear and specific presentation of research findings, integrating the primary data collected into the analysis.

♦ The 'facts' demonstrated by the data are weighted and judiciously used.

♦ Organized thematically to reflect research question(s) and any other issues set out in the Introduction; this section anticipates the Discussion section.

DISCUSSION/CONCLUSIONS

♦ Begins with a summary statement of the research question or purpose of the research and gives a succinct answer to that question.

♦ Integrates the current study into the extant literature. Consistencies are noted and discussed in light of the generalizability of findings this reveals. Inconsistencies are also noted, and the researcher speculates on what the sources of these differences might be. Original contributions of the current research are highlighted.

♦ Engages in final consideration of the strengths and limitations of the research, often with an eye toward making suggestions for further research that will address any limitations/gaps that are identified.

♦ Concludes with general discussion of the implications of the research for other research, related policy, future research possibilities, and so on.

FINISH AT THE BEGINNING

The last thing you write is the element that goes first: the *Abstract*. Abstracts are brief summaries of your paper—normally no more than 150 words—that give an overview of your study's objectives, sample, research site, method(s), main finding(s), and, depending on your objective and the venue of publication, sometimes an implication or two of the findings for policy or practice. The reason for waiting until you finish the paper to write the abstract is that it needs to reflect what is in your paper, and since the paper itself will change to some degree as you redraft and hone its content, it's not until you've finalized the paper that you can summarize it.

There are really two main purposes an abstract serves when it's published in a journal or book. The first is that it gives readers a quick fix on the general thrust and implications of your research, which allows them to decide whether the paper is relevant to them and whether they want to spend time on the whole article. The second is that many researchers catch up on the literature by going through compendia of abstracts of recent research both to get an overall sense of recent developments as well as to locate those articles of special relevance and interest that they can then download or locate in the library, so your abstract should be both concise *and* self-sufficient.

SUMMING UP AND LOOKING AHEAD

The primary purpose of this chapter is to give you some advice on how to write a research report, something many readers of this book will be doing in conjunction with a course on research methods where this book is being used. A central theme of the chapter is that although each part of the paper has a unique purpose and provides unique information, the various parts all are linked and interdependent insofar as each part sets up, anticipates, and speaks to issues that are raised in other sections.

The parts of a research paper and the roles each part fulfills are depicted in Figure 13.2. The way linkages can be accomplished between the various sections of the report was emphasized; each should prepare the ground for the next, i.e., the introduction introduces the issues that are then taken up in the research methods and results section that provides the basis for revisiting and forming conclusions in relation to the issues that were raised in the introduction.

With this chapter finished and your term research projects complete, it is time to pull some themes together and draw the book to a close, which we do in the next chapter.

NOTES

1. For example, Strunk's *The Elements of Style* is available online at www.bartleby.com/141/; there are also many guides to writing research papers you can find online if you apply your favourite search engine using terms such as "writing," "how to," "guide," and "research."

2. This quote comes from Blaise Pascal's *Les Lettres Provinciales*, Letter XVI, 1657 (London: Penguin Books) p. 257. We thank Esther Berry of the University of Sydney for solving the mystery of the source of this quote.

3. Note, by the way, that the same introduction could also serve the opposite purpose in order to make the paper "interesting" by saying that, while most single-parents are women, very little is known about the men who find themselves in that role, and hence that is where the research will take us. Either way, the literature cited in the introduction provides the segue into the next part of the paper, and the themes that are introduced here are the ones—no more and no less—that we should see carried through.

4. The corollary here is that you should *only* report data that bear on your research questions and cut out the excess. This does not mean you should "hide" data that do not say what you like; that would be dishonest. We often gather more data than we actually need—you should not feel compelled to report every single datum you gather just because you gathered it. The question is always what is relevant—whether supportive or not of the interpretation we are offering—to whatever the focus of the paper turns out to be.

MIXED METHODS RESEARCH

Perhaps the biggest surprise for those of us whose interests focus on research methods and their development is how much the research enterprise has changed in a relatively short period of time. Although there are many different areas in which those changes have occurred, a couple stand out for the two of us.

One is in the area of research infrastructure, where digital technologies in particular have had an overwhelmingly pervasive impact on virtually every aspect of how we do research. A mere 20 years ago, when the first edition of *Research Decisions* was published (see Palys 1992), for example, personal computers were still relatively new, the Internet did not yet exist in any publicly available form, and hence the search capabilities that we now take for granted—let alone all the digital content we now search for and the social network sites we are members of—also did not yet exist. While many researchers still seem stuck in 20th century technologies and hence have been slow to consider how the digital revolution has opened up new possibilities for every aspect of the research process (see Palys & Atchison 2009, in press), in this edition of *Research Decisions* almost every chapter includes discussion of the ways the digital revolution is opening doors and providing new opportunities for the ways we can search for relevant literature, contact and recruit participants, and gather, manage, and analyze information.

A second area of change has been in the bourgeoning embrace of greater methodological diversity in many quarters of the social and health sciences. In that regard, it is worth noting that the first edition of *Research Decisions* was the first methods text we know of to actually consider qualitative and quantitative approaches under the same cover and to extol the ways in which the two approaches could complement one another as contributing components of a larger multi-method strategy. Although there are many researchers who remain convinced their preferred approach is the one and only royal road to truth, most researchers (in our circles at least) seem to have put these "paradigm wars" behind them. We are encouraged to see more and more researchers seeking to broaden the range of methodological tools at their disposal and/or who seek to collaborate with others who bring different strategies and perspectives to the table in order to more effectively and comprehensively understand whatever phenomenon happens to be their focus. Although we have mentioned this propensity and the advantages it brings at various points in this book, we bring this edition of *Research Decisions* to a close by discussing mixed methods research in slightly greater detail.

A THIRD WAY?

By now you should be familiar with the differences and similarities among and between various methodological approaches and have a fairly good understanding of their respective strengths and weaknesses. This is crucial for social and health researchers who wish to utilize two or more methods within a single project, a practice commonly referred to as mixed methods approach.

While social and health researchers have been mixing multiple methods of data collection within a single study for well over a century (Maxwell & Loomis 2003), Donald T. Campbell, with various collaborators, is widely regarded as one of the first to formally encourage their use in the more contemporary context. Campbell and Fiske (1959), for example, argued that by using multiple methods (e.g., a paper-and-pencil test, direct observation, a performance measure) to measure multiple 'traits' (i.e., attributes or concepts), researchers could dramatically improve the validity of their observations since they could establish that the measure and not the method was responsible for producing the observed results. They referred to this procedure as a multi-trait–multi-method matrix.

Unobtrusive Measures: Non-Reactive Research in the Social Sciences (Webb, Campbell, Schwartz, & Sechrest 1966) continued this argument by pointing out the benefits to be gained by encouraging and implementing methodological pluralism. In another classic article, Campbell (1969c) encouraged researchers of different disciplines to collaborate and enjoy the benefits that would accrue from the diversity of approaches they would bring, and his notion of the "experimenting society" and quasi-experimentation was based in large part on the analytical power that could be mustered by strategically combining different types and sources of data (e.g., Campbell 1969b; Cook & Campbell 1979).

Denzin (1970, 1978) built upon these ideas when he coined the term **triangulation**, which is a research strategy that permits us to validate our observations by drawing upon multiple sources or perspectives within the same investigation. He suggested there were four distinct ways this triangulation could occur:

- **Theoretical triangulation** involves employing multiple theories throughout the design, collection, and analysis process. Proceeding in this manner would involve a researcher or group of researchers developing research questions from different theoretical vantage points and thereby studying a phenomenon through multiple lenses.

- **Investigator triangulation** refers to the practice of several different researchers contributing in the study to collect, analyze, and interpret data and observations. This practice is thought to improve both the credibility of the observations and the resulting interpretation of the research. One place you see investigator triangulation is in the progressively more common practice of multi-, trans-, and inter-disciplinary research collaboration that brings together teams of researchers from different disciplines in order to research a problem of common interest (e.g., see Campbell 1969c; Leavy 2011).

- **Methodological triangulation** involves employing multiple methods to study a particular phenomenon in order to overcome the deficiencies and biases that may result from employing a single method approach. Certainly *Research Decisions*, which extols the virtue of combining qualitative and quantitative approaches, exemplifies this approach.

- **Data analysis triangulation** refers to the practice of employing several different methods of analyzing and interpreting data in order to improve the validity of the conclusions by ensuring the robustness of one's results.*

These early writings by Campbell and his colleagues in the more quantitative realm and Denzin in the qualitative set the stage for the emergence of what some (e.g., Johnson & Onwuegbuzie 2004; Johnson, Onwuegbuzie, & Turner 2007) have labelled a "third paradigm" of research—mixed methods—which Johnson et al. (2007) define as "the type of research in which a researcher or team of researchers combines elements of qualitative and quantitative research approaches (e.g., use of qualitative and quantitative viewpoints, data collection, analysis, inference techniques) for the broad purposes of breadth and depth of understanding and corroboration" (123).

While use of the term "paradigm" may paint a fairly simple and logical idea—the idea that two heads can be better than one—with an overly

---

* Denzin, N.K. (1970). The research act: A theoretical introduction to sociological methods. Chicago: Aldine. Denzin, N. K. (1978). The logic of naturalistic inquiry. In N. K. Denzin (Ed.), Sociological methods: A sourcebook. New York: McGraw-Hill

grandiose brush (see Kuhn 1970 for the origins of the term), at their base mixed methods approaches are premised on the belief that qualitative and quantitative methods occupy a shared terrain when it comes to objectives, scope, and nature of inquiry, and reflect the desire of many researchers to bridge the 'divide' that had existed between qualitative and quantitative approaches. Researchers adopting this perspective encourage an eclectic approach to the research process that draws upon the complementary strengths of qualitative and quantitative techniques. Proponents believe that the best answers to any research problem come when we consider multiple viewpoints, perspectives, positions, and standpoints instead of one.

One of the most exciting aspects of social and health research is the continued development of mixed methods approaches, which we view as an excellent addition to the research tool belt. However, since mixed methods research designs are more complex than single method projects there are a variety of practical, theoretical, and procedural considerations that should be considered when deciding whether and how to employ them in your particular project. In the remainder of this chapter we will: (1) briefly discuss the philosophical underpinnings of this approach to research; (2) examine the types of questions that mixed methods approaches are particularly well-suited to answer; and (3) assess the unique methodological considerations that researchers thinking of employing this approach need to keep in mind when designing, sampling, collecting, and analyzing the data from mixed methods investigations.

PHILOSOPHICAL UNDERPINNINGS

In Chapter 1 we introduced you to the epistemological traditions of positivism and phenomenologism and noted how social and health researchers working within these traditions have developed different perspectives on what is knowable and how best to study social and health-related phenomena. We illustrated the different perspectives by highlighting what many see as the polar opposite positions of direct, naive, or "classic" realism and constructivism. Recall that this extreme version of realism maintains there is a single reality that exists independent of the researcher that can be understood and discovered through the identification of the "right" theoretical concepts and the testing of these theoretical concepts using the appropriate—most often quantitative—empirical methods. At the other extreme are similarly dogmatic constructivists who believe that knowledge, truth, and reality are socially constructed and thus always in a state of change and never really "knowable" in a finite sense. They argue that the best we can hope for is to arrive at rich qualitative and human-centred description that allows us to understand the processes by which constructions arise and the ways they can be changed.

The distinct differences between these visions of how to define and study truth, knowledge, and reality led many social and health researchers working within each tradition to become increasingly rigid about their preference for, and defence of, either quantitative or qualitative methods. Over time, perspective and method became conflated so that realism became inseparable from quantitative approaches and constructivism became inseparable from qualitative approaches. During the 1970s and 1980s an increasing number of people working within each paradigm began to publish books and articles championing the virtues of their perspective/method while simultaneously calling into question the validity of research conducted within the 'opposing' perspective/method. The realist/quantitative–constructivist/qualitative divide eventually became so pronounced that some observers began to refer to them as the "paradigm wars" or "science wars" (e.g., Ross 1996).

While the "paradigm wars" appear for the most part to have come to an end, there are still some who cling to the belief that fundamental differences in the philosophical underpinnings of qualitative and quantitative research paradigms make the mixing of the two approaches impossible, a position known as the **incompatibility thesis** (Howe 1988). Researchers who are open to mixed methods approaches reject this claim. They feel that social and health-related phenomena are better studied using both qualitative *and* quantitative methods and have sought to ground their approach in an epistemological position that is capable of seeing a middle ground between direct realism and constructivism.

Enter **pragmatism**, which is a philosophical tradition that has its roots in the late 19th century through the works of Charles Saders Pierce, John Dewy, and William James and played a major role in the emergence of symbolic interactionism (e.g., Mead and Cooley). Pragmatism is not committed to any single system of philosophy or view of reality. The central position advanced within pragmatism is the rejection of traditional dualisms of realism *versus* constructivism, free-will *versus* determinism, subjectivism *versus* objectivism, and induction *versus* deduction in favour of taking the position that works best in a particular situation (Johnson & Onwuegbuzie 2004).

Pragmatism is founded on a method of inquiry that is based on an iterative relationship between the processes of discovery and action as opposed to the search for a single truth or correct answer. Pragmatists favour eclecticism and pluralism as opposed to dogmatism when it comes to theoretical, methodological, and analytical approaches to understanding the social world. Pragmatists are results- or outcome-oriented and less concerned with prior knowledges, laws, or rules governing what is to be considered valid knowledge (Maxcy 2003). They are concerned with finding the best or most complete answers to research questions through the best method or combination of methods and they have a strong commitment to praxis (i.e., theory informing practice).

MIXED METHODS RESEARCH QUESTIONS AND OBJECTIVES

Many mixed methods investigations are often simultaneously inductive and deductive, so the types of questions that researchers working within this perspective ask tend to be more layered, nuanced and comprehensive than those that inspire single-method studies. The questions motivating many mixed methods investigations are often concerned with both variance and process. As Maxwell and Loomis (2003) explain, **variance questions** frequently involve describing the frequency with which phenomena of interest occur, and often use aggregate statistics to explain and understand the relationships or predictive capacity of one or more variables or theories related to these phenomena. In contrast, **process questions** are directed at exploring, describing, understanding, and/or explaining the origins, meanings, and relationships connected to particular events, phenomena, or processes—*how* they occur and what they mean to those involved.

For example, in his research with sex buyers, Chris sought to describe and understand how men understood and defined the risks associated with their decisions to purchase sex and to explain how the attitudes and beliefs that these men held about the meanings of risk was related to their sex buying behaviour and the relationships they formed with sex workers. His research questions were both inductive and deductive as he sought a deeper understanding of how risk is defined and understood by men who buy sex, and to explain how variations in the way different sex buyers defined and understood risk resulted in different behavioural outcomes for them and the sex workers. It was clear to Chris that a single-method research design would not be suitable for finding answers to his questions.

Similarly, when Ted and his colleagues sought to understand how police officers in a large urban police department used a state-of-the-art mobile data access system and the impacts it had, their research crossed all the dualisms we have discussed. They wanted quantitative measures of frequency of system use, the circumstances in which it was used, and any outcomes that directly arose from these searches, but at the same time sought to understand officers' perceptions of the system and the meaning it had for the officers and their views of themselves and their job. The project would incorporate both quantitative and qualitative data, include both behavioural and perceptual measures, deductively address their own theoretical interests while looking inductively at the way officers and the police administration understood the system, and look at how attitudes were distributed among patrol officers and relevant others while also trying to understand the basis of those attitudes and their implications for policing. This called for a mixed methods approach to engender a more comprehensive and balanced understanding of the system.

DESIGN ISSUES IN MIXED METHODS RESEARCH

Researchers employing a mixed methods paradigm do so because they believe that bringing together different methodological approaches will give them the best chance of finding comprehensive answers to their specific and multifaceted research questions. Accordingly, while research questions form the foundation upon which mixed methods investigations are built, different projects with their differing objectives and priorities will influence the way the various methods are brought together within the project, although in our experience the way this happens will in most cases involve a mixture of strategic choice and happenstance.

As we have seen throughout the book, a solid research design requires that you pay attention to the relationships among and between various components of your research, and this is particularly so for mixed methods designs. Ideally all of the components will be compatible and "speak" to and complement each other in order to gain the comprehensive understanding being sought. One aspect that may vary is the order in which the different methods are engaged.

Order

Authors in the field suggest there are only two options to choose from—concurrent or sequential ordering (e.g., Morse 1991). However, in our experience the distinction between the two is often more easily made in textbooks than it is in the field, where

pragmatic considerations and project-specific circumstances invariably intervene. We also acknowledge that a priori distinctions between concurrent or sequential strategies are more common in more structured projects that can be proposed completely ahead of time, while more intentionally inductive and emergent strategies often are less concerned with establishing order ahead of time and prefer to enjoy a more ad hoc approach where different sources are sought and embraced as one's understanding of a phenomenon develops and different sources of information are identified. Although the description below maintains this distinction—with our addition of an "ad hoc" category—the main principle you should keep in mind is that the job of the researcher is to bring together all the relevant data one can muster, and not to feel that some source of information is somehow illegitimate or off limits because it was not anticipated at the time you were writing the proposal. The best researchers are data hungry—always looking for new information and new sources of information that will offer a different perspective and more comprehensive understanding of whatever phenomenon or process one is trying to understand.

CONCURRENT MIXED METHOD DESIGNS
Concurrent mixed method designs are said to occur when both qualitative and quantitative data collection occurs at the same time. This approach most frequently occurs with more deductive approaches where researchers bring their theories and/or interests to bear on a site of their choosing, such that one begins with research questions and data sources that are identifiable from the outset. Data-gathering efficiency in such situations may see different members of a coordinated research team working in parallel, each with their separate area of responsibility, and adding their respective contributions to the whole. For example, Chris's research with sex buyers was actually one part of a broader research project that involved other health researchers examining how notions of risk played out in various locations within the sex industry. Thus, while Chris was seeking out both qualitative

and quantitative information from sex buyers regarding their perceptions of the different types of risk their sex buying entailed, others in the team were working with sex workers to better understand these interactions and their consequences from their perspective; a second group was gathering information from the romantic partners of sex workers; a third was focusing on those who "manage" sex workers in venues such as massage parlours, escort agencies, and exotic dance establishments; and a fourth was focusing on the various laws, policies, and legislation that municipal police use to police the sex industry, and the impact of these practices on sex worker health and safety.[1]

Concurrent data acquisition can occur within a specific study as well. For example, in Ted's evaluation of a police department's mobile data system, one part of the study involved doing ridealongs with patrol officers during actual work shifts in order to see firsthand how they used the system. This immediately raised the question of what effect observers' presence in the patrol cars would have on the way officers used the system. Would they use it *more* than usual in order to impress the researchers with how useful it was? Would they use it *less* because of some concern about how their use of it would be viewed? Or might they simply use it *differently*—using some aspects of it and not others—depending on how the researchers or their employers might view their use?

The use of mixed methods allowed Ted to address that issue head on. The mobile data system incorporated eight different "forms" that involved different ways of using the system to access different data sources, and one of the pieces of information captured during the observational sessions was how frequently each one of the "forms" was used. However, the system itself also maintained an ongoing archive of every query that was made in all patrol cars at all times, such that access to this archive would allow the research team to see how frequently each one of the eight forms was used when observers were *not* present, thereby enabling a comparison with the data that were gathered when they *were* present. By examining these two concurrent sets of data, the researchers were able to establish that, with one exception, officers' overall use of the system when observers were in their patrol cars mirrored their use of the system when no observers were present. The one exception was a "comment" form—rather like an early version of email that allowed officers to send typed messages between patrol cars—that was used far less frequently when observers were present than when they were not. Although comforting to know, one limitation to that particular comparison was that, while the researchers could see whether and what differences in overall use did or did not appear, mere examination of the distributions would give no indication of *why* any differences appeared. Nonetheless, by identifying the issue, another research question arose that, not coincidentally, could be addressed by yet another method.[2]

SEQUENTIAL MIXED METHOD DESIGNS

Sequential mixed method designs break the data collection process into stages that follow one another in some logically considered order. This approach is most commonly employed by having a primary data collection strategy followed by collection of supplementary information during a secondary stage that allows you to clarify aspects of the data during analysis. It also happens to be the one that Chris employed in his study of sex buyers. As he explained in his original proposal to the funding agency,

> A mixed method strategy will unfold sequentially in two phases.... The first phase will involve a structured self-administered questionnaire administered via the Internet and the project web site. The second phase will involve in-depth conversational interviews either in-person, on the telephone or online. The combined methods will facilitate a phenomenological investigation of individual attitudes, beliefs and experiences, with a broader investigation of the aggregate patterns of experience and behaviour. They will also provide greater depth and breadth of information than would be available through a single

method approach, and they will enhance our ability to posit a wider range of answers to our research questions.*

Starting with the structured survey was a reasonable thing to do in this case because the main issues he wanted to address were identified ahead of time, and the focus of that phase of the research was largely to generate enough information through a systematic and structured method that would allow him to aggregate the information to create a "big picture" view of a diverse sample of sex buyers and begin to examine statistically the relations among different variables of interest. As he outlined in his proposal,

> We will use a revised version of Atchison, Lowman and Fraser's (1998) instrument to collect data. The instrument consists of a series of open and close-ended questions that measure sex buyers' attitudes, beliefs and experiences. The questionnaire is organized into a series of thematic categories including: general and specific purchasing experience and behaviours; attitudes and understanding of the regulation and structuring of the sex industry; attitudes toward and understandings of sex work; and, personal background and history.†

Notwithstanding the inclusion of some open-ended questions that gave respondents the opportunity to explain and comment at greater length, for the most part the items in the survey were highly structured categorical items that were useful for statistical analysis. Their weakness is that categorical, structured items tend not to be all that informative as to the reasoning or logic that lay behind the choices those categories signify. For that reason, Chris also encouraged those respondents who were willing to engage in a follow-up interview that would allow him to explore in much

greater detail buyers' perceptions of their interactions with sex workers. As he explained in his research proposal,

> We use Plummer's framework of sexual storytelling and Herdt and Stoller's concept of intimate communications to frame the interview. This orientation will lead to a more open discussion and ensure that participants will have the opportunity to define and deliberate on their experiences, concerns, and insights. Respondents will provide personal narratives relating to their positive and negative experiences of paying for sex and with violence, victimization and safety within the context of commercial sex relationships. By using this more open format to the conversation, we will avoid being overly constrained by previous research, and avoid preconceived—perhaps even stereotypical— images of sex buyers.‡

The study that Ted did with the urban police department and their use of their mobile data system also employed a sequential strategy whose ordering went in the opposite direction. In Ted's study, because no one had ever done a systematic evaluation of that sort of system before, the major emphasis initially was on simply watching patrol officers use the system on actual working shifts; gathering archival information from policing "trade" magazines that talked about systems of this type and the hopes and concerns that police officers expressed about them; and using targeted samples of patrol officers, managerial level officers, and radio dispatch personnel to try to ascertain the range of attitudes, and the reasons underlying those attitudes, which patrol officers and others in the police department held about the system. But while these interviews were rich with detail and originated from targeted samples of individuals who collectively represented a useful cross-section of the police department being studied, their main limitation was that the researchers were left with no idea how commonly the different views about the system were held, or how opinions or practices in one sphere were related

*†‡ Atchison, C. (1998). *Men who buy sex: A Preliminary description based on the results from a survey of the Internet-using population*. M.A. thesis, Simon Fraser University

to any other. That was exactly the strength that using a structured survey—eventually administered to a 20 percent sample of all patrol officers in the department—would afford, with all the preliminary exploratory work helping ensure that the survey that was created would address issues that were established to be important, and that would reflect and address officers' beliefs and behaviour in relation to the system.

As these two examples suggest, there is no inherently "right" way to proceed through a multi-method strategy. Which sequence is "best" will depend on many factors such as the amount of prior research in the area, the extent to which the researcher is following a more inductive, deductive, or combined strategy; and/or simply the pragmatics of the situation.

INTEGRATIVE MIXED METHOD DESIGNS

Although our discussion of concurrent and sequential designs depicts an orderly and tidy process of a considered and formally executed design, you also should see hints in the descriptions that suggest it does not always happen that way. In particular, two deviations from those elegant and planned procedures should be noted, which we refer to as **systematic mixed method integration** and *ad hoc* **mixed method integration**.

SYSTEMATIC MIXED METHOD INTEGRATION Do not come away from the above feeling that you must make a decision between pursuing *either* a concurrent *or* a sequential strategy. There is no such requirement. Many multi-method studies incorporate elements of both, and the two projects we describe above are examples of exactly that. In the sex work research project that Chris was involved with, a concurrent strategy was employed insofar as different researchers were gathering data simultaneously from different sources using a variety of methods, while individual researchers, such as Chris, were also employing sequential strategies within their areas of responsibility.

The same mixture of course also can occur *within* any given study, as was evident in Ted's study of the police department's mobile data system. In that research one phase saw several different methods being used concurrently—the in-car observation, archival analysis of the frequency with which different forms were being used, and in-person interviews with a targeted sample of respondents—which were then followed sequentially by a survey that addressed all the relevant issues that had been identified in the earlier phase of that research.

AD HOC MIXED METHOD INTEGRATION The second way that multi-method integration can occur arises from the facts that life involves surprises and does not always proceed as we expect, coupled with our admonition that the main principle in any multi-method study or program of research should be to bring together all the relevant data sources you can. Ted's experience with the mobile data system study is an example of that, as he did not know when that research began that an archive existed of every transaction made over the system. It was only during a preliminary phase of the research that the existence of the archive was noted by one of the computer programmers during casual conversation, with Ted immediately recognizing its significance and the role it could play in helping to deal with one particular rival plausible explanation that would arise in the study.

And finally, no discussion of integrative multi-method strategies would be complete without also paying homage to the *ad hoc* discovery of data sources that is almost inevitable in any field-based research, and is particularly characteristic of more ethnographic or inductively guided qualitative research. Many of the examples we have cited in this text offer examples of that. Recall, for example, the way that Howard Becker's (1993) study of medical students bounced back and forth between interviewing and observation and followed what proved an interesting diversion when one student unexpectedly referred to one of the patients he saw on rounds as a "crock." Similarly, many interview, oral history, and ethnographic studies end up incorporating methods and sources that were not originally planned or foreseen, such as when an interviewee makes note of a diary that was kept during a particular period in their life that we are asking about, or makes mention of the many pictures that were taken during a holiday that we are asking about, or starts pulling out newspaper clippings that reveal how media portrayed a particular episode at the time it was unfolding (see Margolis 1994 for an excellent example of this sort).

SAMPLING ISSUES IN MIXED METHODS RESEARCH

Sampling in mixed methods designs involves considered and often complex mixtures of quantitative and qualitative methodologies relying upon some combination of probabilistic and purposive sampling strategies. As with single-method designs, the type of sampling procedure that is most appropriate is largely determined by your research objectives. If you want to sample from a well-defined population in a manner that will allow you to generalize your results back to that wider population, as is often the case in large-scale descriptive, relational, and explanatory studies, a probabilistic sampling technique is beneficial. If your goal is exploring, describing, or understanding underlying processes in order to identify key aspects of a phenomenon in order to generate new ideas and theories, or you are simply engaging in research where particular identifiable individuals are the best sources for the information that you need—because of their unique experience, or position in an organization, or whatever—then a purposive and targeted sampling technique will be more appropriate.

Multifaceted research questions frequently require that you use multiple and diverse (probability and purposive) sampling techniques to select the people, places, and/or things that are best suited for providing the information necessary to answer your questions. No matter what sampling technique(s) you use, you should keep in mind that overlapping sampling strategies in mixed methods designs normally will need to be congruent. While there is generally no problem with mixing multiple purposive sampling techniques, you often need to be careful when combining probability and purposive techniques within the same investigation.

For example, in most situations it wouldn't make much sense to draw a large convenience sample of participants to complete a self-administered questionnaire and then follow this up by randomly sampling the people who completed the questionnaire to ask them to participate in an in-depth interview. The opposite, however, may well make a lot of sense, e.g., when you begin with a random sample of individuals from some well-defined population in order to see how certain attitudes are distributed in the group as a whole, and then follow this with targeted samples of individuals who represent different constituencies or perspectives within that whole.

For example, during Chris's research with sex buyers he combined network, purposive and quota sampling strategies in order to acquire a sample of Canadian sex buyers to participate in either an in-depth interview or questionnaire. Close to 50 people contacted him after hearing about his research from people in their social network (e.g., family, friends, co-workers, sex workers, other sex buyers). He then used a pre-interview screening process to collect information about each individual's sexual background and experience at paying for sex. Individuals who had a lengthy history of sex buying and who represented particular demographics of buyers were selected and asked to participate in an in-depth interview. Those that did not fit the specifications were directed to the research website and asked to complete the browser-based questionnaire.

Sequential design sampling strategies have the potential to dramatically improve sample selection and solicitation as the technique used in one stage of the research can be used to assist you in identifying and/or contacting the sample for the second stage of the project. This can mean including the participant in both stages of the research or redirecting them to stages that might be more appropriate for them. For example, if you administer a questionnaire via Web browser in a network environment you can use scripts to conduct rudimentary data analysis on your participant's responses while they are completing the survey and when specific types of participants (e.g., extreme cases, deviant cases, theoretically important cases) are identified on the basis of their responses to particular items or sets of items in the questionnaire, they could be presented with a dialogue box, pop-up window, or follow-up email asking them to participate in an interview or focus group.

MIXING METHODS OF DATA COLLECTION AND OBSERVATION

As we have seen throughout the book, there are a wide variety of qualitative and quantitative observation and data collection techniques available to social and health researchers. Some of the quantitative methods we have discussed include questionnaires, structured interviews, structured observation, archival techniques, experiments, and program and policy evaluation. Some of the qualitative strategies we have reviewed include interviews, life and oral histories, case studies, focus groups, field groups, observational studies, ethnographies, archival or document discovery, and program or policy evaluations. We have encouraged you to see these different data collection and observation strategies as tools in your research tool belt with some tools being better suited for certain jobs than others. Remember that in order to determine which tool is best suited for providing the best answers to your particular research question(s), you need to be familiar with the strengths and weaknesses of each. Having a solid understanding of the relative strengths and weaknesses of the various methods is a vital component of mixed methods research.

Tashakkori and Teddlie (1998) assert that the fundamental principle of mixed methods research is that methods should be mixed in order to emphasize the complementary strengths

and non-overlapping weaknesses of the methods. Ideally, a mixed methods design should combine methods in a way that allows you to overcome the weaknesses or limitations of one method by drawing upon the strengths of another. The weaknesses of a particular data collection approach may be in the type, depth, or breadth of data that it can provide. For example, while questionnaires are an excellent method for quickly and efficiently collecting large amounts of data about the relatively static aspects of social and health phenomena, they are a notoriously weak method for acquiring information about context. Similarly, while observational strategies are excellent ways to develop a rich description of context within which attitudes and beliefs are formed and behaviours are displayed, researchers employing these strategies often have no idea where to focus their observations. A sequential mixed methods design that integrates questionnaire and observational strategies would allow you to capture both breadth and depth of description and understanding by capitalizing on the unique strengths of each method.

In addition to helping to neutralize the effects of the inherent weaknesses of any single method, you can use mixed methods observation and data collection strategies to help you develop more reliable and valid instruments. For example, Chris recently became involved in another large interdisciplinary mixed methods study looking at the intersection of gender, conflict, and health within Canada's sex industry. While concepts such as gender, conflict, and health have been defined and measured in a variety of ways, few studies have been done to determine if there are particular definitions and measures that are more valid and reliable than others. In order to determine if there are indeed "better" ways of measuring these concepts, Chris and his research partners have decided to conduct a multi-stage sequential mixed methods investigation. The first stage involves conducting a series of individual and focus group interviews with various stakeholders (e.g., buyers and sellers of sex, healthcare providers, police, social support service providers) in order to identify what each concept means to them and how it impacts their experiences in and around the sex industry. The analysis of the interview data will allow the team to develop a preliminary pool of qualitative and quantitative measures they will then evaluate through a series of tests during the second stage of the study. Once the measures have been thoroughly tested and evaluated in various contexts the team will be in the position to identify which measures will be used in the third and final stage of the research.

Discussions about the integration of methods during data collection and observation often focus on whether a researcher is going to conduct the research sequentially or concurrently. In both cases, the assumption is often that the researcher is relying upon two independent data collection strategies. With some of the advances in computer-assisted observation and data collection techniques we envision a possibility where elements of two different methods can be seamlessly integrated or nested within a single data collection protocol to produce a truly mixed method data collection strategy. For example, using advanced scripting techniques it is well within the realm of possibility to create a data collection strategy that is a hybrid of the browser-based self-administered questionnaire and the conversational interview. As another example, virtual worlds and online gaming environments are ideal spaces in which to integrate quasi-experimental and micro-ethnographic observation seamlessly. The possibilities that network technology offer in this respect are limitless.

While mixing two or more data collection strategies within a single investigation can offer unique advantages, it is important to acknowledge that doing this can also sometimes result in poorer quality data and observations. There are two main situations where the quality of the data could be compromised. The first occurs when a sort of "shotgun" logic prevails that seems governed by the idea that, with so many pellets heading off in the same direction, surely one will hit the target. In methodological terms, this is often manifest in the researcher applying one or all of the methods

less rigorously than would have been the case had s/he opted for a well-aimed, single-method study. Simply throwing all your darts at the board in the hope one will hit the bull's-eye is not a recommended strategy; more often than not they *all* will miss.

The second situation is when you develop the secondary method to "fit" the format and content of the primary method. In this case the secondary method is not used in a way that the research benefits from its unique strengths and the resulting data will likely be severely compromised. For example, it is not unusual for social and health researchers conducting mixed methods research involving questionnaire and interview approaches to simply turn the interview into a researcher-administered version of the questionnaire. In this situation instead of producing rich and nuanced information about the processes underlying the phenomenon under investigation the interviews produce rigid and structured responses that are incapable of revealing the information the researcher would need to answer their qualitative research questions.

ANALYTICAL ISSUES IN MIXED METHODS RESEARCH

All mixed methods investigations require that you bring together the data and observations for your analysis and interpretation. One of the greatest benefits of mixed methods designs comes at the data analysis stage when the different types of data can be brought together and used to shed light on each other. Data from mixed methods investigations are capable of providing you with a much greater diversity of divergent views (Teddlie & Tashakkori 2003), and when divergent views are found it gives you the opportunity to falsify aspects of your theory or to question the assumptions upon which your understanding of a phenomenon are based. Mixed methods analysis allows you to have greater confidence in your research since ideally you will analyze the data in a way that allows you to interrogate more thoroughly the plausibility of your conclusions.

The major issue confronting most researchers is whether to transform one type of data so that it is directly comparable and compatible with the other or to maintain the integrity of each form of data and develop analytical and interpretive techniques that effectively integrate both forms. Since quantitative data are already structured and cannot easily be transformed to become less structured, one of the toughest decisions you have to make during analysis is how you are going to handle your qualitative data. Transforming qualitative data and observations into a more quantitative form by assigning elements of talk, text, or image into static and structured categories can defeat the purpose of collecting the rich qualitative data in the first place. Alternatively, ensuring different types of data "speak" to one another can be very challenging.

At this point there are no analytical techniques we are aware of that have been developed specifically for the simultaneous analysis of qualitative and quantitative data, and there is no single data analysis program that is capable of analyzing both numeric and non-numeric data. While both SPSS and NVivo have the capacity to handle mixed forms of data, neither product offers a complete range of options for analyzing mixed data. Having said this, SPSS can be used to conduct rudimentary analysis of text or "string" data, and datasets can be imported into NVivo for simple analysis and coded and linked to qualitative data. Perhaps with an increasing emphasis on 'convergence' in the technological world we will see this type of integration at some point down the road and SPSS and NVivo will be merged into a single program. For now, sophisticated analyses of mixed data require the researcher to use at least two different programs and then integrate their analysis during the interpretive phase.

SUMMING UP AND LOOKING AHEAD

Johnson and Onwuegbuzie (2004) aptly point out that the epistemological position that a researcher holds does not dictate the methodological and analytical approaches that they must use in order to justify their knowledge claims. Yet there are still many who believe that quantitative and qualitative methodological approaches are fundamentally incompatible—or that only one of the two embodies the qualities of "real" science while the other is hopelessly esoteric and misguided—and that researchers who attempt to combine them in a single project are destined for failure (e.g., compare Gendreau & Bonta 1991 with Smith & Heshusius 1986). We feel that this view of research is an incredibly limiting way of looking at the methodological possibilities for social and health research.

Throughout the book we have urged you to place your research question(s) at the centre of all of your design, sampling and solicitation, data collection, and observation and analysis decisions. We have argued that all methodological and analytic decisions follow from your research questions and that your research decisions should be mindful, *not* mindless, dogmatic or rote. This is also a central tenet of the pragmatic philosophy that underlies mixed methods research.

The decision to undertake a mixed methods investigation in any particular project is not one that you should make without due consideration. While there are obvious advantages to mixed methods research designs, researchers contemplating these types of designs should assess critically whether they are the most appropriate for achieving their specific research objectives. Mixed methods designs are not always your best option; they can be difficult to manage, time consuming, costly, and require that the researcher or research team be thoroughly familiar with the strengths and weaknesses of both qualitative and quantitative methods. Researchers always need to ask themselves if their specific questions could be better answered through a design that relies solely on qualitative or quantitative methods.

In any lengthier program of research, however, we would consider anyone who avoids multi-method inquiry (whether by themselves or in combination with others) as something of a one-trick pony that does an injustice to the phenomena that interest them. For example, we do not understand researchers who engage in statistical analysis of sex offender data in study after study, and make recommendations for policy, without ever having actually spoken to a sex offender. We are equally perplexed when we meet those who engage only in ethnographic or interview-based research and ignore the results of more quantitative studies that would help place their more focused experience in some broader context. What we particularly appreciate about multi-method research is the extent to which it is consistent with a theme we have returned to throughout this book, i.e., that it is one's research questions that should guide inquiry—not some epistemological orthodoxy that happens to be the one thing one learned in graduate school—and that, in the process of addressing those questions, one should leave no stone unturned.

STUDY QUESTIONS

1. What four modes of triangulation were articulated by Denzin (1970)?

2. What do the "paradigm wars" refer to?

3. What is the "incompatibility thesis" and how is it viewed by those who engage in mixed method research?

4. In what sense do mixed methods approaches reflect the philosophical tradition known as pragmatism?

5. Explain how "variance questions" and "process questions" can be viewed as complementary. Which is more allied with qualitative approaches and which is more aligned with quantitative?

6. Explain the difference between concurrent, sequential, and integrative multi-method designs.

7. In what sense might *ad hoc* integration be considered synonymous with qualitative approaches?

8. Do mixed methods strategies favour probabilistic or purposive sampling strategies or "all of the above"? Explain.

9. "When engaged in mixed method research involving surveys and interview methods, the more qualitative interview techniques should always come first." Would you agree with that statement? Explain.

10. In general, the chapter extols the virtues of mixed method approaches because of the enhanced information it produces. But are there circumstances in which it might actually act to *diminish* data quality? Explain.

11. How do mixed methods data assist you at the analytical/interpretive stage of your project? What obstacles currently exist to a more complete integration at that stage of your research?

NOTES

1. The project was actually even more extensive than this. We identify only a few of the concurrent projects here just to give a feel for some of the diversity of sources and methods that were involved.

2. During casual conversation that in-car observers had with officers and in some of the interviews that were conducted, several officers revealed that they had been told by senior officers to minimize their "frivolous" use of the system during the evaluation. The officers told us that they often used the "comment" form to trade off-colour jokes or make other comments that they would not want others to hear, and were avoiding doing so when the observers were present.

APPENDIX A

CRITICAL VALUES OF CHI-SQUARE

	Level of Significance for a Nondirectional Test				
df	.10	.05	.02	.01	.001
1	2.71	3.84	5.41	6.64	10.83
2	4.60	5.99	7.82	9.21	13.82
3	6.25	7.82	9.84	11.34	16.27
4	7.78	9.49	11.67	13.28	18.46
5	9.24	11.07	13.39	15.09	20.52
6	10.64	12.59	15.03	16.81	22.46
7	12.02	14.07	16.62	18.48	24.32
8	13.36	15.51	18.17	20.09	26.12
9	14.68	16.92	19.68	21.67	27.88
10	15.99	18.31	21.16	23.21	29.59
11	17.28	19.68	22.62	24.72	31.26
12	18.55	21.03	24.05	26.22	32.91
13	19.81	22.36	25.47	27.69	34.53
14	21.06	23.68	26.87	29.14	36.12
15	22.31	25.00	28.26	30.58	37.70
16	23.54	26.30	29.63	32.00	39.29
17	24.77	27.59	31.00	33.41	40.75
18	25.99	28.87	32.35	34.80	42.31
19	27.20	30.14	33.69	36.19	43.82
20	28.41	31.41	35.02	37.57	45.32
21	29.62	32.67	36.34	38.93	46.80
22	30.81	33.92	37.66	40.29	48.27
23	32.01	35.17	38.97	41.64	49.73
24	33.20	36.42	40.27	42.98	51.18
25	34.38	37.65	41.57	44.31	52.62
26	35.56	38.88	42.86	45.64	54.05
27	36.74	40.11	44.14	46.96	55.48
28	37.92	41.34	45.42	48.28	56.89
29	39.09	42.69	46.69	49.59	58.30
30	40.26	43.77	47.96	50.89	59.70

The table lists the critical values of chi-square for the degrees of freedom shown at the left for tests corresponding to the significance levels that head the columns. If the observed value of X^2obs [the observed value of chi-square] is greater than or equal to the tabled value, reject H_0 [the null hypothesis]. All chi-squares are positive.

NEL

APPENDIX B

CRITICAL VALUES OF *r*

	Level of Significance for a Nondirectional (Two-Tailed) Test				
df = N – 2	.10	.05	.02	.01	.001
1	0.9877	0.9969	0.9995	0.9999	10.0000
2	0.9000	0.9500	0.9800	0.9990	0.9990
3	0.8054	0.8783	0.9343	0.9587	0.9912
4	0.7293	0.8114	0.8822	0.9172	0.9741
5	0.6694	0.7545	0.8329	0.8745	0.9507
6	0.6215	0.7067	0.7887	0.8343	0.9249
7	0.5822	0.6664	0.7498	0.7977	0.8982
8	0.5494	0.6319	0.7155	0.7646	0.8721
9	0.5214	0.6021	0.6851	0.7348	0.8471
10	0.4973	0.5760	0.6581	0.7079	0.8233
11	0.4762	0.5529	0.6339	0.6935	0.8010
12	0.4575	0.5324	0.6120	0.6614	0.7800
13	0.4409	0.5139	0.5923	0.6411	0.7603
14	0.4259	0.4973	0.5742	0.6226	0.7420
15	0.4124	0.4821	0.5577	0.6055	0.7246
16	0.4000	0.4683	0.5425	0.5897	0.7084
17	0.3887	0.4555	0.5285	0.5751	0.6932
18	0.3783	0.4438	0.5155	0.5614	0.6787
19	0.3687	0.4329	0.5034	0.5487	0.6652
20	0.3598	0.4227	0.4921	0.5368	0.6524
25	0.3233	0.3809	0.4451	0.4869	0.5974
30	0.2960	0.3494	0.4093	0.4487	0.5541
35	0.2746	0.3246	0.3810	0.4182	0.5189
40	0.2573	0.3044	0.3578	0.3932	0.4896
45	0.2428	0.2875	0.3384	0.3721	0.4648
50	0.2306	0.2732	0.3218	0.3541	0.4433
60	0.2108	0.2500	0.2948	0.3248	0.4078
70	0.1954	0.2319	0.2737	0.3017	0.3799
80	0.1829	0.2172	0.2565	0.2830	0.3568
90	0.1726	0.2050	0.2422	0.2673	0.3375
100	0.1638	0.1946	0.2301	0.2540	0.3211

If the observed value of r *is greater than or equal to the tabled value for the appropriate level of significance (columns) and degrees of freedom (rows), reject* H$_0$ *[the null hypothesis]. The degrees of freedom are the number of pairs of scores minus two, or* N – 2. *The critical values in the table are both + and – for nondirectional (two-tailed) tests.*

APPENDIX C

CRITICAL VALUES OF *t*

df	Level of Significance for a Nondirectional (Two-Tailed) Test				
	.10	.05	.02	.01	.001
1	6.314	12.706	31.821	63.657	636.619
2	2.920	4.303	6.965	9.925	31.598
3	2.353	3.182	4.541	5.841	12.941
4	2.132	2.776	3.747	4.604	8.610
5	2.015	2.571	3.365	4.032	6.859
6	1.943	2.447	3.143	3.707	5.959
7	1.895	2.365	2.998	3.499	5.405
8	1.860	2.306	2.896	3.355	5.041
9	1.833	2.262	2.821	3.250	4.781
10	1.812	2.228	2.764	3.169	4.587
11	1.796	2.201	2.718	3.106	4.437
12	1.782	2.179	2.681	3.055	4.318
13	1.771	2.160	2.650	3.012	4.221
14	1.761	2.145	2.624	2.977	4.140
15	1.753	2.131	2.602	2.947	4.073
16	1.746	2.120	2.583	2.921	4.015
17	1.740	2.110	2.567	2.898	3.965
18	1.734	2.101	2.552	2.878	3.922
19	1.729	2.093	2.539	2.861	3.883
20	1.725	2.086	2.528	2.845	3.850
21	1.721	2.080	2.518	2.831	3.819
22	1.717	2.074	2.508	2.819	3.792
23	1.714	2.069	2.500	2.807	3.767
24	1.711	2.064	2.492	2.797	3.745
25	1.706	2.060	2.485	2.787	3.725
26	1.706	2.056	2.479	2.779	3.707
27	1.703	2.052	2.473	2.771	3.690
28	1.701	2.048	2.467	2.763	3.674
29	1.699	2.045	2.462	2.756	3.659
30	1.697	2.042	2.457	2.750	3.646
40	1.684	2.021	2.423	2.704	3.551
60	1.671	2.000	2.390	2.660	3.460
120	1.658	1.980	2.358	2.617	3.373
∞	1.645	1.960	2.326	2.576	3.291

The value listed in the table is the critical value of t *for the number of degrees of freedom listed in the left column for a directional (one-tailed) or nondirectional (two-tailed) test at the significance level indicated at the top of each column. If the observed* t *is greater than or equal to the tabled value, reject* H_0 *[the null hypothesis]. Since the* t *distribution is symmetrical about* t = 0*, these critical values represent both + and − values for nondirectional tests.*

NEL

APPENDIX D

CRITICAL VALUES OF *F*★

Degrees of Freedom in Denominator	Degrees of Freedom in Numerator													
	1	2	3	4	5	6	7	8	9	10	20	50	100	∞
1	161	200	216	225	230	234	237	239	241	242	248	252	253	254
	4052	**5000**	**5402**	**5625**	**5764**	**5859**	**5928**	**5980**	**6022**	**6056**	**6208**	**6302**	**6334**	**6366**
2	18.51	19.00	19.16	19.25	19.30	19.33	19.36	19.37	19.38	19.39	19.44	19.47	19.49	19.50
	98.50	**99.00**	**99.17**	**99.25**	**99.30**	**99.33**	**99.34**	**99.36**	**99.38**	**99.40**	**99.45**	**99.48**	**99.49**	**99.50**
3	10.13	9.55	9.28	9.12	9.01	8.94	8.88	8.84	8.81	8.78	8.66	8.58	8.56	8.53
	34.12	**30.81**	**29.46**	**28.71**	**28.24**	**27.91**	**27.67**	**27.49**	**27.34**	**27.23**	**26.69**	**26.30**	**26.23**	**26.12**
4	7.71	6.94	6.59	6.39	6.26	6.16	6.09	6.04	6.00	5.96	5.80	5.70	5.66	5.63
	21.20	**18.00**	**16.69**	**15.98**	**15.52**	**15.21**	**14.98**	**14.80**	**14.66**	**14.54**	**14.02**	**13.69**	**13.57**	**13.46**
5	6.61	5.79	5.41	5.19	5.05	4.95	4.88	4.82	4.78	4.74	4.56	4.44	4.40	4.36
	16.26	**13.27**	**12.06**	**11.39**	**10.97**	**10.67**	**10.45**	**10.27**	**10.15**	**10.05**	**9.55**	**9.24**	**9.13**	**9.02**
6	5.99	5.14	4.76	4.53	4.39	4.28	4.21	4.15	4.10	4.06	3.87	3.75	3.71	3.67
	13.74	**10.92**	**9.78**	**9.15**	**8.75**	**8.47**	**8.26**	**8.10**	**7.98**	**7.87**	**7.39**	**7.09**	**6.99**	**6.88**
7	5.59	4.74	4.35	4.12	3.97	3.87	3.79	3.73	3.68	3.63	3.44	3.32	3.28	3.23
	12.25	**9.55**	**8.45**	**7.85**	**7.46**	**7.19**	**7.00**	**6.84**	**6.71**	**6.62**	**6.15**	**5.85**	**5.75**	**5.65**
8	5.32	4.46	4.07	3.84	3.69	3.58	3.50	3.44	3.39	3.34	3.15	3.03	2.98	2.93
	11.26	**8.65**	**7.59**	**7.01**	**6.63**	**6.37**	**6.19**	**6.03**	**5.91**	**5.82**	**5.36**	**5.06**	**4.96**	**4.86**
9	5.12	4.26	3.86	3.63	3.48	3.37	3.29	3.23	3.18	3.13	2.93	2.80	2.76	2.71
	10.56	**8.02**	**6.99**	**6.42**	**6.06**	**5.80**	**5.62**	**5.47**	**5.35**	**5.26**	**4.80**	**4.51**	**4.41**	**4.31**
10	4.96	4.10	3.71	3.48	3.33	3.22	3.14	3.07	3.02	2.97	2.77	2.64	2.59	2.54
	10.04	**7.56**	**6.55**	**5.99**	**5.64**	**5.39**	**5.21**	**5.06**	**4.95**	**4.85**	**4.41**	**4.12**	**4.01**	**3.91**
11	4.84	3.98	3.59	3.36	3.20	3.09	3.01	2.95	2.90	2.86	2.65	2.50	2.45	2.40
	9.56	**7.20**	**6.22**	**5.67**	**5.32**	**5.07**	**4.88**	**4.74**	**4.63**	**4.54**	**4.10**	**3.80**	**3.70**	**3.60**
12	4.75	3.88	3.49	3.26	3.11	3.00	2.92	2.85	2.80	2.76	2.54	2.40	2.35	2.30
	9.33	**6.93**	**5.95**	**5.41**	**5.06**	**4.82**	**4.65**	**4.50**	**4.39**	**4.30**	**3.86**	**3.56**	**3.46**	**3.36**
13	4.67	3.80	3.41	3.18	3.02	2.92	2.84	2.77	2.72	2.67	2.46	2.32	2.26	2.21
	9.07	**6.70**	**5.74**	**5.20**	**4.86**	**4.62**	**4.44**	**4.30**	**4.19**	**4.10**	**3.67**	**3.37**	**3.27**	**3.16**
14	4.60	3.74	3.34	3.11	2.96	2.85	2.77	2.70	2.65	2.60	2.39	2.24	2.19	2.13
	8.86	**6.51**	**5.56**	**5.03**	**4.69**	**4.46**	**4.28**	**4.14**	**4.03**	**3.94**	**3.51**	**3.21**	**3.11**	**3.00**
15	4.54	3.68	3.29	3.06	2.90	2.79	2.70	2.64	2.59	2.55	2.33	2.18	2.12	2.07
	8.68	**6.36**	**5.42**	**4.89**	**4.56**	**4.32**	**4.14**	**4.00**	**3.89**	**3.80**	**3.36**	**3.07**	**2.97**	**2.87**

★ *The F-ratio is statistically significant when it exceeds or equals the values above. The .05 level is shown in light type; the .01 level in bold type.*

(continued)

Critical Values of F
(continued)

Degrees of Freedom in Denominator	Degrees of Freedom in Numerator													
	1	2	3	4	5	6	7	8	9	10	20	50	100	∞
16	4.49	3.63	3.24	3.01	2.85	2.74	2.66	2.59	2.54	2.49	2.28	2.13	2.07	2.01
	8.53	**6.23**	**5.29**	**4.77**	**4.44**	**4.20**	**4.03**	**3.89**	**3.78**	**3.69**	**3.25**	**2.96**	**2.86**	**2.75**
17	4.45	3.59	3.20	2.96	2.81	2.70	2.62	2.55	2.50	2.45	2.23	2.08	2.02	1.96
	8.40	**6.11**	**5.18**	**4.67**	**4.34**	**4.10**	**3.93**	**3.79**	**3.68**	**3.59**	**3.16**	**2.86**	**2.76**	**2.65**
18	4.41	3.55	3.16	2.93	2.77	2.66	2.58	2.51	2.46	2.41	2.19	2.04	1.98	1.92
	8.28	**6.01**	**5.09**	**4.58**	**4.25**	**4.01**	**3.85**	**3.71**	**3.60**	**3.51**	**3.07**	**2.78**	**2.68**	**2.57**
19	4.38	3.52	3.13	2.90	2.74	2.63	2.55	2.48	2.43	2.38	2.15	2.00	1.94	1.88
	8.18	**5.93**	**5.01**	**4.50**	**4.17**	**3.94**	**3.77**	**3.63**	**3.52**	**3.43**	**3.00**	**2.70**	**2.60**	**2.49**
20	4.35	3.49	3.10	2.87	2.71	2.60	2.52	2.45	2.40	2.35	2.12	1.96	1.90	1.84
	8.10	**5.85**	**4.94**	**4.43**	**4.10**	**3.87**	**3.71**	**3.56**	**3.45**	**3.37**	**2.94**	**2.63**	**2.53**	**2.42**
25	4.24	3.38	2.99	2.76	2.60	2.49	2.41	2.34	2.28	2.24	2.00	1.84	1.77	1.71
	7.77	**5.57**	**4.68**	**4.18**	**3.86**	**3.63**	**3.46**	**3.32**	**3.21**	**3.13**	**2.70**	**2.40**	**2.29**	**2.17**
30	4.17	3.32	2.92	2.69	2.53	2.42	2.34	2.27	2.21	2.16	1.93	1.76	1.69	1.62
	7.56	**5.39**	**4.51**	**4.02**	**3.70**	**3.47**	**3.30**	**3.17**	**3.06**	**2.98**	**2.55**	**2.24**	**2.13**	**2.01**
40	4.08	3.23	2.84	2.61	2.45	2.34	2.25	2.18	2.12	2.07	1.84	1.66	1.59	1.51
	7.31	**5.18**	**4.31**	**3.83**	**3.51**	**3.29**	**3.12**	**2.99**	**2.88**	**2.80**	**2.37**	**2.05**	**1.94**	**1.81**
50	4.03	3.18	2.79	2.56	2.40	2.29	2.20	2.13	2.07	2.02	1.78	1.60	1.52	1.44
	7.17	**5.06**	**4.20**	**3.72**	**3.41**	**3.18**	**3.02**	**2.88**	**2.78**	**2.70**	**2.26**	**1.94**	**1.82**	**1.68**
100	3.94	3.09	2.70	2.46	2.30	2.19	2.10	2.03	1.97	1.92	1.68	1.48	1.39	1.28
	6.90	**4.82**	**3.98**	**3.51**	**3.20**	**2.99**	**2.82**	**2.69**	**2.59**	**2.51**	**2.06**	**1.73**	**1.59**	**1.43**
200	3.89	3.04	2.65	2.41	2.26	2.14	2.05	1.98	1.92	1.87	1.62	1.42	1.32	1.19
	6.76	**4.71**	**3.88**	**3.41**	**3.11**	**2.90**	**2.73**	**2.60**	**2.50**	**2.41**	**1.97**	**1.62**	**1.48**	**1.28**
∞	3.84	3.00	2.60	2.37	2.21	2.10	2.01	1.94	1.88	1.83	1.57	1.35	1.24	1.00
	6.64	**4.61**	**3.78**	**3.32**	**3.02**	**2.80**	**2.64**	**2.51**	**2.41**	**2.32**	**1.87**	**1.52**	**1.36**	**1.00**

GLOSSARY

Academic freedom: the Canadian Association of University Teachers defines academic freedom as "the right to teach, learn, study and publish free of orthodoxy or threat of reprisal and discrimination" as long as one doesn't violate the ethical standards of one's discipline. Free inquiry is seen as the foundation upon which innovation, creativity and theoretical development can grow. Concern about academic freedom is growing these days as the intervention of third parties into the research process–government, corporations, special interest groups–seems to be increasingly placing constraints on what researchers can do, and universities and colleges administrations themselves seem to be engaging more frequently in micromanagement of their faculty. (p. 21)

Accretion measures: measures that reflect some sort of addition to or building up of products or materials because of our physical presence or activity—documents we produce, products we manufacture, arts and crafts we create, graffiti we write, and so on. Contrasts with **erosion measures**. (p. 218)

***Ad hoc* mixed method integration:** where different data sources and methods are embraced as a result of surprise discoveries that arise during the research process. For example, you might begin a study with interview or oral histories and find during your discussions that an archival set of data also exist that the person you are interviewing will allow you access to. (p. 398)

Adaptive questioning: where answers to specific questions influence the subsequent questions asked. For example, a question early in a survey might ask you to identify your favourite sport. If you respond that it is "hockey," then instead of subsequent questions asking you about "your favourite sport" an adaptive questioning strategy would simply refer to "hockey" given that you have already identified that as your favourite sport. (p. 148)

Aggregated data: data from more than one case that have been combined for analysis. For example, suppose the students in your class each receive a score on the final exam. If we combine ("aggregate") all those scores, we can investigate their distribution, for example, their mean, variability, and so on. If we have other aggregated data on the same people (e.g., how many hours they spent studying or how much emphasis they place on grades), we can look for patterns in the relationships among these bits of information. (p. 6)

Analysis of variance (ANOVA): a probability-based statistical test used to determine whether the means of two or more groups differ from one another. It does so by means of an *F*-test that evaluates the difference between group means relative to the amount of variation that exists within groups. It is similar to using multiple *t*-tests on a given set of data, but controls for error rate in the process. (p. 370)

Analytic control: one of the two general approaches to research that attempts to make inferences about "causes." Contrasts with **manipulative control**, in which the researcher creates or actively intervenes in a situation to create conditions (e.g., as in the classic experiment) and to move people around (e.g., through the creation of control groups and *experimental groups* and through the random assignment of participants to conditions) so that clarity of inference is given the highest priority. In *analytic control,* the researcher takes an existing situation and, through his or her analytical powers alone, tries to "make sense" of the causal patterns that exist. (p. 235)

Analytic induction: a process of theory formulation characteristic of inductive approaches. The researcher begins by making observations and formulating a tentative explanation for those observations. Next, the researcher examines the adequacy of that explanation (does it account for all the data?) and revises the explanation until it successfully accounts for all observed data. Particular attention is paid to negative cases (observations that are inconsistent with the tentative explanatory scheme), since these will suggest revisions. Once an explanatory scheme has been devised that's consistent with all the data gathered to date, the researcher gathers more data to see whether they, too, are consistent with the explanation. If not, the process continues. (p. 288)

Annotation: memos or notes about ones thoughts or insights on a particular passage of qualitative material. In NVivo annotations are virtual sticky notes–that we attach to a particular element (section of text or area of image, video or audio) of any project document. (p. 324)

Anomalies: things that aren't supposed to happen, if indeed a theory is true. For example, early astronomers, who believed that the earth was the centre of the universe, were faced with the anomaly that Mars does not follow a circular or elliptical path around us, but occasionally "wanders" back and forth across the heavens. Recognition of this anomaly was a boon to theory development in astronomy; Copernicus eventually argued for the correctness of *his* theory (that we travel around the sun) because it accounted very simply for what only appeared to be Mars's irregular path, explaining why the illusion occurred. (p. 34)

Anonymize: the process of taking research data and deleting all names and other identifying information that could be used to identify the source of the data. (p. 75)

Archival measures: comprise any information that is contained in "hard copy" or digital records or documents. One might argue that archival measures are nothing more than a particular type of accretion measure, since the documents referred to are products of human activity, but they are sufficiently different and voluminous to be treated as entities worthy of consideration on their own. (p. 217)

Association: a statistical relationship of dependence between two or more variables or measures such that variation in one variable or measure accompanies variation in other variables or measures. The extent to which two or more variables "go together." Statistical measures of association include chi-square, phi-coefficient, the coefficient of contingency, Cramer's V, and Pearsons r. (p. 236)

Assumption of pretest equivalence: the logic of the experiment is, "If two groups are equal to begin with (at the pretest) and treated identically in all respects but one, that one being the presence or absence of the independent (or treatment) variable, then any differences between the groups that is observed at the end of the experiment must be due to the one element on which they differed, that is, the independent variable." Note the phrase "if the two groups are equal to begin with…"; this is the *assumption of pretest equivalence* (that is, that the groups are equal, overall or on average, at the pretest). Violation of this assumption comes from selection biases, which threaten **internal validity**. (p. 244)

Axial coding: see **focused coding**.

Bonferroni technique: a technique that involves splitting the adopted probability required for significance across the entire range of comparisons to be made. For example, if you're adopting a significance level of *p* < .05 and plan to undertake 10 separate *t*-tests (or chi-squares or Pearson correlations), the Bonferroni procedure involves spreading the .05 (known as the *experiment-wise error rate*) across the 10 comparisons, with the result that a .05/10 = .005 significance level would have to be achieved on any given comparison before you'd be prepared to consider it "reliable." (p. 369)

Case study analysis: analysis of a single case. (p. 11)

Case-by-case privilege: a common law method of claiming privilege whereby the researcher argues that the specific relationships that he or she forms with his or her participants within the context of the research is one that demands special protections of communications between the researcher and participant and that s/he should not be obliged to give evidence in court that would identify individual research participants or the data a specific individual supplied. In such cases the researcher must demonstrate that confidentiality was crucial to their specific research project. See also: **class privilege**. (p. 77)

Categorical response item: questionnaire response options where respondents may place themselves in pre-defined categories. The simplest type of categorical question is the **dichotomous** item, a type of categorical response option with only two response alternatives (e.g., the categories of pass or fail). (p. 166)

Categorical variables: variables that differ in kind but have no order or magnitude underlying their differences. For example, you might be counting types of fruit and the your categories might include bananas, apples, and oranges. The three are simply different types of fruit, with none of them being any more or less of a fruit than the others. (p. 334)

Category system: a type of coding scheme that involves using a set of mutually exclusive and exhaustive categories to code any given behaviour we observe. For example, to use a category system to code for violent content in a film, we'd typically begin by breaking the film into units (on, say, a minute-by-minute or a scene-by-scene basis) and code whether the behaviour in each minute or scene is predominantly violent, nonviolent, or whatever. Category systems give a better indication of the *temporal flow* of criterion acts during the observational period than do **sign systems**. (p. 200)

***Caveat emptor* ethic:** "caveat emptor" is a Latin phrase that means "let the buyer beware." The classic example is when you buy a used car: as long as the seller does not mislead you, it is up to you to do whatever testing or assessment that needs to be done to ensure you are not buying a lemon. In the realm of research ethics, it refers to those who believe that by warning people about what they might encounter by participating in research, you have fulfilled your ethical obligations and hence that, if problems arise, you can simply say "Gee, that's too bad but I told you that could happen." As such, it downloads responsibility to the participants, which is antithetical to what research ethics are supposed to be all about, i.e., caring for the research participant, trying to ensure that nothing adverse happens to them as a function of their participation, and taking responsibility in the event anything does happen. (p. 82)

Ceteris paribus: a Latin phrase meaning "all else being equal." This phrase—often explicitly and always implicitly—underlies theoretical statements; that is, variables *X* and *Y* are related to each other, *ceteris paribus*. It's also the cornerstone of the experimentalist methods discussed in Chapters 9 and 10. The true experiment embodies the *ceteris paribus* assumption by testing the effects of certain variables on other variables under conditions in which, overall, all other variables are equalized. (p. 45)

Chi-square: a statistical test of independence used to assess whether two categorical variables are associated beyond what would be expected on the basis of chance variation alone. The chi-square statistic describes deviations between what we'd expect (on the basis of chance, i.e., if the two variables were indeed independent) and what we actually observe. (p. 350)

Class privilege: a relationship–such as that between a lawyer and his or her client–that is recognized and protected under law so that the normal obligation we have to testify what we know when subpoenaed is set aside. A relationship of class privilege means that the court is prepared to assume it exists without the need for the parties of the relationship to prove they deserve to have the confidence of their communications protected every time their confidences are challenged. In such relationships the onus of proof is on those challenging the protected nature of the communications to demonstrate what compelling reasons exist for the privilege to be set aside. (p. 76)

Classic content analysis: classic content analysis is a method of data analysis that allows an analyst to present an 'objective' description of key features of non-numeric data. Demonstrations that the content analytic scheme can be applied reliably and validly are paramount. A central objective of classical content analysis is to present a precise numeric account of the frequency, type, and features of words, ideas, actions, depictions, or other elements of interest present in textual or visual data. A related objective is to also present a thorough analysis of the themes and valuations that are present within the text or images being scrutinized. (p. 307)

Classic experiment: a type of research design, often conducted in a controlled environment such as a laboratory, where the researcher is able to isolate causal relationships between the dependent variable and one or more independent variables. (p. 7)

Cluster analysis: a method of organizing coded material that involves placing similarly thematically coded information (e.g., people, places, events, or social artifacts that share common characteristics) into relational categories that allow the analyst to make distinctions among groupings or clusters of people, places, and so on that are meaningful to the researcher and/or participants. (p. 306)

Coding: a method of data management whereby the analyst attempts to simplify observations by way of assigning them to conceptually or theoretically relevant categories. When an analyst codes the volumes of data they have collected they are in essence organizing and reducing the data into smaller more manageable segments that can be retrieved easily and compared with other coded segments of data. A coded segment might represent or illustrate a specific theoretical or analytic concept, or it can simply reflect elements of the data that we want to highlight or think about further. (p. 304)

Coding scheme: a manual, often prepared prior to the analysis of data that is used to structure the coding of textual, visual, or audio observations in a manner that helps to improve the validity and reliability of the coding classifications made. (p. 199)

Coefficient of contingency: a general class of statistics based in a variation of the chi-square statistic that addresses the degree of association, ranging from -1 to $+1$, between categorically measured variables represented in a contingency table or cross-tabulation. (p. 355)

Common law: law based on legal precedents as established through judicial decisions as opposed to legislative decree. (p. 74)

Comparison group: see **control group**.

Compensatory equalization of treatments: one of several possible threats to internal validity that can emerge in field settings when the treatment or program being evaluated involves goods and/or services considered desirable and where there is a large disparity between groups. Seeing the disparity, administrators, those charged with implementing the treatment, or some of the recipients may reroute some goods or provide access to services among some or all members of the disadvantaged group in an effort to alleviate the disparity. This practice makes the groups less distinct than they would otherwise have been, leading to an erroneous finding of "no difference." (p. 276)

Compensatory rivalry: one of several possible threats to internal validity that can emerge in field settings. If it's known that an evaluation is in progress, one may see compensatory rivalry by the respondents who are receiving the less desirable treatment(s). Knowing that one is in the disadvantaged group may spur a competitive spirit to overcome adversity and perform well. This is particularly likely to be the case in situations where the group already perceives itself as a group (e.g., work teams, crews, classes) and has a lot to lose if a difference is revealed. (p. 276)

Complete observer: one end of the traditional observational continuum. In this role, the researcher identifies himself or herself to the participants as a researcher who's engaged in observational research, either by conducting a study in his or her own setting (e.g., a laboratory or clinic) or by gaining access to another setting (e.g., an organization or a group) after seeking and obtaining permission from someone appropriate. Once in the setting, the complete observer typically does his or her best to remain relatively inconspicuous, doing nothing other than observe with the full knowledge of all who are present that that's why the researcher is there. (p. 190)

Complete participant: one end of the traditional observational continuum. In this role, the observer doesn't reveal himself or herself as a researcher;

from the perspective of those being observed, the researcher *is* a participant. There are two ways this might occur: (1) *post hoc* observation, where a former participant writes his or her account of a setting or event well after the fact, and (2) surreptitious observation, where the researcher observes people without their knowing that they're being observed for the purpose of research. Contrasts with **complete observer** (the other extreme of the role continuum). (p. 190)

Computer-assisted social research (CASR): the practice of using digital or network technologies in order to enhance conventional approaches to observation and data collection. (p. 117)

Computer-assisted telephone interviewing (CATI): a form of telephone interviewing where the researcher uses a computerized script to aid him or her in the administration of the interview and the recording of participant responses. (p. 146)

Conceptual mapping: the act of graphically diagramming the relationships between several theoretically relevant concepts. (p. 58)

Concordance distribution: a listing of the words or phrases that are most often used before or after a word specified in a key-word-in-context (KWIC) analysis. (p. 308)

Concurrent mixed method designs: refers to the situation where one is engaging different methods at the same time. For example, while Ted was doing observational research with police patrol officers on the way that they were using a mobile radio data system, a computer archive was simultaneously being generated that allowed him to compare how officers used the system when he was watching them as opposed to when he was not. (p. 395)

Concurrent validity: a type of validity that involves correlating responses on our measure to some other criterion. Suppose our measure of "romantic love" involves asking two people the question "Are you in love?" We must show that responses to that question are tied to some other independent measure of "love." For example, Zick Rubin's (1973) research on this topic shows that people who say they're "in love" tend to gaze into each other's eyes more often and for longer periods than do couples who do not say they're in love. If we take those measures at approximately the same time, we're engaging in concurrent validation. "Concurrent" means "at the same time"; temporal closeness between the two measures defines concurrent validation. Contrasts with **predictive validity**. (p. 57)

Confidentiality: the ethical right of people to keep information about themselves private or to share it only with those whom they trust to safeguard it. (p. 71)

Confidentiality certificate: a certificate issued by the National Institutes of Health in the United States that provides statutory protection for researchers to ensure that they cannot be forced to disclose identifying research information about participants to any civil, criminal, administrative, legislative or other proceeding. See also **Privacy certificates**. (p. 72)

Consensus model: consensus theoretical models assume that there is general agreement in society about right and wrong, the boundary between criminal and non-criminal activity, the role of government, and so on. They are generally distinguished from conflict models, which assume that views about these issues are not shared and in fact are often hotly contested, which raises questions about just whose interests are being served by government, the laws that are created, and so on. (p. 20)

Constant: something that does not vary or the act of equalizing the influence of the effect of one or more external influences on the experimental condition. This equalization ensures that the researcher can observe the true impact that a specified independent variable has on the dependent variable. (p. 334)

Constructionism: the view that we actively construct reality on the basis of our understandings, which are largely, though not completely, culturally shared. It thus becomes important to understand people's and society's constructions of things, because those constructions will have implications for how we study and make sense of the world. For example, men and women have been "constructed" as active and passive, respectively, for many years. This construction has even spread to our understandings of sexual intercourse and conception. We once envisioned active spermatozoa, released when the man ejaculates, swimming to the woman's ovum, which passively awaits fertilization. As our conceptions of women have changed in recent years, so, too, has our conception of conception. Now researchers bring a more egalitarian perspective to their understanding of the fertilization process: although the spermatozoa are still characterized as swimming to the ovum, the ovum is now considered to play a more active role in "send[ing] out messages to the sperm, participating actively in the process, until sperm and egg find each other and merge" (Flint 1995: D8). (p. 12)

Contingency questions: a question or a subset of questions in an interview or questionnaire that require the respondent to answer only if he or she has answered in a particular way to previously asked questions. (p. 145)

Contingency table: a celled matrix that is used to display the joint (or bivariate) frequencies of the distributions of responses to two nominal or categorical variables. (p. 350)

Control group (or comparison group): a group that is treated identically to the experimental group in *all* respects *except* that it does not receive the independent variable. Its purpose is to control for rival plausible explanations. (p. 241)

Convergent validity: the degree to which your measure is related to other measures to which it is supposed to be related. For example, a measure of how "in love" people are *should* be related to other measures of affection, intimacy, and commitment. If we show that our measure is related to those other indicators, we've demonstrated convergent validity. (p. 56)

Cramer's V: a statistic of association based on chi-square that depicts the strength of association, ranging from 0 to 1, between two categorically measured variables. (p. 355)

Criterion sampling: a type of purposive sampling that involves searching for cases or individuals who meet a predetermined criterion of importance, e.g., that they have a certain disease, meet specific age or language requirements, or have had a particular life experience. (p. 114)

Critical case sampling: a type of purposive sampling where the researcher is looking to extend her/his analysis by looking for a small number of important cases that s/he can use to test or extend her/his theory. (p. 114)

Critical realism: critical realism, or the *critical realist perspective,* can be seen as a midway resolution that acknowledges some truth in both realist and social constructionist perspectives. Like the constructionists, critical realists acknowledge that "reality" is indeed constructed and negotiated, but they also assert that reality is not *completely* negotiable, that is, all explanations are not equally viable. In other words, we *can* be "wrong." But, if we can be "wrong," there must be a reality out there that exists independent of our opinions of it. (p. 20)

Data analysis triangulation: the practice of employing several different methods of analyzing and interpreting data in order to improve the validity of the conclusions by ensuring the robustness of one's results. (p. 392)

De-construct: taking apart a piece of text or image or a concept in order to expose hidden meanings or assumptions. (p. 13)

Deductive approaches: research perspectives characterized by the belief that researchers should begin with theory, from which they then deduce hypotheses, which they then test by gathering data. If the data support the hypothesis, the theory that gave rise to that hypothesis has gained some support, and further tests of the theory (through further hypothesizing and data gathering) are formulated. If the data do not support the hypothesis, the theory's adequacy is questioned, suggesting that the theory should be either rejected or revised. Also known as the hypothetico-deductive method, and sometimes as *"top-down" approaches.* Contrasts with **inductive approaches**. (p. 27)

Deductive coding: where the analyst codes audio, video, or textual data using a well-specified or predefined set of interests or concepts. (p. 304)

Deductive method: see **hypothetico-deductive method**.

Definitional operationism: a play on the term "operational definition" that refers to a type of mono-operationism in which researchers engage in the tautology of operationally defining their variables of interest by definition. For example, a researcher may develop a measure of stupidity but, instead of showing that the measure possesses convergent and divergent validity with respect to other measures, may simply state that the measure is its own definition; that is, what we mean by stupidity is whatever our test measures. Needless to say, that's stupid. (p. 57)

Demographic variables: information about an individual or social group that helps contextualize the person or group, usually in relation to "social facts." It includes variables such as age, sex, race, socioeconomic status, education, and gender. (p. 52)

Dependent variable: in research, the variable we measure in order to assess whether the independent variable exerts any effects. It gains its name because a person's status on the variable (e.g., his or her score) *depends* on whatever effects the independent variable has. Also sometimes known as the *outcome* variable. (p. 237)

Descriptive coding: a basic level of coding that involves creating a summary of the general themes that are present within the material. (p. 304)

Descriptive statistics: statistics that are used to summarize sample data. The major ones included in Chapter 12 are statistics that describe central tendency (the mean, the median, and the mode) and variability (the mean and the standard deviation). (p. 333)

Deviant case sampling: see **extreme case sampling**.

Dichotomy: any division into two parts; an especially popular and appropriate term with respect to classification. A sample might be dichotomized into males and females or into an experimental and a control group. But dichotomies can also be less concrete; qualitative and quantitative approaches to science, for example, represent a dichotomy of research perspectives. (p. 166)

Dichotomous item: a type of categorical response item that contains only two response alternatives. For example, the question "What is your sex?" has only two possible responses for most situations: you can be male or female. (p. 166)

Diffusion (or imitation) of treatment: one of several possible threats to internal validity in field evaluations, where it's not unusual to be faced with intact groups that *cannot* be isolated from one another. Instead of having two (or more) comparison groups that are clearly distinct on the independent variable being considered, we may find that the boundaries between the groups are or become somewhat blurred. For example,

if the groups are differentiated by their access to varying sets of information, any communication between groups about the nature of this information will make each group a little more like the other(s). This diffusion of treatment will act to minimize the groups' separation and heighten their similarity. The independent variable, in other words, doesn't have a real opportunity to "work." (p. 276)

Digital technologies: the full range of computer software, hardware, and architecture that comprise the digital universe. Examples of digital technologies include cellphones, personal computers, digital recorders, digital audio players, gaming systems, wireless access points, and LCD projectors. (p. 22)

Direct realism (or naive realism): is the epistemological position that holds that there is a (i.e., one) reality out there that exists independent of us that can be understood and awaits our discovery. An implication of this view is that, if reality involves a singular truth that exists independent of the observer, it should be able to be understood by different observers in exactly the same way. (p. 4)

Direct relationship: see **positive relationship**.

Disconfirming (or negative case sampling): with this strategy the researcher is looking to extend her/his analysis by looking for cases that will disconfirm it, both to test theory and simply because it is often from our failures that we learn the most. The general principle here is, "If you think your results are not generalizable or the existence of a particular kind of case will undermine all that you 'know' to be true about a phenomenon, then look for that kind of case." See also: **negative cases (or negative case analysis)**. (p. 114)

Disproportional stratified random sample: a probability sampling technique that is used when the researcher is primarily interested in comparing results between strata rather than in making overall statements about the population or when one or more of the subgroups are so small that a consistent sampling ratio would leave sample sizes in some groups too small for adequate analysis. The researcher begins by stratifying the population into subgroups of interest and taking a random sample within each stratum. But a different sampling ratio is used within each stratum, so that equal numbers of units of analysis end up in each of the strata samples. (p. 107)

Divergent validity: involves showing that your measure is not related to other measures to which it's not supposed to be related. For example, a measure of how "in love" people are *should not* be related to independent and different concepts like respect or tolerance (since each of these can exist without love being present). If we show that our measure is independent of (i.e., not correlated with) measures of those other indicators, we've demonstrated divergent validity. (p. 56)

Double-barrelled items: when two questions are presented as a single item or question in a questionnaire or interview. (p. 174)

Ecological validity: a type of external validity that addresses issues of representativeness and generalizability in a slightly different way. Brunswik (1955) first used this term, which refers to the representativeness of the treatments and measures you use in relation to the particular milieu to which you wish to generalize. (p. 246)

Elimination of rival plausible explanations: the process of demonstrating that it is the putative cause per se that is responsible for changes in the dependent measure, rather than related variables, nuisance variables, artifacts, or any of myriad other potential causal agents that might have been present. When the observed relationship between *X* and *Y* is not explained by the presence of other plausible causal agents. One of the three criteria of causality that John Stuart Mill said must be satisfied in order to identify a causal relationship. (p. 236)

Empirical: an approach to the generation of knowledge that maintains that our understanding of the world should come not from philosophizing or speculation, but from data that comes from interacting with and observing the world we seek to understand. (p. 17)

Epistemic relationship: how well your nominal definition and your operational definition demonstrate goodness of fit; that is, how well your operational definition "gets at" or "assesses" what your nominal definition says you're interested in. (p. 50)

Epistemology: deals with the question of how we know what we know and what criteria we bring to the evaluation of whether something is "true" or not. (p. 4)

Erosion measures: measures that reflect some sort of wearing away or removal of products or materials because of our physical presence or activity. The wear on a jacket, worn pathways, and missing objects can all provide the basis for using *erosion measures*. Contrasts with **accretion measures**. (p. 218)

Exhaustive: covering all possible alternatives. A term often used in relation to response options provided in a questionnaire or structured interview such as a CATI. (p. 167)

Experimental operational definitions: creating an operational definition of a construct through the implementation of an experimental condition. (p. 51)

External validity: the *generalizability* of results beyond the specifics of the study, particularly to other people, situations, and times. (p. 246)

Extreme (or deviant case sampling): a purposive sampling technique where extreme cases that represent the purest or most clear cut instance of a phenomenon are selected. For example, if we were interested in studying management styles, it might be most interesting to study an organization that did exceptionally well and/or another that had high expectations but did exceptionally poorly. (p. 113)

Fallibilist realism: a philosophical position that maintains that human beings can be wrong about our beliefs and understandings of the world as a result we must be open to evidence that contradicts our beliefs and understandings. (p. 20)

Focused (or axial coding): creating new thematic categories of meaning by identifying relationships between larger categories and sub-categories of coded textual material. (p. 305)

Funnelling: a technique used in questionnaires and interviews when open-ended and closed or structured questions on the same issue are mixed together. Funnelling involves starting with more general questions and gradually becoming more and more specific. (p. 170)

Gatekeeper: a person who controls access to research participants or other research data such as archival content. Gatekeepers often hold a position of power or status relative to the individuals, groups, organizations, or social artifacts that the researcher is interested in accessing. (p. 86)

Generalizability: the ability to extend the results or findings of the research beyond its original context (i.e., sample) to a more general context (e.g., the population), other people, situations, or times. (p. 97)

Go native: a term used by positivists to mean a researcher's taking on the values and perspectives of the group being studied, so that he or she cannot maintain the detached, analytical stance required, according to positivists, for effectively studying the world. Positivists believe that getting too "involved" with the people we study will destroy our objectivity. (p. 5)

Grounded theory: a term made famous by Glaser and Strauss (1967) that describes theory that's *grounded* in observation. Although most consistent with an inductive approach, the term is not *in*consistent with deductive research: one may wish to test one's grounded theory deductively after it has been formulated. (p. 16)

History: in experimental research, one of many threats to internal validity. In this sense, the term refers to any specific events that occur during the course of the research in addition to the independent variable. To the extent that such other variables exist, they threaten internal validity because those other variables end up being rival plausible explanations for any changes we observe. History is effectively controlled by including a control group, which is a group that's treated identically in all respects to the experimental group (and hence subject to all the same historical factors), except for administration/receipt of the independent variable. (p. 238)

Hypothesis: an unambiguous statement about the results that you expect to occur in a situation if the theory that guides your work is true. Hypotheses are generally associated with deductive inquiry, which believes that "good research" should begin with theory and should be directed toward testing theory. Stating your hypothesis before beginning your research is a bit like placing your bets ahead of time, so that you can't come back later and say, "Oh yes, I knew that was going to happen." If you knew, you should have said so. (p. 7)

Hypothetico-deductive method: the long name given to the process of deduction in social science research. The prefix "hypothetico" points to the role that the *a priori* (before-the-fact) specification of hypotheses plays in this brand of inquiry. Contrasts with **inductive approaches**. (p. 7)

Imitation of treatment: see **diffusion of treatment**.

Incompatibility thesis: the belief that fundamental differences in the philosophical underpinnings of qualitative and quantitative research paradigms make the mixing of the two approaches impossible. (p. 393)

Independent variable: in research, the variable whose effects we wish to identify or assess. Also sometimes known as the *treatment* variable or the *causal* variable. Contrasts with **dependent variable**. (p. 237)

Inductive approaches: research perspectives characterized by the belief that research should begin with observation, since it is only on that basis that **grounded theory** will emerge. Thus, researchers observe, induce empirical generalizations based on their observations, and then, through analytic induction, attempt to develop a full-blown theory that adequately reflects the observed reality. Sometimes known as *"bottom-up" approaches;* contrasts with **deductive** (or "top-down") **approaches**. (p. 11)

Inductive coding: a method of coding textual, audio, or visual data where the analyst either begins with the identification of general themes and ideas that emerge from a very literal reading of the data and then proceeds to either elaborate the category by making finer and finer distinctions or s/he combines specific descriptive coding categories to create more general categories that bring disparate events or descriptions under the same conceptual umbrella. (p. 305)

Inferential statistics: statistics that are used to facilitate drawing conclusions about data–conclusions concerning the extent to which variables are associated and whether differences exist among groups–on the basis of population estimates derived from sample data. The techniques included in Chapter 12 are the *t*-test, the chi-square, and Pearson's product–moment correlation coefficient. (p. 333)

Information sheet: a clearly written and understandable written document that is presented to a research participant prior to their participation in a study that outlines what the nature of what is expected of them as participants, any risks involved, and any promises and safeguards the researcher offers. (p. 69)

Informed consent: an ethical principle that suggests you should not do things to people unless they say it's alright to do so and only when their consent is given on the basis of knowing all aspects of the situation and the possible outcomes that might affect their willingness to participate. Consent cannot be considered binding unless it's given on an *informed* basis. (p. 69)

Instrumentation: one of many possible threats to the internal validity of research, in this instance arising from changes in the way data are collected or organized during the course of a study. For example, if we change the way a certain statistic is gathered, using the "old" way when collecting the pretest data and the "new" way when collecting the posttest data, we don't know whether any differences we observe between pretest and posttest are due to the independent variable or simply to the change in the way we gathered the data. Instrumentation effects also occur when data changes over time because coders or raters become more practised or fatigued or because equipment wears down. (p. 241)

Intensity sampling: a form of purposive sampling that involves sampling people whose interests or vocation makes them experiential experts because of their frequent or ongoing exposure to a phenomenon. (p. 113)

Internal validity: the extent to which differences observed in an experimental study can be *unambiguously* attributed to the experimental treatment itself, rather than to other factors. In other words, to what extent can you be certain that the differences we observe are caused by the independent variable per se, rather than by rival plausible explanations? (p. 237)

Interpretive coding: often distinguished from descriptive coding, which refers to the application of fairly straightforward codes to describe thematic content. Interpretive coding is often a next step that sees the researcher/coder going beyond superficial description to make inferences about underlying qualities or motives. For example, more descriptive categorization might involve coding simply whether a person is "moving" or not. A more interpretive code might ask the researcher/coder to determine whether the person is "in a hurry" or not. Generally speaking, the more interpretive the code, the lower the reliability. (p. 304)

Interquartile range (IQR): a measure of statistical dispersion that highlights the distance between the 25th and 75th percentile of a distribution of scores, this statistic is not influenced by extreme scores since only the middle 50 percent of the distribution of scores are taken into account. (p. 346)

Inter-rater reliability: the degree to which two or more people, using the same coding scheme and observing the same people, produce essentially the same results. Inter-rater agreement must normally be higher than 80 percent in order to be considered acceptable. Compare **test–retest reliability**. (p. 56)

Interval-level measurement: a measure with no true zero point that has rank-ordered ordered attributes with a meaningful distance between them. The most commonly presented example of an interval measure is thermometer readings as the thermometer scale has no true zero point, the intervals between temperature readings go up or down in equal intervals and the interval between 20° and 30° is equal to the interval between 10° and 20°. (p. 335)

Intranet: refers to privately constructed and maintained computer networks that can be accessed only by authorized persons within the company, organization, or institution. Often connected to the Internet, security is maintained by the use of firewalls. Because of their universality of access within the organization, intranets can be used by authorized researchers to gain access to the entire population of the organization, or representative or targeted samples thereof. (p. 118)

Inverse relationship: see **negative relationship**.

Investigator triangulation: refers to the practice of several different researchers contributing in the study to collect, analyze, and interpret data and observations. This practice is thought to improve both the credibility of the observations and the resulting interpretation of the research. (p. 392)

Jackknifing: a technique used when you have a very large number of cases (e.g., 10 times as many cases as you have variables) and want to assess the replicability or reliability of your results. There are several ways to perform this procedure, but the simplest is to randomly split your sample of cases into *two* samples, do the analyses you want to do separately in the two samples, and then focus only on those results that emerge as statistically significant in *both* data sets. (p. 369)

John Henry effect: when participants from the control group in an experimental design actively compete with the experimental group thereby changing their behaviour. This threat to the internal validity of the study is based on an individual by the name of John Henry who, when he learned that his performance was to be compared to that of a steam drill, worked so hard that he outperformed the drill but died in the process. (p. 276)

Key-word-in-context (KWIC) analysis: this type of analysis of textual content involves locating all the places in a document where a particular word or phrase appears and then analyzing the word context surrounding the word or phrase. To do this we generally begin by selecting a word or phrase we are interested in and what range of words surrounding it we will look at in order to determine context. Most analyses of this type select 20–30 words that come before and after the appearance of the selected word. (p. 307)

Likert-type items: a type of structured response item developed by Rensis Likert. Two attributes distinguish a "Likert-type" item. First, the item is an *assertion* (rather than a question). Second, the respondent's task is to indicate the extent to which s/he *agrees* or *disagrees* with the assertion. (p. 164)

Limited confidentiality: when the guarantee of confidentiality that the researcher provides her or his participant is limited by the law as opposed to disciplinary standards. Under limited confidentiality the researcher is saying s/he will divulge information provided by a participant in confidence if s/he is compelled by a court or other legal body to do so. Even in such circumstances, however, the researcher cannot simply wash his/her hands of the situation, because our obligation to minimize harm to our participants remains. To do otherwise would be to engage in ***caveat emptor* ethics**. (p. 81)

Longitudinal research: one of two categories into which research projects fall: *cross-sectional* or *longitudinal*. A cross-sectional study, like a snapshot, provides a glimpse of a sample of people at one point in time. Longitudinal research, in contrast, looks at the same group over time. (p. 63)

Manipulation checks: a common element in experimental designs that involve manipulated independent variables. Because the question being addressed is a validity question, the issue is whether you have indeed created the variable you thought you were creating and/or whether you are assessing the effect of the variable you think you are assessing. (p. 51)

Manipulative control: the active and intentional manipulation of the setting by the researcher in order to maximize clarity of inference by controlling rival plausible explanations. Manipulative control is epitomized by the laboratory experiment, where the experimenter exerts control over every aspect of the setting. Contrasts with **analytic control**. (p. 235)

Matching: a method of intentionally *creating* pretest equivalence. Contrasts with random assignment, which allows you to *assume* pretest equivalence. To use matching, we begin by identifying pairs of individuals who are matched (i.e., as similar as possible) on some variable (e.g., pretest scores), and then randomly assign one person from each pair to the experimental group and the other to the control group. In this way, we're guaranteed groups that are constituted equally with respect to that matching variable. (p. 246)

Maturation: in experimental research, one of many possible threats to internal validity. Defined as processes within the research participants that change as a function of time per se (not specific to particular events), such as growing older, more tired, getting hungrier, and so on. In other words, sometimes changes happen merely because of biological processes that happen over time, and we must be careful to recognize those processes and their effects when we're assessing the effects of other independent variables. (p. 238)

Maximum variation sampling: a type of purposive sampling strategy where the researcher seeks to sample a wide range of extremes of the population to ensure that the resulting sample is as diverse as possible. (p. 114)

Mean: the arithmetic average of a group of scores computed by taking the sum of the values of all scores and dividing them by the total number of scores. (p. 342)

Measured operational definitions: these are contrasted with experimental operational definitions that are created by an experimenter. In the case of measured operational definitions, the research might develop an instrument that simply assesses the extent to which some construct of interest is present. For example, we might operationalize "authoritarianism" by developing an attitude scale that measures authoritarianism, as, for example, Altemeyer (1981) did. (p. 50)

Median: the centermost score in a distribution of scores, the score that splits a distribution of scores in half such that 50 percent of the scores lie above it and 50 percent lie below it. (p. 342)

Memo: a note that we write to ourselves where we elaborate upon the categories of meaning that are beginning to emerge from the research or coding process, just as we might write margin notes in a book we are reading, or include thoughts and other "notes to self" in our field notes as we think of them. (p. 324)

Memoing: a process involved in the analysis of textual, audio, or visual data where the analyst records and reflects upon the observations and insights that s/he has accrued through the research and coding process. (p. 305)

Metaphysics: speculation about the nature of truth and being that goes beyond directly observable truths and into the realm of speculation and abstraction. Positivists, for example, would eschew metaphysics. (p. 4)

Methodological triangulation: employing multiple methods to study a particular phenomenon in order to overcome the deficiencies and biases that may result from employing a single method approach. (p. 392)

Mixed methods approach: defined by Johnson et al. (2007) as "the type of research in which a researcher or team of researchers combines elements of qualitative and quantitative research approaches (e.g., use of qualitative and quantitative viewpoints, data collection, analysis, inference techniques) for the broad purposes of breadth and depth of understanding and corroboration" (123). (p. 3)

Mode: the most typical or frequently occurring score or response in a distribution of scores or responses. (p. 342)

Modus operandi method: a concept advanced by Scriven (1976) to explain the kind of case study analysis that many people (physicians, mechanics, historians, coroners, etc.) do—and do well—all the time. The modus operandi method begins with the creation of a "causal checklist," that is, all those elements that go into producing a certain phenomenon. To explain the phenomenon's presence or absence, we look to that list. If only one element is present (or missing), that element is the cause of the phenomenon's presence or absence. In the event that *more than one* plausible factor emerges, Scriven (1976) suggests that we look for a modus operandi (MO) to help identify the actual cause, just as a detective might identify a criminal by the characteristic manner in which a crime is executed. (p. 286)

Mono-method bias: see **mono-operationalism**.

Mono-operationism and mono-method bias: two potential problems that can be produced when researchers become overly reliant on, respectively, a particular *measure* of a construct or a particular *way* of measuring it. *Mono-operationism* (sometimes called *mono-operation bias*) refers to the problem that develops when we use only one operational definition of a variable (e.g., if we use only IQ tests to measure intelligence, never trying to measure it any other way). *Mono-method bias* refers to reliance on only one method (e.g., self-report interviews) instead of investigating a phenomenon in a number of different ways (e.g., also incorporating observational and/or archival research). See also **definitional operationism**. (p. 52)

"Monte Carlo" computer simulation: a technique that's used to address what occurs when certain assumptions that are required by probability theory are violated. Much of probability theory, on which most social science statistics are based, is based on "long-run" expectations, expectations about what would be true if there were an infinite number of trials. One great advantage of computers derives from the fact that they'll do the same thing over and over again—and do so incredibly quickly—until you tell them to stop. And although you cannot have them process any information an *infinite* number of times (since, by definition, the processing would never end), you can nonetheless instruct a computer to process a set of instructions a *very large* number of times, where "very large" is so large a number that the observed outcomes will closely approximate what you would find if you were to repeat the instructions an infinite number of times. Monte Carlo simulations have been used in this way to evaluate such questions as (a) whether you'd get incorrect results if you violated the assumptions of the *t*-test and found that the dependent variable is not normally distributed in the population; or (b) whether you'd be misled if you accidentally subjected ordinal data to a *t*-test. (p. 337)

Mortality: a situation in which some individuals drop out of the research before it's completed. Single-session, short-term laboratory experimentation virtually precludes mortality as a problem. But in the field, where time-series data and a succession of follow-ups are more likely, the mortality problem increases in relevance. Some individuals who are recorded as participants at the beginning of the study do not return to receive the dependent measure at follow-up; for example, they drop out of therapy, choose to resign from the group, move to another jurisdiction, are released on parole, join another club, get lost, or die. The problem is one of *selection bias*, since the people or units that "survive" to the posttest are no longer the same group that was measured at the pretest. Mortality threatens internal validity and may also limit external validity. (p. 277)

Multiple regression analysis: a statistical technique developed to deal with situations in which one is attempting to correlate many independent variables with some criterion (dependent) measure. This technique allows the analyst to determine how the typical value of the dependent variable changes alongside changes in an independent variable when all other variables are held constant. (p. 370)

Multistage cluster sampling: a probability-based sampling technique that is employed when no sampling frame is available. This technique involves randomly sampling clusters within clusters until one reaches the desired unit of analysis. (p. 108)

Mutually exclusive: the property of a questionnaire item where the categories of response provided do not overlap with one another so that a participant can realistically select only one response option. (p. 167)

Naive realism: see **direct realism**.

Negative cases (or negative case analysis): a crucial part of analytic induction, in which researchers follow iteration after iteration of trying different explanations to see how well those explanations allow them to "make sense" of their data. Negative cases are those instances of the phenomenon that don't "fit" the developing explanation, suggesting that the explanation is not yet complete. Although ignoring negative cases can make one look good, at least temporarily, the qualitative researcher engaged in analytic induction will go out of his or her way to locate them, since they're a most informative source for how an explanation can be improved. See also: **disconfirming (or negative case sampling)**. (p. 114)

Negative (or inverse relationship): refers to a correlation in which one variable increases in value as the other variable decreases. For example, as temperature increases, the number of layers of clothing we wear decreases. (p. 358)

Node: the most basic unit of coding used in the program NVivo. Nodes are short labels representing ideas, themes, personas, places, interests, or concepts. In NVivo nodes are used to store all of the references from the data (e.g., segments of text, image, video, or audio material) that correspond to a particular theme, topic, idea, or concept we identify. (p. 322)

Nominal definition: a statement of what a concept means to the researcher; much like a dictionary definition. Expressing nominal definitions for the key concepts or variables involved in your research allows other researchers to consider whether they would agree with your definition of the term. See also **epistemic relationship**. (p. 48)

Non-probabilistic sampling: a set of sampling techniques in which the probability of selecting each sampling unit is unknown or unknowable. These techniques are optimal when a sampling frame is unavailable, when creative means must be used to locate "closet" samples, and/or when the research objectives would be best fulfilled by a strategically chosen sample. Contrasts with **probabilistic sampling**. (p. 98)

Normal distribution: a symmetrical or bell-shaped continuous probability distribution with a single peak and whose distribution conform to the empirical rule (e.g., where 68 percent of the distribution of scores represented fall within one standard deviation, 95 percent of scores fall within two standard deviations and 99.7 percent fall within three standard deviation points of the mean). (p. 364)

Observer-as-participant: see under **participant-as-observer**.

Open coding: a technique for coding textual, visual or audio content where the analyst identifies general themes and ideas as they emerge from a literal reading of the data. (p. 305)

Operational definition: the way we actually define the variables of interest within the confines of the research project. Suppose you're interested in looking at romantic love. How will you determine whether any two people in your research are actually "in love"? You might decide to ask them, "Are you two in love?" If they say "yes," you will consider them "in love." Their response to the question "Are you in love?" has become the operational definition of the concept of "love" in your research. Contrasts with **nominal definition**. (p. 48)

Ordinal measurement: a measure that has rank ordered attributes that have no meaningful distance between them and no meaningful zero point. An example of an ordinal measure is the typical five-level Likert item asking about a participant's level of agreement (1 = Strongly disagree, 2 = Agree, 3 = Neutral, 4 = Agree, and 5 = Strongly agree) to a particular statement. (p. 335)

Othering: both the physical and the natural sciences have a long tradition of making a distinction between the detached researcher and the object of his or her investigations. For positivists, being "objective" involved remaining detached from the "other" and imposing the viewpoint and value judgments of science. Since "our" standards were "obviously" the "correct" ones, then "our" standards clearly comprised the most appropriate measuring stick to use in assessing and describing "reality." It was *our* job to describe *them*. But several problems arise from that approach, particularly when *they* are a marginalized and misunderstood group, and our description of them imposes our understandings, meanings, and standards in a manner that denies the understandings of, and thereby does an injustice to, the researched group. This process is referred to as othering. (p. 24)

Outcome variable: see **dependent variable**.

Overidentification: a term used by positivists to mean a researcher's taking on the values and perspectives of the group being studied, so that he or she cannot maintain the detached, analytical stance required, according to positivists, for effectively studying the world. Positivists believe that getting too "involved" with the people we study will destroy our objectivity. (p. 5)

Panel studies: a type of longitudinal research in which you identify a particular group (or panel) of people and return to those very same people again and again over time. This contrasts with a *trend study*, for example, where you'd return to the same population each time but take a new sample each time. (p. 150)

Paradigmatic case sampling: a type of purposive sampling where the researcher selects units of analysis based on the fact that they exemplify a particular class. For example, if you were interested in studying the management of professional sports teams, the paradigmatic case in hockey of a successful franchise likely would be the Montréal Canadiens or Detroit Red Wings; for baseball it would be the New York Yankees or the St. Louis Cardinals. (p. 114)

Participant-as-observer and observer-as-participant: the two roles that occupy the middle of the traditional observational continuum. Both involve some participatory and observational aspects; they differ only in which role is emphasized. For the most part, both manifest an effort to reap the advantages of the two roles: their participatory aspects help minimize reactivity, while their observational aspects attempt to minimize ethical difficulties. (p. 197)

Pattern coding: a technique for analyzing textual, audio, or visual data where the analyst identifies and codes content that reoccurs frequently throughout the data. (p. 304)

Pearson product–moment correlation coefficient: a statistical test used to represent the degree to which the values of one variable change as the values of another variable also change. This statistic, also known as **Pearson's r**, is used to summarize the direction (positive or negative) and degree (closeness) of the linear relationship between two variables. The Pearson's r statistic can have a value ranging from −1 to +1. A Pearson's r value of −1 represents a perfect negative association between two variables (i.e., as the value of one variable goes up the other goes down). A value of +1 represents a perfect positive association between two variables (i.e., as the value of one variable goes up so does the value of the other). Finally, a value of 0 means that the two variables are completely unrelated (i.e., as the value of one variable changes the values of the other do not change at all). (p. 357)

Pearson's r: see **Pearson product–moment correlation coefficient**.

Periodicity: a phenomenon produced by the cyclical nature of some lists. Periodicity causes a problem in systematic sampling with random start when the list's cyclical nature becomes confounded with the sampling ratio or interval. (p. 105)

Phenomenologism: an approach to understanding whose adherents assert that we must "get inside people's heads" to understand how they perceive and interpret the world. According to theorists such as Weber, phenomenological understanding is a virtual prerequisite for achieving *verstehen*. (p. 8)

Phi-coefficient: a statistical measure of the strength of the association between two dichotomous categorical measures that is calculated by dividing the chi-square statistic by the sample size and then taking the square root of the resulting quotient. As phi-coefficients are akin to product moment correlation coefficients (Pearson's r), they are interpreted in the same way with the exception that phi-coefficients cannot assume a negative value. (p. 355)

Physical trace measures: a type of data that is based on the effects of human activity or behavior. Physical trace measures can result from the wearing away or removal of products or materials because of our physical presence (erosion) or the addition to or building up of products or materials because of our physical presence or activity (accretion). (p. 217)

Pilot study: a study that takes place prior to the actual study where the researcher is able to test our features of her or his design such as sampling and recruitment strategies or research instruments. (p. 174)

Population: an aggregation of all sampling elements, that is, the total of all the sampling units that meet the criterion (or criteria) for inclusion in a study. The sampling frame, if available, defines the population. (p. 100)

Positive (or direct relationship): refers to correlations between two or more variables where, as one variable increases in value, the other increases in value as well. For example, the more one studies, the higher the grades that one receives. (p. 358)

Positivism: a school of thought marked by a *realist* perspective, an emphasis on quantitative precision, the belief that effective research requires avoiding overidentification, and a search for general truths unearthed through the gathering and analysis of aggregated data. Chapter 1 focuses on "orthodox" or classic positivism, which developed in the 19th and early 20th centuries. (p. 4)

Pragmatism: a philosophical tradition which emerged in the late 19th century through the works of Charles Saders Pierce, John Dewy, and William James and played a major role in the emergence of symbolic interactionism (e.g., Mead and Cooley) that maintains that rejects the idea that there is a single view of reality. In doing this pragmatists reject traditional dualisms of realism versus constructivism, free-will versus determinism, subjectivism versus objectivism, and induction versus deduction in favour of a position that emphasizes adopting the approach that works best in a particular situation. (p. 394)

Predictive validity: a type of validity that involves assessing the extent to which your measure does in fact predict whatever it's supposed to predict. For example, if you develop tests like the LSAT (Law School Admission Test) or GRE (Graduate Records Exam), which are supposed to predict success in law school and graduate school, respectively, then demonstrating the tests' predictive validity would require you to show that scores on the test do indeed relate to later success in law school or graduate school, respectively. See also **concurrent validity**. (p. 57)

Pretest sensitization: see **testing**.

Privacy certificate: a certificate issued by the National Institutes of Justice in the United States that provides statutory protection for researchers to ensure that they cannot be forced to disclose identifying research information about participants to any civil, criminal, administrative, legislative, or other proceeding. See also confidentiality certificate. (p. 72)

Privilege: a term describing the a state of the relationship that exists between researcher and participants whereby the persons in the relationship are exempt from the normal requirement that all of us have to testify when asked to do so in a court of law when and if information discussed in the context of that relationship becomes of interest to the court. The lawyer-client relationship is protected by a privilege, for example, so that you can go and talk freely to your lawyer and seek legal advice without fearing that s/he will get subpoenaed and be on the witness stand the next day giving evidence against you. (p. 74)

Probabilistic sampling: a group of sampling techniques that meet two criteria: the probability of sampling a given individual is known (or at least is theoretically knowable), and each sampling element in the population has an equal probability of being selected. Contrasts with **non-probabilistic sampling**. (p. 98)

Process questions: a class of research questions that are directed at exploring, describing, understanding, and/or explaining the origins, meanings, and relationships connected to particular events, phenomena or processes–*how* they occur and what they mean to those involved. (p. 394)

Project file: the name used to describe the central space in the qualitative data analysis software program NVivo that is used to store all documents (e.g., text, audio, image, or video files), links, and memos that emerge at various stages of the research process from design to reporting. (p. 321)

Proportional stratified random sampling: a type of stratified random sampling where the number of elements sampled in each stratum are proportionate to their numbers in the wider population. For example, if women account for 65 percent of students enrolled in your research methods class and males account for 35 percent drawing a proportionate stratified random sample of students from your class would ensure that 65 percent of your sample are female and 35 percent are male. (p. 107)

Pseudonym: a fictitious name used in order to conceal the real source of an interview or other research data. (p. 75)

Purposive (or strategic) sampling: a general class of sampling techniques that are based on an acknowledgement that the parameters of the population are unknown. Instead of attempting to acquire a statistically representative sample, purposive samples are drawn to achieve a particular theoretical, methodological, or analytical purpose. (p. 113)

Qualitative approaches: research methods characterized by an inductive perspective, a belief that theory should be grounded in the day-to-day realities of the people being studied, and a preference for applying phenomenology to the attempt to understand the many "truths" of reality. Such approaches tend to be constructionist. Qualitative researchers tend to be cautious about numbers, believing that the requirements of quantification distance us even further from phenomenological understanding we should embrace. Qualitative researchers tend to engage most commonly in case study analysis. (p. 3)

Quantitative approaches: research methods that emphasize numerical precision; a detached, aloof stance on the researcher's part (i.e., the avoidance of overidentification); and, often, a hypothetico-deductive approach. Quantitative researchers tend to prefer gathering similar structured data across large samples as this will facilitate their ability to engage in statistical analysis of their data to identify broader patterns across individuals. (p. 3)

Quota sampling: the non-probability equivalent of stratified random sample where the researcher purposively selects participants to fill a pre-determined quota of substantively relevant groups. (p. 116)

Random assignment: a very powerful research procedure that directly addresses the assumption of pretest equivalence: the crucial experimental assumption that your experimental and control groups are equal in all respects *before* the imposition or administration of your independent variable. Given that you have a group of people ready to participate in your research, random assignment is achieved by letting "chance" be the *sole* determinant of which group (i.e., experimental or control) any given person is a member of. Random assignment, coupled with adequate group sizes (i.e., at least 30 per group), allows you to assume, with a reasonable degree of confidence, that the two (or more) groups, on average, are fairly equal on all pre-experimental variables. (p. 244)

Random digit dialing (RDD): a technique for selecting and contacting participants for telephone survey research where the unique identifier portion of the phone number (i.e., the numbers not associated with the area code or exchange) are dialed at random. (p. 146)

Random error: refers to errors that have no systematic biasing effect on a study's results. (p. 102)

Random selection: a type of probabilistic sampling that meets two criteria: (1) nothing but chance governs the selection process, and (2) every sampling element has an equal probability of being selected. If those criteria are met, the resulting sample will be representative of the population included in the sampling frame, within the limits of sampling error. (p. 102)

Range: a measure of dispersion representing the distance between the highest and lowest scores in a distribution. (p. 345)

Rapport: the development of a bond of mutual trust between researcher and participant that is considered to be the foundation upon which access is given and valid data are built. (p. 10)

Rate data: data that are expressed as a frequency per some unit of population, for example, birth rates, crime rates, death rates, unemployment rates, and infant mortality rates. For example, Vancouver's murder rate is currently about 6 per 100,000 per year. Specifying rates rather than raw numbers allows researchers to compare rates in a single location over time or to compare two or more locations despite differences in their population size. (p. 6)

Ratio-level measurement: a measure with an absolute and meaningful zero point and rank-ordered categories of values with meaningful intervals of difference between them. Count or weight measures such as number of years in school or the number of kilograms a baby weighs at birth are common examples of a ratio measure. (p. 335)

Reactive bias: see **reactivity**.

Reactivity (or reactive bias): the degree to which (if at all) the researcher's presence causes research participants to react by changing from their "usual" or "normal" behaviour patterns because they know they're being observed. (p. 151)

Realism: the idea that a reality exists out there independently of what and how we think about it. Contrasts with constructionism and idealism. (p. 12)

Realist perspective: see **realism**.

Reflexive: a process whereby the researcher remains consciously and critically aware of the multiple influences s/he has on the research process while also acknowledging how the research process also influences her or him. (p. 42)

Regression toward the mean: in experimental research, one of many possible threats to internal validity. Unlike testing, where *real* change occurs between pretest and posttest (e.g., because of practice, sensitization to issues, or greater motivation), regression toward the mean involves changes that are more apparent than real. Regression toward the mean refers to the propensity of extreme scorers on the first testing to score closer to the mean (average) of the group on the second testing. This phenomenon arises because of the random error that is present in any measurement and occurs because chance events are unlikely ever to stack up to precisely the same degree on two successive occasions. Also known as statistical regression. (p. 239)

Reliability: the degree to which repeated observation of a phenomenon—the same phenomenon at different times, or the same instance of the phenomenon by two different observers—yields similar results. Underlying this concept are scientific beliefs about the importance of stability and repeatability in the generation of understanding. Two types of reliability are **inter-rater reliability** and **test–retest reliability**. (p. 55)

Replication: the efforts of one researcher to repeat the procedures another researcher has followed in order to ensure that the other researcher's findings are reliable. (p. 32)

Representative sample: a sample is considered representative when the distribution of characteristics in the sample mirrors the distribution of those characteristics in the population. The priority attached to achieving formal representativeness is influenced by your research objectives. (p. 98)

Representative sampling: not to be confused with a representative sample, representative sampling is a purposive sampling strategy where the researcher seeks a sample the represents particular theoretically important characteristics of the wider population. (p. 115)

Researcher–participant privilege: the state of the relationship that exists between researcher and participants whereby the researcher is exempt from the normal requirement that all of us have to testify when asked to do so in a court of law when and if information discussed in the context of that relationship becomes of interest to the court. (p. 73)

Resentful demoralization: one of several possible threats to internal validity that can emerge in field settings. Given the same situation as is described under **compensatory rivalry**—it's known that an evaluation is in progress—participants may demonstrate the opposite response to the discrepancy among groups. With compensatory rivalry, the disadvantaged group rises to the challenge. With resentful demoralization, members of that group perceive the result as adverse and inevitable; they therefore may not even try to compete, and may even intentionally reduce their performance. In this instance, the researcher may *overestimate* the actual potency of the treatment being evaluated. (p. 277)

Rival plausible explanations: alternative factors that might also have accounted for the results you observe. Threats to internal validity, for example,

are all rival plausible explanations. Sound research design aims to minimize these. (p. 17)

Sample: a subset of the population that the researcher wishes to research. (p. 97)

Sampling elements: units or elements about which information will be gathered, they are the "things" you wish to study. Sampling elements can include individuals, groups, organizations or social artifacts. (p. 100)

Sampling error: the degree to which the distribution of characteristics in a sample deviates from the distribution of those characteristics in the population from which the sample was drawn. Estimates of the sampling error can be computed only when random sampling has been done. The two types of sampling error are **systematic error** and **random error**. (p. 100)

Sampling frame: a complete list of all the sampling elements of the population we wish to study. For example, if we want to sample voters in an upcoming election, the voters' lists represent a sampling frame of all eligible voters who have been enumerated. The availability of a sampling frame can influence a researcher's choice of sampling techniques. (p. 101)

Sampling ratio: a way of expressing what proportion of a population is actually sampled. For example, if the population numbers 1,000 people and if you sample 200 of them, your sampling ratio is 200:1,000 (i.e., 200 out of 1,000), or 1:5 (i.e., 1 in 5). (p. 104)

Scatter-plot diagram: a graphic display representing the association or relationship between two continuous variables. A graphic display used to illustrate the bivariate distribution of responses to two variables measured at an ordinal or interval level. (p. 357)

Secondary data: primary research data collected by another researcher for their own purposes that is subsequently made available to other members of the research community for their own purposes. (p. 58)

Selection: one of many possible threats to the internal validity of research, particularly experimental research, because it violates the fundamental premise of pretest equivalence, that is, the assumption that all experimental and control groups are equal before the experiment begins, so that any differences we observe after administering the independent variable must have arisen during the course of the study. See also **assumption of pretest equivalence**. (p. 241)

Selective deposit: a term referring to the fact that some people, groups, and processes have a higher likelihood than others of having their views, lives, and so on made a part of the historical record. Historians can study history based only on what's in the record; thus, our understanding of history is influenced by the factors that influence selective deposit into that record. (p. 157, 219)

Selective survival: a term that reminds us that among those things that are initially put into the historical record (via the already biased process of selective deposit), some have a better chance of surviving the ravages of time than others. For example, stone materials have a better chance of survival than clay or paper materials. (p. 219)

Self-anchoring scale: refers most commonly to a type of scale used by Hadley Cantril (see Chapter 6) in which the end points of the scale are defined by the participant. For example, in his famous international study about people's perceptions of their quality of life, he would first ask participants to think of the worst life situation they could imagine for themselves, and to call that a "1," and then the best situation they could imagine themselves in, and to call that a "10," after which he would ask them to place themselves on the scale "as their life is now." (p. 169)

Semantic differential type item: a type of rating scale questionnaire item originally developed by Osgood, Suci, and Tannenbaum (1957) to assess the meaning associated with particular attitude objects using a set of bipolar adjectives (or dimensions) upon which any given attitude object could be described (e.g., respondents are asked to assess the fairness (fair versus unfair) of being punished for a variety of different behaviours). (p. 170)

Sequential mixed method designs: a type of mixed methods design where the data collection process is broken into stages that follow one another in some logically considered order. This approach is most commonly employed by having a primary data collection strategy followed by collection of supplementary information during a secondary stage that allows you to clarify aspects of the data during analysis. (p. 396)

Serendipity: discoveries that happen purely by accident, as when a prospector strikes oil while searching for gold. The searcher (whether prospector or researcher) must be sufficiently knowledgeable and aware to realize what he or she has found. Many people in history have been perturbed to discover later that a serendipitous discovery had been staring them right in the face but that they'd been too unaware to recognize it at the time. (p. 34)

Sign system: a type of coding scheme in which an observer defines what is of interest to him or her (e.g., instances of violence, prosocial behaviour, or a moral dilemma) and then waits and watches, noting each time one of the predetermined criterion behaviours occurs. Sign systems give a better indication of *how many* prosocial acts are witnessed than **category systems**. (p. 200)

Simple random sampling: the probability sampling technique that allows a researcher to minimize sampling error and allows him or her to calculate the degree of sampling error that probably exists. To perform simple random sampling, in most cases you must have a sampling frame in which every sampling element is listed once and only once. Simple random sampling is then accomplished by merely choosing sample elements at random from the list. This can be done by putting all the names (or whatever) into a hat or drum and pulling them out at random, by numbering all elements in the sampling frame and then using a table of random numbers or random number generator to guide your selection, or using a computer program such as Microsoft Excel® or Open Office Calc® to select randomly from the sampling frame. (p. 101)

Single-response item: a survey response item format that requires the participant to indicate their response to a question in an empty space provided (e.g., In what year where you born? _____). (p. 166)

Snowball sampling: also referred to as network, chain referral, respondent driven, or multiplicity sampling is a purposive sampling technique that involves starting with one or two people and then using their connections, and their connections' connections, to generate a large sample. This technique is especially useful if your target population is a deviant or "closet" population, or isn't particularly well-defined or accessible. (p. 115)

Social facts: life's "big" realities (e.g., the legal and economic system), which wield significant influences on people and are beyond people's control in any direct sense. They are important to positivists because such social realities are believed to exert their effects no matter what we think about them. (p. 6)

Sociology of knowledge: the study of the social origins and social consequences of the processes in a society by which knowledge is constructed. (p. 64)

Stakeholder sampling: a purposive sampling strategy that involves identifying and interview-ing the major stakeholders who are involved in designing, delivering, receiving, or administering a program, policy, or service. (p. 113)

Stakeholders: in relation to social and health research can be any individuals who have a direct interest or concern with a particular aspect of the design, implementation, or outcome of the research. Stakeholders can include research participants, research ethics board members, the individuals, or organizations that sponsor or fund the research, and the researchers themselves. (p. 42)

Standard deviation: a measure of dispersion, expressed in the standard units, that indicates the average distance that any given score in a distribution of scores will be from the mean score in that distribution. A low standard deviation indicates that scores or observations tend to cluster close to the mean while a high standard deviation indicates that scores are spread out from the mean. Standard deviation is calculated by taking the square root of the variance. (p. 349)

Statistical conclusion validity: the determination of whether the test of whether two or more variables are associated more strongly than would be expected on the basis of chance variation alone was done in a reasonable and defensible manner. (p. 246)

Statistical regression: see **regression toward the mean**.

Statistical significance: when an observed correlation or difference is greater than would be expected on the basis of chance variation alone, the correlation or relationship is said to be statistically significant. Statistical significance alone does not imply anything about whether the independent variable caused the difference, or how important the result is. A finding of statistical significance is normally followed by an examination of what the source of the relationship of differences might be. (p. 250)

Statute-based protections: legislative protections for the confidentiality of identifiable information that ensure that research data cannot be used in any legal proceeding without the permission of the participant. In Canada, the only research participants whose information enjoys statute-based protection are those who participate in research conducted by Statistics Canada. The *Statistics Act* gives Statistics Canada employees a privilege to ensure that identifiable information unearthed by research by one portion of government (Statistics Canada) cannot be used by any other branch of government or in any court or other proceedings in a manner that would violate the confidence of any individual respondent. (p. 76)

Strategic sampling: see **purposive sampling**.

Stratified random sample: a probabilistic sampling technique where the researcher divides the population into groupings (or strata) of interest and then samples randomly within each stratum. This technique is used when there is some meaningful grouping variable on which the investigator wishes to make comparisons and where the probabilities of group membership are known ahead of time. (p. 105)

Systematic error: one of two types of sampling error. Systematic error occurs when aspects of your sampling procedure act in a consistent, systematic way, to make some sampling elements more likely to be chosen for participation than others. For example, Chapter 4 describes a 1992 call-in survey in which an American TV program's viewers expressed their opinions about a presidential speech. To participate, respondents had to, among other things, own a touch-tone phone, be interested in and able to understand a TV show dealing with political analysis, and be motivated enough to take the time to express their opinion. These factors created a systematically biased sample: wealthier people, more educated people, and people who wanted to complain were more likely to be represented in that sample than poorer people (who might be unable to afford a touch-tone phone), less educated people (who might be less able to follow the political analysis), and apathetic, uncertain, or contented people (who might have less motivation to call). Contrasts with **random error**. (p. 102)

Systematic mixed method integration: although researchers often consider ahead of time how they will proceed with a mixed method research strategy, and can, for example, decide whether they want to follow a concurrent or sequential strategy, one can also mix the two together. Sometimes this happens because of choices we make–which are referred to as systematic integrative designs–while other times it occurs because of serendipitous or chance events that occur and are not anticipated, in which case we refer to an *ad hoc* integrative strategy. (p. 398)

Systematic sample with random start: a probabilistic sampling technique where the researcher selects a randomly determined starting point within a sampling frame and samples every nth element (based in a sampling ratio) until the desired sample size is reached. (p. 104)

Temporal precedence: one of John Stuart Mill's three criteria of causality that maintains that the cause must come before the effect in time. (p. 235)

Testing: in experimental research, one of many possible threats to internal validity. Testing refers to the effects of taking a test on scores in the second testing. Such effects can operate in several different ways. The first, *pretest sensitization,* involves the fact that taking a test can sensitize you to issues in a way that you wouldn't have been aware of otherwise. It threatens internal validity because, if we observe that your attitudes have changed, we can't be sure whether the change was produced by the independent variable or by the greater sensitization to issues induced by the pretest. Another way in which testing can threaten internal validity is through *practice effects.* If we were trying to assess your abilities, for example, it would be difficult to know in the posttest situation whether you had improved purely because of the practice the pretest gave you or because of the independent variable we had imposed upon you. (p. 239)

Test–retest reliability: the degree to which a measure shows reliability (i.e., consistency) by producing similar results when a test is administered on two successive occasions; that is, where the same group of people are tested and retested. If the test (or scale or other type of measure) is reliable, the two sets of scores should correlate highly: people who score high (or low) on one occasion should also score high (or low) on the second occasion. Compare **inter-rater reliability**. (p. 56)

Theoretical triangulation: employing multiple theories throughout the design, collection and analysis process. Proceeding in this manner would involve a researcher or group of researchers developing research questions from different theoretical vantage points and thereby studying a phenomenon through multiple lenses. (p. 392)

Theory: a set of concepts and a description of how they're interrelated that, taken together, purport to explain a given phenomenon or set of phenomena. The word "theory" is also sometimes used more broadly to refer simply to abstractions; thus, when I look at your behaviour and call you studious, we are making the jump from the concrete (your observable behaviour, i.e., the number of hours per week you spend studying) to the theoretical (the concept of studiousness). (p. 5)

Time-series designs: designs that involve compiling data series that show a dependent measure over time (e.g., monthly, yearly, or whatever time period is meaningful and of interest). The benefit of looking at time-series data (rather than simply looking at singular before/after statistics) is that it helps to put any pre–post changes that are observed in context, so that one can see the overall trend that existed in the data when the

independent variable came into effect. It is particularly useful for identifying threats due to regression toward the mean and for showing the maturation of the trend line. (p. 275)

Treatment variable: see **independent variable**.

Triangulation: a research strategy that permits us to validate our observations by drawing upon multiple theories, methods, investigators or data analysis techniques within the same investigation in order to enhance the validity of the findings. (p. 392)

***t*-statistic:** a measure of whether two group means differ more than would be expected on the basis of chance variation alone. (p. 366)

Typical case sampling: a purposive sampling technique where the researcher selects cases for her or his sample based on the fact that they represent the most usual, average, or normal instances. (p. 113)

Typological analysis: a method of organizing coded material that involves placing similarly thematically coded information (e.g., people, places, events, or social artifacts that share common characteristics) into relational categories that allow the analyst to make distinctions among groupings or clusters of people, places, and so on that are meaningful to the researcher and/or participants. (p. 306)

Units of analysis: the units or elements about which information will be gathered, they are the "things" you wish to study. Units of analysis can include individuals, groups, organizations or social artifacts. (p. 100)

Universe: in the context of sampling, a *theoretical* aggregation of all possible sampling elements. Contrasts with **population**. (p. 100)

Unobtrusive measures: a class of data collection techniques and measures that are not influenced by the direct intrusion of the researcher into the life of participants. Unobtrusive measures are generally divided into two categories: physical trace and archival measures. (p. 217)

Usability: a term employed by graphic and Web designers to refer to the importance of understanding the user interface instead of the system upon which the interface is run. In CASR usability refers to how user-friendly a particular data collection interface such as a browser-based survey is. (p. 147)

Validity: a term that refers, in the most general sense, to whether research measures what the researcher thinks is being measured. This text discusses many kinds of validity, including predictive validity, internal validity, external validity, and ecological validity. All relate to whether you are indeed accomplishing what you think you are. (p. 56)

Variable: stated most simply, anything that varies. For example, in your methods class, "sex" is probably a variable, since the students in your class (unless you go to a sex-specific university or college) probably include both males and females. Variables contrast with *constants,* which are things that do *not* vary. (p. 42)

Variance: a measure of dispersion or spread of scores around the mean. It is calculated by taking the average squared difference of each score from the mean of all scores in the distribution. (p. 348)

Variance questions: a class or research questions that are concerned with describing the frequency with which phenomena of interest occur, and often use aggregate statistics to explain and understand the relationships or predictive capacity of one or more variables or theories related to these phenomena. (p. 394)

Verstehen: a German word, first used in the social sciences by Max Weber, that refers to a profound understanding evidenced by the ability to appreciate a person's behaviour in terms of the interpretive (i.e., phenomenological) meaning he or she attaches to it. (p. 9)

Wallace's wheel: a circular diagram in which Wallace attempted to go beyond the debates about whether inductive or deductive approaches were "best" and to show how the two were actually complementary parts of the same underlying empirical practice of working back and forth between theory and data. (p. 27)

Wigmore criteria: a set of four criteria used by Canadian and U.S. courts to evaluate whether communications in a certain relationship (e.g., researcher–participant, doctor–patient, priest–penitent) should be considered "privileged" and exempt from the normal requirement to testify in a court of law. The criteria require that (1) there be a shared expectation of confidentiality by those in the relationship; (2) confidentiality be essential to the relationship; (3) the relation be an important and socially valued one; and (4) the damage that would be done the relationship by disclosure be greater than the damage to the case at hand by nondisclosure. (p. 74)

Word count analysis: a technique for identifying themes that are present within a particular body of text. This technique assumes that the words that most frequently occur within speech or writing are the ones that represent the concepts or concerns that are most prominent or important to the speaker or author. Identifying the most frequently occurring words allows analysts to identify cognitive-, structural-, and process-related components of talk and text that can be used to gain valuable insights into a variety of social and health related attitudes, beliefs and behaviours. (p. 307)

***z*-scores:** a statistical measure of how far a score deviates from the mean of a group that is expressed as a number of standard deviation units. (p. 364)

REFERENCES

Abramson, P. R., & Hayashi, H. (1984). Pornography in Japan: Cross-cultural and theoretical considerations. In N.M. Malamuth & E. Donnerstein (Eds.), *Pornography and sexual aggression* (pp. 173–185). New York: Academic Press.

ACNielsen. 2004. ACNielsen study finds lower income and older households are closing the gap in PC ownership. [Press release]. Retrieved June 23, 2004, from http://www2.acnielsen.com/news/20040623_ca.shtml.

Adler, P. A., & Adler, P. (1994). Observational techniques. In N. K. Denzin, & Y.S. Lincoln (Eds.), *Handbook of qualitative research* (pp. 377–392). Thousand Oaks, CA: Sage.

Adler, P. A., & Adler, P. (2002). Do university lawyers and the police define research values? In W. C. van den Hoonaard (Ed.), *Walking the tightrope: Ethical issues for qualitative researchers* (pp. 34–42). Toronto: University of Toronto Press.

Alfred, R. (1976). The church of Satan. In C. Glock & R. Bellah (Eds.), *The new religious consciousness* (pp. 180–202). Berkeley, CA: University of California Press.

Altemeyer, R. A. (1970). Adverbs and intervals: A study of "Likert scales." *Proceedings of the 78th annual convention of the American Psychological Association*, 5: 397–98.

Altemeyer, R. A. (1981). *Right-wing authoritarianism*. Winnipeg: University of Manitoba Press.

American Anthropological Association. (1986). *Statements on ethics: Principles of professional responsibility*. Retrieved March 5, 2012, from http://www.aaanet.org/stmts/ethstmnt.htm

American Anthropological Association. (1996). *Final report of the commission to review the AAA statements on ethics*. Retrieved March 5, 2012, from http://www.aaanet.org/cmtes/ethics/Final-Report-of-the-Commission-to-Review-the-AAA-Statements-on-Ethics.cfm

American Political Science Association. (2008). *A guide to professional ethics in political science* (2nd ed.). Washington, DC: Author. Retrieved March 5, 2012, from http://www.apsanet.org/content_9350.cfm

American Psychological Association. (1973). *Ethical principles in the conduct of research with human participants*. Washington, DC: Author.

American Psychological Association. (1994). *Publication manual of the American Psychological Association* (4th ed.). Washington, DC: Author.

American Sociological Association. (1968). Toward a code of ethics for sociologists. *American Sociologist, 3*, 316–18.

American Sociological Association. (1997). *Code of ethics*. Retrieved August 20, 2002, from http://www.asanet.org/members/ecoderev.html

Anderson, K., & Jack, D. C. (1991). Learning to listen: Interview techniques and analyses. In S. B. Gluck & D. Patai (Eds.), *Women's words: The feminist practice of oral history* (pp. 11–26). New York: Routledge.

Andrews, F. M., & Withey, S. B. (1976). *Social indicators of well-being: Americans' perceptions of life quality*. New York: Plenum.

Angrosino, M. V., & Mays de Pérez, K.A. (2003). Rethinking observation: From method to context. In N.K. Denzin & Y.S. Lincoln (Eds.) *Collecting and interpreting qualitative materials*. (2nd Ed.) (pp. 107–154). Thousand Oaks, CA: Sage.

Argyris, C. (1975). Dangers in applying results from experimental social psychology. *American Psychologist, 30*, 469–485.

Aronson, E., & Carlsmith, J. M. (1968). Experimentation in social psychology. In G. Lindsey & E. Aronson (Eds.), *The handbook of social psychology*, Vol. II (2nd ed., pp. 1–79). Reading, MA: Addison-Wesley.

Aronson, E., & Mills, J. (1959). The effect of severity of initiation on liking for a group. *Journal of Abnormal and Social Psychology, 59:* 157–158.

Atchison, C. (1996). Turning the trick: The development and partial implementation of a multi-dimensional research instrument designed for clients of sex sellers. BA (hons.) thesis, Simon Fraser University.

Atchison, C. (1998). Men who buy sex: A preliminary description based on the results from a survey of the Internet-using population. M.A. thesis, Simon Fraser University.

Atchison, C. (1999). Navigating the virtual minefield: Using the Internet as a medium for conducting primary social research. In D. Currie, D. Hay, & B. MacLean (Eds.), *Exploring the social world: Social research in action.* Vancouver: Collective Press.

Atchison, C., Lowman, J., & Fraser, L. (1998). Men who buy sex: Preliminary findings of an exploratory study. In J. Elias, V. L. Bullough, & V. Elias (Eds.), *Prostitution: On whores, hustlers, and johns.* California: Prometheus Press.

Atkinson, P., & Hammersley, M. (1994). Ethnography and participant observation. In N. K. Denzin & Y. S. Lincoln (Eds.), *Handbook of qualitative research* (pp. 248–261). Thousand Oaks, CA: Sage.

Atkinson, T. (1977). *Is satisfaction a good measure of the perceived quality of life?* Paper presented at the annual meeting of the American Statistical Association.

Atlantic Sugar v. *United States.* (1980). 85 Cust. Ct. 128.

Babbie, E. (1989). *The practice of social research* (5th ed.). Belmont, CA: Wadsworth.

Bailey, C. (2007). *A guide to qualitative field research.* (2nd ed.) London: Pine Forge Press.

Bales, R. F. (1970). *Personality and interpersonal behavior.* New York: Holt, Rinehart and Winston.

Barber, B., & Fox, R. C. (1958). The case of the floppy-eared rabbits: An instance of serendipity gained and serendipity lost. *American Journal of Sociology, 54,* 128–136.

Barker, R., Dembo, T., & Lewin, K. (1943). Frustration and aggression. In R. Barker, J. Kounin, & H. Wright (Eds.), *Child behavior and child development* (pp. 441–458). New York: McGraw-Hill.

Barry, D. (2001). Assessing culture via the Internet: Methods and techniques for psychological research. *Cyberpsychology and Behavior,* 4(1), 17–21.

Bauman, S, Airey, J., & Atak, H. (1998). "Effective use of web-based technology: Using the Internet for data collection and communication applications. *Internet Survey Research White Paper.*

Baumrind, D. (1964). Some thoughts on ethics of research: After reading Milgram's "Behavioral study of obedience." *American Psychologist, 19,* 421–423.

Bazely, P. (2007) *Qualitative data analysis with NVivo.* London: Sage Publications.

Becker, H. S. (1958). Problems of inference and proof in participant observation. *American Sociological Review, 23,* 652–660.

Becker, H. S. (1963). *Outsiders: Studies in the sociology of deviance.* New York: Free Press.

Becker, H. S. (1964). Against the code of ethics. *American Sociological Review, 29,* 409–410.

Becker, H. S. (1970). Problems of inference and proof in participant observation. In H.S. Becker, *Sociological work.* Chicago: Aldine.

Becker, H. S. (1979). Do photographs tell the truth? In T. D. Cook & C. S. Reichardt (Eds.), *Qualitative and quantitative methods in evaluation research* (pp. 99–117). Beverly Hills, CA: Sage.

Becker, H. S. (1986). *Writing for sociologists.* Chicago: University of Chicago Press.

Becker, H. S. (1993). How I learned what a 'crock' was. *Journal of Contemporary Ethnography, 22,* 28–35.

Becker, H. S. (1996). The epistemology of qualitative research. In R. Jessor, A. Colby, & R. Schweder (Eds.), *Ethnography and human development: Context and meaning in social inquiry* (pp. 53–71). Chicago: University of Chicago Press. Available online at www.soc.ucsb.edu/faculty/hbecker/qa.html

Becker, H. S. (1998). *Tricks of the trade: How to think about your research while you're doing it.* Chicago: University of Chicago Press.

Becker, H. S., Geer, B., Hughes, E. C., & Strauss, A. L. (1961). *Boys in white: Student culture in medical school.* Chicago: University of Chicago Press.

Benmayor, R. (1991). Testimony, action research, and empowerment: Puerto Rican women and popular education. In S. B. Gluck & D. Patai (Eds.), *Women's words: The feminist practice of oral history* (pp. 159–174). New York: Routledge.

Berg, B. L. (1989). *Qualitative research methods for the social sciences.* Boston: Allyn & Bacon.

Berg, B. L. (2001). *Qualitative research methods for the social sciences* (4th ed.). Boston: Allyn & Bacon.

Berg, B. L. (2007). *Qualitative research methods for the social sciences* (6th ed.). Boston: Pearson.

Berger, T. (1992). *A long and terrible shadow: White values, native rights in the Americas, 1492–1992.* Vancouver: Douglas & McIntyre.

Bhaskar, R. (1986). *Scientific realism and human emancipation.* Bristol, U.K.: Verso (New Left Books).

Black, D. J. (1970). Production of crime rates. *American Sociological Review, 35,* 733–748.

Black, D. J., & Reiss, A. (1970). Police control of juveniles. *American Sociological Review, 35,* 63–77.

Black, M., & Ponirakis, A. (2000). Computer-administered interviews with children about maltreatment: methodological, developmental, and ethical issues. *Journal of Interpersonal Violence, 15,* 682–695.

Blomley, N., & Davis, S. (1998). Russel Ogden decision review. Report to President Jack Blaney of Simon Fraser University. Retrieved March 4, 2002, from http://www.sfu.ca/~palys/ogden.htm

Blumeberg, S. J., Luke, J. V., & Cynamon, M. L. (2006). Telephone coverage and health survey estimates: Evaluating the need for concern about wireless substitution. *American Journal of Public Health, 96,* 926–931.

Blumer, H. (1969). *Symbolic interactionism: Perspective and method.* Englewood Cliffs, NJ: Prentice-Hall.

Bogardus, E. (1925). Measuring social distance. *Journal of Applied Sociology, 9,* 299–308.

Bonta, J., & Gendreau, P. (1990). Reexamining the cruel and unusual punishment of prison life. *Law and Human Behaviour, 14,* 347–372.

Borland, K. (1991). "That's not what I said": Interpretive conflict in oral narrative research. In S. B. Gluck & D. Patai (Eds.), *Women's words: The feminist practice of oral history* (pp. 63–76). New York: Routledge.

Boruch, R. F., & Cecil, J. S. (1979). *Assuring the confidentiality of research data.* Philadelphia: University of Pennsylvania Press.

Bourdieu, P. (1977). *Outline of a theory of practice.* Cambridge: Cambridge University Press

Boyd, N. (1991). *High society: Legal and illegal drugs in Canada.* Toronto: Key Porter Books.

Brajuha, M., & Hallowell, L. (1986). Legal intrusion and the politics of fieldwork. *Urban Life, 14,* 454–478.

Brandt, L. L. (1975). Scientific psychology: What for? *Canadian Psychological Review, 16,* 23–34.

Brantingham, P. J. (1991). Patterns in Canadian crime. In M. A. Jackson & C. T. Griffiths (Eds.), *Canadian criminology: Perspectives on crime and criminality* (pp. 371–402). Toronto: Harcourt Brace Jovanovich.

Brantingham, P. J., & Brantingham, P. L. (1984). *Patterns in crime.* New York: Macmillan.

Broadhead, R.S., & Rist, R.C. (1976). Gatekeepers and the social control of social research. *Social Problems, 23*(3), 325–336.

Brock, D. R., & Kinsman, G. (1986). Patriarchal relations ignored: An analysis and critique of the Badgley report on sexual offenses against children and youths. In J. Lowman, M. A. Jackson, T. S. Palys, & S. Gavigan (Eds.), *Regulating sex: An anthology of commentaries on the findings and recommendations of the Badgley and Fraser reports* (pp. 107–126). Burnaby, BC: School of Criminology, Simon Fraser University.

Bronfenbrenner, U. (1979). *The ecology of human development.* Cambridge, M.A.: Harvard University Press.

Bronskill, J., & Blanchfield, M. (1998, September 20). Canadian convicts used as test subjects in experiments. *Vancouver Sun,* p. 41.

Bruner, J. (1986). *Actual minds, possible worlds.* Cambridge, MA: Harvard University Press.

Brunswik, E. (1955). Representative design and probabilistic theory in a functional psychology. *Psychological Review, 62,* 193–217.

Butterfield, H. (1931). *The whig interpretation of history.* London: G. Bell.

Byrne, D., & Kelley, K. (1989). Basing legislative action on research data: Prejudice, prudence, and empirical limitations. In D. Zillmann & J. Bryant (Eds.), *Pornography: Research advances and policy considerations* (pp. 363–385). Hillsdale, NJ: Erlbaum.

Campbell, D. T. (1957). Factors relevant to the validity of experiments in social settings. *Psychological Bulletin, 54,* 297–312.

Campbell, D. T. (1963). Social attitudes and other acquired behavioural dispositions. In S. Koch (Ed.), *Psychology: A study of a science* (Vol. 6, pp. 94–172). New York: McGraw-Hill.

Campbell, D. T. (1969a). Definitional versus multiple operationism. *Et al., 2*(1): 14–17.

Campbell, D. T. (1969b). Reforms as experiments. *American Psychologist, 24*: 409–429.

Campbell, D. T. (1969c). Ethnocentrism of disciplines and the fish-scale model of omniscience. In M. Sherif & C. W. Sherif (eds.) *Interdisciplinary relationships in the social sciences* (pp. 328–348). Chicago: Aldine.

Campbell, D. T. (1978). Qualitative knowing in action research. In M. Brenner, P. Marsh, & M. Brenner (Eds.), *The social contexts of methods* (pp. 184–209). London: Breem Helm.

Campbell, D. T. (1979). "Degrees of freedom" and the case study. In T. D. Cook & C. S. Reichardt (Eds.), *Qualitative and quantitative methods in evaluation research* (pp. 49–67). Beverly Hills, CA: Sage.

Campbell, D. T. (1984). Can we be scientific in applied social science? In R. F. Conner, D. G. Altman & C. Jackson (eds.), *Evaluation studies review annual* (Vol. 9, pp. 26–48), Beverly Hills, CA: Sage.

Campbell, D. T. (1991). Methods for the experimenting society. *American Journal of Evaluation Research, 12*(3): 223–260.

Campbell, D. T., & Fiske, D. W. (1959). Convergent and discriminant validation by the multitrait-multimethod matrix. *Psychological Bulletin, 56,* 81–105.

Campbell, D. T., & Ross, L. H. (1968). The Connecticut crackdown on speeding: Time-series data in quasi-experimental analysis. *Law and Society, 3,* 33–53.

Campbell, D. T., & Stanley, J. C. (1963). *Experimental and quasi-experimental designs for research.* Chicago: Rand McNally.

Campbell, M. (1994, March 10). Too many immigrants, many say: Federal survey shows relatively less compassion, less tolerance. *Globe and Mail,* pp. A1, A5.

Canadian Institutes of Health Research (CIHR), Natural Sciences and Engineering Research Council of Canada (NSERC), Social Sciences and Humanities Research Council of Canada (SSHRC) (1998, with 2000, 2002, and 2005 amendments). *Tri-Council Policy Statement: Ethical Conduct for Research Involving Humans.* Retrieved May 9, 2006, from http://www.pre.ethics.gc.ca/english/policystatement/policystatement.cfm.

Canadian Institutes of Health Research (CIHR), Natural Sciences and Engineering Research Council of Canada (NSERC), Social Sciences and Humanities Research Council of Canada (SSHRC). (2010). *Tri-Council Policy Statement: Ethical Conduct for Research Involving Humans.* Retrieved May 24, 2012, from http://www.pre.ethics.gc.ca/eng/policy-politique/initiatives/tcps2-eptc2/Default/.

Canadian Psychological Association. (1991). *Canadian code of ethics for psychologists.* Ottawa: Author.

Canadian Psychological Association. (2000). Canadian code of ethics for psychologists (3rd ed.). Ottawa: Author. Retrieved May 22, 2006, from http://www.cpa.ca/cpasite/userfiles/Documents/Canadian%20Code%20of%20Ethics%20for%20Psycho.pdf.

Canadian Sociology and Anthropology Association. (1994). *Statement of professional ethics.* Retrieved February 25, 2002, from http://artsciccwin.concordia.ca/socanth/csaa/englcode.htm#protect

Cantril, H. (1965). *The pattern of human concerns.* New Brunswick, NJ: Rutgers University Press.

Caporaso, J. A. (1973). Quasi-experimental approaches to social science: Perspectives and problems. In J. A. Caporaso & L. L. Roos, Jr. (Eds.), *Quasi-experimental approaches: Testing theory and evaluating policy.* Chicago: Northwestern University Press.

Cassidy, F. (Ed.). (1992). *Aboriginal title in British Columbia: Delgamuukw v the Queen.* Lantzville, BC: Oolichan Books.

Cecil, J. S., & Wetherington, G. T. (Eds.). (1996). Court-ordered disclosure of academic research: A clash of values of science and law. *Law and Contemporary Problems* (special issue), *59* (3).

Chakravartty, A. (2011). Scientific Realism. In E. N. Zalta (Ed.) *The Stanford encyclopedia of philosophy.* Online at <http://plato.stanford.edu/archives/sum2011/entries/scientific-realism/>. Last checked 14 November 2011.

Chambers, E. (2003). Applied ethnography. In N. K. Denzin & Y.S. Lincoln (Eds.) *Collecting and interpreting qualitative materials.* (2nd Ed.) (pp. 389–418). Thousand Oaks, CA: Sage.

Chief Electoral Officer of Canada (2011). *Report of the Chief Electoral Officer of Canada on the 41st general election of May 2, 2011.* Ottawa: Elctions Canada.

Christians, C. (2000). Ethics and politics in qualitative research. In N. K. Denzin & Y. S. Lincoln (Eds). *Handbook of Qualitative Research* (2nd ed., pp. 133–155). Thousand Oaks, CA: Sage.

Churchill, W. (1994). *Indians are us? Culture and genocide in Native North America.* Toronto: Between the Lines.

Cicourel, A. V. (1964). *Method and measurement in sociology.* New York: Free Press.

Clifford, J. (1986). Introduction: Partial truths. In J. Clifford & G. E. Marcus (Eds.), *Writing culture: The poetics and politics of ethnography* (pp. 1–26). Berkeley, CA: University of California Press.

Cohen, S. (1985). *Visions of social control: Crime, punishment and classification.* Cambridge: Polity Press.

Collins, A. (1988). *The sleep room.* Toronto: Lester & Orpen Dennys.

Collins, P. H. (1991). Learning from the outsider within: The sociological significance of black feminist thought. In M. M. Fonow & J. A. Cook (Eds.), *Beyond methodology: Feminist scholarship as lived research* (pp. 35–59). Bloomington, IN: Indiana University Press.

Computer Industry Almanac. (2009). *PCs in-use reached nearly 1.2B in 2008*. Retrieved February 2, 2012, from http://www.c-i-a.com/pr0109.htm.

Computer Industry Almanac. (2010). *Worldwide Internet Users Top 1.8 Billion in 2009*. Retrieved February 2, 2012, from http://www.c-i-a.com/pr072010.htm

Cook, T. D., & Campbell, D. T. (1979). *Quasi-experimentation*. Boston: Houghton Mifflin.

Couper, M. (2000). Usability evaluation of computer-assisted survey instruments. Social *Science Computer Review, 18*, 384–396.

Cowles, M., & Davis, C. (1982). On the origins of the .05 level of statistical significance. *American Psychologist, 37*, 553–558.

Crabb, B. B. (1996). Judicially compelled disclosure of researchers' data: A judge's view. *Law and Contemporary Problems, 59*, 9–34.

Crawford, S., Couper, M. P., & Lamias, M. J. (2001). Web surveys: Perceptions of burden. *Social Science Computer Review, 19*, 146–162.

Cressey, D. R. (1953). *Other people's money: A study in the social psychology of embezzlement*. New York: Free Press.

Culhane, D. (1998). *The pleasure of the Crown: Anthropology, law and First Nations*. Burnaby, BC: Talon Books.

Currey, M. M. (1993). *On the border: An exploratory study of Canadian customs inspector decision-making*. Unpublished master's thesis, Simon Fraser University.

Dahlen, M. (2002). "Learning the web: Internet user experience and response to web marketing in Sweden. *Journal of Interactive Advertising, 3*(1).

Daisley, B. (1994, December 28). Clear evidence needed to invoke Wigmore rules. *The Lawyer's Weekly*.

Darwin, C. (1859). *On the origin of species*. London: John Murray.

Davis, M. (1971). That's interesting! Towards a phenomenology of sociology and a sociology of phenomenology. *Philosophy of the Social Sciences, 1*, 309–344.

Davis, S. (1990). Men as success objects and women as sex objects: A study of personal advertisements. *Sex Roles: A Journal of Research, 23*, 43–50.

Dawes, R. M. (1972). *Fundamentals of attitude measurement*. New York: Wiley.

Delgamuukw v. British Columbia [1991] B.C.J. No. 525.

Delgamuukw v. British Columbia [1997] 3 S.C.R. 1010.

Deloria, V. Jr. (1991). Commentary: Research, redskins, and reality. *American Indian Quarterly*. XV (4): 457–468.

Denzin, N. K. (1970). *The research act: A theoretical introduction to sociological methods*. Chicago: Aldine.

Denzin, N. K. (1978). The logic of naturalistic inquiry. In N. K. Denzin (Ed.), *Sociological methods: A sourcebook*. New York: McGraw-Hill.

Denzin, N. K. (1989). *The research act: A theoretical introduction to sociological methods* (3rd ed.). Englewood Cliffs, NJ: Prentice-Hall.

Denzin, N. K., & Lincoln, Y. S. (1994). Introduction: Entering the field of qualitative research. In N. K. Denzin & Y. S. Lincoln (Eds.), *Handbook of qualitative research* (pp. 1–18). Thousand Oaks, CA: Sage.

Denzin, N. K., & Lincoln, Y. S. (2003). Introduction: The discipline and practice of qualitative research. In N. K. Denzin & Y. S. Lincoln (Eds.) *The landscape of qualitative research: Theories and issues*. (2nd Ed.) (pp. 1–46). Thousand Oaks, CA: Sage.

Deutsch, M. (1973). *The resolution of conflict: Constructive and destructive processes*. New Haven, CT: Yale University Press.

de Vaus, D. (2002). *Surveys in social research* (5th ed.). London: Routledge.

Dingwall, R. (2008). The ethical case against ethical regulation in humanities and social science research. *21st Century Society, 3*(1): 1–12.

Ditton, J. (1979). *Contrology: Beyond criminology*. London: Macmillan Press.

Donnerstein, E., & Berkowitz, L. (1981). Victim reactions in aggressive erotic films as a factor in violence against women. *Journal of Personality and Social Psychology, 41*, 710–724.

Donohue, F. (2008). *The last professors: The corporate university and the fate of the humanities*. Bronx, NY: Fordham University Press.

Dorn, D. S., & Long, G. L. (1974). Brief remarks on the Association's *Code of Ethics. American Sociologist, 9*: 31–35.

Dow Chemical Co. v. Allen. 672 F.2d 1262, 1274-77 (7th Cir. 1982).

Dowbiggin, I. (1997). *Keeping America sane: Psychiatry and eugenics in the United States and Canada, 1880–1940*. Ithaca NY: Cornell University Press.

Doyle, A. C. (1980). *The adventures of Sherlock Holmes.* London: Pan Books. (Originally published 1892.)

Doyle, A. C. (1987). The adventure of Silver Blaze. In A. C. Doyle, *The original illustrated Sherlock Holmes* (pp. 185–200). Secaucus, NJ: Castle Books. (Originally published 1892.)

Dryburgh, H. (2002). Changing our ways: Why and how Canadians use the Internet. Statistics Canada. Available at http://www.statcan.ca/english/ research/56F0006XIE/56F0006XIE.pdf

Duneier, M. (1999). *Sidewalk.* New York: Farrar, Straus & Giroux.

Duran, B., & Duran E. (2000). Applied postcolonial clinical and research strategies. In M. Battiste (Ed.). *Reclaiming Indigenous voice and vision.* (pp. 86–100). Vancouver: UBC Press.

Durkheim, E. (1951). *Suicide: A study in sociology.* (Trans. J. Spaulding & G. Simpson). New York: Free Press.

Durkheim, E. (1968). Social facts. In M. Brodbeck (Ed.), *Readings in the philosophy of the social sciences* (pp. 245–254). New York: Macmillan. (Reprinted from E. Durkheim, 1938, *The rules of sociological method,* New York: Free Press.)

Dutton, D. G., Boyanowsky, E. O., Palys, T. S., & Heywood, R. (1982). *Community policing: Preliminary results from a national study of the RCMP.* Research report prepared for the Research Division of the Solicitor General Canada.

Eichstaedt, J. (2001). An inaccurate-timing filter for reaction time measurement by Java applets implementing Internet-based experiments. *Behavior, Research Methods, Instruments and Computers, 33*(2), 179–186.

Elms, A. C. (1975). The crisis of confidence in social psychology. *American Psychologist, 30,* 967–976.

Epstein, J., & Klinkenberg, W. D. (2001). From Eliza to Internet: A brief history of computerized assessment. *Computers in Human Behavior, 17,* 295–314.

Epstein, J., Klinkenberg, W. D., Wiley, D., & Mckinley, L. (2001). Insuring sample equivalence across Internet and paper-and-pencil assessments. *Computers in Human Behavior, 17,* 339–346.

Etter-Lewis, G. (1991). Black women's life stories: Reclaiming self in narrative texts. In S. B. Gluck & D. Patai (Eds.), *Women's words: The feminist practice of oral history* (pp. 43–58). New York: Routledge.

Farris, G. F. (1969). The drunkard's search in behavioral science. *Compensation and Benefits Review, 1*(2), 29–33.

Faulconer, J. E., & Williams, R. N. (1985). Temporality in human action: An alternative to positivism and historicism. *American Psychologist, 40,* 1179–1188.

Faulkner, R. R., & Becker, H. S. (2008). Studying something you are a part of: The view from the bandstand. *Ethnologie Française, 38*(1), 15–21. Online at http://home.earthlink.net/~hsbecker/articles/ ffbparis.html. Last checked 2 December 2011.

Festinger, L. (1953). Laboratory experiments. In L. Festinger & D. Katz (Eds.), *Research methods in the behavioral sciences* (pp. 136–172). New York: Holt, Rinehart and Winston.

Festinger, L. (1957). *A theory of cognitive dissonance.* Evanston, IL: Row, Peterson.

Festinger, L., & Katz, D. (Eds.). (1953). *Research methods in the behavioral sciences.* New York: Holt, Rinehart and Winston.

Festinger, L., Riecken, H. W., & Schachter, S. (1956). *When prophecy fails.* Minneapolis, MN: University of Minnesota Press.

Filstead, W. J. (1979). Qualitative methods: A needed perspective in evaluation research. In T. D. Cook & C. S. Reichardt (Eds.), *Qualitative and quantitative methods in evaluation research* (pp. 33–48). Beverly Hills, CA: Sage.

Fine, M., Weis, L., Weseen, S., & Wong, L. (2003). For whom? Qualitative research, representations, and social responsibilities. In N. K. Denzin & Y. S. Lincoln (Eds.) *The landscape of qualitative research: Theories and issues.* (2nd Ed.) (pp. 167–207). Thousand Oaks, CA: Sage.

Finney, S. (2001). Real-time data collection in Linux: A case study. *Behavior Research Methods, Instruments and Computers, 33,* 167–173.

Fishbein, M. (Ed.). (1967). *Readings in attitude theory and measurement.* New York: Wiley.

Fishbein, M., & Azjen, I. (1975). *Belief, attitude, intention, and behavior: An introduction to theory and research.* Reading, MA: Addison-Wesley.

Fisher, R. A. (1925). *Statistical methods for research workers.* Edinburgh: Oliver & Boyd.

Fisher, W. A. (1986). The emperor has no clothes: On the Badgley and Fraser Committees' rejection of social science research on pornography. In J. Lowman, M. A. Jackson, T. S. Palys, & S. Gavigan (Eds.), *Regulating sex: An anthology of commentaries on the findings and recommendations of the Badgley and Fraser Reports* (pp. 159–176). Burnaby, BC: School of Criminology, Simon Fraser University.

Fisher, W. A., & Grenier, G. (1994). Violent pornography, antiwoman thoughts, and antiwoman acts: In search of reliable effects. *The Journal of Sex Research, 31*, 23–38.

Fitzgerald, M. H. (2004). Punctuated equilibrium, moral panics and the ethics review process. *Journal of Academic Ethics, 2*, 315–38.

Flint, A. (1995, June 3). The scientists and the radicals square off. *Globe and Mail,* p. D9.

Fonow, M. M., & Cook, J. A. (Eds.). (1991). *Beyond methodology: Feminist scholarship as lived research.* Bloomington, IN: Indiana University Press.

Fontana, A., & Frey, J. H. (1994). Interviewing: The art of science. In N. K. Denzin & Y. S. Lincoln (Eds.), *Handbook of qualitative research* (pp. 361–376). Thousand Oaks, CA: Sage.

Fontana, A., & Frey, J. H. (2003). The interview: From structured questions to negotiated text. In N. K. Denzin & Y. S. Lincoln (Eds.) *Collecting and interpreting qualitative materials.* (2nd Ed.) (pp. 61–106). Thousand Oaks, CA: Sage.

Fox, J., Murray, C., & Warm, A. (2003). Conducting research using web-based questionnaires: Practical, methodological and ethical considerations. *Social Research Methodology, 6*, 167–180.

Fox, N. J. (2008). Induction. In L. M. Given (Ed.) *The Sage encyclopedia of qualitative research methods* (Vol 1, pp. 429–430). Thousand Oaks, CA: Sage.

Fricker, R., & Rand, M. S. (2002). Advantages and disadvantages of Internet research surveys: Evidence from the literature." *Field Methods, 14*, 347–367

Friedson, E. (1964). Against the code of ethics. *American Sociological Review, 29*, 410.

Galliher, J. F. (1973). The protection of human subjects: A re-examination of the *Professional Code of Ethics. American Sociologist*, 8(8), 93–100.

Gendreau, P., & Bonta, J. (1991). Boats against the current: A rebuttal. *Law and Human Behaviour, 15*, 563–565.

Gerard, H. B., & Mathewson, G. D. (1966). The effects of severity of initiation on liking for a group: A replication. *Journal of Experimental Social Psychology, 2*, 278–287.

Gergen, K. J. (1985). The social constructionist movement in modern psychology. *American Psychologist, 40*, 266–275.

Gisday Wa & Delgam Uukw. (1992). *The spirit in the land: Statements of the Gitksan and Wet'suwet'en hereditary chiefs in the Supreme Court of British Columbia, 1987–1990.* Gabriola Island, BC: Reflections Press.

Glaser, B., & Strauss, A. L. (1967). *The discovery of grounded theory: Strategies for qualitative research.* Chicago: Aldine.

Gluck, S. B. (1984). What's so special about women: Women's oral history. In D. Dunaway & W. K. Baum (Eds.), *Oral history: An interdisciplinary anthology* (pp. 221–237). Nashville, TN: American Association for State and Local History.

Gluck, S. B. (1991). Advocacy oral history: Palestinian women in resistance. In S. B. Gluck & D. Patai (Eds.), *Women's words: The feminist practice of oral history* (pp. 205–220). New York: Routledge.

Gluck, S. B., & Patai, D. (Eds.). (1991). *Women's words: The feminist practice of oral history.* New York: Routledge.

Gold, R. L. (1958). Roles in sociological field investigation. *Social Forces, 36*, 217–223.

Gorden, R. L. (1980). *Interviewing: Strategy, techniques and tactics* (3rd ed.). Homewood, IL: Dorsey Press.

Gosling, S., Vazire, S., Srivastava, S., & John, O. P. (2004). Should we trust web-based studies? A comparative analysis of six preconceptions about Internet questionnaires. *American Psychologist, 59*(2), 93–104.

Gravlee, C. (2002). Mobile computer-assisted personal interviewing with handheld computers: The Entryware System 3.0. *Field Methods, 14*, 322–336.

Gray, G., & Guppy, N. (1994). Successful surveys: Research methods and practice. Toronto: Thomson Nelson.

Greene, P. (2001). Review article: Handheld computers as tools for writing and managing field data. *Field Methods, 13*, 181–197.

Greschner, D. (1992). Aboriginal women, the constitution and criminal justice. *University of British Columbia Law Review* (special edition), 338–359.

Hacking, I. (1999). *The social construction of what?* Cambridge, MA: Harvard University Press.

Hagan, F. E. (1989). *Research methods in criminal justice and criminology* (2nd ed.). New York: Macmillan.

Haggerty, K. D. (2004). Ethics creep: Governing social science research in the name of ethics. *Qualitative Sociology, 27*, 391–414.

Hale, S. (1991). Feminist method, process, and self-criticism: Interviewing Sudanese women. In S. B. Gluck & D. Patai (Eds.), *Women's words: The feminist practice of oral history* (pp. 121–136). New York: Routledge.

Hamburger, P. (2005). The new censorship: Institutional review boards. *Supreme Court Review, October 2004 Term*, 271–354.

Hampton, K., & Wellman, B. (1999). Netville online and offline: Observing and surveying a wired suburb. *The American Behavioral Scientist, 43*, 475–493.

Henry, S. (1987). The construction and deconstruction of social control: Thoughts on the discursive production of state law and private justice. In J. Lowman, R. J. Menzies, & T. S. Palys (Eds.), *Transcarceration: Essays in the sociology of social control* (pp. 89–108). Aldershot, U.K.: Gower.

Hoare, T., Levy, C., & Robinson, M. P. (1993). Participatory action research in Native communities: Cultural opportunities and legal implications. *The Canadian Journal of Native Studies* XII: 43–68.

Hoffman, J. E. (1980). Problems of access in the study of social elites and boards of directors. In W. B. Shaffir, R. A. Stebbins, & A. Turowetz (Eds.), *Fieldwork experience: Qualitative approaches to social research* (pp. 45–56). New York: St. Martin's Press.

hooks, b. (1989). *Talking back: Thinking feminist, thinking black*. Boston: South End.

Horn, M. (1999). *Academic freedom in Canada: A history*. Toronto: University of Toronto Press.

Horowitz, I. (1967). *The rise and fall of Project Camelot: Studies in the relationship between social science and practical politics*. Cambridge, MA: MIT Press.

Horowitz, R. (1983). *Honor and the American dream*. New Brunswick, NJ: Rutgers University Press.

Horswill, M., & Coster, M. E. (2001). User-controlled photographic animations, photograph-based questions, and questionnaires: Three Internet-based instruments for measuring drivers' risk-taking behavior. *Behavior Research Methods, Instruments, and Computers, 33*, 46–58.

House, E. R. (1976). Justice in evaluation. In G. V. Glass (Ed.), *Evaluation Studies Review Annual* (Vol. 1, pp. 75–100). Beverly Hills, CA: Sage.

Howe, K. R. (1988). Against the quantitative-qualitative incompatibility thesis, or, dogmas die hard. *Educational Researcher, 17*: 10–16.

Huberman, A. M., & Miles, M. B. (1994). Data management and analysis methods. In N. K. Denzin & Y. S. Lincoln (Eds.), *Handbook of qualitative research* (pp. 428–444). Thousand Oaks, CA: Sage.

Huff, D. (1954). *How to lie with statistics*. NY: Norton (reissued in 1982 and 1993).

Humphreys, L. (1970). *Tearoom trade: Impersonal sex in public places*. Chicago: Aldine.

Inquest of Unknown Female. (1994, October 20). Oral reasons for judgement of the Honourable L.W. Campbell, 91-240-0838, Burnaby, BC.

In re Grand Jury Proceedings: James Richard Scarce. 5 F.3d 397 (9th Cir. 09/17/1993).

In re Michael A. Cusumano and David B. Yoffie [United States of America v. Microsoft Corporation], No. 98-2133, United States Court of Appeals for the First Circuit]. (1998). Retrieved August 20, 2002, from http://www.law.emory.edu/1circuit/dec98/98-2133.01a.html.

International Telecommunication Union. (2009). Measuring the information society – The ICT development index. Retrieved from http://www.itu.int/ITU-D/ict/publications/idi/2009/index.html.

Irwin, J. (1970). *The felon*. Englewood Cliffs, NJ: Prentice-Hall.

Irwin, J. (1980). *Prisons in turmoil*. Boston: Little, Brown.

Irwin, J. (1985). *The jail: Managing the underclass in American society*. Berkeley: University of California Press.

Israel, J., & Tajfel, H. (Eds.). (1972). *The context of social psychology: A critical assessment*. London: Academic Press.

Israel, M. (2004a). Ethics and the governance of criminological research in Australia. Report for the New South Wales Bureau of Crime Statistics and Research. http://www.lawlink.nsw.gov.au/bocsar1.nsf/files/r55.pdf/$file/r55.pdf.

Israel, M. (2004b). Strictly confidential? Integrity and the disclosure of criminological and socio–legal research. *British Journal of Criminology, 44*, 715–740.

Jackson, M., & MacCrimmon, M. (1999). Research confidentiality and academic privilege: A legal opinion. Submission prepared for the Simon Fraser University Ethics Policy Review Task Force. Retrieved August 21, 2002, from http://www.sfu.ca/~palys/JackMacOpinion.pdf.

Jaffee v. *Redmond* (95-266). 518 U.S. 1 (1996).

Jennings, F. (1975). *The invasion of America: Indians, colonialism, and the cant of conquest*. Chapel Hill, NC: University of North Carolina Press.

Johnson, R., & Onwuegbuzie, A. (2004). Mixed methods research: A research paradigm whose time has come. *Educational Researcher, 33*(7): 14.26.

Johnson, R., Onwuegbuzie, A., & Turner, L. (2007). Toward a definition of mixed methods research. *Journal of Mixed Methods Research, 1*(2): 112–133.

Judd, C. M., Smith, E. R., & Kidder, L. H. (1991). *Research methods in social relations* (6th ed.). Fort Worth, TX: Holt, Rinehart and Winston.

Kahneman, D., Slovic, P., & Tversky, A. (1982). *Judgment under uncertainty: Heuristics and biases.* Cambridge: Cambridge University Press.

Karr, L. (2000). New horizons in cross-national experimentation. *Current Research in Social Psychology, 5*(13), 190–205.

Katz, D., & Braly, K. (1933). Racial stereotypes of one hundred college students. *Journal of Abnormal and Social Psychology, 28,* 280–290.

Katz, J. (2007). Towards a natural history of ethical censorship. *Law & Society Review, 41*(4), 797–810.

Kaye, B., & Johnson, T. J. (1999). Research methodology: Taming the cyber frontier: Techniques for Improving online surveys. *Social Science Computer Review, 17,* 323–337.

Kelly, G. A. (1955). *The psychology of personal constructs* (2 vols.). New York: Norton.

Kerlinger, F. N. (1973). *Foundations of behavioral research* (2nd ed.). New York: Holt, Rinehart and Winston.

Kidder, L. H. (1981a). Qualitative research and quasi-experimental frameworks. In M. B. Brewer & B. E. Collins (Eds.), *Scientific inquiry and the social sciences: A volume in honor of Donald T. Campbell* (pp. 226–256). San Francisco: Jossey-Bass.

Kidder, L. H. (1981b). *Research methods in social relations* (4th ed.). New York: Holt, Rinehart and Winston.

Kidder, L. H., & Campbell, D. T. (1970). The indirect testing of social attitudes. In G. F. Summers (Ed.), *Attitude measurement* (pp. 333–385). Chicago: Rand McNally.

Kiesler, S., & Sproull, L. S. (1986). Response effects in the electronic survey. *Public Opinion Quarterly, 50,* 402–413.

Kirk, R. E. (1968). *Experimental design: Procedures for the behavioral sciences.* Belmont, CA: Brooks/Cole.

Kitchin, H. (2002). The Tri-Council on cyberspace: Insights, oversights, and extrapolations. In W. C. van den Hoonaard, (Ed.), *Walking the tightrope: Ethical issues for qualitative researchers* (pp. 160–174). Toronto: University of Toronto Press.

Kline, M. (1994). The colour of law: Ideological representations of First Nations in legal discourse. *Social and Legal Studies, 3,* 451–476.

Knox, R. E., & Inkster, J. A. (1968). Postdecision dissonance at post time. *Journal of Personality and Social Psychology, 8,* 319–323.

Koch, S. (Ed.). (1959). *Psychology: A study of a science* (6 vols.). New York: McGraw-Hill.

Koch, N., & Emrey, J. A. (2001). The Internet and opinion measurement: Surveying marginalized populations. *Social Science Quarterly, 82*(1), 131–138.

Krashinsky, S. (2009 December 17). The future of the magazine. *Globe and Mail.* Retrieved from http://www.theglobeandmail.com/report-on-business/the-future-of-the-magazine/article1404597/.

Kuhn, T. S. (1970). The structure of scientific revolutions (2nd ed.). Chicago: University of Chicago Press.

Lakoff, G. (1987). *Women, fire, and dangerous things: What categories reveal about the mind.* Chicago: University of Chicago Press.

LaPiere, R. T. (1934). Attitudes versus actions. *Social Forces, 13,* 230–237.

Latour, B. (1987). *Science in action.* Cambridge, MA: Harvard University Press.

Leavy, P. (2011). *Essentials of transdisciplinary research: Using problem-centered methodologies.* Walnut Creek, CA: Left Coast Press.

Likert, R. (1932). A technique for the measurement of attitudes. *Archives of Psychology, 140,* 44–53.

Lindesmith, A. (1952). Comment on W. S. Robinson's The logical structure of analytic induction. *American Sociological Review, 17,* 492–493.

Liu, M., Papathanasiou, E., & Hao, Y-W. (2001). Exploring the use of multimedia examination formats in undergraduate teaching: Results from the fielding testing. *Computers in Human Behavior, 17,* 225–248.

Lofland, J. (1971). *Analyzing social settings: A guide to qualitative observation and analysis.* Belmont, CA: Wadsworth.

Lofland, J., & Lejeune, R. A. (1960). Initial interaction of newcomers in Alcoholics Anonymous. *Social Problems, 8,* 102–111.

Lofland, J., & Lofland, L. H. (1984). *Analyzing social settings: A guide to qualitative observation and analysis* (2nd ed.). Belmont, CA: Wadsworth.

Lofland, J., Snow, D., Anderson, L., & Lofland, L. H. (2006) *Analyzing social settings: A guide to qualitative observation and analysis* (4th ed.). Belmont, CA: Wadsworth.

Lofland, L. H. (1973). *A world of strangers: Order and action in urban public space.* New York: Basic Books.

Lombroso, C. (1911). *Crime: Its causes and remedies.* Boston: Little, Brown.

Lord, F. M. (1953). On the statistical treatment of football numbers. *American Psychologist, 8,* 750–751.

Lowman, J. (1983). *The geography of crime and social control.* Doctoral dissertation, Department of Geography, University of British Columbia, Vancouver, BC.

Lowman, J. (1984). *Vancouver field study of prostitution.* Working paper on Pornography and Prostitution (Report #8). Ottawa, ON: Department of Justice.

Lowman, J. (1989). *Street prostitution: Assessing the impact of the law (Vancouver).* Ottawa, ON: Ministry of Supply and Services.

Lowman, J., Atchison, C., & Fraser, L. (1997). *Sexuality in the 1990's: Survey results. [Men who buy sex, phase 2: Internet and British Columbia survey methodology and preliminary results from the Internet survey.]* Retrieved April 26, 2002, from http://users.uniserve.com/%7Elowman/ICSS/icss.htm.

Lowman, J., & Fraser, L. (1995). *Violence against persons who prostitute: The experience in British Columbia.* Research report prepared for Department of Justice, Canada.

Lowman, J., Menzies, R. J., & Palys, T. S. (1987). *Transcarceration: Essays in the sociology of social control.* Aldershot, U.K.: Gower.

Lowman, J., & Palys, T. S. (1991). Interpreting criminal justice system records of crime. In M. A. Jackson & C. T. Griffiths (Eds.), *Canadian criminology: Perspectives on crime and criminality* (pp. 349–369). Toronto: Harcourt Brace Jovanovich.

Lowman, J., & Palys, T. S. (2000). Ethics and institutional conflict of interest: The research confidentiality controversy at Simon Fraser University. *Sociological Practice: A Journal of Clinical and Applied Sociology, 2*: 245–255.

Lowman, J., & Palys, T. S. (2001a). The ethics and law of confidentiality in criminological research. *International Journal of Criminal Justice, 11*: 1–33.

Lowman, J., & Palys, T. S. (2001b). Limited confidentiality, academic freedom, and matters of conscience: Where does CPA stand? *Canadian Journal of Criminology, 43*: 497–508.

M.(A.) v. *Ryan* (1997). 1 S.C.R. 157.

MacInnes, W. J., & Taylor, T. L. (2001). Millisecond timing on PCs and Macs. *Behavior Research Methods, Instruments, and Computers, 33*(2), 174–178.

Malamuth, N. M. (1978). *Erotica, aggression and perceived appropriateness.* Paper presented at the 86th annual convention of the American Psychological Association, Toronto, ON. (Cited in Malamuth 1984.)

Malamuth, N. M. (1984). Aggression against women. In N. M. Malamuth & E. Donnerstein (Eds.), *Pornography and sexual aggression* (pp. 173–185). New York: Academic Press.

Malamuth, N. M. (1989). Sexually violent media, thought patterns, and antisocial behavior. In G. Comstock (Ed.), *Public communication and behaviour* (Vol. 2, pp. 159–204). New York: Academic Press.

Malamuth, N. M., & Donnerstein, E. (Eds.). (1984). *Pornography and sexual aggression.* New York: Academic Press.

Malinowski, B. (1922). *Argonauts of the western Pacific.* London: Routledge & Kegan Paul.

Malinowski, B. (1967). *A diary in the strict sense of the term.* New York: Harcourt Brace Jovanovich.

Malka, A., & Chatman, J. A. (2003). Intrinsic and extrinsic work orientations as moderators of the effect of annual income on subjective well-being: A longitudinal study. *Personality and Social Psychology Bulletin, 29*(6): 737–746.

Manicas, P. T., & Secord, P. F. (1983). Implications for psychology of the new philosophy of science. *American Psychologist, 38,* 399–413.

Manning, P. K. (1991). Analytic induction. In K. Plummer (Ed.), *Symbolic interactionism: Contemporary issues* (Vol. 2, pp. 401–30). Brookfield, VT: Edward Elgar. (Reprinted from R. Smith & P. K. Manning [Eds.], 1982, *Qualitative methods.* Cambridge, MA: Ballinger.)

Margolis, E. (1994). Video ethnography: Toward a reflexive paradigm for documentary. *Jump Cut, 39*: 122–131.

Marquart, J. W. (2001). Doing research in prison: The strengths and weaknesses of full participation as a guard. In J. M. Miller & R. Tewksbury (Eds.), *Extreme methods: Innovative approaches to social science research* (pp. 35–47). Needham Heights, MA: Allyn & Bacon.

Maxcy, S. (2003). Pragmatic threads in mixed methods research in the social sciences: The search for multiple modes of inquiry and the end of the philosophy of formalism." In Tashakkori, A. & Teddlie, C. (eds.) *Handbook of mixed methods in social and behavioral research.* London: Sage.

Maxwell, J., & Loomis, D. (2003) Mixed methods design: An alternative approach. In A. Tashakkori & C. Teddlie (eds.) *Handbook of mixed methods in social and behavioral research.* London: Sage.

McDonald, M. (1998). The Tri-Council policy statement on ethical conduct for research involving humans. *Canadian Bioethics Society Newsletter, 3*(3). Retrieved August 20, 2002, from http://www.bioethics.ca/english/newsletter/3.3/#mcdonald.

McGhee, J. W. (1985). *Introductory statistics.* Los Angeles: West Publishing.

McGinn, M., & Palys, T. S. (2005). *Participants' perspectives on research ethics issues: A research proposal.* Unpublished proposal prepared to seek funding from the Social Sciences and Humanities Research Council and the Research Ethics Boards at Brock University and Simon Fraser University.

McGuire, W. J. (1973). The yin and yang of progress in social psychology: Seven koan. *Journal of Personality and Social Psychology, 26,* 446–456.

McKinlay, A., & Potter, J. (1987). Model discourse: Interpretive repertoires in scientists' conference talk. *Social Studies of Science, 17,* 443–463.

Mead, M. (1960). *Coming of age in Samoa: A psychological study of primitive youth for Western civilization.* New York: Mentor. (Originally published 1928.)

Menzies, R. J. (1989). *Survival of the sanest: Order and disorder in a pre-trial psychiatric clinic.* Toronto: University of Toronto Press.

Menzies, R., & Palys, T. (1999). *Race, ethnicity, and psychiatric regulation in British Columbia, 1875–1950.* Unpublished grant proposal prepared for the Hannah Institute for the History of Medicine Grant-in-aid program. Burnaby, BC: School of Criminology, Simon Fraser University.

Menzies, R. J., & Palys, T. S. (2006). Turbulent spirits: Aboriginal patients in the British Columbia psychiatric system, 1879–1950. In J. E. Moran (Ed.), *Mental health and Canadian society: Historical perspectives* (pp. 149–175). Montreal: McGill–Queen's University Press.

Menzies, R. J., Webster, C. D., & Sepejak, D. S. (1985). Hitting the forensic sound barrier: Predictions of dangerousness in a pretrial psychiatric clinic. In C. D. Webster, M. H. Ben-Aron, & S. J. Hucker (Eds.), *Dangerousness: Probability and prediction,*

psychiatry and public policy (pp. 115–144). New York: Cambridge University Press.

Merton, R. K., & Kendall, P. L. (1946). The focussed interview. *American Journal of Sociology, 51,* 541–557.

Merton, R. K., Fiske, M., & Kendall, P. L. (1956). *The focussed interview.* Glencoe, IL: Free Press.

Miles, M., & Huberman, M. (1994) *Qualitative data analysis.* (2nd ed.) Thousand Oaks, California: Sage.

Milgram, S. (1963). Behavioral study of obedience. *Journal of Abnormal and Social Psychology, 67,* 371–378.

Milgram, S. (1974). *Obedience to authority: An experimental view.* New York: Harper & Row.

Mill, J. S. (1956). *On liberty.* Indianapolis, IN: Bobbs-Merrill. (Originally published 1859.)

Mill, J. S. (1965). *A system of logic.* London: Longman's, Green. (Reprint of 8th edition, originally published 1881; 1st edition published 1843.)

Miller, J. M., & Tewksbury, R. (Eds.). (2001). *Extreme methods: Innovative approaches to social science research.* Needham Heights, MA: Allyn & Bacon.

Mills, A. (1994). *Eagle down is our law: Witsuwit'en law, feasts, and land claims.* Vancouver: University of British Columbia Press.

Mills, C. W. (1959). *The sociological imagination.* New York: Oxford University Press.

Miner, H. (1956). Body ritual among the Nacirema. *American Anthropologist, 58,* pp. 503–507.

Minister, K. (1991). A feminist frame for the oral history interview. In S. B. Gluck & D. Patai (Eds.), *Women's words: The feminist practice of oral history* (pp. 27–42). New York: Routledge.

Mitchell, A. (1994, July 13). Study debunks immigration myths: Harder working, better educated than Canadian-born, Statscan says. *Globe and Mail,* pp. A1, A2.

Mockridge, N. (1968). *The scrawl of the wild: What people write on walls—and why.* Cleveland, OH: World Publishing.

Moloney, M. (2010). *Voices from the grave.* London, UK: Faber & Faber.

Monette, D. R., Sullivan, T. J., & DeJong, C. R. (1994). *Applied social research: Tool for the human services.* Fort Worth, TX: Harcourt Brace.

Monture-Okanee, P. A. (1993). Reclaiming justice: Aboriginal women and justice initiatives in the 1990s. In Royal Commission on Aboriginal Peoples (Eds.), *Aboriginal peoples and the justice system* (pp. 105–132). Ottawa, ON: Canada Communication Group Publishing.

Mook, D. G. (1983). In defence of external invalidity. *American Psychologist, 38,* 379–387.

Morgan, D. L. (1986). Personal relationships as an interface between social networks and social cognitions. *Journal of Social and Personal Relationships, 3,* 403–422.

Morgan, D. L. (1988). *Focus groups as qualitative research.* Newbury Park, CA: Sage.

Morgan, D. L. (2008). Sampling. In L. Givens (Ed.) *The Sage encyclopedia of qualitative research methods.* Sage: Thousand Oaks, CA. Vol. 2, pp. 799–800.

Morgan, D. L., & Spanish, M.T. (1984). Focus groups: A new tool for qualitative research. *Qualitative Sociology, 7,* 253–270.

Morgan, D. L., & Spanish, M. T. (1985). Social interaction and the cognitive organization of health-relevant behavior. *Sociology of Health and Illness, 7,* 401–422.

Morgan, G. (1983). Research as engagement: A personal view. In G. Morgan (Ed.), *Beyond method: Strategies for social research* (pp. 383–391). Beverly Hills, CA: Sage.

Morgan, R. (1980). Theory and practice: Pornography and rape. In L. Lederer (Ed.), *Take back the night: Women on pornography.* New York: William Morrow.

Morse, J. (1991). Approaches to qualitative-quantitative methodological triangulation. *Nursing Research, 40*(2): 120–123.

Morse, J. M. (1994). Designing funded qualitative research. In N. K. Denzin & Y. S. Lincoln (Eds.), *Handbook of qualitative research* (pp. 220–235). Thousand Oaks, CA: Sage.

Napoleon, V. (2005). *Delgamuukw*: A legal straight-jacket for oral histories? *Canadian Journal of Law and Society, 20*: 123–155.

"Native kids used for experiments." (2000, April 26). *Vancouver Sun*, p. A12.

Neuendorf, K., Gore, T., Dalessandro, A., Janstova, P., & Snyder-Suhy, S. (2010) Shaken and stirred: A content analysis of women's portrayals in James Bond films. *Sex Roles, 62*(11-12): 747–761.

Norusis, M. J. (1993). *SPSS® for Windows™: Base system user's guide, Release 6.0.* Chicago: SPSS Inc.

O'Doherty, T. (2011a). Criminalization and off-street sex work in Canada. *Canadian Journal of Criminology and Criminal Justice, 53*(2), 217–245.

O'Doherty, T. (2011b). Victimization in off-street sex industry work. *Violence Against Women, 17*(7), 944–963.

O'Neil, R. M. (1996). A researcher's privilege: Does any hope remain? *Law and Contemporary Problems, 59,* 35–50.

Oakley, A. (1981). Interviewing women: A contradiction in terms. In H. Roberts (Ed.), *Doing feminist research* (pp. 30–61). London: Routledge and Kegan Paul.

Olesen, V. (1994). Feminisms and models of qualitative research. In N. K. Denzin & Y. S. Lincoln (Eds.), *Handbook of qualitative research* (pp. 158–174). Thousand Oaks, CA: Sage.

Olson, K., & Shopes, L. (1991). Crossing boundaries, building bridges: Doing oral history among working-class men and women. In S. B. Gluck & D. Patai (Eds.), *Women's words: The feminist practice of oral history* (pp. 189–204). New York: Routledge.

Osgood, C. E., Suci, G. J., & Tannenbaum, P. H. (1957). *The measurement of meaning.* Urbana, IL: University of Illinois.

Oskamp, S. (1977). *Attitudes and opinions.* Englewood Cliffs, NJ: Prentice-Hall.

Palys, T. S. (1971). *The appeal of the illicit.* Paper presented to the annual meetings of the Manitoba Psychological Society, Winnipeg, MN.

Palys, T. S. (1978). Simulation methods and social psychology. *Journal for the theory of social behavior, 8,* 343–368.

Palys, T. S. (1986). Testing the common wisdom: The social content of video pornography. *Canadian Psychology, 27,* 22–35.

Palys, T. S. (1988, April). The profs and profits picture. *Canadian Business*, pp. 157–158.

Palys, T. S. (1989). Addressing the "third criterion" in experimentalist research: Towards a balance of manipulative and analytic control. In I. Benbasat (Ed.), *The information systems research challenge: Experimental research methods.* Boston, MA: Harvard Business School. (Vol. 2 of the Harvard Business School Research Colloquium Series, J. I. Cash, Jr., & J. F. Nunamaker, Jr. [Eds.].) Online at http://www.sfu.ca/~palys/Palys1989-AddressingTheThirdCriterion.pdf.

Palys, T. S. (1990). *Ideology, Epistemology, and Modes of Inquiry: Aboriginal Issues, Trajectories of Truth, and the Criteria of Evaluation Research.* Paper presented at a meeting of the West Coast Law and Society Group. Online at http://www.sfu.ca/~palys/ideology.htm.

Palys, T. S. (1992). *Research decisions: Quantitative and qualitative perspectives.* Toronto: Harcourt Brace Jovanovich.

Palys, T. S. (1994). *Statement of Dr. Ted S. Palys: Comments on the statement by Dr. Neil Malamuth.* Report prepared for Arvay Findlay, solicitors for Little Sister's Book and Art Emponum, for the case of *Little Sister's v. The Queen.* Last retrieved 23 December 2011, from http://www .sfu.ca/~palys/court.htm.

Palys, T. S. (1996a). *The ethics of ethics: Comments regarding the Tri-Council Working Group's March 1996 draft Code of Conduct for Research Involving Humans.* Personal submission to the Secretariat of the Tri-Council (SSHRC, NSERC, MRC) Working Group on Ethics. (Available online at www.sfu .ca/~palys/codecomm.htm, last checked 23 December 2011.)

Palys, T. S. (1996b). Histories of convenience: Understanding twentieth century Aboriginal film images in context. Paper presented at an international conference regarding Aboriginal peoples and film entitled "Screening culture: Constructing image and identity," York, U.K. (Available online at www.sfu.ca/~palys/).

Palys, T. S. (2008). Purposive sampling. In L. Givens (Ed.) *The Sage encyclopedia of qualitative research methods* (Vol. 2, pp. 697–698.). Sage: Thousand Oaks, CA.

Palys, T. S., & Atchison, C. (2008). *Research decisions: Quantitative and qualitative perspectives.* (4th edition). Toronto: Thomson Nelson.

Palys, T. S., & Atchison, C. (2009). Qualitative research at the gates of the digital age: Obstacles and opportunities. Invited keynote address for the 10th Annual *Advances in Qualitative Methods Conference* of the International Institute for Qualitative Methodology; Vancouver, Canada. Online at http://www.sfu.ca/~palys/Palys&Atchison2009-Obstacles&Opportunities.pdf. Last checked 5 December 2011.

Palys, T. S., & Atchison, C. (in press). Qualitative research at the gates of the digital age: Obstacles and opportunities. *International Journal of Qualitative Methodology.*

Palys, T. S., Boyanowsky, E. O., & Dutton, D. G. (1983). *A behavioural evaluation of the Vancouver Police Department's mobile radio data system.* Research report prepared for the Behavioural Research Group, Department of Communications, Government of Canada, Ottawa, ON.

Palys, T. S., Boyanowsky, E. O., & Dutton, D. G. (1984). Mobile data access terminals and their implications for policing. *Journal of Social Issues, 40*(3), 113–127.

Palys, T. S., Isaac, R., & Nuszdorfer, J. (2012). *Taking Indigenous justice seriously: Fostering a mutually respectful coexistence of Aboriginal and Canadian justice.* Research report prepared for the Executive Director of Vancouver Aboriginal Transformative Justice Services and the Coordinator of Vancouver's Downtown Community Court. Online at http://www.sfu.ca/~palys/PalysEtAl-2012- Aboriginal&CanadianJustice-final.

Palys, T. S., & Lowman, J. (1984). *Methodological meta-issues in pornography research: Ecological representativeness and contextual integrity.* Paper presented at the annual meetings of the Canadian Psychological Association, Ottawa, ON.

Palys, T. S., & Lowman, J. (2000). Ethical and legal strategies for protecting confidential research information. *Canadian Journal of Law and Society, 15*(1), 39–80.

Palys, T. S., & Lowman, J. (2001). Social research with eyes wide shut: The limited confidentiality dilemma. *Canadian Journal of Criminology, 43,* 255–267.

Palys, T. S., & Lowman, J. (2002). Anticipating law: Research methods, ethics and the common law of privilege. *Sociological Methodology, 32,* 1–17.

Palys, T. S., & Lowman, J. (2006). Protecting research confidentiality: Towards a research-participant shield law. *Canadian Journal of Law and Society,* 21, No. 1, 163–185.

Palys, T. S., & Lowman, J. (2010). Going boldly where no one has gone before? How confidentiality risk aversion is killing research on sensitive topics. *Journal of Academic Ethics, 8*(4), 265–284.

Palys, T. S., & Lowman, J. (book in preparation). *Going the distance: The law and ethics of research confidentiality.*

Palys, T. S., Olver, J. O., & Banks, L. K. (1983). *Social definitions of pornography.* Paper presented to the annual meetings of the Canadian Psychological Association, Winnipeg, MN.

Palys, T. S., & Williams, D. W. (1983). *Attitudes regarding capital punishment: On the assessment of false dichotomies.* Paper presented at the annual meetings of the Canadian Psychological Association, Winnipeg, MN.

Park, R. E. (1952). *The collected papers of Robert Ezra Park.* (Vol. 2, *Human communities: The city and human ecology.*) Glencoe, IL: Free Press.

Parsons, T. (1959). Some problems confronting sociology as a profession. *American Sociological Review, 24,* 547–559.

Patai, D. (1991). US academics and Third World women: Is ethical research possible? In S. B. Gluck & D. Patai (Eds.), *Women's words: The feminist practice of oral history* (pp. 137–154). New York: Routledge.

Pearce, M. (2002). Challenging the system: Rethinking ethics review of social research in Britain's National Health Service. In W. C. van den Hoonaard (Ed), *Walking the tightrope: Ethical issues for qualitative researchers* (pp. 43–58). Toronto: University of Toronto Press.

Pedhazur, E. J. (1982). *Multiple regression in behavioral research: Explanation and prediction* (2nd ed.). New York: Holt, Rinehart and Winston.

Peiris, D. R., Gregor, P., & Alm, N. (2000). The effects of simulating human conversational style in a computer-based interview. *Interacting With Computers, 12*, 635–650.

Pepinsky, H. (1987). Justice as information sharing. In J. Lowman, R. J. Menzies, & T. S. Palys (Eds.), *Transcarceration: Essays in the sociology of social control* (pp. 76–88). Aldershot, U.K.: Gower.

Petersen, A. M. (1994). *Waltzing with an elephant: First Nations women's experience in creating a shelter for women in crisis.* Unpublished master's thesis, Simon Fraser University, Burnaby, BC.

Pettit, F. (2002). A comparison of World-Wide Web and paper-and-pencil personality questionnaires. *Behavior Research Methods, Instruments, and Computers, 34*, 50–54.

Pew Research Center. (2010, March 15). *The state of the news media 2010: An annual report on American journalism.* Retrieved from http://www.stateofthe media.org/2010/

Phone has become best friend to us talkative Canadians. (1989, August 12). *Vancouver Sun*, p. F6.

Pirsig, R.M. (1974). *Zen and the Art of Motorcycle Maintenance.* NY: Bantam Books.

Popper, K. R. (1959). *The logic of scientific discovery.* New York: Basic Books.

Preissle, J. (2008). Analytic induction. In L. Givens (Ed.) *The Sage encyclopedia of qualitative research methods* (Vol.1, pp. 15–16), Sage: Thousand Oaks, CA.

Punch, M. (1994). Politics and ethics in qualitative research. In N. K. Denzin & Y. S. Lincoln (Eds.), *Handbook of qualitative research* (pp. 83–97). Thousand Oaks, CA: Sage.

R. v. Gruenke, 3 S.C.R. 263 (1991).

Ragin, C. (1987). *The comparative method.* Berkley, CA: University of California Press.

Ranchhod, A., & Zhou, F. (2001). Comparing respondents of e-mail and mail surveys: Understanding the implications of technology. *Marketing Intelligence and Planning, 19*(4): 254–262.

Ratel, P. (2008). One day at a time: Single parent mothers in academe. In T. Palys & C. Atchison, *Research decisions: Quantitative and qualitative perspectives.* (4th Ed.) (pp. 404–414). Toronto: Thomson Nelson. Online at http://www.sfu.ca/~palys/Ratel.pdf.

Rawls, J. (1971). *A theory of justice.* Cambridge, MA: Harvard University Press.

Reinharz, S. (1992). *Feminist methods in social research.* New York: Oxford University Press.

Richards, L. (1999). *Using NVivo in qualitative research.* London: Sage Publications.

Richards of Rockford Inc. v. *Pacific Gas and Electric Co.* 71 F.R.D. 388 (N.D. Cal, 1976).

Richardson, L. (1994). Writing: A method of inquiry. In N. K. Denzin & Y. S. Lincoln (Eds.), *Handbook of qualitative research* (pp. 516–529). Thousand Oaks, CA: Sage.

Richardson, L. (2003). Writing: A method of inquiry. In N.K. Denzin & Y.S. Lincoln (Eds.) *Collecting and interpreting qualitative materials.* (2nd Ed.) (pp. 499–541). Thousand Oaks, CA: Sage.

Riecken, H. W. (1969). The unidentified interviewer. In G. J. McCall & J. L. Simmons (Eds.), *Issues in participant observation* (pp. 39–43). Reading, MA: Addison-Wesley.

Rigakos, G. (1994). The politics of protection: Battered women, protective court orders, and the police in Delta. Unpublished master's thesis, School of Criminology, Simon Fraser University, Burnaby, BC.

Rigakos, G. (1995). Constructing the symbolic complainant: Police subculture and the non-enforcement of protection orders for battered women. *Violence and Victims, 10*(3), 127–147.

Roberts, J. V., & Jackson, M. (1991). Boats against the current: A note on the effects of imprisonment. *Law and Human Behaviour, 15*(5), 557–562.

Rosenblatt, P. C. (1981). Ethnographic case studies. In M. B. Brewer & B. E. Collins (Eds.), *Scientific inquiry and the social sciences: A volume in honor of Donald T. Campbell* (pp. 226–256). San Francisco: Jossey-Bass.

Rosenhan, D. L. (1973). On being sane in insane places. *Science, 179*, 250–258.

Rosenstock, I. (1974). Historical origins of the health belief model. *Health Education Monographs, 2(4):* 328–335.

Rosenthal, R., & Rosnow, R. L. (1984). *Essentials of behavioral research: Methods and data analysis.* New York: McGraw-Hill.

Ross, A. (ed.). (1996). *Science wars.* Durham, NC: Duke University Press.

Ross, M., Daneback, K., Mansson, S-A., Tikkanen, R., & Cooper, A. (2003). Characteristics of men and women who complete or exit from an on-line internet sexuality questionnaire: A study of instrument dropout biases. *Journal of Sex Research, 40,* 396–403.

Roth, J. A. (1969). A codification of current prejudices. *American Sociologist, 4,* 159.

Rubenstein, S. M. (1995). *Surveying public opinion.* Belmont, NY: Wadsworth.

Rubin, Z. (1973). *Liking and loving.* New York: Holt, Rinehart and Winston.

Rubington, E., & Weinberg, M. S. (Eds.). (1968). *Deviance: The interactionist perspective.* New York: Macmillan.

Russel Ogden v. *Simon Fraser University.* [1998] B.C.J. No. 2288. Burnaby Registry No. 26780. British Columbia Provincial Court (Small Claims Division), Burnaby, British Columbia, Steinberg Prov. Ct. J. June 10, 1998.

Ryan, G. W., & Bernard, H. R. (2003). Data management and analysis methods. In N. Denzin & Y. Lincoln (eds) *Collecting and interpreting qualitative materials.* (2nd ed.) (pp. 259–309). Sage: London.

Saari, L. M., & Judge, T. A. (2004). Employee attitudes and job satisfaction. *Human Resource Management,* 43(4), 395–407.

Salamon, E. (1984). *The kept woman: Mistresses in the '80s.* London: Orbis.

Salazar, C. (1991). A Third World woman's text: Between the politics of criticism and cultural politics. In S. B. Gluck & D. Patai (Eds.), *Women's words: The feminist practice of oral history* (pp. 93–106). New York: Routledge.

Samuels, M., & Ryan, K. (2011). Grounding evaluations in culture. *American Journal of Evaluation,* 32(2): 183–198.

Scarce, R. (1994). (No) trial (but) tribulations: When courts and ethnography conflict. *Journal of Contemporary Ethnography, 23,* 123–149.

Scarce, R. (1999). Good faith, bad ethics: When scholars go the distance and scholarly associations do not. *Law and Social Inquiry, 24,* 977–986.

Schachter, S. (1959). *The psychology of affiliation.* Stanford, CA: Stanford University Press.

Schatzman, L., & Strauss, A. L. (1973). *Field research: Strategies for a natural sociology.* Englewood Cliffs, NJ: Prentice-Hall.

Schmidt, W. C. (2001). Presentation accuracy of Web animation methods. *Behavior Research Methods, Instruments, and Computers, 33,* 187–200

Schmidt, W. C. (2002). A server-side program for delivering experiments with animations. *Behavior Research Methods, Instruments, and Computers, 34,* 208–217.

Schuler, E. A. (1967). Report of the Committee on Professional Ethics. *American Sociologist, 2,* 242–244.

Schultz, D. (2005). The rise of the corporate university. *Logos: A Journal of Modern Society and Culture,* 4(4). Online at http://www.logosjournal.com/issue_4.4/schultz.htm

Schuman, H., & Presser, S. (1981). *Questions and answers in attitude surveys: Experiments on question form, wording and context.* New York: Academic Press.

Schutz, A. (1970). Interpretive sociology. In H. R. Wagner (Ed.), *Alfred Schutz: On phenomenology and social relations* (pp. 265–293). Chicago: University of Chicago Press.

Schwandt, T. A. (1994). Constructivist, interpretivist approaches to human inquiry. In N. K. Denzin & Y. S. Lincoln (Eds.), *Handbook of qualitative research* (pp. 118–137). Thousand Oaks, CA: Sage.

Scriven, M. (1976). Maximizing the power of causal investigations: The modus operandi method. In G. V. Glass (Ed.), *Evaluation Studies Review Annual* (Vol. I, pp. 101–118). Beverly Hills, CA: Sage.

Seidman, D., & Couzens, M. (1974). Getting the crime rate down: Political pressure and crime reporting. *Law and Society Review, 8,* 457–493.

Shadish, W. R., Cook, T. D., & Campbell, D. T. (2001). *Experimental and quasi-experimental designs for generalized causal inference.* NY: Houghton Mifflin.

Shank, G. (2008). Deduction. In L.M. Given (Ed.) *The Sage encyclopedia of qualitative research methods* (Vol 1, pp. 207–208). Thousand Oaks, CA: Sage.

Shea, C. (2000). Don't talk to the humans: The crackdown on social science research. *Linguafranca,* 10 (6), 1–17.

Sheehan, K. B., & Hoy, M. G. (1999). Using e-mail to survey Internet users in the United States: Methodology and assessment. *Journal of Computer Mediated Communication, 4*(3). [On-line]. http://www.ascusc.org/jcmc/vol4/issue3/sheehan.html.

Sherif, M., Harvey, O. J., White, B. J., Hood, W. E., & Sherif, C. W. (1961). *Intergroup conflict and cooperation: The Robber's Cave experiment.* Norman, OK: University of Oklahoma Book Exchange.

Shortt, S. E. D. (1986). *Victorian lunacy: Richard M. Burke and the practice of late nineteenth-century psychiatry.* Cambridge: Cambridge University Press.

Silverman, D. (1985). *Qualitative methodology and sociology.* Brookfield, VT: Gower.

Sinclair, C., Poizner, S., Gilmour-Barrett, K., & Randall, D. (1987). The development of a code of ethics for Canadian psychologists. *Canadian Psychology, 28,* 1–8.

Skogan, W. G. (1975). Measurement problems in official and survey crime rates. *Journal of Criminal Justice, 3,* 17–32.

Smith v. Jones [1999] 1 S.C.R. 455.

Smith, C. B. (1997). Casting the Net: Surveying an Internet population. *Journal of Computer Mediated Communication, 3*(1). Retrieved September 6, 2006, at http://jcmc.indiana.edu/vol3/issue1/smith.html.

Smith, J., & Hashusius, L. (1986). Closing down the conversation: The end of the quantitative-qualitative debate among educational researchers. *Educational Researchers, 15*(4): 4–12.

Smith, L. T. (2001). *Decolonizing methodologies: Research and indigenous peoples.* London: Zed Books.

Smith, R., & Manning, P. K. (1982). *Qualitative methods.* Cambridge, MA: Ballinger.

Social Sciences and Humanities Research Ethics Special Working Committee (SSHWC). (2004). *Giving voice to the spectrum: Report of the Social Sciences and Humanities Research Ethics Special Working Committee.* Report prepared for the federal Interagency Advisory Panel on Research Ethics. Retrieved June 6, 2006, from http://www.pre.ethics.gc.ca/english/workgroups/sshwc/SSHWCVoiceReportJune2004.pdf.

Starr, L. (1984). Oral history. In D. Dunaway & W. K. Baum (Eds.), *Oral history: An interdisciplinary anthology* (pp. 3–26). Nashville, TN: American Association for State and Local History.

Statistics Canada. (2009 June 15). Residential Telephone Service Survey. *The Daily.* Retrieved from http://www.statcan.gc.ca/daily-quotidien/090615/dq090615c-eng.htm.

Steinem, G. (1980). Erotica and pornography: A clear and present difference. In L. Lederer (Ed.), *Take back the night: Women on pornography.* New York: William Morrow.

Stevens, S. S. (1951). Mathematics, measurement, and psychophysics. In S. S. Stevens (Ed.,) *Handbook of experimental psychology* (pp. 1–49). New York: Wiley.

Stinchcombe, A. (1968). *Constructing social theories.* New York: Harcourt Brace Jovanovich.

Strauss, A. L. (1987). *Qualitative analysis for social scientists.* New York: Cambridge University Press.

Strauss, A.L., & Corbin, J. (Eds.) (1997) *Grounded theory in practice.* Thousand Oaks, CA: Sage.

Stricker, L. J. (1967). The true deceiver. *Psychological Bulletin, 68,* 13–20.

Strickland, L. H., Aboud, F. E., & Gergen, K. J. (Eds.). (1976). *Social psychology in transition.* New York: Plenum.

Strunk, W., Jr. (1999). *The elements of style.* NY: Bartleby. (Originally published 1918). Retrieved May 28, 2002, from www.bartleby.com/141

Sudman, S., & Bradburn, N. M. (1982). *Asking questions.* San Francisco: Jossey-Bass.

Surridge, G. (2009, February 10). Say hello! to Canada's magazine sales hit. *Financial Post.* Retrieved from http://www.financialpost.com/story.html?id=1271495.

Tajfel, H. (1972). Experiments in a vacuum. In J. Israel & H. Tajfel (Eds.), *The context of social psychology* (pp. 69–119). London: Academic Press.

Talarico, S. M. (Ed.). (1980). *Criminal justice research.* Atlanta, GA: Anderson.

Tashakkori, A., & Teddlie, C. (1998). *Mixed methodology: Combining qualitative and quantitative approaches.* (Applied Social Research Methods, No. 46). Thousand Oaks, CA: Sage.

Teddlie, C., & Tashakkori, A. (2003). Major issues and controversies in the use of mixed methods in the social and behavioural sciences." In Tashakkori, A. & Teddlie, C. (eds.) *Handbook of mixed methods in social and behavioral research.* London: Sage.

Terkel, S. (1975). *Working.* New York: Avon.

Terry, W. (1984). *Bloods: An oral history of the Vietnam War by black veterans.* New York: Random House.

Thomas, W. I. (1928). *The child in America: Behavior problems and programs.* New York: Knopf.

Thompson, J., Baird, P., & Downie, J. (2001). *Report of the Committee of Inquiry on the Case Involving Dr. Nancy Olivieri, the Hospital for Sick Children, the University of Toronto, and Apotex, Inc.* Ottawa: Canadian Association of University Teachers. Online at http://www.caut.ca/pages.asp?page=199.

Toby, J. (1986). Going native in criminology. *The Criminologist, 11* (May/June), 2.

Traynor, M. (1996). Countering the excessive subpoena for scholarly research. *Law and Contemporary Problems, 59,* 119–148.

Trigger, B. G. (1988). The historians' Indian: Native Americans in Canadian historical writing from Charlevoix to the present. In R. Fisher & K. Coates (Eds.), *Out of the background: Readings on Canadian Native history* (pp. 19–44). Toronto, ON: Copp Clark Pitman.

Tse, A. (1999). Conducting electronic focus group discussions among Chinese respondents. *Journal of the Market Research Society, 41,* 407–415.

Tuckel, P., & O'Neill, H. (2002). The vanishing respondent in telephone surveys. *Journal of Advertising Research, September-October,* 26–48.

Tudiver, N. (1999). *Universities for sale: resisting corporate control over Canadian higher education.* Toronto: Lorimer.

United Nations. (2004). *Information and communications technology (ICT): Vital statistics.* Retrieved September 7, 2004, from http://cyberschoolbus. un.org/Cyber schoolbus/Briefing/Technology/Index.htm.

United States Commission on Obscenity and Pornography. (1970). *The report of the commission on obscenity and pornography.* New York: Bantam Books.

Upton, L. F. S. (1988). The extermination of the Beothuks of Newfoundland. In R. Fisher & K. Coates (Eds.), *Out of the background: Readings on Canadian Native history* (pp. 45–65). Toronto: Copp Clark Pitman.

van den Hoonaard, W.C. (2002). *Walking the tightrope: Ethical issues for qualitative researchers.* Toronto: University of Toronto Press.

van den Hoonaard, W.C (2011). *The seduction of ethics: Transforming the social sciences.* Toronto: University of Toronto Press.

Vidich, A. J., & Lyman, S. M. (1994). Qualitative methods: Their history in sociology and anthropology. In N. K. Denzin & Y. S. Lincoln (Eds.), *Handbook of qualitative research* (pp. 23–59). Thousand Oaks, CA: Sage.

Vidich, A. J., & Lyman, S. M. (2003). Qualitative methods: Their history in sociology and anthropology. In N. K. Denzin & Y. S. Lincoln (Eds.) *The landscape of qualitative research: Theories and issues.* (2nd ed.) (pp. 55–130). Thousand Oaks, CA: Sage.

Wagner, D. G. (1984). *The growth of sociological theories.* Beverly Hills, CA: Sage.

Wahl, A. (2006). Red all over. *Canadian Business, 79*(4), 53–54.

Wallace, W. (1971). *The logic of science in sociology.* Chicago: Aldine-Atherton.

Warwick, D. P., & Lininger, C. A. (1975). *The sample survey: Theory and practice.* New York: McGraw-Hill.

Watson, J. B. (1913). Psychology as the behaviorist views it. *Psychological Review, 20,* 158–177.

Webb, E. T., Campbell, D. T., Schwartz, R. D., & Sechrest, L. (1966). *Unobtrusive measures: Non-reactive research in the social sciences.* Skokie, IL: Rand McNally.

Webb, E. T., Campbell, D. T., Schwartz, R. D., Sechrest, L., & Grove, J. B. (1981). *Non-reactive measures in the social sciences* (2nd ed.). Boston: Houghton Mifflin.

Weber, M. (1968a). Objectivity in social science. In M. Brodbeck (Ed.), *Readings in the philosophy of the social sciences* (pp. 85–97). New York: Macmillan. (Reprinted from M. Weber, 1949, *The methodology of the social sciences,* New York: The Free Press.)

Weber, M. (1968b). The interpretive understanding of social action. In M. Brodbeck (Ed.), *Readings in the philosophy of the social sciences* (pp. 19–33). New York: Macmillan. (Reprinted from M. Weber, 1947, *The theory of social and economic organization,* New York: Oxford University Press.)

Weber, T. (2004). Poorer people closing PC gap. Retrieved June 24, 2004, from https://secure.globe advisor.com/servlet/articlenews/story/rtgam/ 20040623/wcompute0623#.

Weick, K. E. (1968). Systematic observational methods. In E. Aronson & G. Lindzey (Eds.), *The handbook of social psychology* (Vol. 2). Reading, MA: Addison-Wesley.

Weiss, C. H. (1975). Evaluation research in the political context. In E. L. Streuning & M. Guttentag (Eds.) *Handbook of evaluation research* (Vol. 1, pp. 13–26). Beverly Hills, CA: Sage.

Weiss, C. H. (1993). Politics and evaluation: A reprise with mellower overtones. *American Journal of Evaluation Research, 14*(1): 107–109.

Whyte, W. F. (1943). *Street corner society: The social structure of an Italian slum.* Chicago: University of Chicago Press.

Whyte, W. F. (1993). *Street corner society: The social structure of an Italian slum.* (4th Edition). Chicago: University of Chicago Press.

Wiggins, E. C., & McKenna, J. A. (1996). Researchers' reactions to compelled disclosure of scientific information. In J. S. Cecil & G. T. Wetherington (Eds.), Court-ordered disclosure of academic research: A clash of values of science and law. *Law and Contemporary Problems* (special issue), *59*(3), 67–94.

Wigmore, J. H. (1905). *A treatise on the system of evidence in trials at common law, including the statutes and judicial decisions of all jurisdictions of the United States, England, and Canada.* Boston: Little, Brown.

Wilson, S. (2008). *Research is ceremony: Indigenous research methods.* Blackpoint, NS: Fernwood Publishing.

Wilson, W. C. (1973). The emergence of a social issue and the beginning of psychological study. *Journal of Social Issues, 29*(3), 7–18.

Wolcott, H. F. (1992). *Writing up qualitative research.* Newbury Park, CA: Sage.

Wolf, E. R. (1982). *Europe and the people without history.* Berkeley, CA: University of California Press.

Wolf, M. (1992). *A thrice-told tale: Feminism, postmodernism, and ethnographic responsibility.* Stanford, CA: Stanford University Press.

Wolfe, C., & Reyna, V. F. (2002). Using Netcloak to develop server-side Web-based experiments without writing CGI programs. *Behavior Research Methods, Instruments, and Computers, 34,* 204–207.

Woong Yun, W., & Trumbo, C. W. (2000). Comparative response to a survey executed by post, e-mail, and web form. *Journal of Computer Mediated Communication, 6*(1).

Wright, R. (1992). *Stolen continents: The "New World" through Indian eyes since 1492.* Toronto: Penguin.

Yerkes, R. M., & Dodson, J. D. (1908). The relation of strength of stimulus to rapidity of habit-formation. *Journal of Comparative Neurology and Psychology, 18,* 459–482.

Zellerer, E. (1996). Community-based justice and violence against women: Issues of gender and race. *International Journal of Comparative and Applied Criminal Justice, 20* (2): 233–244.

Zimbardo, P. G., Ebbesen, E. B., & Maslach, C. (1977). *Influencing attitudes and changing behavior* (2nd ed.). Reading, MA: Addison-Wesley.

Zimmerman, M. K. (1977). *Passage through abortion: The personal and social reality of women's experiences.* New York: Praeger.

Zinger, I. (1999). *The psychological effects of 60 days in administrative segregation.* Doctoral dissertation: Department of Psychology, Carleton University.

Zinger, I., Wichmann, C., & Andrews, D. A. (2001). The effects of administrative segregation. *Canadian Journal of Criminology, 43,* 47–83.

Znaniecki, F. (1934). Analytic induction. In F. Znaniecki (Ed.), *The method of sociology* (pp. 249–331). NY: Farrar & Rinehart.

INDEX